SPORT PSYCHOLOGY

Nelson-Hall Series in Psychology

Consulting Editor: **Stephen Worchel**
Texas A & M University

Second Edition

SPORT PSYCHOLOGY
An Introduction

Arnold LeUnes
Jack R. Nation
Texas A&M University

NELSON-HALL
PUBLISHERS
CHICAGO

Project Editors: Rachel Schick and Dorothy Anderson
Production/Design: Tamra Phelps
Typesetter: Fine Print, Ltd.
Printer: The Maple Vail Book Manufacturing Group
Illustrations: Bill Nelson
Cover Painting: Ruyell Ho, "Sudden Revelation in a Dark Endless Night"

LeUnes, Arnold D.
    Sport psychology : an introduction / Arnold LeUnes, Jack R.
Nation. — 2nd ed.
      p.   cm. — (Nelson-Hall series in psychology)
    Includes bibliographical references and index.
    ISBN 0-8304-1306-5
    1. Sports — Psychological aspects. I. Nation, Jack. R. II. Title.
III. Series.
GV706.4.L48   1996
796'.01 — dc20   95-41298
                                        CIP

Manufactured in the United States of America

10 9 8 7 6 5 4 3 2 1

Contents

Part Two

Social-Psychological Dimensions 145

Chapter Five

MOTIVATION IN SPORT 147

Chapter Six

LEADERSHIP, COHESION, AND AUDIENCE EFFECTS 199

Chapter Nine

SELECTED ATHLETIC POPULATIONS 353

Chapter Twelve

THE COACH AND SPORT PSYCHOLOGY 481

Chapter Thirteen

SPORT AND PHYSICAL ACTIVITY FOR ALL 523

Preface to the Second Edition

The first edition of this text arose out of a shared belief that the field of sport psychology was in need of a comprehensive book that transcended the narrowness of perspective so common among the available texts. We feel that we accomplished our objective of creating a comprehensive book. However, the passage of time has taken its toll, and the need for a greatly updated and expanded coverage has become obvious. Readers of the second edition will benefit from the continuation of features that worked the first time. At the same time, the field of sport psychology is growing and changing as infants (adolescents?) are prone to do, and updates and alterations are warranted.

Features of this edition that have been retained include:

- *Comprehensive Coverage.* We have covered all topics of concern to sport psychologists and students and, where necessary, have added depth and breadth.
- *A Healthy Balance Between Theory and Application.* In general, the first eight chapters are devoted to theory and research applicable to psychology and sport psychology, whereas the last five chapters are more applied and deal with such topics as psychological assessment, women's sports, youth sport, coaching, and fitness.
- *Topic Coverage.* The coverage devoted to the history of sport and sport psychology is unusual. Some would say that this material is covered elsewhere in the students' coursework. This may be true for some students but we feel that, given the interdisciplinary appeal of sport psychology, coverage of sport history will be new to many. Separate coverage of women in sports is unique. Again, it can be argued, as some have done, that singling females out for elaboration is either superfluous or sexist. It is our contention that the status of women in sport is such that a separate coverage is necessary to deal with the myriad issues affecting females in sport. Some of the same kinds of statements may be relevant to a separate coverage of blacks in sport, but we feel again that the integration of minorities in sport is in its infancy and merits separate attention. Devoting space to high risk athletes is another unusual feature. Finally, a separate handling of the complex issues associated with fitness is unique to our book.
- *Pedagogical Aids.* Chapter outlines, highlighted key terms, thorough chapter summaries, student-oriented suggested readings, and tables, figures, and highlights are offered as a means of furthering student understanding of text material. Highlights are designed to present new developments as well as to provide glimpses into some of the more provocative issues within sport psychology. At the

same time, it is important to note that we have not made our book so "busy" with pictures, boxes, personal glimpses, anecdotes, and other potentially distracting devices that the reader is deprived of content coverage.

- *Test Bank.* Over eight hundred multiple-choice items were created. Many items are new to this edition and others have been recast. Most of the new and recast items have been used with students at Texas A&M University and have been scrutinized statistically for level of difficulty, ambiguous wording, and other possible problems.

- *Thirteen Chapters.* We have retained the thirteen-chapter format, with amendments and additions, which characterized the first edition. It is relatively easy to tie a thirteen- or fourteen-week semester to a text with a similar number of chapters; that tradition we have chosen to continue.

New features include:

- *Updated Chapter One.* The decline in influence of the North American Society for the Psychology of Sport and Physical Activity and the emergence of Division 47 of the American Psychological Association and the Association for the Advancement of Sport Psychology have been pivotal. Also, much work has been done in the areas of credentialing, training, employment, and ethics over the past several years, and advances in these important areas have been addressed.

- *An Expanded Coverage of Performance Enhancement and Anxiety Reduction Techniques.* More emphasis has been placed on behavioral and cognitive behavioral interventions in the establishment and maintenance of desirable sport and fitness

behaviors as well as those applicable to the reduction of anxiety, which interferes with performance.

- *New Chapter Five.* What was once Cognitive Variables in Sport has been recast as Motivation in Sport, and additional emphasis has been placed on the social cognitive models of attribution theory as they apply to sport.

- *Revamped Chapters on Personality and Psychological Assessment.* Personality and assessment have been recast to provide a more cogent handling of the interrelationship between the two areas. Also, some of the tests described in the first edition have been dropped and others which have emerged of late have been added, particularly in the area of sport-specific tests where the state of the art is more fluid and changing.

- *Expanded Coverage of Athletes Who Abuse Drugs.* Most notably in this topic area, the athlete who abuses the anabolic-androgenic steroids is given expanded coverage.

- *Expansion of the Chapter on the Woman Athlete.* Most notable in this regard is the additional coverage granted to the role of the media in promoting or eradicating gender stereotypes in sport, the homophobia literature, and the eating disorders that all too often are found in female athletes.

As was the case with the first edition, there have been clear divisions of labor between the two authors. Arnold LeUnes is responsible for all chapters except 3 and 4, which were written by Jack Nation. At the same time, both authors have interacted on a constant basis to ensure that the content is factual, credible, contemporary, readable, and thought provoking.

Acknowledgments

Texts such as this one could not be written without the contributions made by a vast array of devoted theorists, researchers, and writers who are out there tackling the abundant and knotty problems facing sport psychology. To these dedicated men and women, we offer a hearty thanks. The contributions made by various staff members at Nelson-Hall Publishers have not gone unnoticed either. The support provided by the publisher, Steve Ferrara, is formidable and greatly appreciated. The astute editorial guidance provided by Rachel Schick was invaluable. Rachel responded courteously, promptly, and decisively to all problems that arose in the completion of the second edition, and we owe her a debt of gratitude. The selection of pictures to support the text made by Randall Nicholas was outstanding, and his contribution to the end product is substantial. Dr. Stephen Worchel, the Psychology Editor for Nelson-Hall (and our colleague in the department at Texas A&M), has played a pivotal if behind-the-scenes role in the entire proceedings. It is a delight to work with Steve, and his support is much appreciated. A final professional we would like to thank is Dr.

Carol Oglesby at Temple University who took us to task in a review of the first edition for our failure to properly deal with some facets of the female sport experience. Specifically, Dr. Oglesby pointed out that our first edition was deficient in the number of pictures devoted to women and tended, when women were included, to portray them in a negative or demeaning light. Such a portrayal was most certainly not our intent; these were errors of omission, not commission, and are not repeated in this edition.

As anyone who has undertaken a project of the magnitude of this one will readily admit, there is a price to be paid in terms of family and recreation time while revisions and updates are made. The patience and forbearance of our respective families has been most helpful. Our heartfelt thanks go out to Judy LeUnes, Leslie, Natalie, Chay, Amy, Katie, and Lyndon, and Pat Nation, Derek Nation, and Shannon, Jamie, and Hunter Harris.

A very special thanks goes to Katie Elizabeth LeUnes, born July 3, 1980, for serving as a constant and vivid reminder of the profound importance of the female sport experience.

Basic Concepts and Behavioral Principles

Introduction to Sport Psychology

Sport is adventure, personal and vicarious. It is challenge, endeavor, and relaxation. It is, too, universal, and very few people have not succumbed to its lure, either as participant or spectator.

   (Brasch, 1970)

INTRODUCTION

Our collective fascination with sports and fitness is of epic proportions. On any given Saturday afternoon in early November, hundreds of intercollegiate football teams will tee it up in front of legions of adoring and enthusiastic fans. On Sunday, the professionals will take their turn at punting and passing the proverbial pigskin. At a point geographically removed from the pandemonium of football, the professional golfers will be capping off the tour; players such as Nick Price, Greg Norman, and Fred Couples will earn well over a million dollars. Concurrently, the senior golf tour will produce its own millionaires, luminaries like Lee Trevino and Dave Stockton, Sr. Not to be outdone, seven female professionals in golf and tennis will have earnings of over a million dollars for the year. In another arena, the ageless Carl Lewis will command more than $100,000 to compete in selected track events on the European tour. While these sorts of activities are going on, labor and management negotiators will try to strike an agreement that will allow professional team owners to turn a decent profit while affording their athletically-inclined employees average annual salaries in the $1 million range (most particularly in professional baseball and basketball).

   Another area of athletic expression involves the world community. The Olympic Games, of course, represent the epitome of athletic performance among the nations of the world. Such events as the World Games and the Pan American Games serve as tune-ups for the Olympics. International competition ranging from swimming to luge is virtually an everyday event in tele-vision sports programming. Many dollars and hours of effort are expended on behalf of sport as a manifestation of national pride and prowess, and this is not likely to change in the foreseeable future.

   At another level of amateurism, children and adolescents will be plying their skills each year in a dazzling array of youth programs—city-sponsored soccer leagues, peewee football, Little League baseball, and interscholastic athletics,

Players compete in the national tournament of the Wheelchair Basketball Association in Sacramento, California.

to name only a few of the possibilites. Well over a million children are estimated to play soccer at some level or another; another sizable contingent plays baseball in one of the 8,500 leagues under Little League jurisdiction; yet another 6 million are involved in such interschool competitions as football, basketball, and baseball; the State of Texas, for example, fields almost one thousand public high school varsity football teams.

None of this takes into account the daily games or recreational events that involve so many millions, activities such as racquetball, recreational jogging, and the various aerobics exercises. The relationship of these activities to sport has been the subject of some academic argumentation, but the participants in question likely regard their activity as sport, sport as participant rather than as spectator. For a summary of sport involvement in the United States and elsewhere, see Highlight 1.1.

Clearly, many of us are participants and spectators in the tremendously varied world of sport. The broad field of sport science should therefore do everything it can to enhance understanding and enjoyment of sport of every type and at all levels of complexity. The intent of the remainder of this book is to try to convey to the reader what psychologists and allied sport scientists think they know about sport. Without a doubt, psychologists are relatively new to the scientific analysis of sport. For example, the first documented work of any magnitude relating psychology to sport in the United States was a book written in 1926 by a University of Illinois psychologist, Dr. Coleman Griffith, and entitled *The Psychology of Coaching*. Griffith followed that with a companion volume in 1928 entitled *Psychology and Athletics*. In Europe, things began a bit earlier, but for all intents and purposes sport psychology is a newcomer on the academic and applied scene, worldwide. Perhaps Browne and Mahoney (1984, p. 606) have captured the essence of this youthful state of sport psychology: "Thus raised and nurtured in infancy by the single parent called Sport Sciences, with

Sport Involvement in the United States

Highlight 1.1

ATTENDANCE (IN MILLIONS)

Auto racing　　70.4
Thoroughbred and harness racing　　69.3
College and professional football　　49.9
College and professional basketball　　43.8
Major league baseball　　48.9

TELEVISION VIEWING OF SPORTS (IN MILLIONS)

Professional football　　63.2
Baseball　　62.7
College football　　48.9
Boxing　　37.2
College basketball　　36.2

(Continued next page)

Highlight 1.1 (Continued)

Sport Involvement in the United States

MANAGEMENT

Paul Allen, co-founder of Microsoft Corporation and owner of the Portland Trailblazers, is the wealthiest owner in sport, with an estimated worth of $3.2 billion; Hiroshi Yamauachi, president of Nintendo and owner of the Seattler Mariners, is second in worth at $1.4 billion; Larry Miller, owner of the Utah Jazz, is worth $120 million (fifty-second among all owners) and has been elected to the Softball Hall of Fame as a pitcher.

In 1977, the Toronto Blue Jays and Seattle Mariners cost their respective owners $7 million and $6 million to franchise. In 1993, it cost the owners $95 million to start the Colorado Rockies and Florida Marlins franchises. The cost to team owners for the newest teams in Phoenix and Tampa-St. Petersburg (1998) has been announced at $130 million.

The most valuable franchise in all of sports is the New York Yankees, with an estimated value of $225 million.

The television contract for the 2000 Olympic Games in Sydney cost NBC $715 million; CBS paid $700,000 for the rights to televise the 1960 Rome Olympics.

Gross receipts from the NCAA men's basketball tournament rose from $1.7 million in 1972 to $145 million in 1993.

THE CHANGING FACE OF SALARIES IN PROFESSIONAL SPORTS

Average major league baseball salaries were $600,000 in 1992 and are expected to triple by 1996; twenty players commanded salaries in 1992 above $3.35 million, with Bobby Bonilla tops at $5.8 million.

The average salary in the National Basketball Association (NBA) rose from $260,000 in 1983–1984 to over $1.8 million in 1994–1995, a 700 percent increase over that time period.

Chris Webber, the number one pick in the 1993 NBA draft, signed a contract worth $74.4 million over fifteen years. Glenn Robinson, the number one pick in 1994, signed for $70 million over ten years.

Average player salaries in the National Football League (NFL) jumped from $198,000 in 1986 to $737,000 in 1993; projections are that the average will reach $1 million by 1996.

(Continued next page)

Highlight 1.1 (Continued)

Sport Involvement in the United States

The total purse on the Professional Golf Association (PGA) tour rose from $6.8 million in 1970 to $43 million in 1990; on the ladies tour (LPGA), purses grew from $5.15 million in 1980 to $12.51 million in 1988.

National Hockey League (NHL) salaries averaged $100,000 in 1992–1993 and are expected to go up to $400,000 by 1996; Mark Messier of the New York Rangers commands an annual salary of $6 million.

Sinjin Smith, Randy Stoklos, Karch Kiraly, Brent Frohoff, Tim Hovland, and Kent Steffes (in descending order of earnings) collected nearly $1 million on the professional two-man beach volleyball season in 1990; prize money for this sport has risen 48-fold since 1980.

MISCELLANEOUS

In the 1970s, Nike paid Oregon basketball coach Jim Harter $2,500 for a shoe endorsement deal; Mike Krzyzewski of Duke makes $400,000-plus per year for his deal with Nike. All told, sixty major college basketball programs are listed as "Nike schools."

Bob McAdoo was the highest paid rookie in the NBA in 1972 ($333,000); 1993's top rookie, Shaquille O'Neal, is paid that much money every ten league games.

Heavyweight boxing champion Evander Holyfield made over $60 million in 1991 alone; Mike Tyson earned $31 million that same year.

Basketball legend Michael Jordan made an estimated $40 million in endorsements in 1993, $20 million from Nike and $20 million from other sources. As a further illustration of Jordan's economic impact on sport, corporations whose product he endorsed reported the following surges immediately following the rumor of his pending return to the Chicago Bulls team in early 1995: Nike stock went up 3.3 percent; General Mills, 4.8 percent; McDonald's, 4.6 percent; Sara Lee, 4.4 percent; and Quaker Oats, 1.2 percent. Another indicator of the influence Jordan exerts concerns his drawing power at the gate, even in a sport at which he did not excel, baseball. In 1994, Jordan played minor league baseball for the Nashville, Tennessee, franchise; home game attendance jumped from 277,000 in 1993 to 467,000 the following year, a substantial gain undoubtedly related to his presence on the field.

In 1945, Byron Nelson won eleven consecutive PGA events, earning $30,000 in the process. Winning the same number of corresponding events today would result in earnings of $3 million.

(Continued next page)

Highlight 1.1 (Continued)

Sport Involvement in the United States

At the end of 1993, ten PGA golfers reported career earnings of over $5.5 million, with Tom Kite the leader at $7.7 million. On the LPGA, only Betsy King had surpassed the $5 million figure.

Fifty women's professional tennis players won over $100,000 on the World Tennis Association tour in 1994; Arantxa Sanchez Vicario was tops at $2.05 million. Steffi Graf and Conchita Martinez both won over a million dollars.

The average coaching salary in the NBA in 1992 was $450,000; Pat Riley of the New York Knicks led at $1.2 million.

Six college football coaches were paid nearly $5 million in the early 1990s *not* to coach the remaining years of their respective contracts due to a poor win-loss record; The University of Pittsburgh spent over $2 million in buying out three consecutive unsuccessful coaches.

First round choices in the 1994 NFL draft earned over $60 million in signing bonuses alone; salaries for these twenty-nine players will exceed over $175 million over the eight years of the various contracts.

Thirty-two million viewers watched the 1994 World Cup soccer match between the United States and Brazil.

Overall, sports betting is a $57 billion industry; some estimate the figure to be closer to $100 million due to the difficulty of assessing the magnitude of illegal betting. Gambling on sports in Las Vegas has grown from $360 million wagered in 1980–1981 to almost 1.5 billion in 1989–1990.

Suiting up a high school football player in safe equipment costs $276; a soccer player can be outfitted for $54.

The average tab in 1992 for four people to watch the NBA Los Angeles Lakers play at home was $258, assuming expenditures involving four average-priced tickets, four hot dogs, four soft drinks, two beers, two souvenirs, and parking fees; the league average was $142.

Serious training in ice skating can cost $40,000 per year for coaching fees, costumes, skates, and living expenses.

Over the past three decades, sports franchises have grown from sixteen to thirty in major league baseball, twelve to twenty-seven in the NBA, thirteen to twenty-nine in the NFL, and six to fourteen in the NHL.

Saddle bronc riders Robert, Billy, and Dan Etbauer of South Dakota have combined career earnings of over $1.7 million on the professional rodeo circuit.

Source: *Inside Sports; Sports Illustrated; Time;* and *USA Today.*

a modicum of child support from the (largely unrecognized) parent called Psychology, this exciting toddler named Sport Psychology is now attracting considerable professional and public attention." This youthfulness notwithstanding, let us proceed to some definitional matters that will help us understand just how sport and psychology have become so interrelated.

PSYCHOLOGY DEFINED

Psychology as a scientific discipline began in 1879, in the research laboratory of Wilhelm Wundt in Leipzig, Germany, making it one of the youngest of all the sciences. Some question whether psychology is, in fact, a science at all. These dissenters typically point to the relative sophistication of physics or chemistry to illustrate and strengthen their claims. However, a science is not necessarily measured by the extent of its knowledge base or by its age; rather, the method (the scientific method) used to arrive at its data base should be the critical determinant of what is and what is not a science. Anderson (1966, p. 4) defines the method as "the following of a set of rules for describing and explaining phenomenon: operational definition, generality, controlled observation, repeated observations, confirmation and consistency." Carrying Anderson's definition one step beyond, the role of prediction in science should not be

Table 1.1
Major Subareas of Psychology

Specialty	Major Focus/Interest	Percentage
Clinical	Study causes, diagnose, and treat behavioral disorders.	44%
Counseling	Assist people in dealing with problems of everyday living (i.e., career, education, anxieties, family problems).	11
Educational/School	Assess and remediate behavioral problems in school settings (i.e., special education, emotionally disturbed students, career counseling).	11
Experimental	Conduct basic and applied research in core areas of psychology, such as learning, motivation, cognition, and physiological psychology.	9
Industrial/Organizational	Assist in making the workplace more productive and satisfying for all personnel (i.e., selection, retention, morale, leadership).	6
Developmental	Study life-span issues, such as moral, social, motor, and intellectual development.	4
Social/Personality	Study individual and group differences.	4
Other (Ergonomics, Environmental, Neuroscience, Psychopharmacology, Sport)	Varied activities depending on subarea.	11

omitted or underestimated; indeed, being able to accurately predict future events related to sport would constitute a rather utopian state.

Definitions of psychology prior to the 1950s stressed that psychology was the study of mental activity. Most definitions in the 1950s and 1960s emphasized that it is the scientific study of behavior, human or animal, with the latter contributing to generalizations about the former. Then an interesting transformation in our collective thinking occurred; it became obvious that neither definitional stance was inclusive enough to capture the essence of the human organism. Hence, we witnessed the emergence of a definition that led to a marriage of the two positions:

> Psychology is usually defined as the scientific study of behavior. Its subject matter includes behavioral processes that are observable, such as gestures, speech, and physiological changes, and processes that can only be inferred as thoughts and dreams. (Clark and Miller, 1970)

Benjamin, Hopkins, and Nation define *psychology* similarly, but more succinctly as "the systematic study of behavior and mental processes" (1994, p. 2). They point out that their definition recognizes the significance of objectively studying behavior, yet it allows for the importance of mental processes that are more inferred than observed. They also say that devoting an inordinate amount of time to definitions can be counterproductive, and suggest that "we can get a better idea of what psychology is from looking at what psychologists do" (p. 15). We shall take heed of this admonition and do exactly as they suggest.

Psychologists are called upon today to serve in a diverse number of specialties and in an ever-increasing variety of settings. Table 1.1 and figure 1.1 will give the reader a feeling for this diversity of *specialties within professional psychology.*

Figure 1.1: **Facts about the Profession of Psychology**

Work Settings

36 percent of all psychologists work in academic settings

22 percent work in independent practice

17 percent work in hospitals and/or clinics

12 percent work in business or for governmental agencies

6 percent work in counseling and guidance centers

5 percent work for school systems

2 percent report "Other" as work setting

Gender Issues

30 percent of all Ph.D. holders in psychology are females

50+ percent of all master's degrees in psychology are held by females

50+ percent of all graduate students in psychology are female

36 percent of the membership of APA are females

20 percent of the membership of APA Division 47, Exercise and Sport Psychology, are females

Minority Issues

Blacks, Hispanics, and Asians make up 5 percent of the APA membership

2.2 percent of research psychologists and 2.3 percent of college professors are black

Source: 1993 APA Membership Register.

SPORT DEFINED

Sport is not characterized by a universally accepted definition. The interplay of sport with games, recreation, and play is such that a concise, universally agreed upon definition is difficult to piece together. A summary of the problem of differentiating these various activities is provided by Zeigler (1973, pp. 345–346), who states:

In the 1967 *Random House Dictionary,* for example, the word "sport" is used thirteen ways as a noun, two ways as an adjective, six ways as an intransitive verb, and five ways as a transitive verb. Thus, we will offer here only two definitions which seem to be most applicable to the topic at hand:

1. an athletic activity requiring skill or physical prowess and often of a competitive nature, as racing, baseball, tennis, golf, etc.
2. diversion; recreation; pleasant pastime. The reader can be thankful that play, game, and athletics aren't being defined, as there are 74 ways in which the word "play" is used, and the terms "game" and "athletics" are employed in 23 and three ways, respectively.

On a similar but more elaborate note, Nixon (1984, p. 14) makes distinctions among play, recreation, games, and sport, and these differentiations may be seen in figure 1.2. To Nixon, *play* might be represented by children kicking a ball back and forth or engaging in a snowball fight, the latter being of some historical significance as we shall see in chapter 2. *Recreation* might be personified by jogging or holiday skiing. *Games* are more formalized than either play or recreation, and a "pickup" game of basketball or a soccer match between neighborhood groups would be examples. As for *sport,* he says: "Sport is defined as an institutionalized competitive activity involving two or more opponents and stressing physical exertion by serious competitors who represent or are part of formally organized associations" (p. 13). Nixon further states that an activity is sport when "(a) it is characterized by relatively persistent patterns of social organization; (b) it is serious competition (whose outcome is not pre-arranged) between two or more opponents; (c) it stresses the physical skill factor; and (d) it occurs within a formal organizational framework of teams, leagues, divisions,

Figure 1.2: **Distinctions among Types of Physical Activities**

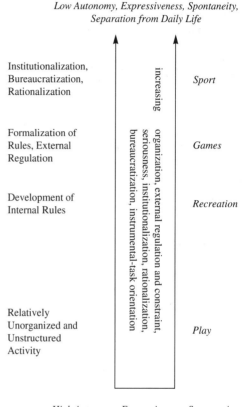

Source: Nixon (1984).

coaches, commissioners, sponsorship, formalized recruitment and replacement of personnel, rule books, and regulatory bodies." A definitional stance that more closely approximates the spirit of this book is offered by Spears and Swanson (1983, p. 3):

> Sport will be considered to be the activities involving powers and skill, competition, strategy and/or chance, and engaged in for

the enjoyment and satisfaction of the participant and/or others. This definition includes both organized sport and sport for recreational purposes. It clearly includes the component of sport as entertainment, which encompasses professional sport.

Harry Edwards (1973, pp. 57–58), the sport sociologist, defines sport as "activities having formally recorded histories and traditions, stressing physical exertion through competition within limits set in explicit and formal governing role and position relationships, and carried out by actors who represent or who are part of formally organized associations having the goal of achieving valued tangibles and intangibles through defeating opposing groups." Singer (1976, p. 40), in a fashion similar to that of Edwards, sees sport as "a human activity that involves specific administrative organization and a historical background of rules which define the objective and limit the patterns of human behavior; it involves competition and/or challenge and a definite outcome primarily determined by physical skill.

If we accept the ideas proposed by Nixon, Spears and Swanson, Edwards, and Singer, certain definitional properties of sport emerge. Among them are:

1. Any definition of sport is going to be possessed of a certain degree of ambiguity.
2. Rules or limits are an important part of the definitional process.
3. The role of history in defining sport seems to be most relevant.
4. The role of victory and defeat is a clear-cut aspect of defining sport.
5. Emphasis is placed on the physical exertion factor in competition.

Although the definitions mentioned to this point have considerable merit, they all fall short of the one we would propose, namely, a definition that incorporates a "*sport for all*" spirit. In a broadly conceived definition, the youngster in peewee football, the high school football star, the collegiate gymnast, the professional athlete, the Olympian, the summer slowpitch softball player who is competing with her friends, and the jogger who is merely trying to maintain fitness are all sport participants. It is in the spirit of "sport for all" that the remainder of this book will proceed.

SPORT PSYCHOLOGY DEFINED

Defining sport psychology is a difficult task at best, and there has not been agreement on the problem to date. Perhaps the first definitional attempt is that of Morgan (1972), who suggests that sport psychology is "the study of psychological foundations of physical activity." In a more expansive mode, Sleet (1972) indicates that sport psychology is not limited to the study of athletes or behavior in athletic competition. Sport psychology research is also interested in acquiring knowledge about crowd behavior, rehabilitation and therapy through physical activity, motor skill acquisition, play group dynamics, readiness, proprioception, motor educability, body image, personality, physical ability, and the phenomenology of movement. Singer (1978) intimates that sport psychology involves the application of the science of psychology to sport. Similarly, Tutko (1979) says that sport psychology in the study of behavior as it relates to sport. Cratty (1983) refers to sport psychology as an applied subdivision of general psychology. While there are points of general agreement among these various definitional stances, Whiting's (1974) reference to the situation as a regular "ragbag" is descriptive even today.

An alternative perspective on this issue, and a reasonably straightforward one, is succinctly

Dr. Norman Shealy (left) *gives lessons on relaxation to the University of Wisconsin football team.*

advocated by Martens (1980), who suggests that we operationally define sport psychology as what sport psychologists do. This simplistic stance is proposed because Martens feels that sport psychology is too premature in its development to worry about a definition that is universally accepted. He further warns us that definitions arising from the podium (academia) are insufficient, and that good solid research in sport settings rather than laboratories should ultimately provide a sounder definition. The biggest flaw in Martens' reasoning, and one that will appear from time to time throughout this book, has to do with the problem of defining just *who* sport psychologists are; certainly no consensus exists on this question.

A lively exchange concerning definitional issues continues. For instance, Dishman (1983) points to an identity crisis in North American sport psychology. He argues that the defining of sport psychology as what sport psychologists do shortchanges the profession and hinders the development of useful theoretical and research models that are needed for the advancement of the discipline. He further calls for the creation of sport-related psychological models rather than a continued reliance on the time-honored clinical or educational models that have dominated sport psychology theory, research, and practice.

In view of the considerable ambiguity and argumentation about definitional matters, we shall accept, with reservations, the definition proposed by Martens. The caveat forwarded by Dishman, however, must be recognized. Clearly, no field of endeavor, inside or external to psychology, can prosper without increasing the sophistication of its theoretical, research, and applied bases. A compelling need exists to press on in the search for sport-related models that define the domain of sport psychology and, in turn, generate research and application that enhances the credibility of sport psychology as a valid scientific undertaking that can make a contribution to sport, worldwide.

WHAT DO SPORT PSYCHOLOGISTS DO?

Granting the acceptance of Martens' definition of sport psychology with all the attendant reservations, it seems appropriate to address our attention to exactly what it is that sport psychologists do. Of course, many teach and conduct research within university environments; others operate in a more applied milieu. One perspective on what both academic and applied sport psychologists do is provided by Nideffer, DuFresne, Nesvig, and Selder (1980, pp. 171–172). They state:

Sport psychologists are being asked to perform the following functions:

1. To *develop performance improvement programs.* This can be accomplished in a number of ways. Techniques like biofeedback, meditation, cognitive behavior modification, attention control training, mental rehearsal, progressive relaxation, autogenic training, hypnosis, and self-hypnosis are used to give the athlete greater control over physiological arousal and concentration.

2. To *use psychological assessment techniques,* including behavioral assessment, paper-and-pencil inventories, psycho-physiological measures, and interviews for the selection, screening, and counseling of athletes.

3. To *improve communication* between athlete–coach, athlete–athlete, and coach–coach through the use of tests, group techniques, and individual consultation. The sport psychologist must be sensitive to the entire system or organizational structure in which both coach and athlete function; that is, they must be sensitive to the needs of each part of the system, yet be able to relate to all parts in an effective and ethical manner.

4. To *provide crisis intervention services.* At critical times, athletes or coaches may be temporarily unable to function, and the sport psychologist may be needed to help them quickly regain control.

5. To *provide consultative and program development services* for coaches, trainers, and others who work directly with athletes. Many times sport psychologists do not have the necessary relationship to provide services directly to athletes. The presence of the psychologist may be threatening and can interfere with the relationship coaches have with their athletes. Under these conditions, the sport psychologist may be more effective by teaching and supervising others in the delivery of service.

6. To *function as a therapist* or clinical psychologist. Frequently sport psychologists are asked to provide clinical rather than educational services. Although sport psychologists should be trained to recognize when an athlete has a severe psychological problem, they should not attempt to treat it. Instead, they should make a referral to a clinical psychologist or a psychiatrist who has experience working with athletes. The needs of the system or team are often in conflict with the needs of a severely disturbed athlete, and the sport psychologist who attempt to serve two masters will end up in a conflict of interest, losing both trust and credibility.

Reasons for Sport Psychology

Why sport psychology? The answers to this question are numerous and reflect world-wide and time-honored fascination with sport and fitness. From the time of the early Greeks, and their emphasis on sport as an expression of beauty, to today, sport has occupied a prominent place in virtually every society. At least six factors have contributed to the evolution of the sport psychology profession.

1. *The pursuit of excellence by athletes.* There are many indications that athletes are open to virtually anything that will allow them to perform at higher and higher levels. Performance enhancement techniques drawn from psychology have been applied widely. Unfortunately, this pursuit of excellence has a down side in the form of steroids, blood doping, and the use of stimulant drugs, to name just a few questionable practices.

2. *Sport as a political tool.* From the time of the first Olympic Games in 776 B.C., athletic achievement has been used as a means of promoting political ends, and the picture remains the same today. Sport psychologists are increasingly being asked by national governing bodies to assist in the development of elite athletes who will serve as international spokespersons for their country.

3. *High salaries in sport.* The fact that sport has become big business, one with a lot of money at stake, has helped propel sport psychology to the forefront. Superstar athletes and athletic organizations have prevailed upon sport psychologists to assist them in their search for excellence.

4. *Recognition gained from sport.* Sport can be viewed as a means of enhancing recognition and resultant feelings of self-worth; there is every reason to believe that sport psychology has something to offer in this regard. One of the proper functions of psychology, and therefore sport psychology, is to assist people in the creation and maintenance of self-esteem.

5. *Spectator interest.* Millions of people are regular viewers of some sort of sport-related activity. The sport psychologist can enhance the value of this facet of sport by helping athletes maximize their talents as well as contributing to spectator enjoyment through, for example, suggestions for controlling violence at sport events. At the same time, efforts must be expended to make participation enjoyable too, so that we do not become a world of watchers rather than doers.

6. *The fitness movement.* Our fascination with athletics tends to obscure a significant facet of the human existence, that of the many manifestations of fitness. The sport psychologist has much to offer in terms of techniques for improving fitness and fitness activities as well as procedures for making the experience enjoyable enough to insure high rates of life-long dedication to personal betterment through exercise.

Obviously, sport psychologists are called upon to possess a myriad of skills, and at least two problems arise as a result. One has to do with training, and the other with ethical provision of services. As the reader has already noted, these are not totally separate issues. However, the training issue is focused on just who a sport psychologist is in terms of educational background. Must one be a Ph.D. with a license to practice psychology in order to function as a sport psychologist? Or can qualified physical educators practice sport psychology? (For the remainder of the book, we shall use physical education to refer to those professionals from assorted departments of kinesiology, sport science, exercise science, movement science, and so forth.) The ethics issue relates more to performing within one's training and capabilities. In any event, these are critical issues that will be dealt with later.

Before we leave this topic, some mention should be made of the U.S. Olympic Committee, which is acutely aware of the demands of

---

Figure 1.3: **U.S. Olympic Committee Recommendations for Sport Psychologist Status**

A group of sport psychologists met in 1982 to make recommendations to the U.S. Olympic Committee (USOC) concerning appropriate sport psychology practice related to those sports under USOC jurisdiction. They concluded that sport psychologists work in three broad areas—clinical, educational, and research—and the academic and training qualifications they recommended for each were as follows:

Clinical Sport Psychologist
- Degree in clinical/counseling psychology or psychiatry from an American Psychological Association accredited or Liaison Committee on Medical Education (LCME) accredited university.
- Meets the standards required for full membership in the American Psychological Association/American Psychiatric Association.
- Psychologists must have a current license/certification. Psychiatrists must have a current license and be board-eligible in psychiatry. In addition, psychiatrists must be prescreened as having met minimum standards set for physicians engaged in USOC Sports Medicine programs.
- Demonstrated experience as an athlete or coach or practitioner in the application of psychological principles to sports.
- A personal interview with a Review Board member(s), if requested.

Educational Sport Psychologist
- A doctorate in psychology or psychiatry or in a related field with background in psychology that would meet the standards required for full membership in the American Psychological Association.
- At least three years of demonstrated postdoctoral experience as an athlete or coach or practitioner in the application of psychological principles to sports.
- Reference letters from recognized institutions/organizations related to the applicant's teaching educational facilitation skills.
- Personal interview with a Review Board member(s), if requested.

Research Sport Psychologist
- A doctorate in psychology or psychiatry or in a related field with a background in psychology that would meet the standards required for full membership in the American Psychological Association in accordance with established guidelines.
- Evidence of scholarly research contributions to the field of sport psychology.
- Reference letters from recognized institutions/organizations related to research conducted by applicant.
- A personal interview with a Review Board member(s), if requested.

Source: U.S. Olympic Committee (1983).

being a sport psychologist and, concurrently, cognizant of the fact that no psychologist is capable of providing all of the services mentioned by Nideffer and his colleagues. More specifically, we are referring to a task force of eminent sport authorities who met in Colorado Springs, Colorado, in 1982 to draw up recommendations for the practice of sport psychology in the sports under the jurisdiction of the U.S. Olympic Committee (U.S. Olympic Committee, 1983). This panel of professionals (Kenneth Clarke, Russell Copelan, Dorothy Harris, Daniel Landers, Rainer Martens, Jerry May, William Morgan, Robert Nideffer, Bruce Ogilvie, Richard Suinn, Denis Waitley, and Betty Wenz) identified three broad areas engaged in by sport psychologists:

Clinical. Helping athletes who experience severe emotional problems and where intervention continues over an extended period of time. Examples of such problems include depression, anorexia, and panic. Clinical services also include crisis intervention, which involves helping an athlete who is in need of immediate intervention for an emotionally severe problem. Examples include helping a team member(s) who is experiencing interpersonal conflicts and an athlete who is experiencing severe stress at the competitive site. Clinical services also include helping individuals achieve personal growth — for example, preparation of career termination, coping with sudden success, and dealing with peer relationships.

Educational. Helping athletes to develop the psychological skills necessary for optimal participation in the sport. Examples include teaching athletes relaxation, concentration, and imagery skills. Educational services also emphasize providing athletes with information that will enhance their participation in the sport. These generally are group-delivered rather than provided through individual athlete training.

Research. Research was designated as a separate component, although it is under-stood that research is inherent in clinical and educational activities. The important role that research plays in the total development of sport psychology activities was recognized. Within the USOC, a Human Subject Review Panel will be used to assure that HEW guidelines are followed. (U.S. Olympic Committee, 1985, p. 5)

Although they state things in a slightly different format, the Nideffer et al. group and the Colorado Springs task force seem to generally agree on the issue of what a sport psychologist does or should be able to do. An elaboration on the USOC-defined areas of expertise can be seen in figure 1.3.

PROFESSIONAL ISSUES IN SPORT PSYCHOLOGY

There are a number of complex and problematic professional issues that must be successfully confronted if sport psychology is to move ahead as a profession. Chief among them are credentialing, training, employment, ethics, and the image of sport psychology. Each issue will be discussed in turn.

Credentialing

Zaichkowsky and Perna (1992) suggest that the nomenclature associated with the credentialing process is confusing, ambiguous, and in need of clarification. Accordingly, they indicate that distinctions can be made between credentialing, certification, registry, and licensure, and it is important to note these distinctions before moving on because they will guide subsequent discussion. *Credentialing* is a broad, generic term used in various professional fields to grant recognition or certification to their respective members. As such, credentialing involves both statutory and nonstatutory designations. *Certification* is generally a nonstatutory designation granted by an organization rather than a statutory body; certification by professional organizations within sport psychology (discussed later in this chapter) serves as an example. *Registry* is a nonstatutory designation indicating professional recognition; the United States Olympic Registry, discussed elsewhere in this chapter, is an example. As for *licensure,* it is a restrictive, statutory process designed to regulate member conduct; the licensing of physicians and psychologists represent two areas in which this process is applicable.

The problem of how to credential sport psychologists and by whom has remained a knotty one within the field, though considerable clarification has emerged over the past several years. Several factors contribute to the credentialing problem. One is the licensure of psychologists. All fifty states and the eight Canadian provinces have implemented licensure laws that greatly restrict psychological practice to those individuals who have relatively narrow academic training in psychology and who have passed the licensing examination. By the nature of the way these laws are written, it would be a rare physical educator within sport psychology who would qualify educationally and experientially to become a licensed practitioner in psychology.

Early on, the licensure problem generated considerable discussion (Brown, 1982; Danish and Hale, 1981; Danish and Smyer, 1981; Dishman, 1983; Gross, 1978; Harrison and Feltz, 1979; Heyman, 1982; Nideffer, Feltz, and Salmela, 1982). The major source of concern expressed by these various authorities centered around potential violations of the licensure laws associated with sport psychology practice; caution was urged pending greater clarification of the licensure issue.

Now that the dust has settled a bit, it appears that the addition of the word *sport* in front of the word "psychologist" does not circumvent the law or render it inapplicable; that is, the word *psychologist*, alone or in combination with other words, is protected by law. Con-

sequently, only licensed psychologists are eligible to call themselves sport psychologists, but this situation is operable only when the psychologist in question is offering his or her services to the public. University professors not offering their services to the public can call themselves sport psychologists and stay within the spirit of the licensure statutes. The net effect of all of this dialogue on licensure is that closure has been obtained about the use of the term *sport psychologist*. However, because of the sizable number of people in the field of sport psychology who come from physical education backgrounds, there exists the potential for disenfranchisement of these valued professionals.

In an attempt to deal with this potential disenfranchisement problem, the Association for the Advancement of Applied Sport Psychology (AAASP), a professional organization for sport psychologists (discussed at greater length later), has created an ambitious alternative to licensure/credentialing. Beginning January 1, 1991, AAASP created a credentialing mechanism for sport psychologists that confers upon qualified persons the title "Certified Consultant, AAASP" ("AAASP passes . . . ," 1990). The AAASP certification process serves a number of useful functions. First of all, it sets a tone that conveys to coaches, athletes, and other concerned individuals or groups that the person possessing certification has met rigorous educational and experiential standards. Secondly, well-trained professionals in the field are granted recognition through the AAASP Registry. Third, the process affords credibility to the profession. Finally, the certification process is a step forward in educating the public about the field, and thus serves as a good public relations vehicle.

The criteria for certification as an AAASP Consultant are numerous and stringent, including:

1. Completion of a doctoral degree from an accredited university.

2. Knowledge of professional ethics.
3. Knowledge of sport psychology subdisciplines, such as intervention/performance enhancement, exercise psychology, and social psychology.
4. Knowledge of biomechanics, exercise psychology, and kinesiology.
5. Knowledge of historical and philosophical roots of sport and physical education.
6. Knowledge of psychopathology.
7. Training in counseling to include course work and supervised practica.
8. Supervision in applied sport psychology under direction of trained person.
9. Knowledge of assessment and intervention techniques.
10. Knowledge of statistics and research design.
11. Knowledge of biological bases of behavior.
12. Knowledge of cognitive/affective bases of behavior.
13. Knowledge of social psychology and sociology of sport.
14. Knowledge of individual differences through course work in areas such as developmental psychology and personality.

As can be seen from the preceding elaboration, the training required for AAASP certification is comprehensive and interdisciplinary. At the same time, it is realistic in terms of what should be required of a person working with athletes and/or teams. In support of this point, Zaichkowsky and Perna indicate that being trained in medicine or psychology is not sufficient grounds for AAASP certification, as some would like to believe; the sport- and exercise-related training must also be there. Zaichkowsky and Perna point to recent certification statistics to substantiate their argument. A review of seventy-two applications for certification in 1991 showed that thirty-two received doctorates in psychology or medicine; only eleven were certified. The other forty applicants received their training in physical education and related areas, and thirty-one were granted certification.

Arriving at these comprehensive standards and getting the approval of the AAASP membership took approximately five years, and approval was granted after much vehement but professional argumentation. Even after the enactment of the AAASP certification process, counterviews have emerged. Chief spokesperson for the counterview is Anshel (1992, 1993), who states that the certification process is perhaps the most controversial issue in contemporary applied sport psychology. Anshel contends that the certification process is flawed on at least two counts, one concerning its exclusionary nature and the other having to do with the past preoccupation with the clinical model as a means of establishing the validity of sport psychology. In summarizing his views, Anshel suggests that professionals in the field need to stop fighting over credentialing issues and get on with the business of providing athletes and coaches with services that are within their competencies. Zaichkowsky and Perna (1992) have taken Anshel to task over his views, throwing their support in the direction of the AAASP certification process. Past AAASP presidents Gould (1990) and Silva (1989) are also highly supportive of the credentialing process, and see it as a major step forward in establishing the overall validity of sport psychology. While siding with some aspects of the dissident view of Anshel, it is our contention that the AAASP standards represent the state of the art at this time in the credentialing of sport psychologists.

Training

Effective training in theory, research, and practice is crucial to the future success of sport psychology. How training is to be accomplished and by whom remains unclear. Departments of psychology have shown little willingness to become involved at any meaningful level, and the variations in training in physical education departments appears to be substantial. There appears to be no consensus as to what constitutes good training; to this point, Lutz (1990, p. 63) says, "the education and training process of sport psychologists has been, for the most part, an unplanned process."

Lutz thinks that training models used in medical schools or colleges of business might have something to offer in training future sport psychologists. Approaches that might be used include the *critical incident method* employed by many medical schools and borrowed from industrial/organizational psychology. Here, critical incidents common to practitioners in the field would be assessed and synthesized to isolate those skills useful to sport psychology. Secondly, the *case study approach* could be used. Major institutions such as Harvard have made much use of this method in their business programs. There is some evidence, according to Lutz, that some medical schools are also making more use of this didactic device. Finally, *mentoring* would be a vital part of the training process. It is used extensively in sport psychology research, but it is Lutz's contention that mentoring is equally applicable to clinical, educational, and consultative activities.

Straub and Hinman (1992) interviewed what they considered to be ten of the leading sport psychologists in North America, and one of the issues addressed was graduate training. One of those interviewed, Bob Nideffer, took the stance that future students wanting to call themselves sport psychologists should all be trained in clinical or counseling psychology, with additional training in the sport science area. Most authorities, however, disagree with Nideffer and suggest that variations in background may be good to the extent that the heterogeneity may serve sport psychologists in academia or research quite well. Several of the individuals interviewed by Straub and Hinman stressed the importance of mentoring, and suggested that students make a concerted effort to match their personalities and professional interests with those of professors with whom they would like to work. Again, these

suggestions are sound but do not constitute a comprehensive solution to the training problem.

One issue that emerges over and over in the literature, and one very much related to training, is that of territoriality. Almost all who write about the future of sport psychology stress the need for harmony and cooperation between psychology and the sport sciences. There are real dangers associated with the sort of mentality alluded to by Dan Gould in his 1989 AAASP Presidential address (Gould, 1990) in which psychologists subtly verbally abuse their physical education cohorts for knowing sport but not much psychology and physical educators blast their psychology counterparts for knowing their psychology but not much about sport and fitness. A climate of backbiting and distrust is created by such pettiness, and does little to advance the profession of sport psychology.

By way of summary, Silva (1989) has suggested an amalgamation of much of what has been said to this point. Critical to the success of the field of sport psychology is the absence of territoriality battles; it is Silva's wish that by the year 2000, no discussion will take place concerning the department in which a sport psychologist is trained. To accomplish this, according to Silva, there should be collaboration among psychology and physical education departments as well as among the various professional organizations with a vested interest in the future of the discipline. Also, there should be diversity in training that takes into account whether an individual wants to be a researcher or a practitioner. For those wanting to work in applied sport psychology, intervention observations, supervised experiences with interventions, and structured internships would be essential. This sort of training model would certainly remedy some of the service delivery problems alluded to by Waite and Pettit (1993).

At this time, a number of generalities are being addressed about training but less is transpiring with regard to specifics. It is our belief that much clarification will take place in this important area over the next decade. The task is a bit daunting, but must be addressed for the betterment of the field.

Employment

Despite evidence suggesting that sport psychology is on the ascent in terms of visibility and general acceptance, the employment picture is less than reassuring. In discussing employment prospects, Gifford (1991) says that there are limited opportunities in the sport psychology field and that obtaining a job is the end product of a combination of ability, training, luck, and considerable self-promotion. Gifford goes on to say that there are a few jobs to be found in academia each year, and an unknown, but undoubtedly small, number in the so-called marketplace. It has been reported by an unknown source at one of the national sport psychology conferences that only six people in the United States are making a living exclusively from money earned in sport psychology. Assuming that this statement is true, it makes for a bleak employment picture, particularly for young people considering careers as sport psychologists.

Though the employment issue is a critical one, surprisingly little enlightenment is found in the available research. In a recent study, Waite and Pettit (1993) conducted a survey of graduates of sport psychology programs for the period 1984–1989, and some interesting observations emerged. After considerable effort to obtain subjects, Waite and Pettit were able to analyze responses from thirty-four individuals equally divided by gender. The following points emerged from their analyses:

1. All but two of the graduates received their doctoral degree from a physical education department.
2. Most of the graduates reported satisfaction with their generally diverse work lives.
3. About half of the respondents were working in some capacity with athletes, though the work was unstable and low in financial return.
4. Almost two-thirds of the work conducted was in teaching and research at the college level.
5. Women made considerably less money than did men in this sample. Overall, women made 74 percent of what men did, with men averaging slightly above $41,000 and women nearly $31,000.
6. There was a marked absence among the respondents of formalized practica supervision in their doctoral training. For example, eighteen respondents reported going through a doctoral program emphasizing intervention or performance enhancement, and eight of them received no practical supervision in their supposed area of expertise as students.
7. 76 percent of the graduates saw no advantage to having licensure, and 47 percent felt no need for AAASP certification.

The Waite and Pettit data suggest several noteworthy conclusions. First of all, there *are* jobs out there for sport psychologists, primarily as academics. It is our suspicion that the other major avenue for becoming engaged in the delivery of sport psychology services is through private practice in psychology, unless one is willing to work at a pay level that is not commensurate with the attainment of a doctoral degree. It is also likely that only a part of the private practice could be devoted to athletes or teams. The marketplace at this time simply will not support much full-time work in sport psychology. Second, there are substantial gender inequities in wages, and these discrepancies need to be addressed. Third, the absence of formal practica training while in graduate school raises serious concerns about whether or not a number of people in sport psychology are truly qualified to work with athletes and teams. Fourth, there is a decided reluctance to support sport psychology efforts in the world external to academia; coaches and athletes want the services, but are quite unwilling to support the enterprise financially. Finally, the lack of concern for licensure or certification among the graduates surveyed is disconcerting, though the fact that many of them were employed in academia somewhat obviates the need for such credentialing. Nevertheless, aspects of these data suggest that credentialing will remain a contentious issue for some time.

Ethics

The establishment, implementation, and oversight of ethical principles to guide psychologists and sport psychologists is not an easy task. Some fifteen years ago, Nideffer (1981) brought the issue to the forefront of sport psychology literature. It was his intimation at that time that ethical guidelines would be unnecessary if all of us were possessed of the highest of ideals and standards of conduct. Given that we do not live in such a perfect world, it is necessary to forge standards of ethical conduct to guide professionals in virtually every professional field. The North American Society for the Psychology of Sport and Physical Activity (NASPSPA) has long been an advocate of accepting those ethical principles set forth by the American Psychological Association (APA). With the creation of the Association for the Advancement of Applied Psychology (AAASP) in 1986, the onerous task of creating ethical principles specific to sport psychology has been a high priority for that organization. As is the case with NASPSPA, the APA ethical principles and code of conduct have emerged as those with which the ethics task force of AAASP can most readily identify. As has been pointed out in a recent AAASP Newsletter, over fifty other organizational codes were studied, including those of the American College of Sports Medicine (ACSM), before settling on a model that fashions itself after the APA

recommendations. It must be understood that the membership of AAASP has not accepted the ethical principle at this point in time, but closure on the issue appears to be near at hand. If accepted, the ethics statement would include a preamble essentially stating that sport psychologists would commit themselves philosophically and in practice to act ethically, encourage ethical behavior in students and allied colleagues, and consult with others should questions arise about proper professional conduct that are not covered in stated ethical guidelines. The proposed ethics document also includes six general principles for ideal professional conduct.

The principles for ideal professional conduct are based on the broad guidelines established by APA. While serving a very useful purpose, the principles are not always specific enough to be useful and are in no way binding until the AAASP membership formally adopts them, assuming such action takes place.

There are a number of stumbling blocks associated with the implementation of ethical principles, particularly the first two, which deal with competence and integrity. With regard to the competence issue, Keith-Speigel and Koocher (1985) are among those who are skeptical of the vague wording that makes it extremely difficult to truly identify incompetent practice. In this connection, Pope and Vasquez (1991) have pointed out that professionals are not particularly reliable evaluators of their own strengths and limitations. Taylor (1994) further highlights concerns about competence related to psychologically based or sport-related skills, which vary considerably among clinical psychologists and physical educators, an ongoing squabble alluded to earlier in this chapter.

Another ethical concern that has drawn a lot of interest of late falls under the second principle, integrity, with a focus on the nagging problem of dual relationships. Buceta (1993), Ellickson and Brown (1990), and Whelan (1994) have been very vocal in their concern about dual

The Six Principles of Professional Conduct for Sport Psychologists

PRINCIPLE A: COMPETENCE

AAASP members strive to maintain the highest standards of competence in their work. They recognize the boundaries of their particular competencies and the limitations of their expertise. They maintain knowledge related to the services they render, and they recognize the need for ongoing education. AAASP members make appropriate use of scientific, professional, technical, and administrative resources. They provide only those services and use only those techniques for which they are qualified by education, training, or experience. AAASP members are cognizant of the fact that the competencies required in serving, teaching, and/or studying groups of people vary with the distinctive characteristics of those groups. In those areas in which recognized professional standards do not yet exist, AAASP members exercise careful judgment and take appropriate precautions to protect the welfare of those with whom they work.

PRINCIPLE B: INTEGRITY

AAASP members seek to promote integrity in the science, teaching, and practice of their profession. In these activities, AAASP members are honest and fair. In describing or reporting their qualifications, services, products, fees, research, or teaching, they do not make statements that are false, misleading, or deceptive. To the extent feasible, they attempt to clarify for relevant parties the roles they are performing and the obligations they adopt. They function appropriately in accordance with those roles and obligations. AAASP members avoid improper and potentially harmful dual relationships.

PRINCIPLE C: PROFESSIONAL AND SCIENTIFIC RESPONSIBILITY

AAASP members are responsible for safeguarding the public and AAASP from members who are deficient in ethical conduct. They uphold professional standards of conduct and accept appropriate responsibility for their behavior. AAASP members consult with, refer to, or cooperate with other professionals and institutions to the extent needed to serve the best interests of the recipients of their services. AAASP members' moral standards and conduct are personal matters to the same degree as is true of any other

(Continued next page)

Highlight 1.3 (Continued)

The Six Principles of Professional Conduct for Sports Psychologists

person, except as their conduct may compromise their professional responsibilities or reduce the public's trust in the profession and the organization. AAASP members are concerned about the ethical compliance of their colleagues' scientific and professional conduct. When appropriate, they consult with colleagues in order to prevent, avoid, or terminate unethical conduct.

PRINCIPLE D: RESPECT FOR PEOPLE'S RIGHTS AND DIGNITY

AAASP members accord appropriate respect to the fundamental rights, dignity, and worth of all people. They respect the rights of individuals to privacy, confidentiality, self determination, and autonomy, mindful that legal and other obligations may lead to inconsistency and conflict with the exercise of these rights. AAASP members are aware of cultural, individual, and role differences, including those due to age, gender, race, ethnicity, national origin, sexual orientation, disability, language, and socioeconomic status. AAASP members try to eliminate the effect on their work of biases based on those factors, and they do not knowingly participate in or condone unfair discriminatory practices.

PRINCIPLE E: CONCERN FOR OTHERS' WELFARE

AAASP members seek to contribute to the welfare of those with whom they interact professionally. When conflicts occur among AAASP members' obligations or concerns, they attempt to resolve those conflicts and to perform those roles in a responsible fashion that avoids or minimizes harm. AAASP members are sensitive to real and ascribed differences in power between themselves and others, and they do not exploit or mislead other people during or after professional relationships.

PRINCIPLE F: SOCIAL RESPONSIBILITY

AAASP members are aware of their professional and scientific responsibilities to the community and the society in which they work and live. They apply and make public their knowledge in order to contribute to human welfare. When undertaking research, AAASP members strive to advance human welfare and their profession while always protecting the rights of the participants. AAASP members try to avoid misuse of their work and they comply with the law.

relationships involving sport psychologists and coaches and athletes. Examples of dual relationships that are considered no-no's if one adheres to the strictest interpretation of the code of ethics include serving simultaneously as coach and sport psychologist, providing psychological services to a student in one's own class, having a beer or two with an athlete, and having out-of-town athletes stay overnight at one's home. It is the considered opinion of each of the preceding authorities that the issue is not vague or ambiguous: the kinds of dual relationships mentioned earlier are not remotely acceptable from the standpoint of ethical behavior.

In an attempt to integrate some data into the discussion of this issue, Petitpas, Brewer, Rivera, and Van Raalte (1994) reported the results of a survey sent to 508 AAASP members, of which 165 responded (28 percent return rate), concerning various ethical issues. There was reasonable consonance between ethical beliefs and actual practices of the respondents. Some issues were widely regarded as difficult judgments, including reporting recruiting violations, reporting gambling by an athlete, reporting an athlete who admitted committing rape in the past, consulting with athletes in objectionable sports such as boxing, socializing with athletes, allowing out-of-town athletes to stay overnight in their home, working with athletes known to use steroids, and working with an athlete known to be involved in illegal activities (other than rape, which was previously mentioned). Finally, while granting the shortcomings of their data, the authors feel that they have shed some preliminary light on ethical concerns, and suggest that AAASP should go ahead and adopt the APA guidelines as amended to fit sport psychology. At the same time, they strongly support ethics training specific to applied sport psychology.

The concern about establishing a workable code of ethics is warranted. Sport psychology, like other professions, is best served by having intelligent and workable guidelines for professional behavior. At this point in time, it appears that the AAASP proposal offers the most in terms of achieving this important goal.

Image

Clearly, the field of sport psychology should project a positive and professional image. However, this has not always been the case. All too often in the past, charlatans and well-meaning but less than competent individuals (many of whom were not trained even slightly in sport psychology) have passed themselves off to professional and other sport organizations as capable of working wonders if given the chance. This sort of incompetence has sent the wrong message to coaches, athletes, and sport administrators. With the increasing professionalization of sport psychology over the past two decades, there is less of this charlatanism and incompetence. Nevertheless, sport psychology has had to exercise ongoing damage control with regard to its image in certain quarters. Perhaps it would make sense to look at the facts of the matter concerning the image of sport psychology from the perspective of athletes, coaches, and professionals within the fields of exercise/sport science and psychology.

With regard to athletes themselves, the media are loaded with everyday references to athletes who are making use of sport psychologists. At various times in the past few years, a number of professional golfers have spoken positively about their interactions with sport psychologists, such as Richard Coop (Greg Norman, Corey Pavin, Payne Stewart), Alan Fine (David Feherty), and Bob Rotella (Dickie Pride, Patti Rizzo). In tennis, Mary Joe Fernandez and Gabriela Sabatini have sung the praises of Jim Loehr in advancing their games. In baseball, John Smoltz has spoken positively of his consultations with Jack Llewellyn. In professional basketball, the efforts of Bruce Ogilvie with the

Miami Heat have been very well-received. In downhill skiing, Richard Suinn has been the recipient of considerable recognition on national television for this work in that sport. Olympic ice skater Nancy Kerrigan has involved herself in a regular mental training program with Cindy Adams. As might be expected, however, there are detractors; Rick Fehr and Scott Hoch in golf and coach Marv Levy of the NFL Buffalo Bills have been less impressed with what sport psychology has to offer. Nevertheless, there is continuing anecdotal evidence that casts a decidedly positive image on the field. As an aside, it has been our experience that these anecdotal accounts have a down side in that they erroneously convey the message to high school and college students that sport psychology is more alive and well than is actually the case. To put it another way, the idea that jobs abound in sport psychology, accompanied by the attendant glory of working with glamorous athletes, is simply misleading.

Additional light is shed on this image issue by results from a study of 1984 Canadian Olympians by Orlick and Partington (1987). These researchers conducted intensive interviews with seventy-five athletes from nineteen different sports. Based on their data, Orlick and Partington were able to draw up composites of good and bad sport psychology consultants. The best consultants were seen as (1) likable and having something very applied and concrete to offer; (2) flexible and knowledgeable enough to meet individual needs; (3) accessible and caring enough to establish rapport with athletes; and (4) facilitative of mental training both before and during competition. The worst consultants were characterized by (1) poor interpersonal skills (were seen as wimpy, domineering, incompatible, expected personal services such as having athletes carry their bags); (2) an inability to apply the various psychological skills to individual sports; (3) an inability to bend to fit individual athlete needs; (4) engaging in limited one-on-one

interactions with athletes (too much group work or lectures); (5) providing inappropriate or intrusive consulting skills at the competition site; and (6) providing little or no feedback. Based on these results, it is evident that care must be exercised in the selection of sport psychology consultants working with elite Olympic athletes. Undoubtedly, the best and worst described by Orlick and Partington are equally applicable in working with athletes in other settings.

Tangentially related to the preceding discussion is the perception of athletes who seek assistance from a sport psychologist. What image does this project of the athletes in question, and what are the ramifications of this perception for the field of sport psychology? Linder, Pillow, and Reno (1989) put these interrelated questions to a test by getting 139 introductory psychology students to respond to a hypothetical situation in which they were asked to evaluate the prospects of two quarterbacks in the professional football draft. One of the hypothetical players went to his coach and the other to a sport psychologist to seek assistance about issues centering around enhancing mental skills. The player who went to his coach for help was viewed as significantly more emotionally stable than his counterpart who sought out the sport psychologist. Additionally, the first player was viewed as much more likely to fit in with management. Overall, seeing a sport psychologist created a negative perception of the athlete and, through guilt by association, the field of sport psychology.

Linder, Brewer, Van Raalte, and De Lange (1991) followed up on this line of research but used hypothetical drafts in baseball, basketball, and football for evaluative purposes. Linder et al. expanded on their 1989 study, adding the perception of psychotherapists to the equation. They again used psychology students as subjects, but were able to obtain results from a sample of Lions Club members attending a regional convention. Derogation of the athletes in all three sports was noted if they sought out a sport psychologist for help with their respective mental games. Also, Lions Club members viewed the issues in a fashion similar to that of college students. Finally, the sport psychologist and the psychotherapist were lumped together perceptually for the most part; that is to say, sport psychologists were viewed pretty much the same as conventional psychology practitioners. This is not all bad; being seen in the same light as practicing mental health professionals may add credibility to what sport psychologists do. However, we are in agreement with Van Raalte, Brewer, Linder, and De Lange (1990), who are convinced that the view students (or Lions Club members) have of sport psychologists as being similar to mental health professionals is, in all likelihood, not a shared perception.

Speaking of mental health professionals and sport psychologists, there has been some interest shown concerning the image of the field of sport psychology among counseling and clinical psychologists as well as exercise/sport science professionals. In this regard, LeUnes and Hayward (1990) mailed out a questionnaire to all 147 chairpersons of APA-approved programs in clinical psychology; 102 (69.4 percent) were returned. Results supported a positive image among this sample with regard to sport psychology, though plans to develop programs in the area were scarce. No real evidence was noted concerning impending turf wars over sport psychology. However, the use of the term *sport psychologist* was seen as contentious, and developments since the survey was conducted have clarified this issue greatly, as noted earlier in this chapter.

Taking a slightly different tack, Petrie and Watkins (1994) reported results of a survey of forty-one APA-approved counseling psychology programs in universities also having physical education departments. Again, the perception of sport psychology among the psychology respondents was favorable. As might be expected, the physical education departments had more

courses in sport psychology, and had more students and faculty with interests in the area. However, over 70 percent of the counseling psychology programs had students with sport psychology interests. Two-thirds of the counseling psychology respondents viewed the restriction of the use of the term *sport psychologist* to licensed psychologists as favorable; only thirty of the physical education respondents agreed with such a stance. As was the case with LeUnes and Hayward, Petrie and Watkins stressed the need for continuing collaboration between psychology and physical education in resolving future professional issues of mutual concern.

A final note related to the image issue concerns three 1995 articles that discussed pros, cons, and problem areas associated with setting up and administering a sport psychology practice (Hays, 1995; Petrie and Diehl, 1995; Petrie, Diehl, and Watkins, 1995). What these authorities have said about working with athletes and teams as a part of a psychology practice is important; however, what may be even more critical is the increased space being devoted to sport psychology issues in the mainline literature of counseling and clinical psychology. The fact that journals such as *Professional Practice: Research and Practice* and *The Counseling Psychologist* are addressing how sport psychology fits into the larger domain of psychological practice suggests a more positive image of the field as a whole.

What we see here is an emerging positive image of sport psychology from both professional and elite amateur athletes. It is clear, however, that the respect of these athletes must be earned. They recognize incompetence in its many manifestations. Insofar as the perception of sport psychology among clinical and counseling psychologists is concerned, there appears to be a very favorable view. With improvements in training, increasing adherence to good ethical practice, and a growing awareness of what sport psychology is all about, it is realistic to expect an upswing in the respect afforded the field by athletes, coaches, athletic administrators, and allied professionals.

SPORT PSYCHOLOGY PROFESSIONAL ORGANIZATIONS

A growing number of professional organizations represent sport psychologists and, at the same time, work for improving the profession for those who use the various services of the membership. Such concerns as credentialing, ethics in both research and practice, and training issues occupy a great deal of time and energy for the leadership in the professional organizations. Eleven rather prominent organizations merit further elaboration; one is international in scope; four are North American societies; four are largely American in membership makeup; and two represent Canadian and Australian sport psychologists.

The International Organization

Many sport psychologists worldwide belong to the *International Society for Sport Psychology (ISSP),* which was founded in 1965 by the late Feruccio Antonelli of Italy. ISSP was formed primarily as a forum for sport scientists from all over the world to engage in communication about sport and fitness, and as a means of breaking down some of the more general barriers that exist between people with differing philosophical and political views. To quote Salmela (1981, p. 45): "The ISSP's main contributions have come from its quadrennial conferences and from its publications." The quadrennial conferences have been held in Rome (1965), Washington (1969), Madrid (1973), Prague (1977), Ottawa (1981), Copenhagen (1985), Singapore (1989), and Lisbon (1993) and have generated considerable interest among sport

psychologists worldwide. ISSP publications are the *International Journal of Sport Psychology* and the *Sport Psychologist,* the latter published in conjunction with Human Kinetics Publishers. In brief, ISSP attempts to bridge the formidable language and political gaps that exist in order to promote the discipline of sport psychology for the world community; in doing so, it serves a most useful purpose.

North American Organizations

An influential organization to which a number of sport psychologists belong is the *North American Society for the Psychology of Sport and Physical Activity (NASPSPA).* NASPSPA has approximately four hundred members, and is subdivided into three areas of member concentration to include sport psychology, motor learning/control, and motor development. The society originated in 1965 with ten charter members and has served since that time as a major force in advancing the knowledge base in sport psychology, primarily through experimental research. The regard with which NASPSPA was once held is summarized by Salmela (1981, p. 121): "NASPSPA is the single most influential academic professional society in the world focusing upon the psychology of sport and physical activity." Salmela's 1981 observation is less true today, but NASPSPA continues to be a force in sport psychology.

The *North American Society for the Sociology of Sport (NASSS)* is another professional force of note, and is composed of some two hundred sport sociologists, social psychologists, and sport scientists in general with professed interests in the ramifications of sport in the broader societal realm. In this context, a tongue-in-cheek quote from Martens (1979, p. 96) offers an interesting historical perspective on the early interface between NASPSPA and NASSS: "Sport psychology will surely be a healthier field when we recognize that the internal psychological processes that occur when people engage in sport must be understood within the societal context of sport. Thus, rather than making war with sport sociologists, we must make love."

Yet another organization of interest is the *North American Society for Sport History (NASSH),* which has over seven hundred members. NASSH serves as the primary vehicle for scholarly interchange with regard to sport history. Given the relative infancy of sport psychology, it follows that we have a brief history. Such is not the case, however, for sport in general, and NASSH devotes much energy to generating information from a historical perspective. Much of what will follow in chapter 2 on historical perspectives is the product of the revelations brought forth by various members of NASSH.

A fourth professional society of consequence is the *North American Society for Sport Management (NASSM).* NASSM held its first annual convention at Kent State University in Ohio in 1986 and attracted more than one hundred professionals interested in various facets of sport management. Members of NASSM are devoted to the application of management theory and practice to sport, exercise, play, and dance settings. Publication of a journal devoted to sport management commenced in 1987 through the combined efforts of NASSM and Human Kinetics Publishers.

American Organizations

As has been noted in earlier discussions of credentialing, training, ethics, and image formation, a major force in propelling sport psychology to the forefront professionally and societally is the *Association for the Advancement of Applied Sport Psychology (AAASP).* AAASP was created in 1985 primarily through the leadership of John Silva, who was able to gather a group of dissidents together at the NASPSPA convention that year. The general feeling at that time was that NASPSPA was not satisfactorily meeting the needs of the more applied side of sport psychology due to its heavy emphasis on research, and an organization with that goal in mind would better serve those sport psychologists working with athletes and teams. AAASP held its first meeting in 1986 in Jekyll Island, Georgia, and has grown to a membership exceeding six hundred (counting student members); there is an approximate fifty/fifty split in the ratio of psychologists to physical educators within the organization. We think it is safe to say that AAASP has ascended to a position of real leadership in sport psychology with its credentialing process and its efforts to set forth standards for training and ethical practice. There is every reason to forecast a bright future for AAASP as a mechanism for advancing the field of sport psychology.

Another organization that has ascended to prominence of late in sport psychology is Division 47, Exercise and Sport Psychology, of the *American Psychological Association* (APA). Division 47 was created in 1986 and now counts one thousand APA members as affiliates; included in that number are twenty-one Fellows, sport psychologists of considerable stature in the field. In view of the considerable financial and political clout of APA coupled with the strength of the division membership itself, it is likely that Division 47 will increasingly be a major player in sport psychology. As an aside, another major organization of psychologists, the *American Psychological Society* (APS), has recently been created. It is not clear at this time, however, just what will transpire within APS with regard to sport psychology.

Perhaps two thousand members of the *American Alliance for Health, Physical Education, Recreation, and Dance* (AAHPERD) report more than a passing interest in sport psychology. The remainder of the AAHPERD membership is devoted to more traditional concerns with exercise, sport science, recreation, and dance.

Though not a professional society in the truest sense of the word, another sport-related enterprise of importance is the *Center for the Study of Sport in Society,* the brainchild of Richard Lapchick. The Center is located at Northeastern University in Boston and was begun as a mechanism to address exploitation of athletes at all levels of sport. The Center has become a major force in dealing with both racism in sport and the interface between athletics and academics. Two publications originate from Lapchick's operation: *Arena Review* and *Journal of Sport and Social Issues.* Their function is to articulate serious societal concerns within sport and to serve as an agent of change to make sport more rewarding and joyous for all involved parties.

Canadian and Australian Organizations

Sport psychology associations are springing up worldwide as the field itself grows. Mentioning them all is prohibitive in terms of space limitations, so only two of the more prominent in Canada and Australia will be discussed here.

Sport psychology in Canada is promoted primarily through the efforts of the *Canadian Society for Psychomotor Learning and Sport Psychology* (CSPLSP). CSPLSP was founded in 1969, though it was a part of the *Canadian Association for Health, Physical Education, and Recreation* (CAHPER) until 1977. CSPLSP represents some two hundred sport psychologists in Canada in the same way that NASPSPA and AAASP serve the interests of their American counterparts. At one time, attempts were made to merge NASPSPA and CSPLSP due to overlapping interests and memberships, but that movement has been discontinued.

In Australia, the *Australian Applied Sport Psychology Association* (AASPA) exists as a forum for advancing sport psychology in that country. AASPA was begun in 1986 and has a very small number of members due to its restrictive requirements. Essentially, AASPA

membership is limited to those Australians who would also qualify for legal registration with the *Australian Psychological Society* (APS). AASPA also works closely with the *Australian Institute of Sport* (AIS), which has a strong sport psychology contingent under the leadership of Jeffrey Bond. Sport psychology in Australia is further strengthened due to its geographical proximity to and shared interests with New Zealand and its small but involved cadre of sport psychologists. The only sport-related journal serving as an outlet for research and application for sport psychologists in that part of the world is the *Australian Journal of Science and Medicine in Sport*; as a result, many articles published in the international or American journals are written by Australians or New Zealanders.

Jeffrey Bond, head of the Australian Institute of Sport (AIS), teaches in Canberra, Australia. Under Bond's leadership, the organization has developed a strong sport psychology contingent and close ties to the College of Sport Psychologists within the Australian Psychological Society (APS).

For those readers with an abiding interest in learning more about the state of sport psychology in the aforementioned countries as well as the rest of the world, John Salmela's 1992 edition of *The World Sport Psychology Sourcebook* is highly recommended.

In addition to their other responsibilities, most of the organizations representing sport psychologists also publish a journal dedicated to furthering the knowledge base in the world of scientific sport. A list of these as well as other publishers and publications is found in table 1.2.

Table 1.2
Major Sport Journals and Publishers

Sport Psychology

Journal of Sport and Exercise Psychology	Human Kinetics
The Sport Psychologist	Human Kinetics
Journal of Applied Sport Psychology	Allen Press
Journal of Sport Behavior	University of South Alabama
International Journal of Sport Psychology	International Society for Sport Psychology

Sports Medicine

Sports Medicine	ADIS Press International
British Journal of Sports Medicine	The British Association of Sport and Medicine
Medicine and Science in Sports and Exercise	American College of Sports Medicine
The Physician and Sportsmedicine	American College of Sports Medicine
Journal of Sports Medicine and Physical Fitness	Federation International de Medicine Sportive
Pediatric Exercise Science	Human Kinetics
Journal of Athletic Training	National Athletic Trainers' Association

Exercise/Sport Science

Research Quarterly for Exercise and Sport	McGraw-Hill
The Physical Educator	Phi Epsilon Kappa

Journal of Physical Education, Recreation and Dance	American Alliance for Health, Physical Education, Recreation and Dance
Quest	Human Kinetics
CAHPER Journal	Canadian Association for Health, Physical Education and Recreation
Canadian Journal of Applied Sport Science	Canadian Association of Sport Sciences

Sport Sociology

Sociology of Sport Journal	Human Kinetics
Journal of Sport and Social Issues	ARENA: Center for the Study of Sport in Society, Northeastern University
ARENA Review	ARENA: Center for the Study of Sport in Society, Northeastern University

Sport History

Journal of Sport History	North American Society for Sport History

Sport Management

Journal of Sport Management	Human Kinetics

Interdisciplinary

Applied Research in Coaching and Athletics Annual	American Press

ORGANIZATION OF THE BOOK

Part One of this book, entitled *Basic Concepts and Behavioral Principles,* is concerned with the issues already discussed to this point, namely attempting to arrive at some degree of closure with regard to what sport is, what sport psychology is, and who may practice the discipline. Another important topic to be addressed in this section will be the history of sport. Sport has a long and fascinating history beginning, for all practical purposes, with the early Greeks. Brief detours into the history of psychology, physical education, and sport psychology itself will also be made. Finally, an intensive discussion of the basic principles of human learning as they relate to sport and physical activity will be conducted. Included in this discussion will be such topics as classical conditioning, operant learning, cognitive learning, anxiety, and intervention and performance enhancement strategies.

Part Two, *Social-Psychological Dimensions,* represents a major thrust of the book. Such topics as attribution theory, need achievement, locus of control, self-concept, leadership, group cohesion, audience effects, and aggression and violence in the realm of sport constitute this portion of the book.

Part Three, *Personality and Assessment,* represents an attempt to look at the interaction between personality theory and research and the measurement of personality traits that may be related to sport performance. In the chapter on personality variables, such topics as sport personology, the black athlete, the high risk athlete, the elite performer, and athletes who abuse steroids and other substances are discussed. With regard to assessment, much of the early sport psychology practice and research involved the measurement of psychological traits and subsequent attempts to relate them to sport performance. Such efforts have fallen into some disrepute. However, an argument can be made

for making better use of assessment techniques that are available as well as creating new and innovative sport-specific tests in an effort to predict how selected individuals will perform at any given moment. It is far too early to abandon this potentially viable area of scientific inquiry.

Part Four, *A Wider Perspective,* allows us to take up selected topics not discussed at length earlier in the book. Certainly, the female performer merits attention; it can be argued that a separate consideration is not necessary, but our contention is that the state of development of women in sport is such that a chapter devoted exclusively to the topic is warranted. Another emerging area of interest is youth sport, in which there has been an explosion of theory, research, speculation, and controversy. Too, the psychological variables that impinge on effective coaching will be an important focal point in this section. Finally, a look at sport and physical activity for all constitutes a logical wrap-up to the book. Millions of recreational joggers, softball players, swimmers, and others take part in health-related activities each day, and there are psychological antecedents and consequences worthy of our consideration.

Summary

1. Sport is big business in this country and the world in general, and psychology has much to offer in terms of our understanding of athletic performance and its enhancement and to the general welfare of athletes at all levels of competitiveness.
2. Psychology is defined as the scientific study of behavior and mental processes, simultaneously emphasizing the necessity for objectively viewing behavioral events and yet recognizing the existence of inferred but not observable mental events that affect human behavior.

3. Psychologists work in a variety of sub-specialties and settings. Those most interested in sport psychology generally are academicians with a clinical, counseling, or educational specialty area.

4. Opinions as to what sport itself actually is are plentiful but not universally accepted. Those that emphasize history, explicit rules, formal organization, defined objectives, and achievement through competition seem to be popular. However, we would like to emphasize a "sport for all" approach as a guiding philosophy for this book.

5. Sport psychology is not easily defined or explained. Martens' succinct definition of "sport psychology being what sport psychologists do" is accepted here with several caveats. Dissent with Martens' point of view is not unknown, and the search for definitional closure goes on.

6. Sport psychologists perform a broad variety of services in academic and athletic settings. They include performance improvement, psychological assessment, communications enhancement, crisis intervention, consultation and program development, and clinical/therapeutic intervention.

7. A number of nagging problems continue to occupy the time and energy of the leadership within sport psychology, including credentialing, training, employment, ethics, and the image projected by sport psychology among coaches, athletes, and various professionals within the field itself.

8. Credentialing is a major problem facing sport psychology. Credentialing is a broad, generic term that encompasses certification, registry, and licensure. The latter term is the most controversial as it is statutory and binding. By law, the term *psychologist* is protected; merely adding "sport" in front of it does not absolve one of adherence to the legalities involved. The Association for the Advancement of Applied Sport Psychology

(AAASP) has reacted to this situation by credentialing involved professionals as *Certified Consultant, AAASP*. AAASP has set up stringent qualifications for granting certification, but the AAASP position on credentialing is not universally accepted.

9. Training of sport psychologists has not been particularly uniform—some people in the field come from traditional clinical or counseling psychology backgrounds and others from more typical physical education programs requiring additional work in the area of psychology. There are potential problems inherent in this situation; the individuals coming from traditional psychology backgrounds may be viewed with suspicion by physical educators in terms of their sport experience. Conversely, the physical educator in sport psychology may be seen as potentially deficient in basic psychology training. It is important that these potential turf battles not be allowed to materialize in view of the detrimental effects such an eventuality could inflict on the field of sport psychology as a whole.

10. The employment picture for sport psychologists is not rosy. There are positions within academia, and private practitioners in clinical or counseling psychology may devote part of their private practices to athletes and teams. Other than those two situations, the employment picture remains problematic.

11. AAASP is working industriously to craft a code of ethics for sport psychology based on the general principles set forth by the American Psychological Association (APA). Issues of competence, integrity, professional and scientific responsibility, respect for individual rights and dignity, concern for the welfare of others, and social responsibility are major ethical concerns within sport psychology.

12. The image of sport psychology appears to be generally good among various athletes,

though room for improvement is a continuing reality. A number of professional athletes have sought the services of sport psychologists, and have reported favorable results. Interviews with Canadian Olympians have shed additional light on the image issue, particularly in identifying characteristics of good and bad sport psychology consultants. The image held by students in several studies of athletes who have sought assistance from sport psychologists is less than gratifying. On the other hand, psychologists from clinical and counseling psychology departments do not appear to harbor negative feelings about the field, thereby suggesting a relative absence in the future of turf wars over the practice of sport psychology.

13. The International Society for Sport Psychology (ISSP) is the leading forum for communication among the world sport psychology community. The *International Journal of Sport Psychology* and the world conferences held every fourth year since 1965 serve as the two major mechanisms for this communication.

14. The North American Society for the Psychology of Sport and Physical Activity (NASPSPA), the North American Society for the Sociology of Sport (NASSS), the North American Society for Sport History (NASSH), and the North American Society for Sport Management (NASSM) are additional professional organizations with North American and Canadian representation.

15. Predominantly American professional societies include the Association for the Advancement of Applied Sport Psychology (AAASP), Division 47 of the American Psychological Association (APA), the American Alliance for Health, Physical Education, Recreation and Dance (AAHPERD), and the Center for the Study of Sport in Society at Northeastern University in Boston.

16. There are also professional organizations in Canada and Australia that represent the interests of sport psychologists in those countries. Many other societies are emerging worldwide with interests in sport psychology.

SUGGESTED READINGS

Allen, M. B. (1994) Authorship in sport psychology: A reference list. *The Sport Psychologist, 8,* 94–99.

> This article includes pertinent readings concerning sport psychology beginning with the major books published in the 1970s and continuing through books published as recently as 1993. Also, there is a listing of published proceedings from the early NASPSPA conferences, the Olympic Scientific Congresses, and those of the ISSP. This collection of major books and related readings serves as a very convenient starting point for someone interested in both the history and the current status of sport psychology as seen through the eyes of book authors from 1970 to 1993.

Andersen, M. B. (1994) Ethical considerations in the supervision of applied sport psychology graduate students. *Journal of Applied Sport Psychology, 6,* 152–167.

> Andersen takes a good look at the status of ethics as related to the supervised experiences of sport psychology students in applied settings. One of the biggest problems noted was that only 20% of those supervising sport psychology graduate students in applied settings had ever undergone training in supervision, thus raising questions about quality control. Andersen goes on to raise other important questions concerning such issues as referring athletes whose problems transcend the training of the sport psychologist, intimacy between supervisor and student, the problem of client exploitation, and homophobia. Three case histories designed to substantiate Andersen's points are also included.

Anshel, M. H. (1990) Commentary: Questioning the quality of sport psychology conference presentations. *The Sport Psychologist, 4,* 205–212.

A major event in the lives of professionals in any field is the annual conference. Such is certainly the case in sport psychology, with the annual meetings of AAHPERD, AAASP, NASPSPA, ISSP, ACSM, and Division 47 of APA, to name a few of the possibilities. Major components of any of these conferences are oral and poster presentation, symposia, and workshops. Anshel has taken the field of sport psychology to task by suggesting that poorly prepared speakers, poor delivery, inappropriate dress, inadequate visual aids, and other shortcomings greatly detract from the utility of these activities. As partial remedies, Anshel suggests that more professional demeanor, higher regard for one's colleagues, and less arrogance are in order if these meetings are to truly serve their informational purpose.

Graham, P. J. (Ed.). (1994) *Sport business: Operational and theoretical aspects.* Dubuque, IA: Brown and Benchmark.

Graham has amassed twenty-nine readings, which cover such broad areas as marketing, strategic planning, sport law, finance and human resource management within the sporting context. Business aspects of the Olympic Games, collegiate athletic departments, and corporate sponsorship of athletic events are a few of the major discussion areas. Such subtopics as trademark licensing, the economics of athletic injuries, salary arbitration, and free agency in major league baseball, drugs in sport, retirement from sport, and the business of sportscasting are addressed in a most readable fashion. This book would be especially useful to students going into the field of sport management.

Granito, V. J., and Wenz, B. J. (1995) Reading list for professional issues in applied sport psychology. *Sport Psychologist, 9,* 96–103.

The authors of this paper have amassed most of the pertinent citations from books, book chapters, and journals dealing with a host of contemporary professional issues confronting sport psychology as it prepares to enter the twenty-first century. The readings list is divided into a "stepping stone" format that addresses major areas: ethics, special ethical issues, education and training, the scope of sport psychology practice, professional identity/credibility, certification and registry, diversity, and practice issues. Most of the relevant bases have been touched by this reading list; the interested reader would find this collection to be very helpful in understanding the problems facing the sport psychology practitioner.

Hardy, C. J. (1994) Nurturing our future through effective mentoring: Developing roots as well as wings. *Journal of Applied Sports Psychology, 6,* 196–204.

This paper is a recapitulation of Hardy's 1993 Presidential Address to the AAASP membership. Every aspect imaginable related to professional mentoring is touched upon, and a number of areas of psychology are drawn from for the presentation. Highlights of the address include such ideas as sharing power, sharing competence, and sharing self in defining the mentoring process; and defining the mentor as one who can *m*anage, *e*ncourage, *n*urture, and *t*each *or*ganizational *r*esponsibility. Ideal mentor and protege qualities are discussed, as are the benefits to be gained for involved parties in a mentoring relationship. This article is exceptional in presenting the topic of professional mentoring.

Johns, D. (1993) Nutritional needs or athletic overconformity: Ethical implications for the sport psychologist. *The Sport Psychologist, 7,* 191–203.

Johns notes that nutrition and dietary issues are common in athletics, and suggests that there are times when weight control can raise some serious ethical issues for all concerned. If the sport psychologist is working with a particular athlete where the weight control program goes beyond what appears to be normal and healthy, ethical compromise is possible. Sport psychologists are an important part of the sport science support system for athletes, but must protect themselves and athletes against unethical practices. Helping athletes understand the ramifications of their decisions is part and parcel of the job description of the sport psychologist, and prevents the sport psychologist from becoming what Hughes and Coakley in a 1992 *Sociology of Sport Journal* article call a "high tech pimp."

Jones, D. G., and Daley, E. L. (1992) *Sports ethics in America.* Westport, CT: Greenwood Press.

This is primarily a bibliography on sport ethics drawn from a variety of professional fields. The volume has five major sections: (1) general works and philosophy; (2) the team, players, and coaches; (3) the game, competition, and contestants; (4) sport and society; and (5) reference works. This compilation can serve as a point of departure for looking more intensively at ethical concerns in sport.

LeUnes, A., and Moseley, D. (1990) Frequently cited references in texts in sport psychology. In W. Simpson, J. S. Picou, and A. LeUnes (Eds.), *Applied Research in Coaching and Athletics Annual, 1990.* Boston: American Press.

Seven textbooks in sport psychology published prior to 1990 (Bird and Cripe, Butt, Cox, Gill, Iso-Ahola and Hatfield, LeUnes and Nation, and Silva and Weinberg) were analyzed to identify commonly cited references. Sixty-seven references were cited by at least five authors, and were further scrutinized. Forty-seven of the sixty-seven citations were journal articles, most commonly from the *Journal of Sport Psychology/Sport and Exercise Psychology, Research Quarterly, Journal of Personality and Social Psychology,* and *Psychological Review.* Martens, Landers, Carron, Passer, R. E. Smith, and Weinberg were the most commonly cited authors. Arousal/anxiety, group cohesion, and youth sport were the most frequently cited research domains. These findings are discussed in terms of their role in helping to define the knowledge and research base in sport psychology.

LeUnes, A., Wolf, P., Ripper, N., and Anding, K. (1990) Classic references in *Journal of Sport Psychology, 1979-1987. Journal of Sport and Exercise Psychology, 12,* 74–81.

In an attempt to isolate those reference works that are critical in defining the field of sport psychology, the authors analyzed the references sections of every paper published in JSP from 1979 through 1987. Fifty-seven citations (thirty-nine articles, nine books, nine edited readings/book chapters) were chosen as a function of numeri-cal frequency to be included as sport psychology "classics," publications most often cited by other authors in the field. Prominent authors and common topics were also noted. This article should be useful in guiding professionals and students alike through the pertinent literature for that period as cited in the top journal in sport psychology.

Wilcox, R. C. (Ed.). (1994) *Sport in the global village.* Morgantown, WV: Fitness Information Technology, Inc.

This edited reader incorporates the latest thoughts of a number of historians, political scientists, and sociologists with regard to a world-wide sport perspective. The global significance of sport is treated in a most scholarly fashion. The end result is a significant reader that addresses the role of sport and its contribution to improved global understanding, cross-cultural literacy, and betterment of the human condition.

REFERENCES

AAASP passes certification criteria. (1990) *AAASP Newsletter, 6*(1), 3–4.

Anderson, B. (1966) *The psychology experiment.* Belmont, CA: Wadsworth.

Anshel, M. H. (1992) The case against the certification of sport psychologists: In search of the phantom expert. *The Sport Psychologist, 6,* 265–286.

Anshel, M. H. (1993) Against the certification of sport psychology consultants: A response to Zaichkowsky and Perna. *The Sport Psychologist, 7,* 344–353.

Benjamin, L. T., Hopkins, J. R., and & Nation, J. R. (1994) *Psychology* (3d ed.). New York: Macmillan.

Brasch, R. (1970) *How did sports begin?* New York: David McKay.

Brown, J. M. (1982) Are sport psychologists really psychologists? *Journal of Sport Psychology, 4,* 13–18.

Browne, M., & Mahoney, M. (1984) Sport psychology. *Annual Review of Psychology, 35,* 605–625.

Buceta, J. M. (1993) The sport psychologist/athletic coach dual role: Advantages, difficulties, and ethical considerations. *Journal of Applied Sport Psychology, 5,* 64–77.

Clark, K., & Miller, G. (Eds.). (1970) *Psychology.* Englewood Cliffs, NJ: Prentice-Hall.

Cratty, B. J. (1983) *Psychology in contemporary sport (2d ed.).* Englewood Cliffs, NJ: Prentice-Hall.

Danish, S. J., & Hale, B. (1981) Toward an understanding of the practice of sport psychology. *Journal of Sport Psychology, 3,* 90–99.

Danish, S. J., & Smyer, M. (1981) Unintended consequences of requiring a license to help. *American Psychologist, 36,* 13–21.

Dishman, R. K. (1983) Identity crisis in North American sport psychology: Academics in professional issues. *Journal of Sport Psychology, 5,* 123–134.

Edwards, H. (1973) *Sociology of sport.* Homewood, IL: Dorsey Press.

Ellickson, K. A., & Brown, D. R. (1990) Ethical considerations in dual relationships: The sport psychology-coach. *Journal of Applied Sport Psychology, 2,* 186–190.

Gifford, R. (1991) *Applied psychology: Variety and opportunity.* Boston: Allyn and Bacon.

Gould, D. (1990) AAASP: A vision for the 1990's. *Journal of Applied Sport Psychology, 2,* 99–116.

Gross, S. (1978) The myth of professional licensing. *American Psychologist, 33,* 1009–1016.

Harrison, R., & Feltz, D. L. (1979) The professionalization of sport psychology: Legal considerations. *Journal of Sport Psychology, 1,* 182–190.

Hays, K. F. (1995) Putting sport psychology into (your) practice. *Professional Psychology: Research and Practice, 26,* 33–40.

Heyman, S. R. (1982) A reaction to Danish and Hale: A minority report. *Journal of Sport Psychology, 4,* 7–9.

Keith-Speigel, P., & Koocher, G. P. (1985) *Ethics in psychology.* New York: Random House.

LeUnes, A., & Hayward, S. A. (1990) Sport psychology as viewed by chairpersons of APA-approved clinical psychology programs. *The Sport Psychologist, 4,* 18–24.

Linder, D. E., Brewer, B. W., Van Raalte, J. L., & De Lange, N. (1991) A negative halo for athletes who consult sport psychologists: Replication and extension. *Journal of Sport and Exercise Psychology, 13,* 133–148.

Linder, D. E., Pillow, D. R., & Reno, R. R. (1989) Shrinking jocks: Derogation of athletes who consult sport psychologists. *Journal of Sport and Exercise Psychology, 11,* 270–280.

Lutz, D. J. (1990) An overview of training models in sport psychology. *The Sport Psychologist, 4,* 63–71.

Martens, R. (1979) About smocks and jocks. *Journal of Sport Psychology, 1,* 94–99.

Martens, R. (1980) From smocks to jocks. A new adventure for sport psychologists. In P. Klavora & K. Wipper (Eds.), *Psychological and sociological factors in sport* (pp. 20–26). Toronto: The University of Toronto.

Morgan, W. P. (1972) Sport psychology. In R.N. Singer (Ed.), *The psychomotor domain* (pp. 193–228). Philadelphia: Lea and Febiger.

Nideffer, R. M. (1981) *The ethics and practice of applied sport psychology.* Ithaca, NY: Mouvement Publications.

Nideffer, R. M., DuFresne, P., Nesvig, D., & Selder, D. (1980) The future of applied sport psychology. *Journal of Sport Psychology, 2,* 170–174.

Nideffer, R. M., Feltz, D. L., & Salmela, J. H. (1982) A rebuttal to Danish and Hale: A committee report. *Journal of Sport Psychology, 4,* 3–6.

Nixon, H. (1984) *Sport and the American dream.* New York: Leisure Press.

Orlick, T., & Partington, J. (1987) The sport psychology consultant: Analysis of critical components as viewed by Canadian Olympic athletes. *The Sport Psychologist, 1,* 4–17.

Petitpas, A. J., Brewer, B. W., Rivera, P. M., & Van Raalte, J. L. (1994) Ethical beliefs and behaviors in applied sport psychology. *Journal of Applied Sport Psychology, 6,* 135–151.

Petrie, T. A., & Diehl, N. S. (1995) Sport psychology in the profession of psychology. *Professional Psychology: Research and Practice, 26,* 288–291.

Petrie, T. A., Diehl, N. S., & Watkins, C. E. (1995) Sport psychology: An emerging domain in the counseling profession? *The Counseling Psychologist, 23,* 535–545.

Petrie, T. A., & Watkins, C. E. (1994) A survey of counseling psychology programs and exercise/

sport science departments: Sport psychology issues and training. *The Sport Psychologist, 8,* 28–36.

Pope, K. S., & Vasquez, M. J. T. (1991) *Ethics in psychotherapy and counseling.* San Francisco: Jossey-Bass.

Salmela, J. H. (1981) *The world sport psychology sourcebook.* Ithaca, NY: Mouvement Publications.

Silva, J. M. (1989) Toward the professionalization of sport psychology. *The Sport Psychologist, 3,* 265–273.

Singer, R. N. (1976) *Physical education foundations.* New York: Holt, Rinehart and Winston.

Singer, R.N., (1978) Sport psychology: An overview. In W.F. Straub (Ed.), *Sport psychology: An analysis of athletic behavior* (pp. 3–14). Ithaca, NY: Mouvement Publications.

Sleet, D. (1972) Sport psychology. In *Psychosources. The psychology resources encyclopedia.* Del Mar, CA: CRM books.

Spears, B., & Swanson, R. (1983) *History of sport and physical education in the United States* (2d ed.). Dubuque, IA: Wm. C. Brown.

Straub, W. F., & Hinman, D. A. (1992) Profiles and professional perspectives of 10 leading sport psychologists. *The Sport Psychologist, 6,* 297–312.

Taylor, J. (1994) Examining the boundaries of sport science and psychology trained practitioners in applied sport psychology: Title usage and area

of competence. *Journal of Applied Sport Psychology, 6,* 185–195.

Tutko, T. A. (1979) The identity of the sport psychologist. In P. Klavora & J. V. Daniel (Eds.), *Coach, athlete, and the sport psychologist* (pp. 40–43). Toronto: University of Toronto.

U.S. Olympic Committee (1983) USOC establishes guidelines for sport psychology services. *Journal of Sport Psychology, 5,* 4–7.

Van Raalte, J. L., Brewer, B. W., Linder, D. E., & De Lange, D. (1990) Perceptions of sport-oriented professionals: A multi-dimensional scaling analysis. *The Sport Psychologist, 4,* 223–234.

Waite, B. T., & Pettit, M. E. (1993) Work experiences of graduates from doctoral programs in sport psychology. *Journal of Applied Sport Psychology, 5,* 234–250.

Whelan, J. P. (1994) Considering ethics. *AAASP Newsletter, 9,*(1), 14.

Whiting, H. T. A. (1974) Sports psychology in perspective. In J.D. Brooke (Ed.), *British proceedings of sports psychology* (pp. 1–11), Salford, England: University of Scotland.

Zaichkowsky, L. D., & Perna, F. M. (1992) Certification of consultants in sport psychology: A rebuttal to Anshel. *The Sport Psychologist, 6,* 287–296.

Zeigler, E. F. (Ed.). (1973) *A history of sport and physical education to 1900.* Champaign, IL: Stipes.

Chapter Two

A Historical Perspective on Sport

INTRODUCTION

Sport, no doubt, preceded recorded history. However, the first Olympic Games staged in Greece in 776 B.C. represent an accepted landmark for the continuing inquiry into sport history. Prior to that time, there is only fragmentary evidence for the existence of sport.

Much of what we know about the history of sport is fragmentary and suppositional. *Archeological findings* have yielded mosaics, frescoes, paintings, textiles, works of art and sculptures, architecture, seal stones, ornaments, tablets, and other sources from which we have inferred much about sport history. Also, works such as Homer's *The Iliad* and *The Odyssey* are considered landmark pieces of literature to sport historians. Much later, church records tell us something about sport history in Roman times and beyond. Indeed, a rich legacy of materials exists from which to draw inferences but, in the final analysis, our earliest sport history must be considered suppositional or speculative. In any event, there is considerable sport history to review.

THE ANCIENT WORLD

Palmer and Howell (1973) indicate that the first archeological evidence for sport and games comes from the *Sumerian civilization* of 3000 to 1500 B.C., a society that arose between the Tigris and Euphrates rivers. Artifacts found there seem to indicate participation in boxing and wrestling events. Board games have also been discovered from this time period.

In reviewing a host of pertinent studies related to the *Egyptian civilization* (3000–1100 B.C.), Palmer and Howell cite evidence for the existence of acrobatics, tumbling, resistance exercise, yoga, tug-of-war, a kicking game, crawling games, and ball games. Simri (1973) mentions some evidence as early as 1500 B.C. for the existence of ball games. He cites a relief showing what appears to be a pharaoh holding a bat and ball (while two priests await a catch), knife throwing, wrestling, the swinging of weights, swimming, board games, and a host of other activities that are indicative of considerable interest in sport and physical activity on the part of the early Egyptians. An inference made from findings in various tombs is that these activities were viewed as more suitable for the nobility, namely, kings, pharaohs, and noblemen. However, poor people did not leave tombs and artifacts to be pored over, so little is known about whether, in truth, only the nobility engaged in these activities and what their attitudes might have been about sport and games for the economically less fortunate.

Evidence from *ancient China* is supportive of the existence of sports. According to Sasijima (1973), ancient Chinese history begins around 1700 B.C. and can be broken into four dynasties as follows: Yin, 1700–1100 B.C.; Chou, 1100–256 B.C.; Chin, 221–207 B.C.; and Han, 202 B.C.–A.D. 8, A.D. 25–221. Of particular relevance is the *stage of Chou*; as part of the proper education of its young people at that time, children were expected to be trained in the *six virtues* (wisdom, benevolence, goodness, righteousness, loyalty, and harmony), in the *six good actions* (honoring parents, being friendly to brothers, polite to relatives by marriage, neighborly, trustful, and sympathetic), and the *six arts* (rituals, music, archery, charioteering, writing, and mathematics) (Zeigler, 1973b). However, it appears that Chinese enthusiasm for physical activity was tempered in part because of the more quiet, cerebral, studious nature of the dominant religions in the East, namely, Taoism, Buddhism, and Confucianism. However, the founder of Buddhism, Prince Siddhartha (later known as Buddha) was, according to Rajagopalan (1973, p. 51), a "sportsman of no mean order." The prince was said to have excelled in a number of games and sports.

Rajagopalan further informs us of evidence in *India* for the existence of hunting, fishing, archery, wrestling, boxing, the javelin throw, running, swimming, jumping, digging, and dancing as early as 1500 B.C. As food for thought, he also mentions that marbles dating back to Neolithic times have been unearthed. Whether these marbles were used for recreation purposes, as weapons, or were valued for their aesthetic properties is not known.

A significant contribution to our understanding of sports in antiquity was made by the unearthing of the *Palace of Minos* in 1871. The Minoan times ran from roughly 3000 to 1200 B.C., and Minoans were people living on the isle of Crete during that period. Significant evidence was obtained from a variety of sources that points to the existence of such activities as tumbling, acrobatics, dancing, boxing, wrestling, hunting, archery, running, swimming, table games, sailing, and a host of so-called "*taureador*" sports (Howell, 1969; Palmer and Howell, 1973). The "taureador" sports were those that related to bull grappling, bull vaulting, and other possible acrobatic events involving the bull. Bull grappling we now recognize as steer wrestling in our modern day rodeo! The "taureador" sports were apparently so dominant with the Minoans that Palmer and Howell (1973, p. 69) say: "The representations of the bull games far outnumber any other games in the Minoan period. The bull is a common subject of Minoan artists, and is shown to us on seal stones, frescoes, rhytons, plaster reliefs, bronze, rings, pendants, and vases." A particularly revealing source of information, and a neglected one, has been the seal stones that were essentially carved or engraved on clay. Not all dealt with physical activity but Howell (1969) found twenty-five in the Ashmolean collection at Oxford University that were related to the various sporting events suggested earlier.

THE GREEK CONTRIBUTION

Though the subject of considerable debate among historians, it appears that the Minoan civilization was destroyed by the Mycenaeans, or early Greeks, around 1400 B.C. Some two hundred years later, the Mycenaeans attacked and destroyed Troy. The Mycenaeans in turn, were vanquished by the Dorians. With the ascent to power of the Dorians, a "dark age" in Greek history began. Much of what we do know about the Dorian era has been generated by the epics and stories of and about the period, not the least of which were those by a blind Ionian poet named *Homer*. The writings of Homer have led sport history authorities (for example, Harris, 1973; Van Dalen, Mitchell, and Bennett, 1953; and Zeigler, 1973a, among others) to refer to this period, roughly 1200 to 700 B.C., as the *Homeric Age*. In actuality, Van Dalen et al. see the Homeric period in Greek history as running from prehistoric times to 776 B.C., the time of the first Greek Olympiad. They further break Greek history into the following three periods:

1. *Early Athenian.* This encompassed the period from 776 B.C. to the end of the Persian War in 480 B.C.
2. *Spartan.* This ran throughout the history of Sparta, roughly from the eighth century B.C. to the Macedonian conquest in 338 B.C.
3. *Later Athenian.* This was the period from 480 B.C. to the ultimate conquest of the Greek city–states by the Macedonians in 338 B.C. Except for its later stages, this has been called the "Golden Age of Greece."

Homeric Greece

Homer is believed to have written *The Iliad* and *The Odyssey* around 850 B.C. He essentially took various tales and legends transmitted by word of mouth and created our earliest documented literature. As a result, much of what is known about Greek life at the time of the Trojan War (1194–1184 B.C.), a ten-year struggle between the Greeks and the Trojans of Troy, is attributable to Homer. *The Iliad* has been called variously a "classic epic of war" (Stull, 1973, p. 121) and the "basic source of the Greek concept of manhood" (Stull and Lewis, 1968). These writers further suggest that *The Iliad* indeed is the first written account for sport historians to peruse. One of the unique features of *The Iliad* is its description of the so-called *funeral games,* so named because they were started by Achilles in honor of his slain companion and friend, Patroclus. The games were called to give the involved warriors a brief respite from war and to lift their mourning through physical competition. Such activities as wrestling, boxing, archery, chariot racing, sword fighting, javelin and discus throwing, and footracing characterized the funeral games.

As for *The Odyssey,* it recounts the trials and tribulations of Odysseus, a Greek hero at the battle of Troy who was absent from his Ithaca home for twenty years. The final forty-one pages are rich in information for the sport historian. Wrestling and boxing are prominently mentioned, as is an amalgam of the two, an event known as the *pankration* (pancratium). Harris (1972) parallels the pankration to judo while Binfield (1948) and Hackensmith (1966) interpret it as quite similar to jujitsu. Henry (1976) says that if historians are correct in their interpretation of the event, it "more closely resembles a gutter brawl than an athletic event" (p. 16). Also mentioned in *The Odyssey* are the diskos (discus) or weight throw, the javelin, ball games, the footrace, and archery.

Despite their allegedly apocryphal nature, *The Iliad* and *The Odyssey* must be regarded as brilliant works that have contributed significantly to our understanding of ancient Greece and its many facets, one very important aspect of which was sport. The ancient Greeks placed much value on sporting and physical activities, and their love for them influenced generations of Greeks, Romans, Macedonians, and others who were to follow them historically.

The Early Athenians

Nowhere can this reverence for sport and competition be better viewed than in the concept of the Olympic Games, first held in Olympus in 776 B.C. The initial games consisted of the *stadion,* or single course race, and they continued that way until the fourteenth Olympiad in 724 B.C., at which time a double course race, the *diaulos,* was added. A long course race, the *dolichos,* was added in 720 B.C., and wrestling and the pentathlon were added during the eighteenth games in 708 B.C. Twenty years later, boxing was added. The twenty-fifth Olympiad (680 B.C.) saw the addition of chariot racing. In the thirty-third games, horse racing and the pankration were added. In the sixty-fifth games (520 B.C.) the race in armor was included and, with minor variants, the games were to remain pretty much the same until their demise some one thousand years later (Yalouris, 1979). The typical Olympic events and a representative program from 520 B.C. to the end in A.D. 394 are summarized in table 2.1.

The early Olympic Games were characterized by *several unique features.* One is that the only material award for winners was a *crown of wild olive leaves.* However, Olympic heroes were greatly admired for their skills and the fame they brought to their home states, and rewards above and beyond the olive leaf crown were most certainly given to the top athletes once they returned to their homes upon completion of the games. Another interesting feature is that contestants after the fifteenth games (720 B.C.) *competed in the nude.* Harris (1972) offers two plausible explanations for what may seem to be an oddity to those of us of more modest inclinations. One is that in Homeric Greece, nude competition was not in vogue, but one runner lost his shorts in the middle of a race and proceeded to win handily, thereby setting a trend for his colleagues. Perhaps superstitious behavior is not the invention of the modern athlete! A second explanation

Table 2.1
Typical Olympics, 520 B.C. to A.D. 394

Three combat events	*Four running events*	*Pentathlon*
Boxing	200 yards	Javelin
Wrestling	400 yards	Discus
Pankration	Distance	Long jump
	Race in armor	200-yard race
		Wrestling

A Typical Program of Events

Day One

Morning. Swearing-in ceremony for competitors and judges in the *Bouleuterion* (Council-House) before the altar and statue of *Zeus Horkios* (Zeus of the Oaths); contests for heralds and trumpeters held near the stadium entrance; boys' running, wrestling and boxing contests; public and private prayers and sacrifices in the Altis; consultation of oracles.

Afternoon. Orations by well-known philosophers and recitals by poets and historians; sightseeing tours of the Altis; reunions with old friends.

Day Two

Morning. Procession into the hippodrome of all those competing there; chariot- and horse-races.
Afternoon. The pentathlon: discus, javelin, jumping, running, and wrestling.
Evening. Funeral rites in honor of the hero Pelops; parade of victors round the Altis; communal singing of victory hymns; feasting and revelry.

Day Three

Morning. Procession of the *Hellanodikai* (judges), ambassadors from the Greek states, competitors in all events, and sacrificial animals round the Altis to the Great Altar in front of the Temple of Zeus, followed by the official sacrifice of one hundred oxen given by the people of Elis.
Afternoon. Foot-races.
Evening. Public banquet in the Prytaneion.

Day Four

Morning. Wrestling.
Midday. Boxing and the *pankration.*
Afternoon. Race-in-armor.

Day Five

Procession of victors to the Temple of Zeus where they are crowned with wreaths of wild olive by the Hellanodikai, followed by the *phyllobolia* (when the victors are showered with leaves and flowers); feasting and celebrations.

Sources: Hackensmith (1966); Swaddling (1980); Yalouris (1979).

has to do with a runner losing his shorts, an event that caused him to trip. He was killed in the subsequent fall, thereby causing the presiding magistrate to ban shorts for the remainder of that and later games. A third, and more plausible explanation is offered by Swaddling (1980); she suggests that the nudity was driven by the motivation to show off a sleek, powerful, and muscular physique.

A third interesting feature of the early competition was the *stadium* itself. Archaeological evidence indicates that the typical Greek stadium was rectangular, perhaps 200 yards long and 25 to 40 yards wide, with a turning post at each end. Longer runs added to the Olympic Games in 724 and 720 B.C. required the contes-

tants to make a series of abrupt turns at each end of the stadium. This was particularly true of the long event added in 720 B.C., which has been reported to be 2 to 3 miles (Binfield, 1948), or as long as 3,850 meters (Yalouris, 1979), and approximately a mile or perhaps even longer (Henry, 1976).

A final aspect of note is that *women were not allowed to participate* or, in most instances, even view the activities. Exceptions apparently were made in cases of virgins, who were allowed to be spectators. The penalty for violating this prohibition against female spectators was to be flung from the highest cliffs of Mount Typaion (Yalouris, 1979). The one instance in which a female could be awarded an Olympic prize was

This detail from a sixth century B.C. vase painting reveals two characteristics of the Olympic games in ancient Greece: no women and no uniforms.

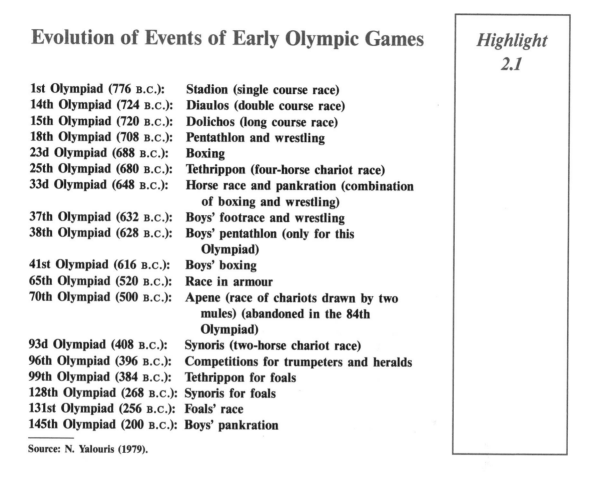

Evolution of Events of Early Olympic Games

*Highlight
2.1*

1st Olympiad (776 B.C.):	**Stadion (single course race)**
14th Olympiad (724 B.C.):	**Diaulos (double course race)**
15th Olympiad (720 B.C.):	**Dolichos (long course race)**
18th Olympiad (708 B.C.):	**Pentathlon and wrestling**
23d Olympiad (688 B.C.):	**Boxing**
25th Olympiad (680 B.C.):	**Tethrippon (four-horse chariot race)**
33d Olympiad (648 B.C.):	**Horse race and pankration (combination of boxing and wrestling)**
37th Olympiad (632 B.C.):	**Boys' footrace and wrestling**
38th Olympiad (628 B.C.):	**Boys' pentathlon (only for this Olympiad)**
41st Olympiad (616 B.C.):	**Boys' boxing**
65th Olympiad (520 B.C.):	**Race in armour**
70th Olympiad (500 B.C.):	**Apene (race of chariots drawn by two mules) (abandoned in the 84th Olympiad)**
93d Olympiad (408 B.C.):	**Synoris (two-horse chariot race)**
96th Olympiad (396 B.C.):	**Competitions for trumpeters and heralds**
99th Olympiad (384 B.C.):	**Tethrippon for foals**
128th Olympiad (268 B.C.):	**Synoris for foals**
131st Olympiad (256 B.C.):	**Foals' race**
145th Olympiad (200 B.C.):	**Boys' pankration**

Source: N. Yalouris (1979).

in the equestrian events; owners rather than riders were crowned as victors.

While the Olympic Games have survived for nearly three thousand years (minus the afore-mentioned 1,600-year hiatus), there were other premier athletic competitions conducted during the early Greek period (Sweet, 1987; Yalouris, 1979). As has been duly noted, the first Olympic Games were held in 776 B.C. In 582 B.C., the Pythian Games emerged, and were held in Delphi during the year prior to the next Olympic Games. In 581 B.C., the Isthmian Games began in Corinth, and were held every two years. Eight years after the institution of the events in Corinth, the Nemean Games began in Nemea, and also were conducted every two years. The Olympic, Pythian, Isthmian, and Nemean Games composed what was known as the Panhellenic Games. While the Panhellenic competitions were of prime importance, additional testimonial to the significance of athletics in Greece is provided by the fact that there were at least nineteen other major competitions held in places like Alexandria, Athens, Pergamon, Sardis, Thespai, and on the island of Kos. Another of these so-called lesser games, the Leukophrynia at Magnesia on the Maiandros, was probably of the status of the Pythian Games.

The Spartan Period

The *Spartans,* according to Yalouris (1979), probably never numbered more than five thousand people (Van Dalen et al. place the number at nine thousand). Yet they were a dominant military force for several centuries, an attestation to their desire to produce the perfect warrior.

The Spartans lived among a group of slaves or·serfs known as *helots,* numbering perhaps as high as 250,000, and unrest among these helots as well as the threat of outside invasion made it necessary for the Spartans to be fit and prepared for combat. Their excessive emphasis on militarism was undoubtedly warranted.

Physical activity to the Spartans was seen to be of value only in terms of its contribution to this *perfect warrior* concept. Unlike the Athenians, who saw physical competition as a beautiful and

---

Highlight 2.2

Milos of Kroton

The athletic world has a penchant for elevating its heroes to larger-than-life proportions, and the ancient Greeks apparently were no exception. The legendary wrestler, Milos of Kroton, represents a case in point. Milos (also variously cited as Milo and Milon) lived in Kroton, a Greek colony on the Italian boot, during the sixth century B.C. Milos won six consecutive Olympic wrestling championships from 536 to 512 B.C.; in addition, he was victorious in an additional twenty-six instances at the Isthmian, Nemean, and Pythian games, giving him a total of thirty-two national titles during his wrestling career.

As might be suspected, much folklore surrounded this heroic figure. Unbelievable feats of strength and equally unfathomable gastronomic excesses were attributed to him. Legend has it that Milos once carried a bull (or heifer) around the stadium at Olympia, slew it with his fists, and devoured it in its entirety before the day was over. Milos was also said to have eaten twenty loaves of bread at one meal; in another instance, he consumed the equivalent of nine liters of wine in a short time in order to win a bet.

In addition to his feats of strength and gastronomic excess, Milos was a student of Pythagoras and wrote a number of scholarly treatises of some importance. Too, he took up arms on occasion in order to defend Kroton from its enemies and was said to have been heroic in battle.

Milos' strength ultimately did him in. He apparently ventured one day into a nearby forest and noticed a partially cut tree into which wedges had been driven. Milos tried to topple the tree, but managed only to get his hands trapped where the wedges once were. Unable to extricate himself from his inadvertent but self-imposed trap, Milos was attacked and killed by wild beasts.

Sources: Brasch (1970); Harris (1972); Whorton (1981); Yalouris (1979).

harmonious extension of oneself, the Spartans subjugated personal goals and achievements in order for the city–state (Sparta) to survive. In effect, there is a selflessness here that speaks well for the Spartan point of view.

Lest one thinks that the Spartan search for the perfect warrior was a narrow and one-sided effort, it should be noted that the Spartans were very successful in Olympic competition. Yalouris tells us that the first apparent Spartan victor was Akanthos, who won the *dolichos* (long course race) in the fifteenth Olympiad (720 B.C.). Further, eighty-one winners in the games between 720 and 576 B.C. were Spartans. Twenty-one of the thirty-six winners of the *stadion* (single course race) were Spartans. Interestingly, it was the Spartans who introduced nakedness among the Olympic competitors and also the practice of anointing themselves with oil prior to competition, a ritual that became quite common in later games.

In order for the Spartan citizen to meet the demands of the perfect warrior concept, training began early. At birth, children were taken before their elders for judgment, and the sickly were left on Mount Taygetus to die or be rescued by slaves (Hackensmith, 1966; Van Dalen et al., 1953). Spartan males were educated at home until their seventeenth birthday, at which time they became wards of the city-state for gradual training in the arts of manhood and good citizenship. Military training was intensified each year and actual engagement in combat was not unusual by age twenty. A big part of all this preparation, of course, was in the physical domain. The Spartan citizen-soldier was expected to engage daily in a regimen of physical exercise until age thirty. At age fifty, retirement was allowed if military conditions were favorable for such an action. In addition to military training, a rather exacting regimen of diet and clothing was imposed. The boys went barefoot, wore the same tunic all year irrespective of hot or cold weather, and were fed meager rations.

Stealing to supplement the diet was encouraged, as craftiness in such matters would be valued militarily. Bathing was not acceptable though swimming in nearby rivers or streams was apparently condoned. Beatings and flogging were commonplace as a means of character training.

Women were less regimented than men but were expected to take part in physical activities of a public nature until age twenty. At all times, women were expected to place a premium on personal fitness and appearance. Their exercise program was similar to that of the young men, that is, wrestling, javelin, discus, running, jumping, dancing, and a host of other conditioning games.

The fascination with fitness, competition, and militarism was not without cost. Rice, Hutchinson, and Lee (1969, p. 17) sum it up well:

> The Spartan system of physical and military training obtained the desired results: the army was the best in the world. Spartans never made the mistake of substituting specialization in athletics for the ultimate goal of specialization for war. For this preeminent military position they sacrificed personal liberty, individualism, home life, and the achievements of peace. Sparta did not contribute great drama, immortal verse, models of architecture, and inimitable sculpture but left such accomplishments to her more cultured neighbor, Athens.

Adding support to the claims of Rice and his colleagues is a statement from Forbes:

> The Spartan system of physical education achieved its limited aim and in that sense was a resounding success. Nearly every Spartan could glory in a splendid physique and in health unequaled elsewhere in Greece. Spartan courage, tenacity, and obedience were proverbial. If the battle of Waterloo was won on the playing-fields of Eton, surely Sparta's many battles were won on the playing-fields by the River Eurotas. Speaking of New Hampshire, Daniel Webster once said, "The

Granite State makes men." Sparta made men.

But the cost was high. Sparta deliberately neglected the education of the mind. In a country astonishingly rich in philosophers, Sparta had none. Poets were few—none of note after the seventh and sixth centuries. Books that deal in generalizing terms with the cultural contribution of Greece have little to say about Sparta. Such were the results of a one-sided educational system in the world's first totalitarian state. (1973, p. 138)

The Later Athenians

The later Athenian period, particularly the earliest portion, has been referred to as the *"Golden Age of Greece."* With the rather amazing defeat of a seemingly superior Persian army in 480 B.C., nearly fifty years of peace and unprecedented growth began. The city–state concept was in full force and was most effective; Sparta had achieved great status as a military power and Athens had become a mecca for artists, poets, writers, and the intelligentsia in general. Greece became, as a result of the Persian War and the ensuing good times, about as cohesive a "nation" as it ever had been in the past or would be in the future. A spirit of unity prevailed. In Athens, a greater expansion of the concept of democratic government gave the masses a larger say in matters related to their welfare. The base of wealth was ever-expanding and many citizens of Athens profited from this economic bonanza. Tremendous emphasis in Athenian education was placed on greater enhancement of individual freedom, a fact that has not gone unchallenged as a contributor to the eventual fall of the Greek civilization.

Physical education became a matter of self-enhancement and self-expression; the utilitarian aspects of physical and military preparedness were overlooked. The individual took precedence over the welfare of the state. Rampant professionalism dominated sporting events, thereby encouraging spectatorism rather than participation. Amusement of the masses became preeminent. Plato (427–347 B.C.), a student of Socrates (470?–399 B.C.) and a leading social critic of his time, was particularly outspoken in his views of the decline of Greek values. He saw the real value of physical activity to lie in its moral education properties. Also, he was quite opposed to the professionalization of athletes. In any event, life was good for the Athenian of that period and the gradual softening of the city–state fiber went largely unnoticed until it was too late.

Prosperity was not to prevail for long. Athens, under the influence of Pericles, became involved in wars of aggression with other city-states, a situation that was to persist over a period of twenty-seven years beginning in 431 B.C. Eventually, the Spartans prevailed over the Athenians, who fell under Spartan domination. Meanwhile, a costly internecine conflict between the various city-states under Spartan rule and the Spartans themselves led to a rebellion in which the Spartans fell to a coalition army of city-states led by Thebes. The Spartans were subdued in 371 B.C., ending almost a century of Panhellenic internal conflict. This costly, long-term war rekindled the spirits of the aggressive Persians. In order to deal with this threat, Phillip II (382–336 B.C.), king of Macedonia in northern Greece, invaded what was left of the vulnerable Spartans and Athenians, thereby bringing them under Macedonian domination. The Greek empire effectively came to an end in 338 B.C. The legacy it provided, however, would influence sport and physical activity throughout the next seven hundred years and, ultimately, throughout the broader historical context.

While preparing to deal with the ominous Persians, King Phillip was assassinated and his son, Alexander the Great (356–323 B.C.), took charge of the Macedonians. Though only twenty-three years old, he was able to marshal forces that not only dealt effectively with the Persians but also were able to conquer Asia Minor, Egypt,

Quotes about Sport and Exercise from Prominent Men of the Early Greek Period

Highlight 2.3

Socrates: "No citizen has a right to be an amateur in the matter of physical training; it is a part of his profession as a citizen to keep himself in good condition, ready to serve his state at a moment's notice."

Plato: "Gymnastics as well as music should receive careful attention in childhood and continue through life."

Plutarch: "The exercise of the body must not be neglected; but children must be sent to schools of gymnastics. This will conduce partly to a more handsome carriage and partly to an improvement of their strength."

Aristotle: "The education of the body must precede that of the intellect."

Galen: "He is the best physician who is the best teacher of gymnastics."

Euripides: "Of all the countless evils through Hellas, there is none worse than the race of Athletes."

Source: Rice, Hutchinson, and Lee (1969).

and India. Alexander was consolidating his empire when he was stricken with a disease that took his life at the age of thirty-four. Significantly, in his eleven-year odyssey sports and competition and Greek culture in general were spread far and wide by his troops. Alexander himself was reportedly a good athlete, although he seldom competed because he felt that kings should compete only against other royalty. As his conquests grew, so did the Hellenization of the lands to the east, and soon sport arenas and athletic festivals sprang up in profusion.

THE ROMANS

By 500 B.C. there were two thriving civilizations in Italy, the *Etruscan* and the Greek. The Greeks occupied, as part of their expansionist policy, the southern part of Italy, while the Etruscans occupied that part of Italy generally north of the Tiber River. Little is known of the origin of the Etruscans and none of their literature has survived; what we know of them comes from the Roman and Greek writers and from the elaborate and ornately decorated tombs in which the Etruscans buried their dead.

Wall paintings and sculptured reliefs clearly indicate that the Etruscans held the Greeks in high esteem and were attracted to their love of sport. Harris (1972) tells us that the Etruscans did not slavishly follow the Greek sporting traditions as exemplified by the fact that their athletes apparently competed in clothes. Also, they possessed more of a streak of cruelty as indicated by their interest in gladiatorial fights and what Harris calls wild beast shows. Howell and Sawula (1973) point out that the most popular activity for the Etruscans was chariot racing, but dance, music, javelin, discus, boxing, wrestling, jumping, running, horse racing, acrobatics, and table games were also significant to them. They make no mention of the wild beast shows mentioned by Harris, and so no firm conclusion can be drawn about the importance or even the presence of such events. The Etruscans ceased to be a major power by the end of the fourth century B.C., but their influence on the Romans was considerable.

In 500 B.C. no one could have envisaged the *Romans* dominating the Mediterranean world within three hundred fifty years. In a long series of acts of aggression against their neighbors, including the Etruscans, the Romans enhanced their base of power. By 275 B.C. they had dominated their neighbors and set up a city–state rule that would have been the envy of the less unified Greeks. Corsica, Sicily, Sardinia, and Spain came under Roman rule in the Punic Wars. Finally in 146 B.C., the Greeks fell to the Romans.

By the time the Greeks fell, much of their creative genius had degenerated. The energetic, industrious Romans, at the peak of their power and prosperity, revived much of this lost vitality. Van Dalen et al. (1953) draw a nice comparison between the people of the two cultures:

> The Latin possessed a serious, industrious personality and a natural executive ability. On the other hand, he lacked the sparkling, aesthetic genius and the capacity for deep philosophical contemplation of the Greek. The empire builders were not proficient in pure art forms, did not fashion new lights of philosophical thought, or evolve new concepts of scientific truths. Nevertheless, the Western world is deeply indebted to the Romans for their practical contributions to mankind. Although the Greeks were the more profound and versatile thinkers, the Romans were the more energetic and efficient "doers." (P. 76)

For the early Romans, particularly in those years of military conquest, physical education was aimed at producing a better soldier. The Greek preoccupation with aesthetics, grace, beauty, and harmony was looked upon as a bit frivolous and not at all conducive to developing toughness and strength of character. Unlike the Spartan youth educated in military barracks or the Athenian educated in the gymnasium, the Roman child was constantly under parental tutelage. Around age seventeen, the males were expected to join the military service for a period of thirty years. At all times, physical fitness was expected. Work at activities (i.e., farming) that were intrinsically physically taxing contributed to fitness, but it remained the responsibility of the family to insure the fitness of their offspring.

Popular activities at the time included table games, ball games, horse races, chariot races, dancing, running, jumping, fencing, and javelin throwing. Of particular interest were the ball games. Roman youth appear to have engaged in an early version of what is now known as handball. The name used for the game was *harpastum,* also known as *phaininda* (Van Dalen et al., 1953; Young, 1944). Evidence indicates that involved youths would hit a ball with an open hand against a wall for the eventual return by one or more of the other competitors.

As the Roman Empire expanded, a period of great prosperity was achieved. People had more money and leisure time than in the past, and their demand for leisure activities increased. Self-serving individualism, unrest among the masses, governmental corruption, outright despotism, and a decay in morality and religious values were at work in creating the decadence that would eventually doom the proud Romans.

Physical fitness took on a new look. Professionalization of both the military and the athletes led to a rather fragmented philosophy about the whole issue. Fitness for the military and for athletes seemed sensible, but little incentive was seen by the ordinary citizen for more than the most cursory fitness. The Romans, like the Greeks earlier, became spectators rather than participants.

Nero as Athlete

The typical perception of the character of the Roman emperor, Nero, is quite negative; almost invariably, his name is associated with evil. Stories about his propensities for cruelty, both true and apocryphal, do him no favor; this is particularly true where the early Christians were concerned. However, it is the contention of Mouratidis that historical accounts of the life of Nero are distorted because they have been written almost exclusively by his enemies, hardly an impartial panel. His negative image has been furthered by the fact that he avidly embraced the Greek love and admiration for athletic glory, thereby offending many Romans who were not Christians. The combination of offending both the Christians and the Roman power structure led, according to Mouratidis, to a less than objective accounting of Nero's behavior.

Nero was born in A.D. 37, ascended to power as emperor seventeen years later, and died at age thirty in the year A.D. 68. During his short reign, he tried to Hellenize sport (and Roman life in general) by bringing it into line with earlier Greek philosophy and practice. He instituted schools for athletic participants and masterminded the construction of a magnificent gymnasium for athletic expression. Nero also attempted to humanize the gladiatorial event by ruling that no combat be conducted to the death of one of the participants. As a participant himself, Nero was fascinated with chariot racing and wrestling, events in which he apparently made periodic public appearances, much to the chagrin of the ruling class and to the glee of the proletariat in Rome. This catering to the masses while offending both the ruling class in Rome and the increasingly numerous and powerful Christians, in the name of Hellenizing sport and the arts in Rome, played a role in his ultimate demise, both physically and historically.

Source: Mouratidis (1985).

The ever-increasing decay of national values and the lowered emphasis on participation led to events that appealed to many Romans, events that still serve as measures of how decadent a society can become. A small indicator can be found in the general rejection of Greek sporting tradition by the Romans. As an example, running, throwing, and jumping were generally boring to the Romans, but wrestling, boxing, and the pankration were more exciting. To enhance the thrill of boxing, the gloves were "enhanced" by adding pieces of lead or iron, and two or three potentially lethal spikes were added to the glove knuckles. One of the more dramatic events was *chariot racing*. Though conceived in a high spirit, it reached new depths in Rome. Cheating, pushing, cutting in front of opponents, and hitting opponents when possible were all acceptable behaviors. Because of the nature of the various dangerous sports engaged in by the Romans, there were many injuries and deaths. Substantial gambling added to the drama of these events (and perhaps to the decadence). Race drivers, perhaps above all others, were revered in all of Rome; Rice et al. (1969) tells us that if a slave somehow became a highly successful driver, he was given freedom. If a free man, he was given monetary rewards. *Diocles,* a Spaniard, was cited as an example of what could lie in store for the successful driver (called an auriga). Diocles won

the equivalent of almost $2 million over a twenty-four-year period in which he won 1,462 of 4,257 races!

A step up in appeal to our most primitive side and a step down in terms of the values of sportsmanship was the *gladiatorial event.* Though the events were popular among the Etruscans, the Romans did not revive them until the middle of the second century B.C. At first, the gladiatorial competition was restricted and was conducted for the entertainment of the wealthy and engaged in primarily by prisoners

"Thumbs down!" is the crowd's verdict in this nineteenth century interpretation of gladiatorial combat in ancient Rome. Insatiable Romans continually sought variations on their bloodthirsty theme: dual combat was soon replaced by battles involving hundreds of gladiators and later by combat between humans and wild animals.

of war who preferred risking death to slavery. However, demand became so high that schools for gladiators were instituted, and professionalization of the combat was under way. As time went on, watching two combatants fight it out to the death was not enough, so new wrinkles were added. Scores of men were pitted against each other; the arena was flooded and mock naval battles were staged in which many were killed; wild animals were brought in and killed by their natural predators; eventually men and animals were pitted against each other. These latter two events were named the *venationes*, or the hunt for wild beasts. Buchanan (1975) actually cites figures related to animals killed in the Roman amphitheaters; the Emperor Augustus is said to have boasted of having thirty-five hundred animals killed in his shows. Not to be outdone, several years later, Titus had five thousand animals killed in one day. Another example of excess is the celebration marking the one-thousandth year of the Roman Empire in 249 A.D.; the Emperor Philip had thirty-two elephants, ten elks, ten tigers, sixty tame lions, thirty tame leopards, ten hyenas, six hippos, one rhinoceros, ten zebra, ten giraffes, twenty wild asses, and forty wild horses put to death in a one-day beast hunt.

The Roman Empire began in 31 B.C. and ended in A.D. 476, a period of more than five hundred years. The decline of the Roman Empire, according to Rice et al. (1969), can be attributed to a number of interrelated factors. Depopulation due to a lowered birth rate brought about by instability of the institution of marriage, gladiatorial game deaths, incessant civil wars, and a high suicide and homicide rate all were instrumental in weakening the structure of the civilization. Add general physical and moral decay and economic ruin to the preceding liabilities and all the ingredients for decline are present. Too, the rise in influence of Christianity was a factor of considerable importance. The final nail was driven in the Roman Empire coffin by the Teutonic barbarian invaders from Northern Europe.

THE MIDDLE AGES

With the fall of Rome, a period of historical darkness began. Not until the discovery of the New World one thousand years later was the darkness essentially lifted.

One beacon of brightness in the gathering twilight of culture was found in the *Byzantine Empire* to the east. Much of the Greek culture, language, and love of sport had been preserved in Constantinople. At the same time, much of the Roman approach to law and governance was subscribed to. Christianity was the dominant religion of the Byzantines. Obviously, they borrowed from the Greeks, Romans, and Christians alike. The Byzantine Empire endured from approximately the fourth century A.D. to 1453, when Constantinople fell to invading forces.

Among the favorite activities of the Byzantines was chariot racing, an activity that was to last until the twelfth century. Much of what was done in Constantinople was copied from the model provided by the Romans. To quote Schrodt (1981, p. 44): "Chariot races were the most important events in the life of the ordinary Byzantine citizen, and race days were occasions for excessive gambling, roistering, eating, and shouting—providing a particular kind of excitement and entertainment not available to him in any other facet of his life." Shades of our Super Bowl weekend!

The hippodrome in which the chariot races were held was also used for public executions. Understandably, the Christian leaders were not fond of any of the proceedings in the hippodrome, whether races or executions.

By the fifth century A.D. the Byzantines had lost their fascination with gladiatorial contests and *venationes*, and these activities ceased to be. Schrodt indicates that even at their acme, the *venationes* of the Byzantines appeared to be more acrobatic and less sadistic and cruel than the Roman versions.

Within the Byzantine time and territorial purview came the *demise of the Olympic Games.* It is generally agreed that Theodosius I (346?-395) decreed that the games be ended in 394 because of what he viewed as pagan idolatry. The games were not to take place again until 1896, a period of more than one thousand five hundred years. Theodosius, himself a Christian, felt that the games glorified the paganism of body worship associated with the Greeks and should be abolished. This assertion by Theodosius has led Brasch (1970, p. 414) to say: "While one religion had given birth to the Olympic Games, in the name of another they were destroyed."

In the West, the barbaric Teutons were establishing themselves; during the fifth century, the Visigoths occupied Spain, the Vandals seized North Africa, Gaul came under the domination of the Franks and Burgundians, and the Anglo-Saxons took over Britain. The result of this influx of barbarians was the creation of an intellectual vacuum in a previously cultured world; language and learning languished. Civilization as it was known at that time was in decline. The barbarians lived in crude dwellings, wore equally crude clothes, and were essentially farmers and herders of sheep and cattle. What these invaders lacked in language and worldly sophistication, however, was compensated for by a stable family life, industriousness, physical vitality, and intense loyalty to friends and an equal capacity for cruelty to those whom they disliked. The barbarians infused a physical vigor into the decadent Roman life. The Teutons were to eventually acquire the more aesthetic skills for which the Romans and, more particularly, the Greeks were known, and the combination of physical vitality and intellectual growth created a backdrop for the development of Western Europe and, ultimately, the New World. Many

of us in the Western Hemisphere are descendants of these early barbarians.

While the barbarians were dominant in the West and the Byzantines were a force to reckon with in the East, a movement of major influence was itself showing strength, and this was *Christianity.* Most of the early Christians were unshakable in their belief in Jesus as savior; they believed strongly in a better life hereafter, and suffering in this life was immaterial or expected. Martyrdom in the name of Christianity was a virtue. These Christians also firmly rejected the debauchery and degradation of the Romans; they felt that life was best lived in service to the soul, not the body. This early belief pattern was to have profound repercussions for physical activity for more than one thousand years, and even today we find people who are guilt-ridden if they have a good time, as if there were something evil about worldly pleasures.

Because their belief patterns ran counter to the licentiousness of the Romans, many Christians suffered indignities and cruelties that only served to reinforce rather than dissipate their piety. The end result of much of this piety was an increasing disenchantment with the physical side of man, and nowhere is this better seen than in the extremism of the *ascetics* of the early Middle Ages, which roughly covered the period from the sixth to tenth centuries. The ascetics personified the ultimate in Christian rejection of bodily worship and, conversely, the acceptance of sacrifice and suffering. The ascetics lived as hermits in caves or other primitive surroundings where suffering could be maximized; they fasted, prayed, and meditated; they tormented themselves with physical discomfort by sleeping on beds of nails or by beating themselves into exhaustion. It is no small wonder that their fanaticism often led them to bizarre behavior fed by hallucinations brought on by the interaction of prolonged meditation, contemplation, pain, sleeplessness, and virtual starvation. Needless to say, physical activity of a healthful nature had no place in the lives of the ascetics.

A more rational approach to worship was seen in the *monasteries* organized in Europe by Saint Benedict in the early part of the sixth century. These monasteries were set up so that those who wished to live a holy life minus the distractions of the secular world could do so. Strict discipline centered around manual labor, reading, study, and prayer. Work was seen as meeting their physical needs, and much of their labor centered around construction of the monasteries themselves. Again, physical education per se had no place. Historians and historians of sport should be thankful to the monks, however, because much of what we know about significant periods of our history is available to us as a result of their thorough record keeping and preservation of previously generated literature.

In the latter part of the Middle Ages, approximately the eleventh to the thirteenth century, the *Age of Chivalry* came to the fore as an influential force in reviving interest in physical activity. The feudal estates of the Age of Chivalry, which probably originated with the Germanic tribes of the tenth and eleventh centuries, were presided over by landlords who placed much emphasis on fitness for military and competitive tournament purposes; physical preparedness for combat and competition was the order of the day. Broekhoff (1968, p. 24) points to the interplay of militarism and physical activity: "Physical education has always been held in high esteem at times in which a society recognizes the need for physical action." The core of chivalric training was physical education, with the intellect virtually neglected; many of the knights were poorly educated or illiterate (Moolenijzer, 1968). Early education took place at home; at age seven, a son of the nobility was taken from his home to serve a baron or king as a page; at fourteen, he became a squire and served an apprenticeship to a knight by caring for his horse and acting as shield bearer in combat. At age twenty-one, he became a full-fledged knight. Preparatory to knighthood, some emphasis was placed on the arts and social graces, but the majority of the time from age seven on was devoted to horsemanship, swordsmanship, and hunting. Perhaps the best summary of what was expected in the training for knighthood is reflected in a prose passage by Rothe near the end of the fifteenth century (Neumann, 1936):

> The arts all seven which certainly at all times a perfect man will love are: he must ride well, be fast in and out of the saddle, trot well and canter and turn around and know how to pick something up from the ground.
>
> The other, that he knows how to swim and dive into the water, knows how to turn and twist on his back and on his belly.
>
> The third, that he shoots well with crossbows, arm, and handbows; these he may well use against princes and dukes.
>
> The fourth, that he can climb fast on ladders when necessary, that will be of use in war, in poles and ropes it is also good.
>
> The fifth art I shall speak of is that he is good in tournament, that he fights and tilts well and is honest and good in the joust.
>
> The sixth art is wrestling also both fencing and fighting, beat others in the long jump from the left as well as from the right.
>
> The seventh art: he serves well at the table, knows how to dance, has courtly manners, does not shy away from board games or other things that are proper for him.

Obviously, the prospective knight was expected to be proficient in various aspects of horsemanship, swimming and diving, archery, climbing, fencing, wrestling, jumping, dancing, and table games.

One outgrowth of all this fascination for readiness for war and fitness for competition was the *joust* (bouhourt). In its original form, both the horse and the rider were as protected as was possible considering that the purpose of the event was to dislodge one's competitor from his horse. As time went on, a simple joust was not sufficient; blunt instrumentation was replaced with sharp and lethal lances and all other safe-guards were largely dropped. Also, touring professionals, called "jousting bums" by Moolenijzer, started taking over the event, lead-ing, in part, to its demise as a sporting event in the first part of the sixteenth century.

The overall effect of chivalry, however, was to elevate physical activity to a position of impor-tance again; it remained for subsequent genera-tions to arrive at a balance between the physical and intellectual so revered by the early Greeks.

THE RENAISSANCE

During the fourteenth to sixteenth centuries, there was a major reawakening of interest in language, culture, arts, and education, and this renaissance had considerable influence on sport and physical activity. A major part of this rebirth was the estab-lishment of universities, such as those found in Paris, Salerno, and Bologna. Loosely structured and attended by a rather ragtag clientele, these early universities placed much emphasis on gram-mar, logic, mathematics, and scholarly debate and essentially accorded no place for organized phys-ical activities. As a consequence, much youthful energy was spent in confrontations with the local populace, pranks, fights among themselves, and other shenanigans. All in all, however, these universities presaged an age of intellectual inquiry that was to end the Dark Ages.

Concomitant with this reawakening of interest in knowledge was the growth of free trade and mercantilism, the lessening of the strength of the feudal estates, and an increasing secularism. Gunpowder was developed and this was to change the course of warfare drastically; the printing press was invented by Gutenberg; Columbus sailed to the New World; and his Por-tuguese and Spanish peers were quite involved in their various discoveries all over the globe.

Though still fettered with much ecclesiasti-cism and the remnants of chivalry, break-throughs in thinking and to some extent in phys-ical activity were being made in Italy by Vittorino da Feltra (1378–1446), Martin Luther (1483–1540) in Germany, Juan Luis Vives (1492–1540) in Spain, Michel de Montaigne (1533–1592) and François Rabelais (1490–1553) in France, Sir Thomas Elyot (1490?–1546) in England, Paracelsus (1493–1541) in Switzerland, and Copernicus (1473–1543) in Poland. These influential scholars were not rabid proponents of physical exercise in the early Greek and Roman sense, but they did see a place for physi-cal fitness in the scheme of things for the healthy, well-rounded individual. This stance, of course, was a big departure from the asceticism and monasticism of the early Middle Ages.

THE REFORMATION

In addition to the continuing influence of the writings of each of the great thinkers of the Renaissance period, the rapidly enlarging world was starting to feel the effects of people like Galileo (1564–1642) with his popularization of the telescope (among other things), Isaac New-ton (1642–1727) and his concept of gravity, and the eloquence of Sir Francis Bacon (1561–1626) on educational issues. Also, John Milton (1608–1674), John Locke (1632–1704), and Jean Jacques Rousseau (1712–1778) bridged the gap between the Age of Reformation and the Age of Enlightenment. Though not much was hap-pening during this period with regard to physi-cal activity, the Reformation is clearly an important historical period.

THE AGE OF ENLIGHTENMENT

Recognition of the dignity and rights of each person and emphasis on the ability to think ana-lytically and critically marked the Age of

Enlightenment. England was operating under a form of democracy, making it unique at that time. The French and the new Americans in New England were becoming aware that education for all was a worthy goal, and it should be neither a responsibility of the church nor the right of only the wealthy or noble. These flames were fanned by educational reformers such as Rousseau, Johann Heinrich Pestalozzi (1746–1827), and Pestalozzi's European disciples: Friedrich Froebel (1782–1852), Johann Friedrich Herbart (1776–1841), and Phillip Emanuel von Fellenberg (1771–1844).

Rousseau's beliefs, summarized in *Emile* (1762), were a break with tradition. He opposed the formal learning so characteristic of schools of that time, which stressed Latin, Greek, and mathematics; and Rousseau heretically insisted that play, games, manual arts, and nature studies would be more educational. Unlike Locke and Rabelais, who were proponents of physical education in the schools, but for military and health reasons, Rousseau viewed such a requirement as part of the total development of the child and young adult of school age. It is also interesting to note that Rousseau, according to Gerber (1968), was also a proponent of sport as a means of promoting national unity.

Even more heretical than his opposition to formal learning was Rousseau's insistence that the nature of man is good and not sinful, as had been emphasized for so many previous centuries. He was to have a profound impact on education and philosophy beyond anything he could ever imagine.

Pestalozzi, in turn, was greatly influenced by Locke and Rousseau, and he passed down to his disciples his emphasis on physical education within the total school curriculum. Though all of these disciples practiced variations of what Locke and Rousseau had suggested, they were *in toto* proponents of games and physical activity within the academic life of the child.

Thanks in part to the collective efforts of many, from Copernicus and Rabelais to Locke and Rousseau, there developed a veritable explosion of activity all over Europe in the eighteenth and nineteenth centuries. The Germans, under the guidance of physical educators such as Johann Christoph Friedrich Guts Muth (1759–1839), Friedrich Ludwig Jahn (1778–1852), and Adolf Spiess (1810–1858), developed active programs in *gymnastics,* which were, in reality, broadly based programs of physical fitness. The Germans also contributed the *playground movement* in the latter part of the nineteenth century. The Danes and the British were also very active in the promotion of play, games, and various physical activities.

COLONIAL AMERICA

The settling of Jamestown, Virginia, in 1607 and Plymouth, Massachusetts, in 1620 signaled the beginning of the *colonial period* in American history. Though Leonard (1984) says the times were not as stark and monotonous as some would have us believe, the period nevertheless had its rigors; the soil had to be tilled, the forests cleared, houses built, and protection against the elements had to be generated. Strong prohibitions were placed on play and sport, partially due to persistent threats to survival and because of religious admonitions to avoid idleness and abuse of precious work time.

Among the early settlers were the *Puritans,* who were particularly opposed to sports because of their interference with what the Puritans considered proper piety. In some ways, the Puritans were a throwback to the ascetics of the Middle Ages; they truly resented the "worldliness" of sport. To counter their influence in England prior to their departure to the New World, King James I issued a proclamation known as the *Book of Sports,* which was a statement that parts of divine services of any kind should be devoted to games, play, feasts, and physical activity. Puritans in both England and the colonies tenaciously fought the *Book of Sports,* continually trying to protect the Sabbath from levity.

Though influential, the Puritans were not the only *Sabbatarians;* evangelical groups neither Anglican nor Puritan sprang up all over the colonies, not the least of which was the Society of Friends (Quaker) sect, founded by George Fox in the early eighteenth century. The Quakers, the Puritans, and other evangelicals were powerful forces in opposing sports and physical activity.

Nevertheless, sports and games flourished. Influential men of the period, such as Benjamin Franklin (1706–1790) and Samuel Moody (1727?–1795), called for physical activity as a health and character builder. The *taverns,* much to the chagrin of the Puritans, became a focal point for social life and sponsored card games, billiards, bowling, and rifle and pistol competitions. Cockfighting and horse racing were not unknown in the colonies. Other popular activities were skittles (bowling), cricket, football (more soccer than football as we now know it), golf (called "goff"), shinny, rounders, ninepins, swimming, and tennis (Rice et al., 1969; Struna, 1981).

In Maryland, the colonials paid lip service to Sabbatarianism, generally going their merry way, enjoying fox hunting, yachting, and "ball and long bullets," the latter a game involving the throwing of cannonballs for distance (Kennard, 1970, p. 393). Gambling related to these sporting events was not at all unusual; particularly prominent was betting on horse races. Rader (1983) tells of a southern colonial named William Byrd III who was such an inveterate gambler that, after depleting the considerable family fortune amassed by his father, he committed suicide at an early age.

In 1732, the first sport social club, the Schuylkill Fishing Company, was organized in Philadelphia for purposes of allowing its members to hunt and fish on the Schuylkill River and to demonstrate that work and play could in fact be mutually advantageous to individual well-being.

A significant part of the colonial period was the Revolutionary War, fought from 1775 to 1783. According to Ledbetter (1979), several features characterized the games, play, and sport of the warriors of the Revolution. One is that most of what we know is gleaned from diaries and records of officers; few enlisted men kept notes on their activities. A second feature is that the army had no specific athletic and recreation program so that the soldiers had to improvise as they went. Also, competition between units was not stressed as a means of maintaining morale. A third feature is that most of the war effort was curtailed in the cold months, so that much spare time was available for recreational purposes. A fourth feature is that seldom did winning or losing matter; competition for the sake of recreation was paramount and there was much spontaneity in the generation of diversions.

According to Ledbetter, games and sports of the Revolutionary War included wicket, cricket (an ancestor of baseball), shinny (a cousin of field hockey), football, fives (handball), ninepins, billiards, shuffleboard, boxing, horse racing, cockfighting, sleighing, snowball fighting, skating, swimming, sailing, and wrestling.

THE CIVIL WAR PERIOD

Between the Revolutionary War and the Civil War, sports clubs similar to the Schuylkill Fishing Company proliferated; universities such as Harvard instituted wrestling and football, boxing clubs were springing up, and various forms of racing gained in popularity. The fervor associated with horse racing gave impetus to Stephen Foster (1826–1864) to extol its virtues in his popular song, "Camptown Races," generally considered to be the first popular song with a sport theme (Leonard, 1984).

In 1843, Yale University started a collegiate rowing club, and a year later Harvard did the same. This interest in rowing eventually led to

America's first intercollegiate sport, boating, in 1852 (Lewis, 1967; Spears and Swanson, 1983). The first competitive race was held on Lake Winnipesaukee in New Hampshire and was won by Harvard. These regattas continued to grow in popularity, and a number of other universities created competitive teams. The sport of boating was to set a precedent for intercollegiate competition that has now reached staggering proportions.

The Civil War, despite its immense brutality, had numerous moments of levity insofar as sport goes. Sport at the outbreak of the fighting was in a period of unprecedented acceptance. Many of the Puritan and Pietist proscriptions against sport had been diluted or ignored. Great surges in inventions, wealth, urbanization, and industrialization were at hand, and were altering our society greatly (Lucas, 1968). So it seems natural that sports should be such a big part of the nonfighting aspect of the life of the Civil War soldier.

According to Fielding (1977a): "In the beginning, the Civil War was a holiday which freed

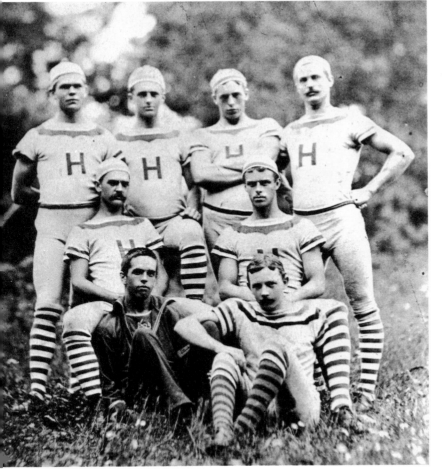

Boating was the first intercollegiate sport to gain widespread popularity. By the time members of Harvard's crew posed for this photo in 1875, Harvard and Yale had been competing in regattas for almost twenty-five years.

American youth from the shackels [sic] of responsibility. The soldier was recruited amidst a revival atmosphere. In his home town the call went out, the speeches were made and the whiskey flowed" (p. 145). In this atmosphere, it should not be surprising that the typical recruit had little patience with drill, ceremony, pomp, circumstance, and military maneuvers.

Fielding (1977b) conveniently divides the life of the Union soldier into four aspects, and talks of the typical activities that took place in each. The initial conscription into the army was arduous but boredom crept in when training was light. Competitive activities engaged in generally had a military purpose, hence shooting, horse races, and drilling were emphasized. Later, boxing, wrestling, footraces, fencing, and football were allowed. In addition to assisting training and relieving boredom, the various activities also enhanced group solidarity, which was a real plus for the trainers of the raw recruits. Holidays on or near the battlefield were a second part of the soldier's life, and recreation was generally similar to that of the boot camp period. One sport that was added here that did not seem to be present in early training was baseball. According to Crockett (1961, p. 341), it was a welcome addition: "Baseball appears to have been the most popular of all action sports engaged in by 'Billy Yank' and 'Johnny Reb.'" Betts (1971) indicates that prisoners of war passed time playing baseball. He also cites a case of a $100 challenge game played in Virginia between Army of the Potomac factions from New York and New Jersey. Betts further mentions a game between Union soldiers in Texas who were playing outside friendly lines. Rebel soldiers attacked them, wounding and capturing the centerfielder and scattering the other participants.

A third dimension of soldiering was the winter camp experience. In cold weather, soldiering diminished considerably and free time escalated. Cockfights were popular, but perhaps the most exciting events for the soldiers were snow-ball fights (Crockett, 1961; Fielding, 1977b). These snowball fights became so sophisticated in certain instances that complex plans of attack along military lines were developed and weapons stockpiled. Some of these battles were quite long and so bitterly fought that serious injuries became commonplace, and the activity had to be reduced in intensity or stopped.

The final facet of soldier life was centered around lulls in the fighting. Cockfights, football, and baseball were quite popular, along with most of the activities mentioned in the other phases. Crockett (1961) says the soldiers of the Union and Confederacy alike engaged in thirty-four different sports and recreation practices during the conduct of the war. The typical Civil War firefight was at close quarters due to limitations in the accuracy of the rifles and pistols and as a result of much use of swords and knives. In the infighting process, many verbal exchanges accompanied the fighting, and tempers flared as a result. Fielding (1977b) cites several instances in which combat was actually stopped so that combatants angered by these verbal exchanges could settle their disputes on neutral ground between the Union and Confederate soldiers through boxing. Once the issue was settled by fisticuffs, the war would be resumed.

THE TECHNOLOGICAL REVOLUTION

Prior to the Civil War and, more particularly, in the forty years that followed it, great changes took place in the American way of life. Population explosion was to take place; 17 million people lived in the United States in 1840 whereas there were 50 million by 1880 (Spears and Swanson, 1983). Immigration was rampant, initially by northwestern Europeans and later by Catholics and Jews from Southern and Eastern Europe (Rader, 1983). The blacks freed by the Emancipation Proclamation of 1863 were yet to be assimilated. North-South relations were strained. The effects of the techological revolution were being felt throughout the fabric of America. And sport was not exempt from these reverberations.

A particularly informative handling of these various social forces is provided by Betts (1953). He states that a number of factors contributed to the new direction in sport from 1850 to 1900, and among them were the decline of Puritan orthodoxy, the influence of the new immigrants, frontier emphasis on manliness and strength, the English athletic movement, and the contributions of energetic sportsmen. In figure 2.1, Betts further cites a number of products of this new technology as shaping the direction of sport.

Significant athletic events of the era included the founding of the New York Athletic Club in 1868, which was the first attempt to bring amateur athletics under a unified umbrella and led ultimately to the formation of the *Amateur Athletic Union (AAU)* in 1888. The first professional baseball team, the Cincinnati Red Stockings, was founded in 1869; tennis was introduced to the country in 1874; the National Baseball League was formed in 1876 with eight original participants; the United States Lawn Tennis Association was formed in New York in 1881; basketball was invented in 1891 by Dr. James Naismith of Springfield, Massachusetts; the first relay race in track and field was run in 1893, and this event was America's unique contribution to the sport; and the first American marathon race was held in Massachusetts in 1897.

A particularly noteworthy event of the time was the *reinstitution of the Olympic Games* in Athens, Greece, in 1896. The modern games were the product of the leadership of a Frenchman, Pierre de Fredy, Baron de Coubertin. Spears and Swanson (1983) indicate that he was by no means the first to try, merely the one who succeeded. With the exception of the war years in 1940 and 1944, the games have continued to be held and

Figure 2.1: **Impact of Technological Advances on Sport**

1. *Railroads.* The railroad companies made fairly extensive travel distinctly possible. The various railroad companies sponsored travel to athletic events in order to spur ticket sales. The Harvard–Yale boat races were put together by a railroad company that promised to transport and defray all expenses of the participants (Lewis, 1967). The rail companies were also instrumental in popularizing baseball, horse racing, and boxing.
2. *Telegraphy.* The development of telegraphy led to a great expansion in the transmission of sport information between cities, and by 1870 many metropolitan newspapers reported sport news. The first sport section in a newspaper was created in New York by William Randolph Hearst just before the year 1900.
3. *Innovations in printing.* Various improvements in the printing process allowed for better newspapers, journals related to sport only, and books with sport themes.
4. *Sewing machine.* The sewing machine allowed for more diverse and higher quality athletic goods.
5. *Incandescent lighting.* Improved quality of lighting expanded the sport day by allowing for nighttime events at a higher quality than that provided by gas lighting. Electrification created the environment for the growth of basketball and volleyball.
6. *Vulcanization of rubber.* The advent of vulcanized rubber had far-reaching consequences for the development of the ball so central to most sports. Pneumatic tires revolutionized cycling and harness racing and were to ultimately have great impact on automobile racing in the 1900s.
7. *Miscellany.* The stop watch, percussion cap, ball bearings, camera, movies, telephone, typewriter, and phonograph are just a few other products of the industrial revolution that were to enlarge the role of sport in the life of the American participant and spectator.

Source: Betts (1953).

Fashionable New Yorkers took quickly to the new game of lawn tennis after 1880. Here, a quartet of well-dressed women enjoy the game in Brooklyn's Prospect Park.

have, despite many political problems, grown in popularity.

All in all, the period from 1850 to 1900 was one of the dramatic changes in the American way of life and one of great growth in all facets of sporting events.

1900 TO THE PRESENT

At the risk of neglecting the past ninety years, only a few high spots will be touched upon from this period. The historical antecedents of most of the topics we will be dealing with in the remaining chapters have short histories, almost always from some point in the 1900s, so much

of the history of this period will be woven into the various topical elaborations in chapters to follow. There are, however, some high points that merit immediate attention.

America went from a concern with national issues only to a nation of great worldwide influence in the 1900s, and this assumption of power was to affect sport. Olympic participation was only one case in point; others include the creation of the Davis Cup competition in tennis and international pistol competition in 1900.

Internally, a crisis of major proportions was brewing in intercollegiate football that eventually necessitated intervention by *President Theodore Roosevelt* (1858–1919) in 1905 in order to arrive at some determination of the future of that game, which had become so brutal in the eyes of many critics. Lewis (1969) covers the situation well, but issues a warning that Roosevelt's role has been reported so variously by so-called authorities that one must use caution in adopting a doctrinaire view of just what the President actually did. Roosevelt, of course, believed strongly in the value of physical activity and saw football as "the most valuable of all team sports because it provided each individual with opportunities to test his courage" (Lewis, 1969, p. 719). Yet there were many dissenters because of injuries, deaths, cheating, and general brutality associated with the sport. After a number of meetings with interested parties from Yale, Harvard, Princeton, New York University, and members of the rules committee of the Intercollegiate Athletic Association of the United States, agreements were reached as to the future of football in what Lewis describes as "probably the single most important event in the history of intercollegiate sport" (p. 724). Lewis goes on to point out that President Roosevelt's role in the discussions was significant but not crucial and that he did not, as some would have us believe, save the game because it was never really threatened; the desire to reform the game was there, not an intent to abolish it. During the course of the various discussions, the president's son, Theodore, Jr., a freshman at Harvard, suffered a broken nose and facial cuts and bruises while playing the Yale game. Despite these injuries to his son, President Roosevelt remained steadfast in affirming the value of football (Lewis, 1969). Four years after the tempest, the *National Collegiate Athletic Association (NCAA)* was formed (in 1910) and is the prime governing force in college athletics at present.

Another interesting issue of the times had to do with prohibitions against Sunday participation in sport, the so-called *Blue Law of 1794,* which was a holdover from the days of the Puritans and the evangelicals of the colonial period. After World War I, sports became a virtual

obsession with Americans, and increasingly were engaged in on the Sabbath. Jable (1976) relates that in 1919 the Philadelphia Park Commission started allowing sports such as baseball, tennis, and golf to be played on Sundays in parks under its jurisdiction. The Philadelphia Sabbath Association took the issue to court, and the battle was on.

A big test of the Blue Law was made by the Philadelphia Athletics professional baseball team when they scheduled a Sunday afternoon game in August of 1926. The game was played and was viewed as a success by the team management, but the Sabbatarians promptly took them to court for their violation of the Sabbath and won an injunction against any further such indiscretions.

The stock market crash of 1929 put a well-documented strain on the economy of the country and, in the search for relief from the economic plight of their citizens, Philadelphia and Pennsylvania politicians and other officials turned again to Sunday sport as a partial solution. Again, Sabbatarians, such as the Friends of the Proper Observance of the Sabbath, took umbrage at this increasing encroachment on the sanctity of the final day of the week. However, laws were passed that allowed local option voting on Sunday sports. Philadelphia and Pittsburgh voters approved the option by a 7 to 1 majority, and on November 12, 1933, the Pittsburgh Steelers (known then as The Pirates) lost to a team from Brooklyn 32–0 before 12,000 supporters while the Eagles of Philadelphia were playing the vaunted Chicago Bears to a 3–3 tie before 20,000 fans. The Blue Law of 1794 was defeated to the dismay of the Sabbatarians. Perhaps the issue was best summed up by Jable (p. 363): "Eighteenth-century customs were not compatible with twentieth-century behavior."

Another historical landmark is chronicled by Zingale (1977), who summarizes much of what *Dwight D. Eisenhower (1890–1969)* did for public attitudes and behaviors related to physical

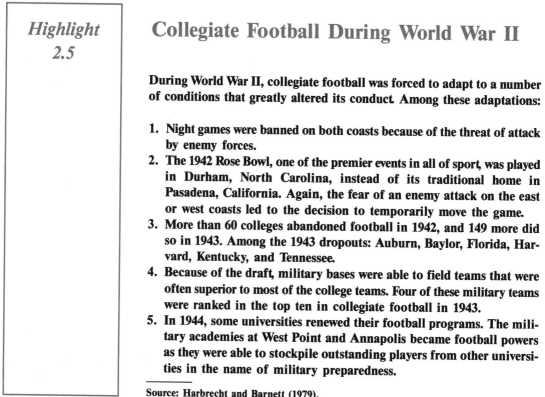

Highlight 2.5

Collegiate Football During World War II

During World War II, collegiate football was forced to adapt to a number of conditions that greatly altered its conduct. Among these adaptations:

1. Night games were banned on both coasts because of the threat of attack by enemy forces.
2. The 1942 Rose Bowl, one of the premier events in all of sport, was played in Durham, North Carolina, instead of its traditional home in Pasadena, California. Again, the fear of an enemy attack on the east or west coasts led to the decision to temporarily move the game.
3. More than 60 colleges abandoned football in 1942, and 149 more did so in 1943. Among the 1943 dropouts: Auburn, Baylor, Florida, Harvard, Kentucky, and Tennessee.
4. Because of the draft, military bases were able to field teams that were often superior to most of the college teams. Four of these military teams were ranked in the top ten in collegiate football in 1943.
5. In 1944, some universities renewed their football programs. The military academies at West Point and Annapolis became football powers as they were able to stockpile outstanding players from other universities in the name of military preparedness.

Source: Harbrecht and Barnett (1979).

fitness and sports during his presidency from 1952 to 1960. Himself an athlete at the United States Military Academy at West Point (member of the baseball and football squads), Eisenhower maintained a lifelong love of sport and fitness. Testing conducted by physical educators during the early 1950s revealed then 58 percent of young people in the United States were deficient in one or more of six aspects of strength and flexibility, compared to only 9 percent of their European counterparts. Dismayed by these findings, the president called for a convention of experts on fitness. In June, 1956, the conference on Youth Fitness was convened, and a number of far-reaching recommendations were made. Also, the *President's Council on Youth Fitness* was formed. This infusion of presidential clout

into the fitness realm must be regarded as a landmark event. The subsequent involvement on the part of President John F. Kennedy (1917–1963) was significant also.

The years since the 1950s, which Twombly (1976) calls the *Electronic Age* of sport, have seen an amazing involvement in physical activity. The growth of interest and involvement has been spectacular, as has a preoccupation with being a spectator rather than a participant. The latter situation is a source of considerable concern for critics of our modern lifestyle; references from neophytes and experts alike are constantly being made to the parallels between contemporary physical softness and that of the decadent Romans of two thousand years ago. The growth of collegiate and professional sport has been phenomenal in the past thirty years. Equally dramatic has been the rise in the sophistication and influence of television; many see television as a corrupting force in sport in a variety of ways.

All things considered, sport and physical activity are a big and fascinating business today, far removed in many ways from their origins, but nevertheless a powerful social force.

A BRIEF HISTORY OF PHYSICAL EDUCATION

Paralleling and interacting with the history of sport and physical activity is the *physical education movement* in the United States. Though there were proponents of what might be construed as physical education among the early colonists, perhaps the early German and Swedish immigrants who brought with them an enthusiasm for gymnastics in the early 1800s were our earliest physical educators. Catharine Beecher (1800–1878), daughter of the well-known preacher Lyman Beecher, sister of Harriet Beecher Stowe, the author of *Uncle Tom's Cabin,* and sister of the renowned reformer Henry Ward Beecher, was an early proponent of physical activity for women. She wrote two books advocating fitness in women, *Course of Calisthenics for Young Ladies* (1832) and *A Manual of Physiology and Calisthenics for Schools and Families* (1856). Among other things, her work was instrumental in the creation of the *first physical education program for women* at Vassar College, in 1865.

In 1861, the *first collegiate men's physical education program* had been established at Amherst College and, significantly for the time period, was called the Department of Physical Education. It was not until the 1920s that physical education would completely supplant physical culture as the preferred term for addressing these kinds of activities and departments. In any event, the department was chaired by Dr. Edward

Hitchcock (1828–1911), and the program stood alone for twenty years as an example for all to emulate. By 1965, there would be 539 colleges and universities offering professional preparation in physical education (Lee, 1983).

Another significant milestone for 1861 was the publication of the first physical education journal by Diocletian (Dio) Lewis (1823–1886), an eminent physical educator of the time, which was entitled *Gymnastics Monthly and Journal of Physical Culture.* A year later, Lewis published a significant book, *The New Gymnastics for Men, Women, and Children.* Another significant publication for professionals in the field was the *American Physical Education Review* (1896), which later became the *Journal of Health and Physical Education* in 1930, the *Journal of The American Association for Health, Physical Education, and Recreation* in 1949, the *Journal of Health, Physical Education, and Recreation* in 1955, the *Journal of Physical Education and Recreation* in 1976, and the *Journal of Physical Education, Recreation and Dance (JOPERD)* in 1982. Another significant physical education journal, the *Research Quarterly,* was founded in 1930 and became the *Research Quarterly for Exercise and Sport* in 1980; the interested reader is referred to an article by Park (1980) that summarizes its first fifty years. A journal for coaches, the *Athletic Journal,* began publication in 1919.

On the educational front, the *first state to pass a law requiring physical education in the public schools* was California in 1866, primarily as a result of the efforts of John Swett of the Rincon School (Hoepner, 1970). It was quite a while before other states followed suit; by 1930, 36 states had laws requiring physical education in the schools. By 1916, however, physical education had reached a level of importance that allowed for the appointment of the first state supervisor of physical education, Dr. Thomas Storey (1875–1943) of New York. Not coincidentally, New York University and Columbia University conferred the first Doctor of Philosophy degrees in physical education in 1924.

As events unfolded, there was a growth in the number and influence of professional organizations within physical education. In 1885, the American Association for the Advancement of Physical Education was created; in 1903, it became the American Physical Education Association; in 1937 the name was changed to the American Association for Health and Physical Education; the word "Recreation" was added to the title in 1938; the word "Association" was replaced by "Alliance" in 1975; and the official name as of now is *The American Alliance for Health, Physical Education, Recreation, and Dance (AAHPERD)*. Another organization, the College Physical Education Association (CPEA), was formed in 1897, followed by Amy Homans' (1848-1933) creation, the National Association for Physical Education of College Women in 1910, and Phi Epsilon Kappa, the professional fraternity of physical educators, in 1913. At the same time these organizations were lending their influence to the cause of physical fitness, organizations such as the Playground Association of America (1906), the Boy Scouts (1910), the Girl Scouts (1912), and the Campfire Girls (1912) were springing up to further emphasize the broad concepts of fitness and recreation.

Though the list of leaders is virtually endless, we would be remiss if a few of the more eminent contributions were not mentioned. In 1880, Dr. Dudley Sargent (1849-1924) was appointed Director of Hemenway Gymnasium at Harvard. Dr. Sargent, a physician (as were most of the early pioneers in physical education), was an early promoter of strength testing and was said to have administered 50,000 anthropometric tests in his career (Hackensmith, 1966). In 1890, Dr. Luther Gulick (1865-1918) devised the first athletic achievement test, which dealt with the pentathlon event in track. In 1904, *R. Tait McKenzie* (1867-1938) became head of the Department of Physical Education at Pennsylvania University,

where he distinguished himself for twenty-seven years. In addition to his scholarly and leadership qualities, McKenzie was a most accomplished sculptor, and he was perhaps the first since the early Greeks to use athletics as a subject. His works became world famous, leading Lee (1983, p. 203) to say: "No one of modern times has bound the profession of physical education to the glories of its ancient heritage as did R. Tait McKenzie through his art work."

Two other leaders of note, Clark Hetherington (1870-1942) and Jesse Feiring Williams (1886-1966), published books in 1922 that called for a movement away from the militaristic and moralistic gymnastic influence of the Germans and Swedes and toward the establishment of a physical education by and for the United States, one that educated the whole person. This call ushered in a new era for physical education. Also, the influence of eminent educators, psychologists, and philosophers of that time was instrumental in shaping not only our views of physical education but also our vision of education and life in general. Among them were people like John Dewey (1859-1952), G. Stanley Hall (1846-1924), William James (1842-1910), and E. L. Thorndike (1874-1949).

The cause of physical education was greatly served by the events of World Wars I and II. The fitness deficiencies among our youth that were so graphically illustrated by medical exams, coupled with the need for fitness for those accepted into military life, gave added impetus to the physical education movement. Also, events of the Korean War and fitness test results amassed by physical educators in the 1950s and 1960s and presented to Presidents Eisenhower and Kennedy only served to strengthen the case.

Two other recent events that have been most salient in their far-reaching effects are the *Civil Rights Act of 1964* and *Title IX* of the Educational Amendment Act of 1972. These acts militated against discrimination due to race or sex and have facilitated the integration of women and minorities into the mainstream of American life, including physical activity and sport.

A BRIEF HISTORY OF PSYCHOLOGY

Most historians in psychology attribute the beginning of psychology as a scientific endeavor to the year 1879. At that time the German Wilhelm Wundt (1832–1920) had started a laboratory in Leipzig aimed primarily at the study of psychophysiological phenomena. According to Roediger, Rushton, Capaldi, and Paris (1984), Wundt was a prolific writer who published some 50,000 pages of professional papers.

Prior to the establishment of the Leipzig laboratory, German scientists such as Hermann Ebbinghaus (1850–1909), Hermann von Helmholtz (1821–1894), and Gustav Fechner (1801–1887) were systematically studying various psychophysical phenomena. Fechner published a book, *Elements of Psychophysics*, in 1860, and this is considered to be one of the earliest of all psychology texts.

In 1870, Sir Francis Galton (1822–1911), an Englishman, published *Hereditary Genius*, a book that was to spur eventual interest in the development of psychological tests. In 1880, another prominent figure, G. Stanley Hall, was appointed president of Clark University. Hall was the leader of a child-study movement that had considerable impact on educational practices; he also started in 1887 the first psychology journal, the *American Journal of Psychology*, which still exists today. In 1890, William James published his two-volume work entitled *Principles of Psychology*, a twelve-year labor of love (Benjamin, Hopkins, and Nation, 1994). Out of James' work would grow a historical school of thought known as *functionalism*. Functionalism, as opposed to the structuralist camp of the early psychophysicists with their emphasis on the elements of mental life, was more interested in the uses or functions of the mind. John Dewey, who administered an influential experimental school at the University of Chicago from 1896–1903, was also a leading functionalist.

An alternate method of looking at human behavior was proposed in 1913 by John B. Watson (1878–1958). Watson outlined his revolutionary *behavioristic approach* in a paper entitled "Psychology as the Behaviorist Views It." He advocated that scientists should study observable behavior not unobservable mental processes or the murky mystical mentalisms of the structuralists and functionalists. Reinforcement of a sort was provided for Watson's viewpoint in the same year (1913) by E. L. Thorndike, who outlined his behavioristic notions in a treatise entitled *Educational Psychology*. Subsequent behaviorists, including Clark Hull (1884–1952), Edward Tolman (1886–1961), and Edwin Guthrie (1886–1959), provided further fuel for the behaviorist fires with their varied but behavioral theories. The most contemporary leader of the behavioral movement was the eminent Harvard psychologist, B. F. Skinner (1904–1990). Skinner eloquently outlined his position in such offerings as *Behavior of Organisms* (1938), the fictional *Walden Two* (1948), and *Beyond Freedom and Dignity* (1971). All of these American behaviorists are indebted to the work of the Russian physiologist, Ivan Pavlov (1849–1936), who demonstrated the nature of classical conditioning in the late 1800s.

Another powerful force in the history of psychology has been the *psychoanalytic model* of Sigmund Freud (1856–1939). Over the past eighty years much has been said on both points of view as to the efficacy or validity of psychoanalysis, but it has served to spur much research into personality theory, psychopathology, and psychotherapy techniques.

As a protest to the pessimism of the analysts, American psychologists such as Abraham Maslow (1908–1970) and Carl Rogers

Time Line

B.C.

850	Homer writes the *Iliad* and the *Odyssey*.
776	First Olympic Games are conducted.
520	Sixty-fifth Olympic Games establishes format for rest of competitions until games end in A.D. 394.
146	Greek Empire falls to the Romans.

A.D.

394	Theodosius I declares that the Olympic Games must cease because of their glorification of bodily paganism.
476	Roman Empire falls to the invading Teutons.
1000–1200	Age of Chivalry places much emphasis on knightly combat as sport.
1300–1500	The Renaissance period is characterized by reawakening of interest in physical activity, though it is largely informal.
1618	King James I issues proclamation known as *Book of Sports*.
Eighteenth century	Rousseau espouses virtues of physical activity as part of total development of the person: he is also a proponent of sport as a means of promoting national unity. The roots of the German playground movement are established.
1732	Schuylkill Fishing Club is established in Philadelphia, and remains the oldest sporting organization in America.
1810	Tom Molineaux, a black, engages Tom Cribb in first interracial boxing title fight in history.
1831	*Course of Calisthenics for Young Ladies,* by Catherine Beecher, is published.

1846	First recorded baseball game is played in Hoboken, New Jersey.
1852	First intercollegiate sporting event takes place between rowing crews from Harvard and Yale.
1861	First college physical education program for men is instituted at Amherst College.
1865	First physical education program for women is started at Vassar College.
1866	California becomes the first state to pass a law mandating physical education in public schools.
1868	New York City Athletic Club is formed.
1869	Rutgers and Princeton play the first intercollegiate football game.
1871	Palace of Minos is unearthed, yielding valuable artifacts for sport historians and others.
1872	Bud Fowler is the first black professional baseball player.
1874	Tennis is introduced to America.
1876	The first intercollegiate track meet is conducted in Saratoga, New York.
1876	A. G. Spalding becomes the first major sporting goods corporation.
1882	Handball is introduced to the United States.
1883	Moses Fleetwood Walker becomes the first black major league baseball player.
1886	*Sporting News* is published for the first time.
1887	Legal betting takes place at a racetrack in New York State.
1888	The Amateur Athletic Union (AAU) is formed.
1889	Walter Camp selects the first college football all-American team.
1891	Basketball is invented by Dr. James Naismith in Springfield, Massachusetts.

(Continued next page)

Time Line *(continued)*

1891	A world high jump record is set by W. B. Page at 6 feet 4 inches.
1895	William Randolph Hearst starts the first newspaper sport page.
1896	The Olympic Games are reinstituted in Athens, Greece.
1897	The first American marathon race is run in Massachusetts.
1900	Women take part in Olympics for the first time.
1901	The first bowling tournament is held in Chicago, Illinois.
1903	The World Series in major league baseball is played for the first time.
1904	The Olympic Games are held for the first time in America in St. Louis.
1905	The Intercollegiate Athletic Association is formed, laying the groundwork for creation of the National Collegiate Athletic Association (NCAA).
1905	President Teddy Roosevelt convenes a meeting of major university presidents to reduce violence in football.
1911	The first Indianapolis 500 takes place.
1913	Jim Thorpe is stripped of medals won in the 1912 Olympics because he had played professional baseball in 1909 and 1910.
1913	The forward pass is introduced in football.
1916	The Professional Golfer's Association (PGA) is formed.
1917	The National Hockey League (NHL) is created in Canada.
1919	The first coaching journal, *Athletic Journal,* is published.
1920	The first play-by-play account of a football game takes place as Station WTAW of College Station, Texas, broadcasts Texas-Texas A&M game.

1926	Gertrude Ederle becomes the first woman to swim the English channel.
1928	Women take part in track and field at the Olympics for the first time.
1928	The United States Volleyball Association is formed.
1932	Mildred (Babe) Didrikson dominates women's track and field at the Olympic Games.
1933	Didrikson makes her debut in professional basketball.
1935	The first night game in major league baseball is played in Cincinnati.
1935	Hialeah (Florida) Race Track employs an electronic eye to determine race winners.
1936	The Rodeo Cowboy Association is formed under the name of Cowboy's Turtle Association.
1938	The first intercollegiate gymnastics championships are held.
1939	Little League baseball begins.
1939	A college basketball game between Columbia and Princeton becomes the first televised sport event.
1940	The Olympic Games are cancelled until 1948 because of World War II.
1941	Ohio State University hosts the first college fencing championships.
1945	Five college players from Brooklyn College admit taking bribes to throw a basketball game.
1947	Jackie Robinson breaks the color barrier in professional baseball.
1947	Babe Didrikson Zaharias wins the British Open golf championship.
1948	Fred Morrison invents the Frisbee.
1949	The National Basketball Association (NBA) is formed from two other leagues.

(Continued next page)

Basketball inventor James Nai-smith takes a shot at the first "hoop"—a peach basket.

Gertrude Ederle dons a thick coat of grease to ward off the cold before swimming the English Channel in 1926. Ederle, the first woman to brave the channel, beat the men's record by nearly two hours.

Time Line *(Continued)*

1949	The Ladies Professional Golfer's Association (LPGA) is formed.
1950	Black players are admitted to professional basketball.
1951	The Soviet Union files to take part in the 1952 Olympics.
1954	*Sports Illustrated* begins publication.
1954	The Fellowship of Christian Athletes (FCA) is initiated.
1954	Roger Bannister posts the first mile run in under four minutes in Oxford, England (3:59.4).
1961	Mickey Mantle becomes the highest paid player in the American League at $75,000.
1962	Wilt Chamberlain scores 100 points in an NBA game.
1965	The so-called eighth wonder of the world, the Astrodome, opens in Houston.
1966	The first football Super Bowl is staged.
1971	The Association for Intercollegiate Athletics for Women (AIAW) is formed.
1972	Title IX of the Educational Amendments Act opens up sports for females.
1972	The Boston marathon has its first female entrant.
1973	A New Jersey court allows girls to play Little League baseball.
1975	Frank Robinson is hired as the first black manager in major league baseball.
1976	Janet Guthrie is the first woman to compete in the Indianapolis 500.
1979	Women reporters are allowed in athletic dressing rooms after games for interviews.
1980	Olympic Games are held in Russia, the first time they have been hosted by a Communist country. The United States boycotts the games.
1980	Entertainment and Sports Programming Network (ESPN) begins broadcasting television.
1982	Commemorative stamps honoring Bobby Jones and Babe Didrikson Zaharias are issued by the U.S. Postal Service.
1984	Olympics are held in Los Angeles, and Russians return the U.S. boycott of the 1980 Games in Moscow.
1987	Ben Johnson of Canada runs 100 meters in world record time of 9.84 seconds; he is later stripped of the record for steroid abuse.
1989	Pete Rose of the Cincinnati Reds baseball team is banned from baseball for life, thereby jeopardizing his place in the Hall of Fame.
1991	Carl Lewis sets the world record for 100 meters at a meet in Tokyo; his time was 9.86 seconds. Over the course of the next year eleven world records are set in track and field.
1991	Earvin "Magic" Johnson of the Los Angeles Lakers announces that he has tested positive for HIV, the virus that causes AIDS.
1992	The so-called USA Dream Team runs roughshod over the basketball competition at the Summer Olympics, winning the championship over Croatia 117–85.
1992	Raybestos Brakettes of Stratford, Connecticut, wins the women's national fastpitch softball championship for the twenty-fifth time since 1958.
1993	Tennis great Arthur Ashe dies at age forty-nine of AIDS.
1993	Michael Jordan prematurely retires from professional basketball; he takes up professional baseball the next year.
1994	The Silver Bullets, a touring women's baseball team, is created.
1994	Major League baseball goes on strike in August; the World Series is cancelled for the first time ever.

(1902–1987) have championed the *humanistic movement,* an approach with strong emphasis on optimism and individual initiative. The humanists, like most psychologists, owe a heavy debt to philosophy; humanism is traceable to the works of Rousseau.

On a more atheoretical tack, the *testing movement* has been influential. In 1902 two French physicians, Alfred Binet (1857–1911) and Theodore Simon (1873–1962), created the first paper-and-pencil test of intelligence. This objective measure of intelligence sparked a revolution that was to generate literally thousands of tests designed to measure every psychological trait and capability imaginable. Many of the significant tests pertinent to sport psychology are discussed in chapter 8.

A modern point of emphasis in the field of psychology includes the study of physiological bases for behavior and investigation of mental or cognitive events that shape behavior. The structuralists and functionalists are essentially defunct; the Freudians are small in number and suspect in scientific validity; the humanists, though a bit fuzzy scientifically, have their devotees, and behaviorism is thriving though modified to place more credence in less observable behaviors, that is, mental events.

SUMMARY

1. Much of what we know about sport in ancient times has been gathered from analysis of various archeological findings that include mosaics, frescoes, paintings, textiles, works of art, sculpture, ornaments, tablets, architecture, and seal stones.
2. Artifacts dated to the period 3000–1500 B.C. seem to indicate that boxing, wrestling, and board games were engaged in by the Sumerians. An even broader representation of activities is yielded by the Egyptians of the same time period. The early Chinese were apparently avid participants in sport, as were the Indians of 1500 B.C.
3. The unearthing of the Palace of Minos in 1871 showed that the Minoans of 3000 to 1200 B.C. engaged in many activities, but the so-called "taureador" sports (bullgrappling and related activities) seemed to dominate their interest.
4. Much of what we have learned about early Greek activities has been gleaned from the *Iliad* and the *Odyssey,* twin creations of the blind Ionian poet, Homer. It is generally agreed that they were written about 850 B.C., and both reveal the Greek love of sport.
5. The date of the first Olympic Games has been fixed as 776 B.C. It was not until the fourteenth Olympics that more than one event was held; a second running event was added in 724 B.C., and a long race was added in 720. By the sixty-fifth games in 520 B.C., the games had been enlarged to include wrestling, boxing, the pankration, four running events, and the pentathlon. This format was to last until the demise of the games in A.D. 394.
6. Olympic winners won a crown of wild olive leaves for their victories. They competed in the nude (after 720 B.C.), and women were, with few exceptions, not allowed to compete in or view the games. The penalty for violating this rule was death to the offender.
7. The people of the city–state of Sparta, unlike their contemporaries in Athens who saw physical activity as a glorification of the entire human organism, viewed physical activity as a means of furthering military preparedness. They emphasized the "perfect warrior" concept, and physical activity was aimed at meeting this ideal. In the process, many Spartan athletes were successful in the Olympic Games and other sports events.
8. The defeat of the Persians in 480 B.C. ushered in the "Golden Age of Greece." Great harmony existed between the various

Greek city–states. As time wore on, internecine wars broke out. Energies and resources were strained, and the Greeks could not withstand external invasions, falling to the Macedonians. The Greek empire ceased to exist as a power in 338 B.C., though the overall effect it had on culture has never ceased.

9. The Romans ascended to power over all of the Mediterranean world in 146 B.C. The early Romans, much like the Spartans, viewed physical activity as a means of preparing men for combat. Many sports and games were played; one of them, harpastum, appears to be the earliest version of what is now known as handball. As time wore on, the Romans came to view activity and fitness as the province of the professional army and the full-time athletes. A period of physical neglect set in and, coupled with a deterioration in the overall quality of life values, laid the framework for the ultimate demise of the Romans.

10. Gladiatorial events and *venationes,* fights between animal predators or man and predator, became very popular in meeting the decadent needs of the later Romans. The Roman Empire ended in A.D. 476, when the barbarian Teutons from the north took over.

11. The Middle Ages was a period of about one thousand years characterized by the development of Christianity, many wars, devastating diseases, and a dearth of intellectual advancement. One early exception was found in the Byzantines in the East; they carried on many of the Greek aesthetic and athletic traditions. Chariot racing was most popular, though gladiatorial events and *venationes* were well-received; apparently they were not as violent as those staged by the Romans, however. The Olympic Games died at the decree of the Byzantine ruler, Theodosius I, in A.D. 394 because of their supposed worship of pagan practices.

12. The growth of Christianity led to a rejection of most of the Greek and Roman worship of sport and physical activity. The body was seen as secondary to the soul; the ultimate here can be seen in the self-imposed pain and indignities of the ascetics, and the quiet, monastic, worshipful, reflective lifestyle of the monks of the sixth century A.D.

13. The Age of Chivalry, from the eleventh to the thirteenth century, was an important time for physical competition. Swordsmanship, horsemanship, and physical preparedness for competition and combat were greatly valued as a part of chivalric training.

14. The Renaissance — the age of Martin Luther, Paracelsus, and Rabelais — was a period of rebirth of ideas but not a major period in sport and physical fitness. Jousting, however, was prominent.

15. The Reformation, dominated by ideas from Galileo, Newton, Bacon, and Locke, was not marked by great advances in physical activity, though the stage was being set for a veritable explosion of such endeavors.

16. The Age of Enlightenment was dominated by Pestalozzi, Rousseau, Froebel, and Herbart, all of whom espoused to varying degrees and in different ways the importance of physical activity to the overall well-being of a child. Their influence over the past two hundred years has been inestimable; physical educators continue to pay homage to these pioneers.

17. The early colonials in America were consumed with concerns of safety and piety, and all physical activities had to conform to these demands. However, by 1700, games and sports were flourishing; taverns became a focal point for social life, offering a broad array of games, sports, and gambling activities. This profligacy offended the Pietists and Sabbatarians of various religious persuasions, and the conflict between fun and

the forces of evil was on, a conflict that is still being staged today.

18. The Revolutionary War was a time of immense interest in recreational diversions and fitness for both military preparedness and for relief from the boredom of a war.

19. The Civil War, despite its bloodshed and well-documented inhumanity, was replete with sport and physical activity. Baseball was popular among troops on both sides. Competition within and sometimes between the armies was continual.

20. Prior to the Civil War, and most certainly afterward, a technological revolution of major proportions took place, with multiple effects on the face of sports. Population growth, rapid urbanization, and the development of the sewing machine, the light bulb, the camera, vulcanized rubber, the railroad, telegraphy, and innovations in printing revolutionized the face of America and its sport involvement.

21. The development of intercollegiate sports, the creation of professional baseball leagues, the increasing fascination with football, the development of the Amateur Athletic Union (AAU), and the reinstitution of the Olympic Games in 1896 are only a few of the sports landmarks between 1850 and 1900.

22. A crisis in American football required the intervention of President Theodore Roosevelt in 1905. Attacks were being made in Pennsylvania against laws that prohibited Sunday sport involvement. The two world wars signaled more need for physical fitness in American youth. All of these affected modern sports. Also, the expansion of sports created by television and professional sports becoming a big business have had significant effects.

23. The history of physical education is one of significant events and of people who have moved the field along to its present state of importance.

24. Psychology, officially beginning in 1879 with Wundt in Leipzig, has been influential in many spheres of American life, and its influence on sport and physical activity is significant.

SUGGESTED READINGS

Berryman, J. (1982) Important events in the history of American sports: A chronology. In R. Higgs (Ed.), *Sports: A reference guide* (pp. 227–267). Westport, CT: Greenwood Press.

> Berryman has compiled a thorough and readable chronology of sport events from 1618 to mid-1981. The reader can quickly become familiar with sport history by reading Berryman's work.

Brasch, R. (1970) *How did sports begin?* New York: David McKay.

> Brasch details the development of forty-three separate sports and the Olympic Games in this 434-page volume.

Higgs, R. (1982) *Sports: A reference guide.* Westport, CT: Greenwood Press.

> In addition to a chapter on the history of sports, Higgs has chapters on sports and art and literature, as well as an excellent appendix on important research centers, collections, and directories within the United States and Canada.

Sears, H. D. (1992) The moral threat of intercollegiate sports: An 1893 poll of ten college presidents, and the end of "the champion football team of the great west." *Journal of Sport History, 19,* 211–226.

> Though football came under close scrutiny during the deliberations of President Theodore Roosevelt in 1905, an earlier attack was launched by the ministers of the Kansas Methodist Conference in 1894. The center of the controversy was Baker University in Kansas; the institution had somehow amassed a great pool of football talent by recruiting students and nonstudents alike to take part in the sport; because of their record, they were referred to as the Best in the West among football teams of the period. It appears

that the game itself and the way that Baker went about the process of winning offended the sensibilities of the pietist Christian advocates who had helped form the Kansas Methodist Conference of which Baker was a part. Sears says that the game itself was viewed by the pietists as being "inextricably linked to alcohol, sabbath-breaking, gambling, de-civilizing public violence, and the sinful waste of youthful blood and time" (p. 211). Ultimately, football was banned in the conference in 1894 due to pietist opposition.

Twombly, W. (1976) *200 years of sport in America: A pageant of a nation at play.* New York: McGraw-Hill.

    Twombly divides the history of sport into four ages, Pastoral (1776–1865), Passionate (1866–1919), Golden (1920–1945), and Electronic (1946–1976), and provides approximately fifteen vignettes per age in both prose and pictures as a means of documenting the progression of sport over the past two hundred years.

Yalouris, N. (1979) *The eternal Olympics: The art and history of sport.* New Rochelle, NY: Caratzas Brothers, Publishers.

    The prose in this book is informative and the pictures captivating. There are 156 illustrations, primarily from early Greek times and secondarily from the Roman era. A list of all known Olympic winners from 776 B.C. to A.D. 369 is also provided.

REFERENCES

Benjamin, L. T., Hopkins, R., & Nation, J. R. (1994) *Psychology.* (3d ed.) New York: Macmillan.

Betts, J. (1953) The technological revolution and the rise of sport, 1850–1900. *Mississippi Valley Historical Review, 40,* 231–256.

Betts, J. (1971) Home front, battlefield, and sport during the Civil War. *Research Quarterly, 42,* 113–132.

Binfield, R. (1948) *The story of the Olympic Games.* London: Oxford University Press.

Brasch, R. (1970) *How did sports begin? A look at the origins of man at play.* New York: David McKay.

Broekhoff, J. (1968) Chivalric education in the Middle Ages. *Quest,* Monograph XI (Winter), 24–31.

Buchanan, D. (1975) *Roman sport and entertainment.* Essex, England: Longmans.

Burns, E. (1985) Perspective. *Sports Illustrated.* December 2, 8–12.

Crockett, D. (1961) Sports and recreational practices of Union and Confederate soldiers. *Research Quarterly, 32,* 335–347.

Fielding, L. (1977a) Sport as a training technique in the Union Army. *The Physical Educator, 34,* 145–152.

Fielding, L. (1977b) Sport and the terrible swift sword. *Research Quarterly, 48,* 1–11.

Forbes, C. (1973) The Spartan Agoge. In E. F. Zeigler (Ed.), *A history of sport and physical education to 1900* (pp. 133–138). Champaign, IL: Stipes.

Gerber, E. (1968) Learning and play: Insights of educational protagonists. *Quest,* Monograph XI (Winter), 44–49.

Hackensmith, C. (1966) *History of physical education.* New York: Harper & Row.

Harbrecht, T., & Barnett, C. R. (1979) College football during World War II: 1941–1945. *Physical Educator, 36,* 31–34.

Harris, H. A. (1972) *Sport in Greece and Rome.* Ithaca, NY: Cornell University Press.

Harris, H. A. (1973) The spread of Greek athletics. In E.F. Zeigler (Ed.), *A history of sport and physical education to 1900* (pp. 139–153). Champaign, IL: Stipes.

Henry, B. (1976) *History of the Olympic Games.* New York: Putnam's.

Hoepner, B. (1970) John Swett's experience with physical exercise at the Rincon School: Foundation for the first state physical education law in the U.S. *Research Quarterly, 41,* 365–370.

Howell, M. (1969) Seal stones of the Minoan period in the Ashmolean Museum, Oxford, depicting physical activities. *Research Quarterly, 40,* 509–517.

Howell, M. L., & Sawula, L. W. (1973) Sports and games among the Etruscans. In E.F. Zeigler (Ed.), *A history of sport and physical education to 1900* (pp. 79–91), Champaign, IL: Stipes.

Jable, J. T. (1976) Sunday sport comes to Pennsylvania: Professional baseball and football triumph over the Commonwealth's archaic blue laws, 1919–1933. *Research Quarterly, 47,* 357–365.

Kennard, J. (1970) Maryland colonials at play: Their sports and games. *Research Quarterly, 41,* 389–395.

Ledbetter, B. (1979) Sports and games of the American Revolution. *Journal of Sport History, 6,* 29–40.

Lee, M. (1983) *A history of physical education and sports in the USA.* New York: Wiley and Sons.

Leonard, W. (1984). *A sociological perspective of sport* (2nd ed). Minneapolis: Burgess.

Lewis, G. (1967) America's first intercollegiate sport: The regattas from 1852 to 1875. *Research Quarterly, 38,* 637–648.

Lewis, G. (1969) Theodore Roosevelt's role in the 1905 controversy. *Research Quarterly, 40,* 717–724.

Lucas, J. A. (1968) A prelude to the rise of sport: Antebellum America, 1850-1860. *Quest,* Monograph XI (Winter), 50–57.

Moolenijzer, N. (1968) Our legacy from the Middle Ages. *Quest,* Monograph XI (Winter), 32–43.

Mouratidis, J. (1985) Nero: The artist, the athlete, and his downfall. *Journal of Sport History, 12,* 5–20.

Neumann, H. (Ed.). (1936) *Der Rittterspiegel.* Halle, Germany: Max Niemeyer.

Palmer, D., & Howell, M. L. (1973) Sports and games in early civilization. In E.F. Zeigler (Ed.), *A history of sport and physical education to 1900* (pp. 21–34). Champaign, IL: Stipes.

Park, R. (1980) The *Research Quarterly* and its antecedents. *Research Quarterly for Exercise and Sport, 51,* 1–22.

Rader, B. (1983) *American sports from the age of folk games to the age of spectators.* Englewood Cliffs, NJ: Prentice-Hall.

Rajagopalan, K. (1973) Early Indian physical education. In E.F. Zeigler (Ed.), *A history of sport and physical education to 1900* (pp. 45–55). Champaign, IL: Stipes.

Rice, E., Hutchinson, J., & Lee, M. (1969) *A brief history of physical education* (5th ed.). New York: Ronald.

Roediger, H., Rushton, J., Capaldi, E., & Paris, S. (1984) *Psychology.* Boston: Little, Brown.

Sasijima, K. (1973) Early Chinese physical education and sport. In E.F. Zeigler (Ed.), *A history of sport and physical education to 1900* (pp. 35–44). Champaign, IL: Stipes.

Schrodt, B. (1981) Sports of the Byzantine Empire. *Journal of Sport History,* 8, 40–59.

Simri, U. (1973) The ball games of antiquity. In E.F. Zeigler (Ed.), *A history of sport and physical education to 1900* (pp. 93–99). Champaign, IL: Stipes.

Spears, B., & Swanson, R. (1983) *History of sport and physical activity in the United States* (2d ed.), Dubuque, IA: Wm. C. Brown.

Struna, N. (1981) Sport and colonial education: A cultural perspective. *Research Quarterly for Exercise and Sport, 52,* 117–135.

Stull, G. A. (1973) The athletic events of *The Odyssey.* In E.F. Zeigler (Ed.), *A history of sport and physical education to 1900* (pp. 121–131). Champaign, IL: Stipes.

Stull, G. A., & Lewis, G. (1968) The funeral games of the Homeric Greeks. *Quest,* Monograph XI (Winter), 1–13.

Swaddling, J. (1980) *The ancient Olympic Games.* Austin, TX: The University of Texas Press.

Sweet, W. E. (1987) *Sport and recreation in ancient Greece.* New York: Oxford Press.

Twombly, W. (1976) *200 years of sport in America: A pageant of a nation at play.* New York: McGraw-Hill.

Van Dalen, D., Mitchell, E., & Bennett, B. (1953) *World history of physical education.* Englewood Cliffs, NJ: Prentice-Hall.

Whorton, J. C. (1981) Muscular vegetarianism: The debate over diet and athletic performance in the progressive era. *Journal of Sport History,* 8, 58–75.

Yalouris, N. (Ed.). (1979) *The eternal Olympics: The art and history of sport.* New Rochelle, NY: Caratzas Brothers, Publishers.

Young, N. (1944) Did the Greeks and the Romans play football? *Research Quarterly,* 15, 310–316.

Zeigler, E. F. (Ed.). (1973a) *A history of sport and physical education to 1900.* Champaign, IL: Stipes.

Zeigler, E. F. (1973b) Historical foundations: Social and educational. In E.F. Zeigler (Ed.), *A history of sport and physical education to 1900* (pp. 11–19). Champaign, IL: Stipes.

Zingale, D. (1977) "Ike" revisited on sport and physical fitness. *Research Quarterly,* 48, 12–18.

Behavioral Principles and Applications

INTRODUCTION

An athlete rarely excels in a given sport due only to his or her natural gifts. The natural endowment surely plays a major role as a determinant of athletic performance, but skill development is equally essential to establishing a competitive profile. Basic to the notion of athletic development is the idea that the environment shapes, polishes, and directs the course of sport behaviors. In other words, what we learn about a sport often dictates how we perform in a sport, and ultimately it determines at what level we participate in sport activities. In this chapter we shall discuss some of the basic learning processes that underlie the acquisition of selected athletic skills. And we shall see that in many instances trainers and coaches can intervene to alter these processes and thereby produce a more talented sport performer.

In psychology, the term "learning" is a generic label embracing a wide range of environmental conditions that function to change behavior through experience (Tarpy, 1983). Our coverage will focus on three major types of learning and examine the role of each in sport. The three learning categories are: *classical conditioning, operant learning,* and *cognitive learning.*

CLASSICAL CONDITIONING

Classical conditioning is a form of learning that has its scientific roots in Russia. The renowned physiologist Ivan Pavlov was among the first investigators in this area and classical conditioning is most commonly associated with his name (Pavlov, 1927). Traditionally, the procedure shown in figure 3.1 is used to describe the conditions that are necessary for learning to take place. First, a primary eliciting stimulus, called an unconditioned stimulus (UCS), is presented. It reflexively evokes a response, labeled appropriately an *unconditioned response* (UCR). Note that this relationship is biologically prepared; that is, experience is not necessary for the occurrence of the behavior. Subsequently a neutral event called a conditioned stimulus (CS) is paired

---

Figure 3.1: The Procedure for Obtaining Classical Conditioning

A. Before Conditioning

(*Metronome*)
Conditioned Stimulus [CS] ——————▶ No Response

(*Meat Powder*)   (*Salivation*)
Unconditioned Stimulus [UCS] ——————▶ Unconditioned Response [UCR]

B. During Conditioning
Metronome
Conditioned Stimulus [CS]
Followed by

(*Meat powder*)   (*Salivation*)
Unconditioned Stimulus [UCS] ——————▶ Unconditioned Response [UCR]

C. After Conditioning

(*Metronome*)   (*Salivation*)
Conditioned Stimulus [CS] ——————▶ Conditioned Response [CR]

with the UCS, and after several such pairings the CS comes to produce a conditioned response that it did not previously trigger. In Pavlov's original investigations using dogs as subjects, for example, the introduction of a food pan containing meat powder (UCS) automatically elicited a flow of saliva (UCR) from the parotid gland. When a metronome (a timing device that marks exact time by emitting sounds at regular intervals) was presented repeatedly (the CS) just prior to introducing the meat powder, it too came to elicit a salivation reaction (the CR).

Despite the enormous popularity of classical conditioning as a subject area for experimental psychologists, there has not been widespread application of classical conditioning techniques in the sport and physical education realms. When applications are made, they generally fall in the area of stress alleviation or some other method of controlling the discomfort that sometimes comes with competition (see Smith, R. E., 1984). For instance, it is not uncommon to find immensely gifted sport competitors who become so acutely anxious before a big meet, or a critical game, that they lose sleep, vomit, and so forth. Such reactions lower the physical and mental status of the athlete to a point at which his or her ability to perform is compromised. When this sort of misery occurs, a form of classical conditioning called *reciprocal inhibition* may prove helpful (Craighead, Kazdin, and Mahoney, 1981). This counterconditioning technique involves training the athlete to think about the upcoming competition in a supportive, relaxing context. By pairing the stressful thoughts with behavioral events that are incompatible with the anxiety reaction, the former anxiety-eliciting mental events (thinking about the gymnastics routine, rehearsing the game strategy) evoke relaxation and an attitude of confidence. Now, instead of discomfort, the athlete feels comfortable when he or she thinks about the approaching competition. Such approaches have been used successfully in helping many different types

of athletes (Cox, 1985). We discuss this topic in greater detail in chapter 4.

Other possible uses of classical conditioning methodologies in sport include memory aids and cues that might facilitate recall of particular performance strategies. Along these lines, the importance of the learning context becomes apparent (Smith, S. M., 1979, 1984). For example, psychologists have known for years that we remember better when we recall information under the precise conditions under which it was learned (see Smith, S. M., 1979). Trouble arises when we learn in one situation and perform in another. Perhaps this is because the requisite behaviors have been classically conditioned to relevant stimuli in the environment. When the stimuli are reinstated, performance improves due to the added benefits associated with multiple retrieval cues. For the athlete, this may translate into better execution and a more effective competitive posture. It follows that coaches and trainers would be wise to make special arrangements for their athletes to acquire basic skills under fundamentally the same circumstances of their expected uses. This might mean practicing on the game field as opposed to a remote practice area, working out with an audience present, and wearing the same uniform for practice as in actual competition.

Unfortunately, systematic studies of the viability of such classical conditioning applications have not been undertaken. Perhaps a serious test of these predictions would be excessively expensive and logistically cumbersome. Nonetheless, classical conditioning is a learning system that likely has greater relevance to sport than heretofore realized, and future developments in this important area are needed.

OPERANT LEARNING

In contrast to the paucity of research on classical conditioning and sport, there has been a veritable explosion of experimental work on the application of operant techniques in sport and exercise (see Donahue, Gillis, and King [1980] and Leith and Taylor [1992] for reviews). Operant learning, or operant conditioning as it is also called, is a set of principles set forth by the late B.F. Skinner at Harvard University. Unlike classical conditioning, for which the important feature for learning is temporal contiguity, for operant learning it is the consequence or outcome of responding that dictates behavioral development (Schwartz, 1984).

Basic Principles

Although operant behavior and the vast research that relates to it are exceedingly complex, the basic tenets of the operant position can be expressed rather simply (see figure 3.2). First, there is the common reward procedure that is known in psychology circles as *positive reinforcement.* Positive reinforcers are events (stimuli)

that, when produced by a response, increase the probability of occurrence of that response. An example is when someone performs well on a given task and receives praise or recognition. According to the principle of positive reinforcement there is a good chance he or she will behave similarly in the future. *Negative reinforcement,* by contrast, is a second operant procedure wherein behavioral probability increases when the response prevents or terminates an aversive stimulus. Performing at a certain level to avoid the unkind remarks of an excessively harsh and wrathful coach illustrates the use of negative reinforcement. Opponent processes to these reinforcement techniques are *punishment* and *omission* training, each of which operates to weaken behavior. The former involves the delivery of aversive stimulation contingent upon some behavior; the latter is said to take place when a response results in the loss of a scheduled reward event. In either case, the impact is a negative one that is designed to diminish the strength of responding.

Figure 3.2: **Four Basic Training Procedures Used in Operant Conditioning**

	Positive (e.g., food)	Negative (e.g., shock)
Effect of the Response on the Stimulus — *Produces Stimulus*	Positive Reinforcement	Punishment
Effect of the Response on the Stimulus — *Prevents or Eliminates Stimulus*	Omission Training	Negative Reinforcement

Type of Stimulus

Behavior Coaching Techniques

Although the application of operant conditioning concepts has been made under a variety of labels, one of the more elaborate descriptions of the potential uses of such methods was introduced by Martin and Hrycaiko (1983) under the rubric of "effective behavioral coaching." The definition of effective behavioral coaching (EBC) is "the consistent application of principles of behavioral psychology for the improvement and maintenance of athletic behavior" (p. 10). A cardinal operant principle endorsed by EBC is the identification of target behaviors. In this case, this means the specific detailed measurement of selected athletic performances. Rather than rely on impressions and poorly defined criteria for evaluating the effectiveness of certain training strategies, a coach should prepare a preliminary list of behaviors that are the goal of the training manipulation. Such precision provides better clues to the validity of new techniques. Martin and Hrycaiko suggest the following as an example list for a coach of a group of young persons in an age-group competitive sport:

I. Desirable behaviors by athletes at practices:
   A. Attendance at practice
   B. Good listening to instruction (in groups and individually)
   C. Practice of proper skill technique following instruction
   D. Practice of proper components of good technique during endurance training
   E. Continuous repetition of skill without frequent stopping
   F. Practice of skills with the intensity and speed at least equal to that required in the final desired performance
   G. Practice of relaxation techniques and imagery (so that they might be used just prior to competition)

II. Desirable behaviors by athletes at competition:
   A. Muscle relaxation and imagery to prepare to compete
   B. Good skill performance leading to measurable performance improvement (e.g., time, distance)
   C. Good team spirit and mutual support of group members
   D. Desirable sportsmanlike behaviors and minimal behavior problems (e.g., shaking hands, emotional control after losing or poor officiating). (Martin and Hrycaiko, 1983, p. 11)

Once the specific target behaviors have been identified, the appropriate reinforcement procedure should be implemented. It is the consequence of responding that is thought to regulate future response probabilities. Therefore, the coach or trainer should provide the appropriate positive or negative experiences consequent to the performance of desired or undesired athletic responses.

An elegant report demonstrating the potential use of behavioral coaching methods has been provided by Allison and Ayllon (1980). These researchers examined the efficacy of the behavioral coaching method relative to standard methods of coaching youth football. The procedure for behavioral coaching involved the use of verbal instructions and feedback in a systematic way with four male athletes. When the athlete executed a blocking motion properly, the coach blew a whistle and told the player, "great, way to go." Incorrect blocking techniques were met with verbal reprimands while the player was in a frozen position. Furthermore, the player was given explicit instruction using the coach as a model and later was asked to imitate the proper techniques. This behavioral method contrasted with the standard method primarily in terms of consistency. In the standard method, the coach did not often provide encouragement and when

Figure 3.3: **The Percentage of Trials in Which Football Blocks Were Executed Correctly as a Function of Standard Coaching and Behavioral Coaching Techniques**

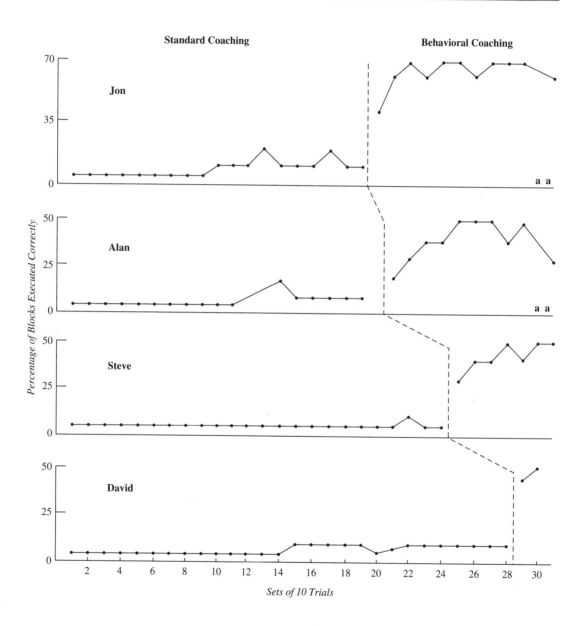

Source: Allison and Ayllon (1980).

verbal rewards were given they were not enthusiastically offered.

Figure 3.3 shows the results of this attempt to judiciously apply an operant learning strategy. Obviously, the four individuals tested performed better when they received behavioral coaching than standard coaching. The praise following the desirable response can be interpreted as positive reinforcement in this case. Similarly, the verbal reprimands can be interpreted as punishment for the incorrect response. The idea is that these environmental events were contingently related to selected target behaviors.

The comparative effectiveness of positive reinforcement and punishment was assessed in a differential reinforcement study of coaching tennis skills (Buzas and Ayllon, 1981). Under one set of conditions, three female students (ages thirteen to fourteen) from a physical education class at a junior high school were corrected with rou-

tine criticism when they made errors in executing three tennis skills—forehand, backhand, and serve. Performance under this correction procedure defined *baseline,* an operant term used to describe stable response rates when a specified set of conditions is employed. After a period of time, a *differential reinforcement* procedure was introduced whereby the coach selectively ignored errors but systematically praised correct performance. The results of this study revealed that all three girls increased in the execution of appropriate tennis skills by two to four times the baseline rates when coached using this differential reinforcement approach. Positive reinforcement was a more desirable tactic than punishment. Although different findings might occur with older age groups or other special populations, it is doubtful that aversive training procedures ever are preferred over positive techniques, at least when they are used in isolation (see highlight 3.1).

Why Punish?

Highlight 3.1

As a defensive end for a high school football team in the Midwest, Jason R. was no standout, but he was a reliable player with good judgment. At least this was the usual pattern, but one that Jason failed to conform to during last Friday night's game against an opponent from a neighboring town. It was an absolutely horrid evening with a spate of missed assignments, poor tackling techniques, and penalties. Now it is Monday afternoon practice, and experience tells Jason that he will pay the price for his shortcomings; he must suffer the physical abuse of his coach, and the embarrassment of being singled out for punishment.

"You're worthless, kid," the coach screamed. "I might as well have stood a dummy out there. You let that jerk beat you all night long. Do you know what it means to hit somebody? Try this sometime!" (Jason is flattened by the enraged coach.)

"I'm warning you, you execute the way you did Friday night, and I'll execute you. I'll be on the sideline waiting for you. Count on it!" the coach wailed.

(Continued next page)

Highlight 3.1 (Continued)

Why Punish?

For the uninitiated, this vignette may sound farfetched, but for anyone who has participated in athletics, it is likely all too familiar. It is just another example of the use of a coaching strategy predicated on fear and intimidation. How many times have we seen a coach shout negative comments to a player when a mistake is made, only to quietly look past positive performances? The player under such circumstances putatively learns through relief, and perhaps the system works. But the truth is that virtually no systematic research on this style of behavioral intervention has been attempted (Donahue et al., 1980). In one or two of the few studies that include a negative condition approximating this approach, more desirable results were obtained with positive reinforcement. Then why the widespread use of harsh tactics? Perhaps years of modeling aggressive coaches who win has spawned a generation of athletic trainers and coaches who have adopted the policy of "Do it right, or else!" Whatever the reasons for their use, a more serious scientific look into the use of popular aversive conditioning techniques is badly needed.

Even if the gap between research and practice were lessened in the area of aversive control, we must nonetheless question the wisdom of continuing to use an approach that creates stress and negative self-images. How is Jason likely to feel after being publicly disgraced in front of his teammates? Even if his performance does improve, he is not likely to forget the ridicule and open contempt heaped on him by his coach. Along these lines, the famous Harvard behaviorist B.F. Skinner cautioned against excessive use of punishment and negative reinforcement in controlling behavior (Skinner, 1971) on the grounds that such procedures evoke unwanted emotional by-products. Along with control come anger and aggression; although these traits may be only moderately destructive within the bracketed framework of certain sport environments, they clearly may have a more negative impact on civilized society as a whole. To even the most ardent supporter of sport, aversive techniques that achieve the desired results would not likely appear useful when they sacrifice personal dignity and perceptions of self-worth. Perhaps coaches would be better advised to employ positive reinforcement techniques. As philosopher Henry David Thoreau remarked, "There are few exceptions where it is better to punish a sin than to reward a virtue."

Sources: Donahue, Gillis, and King (1980); Skinner (1971).

In another area of athletic competition, Shapiro and Shapiro (1984) extended the use of behavioral coaching techniques to include skill acquisition in track. Using the previously described procedures employed by Allison and Ayllon (1980), conditioning, form, and starts in the blocks improved for high school track athletes. The end result was decreases in running times for two events (100m and 200m).

Elsewhere, the development of swimming skills has been the focus of attention for operant applications including behavioral coaching techniques. The procedure of shaping was used to modify the form of an incorrect kicking motion in the front crawl swimming motion of a novice swimming student at Dalhousie University (Rushall and Siedentop, 1972). *Shaping* is an operant technique that involves the selective reinforcement of successive approximations to a goal behavior. When teaching an animal to press a lever to receive food, for example, it is most improbable that the animal will begin pressing the lever immediately upon placement in the apparatus. Typically, the animal is given reinforcement (food) for just moving toward the lever, then for touching the lever with some part of its body, and eventually the criterion for an actual lever press is introduced. Gradually, the animal is shaped into performing the desired response. Similarly, the young swimmer mentioned above was shaped into executing a more acceptable flutter style kick. The specific operant procedure used to accomplish the intended result is described below:

> The desired terminal behavior was to effect an acceptable form of the flutter kick. The consequences used were (1) a light was shone in the swimmer's face every time he performed an incorrect kick, (2) only lengths performed to criterion were recorded on the swimmer's progress chart each being worth double the normal amount, and (3) the coach discussed the subject's performance after each session. The performance criterion was gradually made more stringent for the subject to record a satisfactory length. Initially, four [unacceptable] kicks per length were allowed to be deemed satisfactory. This was reduced to a complete absence of kicks in the fourth practice session. The most attention time required of the coach for the process was to observe 20 laps of swimming in each of the four sessions. (Rushall and Siedentop, 1972, p. 149)

The findings showed that the number of incorrect swimming kicks systematically decreased with increasing sessions and the associated elevated criteria. Closer inspection of exactly what happened in this study perhaps would be instructive. The shaping component of the operation, of course, is contained in the more stringent performance criterion implemented gradually over sessions. That is, initially reinforcement (gaining a satisfactory evaluation) was attainable when as many as four errors were made, but eventually performance had to be error free. But there is another principle at work here. Can you identify it? What is the operant procedure being used to control the swimming of the student? Recall that in earlier discussions we said that *omission training* involves the removal of a scheduled reinforcement contingent upon the occurrence of an unwanted behavior. Under such circumstances, reinforcement is given when the response is not present; that is, when it is omitted. This is basically what was required of the swimmer. Reinforcement was given not for executing a certain number of correct actions, but rather it was given for the absence of incorrect actions. Such a modification procedure clearly illustrates the uses and advantages of applying one of the several types of operant methods described earlier.

Koop and Martin (1983) have used a behavioral coaching strategy to teach swimming that emphasized negative consequences of incorrect performances as well as positive consequences of correct performances. Specifically, three male and two female swimmers ranging from seven to twelve years of age received a tap on the shoulder with a padded stick when errors in specific strokes were made during a lap. In addition, when laps were swum correctly, the trainer shouted "Good" or "That's great! You're really getting that arm right." This technique produced a systematic decrease in errors of selected swimming strokes. So, at least for swimming, a variety of behavioral coaching methods appear to produce performance benefits.

Another sport in which behavioral coaching techniques have proven to be effective is gymnastics. Allison and Ayllon (1983) were able to identify six female gymnasts on a high school team who demonstrated either no proficiency or no higher than 20 percent proficiency on basic routines such as backward walkovers, front handsprings, and reverse kips. The format for teaching the gymnastic skills using behavioral coaching was very similar to that used by Allison and Ayllon in the football study mentioned earlier in this section, that is, executing the skill, judging correct position, describing the incorrect position, modeling the correct position, and imitating the correct position. Each step in the process was handled by the coach using his own words to shape behavior. Incorrect landings on the mat were met with the word "freeze" followed by corrective instruction; properly executed landings were exempt from the "freeze" admonition. In the standard coaching condition, instructions on proper execution were given, skills were modeled by the coach or another gymnast, verbal feedback was given regarding errors, and praise and threats were used where deemed appropriate by the coach. As might be predicted, the behavioral coaching procedure was more effective in imparting all three skills to the young gymnasts.

In a later study with a slightly variant theme, Wolko, Hrycaiko, and Martin (1993) compared standard coaching versus standard coaching plus behaviorally-based self-regulation with five female gymnasts ages ten to thirteen years. There were three experimental conditions manipulated: a baseline condition with standard coaching only, a treatment condition (T1) that combined elements of standard coaching with public self-regulation, and a treatment condition (T2) that combined standard coaching with private self-regulation components. Conditions T1 and T2 are important in that there is controversy among psychologists as to the merit of public versus private self-regulation strategies, such as self-monitoring, goal setting, and self-evaluation. Bandura (1977) is one advocate of the privacy point of view while Hayes and associates (Hayes, Rosenfarb, Wulfert, Munt, Korn, and Zettle, 1985; Hayes, Munt, Korn, Wulfert, Rosenfarb, and Zettle, 1986) are convinced of the efficacy of a public component in self-regulation strategies. (We shall return to this point briefly when discussing public recordings.) In this context, Wolko et al. looked at private versus public self-regulation in an effort to improve balance beam proficiency among the gymnasts in question. Setting performance goals, behavior recording, displaying the results, rewarding goal attainment, and providing frequent and immediate feedback concerning the desired behavior were some of the techniques used to shape performance. In general, the T2 condition was the most effective of the three treatments, though the effect was not particularly pronounced. Overall, the Wolko et al. research did support the utility of adding a behaviorally based self-management component to standard coaching. The net effect of all this is supportive of the use of behavioral coaching procedures to enhance skill acquisition in gymnastics.

Public Recordings

The performance of swimming athletes has also been studied using a "public recording" reinforcement procedure (Donahue et al., 1980). Public recordings are essentially just that; they are the displaying of formal evaluations in such a fashion that how well the athlete did, or how poorly, is apparent to all. When we do something well, generally speaking, we want someone to know about it, and athletics is no exception. The positive reinforcement is in the satisfaction that goes with posting a good score on the public record.

An investigation by McKenzie and Rushall (1974) evaluated the impact of checking off completed work units on a program board that was presented publicly. Eight members of a swimming team were asked to record the number of laps they swam during successive 1-minute periods in a series of uninterrupted swims. When a certain level of output was achieved, the swimmers checked off the appropriate box on a program board located where other swimmers could see it. In this particular investigation, the intervention strategy (the public recording manipulation) was introduced after a baseline control period, and then it was discontinued. This design, called an *ABA design,* permits the experimenter to evaluate the effectiveness of the modification procedure. Specifically, one would expect that to the extent to which the intervention (B) produced superior results relative to baseline conditions (A), then there should be a pattern of improvement under B but a subsequent decline under A. Otherwise, the improvement registered during the period of intervention might just reflect practice efforts or something else unrelated to the behavioral manipulation. Regarding the findings reported by McKenzie and Rushall (1974), the results were in the expected direction. Specifically, all eight swimmers had 20 to 30 percent more work output in the intervention phase than the baseline period. Moreover, when the public recording procedure was discontinued the output of seven of the eight swimmers decreased substantially.

Displaying formal evaluations is often utilized by swimming athletes and is an example of "public recording" reinforcement processes.

The use of public recordings as an applied operant technique raises some interesting theoretical questions. Not the least of the issues here relates to the very nature of the reinforcement process. Is the intervention grounded to positive reinforcement or negative reinforcement? At first glance, it appears to be positive in nature, because the person enjoys the satisfaction of showing the world how well she or he performed. But there is also the possibility that a negative incentive is the true motivational source responsible for any noticed improvement in performance. Surely the person does not want to suffer the embarrassment and potential ridicule attendant to a poor showing. To avoid the possibility of such derisive experiences, an athlete may perform at a high level not to gain recognition but to insure his or her acceptance into a support group. In other words, the response avoids an aversive situation that would otherwise occur. This is clearly negative reinforcement, and many psychologists have suggested that this sort of control is stronger than that accomplished by positive means (Geen, Beatty, and Arkin, 1984).

Regardless of the exact nature of the social reinforcement process underlying the effects observed in coaching swimmers by McKenzie and Rushall (1974), even more dramatic results may occur with material rewards. Rushall and Pettinger (1969) found that thirty-two members of a swimming team increased lap production more when the rewards involved candy or money than they did when the coach's attention served as reward. Thus, while many incentives can be used to modify athletic performance, evidently some consideration should be given to the selection of the particular events that are to function as reinforcement outcomes.

Changing Coaching Behaviors

Operant procedures can be used to modify the behavior of coaches as well as athletes. Indeed, Dickinson (1977) has expressed forcefully the need to implement techniques for changing coaching behavior. Among the recommendations for change are increases in the frequency with which positive comments are offered and greater clarity with regard to specific sport behaviors that are required for excellence. In other words, coaches should use more positive reinforcement and provide better instruction.

Rushall and Smith (1979) attempted to show that the quality and quantity of feedback statements could be increased through self-recording techniques. The subject in this investigation was a thirty-two-year-old senior male swimming coach. Self-recording of "reward and feedback behaviors" was accomplished with the use of sheets that contained columns indicating types of feedback (effort, skill, task execution, performer interaction), and thirty-one key words, all of which could be checked. During several coaching sessions, the subject was signaled at the end of successive 5-minute intervals to count the frequency with which he was giving verbal rewards and relevant feedback. This self-recording process, which in essence is reinforcing the coach for performing goal behaviors that define high quality coaching, produced the desired result. The frequencies of emission of verbal comments and feedback increased dramatically over the course of the study.

An adjunctive element to the Rushall and Smith (1979) project is worthy of mention. Realistically, one cannot expect a coach to continue to keep detailed personal records indefinitely. It is just too time consuming to keep track of the frequency with which specific verbal remarks are registered, and so forth. So how can we expect the target behaviors to survive when the intervention processes are removed? Fortunately, operant conditioners have perfected a procedure called *fading*, which assures persistence even beyond the point at which the behavioral manipulation is discontinued. The fading strategy used by Rushall and Smith involved gradually "leaning" or stretching the reinforcement schedule so that the required

5-minute interval counts became less and less frequent. The high production of the target behavior continues in such a case but the control of the higher quality coaching performance falls under the influence of other stimuli, such as witnessing improvement in the athletes themselves, greater comradeship, and so forth. In effect, a temporary control device is exchanged for a more enduring one. A follow-up period of observation conducted by Rushall and Smith indicated that their fading techniques were successful in achieving the purpose of transferring stimulus control from the checklist to the performance of the swimmers.

Conditioned Reinforcement

Yet another operant procedure that may prove useful for training athletes is *conditioned reinforcement*. Conditioned reinforcers are stimuli that, when paired with a primary reinforcer, come to possess the same control properties as the primary reinforcer (Martin and Pear, 1992). An example in a more traditional laboratory setting is when a tone is paired with a primary reward object such as food, and then the previously neutral tone acquires the ability to strengthen behavior it is made contingent upon. That is, the subject works for the previously neutral event (the conditioned reinforcer) because it has been correlated with reward.

In applied situations, a common training rationale based on conditioned reinforcement is the *token system* (Kazdin, 1977; Thomas and Miller, 1980). In such a system, an object of some sort is given to the subject when the appropriate behavior is executed. For example, a plastic disk might be given to a child suffering from a speech difficulty upon the successful production of a word phase. At some point, the token (the disk) can be exchanged for a more meaningful object such as a toy or food. Research has shown that this form of conditioned reinforcement is an effective way to modify behavior, and it has the advantage of not satiating the subject (Martin and Pear, 1992).

Two investigations have indicated that token systems can be used to alter athletic skills. In a study by Jones, reported in Donahue et al. (1980), the subjects of the manipulation were participants in a basketball camp. Because the objective of most basketball coaches is to outscore the opponent, it seemed reasonable to select "points scored" as the target behavior. The staff employed three different training routines. First, all members of a given basketball squad were rewarded with an "Olympic ring" each time their team scored 20 points. With 80 points in a single game, four rings were given to each player on the team. Later, these rings could be redeemed for food or rewards. Secondly, the players were placed on the same sort of token system, but it was predetermined that no rings would be dispensed. A third condition simply scored the games in the standard way, and no token system was even suggested. The findings from this study revealed that players scored more points under the Olympic ring contingency than either of the other conditions. Evidently, the operant strategy of token reinforcement was an effective behavioral control device.

Nine members of a professional basketball team were subjects in a token system intervention that used money as the conditioned reinforcer (money, after all, is a sort of token because it has value only when it can be exchanged for something of greater worth). The players were given financial rewards for efficient offensive performance. An efficiency average (EA) served as the target measure. In this study, an *ABAB* design was used in which the intervention following the initial baseline was discontinued but subsequently reinstated. Each time the token intervention was instituted, three players with the highest EAs received monetary payments. The result showed that six of the nine players increased their offensive production during the first intervention and of these six, four decreased in performance during the return to baseline. All four players subsequently improved again when the final intervention was introduced. So, consistent with findings in other studies using token systems, conditioned reinforcers did have a positive influence on athletic performance.

Although it seems clear that token systems have a legitimate place in the development of sport skill, the use of such tangible rewards to control behavior is not without opposition. The concern over the use of such techniques stems from evidence indicating that, following the removal of a recently introduced reward, response rates decline to levels below those consistently maintained prior to the introduction of the rewarding event (Lepper, Greene, and Nisbett, 1973). For instance, consider what may happen with the aforementioned use of rings to reinforce high point production in basketball games. How will the athletes react when their high outputs no longer render the rings? Will they abandon the activity altogether because the payoff is no longer there? Unfortunately, there is a good chance that this will be the case.

Lepper and Greene (1978) have suggested that such negative patterns following reward removal may in fact relate to *overjustification*. According to this view the introduction of an external reward forces a person to review the value of the activity, and the amount of worth attached to the behavior often is defined according to the degree of extrinsic gain. Ultimately, when the external reward is taken away, the person concludes that the entire reason for responding is gone. What this may mean to a coach is that, if external reinforcement manipulations are to be used, some agenda should exist for shifting to more realistic controlling stimuli. Earlier in this chapter we talked about fading as a psychological principle. Here is another instance in which such a procedure could prove useful.

A specialized application of conditioned reinforcement in sport is chaining. According to Martin and Pear (1992), a stimulus-response chain is a series of stimuli and responses in which each response except the last serves as a stimulus or

signal for the next response in a required sequence. The last response in the chain is followed by a reinforcer. Accordingly, there are three kinds of chains possible: total, forward, and backward. In the total chain, the person attempts all steps from the beginning to the end of the chain on each trial and continues with total task trials until all steps are mastered. In forward chaining, the first step in a sequence is mastered, then steps one and two, then steps one, two, and three, and so forth until the entire chain is acquired. In backward chaining, the reverse is true; that is, the last step in a chain is established, then paired with the next to last step, and so forth with progression to the beginning of the chain. Two sport-related examples of backward chaining have been used by Killian (1988) with swimmers and by O'Brien and Simek (1983) with golfers. Killian's article is a "how-to-do-it" type presentation, and focuses on a backward chain sequence for teaching the back float, the prone float, and the crawl stroke. Using the back float as an example, the swimmer first crouches in chest-deep water, lays the head back until the ears are submerged, and immediately recovers to the standing position. The second step in the chain begins with the ears submerged followed by rising to the tiptoes and recovery to the standing position. The next step begins with the ears submerged followed by the extension of one leg off the bottom of the pool and recovery to the standing position. Step four in the sequence begins in a crouch position with the ears submerged and one leg extended, followed by a gradual lifting of the supporting leg from the bottom of the pool and recovery to the standing position.

In the case of golf, the reverse or backward sequencing would first focus on putting on the green. Putting the ball in the hole in the smallest number of strokes is the goal in golf, and the successful putt should therefore be reinforcing. In step two, chipping onto the green is the focus, and putts are made as reinforcement. Step three is the fairway shot, followed by a successful chip and equally successful putt. Step four involves driving the ball off the tee box, followed in turn by successful completion of steps one, two, and three. The utility of backward chaining was the focus of the O'Brien and Simek study; its superiority over traditional coaching methods was demonstrated with twelve novice golfers divided into two groups of six for experimental purposes. Of particular interest in the latter regard were the scores of the golfers on their first full round of golf upon completion of the chaining versus traditional coaching sequences; the chaining group scored 17.33 points better than the traditionally coached control group, or almost one stroke per hole for eighteen holes.

In a separate study, Simek, O'Brien, and Figlerski (1994) applied their chaining-mastery approach outlined in *Total Golf* (Simek and O'Brien, 1981) in hopes of improving the performance of fourteen collegiate golfers. Simek and O'Brien started with the idea of conducting a four-week training program. Week one was devoted to establishing a baseline of golf performance by having all subjects complete three rounds of play. Step two involved completing the first nine segments of a nineteen-step backward chaining sequence, primarily involving putting at ever-increasing distances. Also, three more rounds of golf were played for purposes of later comparisons. Step three involved completing steps eleven through nineteen of the chain, and dealt with short iron play. Again, three more rounds of golf were played to check on progress. Simek and O'Brien were able to improve scores by 3.4 strokes per eighteen holes after the brief training. For a variety of reasons, at the end of the third week of the study, the team coach was unable or reluctant to follow through on the reward system originally agreed upon (i.e., spots on the golf team for upcoming matches and/or new golf balls), and performance deteriorated in the face of the extinction condition thus imposed. Steps twenty through twenty-three, which were to involve hitting long irons and

woods, were never instituted. However, even after that unfortunate coaching decision was made (at least in terms of research design), team performance remained above baseline achieved prior to the introduction of the chaining-mastery program. Despite some obvious limitations, the 1994 Simek, O'Brien, and Figlerski study lends further support to the validity of chaining, and particularly the backward variety, as a means of improving athletic performance.

Premack Principle

When tokens or other types of tangible rewards are not used for behavior modification, the opportunity to engage in a preferred activity can act as reinforcement. In learning circles this approach is often referred to as the *Premack Principle* (Premack, 1962). The idea is that any behavior that is independently more probable than some other behavior can be used as a reward to strengthen the lower probability response. For example, a child presented with the task of completing his or her arithmetic assignment may be offered the chance to play with the classroom gerbil, subject to meeting the academic contingency. Basically, the behavior is the reinforcer in this procedure and in that sense the Premack Principle departs somewhat from the traditional operant format.

The potential effectiveness of a Premack training operation in the area of athletics and sport is evident from a study by Kau and Fisher (1974). The purpose of this research was to demonstrate that the preferred activity of engaging in various social activities could be used as a reinforcement for the less probable activity of jogging in an aerobics program. The results of the study indicated that over a four-week course, sharp increases in jogging were apparent. Interestingly, weight loss and other natural reinforcers took over and the program was judged to be successful beyond the point of the intervention. At any rate, in at least some cases the opportunity to perform a response that is deemed desirable can be used successfully as a behavioral method for athletic training.

One of the great advantages of the Premack approach is that the program is individually tailored to meet the needs of each person. Not all people enjoy doing the same things. For some people, the opportunity to immerse themselves in a social situation may be outright offensive. Rather than be forced to engage in what he or she views as trivial social interactions, the person may prefer a private moment in a sauna. The point is that, according to the Premack Principle, targeted behavioral rates can be increased in both individuals as long as the responses occasion the opportunity to do what they enjoy. The bottom line for the coach is: Find out what the athlete likes to do and make the opportunity to do it contingent upon the execution of the desired sport skills.

Response Cost

One operant technique not yet mentioned is *response cost*. Response cost is a procedure whereby undesirable behaviors are penalized by taking away a reward object already in the possession of the person. The rewards are regained when appropriate behaviors are exhibited. This approach differs slightly from omission training in that reponse cost involves rewards that have already been obtained, whereas omission training involves scheduled rewards that were never given. A response cost procedure used by Wysocki, Hall, Iata, and Riordan (1979) was successful in getting seven of eight college students to increase aerobic exercising, and the benefits were still apparent at a twelve month follow-up.

Feedback

We have seen that a number of different applications of operant learning are possible in the world of sport. Curiously, all of the studies reported in this chapter have one feature in common. That feature is *feedback*. There was always knowledge of results, whether it was in the form of a public record, a tangible object, attention, or the chance to engage in a preferred activity. Considering the demonstrated utility of providing feedback to athletes in controlled experimental settings, it is not altogether a surprise that coaches and trainers have used films and the even more immediate feedback afforded by videotaping (Penman, 1969). When an athletic participant receives information about what and how he or she has done, in whatever form, chances are that person's skill development will benefit.

Also, we note that in another study of feedback that examined endurance in a laboratory setting, Hall, Weinberg, and Jackson (1987) found that the nature of the feedback stimulus is important in determining performance. Specifically, feedback given during training is preferred to feedback given at the end of training. Apparently, the value of moment-to-moment results is greater than the final result, at least as it relates to athletic performance as an adjunct of behavior.

Training Variables

Session Length

Training variables that are known to affect operant performance have also attracted the interest of applied sport psychology investigators. One such variable with the potential for having profound impact on the acquisition of sport skill is the length and spacing of practice sessions. What are the optimal durations for teaching new skills? Should the practice sessions occur close together or should they be widely spaced with long rest intervals? These were a few of the questions taken under consideration in an article by Sanderson (1983). The psychology of learning literature would argue that *distributed practice* (widely spaced training trials with long periods of rest) should be superior to *massed practice* (cramming training sessions into a short time frame). But as Sanderson notes, the only conclusion that can be drawn for the development of sport skill is that "somewhere between too little rest and too much lay off is the desired condition for practice" (p. 121). A great deal depends on the skill being developed and the nature of the instruction process. In general, it is safe to say that aspects of performance requiring gross motor skills (catching a baseball, blocking technique in football, and so forth) survive over longer periods of time than events that have mental components (reading keys, using appropriate cognitive strategies, and so forth). Accordingly, coaches should be alert to the different types of training programs that may be most suitable for introducing a particular skill.

Schedules of Reinforcement

Another variable that may influence the efficacy of athletic training operations is *schedule of reinforcement*. It is widely accepted that *intermittent reinforcement* occasions greater persistence than *continuous reinforcement* (Nation and Woods, 1980). This means that when a target response is rewarded half the time but is not rewarded on the other half of the trials (intermittent reinforcement), the response will continue for a greater time period after reward is no longer available than would be the case had the response been rewarded every time it occurred. An example is the child who learns to throw a tantrum in order to get what he or she wants

Young tennis players practicing their swing learn from experience that not every contact they make with the ball will be on target. According to the concept of intermittent reinforcement, the ability to accept occasional failure serves to instill perseverance in their game.

from a parent. If the parent is inconsistent, that is, occasionally he or she gives in but not always, the child is essentially on an intermittent reinforcement schedule. Be assured that the parent will have greater difficulty extinguishing this tantrum behavior by finally ignoring it altogether than would have been the case had the tantrum response consistently been reinforced (had the child always got his or her way).

To date only a few studies of sport behavior have examined the possible utility of intermittent reinforcement as a tool for insuring response persistence (see Donahue et al., 1980). But there is little doubt that such schedules can serve the coach or training staff. An offensive lineman who learns that he will fail once in awhile, nonetheless learns to keep trying. A tennis player, having learned that most but not every strategically placed serve will be a winner, acquires an attitude of perseverance. To be sure, intermittent reinforcement schedules are accomplished to some degree according to the natural order of competition. But training experiences in this area need not be haphazard; rather, schedules can be judiciously programmed to produce the intended result.

Learned Helplessness

Perhaps one of the most exciting links between operant phenomena and the sport realm rests with the concept of *learned helplessness*. Learned helplessness is said to occur when an organism previously exposed to an aversive noncontingency exhibits a deficit in the acquisition of a subsequent operant behavior (Maier and Seligman, 1976). This means that when animals or people are placed in situations in which they have no control over their success or failure rate, they do poorly on other unrelated tasks even though their chances for success might be good. An example in the animal laboratory is the rat that is exposed to shock and cannot turn the shock off regardless of its activity. Later, when

this animal is exposed to shock in another environment in which the shock could be terminated by something as simple as a lever press, no responses are attempted (Seligman and Beagley, 1975). It's as if the rat has learned that it is helpless with respect to controlling the environment and carries this expectancy of uncontrollability with it into new learning situations even though the reward conditions have improved dramatically. Similarly, humans often show depression and other types of performance anomalies once they have experienced a series of failures due to circumstances they view as largely outside their control (Abramson, Seligman, and Teasdale, 1978). The person comes to expect failure and, not surprisingly, does fail.

Psychologist Carol Dweck has written on the potential parallels between learned helplessness as a laboratory phenomenon and certain problem athletes (Dweck, 1980). The issue seems to center on how the sport participant reacts to his or her own encounters with failure. When a person becomes preoccupied with failure and assumes personal responsibility for it, chances are greater for helplessness. Dweck uses the example of heavyweight boxer Dwayne Bobick, who had a near perfect record but eventually was knocked out in the first round. He subsequently lost every fight. According to helplessness theory (cf. Abramson et al., 1978), such a result in a "success only" person is not unexpected. Because there has been no experience with failure and interpolated success, failure signals only more setbacks, and negative forecasts only build on themselves. Ultimately, a losing attitude (helplessness) emerges.

What is preferred may be a mastery-oriented attitude toward failure. When a person uses a personal disappointment as a "psyching-up" mechanism, and struggles even harder, then the chances for an eventual triumph increase appreciably. It has been recommended that intermittent reinforcement schedules of the sort described earlier could help immunize individuals against feelings of helplessness (Nation and Massad, 1978). The belief is that failure experienced in the context of aggregate success builds an attitude of persistence, and therein preempts helplessness. One has only to look to Dweck's example of Ben Hogan to appreciate what a positive attitude in the face of adversity can do for a competitor. Despite a conspicuous lack of natural talent, years of defeat, and a severe auto accident that nearly killed him, a dedicated Hogan came back to become perhaps the greatest golfer ever. Clearly, failure is perceived differently by different people.

On a purely commonsense level, all of this points to the need to make players, especially young ones, feel as if they are winners. A young athlete constantly berated and criticized by a coach or parent will think only of losing and feel helpless about winning. In highlight 3.1 we addressed the issue of aversive control and concluded that, even though it may be effective, it is also potentially destructive, both to the individual and society. Rather than criticize, a better strategy might be to build real confidence by teaching children how to handle failure in a realistic fashion.

COGNITIVE LEARNING

Over the past several decades the psychology of learning has witnessed a resurgence of interest in the uniquely mental aspects of behavior (Kirschenbaum and Wittrock, 1984). Several years ago, terms such as "the mind," "beliefs," and "mental activity" were considered unobservables and therefore were events outside the purview of scientific psychology. More recently, psychologists have been more accepting of the cognitive position, and processes such as imagery, rehearsal, and causal ascription have become primary areas of focus (see Weinberg, 1984). Evidence even indicates that such cognitive events are crucial for the elite athlete (cf. Mahoney, Gabriel, and Perkins, 1987).

Imagery

Cognitive learning theory and its applications have certainly gained increased visibility in the sport environment in recent years. One outgrowth of the cognitive approach to learning is what Mahoney (1977) calls the cognitive skills, which include self-efficacy, arousal regulation, attentional focus, and imagery. We shall focus here on imagery; the other cognitive skills Mahoney cites will be discussed in other chapters. According to Solso (1991, p. 267), mental imagery refers to "a mental representation of a nonpresent object or event." Moran (1993) takes this definition a step further by suggesting that the representation need not be confined to the visual sense but may actually be manifested in "hearing a favorite tune" or "feeling a favorite fabric." However, as has been pointed out by Porter and Foster (1988), the focus of attention within sport psychology has largely been on the visual representation, or what is called "the mind's eye."

Imagery has been a focus of scientific interest for over one hundred years. John Hughlings Jackson wrote that "the posterior lobe of the right side of the brain . . . is the chief seat of the revival of images" (Jackson, 1874/1932). Tippett (1992) further suggests that there is evidence of case studies concerning the use of imagery dating back to the nineteenth century. In the realm of motor behavior and athletics, Woolfolk, Parrish, and Murphy (1985) indicate that imagery has been used for almost sixty years. An article by Feltz and Landers (1983) isolated ninety-eight studies related to mental practice and motor performance. Since that time there has been a veritable explosion of research activity related to imagery, covering such sports as basketball (Predebon and Docker, 1992; Wrisberg and Anshel, 1989), golf (Martin and Hall, 1995; Woolfolk, Murphy, Gottesfeld, and Aitken, 1985), ice skating (Rodgers, Hall, and Buckholz, 1991), racquetball (Gray, 1990), softball (Hecker and Kaczor, 1988), and track and field (Machlus and O'Brien, 1988). Earlier success stories using imagery have been reported for downhill skiing (Suinn, 1972), gymnastics (Meyers, Schleser, Cooke, and Cuvillier, 1979), volleyball (Shick, 1970), and weightlifting (Hale, 1982).

As noted earlier, basketball is a sport in which imagery training has been utilized on a fairly frequent basis. In an early study, Meyers and Schleser (1980) used imagery training in an effort to improve the shooting performance of a male collegiate basketball player. In actual game situations, the following coping mechanisms were used: coping instructions patterned after Meichenbaum (1977) (refer to chapter 4)

were implemented so that self-reinforcement statements were given for successful performances, attribution for failure was shifted from self-blame to effort requirements and external demands, and so forth. Also, the athlete was taught to relax and imagine successful scenes in increasingly problematic situations. The athlete imagined failure situations as well, but he was able to cope with the setbacks during the imagery session. These procedures were practiced first in a noncompetitive environment, but later prior to pregame warmups and even during the game when there was a break in the action. Figure 3.4 shows the points-per-game record for the basketball player before the cognitive intervention

Figure 3.4: **Points per Game for the 28-Game Season Before (Pretreatment) and After (Post-treatment) the Introduction of a Cognitive Intervention Technique**

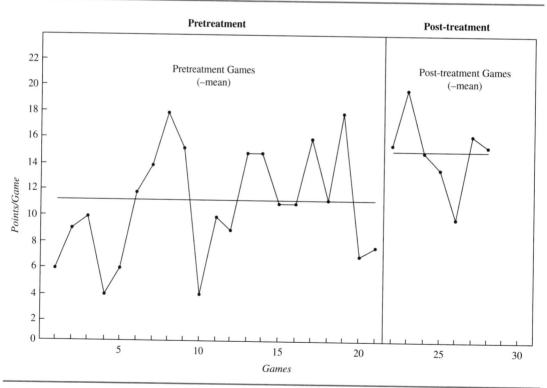

Source: Meyers and Schleser (1980).

(pretreatment) and after the intervention (post-treatment). Clearly, significant improvement in performance did occur following the introduction of the cognitive strategies. Although not reflected in figure 3.4, shooting percentage (field goal) increased from 42 percent to almost 66 percent.

A number of recent studies of imagery and basketball have focused on improving free throw performance. For example, Wrisberg and Anshel (1989) noted that mental imagery played a substantial part in assisting young boys at a summer camp to improve free throw performance. These data were replicated by Predebon and Docker (1992) in a study of thirty experienced male basketball players in Australia; their imagery plus preshot routine group significantly outperformed physical routine and no routine groups, thereby lending credibility to both imagery and the institution of a preshot routine in assisting athletes in dealing with distracting performance influences. However, in a disclaimer, Lamirand and Rainey (1994) failed to find any benefits to imagery in their study of eighteen female college basketball players, but did point to small sample size and unforeseen methodological shortcomings (i.e., failure to assess imagery ability of subjects, lack of individualized interventions, no actual check on whether subjects were practicing imagery) as problematic in their study.

In a related study that also failed to show the efficacy of imagery, this time in field goal shooting, Weinberg, Hankes, and Jackson (1991) introduced 105 college students to a basketball task requiring a fifteen-foot perimeter shot. After a performance baseline was established, the subjects were randomly assigned to a one-minute, a five-minute, or a ten-minute mental preparation condition not restricted to, but most commonly employing, imagery. Also, the subjects were again randomly assigned to groups in which mental practice took place either prior to or after a three-minute physical practice preparatory to

the actual shooting task. Thus, six experimental conditions were created; these were created by combining the amount of mental preparation time (one minute, five minutes, ten minutes) and the temporal location of the mental practice (either before or after a three-minute physical practice period prior to performing the basketball shooting task). In addition, there was a physical practice only control group. Interestingly, none of the mental preparation groups shot field goals any better than the practice only group. Also, the temporal location of the mental practice was of no significance. Perhaps the failure to achieve the expected results in this instance is best explained by the fact that, in addition to imagery, the subjects were allowed to use other mental preparation strategies of their choice (i.e., attentional focus, relaxation, positive self-statements, preparatory arousal), thus diluting the imagery effect. This confounding of effects noted in the Weinberg et al. study is not unusual in the imagery literature because of the obvious overlap in mental preparation strategies. In this regard, Kendall, Hrycaiko, Martin, and Kendall (1990) reported difficulties in teasing out the relative merits of imagery versus relaxation and positive self-talk in explaining the success of their intervention package in improving the defensive play of four female collegiate basketball athletes.

Though the available research has produced equivocal results, there is every reason to believe in the utility of imagery in improving motor skill performance. Clearly, there is need for more sophisticated studies on imagery and related mental preparation procedures.

A modification of the basic imagery procedure has been developed by Richard Suinn (Suinn, 1972), and is called *visuomotor behavioral rehearsal* (VMBR), According to Suinn (1993, p. 499), VMBR is "a covert activity whereby a person experiences sensory-motor sensations that reintegrate reality experiences, and which include neuromuscular, physiological, and emotional involvement." As such, there are three major components to VMBR: relaxation training, imagery rehearsal of athletic performance under stress, and skill performance in a simulated environment. As opposed to the more typical mental practice instruction of "close your eyes and try to imagine yourself making the free throw," VMBR seeks a full-dimensional re-experiencing of the event:

> Be there in the situation again . . . so that you are aware of where you are, what's around you, who's with you . . . you're actually on the basketball court again, the home court . . . score is all tied, the crowd is especially vocal, you have the ball in your hands, breathing a little shallowly . . . you bounce it several times, can feel the firmness . . . take a deep breath to settle down . . . focus on the rim. . . . (Suinn, 1993, p. 499)

Suinn stresses that VMBR is not random in content; it is a well-controlled copy of experience and is subject to conscious control. He further suggests that the strength of VMBR over many other mental practice schemes lies in the fact that it is a standardized training method that is subject to replication in practice and research; as we shall see, VMBR has in fact been the subject of considerable investigation. It is also efficacious because it does not require the sort of specialized training associated with the use of imagery through hypnosis. Prominent athletes of the past two decades who have used VMBR to their competitive advantage include Jean Claude Killy in Alpine skiing, Jack Nicklaus in golf, Dwight Stones in high jumping, and Chris Evert in tennis, to name just a few (Suinn, 1993).

Perhaps the first study involving VMBR was reported by Titley (1976), who employed the technique with a football field goal specialist who had missed three crucial kicks from 35 yards, all of which made the difference between a win and a loss or tie. Following VMBR, the kicker became more consistent, and he ended up setting fourteen records at his university as well

as kicking a personal best and NCAA record 63-yard field goal. Similar kinds of successes using VMBR have been reported for baseball (Gough, 1989), bowling, tennis, and basketball (Winning Associates, 1978), golf (Kirschenbaum and Bale, 1980), and pistol shooting (Hall and Hardy, 1991).

VMBR has been used often in basketball. One very interesting application of VMBR was made by Schleser, Meyers, and Montgomery (1980) with two female basketball players. One player was a center with problems in shooting free throws, the other a forward who needed assistance with field goal shooting. Using VMBR in conjunction with several other mental skills techniques, Schleser et al. were able to improve the accuracy of free throw shooting by the center from a baseline of 41 percent to 55 percent; no perceptible change in field goal accuracy was noted. In the case of the forward, her field goal average improved from 37 percent to 52 percent while her free throw percentage remained stable at 68 percent. Such real-life research with athletes is often fraught with difficulties; in this case, the center withdrew from the treatment program after the seven-game baseline and the thirteen-game intervention period. The remaining eleven games offered a rare opportunity, methodologically, to follow up on the center; interestingly, she hit slightly below 29 percent of her free throws during that time frame. Perhaps the noticeable performance decrement is not an indictment of the training the center underwent, but rather may be attributable to a motivational deficit for the last part of the season. Regardless of interpretation, Suinn (1993) suggests that data like these underscore the fact that compliance with mental training is as important as compliance with physical training in athletics.

In another basketball study, Hall and Erffmeyer (1983) employed VMBR in an attempt to enhance free throw accuracy among ten highly skilled female members of an intercollegiate basketball team. In their research (rare in that an actual control manipulation was carried out), a group of women was trained to relax and visualize excellent foul shooting. A second group (the VMBR condition) viewed a color videotape of a model female basketball player executing ten consecutive foul shots with perfect form. Because the model was viewed from behind, it was relatively easy for each woman to imagine that she was the one actually shooting the free throws. After the tape, those in the VMBR condition were asked to close their eyes and again view themselves as shooting without errors in form or consequence.

The findings from this interesting study indicated that watching a tape had a more dramatic impact on performance than imagery training alone (see figure 3.5). Specifically, the percent of free throws made rose sharply during a five-day post-test period following treatment for the VMBR athletes, but there was no corresponding increase among the players who had merely learned to relax and use visual imagery (no

Figure 3.5: **A Comparison of Pretest and Post-Test Foul-Shooting Percentages of Groups Experiencing a Visuomotor Behavioral Rehearsal (VMBR) Intervention or Relaxation Training Only**

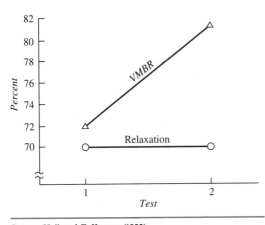

Source: Hall and Erffmeyer (1983).

modeling). These findings are of special significance because they suggest that the use of more traditional imagery techniques may be limited. Certainly such approaches may be at a disadvantage without some sort of visual aid that may assist in the process of image formation.

To this point, we have reviewed a body of literature that is generally supportive of the utility of imagery and VMBR. It appears that imagery-based mental training techniques can be of use to sport psychologists, coaches, and athletes. However, there are a number of factors to be considered in using imagery that make the process even more effective, and they are reviewed in highlight 3.2.

Psyching-Up Strategies

Of all the intervention strategies that are rooted to the traditions of cognitive psychology, perhaps none has received more attention than psyching-up techniques. The term "psyching-up" is often used in athletic circles by coaches, players, and others close to the competition. Despite the nebulous features associated with such an unscientific term, it connotes some very specific ideas. When a player "psychs up," a state of cognitive and mental readiness is gained that affords the athlete a psychological advantage. Cognitive elements are brought forth in such polished form that physical precision results. Tension, alertness, and even nausea have all been shown to contribute to optimum behavioral expression in sport. In conventional vernacular, the player must develop "a winning attitude."

Only recently has the systematic literature on psyching-up begun to take shape. Weinberg (1984) has proposed that the varied techniques that form the corpus of this literature can be categorized as invoking (1) attentional focus, (2) self-efficacy statements, (3) relaxation, (4) imagery, or (5) preparatory arousal. While some approaches are characterized by more than one area, others focus exclusively on one dimension.

The seminal paper on psyching-up was written by Shelton and Mahoney (1978). In a test of influence of the psyching-up strategy on motor performance, thirty Olympic-style weightlifters were instructed to psych up or simply count backward prior to performing on a hand dynamometer task designed to measure grip strength. The results indicated that the athletes who were permitted to use their own methods for getting themselves psyched up showed dramatic increases in performance, whereas their control counterparts (the counting backward condition) either registered no improvement or actually exhibited performance decreases.

These findings were extended by Weinberg, Gould, and Jackson (1980) in a study that examined task specificity and psyching-up. Three different motor tasks (isokinetic leg strength, stabilometer balance, speed-of-arm movement) were employed and careful measurements were taken on each task after a psych-up manipulation. The results indicated that while isokinetic leg-strength performance was facilitated by the psych-up strategy, the other two behaviors were largely unaffected by this intervention. It would seem, therefore, that only certain types of response systems are likely to benefit from psych-up techniques.

Along other lines, Weinberg, Gould, and Jackson (1981) have observed that the changes in the motor systems affected by psych-up strategies are relatively independent of the duration

A football player psychs up before a game by meditating. A well-known study gives credence to the idea that athletes who are permitted to use their own methods for getting themselves psyched up show dramatic increases in performance.

Sport Imagery Training

Although both elite performers and beginners may practice imagery training to some extent, not many people are ever likely to develop this skill to its potential. For one thing, it is often self-taught, and for another it is not likely to be systematized. The practical use of sport imagery training could perhaps be enhanced by directing greater attention to the conditions that facilitate its development. Some of the more important conditions are suggested below.

1. *Vividness and controllability.* Images are likely to prove most beneficial when they are colorful, realistic, and involve the appropriate emotions. Actual recollections of previous performances provide an anchor for building comparisons, and they make images of future performances seem more believable. It may well be that vividness and controllability are themselves mediated by having the athletes use images that are personally meaningful to them; the utility of such a point has been noted by Hecker and Kaczor (1988) and Lee (1990). When the downhill skier really sees the slope, his or her mental executions are more likely to result in real improvements. Also, it is essential that the skier be able to control the presence of the image. That is, he or she must be able to turn it on and off in order to use it to advantage. In certain circumstances, images may be distracting and divert the athlete's focus from the task immediately at hand. Knowing when to use imagery is as important as knowing how to use it.

2. *Practice.* Imagery is a skill that can be learned. Although some people are better at visualizing events than others, everyone can improve his or her mental functioning along these lines. This is not to say, however, that improvement is likely to come about quickly or without effort. Often, athletes must mentally practice for months before they become proficient in the use of imagery techniques. Short sessions with long rest intervals are preferred; repetition is absolutely required. Weinberg (1982) has suggested that imagery practice sessions should be at least one minute long but should never exceed five minutes in duration.

3. *Attitude and expectation.* Imagery is most likely to benefit those who believe in it (Harris and Robinson, 1986). If an athlete rejects the approach as nontraditional, it is not likely to be of much value. If used at all, the technique should be approached with the recognition that it is a legitimate skill and, like any other skill, can be learned in time, within the ability of the learner.

(Continued next page)

Highlight 3.2 (Continued)

Sport Imagery Training

4. *Previous experience.* **Some evidence exists that experienced athletes may gain more than beginners from imagery training (Howe, 1991). The reason is not clear. It may be because the more experienced performer has already mastered basic physical skills and thus is able to allocate more attention to mental processes.**

5. *Relaxed attention.* **A relaxed state of mind during imagery training seems to facilitate the effectiveness of training (Lanning and Hisanga, 1983). A person who is fully relaxed is better able to attend to the integrity of an image, with the result that images are more vivid and easier to control.**

6. *Internal versus external imagery.* **Although the scientific evidence is still out (Suinn, 1993; Whelan, Mahoney, and Meyers, 1991), the notion that an internal perspective results in more favorable images than an external one has intuitive appeal. To see someone else perform successfully is one thing; it is something else again to visualize oneself accomplishing the same feat. If for no other reason, the image should likely include oneself because it is desirable for the image to overlap as much as possible with the real-life situation.**

7. *Age.* **It is generally believed that older athletes are better able to use imagery, and not totally due to differences in relative level of skill development. However, there is recent evidence that young children can in fact become good imagers. Partington (1990) demonstrated that young figure skaters (ages ten to fourteen years) and gymnasts (eight to eleven years) could profit substantially from mental imagery training. Similarly, Li-Wei, Qi-Wei, Orlick, and Zitzelsberger (1992) reported significantly greater improvement in table tennis skills among Chinese seven- to ten-year-olds who were imagery-trained when they were compared with nontrained controls. Though studies such as these are encouraging and suggestive of the need for more research, it still appears at this time that there exists a positive correlation between experience and ability to profit from imagery.**

Sources: Harris and Robinson (1986); Hecker and Kaczor (1988); Howe (1991); Lanning and Hisanga (1983); Lee (1990); Li-Wei, Qi-Wei, Orlick, and Zitzelsberger (1992); Partington (1990); Suinn (1993); Weinberg (1982); Whelan, Mahoney, and Meyers (1991).

of the interval during which the psyching-up takes place. Specifically, while leg-strength performance increased above a baseline level following instructions to use whatever psych-up technique the subject might select, the length of time the subject engaged in this exercise was of little consequence. Such findings are of interest because they are at odds with much of the traditional psychological literature on arousal and performance.

Documentation of the validity of psyching-up strategies for increasing athletic performance in field situations is provided by Caudill, Weinberg, and Jackson (1983). Using college sprinters and hurdlers off the North Texas State University track team (now the University of North Texas), performance was evaluated for each of sixteen athletes under both psych-up and control conditions. The findings revealed that significantly better performances did occur for fifteen of the sixteen athletes under the psych-up as opposed to the control condition. Apparently, the increased effectiveness associated with psyching-up, assumed by coaches, players, and sport practitioners, is genuine and confirmable.

Further Considerations

Prior studies have focused on the range and scope of influence of cognitive techniques. Increasing evidence indicates that cognitive approaches are most likely to be effective when the athletic skill has a large cognitive component. Ryan and Simons (1983), for instance, found that mental practice facilitated learning of a low motor task with a heavy cognitive component but had no effect when the cognitive aspects of the task were reduced. Such findings imply that some athletic tasks such as tackling in football, or serving in volleyball or tennis, may not benefit from cognitive learning interventions. Or, as Feltz and Landers (1983) note, if positive effects are to be achieved in such sports using cognitive methods, then considerably more time should be allocated to the intervention (p. 46).

Another topic of heated debate has centered on what Schmidt (1982) has labeled "the initial learning hypothesis." The position taken here is that cognitive interventions are most likely to enhance performance during the early stages of skill acquisition. Perhaps this could be due to a greater reliance on cognitive components at this stage; that is, you still have to think about it before you execute it. In any case, the implication is that elite athletes (athletes already performing at a high level of efficiency) would be better off invoking an alternative strategy. And this notion does have some support (Schmidt, 1982, pp. 458–462). But the findings are far from conclusive in this area and any remarks made must be considered tentative.

Even if externally imposed cognitive intervention strategies are shown to be of limited value for elite athletic performers, there can be little doubt that internal cognitive processes are important to performance of truly gifted athletes. Indeed, there is even evidence that internally based cognitive strategies can be used to differentiate more successful competitors from their less successful counterparts (Mahoney and Avener, 1977). Several years ago, a suspicion among researchers was that many world class long distance runners were using "dissociative" strategies that permitted them to block out the pain and torment of the final, most stressful part of the race. For example, for the closing few miles a marathoner might count backward from some set value, or think about an unrelated, pleasant activity, and thereby shut out the agony associated with finishing. It was left to Morgan and Pollack (1977) to assess scientifically the validity of such dissociative processes among elite long distance runners. Contrary to what many people in sports expected, the better runners adopted an "associative" task-demand/body-monitoring cognitive strategy, and it was the less talented runner who was more likely to dissociate. The more competent runner, it seems, is more likely to "stay in tune with bodily signals."

That is, should something go wrong it is advantageous to detect the problem immediately so that appropriate corrective action can be taken. This may mean engaging in some sort of compensatory mechanism or ceasing any further activity altogether in order to avoid irreparable damage.

Elsewhere, greater concentration ability, success in dreams, reported self-confidence, and self-instructional behavior have been reported by successful gymnasts (Mahoney and Avener, 1977) and by racquetball players (Meyers, Cooke, Cullen, and Liles, 1981), at least relative to less successful athletes in the same sport. Also, it seems that "champion" status athletes in these sports handle situational anxiety better than the less skilled athlete. So, even though the value of cognitive learning manipulations introduced by coaches or trainers may occasionally be questioned, there is clearly evidence to indicate that internal cognitive mechanisms are important to the ultimate success of even the most gifted athletic participant.

We have now discussed some of the possible sport applications of learning processes in three major areas: classical conditioning, operant learning, and cognitive learning. Each of these areas has an immense basic literature, and only a few of the many uses of the knowledge base in this area have been suggested by sport psychologists. Oversights are especially great in the areas of classical conditioning, considering the demonstrated value of procedures in this area regarding other attempts at human behavior modification (see Wolpe, 1982). Finally, the technology of behavioral psychology must be appreciated by coach and player alike for the athlete to reach his or her athletic potential.

SUMMARY

1. Classical conditioning, operant learning, and cognitive learning are three major types of learning that have influenced sport.

2. In classical conditioning, a primary eliciting stimulus called an unconditioned stimulus (UCS) reflexively produces a response called an unconditioned response (UCR). When a neural stimulus, called a conditioned stimulus (CS), is paired with the UCS, the CS comes to evoke a conditioned response (CR) similar to the UCR.

3. Despite a large literature on classical conditioning, it has been an overlooked area in the psychology of sport.

4. In operant learning, positive reinforcement refers to the strengthening of behavior by presenting an event following responding. Conversely, negative reinforcement refers to the strengthening of behavior by removing an event following responding. Punishment and omission training both weaken responding, but different operations are involved with each procedure.

5. Behavioral coaching techniques involve the application of learning principles to situations involved with training athletic competitors. Differential reinforcement, shaping, and reinforcement are a few of the learning principles that have been used in this area.

6. Public recordings involve the placement of formal evaluations in a display in an effort to reward or punish athletic performances.

7. In addition to emphasizing behavioral techniques for the purpose of changing the athlete's performance, behavioral manipulations can also be used to modify the behavior of coaches. Feedback statements about the frequency with which positive and negative criticism is given especially have produced positive results.

8. Conditioned reinforcers are neutral stimuli that, when paired with primary reinforcers, come to act as primary reinforcers. Token systems illustrate one potential use of conditioned reinforcers. Another application of conditioned reinforcement involves chaining, whereby each response in a stimulus-response

chain serves as a signal for the next response; the last response in the chain is a reinforcer. Swimming and golf are two sports in which chaining has been used effectively in skill development.

9. The Premack Principle states that a high probability behavior can be used as a reward for the occurrence of a lower probability response. The advantage of this approach is that rewards are defined on an individual basis.

10. Session length and schedules of reinforcement are two training variables discussed in the chapter. As a rule, widely spaced trials work better when gross motor skills are the target of training. Also, persistence in responding is greater when intermittent rather than continuous reinforcement is used.

11. Learned helplessness occurs when an expectancy of uncontrollability emerges following exposure to an aversive noncontingency. Many athletes fail because they anticipate failure. One way to prevent learned helplessness is to incorporate success and failure experiences into the training program.

12. Cognitive learning theory involves the study of the mental aspects of behavior. Recently, sport psychology has witnessed an increased interest in cognitive learning as it relates to treatment intervention and performance enhancement. Imagery and visuomotor behavioral rehearsal (VMBR) are two cognitive learning approaches that have been used widely and well in performance enhancement with athletes in many sports.

13. Mental practice techniques that make use of cognitive manipulations have produced positive results, but a number of issues are yet to be reconciled. Among them are the restrictions on *when* and *where* the techniques can be applied in sport, and there is some question about the usefulness of the approach when the elite athlete is being trained.

SUGGESTED READINGS

Martin G., & Pear, J. (1992) *Behavior modification: What it is and how to do it.* (4th ed.). Englewood Cliffs, NJ: Prentice-Hall.

This book is one of the best of the various texts on behavior modification. The basics of conditioning and learning are presented in a most comprehensive and readable fashion. Discussions of such topics as positive and negative reinforcement, conditioned reinforcement, chaining, punishment, token economies, and cognitive behavior modification are particularly salient within the context of the topics discussed in this chapter. Also, the examples used from time to time from athletics should be of particular interest to students of sport psychology.

Moran, A. (1993) Conceptual and methodological issues in the measurement of mental imagery skills in athletes. *Journal of Sport Behavior, 16,* 156–170.

In this timely article, Moran discusses the relative strengths and weaknesses of a variety of tests that purport to assess aspects of mental imagery. This is a particularly relevant article because it addresses an issue that appears to be a weak link in imagery research in sport: assessment. Mental imagery tests discussed include the Questionnaire on Mental Imagery (QMI), a shortened version of the QMI (SQMI), Vividness of Mental Imagery Questionnaire (VVIQ), and the Movement Imagery Questionnaire (MIQ). The latter three instruments do have some history of usage within the sporting context. The author suggests that the ephemeral nature of imagery itself contributes to validity problems with the various scales, thus creating a confused picture concerning mental imagery assessment.

Peterson, C., Maier, N. F., & Seligman, M. E. P. (1994) *Learned helplessness: A theory for the age of personal control.* New York: Oxford University Press.

This book extends and updates the earlier work of Seligman on learned helplessness as the end result of a lack or perceived lack of controllability in one's life. The book focuses on updating the literature on learned helplessness; at the same time, applications are made with regard to contemporary culture. Future directions as seen by the authors are also delineated. The student who has read this volume and the 1977 Seligman book will be well-versed in theory and application in relation to learned helplessness.

Porter, K., & Foster, J. (1990) *Visual athletics*. Dubuque, IA: Wm. C. Brown.

Mental skills essential to skill development in such sports as baseball, basketball, golf, running, soccer, tennis, and triathlon are discussed by the authors. Step-by-step visualization exercises are provided for the preceding sports. In addition to the heavy emphasis on visualization, other mental skills such as relaxation and goal setting are addressed. This book is very readable and is designed to help the athlete learn to flex his or her mental muscles.

Savoy, C. (1993) A yearly mental training program for a college basketball player. *The Sport Psychologist, 7*, 173–190.

In this case study of a female collegiate basketball player, the author demonstrates how to apply mental skills training to performance enhancement in an already skilled athlete. Various psychological tests and an interview were used with the athlete prior to devising a collaborative training program involving imagery, centering, focusing, and energizing. An end-of-the-year follow-up on the athlete showed less pregame anxiety and an overall improvement in game and practice statistics as well as performance rating by the coach.

Seligman, M. E. P. (1975) *Helplessness*. San Francisco: W.H. Freeman

This is a nonacademic coverage of the concept of helplessness as it relates to depression and the stresses of everyday life. It is tied to research, but the reader need not be a student of experimental psychology to understand it. The basic notion that lack of control resulting from an environmental noncontingency can produce deficit performance is linked to a variety of phenomena in everyday life, and even to death, in some instances.

Sherman, C. (1995) Shaping and chaining motor skills. *Track Technique, 130*, 4148–4150.

This article provides the reader with a concise and highly readable introduction to the behavioral concepts of shaping and chaining as applied to track. A specific example of shaping is applied to the hurdles, and chaining is demonstrated for the shot put. Also, a good review of the literature and pertinent references related to the use of shaping and chaining in a variety of sport/motor skills areas are provided.

Skinner, B. F. (1971) *Beyond freedom and dignity*. New York: Knopf.

The classic work by one of the foremost authorities on learning addresses the problems associated with the use of aversive control techniques. The author calls into question the wisdom of using punishment and negative reinforcement when other procedures are available. The implications of this work for coaching and other areas that make use of aversive techniques become clear as the author spells out the unfortunate consequences associated with negative stimulation. The recommendation by Skinner is that we substitute positive reinforcement for negative reinforcement and omission training for punishment.

Tippett, L. J. (1992) The generation of visual images: A review of neurophysiological research and theory. *Psychological Bulletin, 112*, 415–432.

This literature review is intended for a high-level audience with some sophistication in neuropsychology. Within those confines, however, Tippett has done an excellent job of giving her readers a good view of the biological mechanisms that are at work in influencing mental imagery. Tippett concludes her article by stating that imagery is a multicomponent process as opposed to a very unidimensional or simplistic one and that mental images appear to be generated in the left as opposed to the right hemisphere of the brain, challenging long-held beliefs. The latter point, however, remains open to scientific study for ultimate verification.

REFERENCES

Abramson, L. Y., Seligman, M. E. P., & Teasdale, I. D. (1978) Learned helplessness in humans: Critique and reformulation. *Journal of Abnormal Psychology, 87,* 49–74.

Allison, M. G., & Ayllon, T. (1980) Behavioral coaching in the development of skills in football, gymnastics, and tennis. *Journal of Applied Behavior Analysis, 13,* 297–314.

Allison, M. G., & Ayllon, T. (1983) Behavioral coaching in the development of skills in football, gymnastics, and tennis. In G. L. Martin and D. Hrycaiko (Eds.), *Behavior modification and coaching: Principles, procedures, and research* (117–145). Springfield, IL: Charles C. Thomas.

Bandura, A. (1977) Self-efficacy: Toward a unifying theory of behavioral change. *Psychological Review, 84,* 191–215.

Buzas, H. P., & Ayllon, T. (1981) Differential reinforcement in coaching tennis skills. *Behavior Modification, 5,* 372–385.

Caudill, D., Weinberg, R., & Jackson, A. (1983) Psyching-up and track athletes: A preliminary investigation. *Journal of Sport Psychology, 5,* 231–235.

Cox, R. H. (1985) *Sport psychology: Concepts and applications.* Dubuque, IA: Wm. C. Brown.

Craighead, W. E., Kazdin, A. E., & Mahoney, M. J. (1981) *Behavior modification: Principles, issues, and applications.* Boston: Houghton Mifflin Company.

Dickinson, J. A. (1977) *A behavioral analysis of sport.* Princeton, NJ: Princeton University Press.

Donahue, J. A., Gillis, J. H., & King, K. (1980) Behavior modification in sport and physical education: A review. *Journal of Sport Psychology, 2,* 311–328.

Dweck, C. S. (1980) Learned helplessness in sport. In K.M. Newell & G.C. Roberts (Eds.), *Psychology of motor behavior and sport—1979* (pp. 1–11). Champaign, IL: Human Kinetics.

Feltz, D. L., & Landers, D. M. (1983) The effects of mental practice on motor skill learning and performance: A meta-analysis. *Journal of Sport Psychology, 5,* 25–57.

Geen, R. G., Beatty, W. W., & Arkin, R. M. (1984) *Human motivation: Physiological, behavioral and social approaches.* Boston: Allyn and Bacon.

Gough, D. (1989) Improving batting skills with small-college baseball players through guided visual imagery. *Coaching Clinic, 27,* 1–6.

Gray, S. W. (1990) Effects of visuomotor rehearsal with videotaped modeling on racquetball performance of beginning players. *Perceptual and Motor Skills, 70,* 379–385.

Hale, B. D. (1982) The effects of internal and external imagery on muscular and ocular concomitants. *Journal of Sport Psychology, 4,* 379–387.

Hall, E. G., & Erffmeyer, E. S. (1983) The effects of visuo-motor behavior rehearsal with videotaped modeling on free-throw accuracy of intercollegiate female basketball players. *Journal of Sport Psychology, 5,* 343–346.

Hall, E. G., & Hardy, C. J. (1991) Ready, aim, fire . . . Relaxation strategies for enhancing pistol marksmanship. *Perceptual and Motor Skills, 72,* 775–786.

Hall, H. K., Weinberg, R. S., & Jackson, A. (1987) Effects of goal-specificity, goal difficulty, and information feedback on endurance performance. *Journal of Sport Psychology, 9,* 43–54.

Harris, D. V., & Robinson, W. J. (1986) The effects of skill level on EMG activity during internal and external imagery. *Journal of Sport Psychology, 8,* 105–111.

Hayes, S. C., Munt, E., Korn, Z., Wulfert, E., Rosenfarb, I., & Zettle, R. D. (1986) The effects of feedback and self-reinforcement instructions on studying performance. *Psychological Record, 36,* 27–37.

Hayes, S. C., Rosenfarb, I., Wulfert, E., Munt, E. D., Korn, Z., & Zettle, R. D. (1985) Self-reinforcement effects: An artifact of social standard setting? *Journal of Applied Behavioral Analysis, 18,* 201–214.

Hecker, J. E., & Kaczor, L. M. (1988) Application of imagery theory to sport psychology: Some preliminary findings. *Journal of Sport and Exercise Psychology, 10,* 363–373.

Howe, B. L. (1991) Imagery and sport performance. *Sports Medicine, 11,* 1–5.

Jackson, J. H. (1932) On the nature of the duality of the brain. In J. Taylor (Ed.), *Selected writings of John Hughlings Jackson: Vol. 2. Evolution and dissolution of the nervous system* (pp. 129–145). London: Hodder & Stoughton (Reprinted from *Medical Press and Circular,* 1874, *1,* 19.

Kau, M. L., & Fisher, J. (1974) Self-modification of exercise behavior. *Journal of Behavior Therapy and Experimental Psychiatry, 5,* 213–214.

Kazdin, A. E. (1977) *The token economy: A review and evaluation.* New York: Plenum.

Kendall, G., Hrycaiko, D., Martin, G. L., & Kendall, T. (1990) The effects of an imagery rehearsal, relaxation, and self-talk package on basketball game performance. *Journal of Sport and Exercise Psychology, 12,* 157–165.

Killian, K. J. (1988) Teaching swimming using a backward chain sequence. *Journal of Physical Education, Recreation and Dance, 59*(5), 82–86.

Kirschenbaum, D. S., & Bale, R. M. (1980) Cognitive-behavioral skills in golf: Brain power golf. In R. Suinn (Ed.), *Psychology in sports: Methods and applications* (pp. 334–343). Minneapolis, MN: Burgess.

Kirschenbaum, D. S., & Wittrock, D. A. (1984) Cognitive-behavioral interventions in sport: A self-regulatory perspective. In J. Silva & R. Weinberg (Eds.), *Psychological foundations of sport* (pp. 81–98). Champaign, IL: Human Kinetics.

Koop, S., & Martin, G. L. (1983) Evaluation of a coaching strategy to reduce swimming stroke errors with beginning age-group swimmers. *Journal of Applied Behavioral Analysis, 16,* 447–460.

Lamirand, M., & Rainey, D. (1994). Mental imagery, relaxation, and accuracy of basketball foul shooting. *Perceptual and Motor Skills, 78,* 1229–1230.

Lanning, W., & Hisanga, B. (1983) A study of the relationship between the reduction of competitive anxiety and an increase in athletic performance. *International Journal of Sport Psychology, 14,* 219–227.

Lee, C. (1990) Psyching up for a muscular endurance task: Effects of image content on performance and mood state. *Journal of Sport and Exercise Psychology, 12,* 66–73.

Leith, L. M., & Taylor, A. H. (1992) Behavior modification and exercise adherence: A literature review. *Journal of Sport Behavior, 15,* 60–74.

Lepper, M. R., & Greene, D. (1978) *The hidden cost of reward: New perspectives on the psychology of human motivation.* New York: Halsted.

Lepper, M. R., Greene, D., & Nisbett, R. E. (1973) Understanding children's intrinsic interests with intrinsic awards: A test of the "overjustification" hypothesis. *Journal of Personality and Social Psychology, 28,* 129–137.

Li-Wei, Z., Qi-Wei, M., Orlick, T., & Zitzelsberger, L. (1992) The effect of mental-imagery training on performance enhancement with 7-10-year-old children. *The Sport Psychologist, 6,* 230–241.

Machlus, S. D., & O'Brien, R. M. (1988) Visuo-motor behavior rehearsal and preparatory arousal in improving athletic speed. Paper presented to the Annual Meeting of the American Psychological Association, Atlanta, Georgia.

Mahoney, M. J. (1977) Cognitive skills and athletics performance. Paper presented at the Eleventh Annual Meeting of the Association for the Advancement of Behavior Therapy, Atlanta, Georgia.

Mahoney, M. J., & Avener, M. (1977) Psychology of the elite athlete: An introductory study. *Cognitive Therapy and Research, 1,* 135–141.

Mahoney, M. J., Gabriel, T. J., & Perkins, T. S. (1987) Psychological skills and exceptional athletic performance. *The Sport Psychologist, 1,* 181–199.

Maier, S. F., & Seligman, M. E. P. (1976) Learned helplessness: Theory and evidence. *Journal of Experimental Psychology: General, 105,* 3–46.

Martin, G. L., & Hrycaiko, D. (1983) Effective behavioral coaching: What's it all about? *Journal of Sport Psychology, 5,* 8–20.

Martin, G. L., & Pear, J. (1992) *Behavior modification: What it is and how to do it* (4th ed.). Englewood Cliffs, NJ: Prentice-Hall.

Martin, K. A., & Hall, C. R. (1995) Using mental imagery to enhance intrinsic motivation. *Journal of Sport and Exercise Psychology, 17,* 54–69.

McKenzie, T. L., & Rushall, B. S. (1974) Effects of self-recording on attendance and performance in a competitive swimming training environment. *Journal of Applied Behavior Analysis, 7,* 199–206.

Meichenbaum, D. (1977) *Cognitive behavior modification.* New York: Plenum.

Meyers, A. W., Cooke, C., Cullen, J., & Liles, L. (1981) Psychological aspects of athletic competitors: A replication across sports. *Cognitive Therapy and Research, 5,* 29–33.

Meyers, A. W., & Schleser, R. (1980) A cognitive behavioral intervention for improving basketball performance. *Journal of Sport Psychology, 2,* 69–73.

Meyers, A. W., Schleser, R., Cooke, C., & Cuvillier, C. (1979) Cognitive contributions to the development of gymnastic skills. *Cognitive Therapy and Research, 3,* 75–85.

Moran, A. (1993) Conceptual and methodological issues in the measurement of imagery skills in athletes. *Journal of Sport Behavior, 16,* 156–170.

Morgan, W. P., & Pollack, M. L. (1977) Psychology characterizations of the elite distance runner. *Annals of the New York Academy of Sciences, 301,* 382–403.

Nation, J. R., & Massad, P. (1978) Persistence training: A partial reinforcement procedure for reversing learned helplessness and depression. *Journal of Experimental Psychology: General, 107,* 436–451.

Nation, J. R., & Woods, D. J. (1980) Persistence: The role of partial reinforcement in psychotherapy. *Journal of Experimental Psychology: General, 109,* 175–207.

O'Brien, R. M., & Simek, T. C. (1983) A comparison of behavioral and traditional methods for teaching golf. In G.L. Martin & D. Hrycaiko (Eds.), *Behavior modification and coaching: Principles, procedures, and research.* Springfield, IL: Charles C. Thomas.

Partington, J. (1990) Personal knowledge in imagery: Implications for novice gymnasts, figure skaters, and their coaches. Paper presented to the Annual Conference of the Canadian Society for Psycho-Motor Learning and Sport Psychology, Windsor, Ontario.

Pavlov, I. P. (1927) *Conditioned reflexes.* London: Oxford University Press.

Penman, K. (1969) Relative effectiveness of teaching beginning tumbling with and without an instant replay videotape recorder. *Perceptual and Motor Skills, 28,* 45–46.

Porter, K., & Foster, J. (1988, Jan.) In your mind's eye. *World Tennis,* 22–23.

Predebon, J., & Docker, S. B. (1992) Free-throw shooting performance as a function of preshot routines. *Perceptual and Motor Skills, 75,* 167–171.

Premack, D. (1962) Reversability of the reinforcement relation. *Science, 136,* 235–237.

Rodgers, W., Hall, C., & Buckholz, E. (1991) The effect of an imagery training program on imagery ability, imagery use, and figure skating performance. *Journal of Applied Sport Psychology, 3,* 109–125.

Rushall, B. S., & Pettinger, J. (1969) An evaluation of the effect of various reinforcers used as motivators in swimming. *Research Quarterly, 40,* 540–545.

Rushall, B. S., & Siedentop, D. (1972) *The development and control of behavior in sports and physical education.* Philadelphia: Lea and Febiger.

Rushall, B. S., & Smith, K. C. (1979) The modification of the quality and quantity of behavioral categories in a swimming coach. *Journal of Sport Psychology, 1,* 138–150.

Ryan, E. D., & Simons, J. (1983) What is learned in mental practice of motor skills: A test of the cognitive-motor hypothesis. *Journal of Sport Psychology, 5,* 419–426.

Sanderson, F. H. (1983) Length and spacing of practice sessions in sport skills. *International Journal of Sport Psychology, 14,* 116–122.

Schleser, R., Meyers, A. W., & Montgomery, T. (1980) A cognitive behavioral intervention for improving basketball performance. Paper presented to the Association for the Advancement of Behavior Therapy, New York.

Schmidt, R. A. (1982) *Motor control and learning: A behavioral emphasis.* Champaign, IL: Human Kinetics.

Schwartz, B. (1984) *Psychology of learning and behavior.* New York: W.W. Norton and Company.

Seligman, M. E. P., & Beagley, G. (1975) Learned helplessness in the rat. *Journal of Comparative and Physiological Psychology, 88,* 534–541.

Shapiro, E. S., & Shapiro, S. (1984) Behavioral coaching in the development of skills in track. In J. Silva & R. Weinberg (Eds.), *Psychological foundations of sport* (pp. 81–98). Champaign, IL: Human Kinetics.

Shelton, T. O., & Mahoney, M. J. (1978) The content and effect of "psyching-up" strategies in weight lifters. *Cognitive Therapy and Research, 2,* 275–284.

Shick, J. (1970) Effects of mental practice in selected volleyball skills for college women. *Research Quarterly, 51,* 88–94.

Silva, J. M. (1982) Competitive sport environment: Performance enhancement through cognitive intervention. *Behavior Modification, 6,* 443–463.

Simek, T. C., & O'Brien, R. M. (1981) *Total golf: A behavioral approach to lowering your score and getting more out of your game.* Bethpage, NY: B-Mod Associates.

Simek, T. C., O'Brien, R. M., & Figlerski, L. B. (1994) Contracting and chaining to improve the performance of a college golf team: Improvement and deterioration. *Perceptual and Motor Skills, 78,* 1099–1105.

Skinner, B. F. (1971) *Beyond freedom and dignity.* New York: Knopf.

Smith, D. (1987) Conditions that facilitate the development of sport imagery training. *The Sport Psychologist, 1,* 237–247.

Smith, R. E. (1984) Theoretical and treatment approaches to anxiety reduction. In J. M. Silva & R. S. Weinberg, (Eds.), *Psychological foundations of sport* (pp. 157–170). Champaign, IL: Human Kinetics.

Smith, S. M. (1979) Remembering in and out of context. *Journal of Experimental Psychology: Human Learning and Memory, 5,* 460–471.

Smith, S. M. (1984) A comparison of two techniques for reducing context-dependent forgetting. *Memory and Cognition, 12,* 447–482.

Solso, R. L. (1991) *Cognitive psychology* (3d ed.). Boston: Allyn & Bacon.

Suinn, R. M. (1972) Behavioral research for ski racers. *Behavioral Therapy, 3,* 519–520.

Suinn, R. M. (1993). Imagery. In R. N. Singer, M. Murphey, & L. K. Tennant (Eds.), *Handbook on research in sport psychology* (pp. 492–510). New York: Macmillan.

Tarpy, R. M. (1983) *Principles of animal learning and motivation.* Glenview, IL: Scott, Foresman and Company.

Thomas, D. L., & Miller, L. K. (1980) Helping college students: Democratic decision-making versus experimental manipulation. In G. L. Martin and J. G. Osborne (Eds.), *Helping in the community: Behavioral applications* (pp. 180–240). New York: Plenum.

Tippett, L. J. (1992) The generation of visual images: A review of neuropsychological research and theory. *Psychological Bulletin, 112,* 415–432.

Titley, R. W. (1976) The loneliness of the long distance kicker. *Athletic Journal,* September, 74–80.

Weinberg, R. S. (1982) The relationship between mental strategies and motor performance: A review and critique. *Quest, 32,* 195–213.

Weinberg, R. S. (1984) Mental preparation strategies. In J.M. Silva and R.S. Weinberg (Eds.), *Psychological foundations of sport* (pp. 145–156). Champaign, IL: Human Kinetics.

Weinberg, R. S., Gould, D., & Jackson, A. V. (1980) Cognition and motor performance: Effects of psyching-up strategies on three motor tasks. *Cognitive Therapy and Research, 4,* 239–245.

Weinberg, R. S., Gould, D., & Jackson, A. V. (1981) Relationship between the duration of the psych-up interval and strength performance. *Journal of Sport Psychology, 3,* 166–170.

Weinberg, R. S., Hankes, D., & Jackson, A. (1991) Effect of the length and temporal location of the mental preparation interval on basketball shooting performance. *International Journal of Sport Psychology, 22,* 3–14.

Whelan, J. P., Mahoney, M. J., & Meyers, A. W. (1991) Performance enhancement in sport: A cognitive behavioral domain. *Behavior Therapy, 22,* 307–327.

Winning Associates. (1978) *Athlete's homework manual.* Morgantown, WV: Winning Associates.

Wolko, K. L., Hrycaiko, D. W., & Martin, G. L. (1993) A comparison of two self-management packages to standard coaching for improving performance of gymnasts. *Behavior Modification, 17,* 209–223.

Wolpe, J. (1982) *The practice of behavior therapy.* New York: Pergamon.

Woolfolk, R. L., Murphy, S. M., Gottesfeld, D., & Aitken, D. (1985) Effects of mental rehearsal of task motor activity and mental depiction of task outcome on motor skill performance. *Journal of Sport Psychology, 7,* 191–197.

Woolfolk, R. L., Parrish, M. W., & Murphy, S. (1985) The effects of positive and negative imagery on motor skill performance. *Cognitive Therapy and Research, 9,* 335–341.

Wrisberg, C. A., & Anshel, M. H. (1989) The effect of cognitive strategies on the free throw performance of young athletes. *The Sport Psychologist, 3,* 95–104.

Wysocki, T., Hall, G., Iata, B., & Riordan, M. (1979) Behavioral management of exercise: Contracting for aerobic point. *Journal of Applied Behavior Analysis, 12,* 55–64.

Chapter Four

Anxiety, Arousal, and Intervention

INTRODUCTION

Virtually every person who has been intimately involved with sport recognizes the importance of motivational influences on athletic performance. Both coaches and players commonly attribute success to "being up" or failure to "being down." Intensity, commitment, and level of alertness often dictate the style and eventual outcome of sport performance.

Despite the obvious advantage of individual readiness and determination, the negative consequences of extreme excitement cannot be ignored. As we shall see, gearing up for an athletic contest will produce benefits up to a point and then further increases in motivation may actually be counterproductive. To better understand this basic principle, one needs to focus on the subtle but exceedingly important difference between arousal and anxiety. *Arousal*, as it is commonly invoked, refers to an all-inclusive, well-ranging continuum of psychological activation (Sonstroem, 1984). By way of contrast, *anxiety* is generally regarded as a negatively charged emotional state that is characterized by internal discomfort and a feeling of nervousness. This is not to say that anxiety is independent of arousal; quite to the contrary, anxiety contributes to the overall arousal state, but anxiety in many instances must be dealt with as a special case of activation. For example, the impact of anxiety in sport is apparent from empirical studies of national championship wrestlers who reported they felt excessive stress prior to competition (Gould, Horn, and Spreeman, 1983), as well as numerous anecdotal accounts of the debilitating effects of tension.

In this chapter, we shall explore the determinants of arousal and anxiety, the effect of these variables on sport performance, and finally strategies designed to promote performance via the alleviation of anxiety.

DETERMINANTS OF ANXIETY AND AROUSAL

"I'm scared when I play tennis. I fear failure at every corner, and until I rid myself of that attitude, I know I'll never attain my goals, winning a Wimbledon or a U. S. Open."

> **Pam Shriver, World class tennis player, talking of her own performance anxieties in 1985**

Because of the diverse nature of anxiety formation, both physiological and psychological causes must be considered. Each of these aspects of anxiety and arousal is important to the ultimate expression of the behavior—biological and mental events work in concert to produce changes in athletic performance. With a better grasp of this interaction, we are in a position to improve our knowledge of how to manipulate arousal so that sport performance is enhanced.

Neurophysiological Mechanisms

Although a detailed description of the body components that comprise the physiological substrate of anxiety is beyond the scope of this book, two of the major contributors to arousal phenomena can be specified: brain mechanisms and the autonomic nervous system (ANS). Curiously, as noted by Hatfield and Landers (1983), only recently have sport psychologists come to recognize the importance of studying these systems. Although the intricate workings of the central nervous system (CNS), of which the brain is a part, remain a mystery for neuroscientists, the peripheral nervous system (PNS), which includes the ANS, is much better understood. Nonetheless, theory and methodology in sport psychology have only recently made advances in extrapolating basic psychophysiologic research findings to the athletic realm.

Commonly Used Measures of Arousal

The measurement of arousal has typically been conducted through assessing physiological indicators or through psychological self-report questionnaires. One advantage of physiological measurement is its independence from verbal expressive ability. Another is its utility with almost any kind of person; the capacity for self-observation is not a prerequisite. Finally, almost all of the physiological measures can be used continuously, parallel to actual behavior.

Disadvantages of using physiological measures center around their complexity. For one thing, they do not correlate highly with each other, which represents a substantial drawback to such assessment. Also, why athlete A responds to stressful competitive situations with heart rate changes and athlete B reacts to the same situation with increased gastrointestinal activity is perplexing to researchers in this area. On the whole, it appears that there is much to be learned about how to make the most effective use of physiological indicators of arousal.

As for psychological measures, they offer ease of administration and analysis. However, they are also subject to unwanted effects, such as social desirability; for example, instead of answering honestly, the athlete gives responses according to what he or she thinks the examiner (or coach) may desire. Also, questionnaires often necessitate sizable samples in order to control for subject variability, and many athletic teams are not made up of large numbers of players.

Overcoming these inherent drawbacks to each approach is a daunting task. However, the use of multiple physiological indicators as opposed to a single marker may be a fruitful way to proceed. The trend toward more sophisticated, more portable, and less expensive hardware can only facilitate the process of physiological assessment in the future. As for the psychological measures, there is a trend toward more multidimensional arousal measures as well as ones with a more sport-specific orientation. Both of these advances can only assist the process of psychological assessment.

A summary of some of the more commonly used physiological and psychological assessment techniques is provided for us by Hackfort and Schwenkmezger (1989), Landers and Boutcher (1993), and other researchers.

PHYSIOLOGICAL

Assessment techniques for measuring arousal of the central and autonomic nervous system include:

(Continued next page)

Highlight 4.1 (Continued)

Commonly Used Measures of Arousal

1. *Electroencephalography (EEG).* Here, the emphasis is on assessment of brain waves. Alpha state is indicative of relaxation and beta state is suggestive of arousal.
2. *Electrical properties of the skin.* Skin conductance or resistance to an electrical current is measured. Arousal causes increased perspiration, which increases flow of the current.
3. *Heart rate (HR).* Increases in heart rate or changes in patterns may indicate arousal.
4. *Blood pressure.* Increases in blood pressure are associated with arousal.
5. *Electromyography (EMG).* Muscular tension is measured, and increases in tension are indicative of arousal.
6. *Epinephrine, norepinephrine, or cortisol.* All of these biochemical agents are released during stress, and can be measured through blood or urine.

PSYCHOLOGICAL

Psychological measurement techniques to measure arousal include the following questionnaires:

> State-Trait Anxiety Inventory
> Competitive State Anxiety Inventory-II
> Sport Competition Anxiety Test
> Cognitive-Somatic Anxiety Questionnaire
> Sport Anxiety Scale
> Endler Multidimensional Anxiety Scales

Of particular relevance to our discussion at this time are the last three scales; the initial three have either been discussed earlier or will be in chapter 8, Psychological Assessment. The Cognitive-Somatic Anxiety Questionnaire (CSAQ) was created by Schwartz, Davidson, and Goleman (1978) and is composed of fourteen items; it measures both the cognitive and somatic aspects of anxiety. The Sport Anxiety Scale (SAS) was created by Smith, Smoll, and Schutz (1990) and represents a variant of the cognitive-somatic theme; there is a somatic scale, but the cognitive trait anxiety scale is broken into two components—worry and concentration disruption. Smith et al. believe that their three-part assessment scheme

(Continued next page)

Highlight 4.1 (Continued)

Commonly Used Measures of Arousal

allows for more precise measurement and more creative and effective treatment programs for anxiety alleviation. The third questionnaire, the Endler Multidimensional Anxiety Scales (EMAS) presented by Endler, Parker, Bagby, and Cox (1991), represents a factorial approach to anxiety assessment that is based on an interactional perspective on personality; anxiety is a multiplicative function of the person X situation interaction. The EMAS scales are composed of sixty items measuring trait anxiety and twenty purporting to assess state anxiety. Data analysis by Endler et al. supports the distinction between state and trait anxiety, and the two Endler scales measuring each anxiety component appear to be psychometrically sound. Endler and his associates also make a case for the multidimensionality of both trait and state anxiety, thereby suggesting that each is actually made up of several subcomponents. The EMAS scales may have much to offer the sport psychologist interested in anxiety assessment. Certainly, it appears to be a promising companion to Spielberger's State-Trait Anxiety Inventory (STAI).

Sources: Endler, Parker, Bagby, and Cox (1991); Hackfort and Schwenkmezger (1989); Landers and Boutcher (1993); Schwartz, Davidson and Goleman (1978); Smith, Smoll, and Schutz (1990).

Regarding brain structure and functions, the *cerebral cortex,* the *hypothalamus,* and the *reticular formation* represent the most critical substructures related to anxiety and arousal (Carlson, 1991). The cerebral cortex is the convoluted mass of neural tissue shown in figure 4.1 that makes up the outer covering of the brain. Cortex comes from the Latin word meaning "bark," and it has the same rough appearance. Here, higher intellectual functions take place, and cognitive representations of anxiety are fashioned. When a gymnast mulls over his or her nervousness prior to a vault, cortical activation determines the manner by which the arousal state is translated into constructive determination and focus. It is at the cortical level that the experience of anxiety is interpreted as a relevant emotional phenomenon.

Figure 4.1: **Human Brain Structures Important for Arousal and Anxiety**

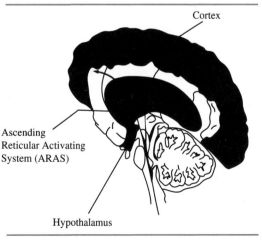

Cortex

Ascending Reticular Activating System (ARAS)

Hypothalamus

The hypothalamus is another forebrain structure that has been linked to arousal. When certain areas of the hypothalamus are surgically destroyed, a decrease in the level of behavioral action occurs, and sleep often ensues. Conversely, electrical stimulation of discrete regions within the hypothalamic area have been shown to cause increased excitement (Benjamin, Hopkins, and Nation, 1994). Although a few studies of the role of the hypothalamus in sport behavior have been conducted, the fact that this structure is so integrally involved in the control of the endocrine system (which prepares the body for both psychologically and physically demanding circumstances) would suggest that hypothalamic functions are vital determinants of athletic proficiency.

The reticular formation is a complex system of ascending and descending pathways that extend from the lower brain stem throughout the midbrain area. Although the precise function of the reticular formation is difficult to ascertain, the available evidence suggests that it serves as an alarm system to awaken the rest of the brain (Cotman and McGaugh, 1980). When an incoming signal arrives at the level of the reticular formation, cortical centers are alerted that new information is on the way. Appropriately, when the reticular formation functions appropriately, new (sensory) information is processed attentively and arousal results (Lykken, 1968). Yet, when the reticular formation is rendered dysfunctional, loss of attention and even sleep occurs. It follows from these observations that the reticular formation should be involved in any situation in which alertness is at a premium, as is the case for athletic participation.

As indicated, the autonomic nervous system (ANS) is also very much involved in arousal functions. It is largely through this ANS network of neural fibers that bodily reactions to environmental stressors are expressed. Of special interest is the interaction between the ANS and the endocrine system, which consists of glands such as the adrenals, thyroid, and the master controlling gland called the pituitary. They release their respective secretions (hormones) into the bloodstream in order to prepare the body for emergency situations. The provocation for this hormonal discharge often comes from stress-mediated ANS activation. For example, immediately prior to a critical dive in an aquatics competition, a participant may feel anxious and nervous. Consequently, the ANS excites the adrenals, forcing the systematic distribution of the hormone epinephrine. Also known as adrenalin, epinephrine energizes the person and accents his or her state of physical and mental readiness. Accordingly, the interplay between the nervous system and the endocrine system serves to enhance performance. In this instance anxiety and arousal increase the chances for success by triggering physiological reactions that contribute to a positive individual athletic profile.

Psychological Mechanisms

Although biological processes are central to the experience of anxiety, clearly cognitive and behavioral aspects of stress reactivity also must be addressed (Borkovec, 1976). How athletes think about threatening events may determine both the level of felt discomfort and the course of action for alleviating the tension. Occasionally, people become so preoccupied with their negative thoughts that they are unable to resolve even routine life events, with the end result that their confidence about handling stress diminishes (Meichenbaum, 1977). Of course, this process evolves into a negative circular spiral in which one disastrous encounter precipitates yet another, and on it goes. The ultimate fate of such recurrent episodes is a form of emotional debilitation that may require psychological intervention. Further discussion of this topic will appear later in the chapter.

With respect to coping strategies, it is important to distinguish between two different types

A professional tennis player who feels at ease on his or her home court may experience situational apprehension, or state anxiety, when confronted for the first time by Wimbledon's crowds of spectators.

of anxiety. *State anxiety,* as defined by Spielberger (1972), is a transitory form of apprehension that varies in intensity, commensurate with the strength of the fear-eliciting cue. When a young girl is required to perform a recital in front of a live audience for the first time, she may exhibit obvious signs of nervousness, including trembling, perspiration, and high distractibility. Similarly, a professional tennis player who has never before played at Wimbledon may be overwhelmed by the crowds at center court, and his or her performance may be adversely affected. In instances such as these when highly skilled performers suffer bouts of anxiety, the emotional reaction is one that is likely to be peculiar to that specific circumstance. The young pianist may have no difficulty performing in small groups or in front of friends, and surely the professional tennis player feels at ease amidst more familiar surroundings. This sort of situational apprehension occurs in all of us from time to time.

Recent developments in the state anxiety literature have focused on the multidimensional

nature of the phenomenon. Specifically it has been proposed that state anxiety actually consists of two components, *cognitive state anxiety* and *somatic state anxiety.* The former is characterized by worry and emotional distress whereas the latter is more physiologically based, i.e., rapid heart rate, clammy hands, and so on.

A significant development in the assessment of cognitive and somatic state anxiety is the Competitive State Anxiety Inventory II (CSAI-II) (Martens, Burton, Vealey, Smith, and Bump, 1989). The scale is composed of twenty-seven items arranged on a four-point Likert format. In support of the proposal by Martens et al. that these two aspects of state anxiety be dealt with as independent constructs, both Burton (1988) with swimmers and Gould, Petlichkoff, Simons, and Vevera (1987) with pistol shooters have shown that athletic performance is differentially affected by the type of anxiety being measured. In both the Burton and Gould et al. studies, performance was linear and inversely related when the cognitive type of anxiety was assessed and quadratically related (i.e., the inverted-U) when the somatic scale was measured. A representation of these effects can be seen in figure 4.2.

Figure 4.2 suggests that as cognitive anxiety increases, performance deteriorates; this means that even a little anxiety is not productive if it is of the cognitive variety. This flies in the face of the old coaching axiom that a bit of anxiety is good for the athlete. On the other hand, if the anxiety is of the somatic variety, the coaching axiom is supported, but only up to an optimal and not always predictable level, which is suggested by the inverted-U relationship. Coaches and athletes need to be aware that when dealing with anxiety and performance, they are really talking about two very different things, according to the Gould et al. anxiety dichotomy. We are of the opinion that an awareness of the differences between cognitive and somatic anxiety offers much to coaches and athletes in terms of dealing with precompetitive anxiety symptoms. Self-doubt and worry are manifestations of cognitive anxiety, and are detrimental to performance unless intervention is made by either the athlete or his or her coach.

Figure 4.2: Effects of State Anxiety on Athletic Performance

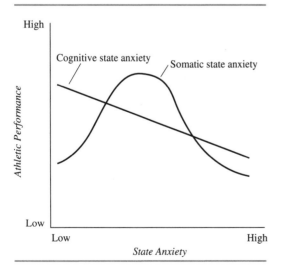

At the same time, optimal levels of somatic anxiety need to be encouraged in view of the facilitative effects it has on performance.

In any event, there is reason to suspect that state anxiety as it relates to sport is a multidimensional issue, and future work in this area should help clarify the relationship that each of these components has with competitive athletic behavior.

Compared to state anxiety, *trait anxiety* is a more enduring form of anxiety (Spielberger, 1972). Persons with trait anxiety (A-trait persons) project a profile that reflects nonspecific anxiety proneness. A broad range of life situations are perceived as threatening, and the individual's reaction to such events is commonly disproportionate to the actual fear properties of the stimulus. With this type of anxiety disturbance, the person may be haunted by fears of the most trivial phenomena. In its extreme form, the A-trait condition may render the individual dysfunctional and incapable of responding at all.

In terms of the relations between state and trait anxiety and competitive athletic performance, one theoretical formulation that has guided research in this area has been proposed by Martens, Gill, Simon, and Scanlan (1975). The theory posits that state anxiety registered by a person in a competitive situation is determined by the person's perception of the likelihood of success. The prediction is that when sport outcomes are contingent on lower levels of anxiety, athletes who are uncertain of their ability, and thus more likely to feel anxious, are also more likely to perform poorly. Consistent with this prediction Gerson and Deshaies (1978) examined batting averages of female varsity intercollegiate softball players participating in the National Women's Intercollegiate Softball tournament and found that, indeed, higher precompetitive state anxiety was associated with lower batting averages. Perhaps the expectancy of performing poorly more than lack of ability per se leads to the athlete's poor performance.

Supporting evidence also comes from field investigations of golf performance (Weinberg and Genuchi, 1980). Because golf is a game that requires precision, coordination, and the integration of fine muscle movements, it is especially appropriate for studying the effects of anxiety on athletic performance. Excessive levels of anxiety may interfere with the execution of golfing responses that must occur within a relative narrow range of expertise. Weinberg and Genuchi found that high A-trait persons were more likely to experience elevated state anxiety on Day 1 and Day 2 of a competitive collegiate golf tournament than persons low in trait anxiety. Further, it was shown that high state anxiety levels and expectations of performing poorly were related to how well the golfers did in the tournament. Better performances were associated with low anxiety and worse performances were associated with high anxiety.

Additional evidence that favors the idea that competitive anxiety may be a principal determinant of athletic proficiency comes from studies of youth sport (Passer, 1983). When 316 male youth soccer participants were evaluated with respect to competitive trait anxiety, it was discovered that players' performance expectancies, anticipated affective reactions to success-failure, and expectancies for criticism, were all influential in determining how well the child played. The greater the anxiety (i.e., the more dismal the expectations for being successful), the less effective were the youth participants, at least as rated by their coaches with respect to overall ability. Moreover, failure seems to be potentially more devastating, psychologically speaking, for youngsters who demonstrate high competitive trait anxiety. Such children worried more about their performance and were more apprehensive about evaluations by peers than children who registered low anxiety. The disquieting aspect of these findings, of course, is that a vicious cycle may form. The child who is anxious and expects to perform poorly does so, and consequently experiences greater perceived ridicule, which leads to increased apprehensiveness about competitive situations.

Brustad and Weiss (1987) extended Passer's (1983) research on patterns of competitive trait anxiety by examining female athletes and male athletes in different sports. Interestingly, when male baseball players were evaluated, those who registered high competitive trait anxiety reported lower levels of self-esteem and more frequent worries, in much the same fashion as the youth soccer players mentioned earlier. For female softball players, however, no significant relationships were found between levels of competitive trait anxiety and cognitive variables. Apparently, competition in sport takes on different meanings for males and females, a point we will return to in greater detail in later chapters.

Two other important variables that seem to be important with respect to modulating the intensity of anxiety reactions in children and adult competitors are the skill level of the competition and the relative time to competition (see Huddleston and Gill, 1981, for a review). In a study of parachutists (Fenz, 1985), for instance, it was observed that highly skilled parachutists actually exhibit low levels of anxiety immediately prior to a jump. Conversely, parachutists who are not yet accomplished jumpers experience extreme levels of anxiety just before the jump. The studies discussed earlier, beginning with Martens et al. (1975), would lead us to believe that the high anxiety before the jump may prevent the poor parachutists from gaining in skill development. Additional work by Fenz (1985) and Mahoney and Avener (1977) indicates that the discrepancies in skill level that foster differential anxiety reactions in athletes are particularly important as the person approaches closer to the competition. However, Huddleston and Gill (1981) failed to confirm this idea. In their study involving track and field competitors, athletes did show greater levels of anxiety as their respective events drew nearer, but this was uniformly true for highly skilled athletes (those who reached national qualifying standards during the season) and for less skilled athletes.

At odds with the relatively large literature that argues that competitive trait anxiety negatively affects athletic performance, Scanlan and Passer (1979) have shown that competitive performance expectancies, but not competitive trait anxiety, relate to athletic ability. In a field study involving ten- to twelve-year-old female soccer players, intrapersonal factors affecting players' pregame personal performance expectancies were first identified. Subsequently, the impact on each player of winning or losing the game was determined, and the interaction of the game outcome with intrapersonal variables was assessed by determining each player's expectations for a hypothetical rematch, ostensibly with the same opponent. The results showed that winning players held higher expectancies for themselves and their team than did losing players or players who had tied. Similarly, players with greater ability were higher in self-esteem than their less proficient counterparts. But high and low competitive trait-anxious players evidenced similar profiles with respect to performance expectancies. This pattern of results calls into question the validity correlated with athletic competency. Performance expectancies and general self-attitude would appear to be more directly related to how well an athlete performs than the anxiety events they are purported to mediate (Martens, 1974).

Drive Theory and the Inverted-U Hypothesis

Two important psychological theories which focus on this arousal-performance relationship are Hullian drive theory and the inverted-U hypothesis, and we shall discuss each in turn. As noted previously, somatic anxiety seems to be related to performance in a curvilinear fashion.

The idea that increases in anxiety, and ultimately in arousal, increase performance up to a point, and that further anxiety impairs performance, is an important consideration for the *drive theory* of learning and behavior first advanced by Yale psychologist Clark Hull more than fifty years ago (cf. Hull, 1943). This formulation states that behavior potential $_sE_r$ is a multiplicative function of drive (D) and habit strength ($_sH_r$); specifically:

$$_sE_r = D \times {_sH_r}$$

In the Hullian tradition, the concept of *drive* related to a nonspecific motivational force that served to energize responding. At the animal level, drive was defined operationally as the number of hours of deprivation of food, water, sex, and so forth. But in dealing with humans, drive functions were often interpreted within the broad realm of arousal (cf. Benjamin, Hopkins, and Nation, 1994). Sources of drive included conflict and tension (anxiety) that inspired the person to seek their reduction. Within this context, motivational (drive) variables were viewed as intervening states, the expression of which was observed in overt actions. Consequently, linear increases in performance would be expected commensurate with increases in anxiety and arousal.

By way of contrast, habit was viewed as associative as opposed to a motivational variable. This means that habit is determined by learning principles, which include the process of reinforcement as described in detail in chapter 3. Notice the *s* and *r* subscripts on the symbol for habit. This suggests that habit strength is peculiar to a specific stimulus (*s*) and response (*r*). Because different habits are likely to vary in strength due to different learning experiences, they are predictably going to interact with a given amount of drive. Habits that are strong, and thus high in the habit hierarchy, will contribute to substantially greater values of $_sE_r$ (the tendency to make the response) than lesser habit values, due to the multiplicative nature of the drive and habit relationship. Consequently, when there are clear discrepancies in habit strength, increased drive should have a facilitating effect by pushing the excitatory potential values ($_sE_r$) of correct responses (high habit) well above some threshold for responding, while incorrect responses (low habit) and their corresponding excitatory potential values remain below threshold.

A quite different picture emerges, however, when the different habits involved in a situation are of similar strength. In such cases higher drive levels may interact with habit to produce excitatory potential products that are all above threshold. Thus, response competition would occur and behavioral interference would be expected. A better strategy might be to keep drive levels low, so that the movement of specific habits (and the excitatory potential values linked to them) across the threshold could be controlled.

This complex prediction of the Hullian rationale was empirically tested many years ago by one of Hull's most distinguished students, Kenneth Spence. Spence reasoned that in an easy task, in which the habit differentiates between correct and incorrect responses are likely to be sizable, higher drive level should result in better performance. Conversely, in a difficult task, in which the respective habit strengths for correct and incorrect behaviors are not likely to be great, high drive should produce worse performance, because of the behavioral interference alluded to in the preceding paragraph. The formal test of this important line of thought came from Spence, Farber, and McFann (1956). In this study, subjects were presented with easy or difficult word lists. Anxious (high anxiety) subjects learned the easy list faster whereas nonanxious (low anxiety) subjects learned the difficult list faster.

These data confirmed some of the precise predictions of the Hullian model. But they further challenged some of the assertions made by a doctrine that had its origins much earlier. As long ago as 1908, Yerkes and Dodson described the relation between psychological activation and performance as an inverted-U (see figure 4.3). This *inverted-U hypothesis* states that there is an optimal level of arousal for every behavior, values above and below which are likely to create poor performance. It follows that in some cases intensely motivated performers are going to do well, but in other cases those same individuals are going to have trouble.

As it relates to sport, the inverted-U hypothesis predicts that athletes may become so "psychologically charged" that they are unable to perform efficiently (Bunker and Rotella, 1980). Precompetitional hype is a familiar tool used by sport practitioners, ostensibly to "get athletes ready to play." But implicit in the message of the inverted-U formulation is the notion that such a strategy can be excessively used and it may actually backfire. When a long jump competitor gets so psyched up that he or she "ties up" going down the runway, arousal is translated as anxiety and it becomes counterproductive. A preferred approach would be to relax so that the appropriate response could be executed. This is

Figure 4.3: **The Relation between Arousal and Performance as Expressed by the Yerkes-Dodson Law**

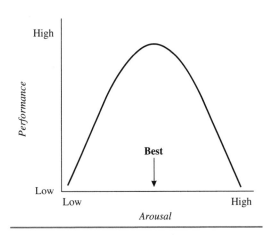

not to say that motivational enhancement techniques are valueless, of course, because a moderate level of excitement may be needed to maintain attention and generate the best performance.

Because the basic tenet of the inverted-U hypothesis proposes that the optimum point of arousal varies as a function of task characteristics, different sports are likely to demand different levels of arousal for the best results. In a game such as golf, in which fine motor behaviors are at a premium, a lower point of optimal arousal is expected relative to, say, wrestling, in which delicate performances are not judged to be so critical. Even for the same sport, the nature of the requisite behaviors may dictate different levels of psychological activation for the best result. In football, for instance, a highly aroused defensive lineman capering before an opponent may be appropriately cast. But a quarterback who must make instantaneous decisions may not be served so well by high levels of arousal. The essential point here is that individual demand characteristics of each sport may dictate, to a large extent, the optimal level of arousal necessary for good performance; a representation of this relationship can be seen in figure 4.4.

Also, as graphically depicted in figure 4.5, skill level is likely to dictate disparate points of optimal arousal. For a beginning athlete, the inverted-U account of the relation between arousal and performance predicts a lower optimum range than would be the case for intermediate or advanced players. When a shooter in a rifle competition is new to the sport, high levels of excitement may have a diverting influence and make it difficult to sustain a steady aim. For a more experienced participant, however, the same high level of arousal may channel attention and contribute positively to the task.

A considerable amount of space in the literature on arousal/performance interactions has been devoted to professed differences in the predictions made by either drive theory or the inverted-U hypothesis (see Sonstroem, 1984). The common assertion is that drive theory predicts that well-learned tasks involving established habits should always reflect performance facilitations as anxiety (arousal) increases. On the other hand, the inverted-U hypothesis argues that behaviors, however well they are learned, will be impaired at some point, given a sufficiently high level of anxiety and arousal.

Clearly, great numbers of research articles can be brought forth in support of each of the claims. Wankel (1980), for instance, studied drive

Figure 4.4: Optimal Arousal Level Required for Various Sports

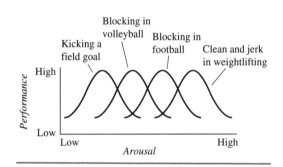

Figure 4.5: Application of Yerkes-Dodson Law to Rifle Shooters of Various Skill Levels

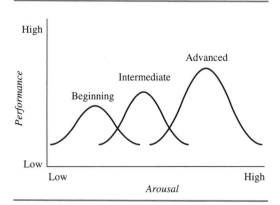

manipulations in motor performance tasks by varying audience size. In this sort of investigation modeled after Zajonc's social facilitation theory (Zajonc, 1965), increased numbers of observers are alleged to increase drive (anxiety) and therein facilitate responding. But the report by Wankel revealed that audience size had no effect on pursuit rotor tracking. Further, dispositional differences in anxiety were negatively correlated with performance; high anxious subjects performed more poorly than low anxious subjects. Yet despite such reports, Landers (1980) comments that "[an] obstacle in the way of advocating abandonment of drive theory is the overall success this theory has had in the area of social facilitation research." Such statements are vigorously in agreement with the predictions of drive theory as it is described earlier.

In terms of explicit tests of the validity of the position taken by the inverted-U hypothesis in the sports world, Martens and Landers (1970) assigned high, moderate, or low anxious male youths to a motor tracking task under conditions of high, moderate, or low stress. Supporting evidence from physiological measures (heart rate, palmar sweating) confirmed the differences in the three different stress conditions. The overall pattern of results was highly favorable to an inverted-U type model. Specifically, it was shown that the moderate stress condition was associated with better motor performance than either low- or high-stress conditions. Further, Martens and Landers observed that boys with moderate A-trait scores performed better on the tracking task than either low A-trait or high A-trait boys.

Similar findings were reported by Klavora (1977) in a field study that used Canadian male high school basketball players as subjects. Precompetition state anxiety scores for 145 boys were obtained for each player throughout the second half of a season. Following the completion of each of the games, the respective coaches were asked to rate the performance of each basketball player in terms of whether his perfor-

mance could be described as poor, average, or outstanding. When the performance ratings were presented as a function of the individual athlete's level of state anxiety, a profile emerged that was of the general form of the inverted-U. That is, the rating of outstanding was most likely to be achieved when the player reported a moderate level of stress. When players indicated either low or high levels of state anxiety, they were more likely to perform at a poor or average level.

To date, one of the more compelling articles related to establishing the validity of the inverted-U curve has been written by Sonstroem and Bernardo (1982). In this study that involved thirty female university varsity basketball starters of six different teams, an athlete's lowest, median, and highest pregame state anxiety values across three games of a double-elimination basketball tournament held at Brown University were used to define low, moderate, or high anxiety levels. Also, the effects of trait anxiety were investigated. Performance during the competition was determined by total points scored and an overall value that was generated for each player by the linear combination of shot percentage, rebounds, points, assists, steals, fouls, and turnovers committed. As with the previous studies, the performance measures were examined as a function of registered anxiety. The intrasubject results appeared to be remarkably consistent with the inverted-U hypothesis. Not only did total points and game performance (see figure 4.6) follow a quadratic trend (first increasing, then decreasing) as a function of state anxiety, but this general pattern held across low, moderate, and high trait anxiety comparisons. Thus, the robustness of the effect of anxiety, and therein arousal, would seem to be substantial.

Although there is considerable support for the viability of the inverted-U relationship between arousal and performance, some are critical of the hypothesis. Chief among them is Neiss (1988), who has raised objections on a number of fronts. First of all, Neiss objects to the

Figure 4.6: **The Effect of Trait and State Anxiety on Individual Game Performance (Standard Scores)**

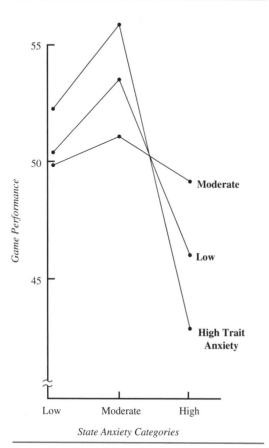

State Anxiety Categories

Source: Sonstroem and Bernardo (1982).

but the simplest of performance behaviors. Finally, Neiss believes the inverted-U hypothesis to be an impediment to the attainment of a sound understanding of individual differences in performance.

Another critic of the inverted-U hypothesis is Jones (1990), who indicates that the arguments against the theory appear to be overwhelming. Jones' criticisms are echoed by King, Stanley, and Burrows (1987, p. 11), who refer to the inverted-U as a "terrible myth," and Hardy and Fazey (1987), who refer to it as a "catastrophe for sport psychology." Gould and Krane (1992) argue that the inverted-U hypothesis is too simplistic and vague to be of much value in explaining the complex relationship between arousal and performance.

However, the weight of the evidence suggests that the inverted-U hypothesis is indeed of value to the sport psychologist. Studies supportive of the construct are numerous, as has been indicated in discussion earlier in this chapter. Recent summaries by Anderson (1990) and Landers and Boutcher (1993) are also supportive. Landers and Boutcher make their case based on two points, one being the apparent generalizability of the inverted-U across field and experimental situations and the other having to do with similarities in performance patterning for arousal that are induced either psychologically or physically through drugs, exercise, or muscle tension. Anderson, in a rejoinder to the critical article by Neiss, argues for the utility of the inverted-U hypothesis. She indicates that Neiss's 1988 arguments against the hypothesis are unwarranted on both logical and empirical grounds. She sums up her views (and ours) of the hypothesis as follows: "Although the ultimate value of the hypothetical, conceptual construct of arousal is as yet unresolved, substantial evidence does favor its pragmatic usefulness and hence its continued investigation" (p. 99). We fully expect to hear more about the inverted-U hypothesis in future deliberations in sport psychology concerning

inverted-U because it is descriptive rather than explanatory. Secondly, he sees the inverted-U hypothesis as immune from falsification; that is, because of definitional and methodological difficulties inherent in most research of the construct, almost any results could be interpreted or otherwise explained away as supportive. This situation renders the theory unfalsifiable. Thirdly, Neiss suggests that even if the hypothesis were true, it is trivial in terms of explaining anything arousal and performance. At the same time, it is evident that the inverted-U hypothesis has supplanted Hullian drive theory due to the latter's unidimensional and oversimplified explanation of the arousal-sport performance relationship.

INTERVENTION STRATEGIES: ANXIETY ALLEVIATION

In the first section, we have reviewed some of the biological and psychological features that are believed to be most important to the formation of anxiety. Additionally, we have seen that anxiety viewed as a source of arousal can have a positive effect in the sport arena. But there is no dismissing the debilitating impact that intense stress and excessive emotional reactivity can have on an amateur or professional career. In this section, we shall discuss several of the treatment strategies that have been used as intervention techniques designed to alleviate excess tension. For the sport psychologist, the ability to lower and control anxiety within tolerable limits is one of the most important services that he or she can provide.

For some athletes, even the most stressful situations are approached with the same emotional outlook as a walk in the park. In a nationally televised college basketball game between two of the nation's top twenty ranked teams, a point guard was observed to yawn during a timeout 3 seconds before the game's end. With the team leading by only one point, his relaxed style would seem to be unexpected, especially because this same guard had to convert two free shot opportunities following the timeout in order to assure a victory for his team. He made both free throw attempts and withdrew to the locker room without ceremony.

Such examples are common in the lore of amateur and professional athletics, but the truth is that a sizable number of highly skilled players are prone to anxiety bouts that prevent them from performing at the highest level of their ability. When a player "chokes" in a game situation, the effect may be to make it more difficult to execute freely when a similar circumstance is reinstated. The resulting vicious loop in which anxiety precludes success and failure increases anxiety may render the athlete dysfunctional unless something is done to break the cycle. In some instances this intervention may take the form of a program designed to increase the player's mental toughness. In other types of treatment, conditioning techniques can be used that produce the desired behaviors independent of cognitive mediation. The models discussed in the next few pages represent some of the more popular methods available for changing mental or behavioral reactions to anxiety-evoking situations.

Classical Conditioning Techniques

One of the oldest and most widely accepted accounts of the causes of anxiety is predicated on the principles of classical conditioning (Mowrer, 1960). Recall from our discussion in chapter 3 that classical conditioning involves the continuous association of an unconditional stimulus (UCS) and a conditioned stimulus (CS). Regarding fear (anxiety) development, a CS is believed to be paired with a fear-eliciting UCS; consequently the CS acquires the ability to elicit a conditioned fear reaction (the CR). Fear, then, mediates performance by virtue of occasioning behaviors that are compatible with or oppositional to selected voluntary behaviors.

In terms of what this conditioned fear mechanism means in sport, apprehensiveness is likely to be engendered when a competitor associates poor performance in pressure situations with peer disappointment and even ridicule. Especially in sports like rifle shooting and golf, which require highly skilled fine motor behaviors, the situation (the CS) evokes a level of anxiety (the CR) that in turn produces muscle tightness, nervousness, an unsteady hand, and other reactions that prevent the synchronous flow of the appropriate movements. Here, the fact that anxiety occurs at all runs counter to successful performance. What is necessary is a strategy designed to disrupt the chain of events that has produced the anxiety, or conditioned fear, as it is more often referred to in the psychology literature.

Extinction

From a learning point of view, one of the surest ways to eliminate classically conditioned fear is to place it on *extinction*. This process would mean presenting the conditioned fear-eliciting cue (the CS) in the absence of the threatening event (the UCS). Because the CS is inherently neutral, repeated exposure with no UCS pairing will result in the diminution of the response strength of the CR. Simply stated, the CS cannot stand alone. When this extinction approach is employed in a therapeutic realm it is called *flooding* (refer to Martin and Pear, 1992, for a more detailed discussion).

Flooding has been used extensively in the treatment of phobias such as claustrophobia or a fear of flying; in the first instance, the client may be put in a closet for several hours, at which point the fear of closed places should subside. In the case of fear of flying, the client might be exposed to a real, aborted jet takeoff and subsequent flight (Serling, 1986). The idea in both cases is that the subject will experience a vivid terror response followed by gradual relaxation in the face of the fear-producing stimulus/stimuli. Crafts, Schneirla, Robinson, and Gilbert (1938) reported an interesting case of a young woman with a phobic response to travelling in an automobile. The physician in the case ordered her to drive the fifty miles to his office; by the time she arrived, a cure had been effected. Though suffering intensely at first, she gradually calmed down and manifested little fear of driving or riding in the car. One of the strengths of flooding is that it forces the person being treated to stay in a phobic situation while con-

currently demonstrating to them that catastrophe does not result by doing so. In one study of the efficacy of flooding, Marks, Boulougouris, and Marset (1971) reported that 75 percent of a group of seventy phobics remained in an improved state four years after treatment by the flooding procedure. Carson and Butcher (1992), however, do issue a caution concerning flooding; they have reviewed research on the technique and have concluded that it is a very useful procedure for some people, neutral for others, and actually harmful in a few instances. By way of illustration of the potentially harmful consequences of flooding, Carson and Butcher cite a study by Emmelkamp and Wessels (1975), in which a client with an exaggerated fear of wide open places (i.e., agoraphobia) cowered in a cellar rather than face the ninety minutes of exposure to the outside world dictated by the therapist in the case.

Because flooding is an intervention technique that is likely to provoke extremely high levels of anxiety, especially in the early stages of treatment, it must be used cautiously (Smith, 1984). Consider what a 30- to 40-minute flooding session may involve. As a professional baseball player you are asked to imagine that you are batting in the bottom of the ninth inning with your team trailing by a single run. The count is three balls and one strike. You swing and miss; fans shout derisive remarks, players on the field taunt you, and you sense the complete rejection of other team members. Again you swing and again you miss the ball, which clearly was thrown out of the strike zone. The game is over, you have failed, and you are alone.

The purpose of such forced exposure to unkindness, of course, is to permit the patient (player) to encounter such thoughts within the relatively safe confines of the therapy environment. Ultimately, the amount of fear and anxiety that are triggered by such threatening images should diminish. But intense unpleasantness is surely going to be the rule in the initial treatment sessions, and judiciousness on the part of the therapist is essential.

A variant of flooding that is preferred by many psychologists is *implosive therapy* (Stampfl and Levis, 1967). This technique incorporates many of the same features of flooding but it includes a hierarchy of fear-eliciting images that each person judges to reflect those aspects of his or her personal situations that are most and least threatening. Accordingly, the therapist is free to systematically work through the list, extinguishing the anxiety to items lower in the hierarchy before proceeding to more tension-laden images. Using this technique combined with clinical insights into the psychodynamic undercurrents that contribute to the disorder, the successful practitioner can help alleviate stress symptoms (Foa et al., 1983), and this can be accomplished without undue felt anxiety.

Despite the widespread use of extinction techniques in applied settings in general, few attempts have been made to employ the treatment regimen in sport settings, either in laboratory or field studies (Smith, 1984). Many sport psychologists are disinclined to use an approach that is so fundamentally geared to aversive conditioning. Nonetheless, flooding and implosion have on occasion produced real benefits when alternatives have failed to reduce anxiety and they should be considered as part of the arsenal for effecting behavior change.

Counterconditioning

A classical conditioning therapy procedure that is favored over the extinction approaches, at least by sport psychologists, is *counter-conditioning*. In counterconditioning, there is no attempt to eliminate the anxiety evoked by the CS. Rather the objective is to use an antagonistic UCS to condition competing responses to the CS that will interfere with the existing CR (fear, anxiety). If a person is given sufficient retraining, or counterconditioning, the newly acquired conditioned behaviors will replace the older fear reaction as the dominant response tendency. The basic components of counterconditioning are graphically illustrated in figure 4.7.

Figure 4.7: **The Basic Model of Counterconditioning Used in Behavior Therapy**

Note: (A) The original associations involve a weaker stimulus-response connection (e.g., anxiety reaction) and a stronger stimulus-response connection (e.g., relaxation). (B) When the stimuli that cause each response are paired, the stronger of the two responses begins to connect to the weaker stimulus as well as the stronger stimulus. (C) Eventually, the originally weaker response is replaced with the new, stronger response (e.g., the previously anxiety-eliciting stimulus now evokes relaxation).

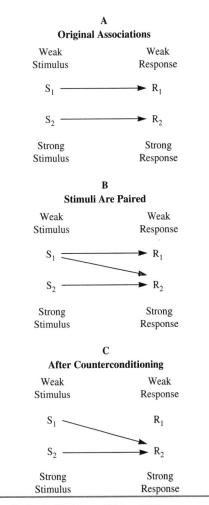

Source: Benjamin, Hopkins, and Nation (1994).

The aim of any counterconditioning treatment initiative is redefining the behavioral consequences of anxiety. For the athlete, this means changing habits with respect to how stressful situations are handled. Consider the apocryphal case of Vernon Smith. Vernon is a nineteen-year-old male on the college varsity track team. He is an immensely talented high jumper who has the potential for developing into a national class competitor. Yet his performance is often erratic, and he seems to especially have trouble in those meets that would bring him the greatest recognition. Closer inspection reveals that a major factor in Vernon's mercurial performance record is stress. He suffers intense feelings of discomfort and tension in big meets. He imagines that he will embarrass himself by stumbling on his approach to the bar, and that thousands of people will see him as foolish and miscast. To ensure that he does not fall, he approaches the bar tentatively, thus avoiding shame but guaranteeing a substandard jump.

Treatment in this case involves *relaxation training*. In this procedure, the person learns to make a series of physiological reactions that include decreased muscle tone, lowered heart rate, slower respiration, and an increase in the production of alpha brain wave patterns. With respect to the treatment of Vernon, once he has mastered the art of relaxation, he is enjoined to think about a competitive scene that creates anxiety. When the anxiety is superordinate, Vernon is asked to switch off that scene and focus again on relaxing. According to the basic tenets of counterconditioning, the relaxation response will eventually bond to those stimulus events that previously were associated with tension. When Vernon begins a jump, thoughts of disaster that previously caused him to tighten up, now evoke relaxation, and performance should improve.

An assortment of relaxation techniques such as the one prescribed for Vernon are used in modern behavior therapy, and all are variations of the *progressive relaxation procedure* originated by Edmond Jacobson (1938). In this technique, which begins with each patient lying on his or her back with arms extended to the side, selected muscle groups are first tensed and then slowly relaxed. Then the same procedure shifts to other major muscles. The purpose of this approach is to help patients identify the various muscle systems within the body and to teach them to discriminate between tense and relaxed muscle conditions. Most of the time during the session should be devoted to relaxation training, which is more difficult to accomplish. Acquisition may be slow at first, but after a few months athletes and most other patients learn to evoke a relaxation response in just a few seconds (Nideffer, 1981).

Although relaxation is a common component of many counterconditioning operations, numerous other behaviors are suitable for treating anxiety disorders. Humor, sexual arousal, and incongruous images have all been used successfully to alter a person's reaction to a fear-eliciting situation. Indeed, one of the more popular versions of counterconditioning therapy, known as *systematic desensitization,* recommends the inclusion of a range of responses that formally compete with anxiety (Wolpe, 1982). The systematic desensitization model appeals to many treatment specialists because it embraces a hierarchical arrangement of anxiety arousing events, with low anxiety items at the bottom of the list and high anxiety items at the top. One example of such a list has been presented by Smith (1984). The case (a hypothetical one) involves an acute anxiety reaction experienced by a male basketball player when presented with high pressure game situations. The hierarchy in this existence was of the form:

5. Preparing to shoot a free throw, with 1 second left in the championship game and your team trailing by 1 point (high anxiety scene)

4. Sitting in the locker room before the game as your coach tells you how important this game is (moderately high anxiety scene)

3. Walking toward the arena where the game will be played (moderate anxiety scene)

2. Getting up from bed in the morning and thinking of the game that evening (moderately low anxiety scene)

1. Thinking about the fact that the game will be played in two days (low anxiety scene)

Treatment would involve taking the lowest anxiety scene and pairing it with relaxation, or an amusing idea, or some other conflicting behavior. Once the scene no longer evoked an anxiety response, and instead produced the relevant counterconditioned behavior, treatment would proceed to the next step (moderately low anxiety scene) and the process would be recapitulated. Eventually, the patient would work upward through the list until completion. The advantage of such a strategy is that it makes counterconditioning easier to achieve. Because items low on the list necessarily evoke minimal fear and tension, they are more susceptible to disruption. In classical conditioning terms this means that the CR strength is likely to be low relative to that of the competing response elicited by the antagonistic UCS (refer back to figure 4.7). Further attempts at counterconditioning involving more intense fear-eliciting cues will be accomplished with greater ease because of the gains made lower in the hierarchy.

To summarize the application of classical conditioning techniques in treating sport-related anxiety disorders, one approach (extinction) is intended to eliminate anxiety altogether, whereas the other (counterconditioning) aims to replace the conditioned anxiety reaction with a more tolerable alternative. Although the extinction procedures have the advantage of total removal of anxiety, the counterconditioning techniques have been more thoroughly investigated (see Winter, 1982). With either approach, athletic

performance should be facilitated and life should be a bit more comfortable in general for participants.

Instrumental Conditioning Techniques

Previously, we have considered only treatment regimens that are based on classical conditioning principles. In this section we discuss the relevance of instrumental procedures (refer to chapter 3) for treating anxiety reactions that actively interfere with the execution of motor behaviors in sport.

Reinforced Practice

The procedure known as *reinforced practice* (refer to Leitenberg, 1976) is one instrumental approach that has been used with success in the treatment of anxiety related disorders. The central idea underlying this approach is that reinforcement can be administered in such a fashion that responses incompatible with the typical anxiety behaviors are strengthened. For example, a person who has a fear of snakes may be asked to approach a snake that is placed in a glass enclosure at a set distance across the room. Successively closer steps toward the snake are identified by numbered strips of tape on the floor. A 1 may correspond to an initial step, a 2 to the next, and so on up to, say, 14, which is at the point of the enclosure. Each time the patient moves closer to the snake he or she is rewarded by the therapist with verbal praise or some tangible evidence of approval. A record is kept of the patient's progress, and he or she sees the graphic representation reflecting improvement. By learning to approach a feared object, the patient loses his or her phobia.

Although this procedure has not been applied in any systematic way in a sports setting, it could easily be adapted to fit the demands of the athletic environment. Rewarding mental approaches to a crowded area, for instance, may prove to be helpful for a gymnast who fears a large audience. Or reinforcing a young batter who fears a pitched baseball for making increasingly more aggressive swings may decrease anxiety and may increase hitting performance in the process. This is a potentially rich area for sport psychology research and some worthwhile information along these lines clearly is needed.

Biofeedback

Perhaps the most common intervention technique based on the principles of instrumental learning is a procedure known as *biofeedback.* Known in the experimental psychology literature as "instrumental conditioning of autonomic behaviors," this area had its origins with Neal Miller at Rockefeller University (Dicara, 1970; Miller, 1978). Challenging a long-standing axiom that instrumental techniques were restricted to voluntary, somatically controlled responses, Miller and his colleagues observed under a variety of experimental conditions that animals could learn to control heart rate, digestive procedures, salivation output, and other internal responses. Before long, practitioners were employing reinforcement techniques to treat everything from migraines to excess muscle tension caused by stress.

The popularity of biofeedback is due in part to the fact that the various procedures are the by-products of sound experimental procedures in psychology and psychophysiology. Other factors contributing to the general acceptance of biofeedback in medicine and psychology include its applicability to conditions for which there is no medical or surgical alternative, its freedom from demonstrable toxicity, and its cost effectiveness compared to many other alternative treatments (Sandweiss, 1985).

Sandweiss and Wolf (1985) point out that in sport, three areas of application have been identified by a task force supported by the Biofeedback Society of America: stress management for athletes, rehabilitation of sport-related injuries, and performance enhancement training.

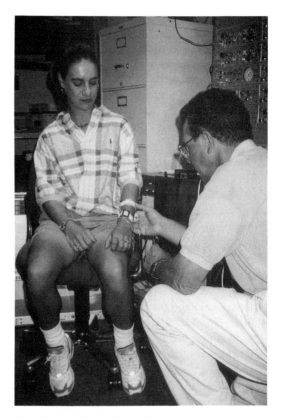

A senior member of a collegiate golf team undergoes biofeedback response assessment preparatory to anxiety management training.

Often biofeedback training involves the inclusion of some sort of electronic gadgetry that signals the patient that an appropriate autonomic response has occurred. And the use of such biofeedback devices in treating athletes has produced convincing results. DeWitt (1979), for example, used an electromyographic procedure to assist football players in learning to relax. The electromyograph is equipped with electrodes that can be placed at selected muscle sites. These electrodes sense the degree of muscle contraction, and the information is presented in either digital or analog form on a display screen. By focusing on the feedback from the screen, players were able to decrease muscle tension and preempt excessive arousal.

In another investigation by DeWitt (1980), cognitive therapy was combined with biofeedback training in an attempt to lower stress among university football and basketball players. Cognitive approaches to treatment focus on restructuring thought processes and self-perceptions and as a rule have been valuable treatment tools in traditional clinical settings. Using the techniques of mental rehearsal and cognitive restructuring along with electromyographic feedback, DeWitt decreased muscle tension in a laboratory setting for six varsity football players and twelve varsity basketball players. Moreover, the players' performance efficiency improved dramatically following the intervention. Although this study provides no clues as to the differential effects of cognitive therapy versus biofeedback training, it does provide evidence that performance increases parallel reductions in muscle tension brought about by biofeedback sessions.

Elsewhere, Daniels and Landers (1981) conducted an investigation of a squad of shooters who were given either verbal instructions or auditory biofeedback training. The findings revealed that the shooters who were given biofeedback training improved more and maintained greater consistency than their counterparts who received only verbal statements about their performance. Additionally, the biofeedback groups exhibited greater control over the automatic pattern, thus validating the relation between internal autonomic control and enhanced shooting performance.

Despite forceful arguments by many sport practitioners about the desirability of using biofeedback techniques (Bird and Cripe, 1986; Zaichkowsky and Fuchs, 1989), only a few experimental demonstrations of potency of the approach have occurred in actual field studies. Although supporting evidence from well-controlled laboratory investigations of motor performance are somewhat helpful (French, 1978), what is needed are experiments with athletes who are actually attempting to function under intense stress. Also, there is the very serious issue of the reliability of the effects (see highlight 4.2).

Does Biofeedback Really Work?

*Highlight
4.2*

The appropriateness of biofeedback as an intervention technique is complicated by a report by Dworkin and Miller (1986) that reverses the position taken by the founder of the area. Miller and his colleagues ran more than two thousand animals in a series of experiments designed to replicate some of the seminal biofeedback studies, and the result was an inability to reproduce the earlier effects. The unreliability of biofeedback as an intervention procedure with human behavior disorders has also been an item for fiery debate.

Certain treatment specialists seem to be more likely than others to obtain positive results. Although differing techniques and levels of expertise may contribute to the discrepant results to some degree, it is most remarkable that many therapists never report improvement for their patients on a consistent basis. This has triggered a steady flow of accusations about fraudulent reporting and embellished accounts of the successes of biofeedback training.

This biofeedback controversy is no less heated in the realm of sport intervention. In a report on enhancing human performance (Druckman and

(Continued next page)

Highlight 4.2 (Continued)

Does Biofeedback Really Work?

Swets, 1987), quite negative conclusions were reached about the efficacy of biofeedback training techniques. It seems that when a positive result is obtained it often turns out to be a fluke. Because performance enhancement is noted in one instance, or in one individual, does not mean that it will be seen again in the same situation or with other performers. The lack of reliable findings from case to case has caused many treatment specialists to turn away from biofeedback and pursue other behavioral change strategies.

Still, it likely would be a mistake to presume that biofeedback is contraindicated as an intervention technique in sport. As shown elsewhere in this chapter, biofeedback training apparently is valuable in certain situations. Perhaps it would be a better idea to drop the indictment and focus on defining the boundaries and conditions under which the technique actually does work.

To this end, Zaichkowsky and Fuchs (1989) suggest that biofeedback alone or in conjunction with other self-control methods can be useful in teaching athletes to self-regulate their psychophysiological stress responses and related sport performance. They are quick to point out, however, that there are problems to be addressed. One has to do with the fact that elite athletes have not been used in biofeedback studies. Another shortcoming has to do with the fact that seldom has the mastery of self-regulation actually been demonstrated in the available research. Inferences made from small samples of athletes represent yet another difficulty; Zaichkowsky and Fuchs call this forcing of small numbers of subjects into experimental designs that traditionally call for large sample sizes the "shoe-horn" procedure. As an antidote to the last criticism, the authors suggest the use of single-subject experimental designs with proper monitoring and careful follow-up. Finally, authors of future studies should be careful in specifying whether they are studying a particular biofeedback procedure or a combination of intervention modalities.

In this connection, Lehrer, Carr, Sargunaraj, and Woolfolk (1994) conducted a comprehensive review of the literature on stress management techniques to include certain types of biofeedback. It is their contention that cognitively oriented stress management techniques have specific cognitive effects, specific autonomic effects arise from autonomically oriented methods, and specific muscular effects are generated from muscularly oriented methods. Their conclusion that electromyographic (EMG) feedback is very effective with particular muscle groups may point to its efficacy as a biofeedback treatment of choice in a number of sport situations.

Sources: Druckman and Swets (1987); Dworkin and Miller (1986); Zaichkowsky and Fuchs (1989); Lehrer, Carr, Sargunaraj, and Woolfolk (1994).

Cognitive Techniques

Whereas the foregoing interventions focused on behavioral techniques evolving out of the basic literature on classical conditioning and instrumental learning, cognitive intervention strategies are designed to restructure the way the athlete thinks about competition. Attitudes, impressions, and other covert mental operations are not only acknowledged to exist, they are the targets of change. Thus, rather than attempt to modify the behavior, cognitive approaches aim to alter thought processes (cognitions) and therein influence responding (athletic performance).

Stress Inoculation Training

One cognitive strategy that is grounded to an empirical treatment framework is called *stress inoculation* therapy (SIT) (Meichenbaum, 1977). With this regimen the person learns an appropriate coping strategy for dealing with the negative emotional fallout that comes with periodic bouts of acute anxiety. Typically, a person who suffers from debilitating stress becomes preoccupied with self-deprecating personal statements and the feeling that his or her defense system is collapsing. In the stress inoculation approach, the idea is to get the patient to recognize the pattern of events that characterizes the anxiety attack and then to use those cues as signals for making adaptive coping responses. Such a treatment is designed to redirect anxiety-mediated behavior and to formally teach a patient how to deal with stress. Three stages are generally involved in the retraining experience: (1) the experiential conditions of anxiety are clarified for the patient, so that the onset of the negative mood state is easier to identify; (2) re-education regarding the determinants and dynamics of the stress response must take place; and (3) appropriate coping behaviors are practiced, and then used when stress occurs. Thus, stress becomes a stimulus for the execution of functional behavior.

In athletics, the original SIT format has been altered only slightly to produce four stages (see Long, 1980). In the initial phase, discussions are held with the athlete about the particular feelings he or she has in certain competitive situations. The therapist explains the impact that such feelings are likely to have on performance. The intent of this period is to increase the athlete's awareness of the unique physical and mental reactions that constitute stress. In the second phase, the educational program is intensified and the athlete learns about the basic self-regulation skills. It is not unusual during this period to administer the training in small groups. During the third phase, specific coping behaviors are prescribed and the athlete is taught to transform negative thoughts into positive self-statements. For instance, a player might be instructed to react to an image of choking under pressure with a private statement such as, "Just relax, you can do this. You have handled tougher situations, so just get on with doing your job." By converting negative self-statements to positive verbal commands, the individual develops a more practical coping style. Finally, in the fourth and last stage recommended by Long's version of stress inoculation training, the athlete has a chance to implement his or her new strategy in graded stress situations. Successively more threatening competitive circumstances are presented in imaginal form, and than actual athletic situations are instated. Even though the athlete's fears may not subside, his or her reaction to them may be dramatically changed.

Another application of SIT to athletics is highlighted in a series of reports by Mace and several colleagues. Mace, Eastman, and Carroll (1987) demonstrated the efficacy of SIT in remediating the performance difficulties of a male Olympic gymnast with concentration problems brought on by debilitating anxiety and self-doubt. Twelve SIT sessions involving relaxation, visualization, and positive self-statements were employed with the gymnast, and highly positive performance in subsequent gymnastics meets was reported. Others successes using SIT have been noted with squash players (Mace and Carroll, 1986). Meichenbaum (1993), in a twenty-year update on the use of SIT, cites a dozen studies from 1980 through 1989 in which SIT was successfully employed with athletes from at least five different sports. He further cites over two hundred additional studies of the utility of using SIT in a variety of school, medical, psychiatric, and other treatment settings.

Meichenbaum sees SIT with athletes as an educational program in self-control and not as a form of psychotherapy. Smith (1980) refers to the kinds of things that are part and parcel of SIT as "mental toughness training." Perhaps the best way of summarizing what SIT has to offer coaches, athletes, and sport psychologists is provided in the following quote by Meichenbaum (1993, p. 374):

> SIT is not a panacea. Rather, it is a heuristically useful way to conceptualize both the distress that individuals experience and the factors leading to their behavioral change, as well as a clinically sensitive way to provide help on both treatment and a preventative basis. SIT does not represent a treatment formula that can be routinely applied to distressed individuals; it is a set of general guiding principles and accompanying clinical procedures that must be individually tailored to the unique characteristics of each case.

Cognitive Control

Successful athletes, in comparison to their less successful peers, are invariably more positive and confident in outlook. Part of this optimism, or what Seligman (1991) calls "learned optimism," is attained because they are in control of their thought patterns relating to performance. Bunker, Williams, and Zinsser (1993, p. 225) sum up this proposition as follows:

Confident athletes think they can and they do. They never give up. They typically are characterized by positive self-talk, images, and dreams. They imagine themselves winning and being successful. They say positive things to themselves and never minimize their abilities. They focus on successfully mastering a task rather than worrying about performing poorly or the negative consequences of failure. This predisposition to keep one's mind on the positive aspects of one's life and sport performance, even in the face of setbacks and disappointments, is a hallmark of the successful athlete. . . ." Critical to this control of cognitions is self-talk, and the key is to always accentuate the positive and not engage in self-defeating cognitions. At the same time, it is important to realistically assess successful and unsuccessful behaviors without engaging in counterproductive cognitive attacks on the self. It is okay to be critical of poor performance, say on a classroom test; "I did poorly because I failed to grasp some key concepts" is far preferable to judgmental thoughts like "I am obviously stupid or I would have done better on the test." Again, keep the emphasis on assessing behavior and stay away from self-condemnation; nothing constructive comes from such ideation.

It is important to realize that too much thinking in and of itself can be detrimental to performance; to paraphrase baseball legend Yogi Berra when asked what he thought about when he was at the plate preparing to hit: "I don't think 'cause I can't think and hit at the same time." As sport behaviors become stamped in, less and less cognitive activity is necessary. Still, there are times when things go wrong and self-defeating thoughts may appear. At this point, positive self-talk is essential.

Self-talk can be used for a variety of purposes, including enhancing skill acquisition, changing bad habits, assisting in maintaining proper focus, creating a positive mood state, changing already existing negative affective states, controlling effort, and building self-efficacy (Bunker et al., 1993). Three of the more effective methods for controlling self-talk are thought stoppage, countering, and reframing. In thought stoppage, counterproductive or distracting cognitions are eliminated through the use of mental or physical triggers such as uttering or thinking the word "Stop" or snapping the fingers. Each athlete should choose the trigger that is least obtrusive and most useful to him or her. Bunker and Owens (1985) report an interesting application of thought stoppage with a golfer. The golfer in question was asked to put one hundred paper clips into her pocket prior to beginning a round of golf. As a negative thought entered her mind she was to move a clip to her back pocket. At the end of 18 holes, her score was 84, and she had moved 87 clips to the back pocket; the accumulation of paper clips served as a poignant indicator to the golfer of just how many negative thoughts she had during a typical round and how thought stoppage might help in dealing with the problem.

Countering represents an internal dialogue using facts and reasons to refute negative thinking; it is important in countering to remember that just challenging negative thoughts may not be enough to turn things around in terms of confidence. It may actually require complex cognitive activity armed with facts and data to change a negative mindset that has some basis in fact and is firmly entrenched. Examples of negative thoughts and some useful counters to them are provided in table 4.1.

As for reframing, it is described as the creation of alternate frames of reference or ways of looking at the world (Gauron, 1984); essentially,

Table 4.1
Examples of Countering

Self-Defeating Thoughts	Countering Thoughts
I can't hit her. She throws too hard!	Yes, she throws hard, but I have worked hard on my hitting. I will hit!
I wish they wouldn't use the off-colored balls, as I have trouble picking them up off of the bat.	The color of the ball is the same for everyone, and I'm as good as anyone else.
I can't stand the pressure. I'm about to choke, and that is a sign of failure.	Really, the pressure is a sign that I care about the match, and is merely a prelude to a peak performance.
If I walk this batter, things will go downhill from there.	Just throw strikes like you almost always do. And they won't banish you to Rwanda or Siberia if you fail.
The officiating stinks and we can't win because of it.	Officials almost never make a difference in who wins, so I'll play my best and let the chips fall where they may.
She runs the 100 in 11.3 seconds. There's no way I can beat her.	I am well-trained in the sprints, and she's probably exaggerating her times anyway.
If I try to catch the fly and miss, I will look silly.	Looking silly is irrelevant; I owe it to myself and my teammates to give it my best effort.

Champion gymnast Dominique Dawes readying for the high beam. Dawes has learned to handle anxiety by thinking about the enjoyable festivities that follow the competition as a reward for focusing on the event at hand.

the athlete can take negative cognitions and reframe them as positives. Performance decrements, such as slumps in hitting in baseball or shooting free throws in basketball, can be reframed as periods of rest and renewed dedication. Feelings of arousal prior to competition, such as "butterflies" prior to the kickoff in football, can be reframed as excitement and readiness as opposed to tension and anxiety. As is pointed out by Bunker et al. (1993), an important element of reframing is that it does not bring into play any denial or downplaying of expressed concerns; rather, it involves a conscious awareness of reality and subsequent cognitive restatement that can be used to the advantage of the athlete.

Hypnosis

Hypnosis has been defined as an altered state of consciousness characterized by increased acceptance of suggestion. Despite connotations of voodoo and deception, hypnosis has a lengthy history that suggests it is an effective method for controlling anxiety (Rotella, 1985). Yet scientists remain uncertain about how this mysterious procedure benefits patients suffering from anxiety disorders. Some argue that hypnosis is nothing more than increased concentration, whereas others advocate that trance states alleviate basic tensions arising out of underlying psychic conflicts. Whatever the mechanism, sport psychologists have shown that hypnosis is a viable technique for inducing a relaxed state that is crucial to success in sport.

Krakauer (1985) reports a long list of professional athletes who have been helped with hypnotic procedures. Former heavyweight boxing champion Ken Norton used a hypnotist to help him prepare for his fight with Muhammad Ali, a fight that he won. In baseball, hypnotist Harvey Misel has intervened on behalf of more than fifty major league players, among them Bill Buckner when he was playing for the Chicago Cubs. Buckner had been in a batting slump that had brought his average 20 points below his normal performance. After a few sessions with hypnosis, Buckner increased his batting performance so dramatically that he was named National League Player of the Month. Elsewhere, Heyman (1987) reported the successful use of hypnosis in a case study of an amateur boxer suffering from anxieties and lowered performance brought about by crowd behavior and noise. Heyman's intervention with hypnosis assisted the boxer in coping more effectively with the crowd-related distractions. As a result of the treatment regimen, the boxer was able to perform his sport at a higher level of proficiency. Schreiber (1991) has demonstrated the utility of hypnosis in improving shooting performance of female collegiate basketball players.

A number of analysts of therapeutic models in sport have advanced the notion that the true strength of hypnosis rests with the athlete's belief that the procedure works (Rotella, 1985). If the athlete approaches the competitive situation with a positive frame of mind, confidence is increased, and as we observed in earlier discussion, this in itself can improve performance efficiency. Still, negative scientific reports failing to confirm the alleged usefulness of hypnosis in sport are not uncommon (Greer and Engs, 1986), so that skeptics continue to question the validity of the procedure.

Cox, Qiu, and Liu (1993) have perused literature reviews by Johnson (1961), Morgan (1972),

and Morgan and Brown (1983) and have arrived at a set of generally agreed upon conclusions about the status of hypnosis and motor performance:

1. General arousal techniques are more useful in enhancing muscular strength and endurance than hypnotic suggestions.
2. Negative suggestions invariably work to the detriment of the performer.
3. Hypnosis can help a successful athlete, but it cannot make a good performer out of a poor one.
4. Hypnotizing athletes may do more harm than good, underscoring the importance of a trained psychotherapist.
5. The deeper the hypnotic trance, the more likely it is that the trance will work to improve performance.
6. Dependency problems involving the therapist can be circumvented by autohypnosis.

One additional point concerning hypnosis and its relationship to other relaxation procedures is offered by Schwartz (1993); he is of the opinion, after reading a thorough assessment of the literature by Lehrer and Woolfolk (1993), that persons low in hypnotic susceptibility respond better to EMG biofeedback and progressive muscle relaxation, whereas hypnosis is more efficacious with individuals who are high in hypnotic susceptibility. Hypnotic susceptibility appears to be associated with responsiveness to treatment with most relaxation techniques, though this does not extend to biofeedback. Schwartz goes on to conclude that hypnosis and biofeedback may be mutually incompatible as self-management interventions. Such a conclusion should offer fertile grounds for additional research.

Yoga, Zen, and TM
Even more controversial than hypnosis are meditation procedures such as *yoga, Zen,* and

transcendental meditation (TM). Such procedures teach people to relax by excluding distracting images from consciousness. By narrowing the concentration of the individual and restricting the range of mental activity, task requirements are given greater attention and performance should improve accordingly. Yet, because the precise goals of intervention are not clearly delineated in such procedures, gauging psychological growth during treatment is often difficult. Consequently, it is virtually impossible to determine parallels between performance changes and mental progress. Not surprisingly, there has been a scarcity of empirical reports that establish the role that TM and other meditational procedures may play in the treatment of anxiety disturbances among athletes.

A FINAL NOTE

In this chapter we have seen that techniques are available that decrease arousal with the result that better sport performances occur. But arousal levels can fall too low, and performance deteriorates. The real issue for the coach or practitioner is identifying the level of tension that maximizes the athlete's attention and maintains his or her concentration. At what point do we pull in the reins, and how much control is required? Has the player peaked too soon, and how long can optimal arousal levels be expected to be sustained? As most coaches know already, the answers to these questions are individually determined. Nonetheless, some of the features covered in this chapter may help with respect to improving our judgments about arousal and athletic performance.

SUMMARY

1. Arousal is an all-inclusive term referring to psychological activation. Anxiety is gener-

ally regarded as a negatively charged emotional state.

2. The cerebral cortex, the hypothalamus, and the reticular formation are brain structures important to the expression of anxiety.

3. State anxiety is a transitory form of apprehension that varies in intensity. Trait anxiety is a more enduring variable that reflects nonspecific anxiety proneness. A sport-related measure of state anxiety that offers considerable promise is the Competitive State Anxiety Inventory-II (CSAI-II) by Rainer Martens and associates. The CSAI-II measures cognitive state anxiety, somatic state anxiety, and sport self-confidence. Particularly detrimental to sport performance is cognitive state anxiety.

4. The drive theory of learning and performance posits that arousal will interact positively with well-established behaviors but negatively influence behaviors with weaker habit strength. By contrast, the inverted-U hypothesis states that all behaviors (low or high habits) will increase as arousal increases, up to a point; further increases in arousal will result in performance deterioration. Research in sport has demonstrated that optimal arousal is not uniform across all sports; the level of arousal necessary to bench press 350 pounds is very different from that needed for hitting a six-foot putt. Another outgrowth of research inside and external to sport psychology has led to some skepticism concerning the inverted-U hypothesis, though it is viewed as superior to the more simplistic Hullian drive theory.

5. Flooding and implosive therapy are two intervention techniques based on the principles of classical conditioning. In each of these procedures, extinction is used as a method for anxiety alleviation.

6. Relaxation training employs the technique of counterconditioning to replace anxiety reactions to fear-eliciting cues with calmness.

The end result is that the athlete's performance improves. A variant of this procedure is called systematic desensitization.

7. Reinforced practice is an intervention procedure based on the principles of instrumental conditioning. The idea is to reward the person for systematic approaches toward an anxiety-provoking stimulus.

8. One of the most popular methods for treating anxiety is an instrumental technique known as biofeedback. Ostensibly, this approach uses reward outcomes (feedback) to change the probabilities of autonomic behaviors. However, recent research questions the validity of the early claims along these lines.

9. One of the better known of the cognitive techniques for dealing with anxiety is stress inoculation therapy (SIT), the treatment strategy devised by Donald Meichenbaum. The utility of SIT has been demonstrated in a number of sport-related studies.

10. Cognitive control techniques include thought stoppage, countering, and reframing, all of which place heavy emphasis on positive self-talk in the face of competitive stress. They have been used very effectively with athletes in anxiety management.

11. Another well-known and controversial cognitive procedure is hypnosis, which has been used successfully with a variety of athletes. However, hypnosis does not work in every case and should always be carried out by skilled psychotherapists.

12. Yoga, Zen, and Transcendental Meditation (TM) are other well-known relaxation procedures, though their efficacy with athletes has not been demonstrated at this point in time.

SUGGESTED READINGS

Academy releases report on boosting human performance. (1994) *APS Observer, 7* (5), 1–19.

Though this article is not directed specifically at a sport psychology audience, its ramifications are significant for the field. The report is a summary of the conclusions generated by the National Research Council's (NRC) Committee on Techniques for the Enhancement of Human Performance. Two of the eleven members of the committee figure prominently in sport psychology, Deborah L. Feltz and Robert B. Zajonc. In view of the never-ending search for excellence in performance, many techniques have emerged from psychology, and the committee thoroughly analyzed a number of them. Included were such topics as building self-confidence, thought suppression, hypnosis, restricted environment stimulation (REST), and meditation. The committee findings generally support those techniques possessing a solid theoretical and experimental foundation. Also summarized in the report are findings from 1987 and 1991 on other psychological topics such as sleep learning, extrasensory perception, mental practice of motor skills, stress reduction, some aspects of personality testing, modeling, and yoga.

Kleine, D. (1990) Anxiety and sport performance: A meta-analysis. *Anxiety Research, 2,* 113–131.

Kleine has applied the meta-analytic statistical procedure to the available literature on anxiety and sport. Fifty studies published between 1970 and 1988 met the criteria set by Kleine for inclusion in his study. The relationship between anxiety and performance was also looked at from the standpoint of age, sex, gender, anxiety inventories used, sport task characteristics, and the inverted-U hypothesis. In the case of the inverted-U, ten studies of the hypothesis were reviewed; Kleine concludes that evidence for the inverted-U relationship is scarce. He was particularly intrigued that the majority of the studies failed to test for or discuss the linearity versus curvilinearity issue related to the inverted-U.

Lehrer, P. M., & Woolfolk, R. L. (Eds.) (1993) *Principles and practice of stress management* (2d ed.). New York: Guilford.

Though cited several times in the text of this chapter, there is much more of value in this edited reader for the student of stress management. Readings on progressive relaxation, yoga, meditation, hypnosis, autogenic training, biofeedback, cognitive approaches to stress management, stress inoculation training, music therapy, aerobic exercise and stress management, pharmacology, and comparisons of the effectiveness of the various stress management procedures are all discussed at great length. This edited reader is invaluable as a resource for those interested in the many stress management treatments that are available for use by therapists and sport psychologists.

Petruzello, S. J., Landers, D. M., & Salazar, W. (1991) Biofeedback and sport/exercise performance: Applications and limitations. *Behavior Therapy, 22,* 379–392.

The authors provide a good review of some of the literature on various biofeedback procedures; in the process, they have dichotomized the various areas into those with known and those with unknown effects. In the former instance, the authors feel that heart rate (HR), respiration, and slow potentials have been sufficiently researched and demonstrated to be effective in performance enhancement. In the latter case, they feel that electromyographic (EMG) and EEG or alpha feedback procedures have been investigated the most but have produced the least convincing effects. This reading represents a synopsis of what we think we know about biofeedback in its various manifestations.

Prapavessis, H., Grove, J. R., McNair, P. J., & Cable, N.T. (1992) Self-regulation training, state anxiety, and sport performance: A psychophysiological case study. *The Sport Psychologist, 6,* 213–229.

A single-subject research design was applied to test the efficacy of cognitive-behavioral interventions in assisting a small-bore rifle shooter to perform more effectively. A variety of procedures to include relaxation, thought stoppage, refocusing, positive coping statements, and biofeedback were used with the shooter. Decreases in cognitive and somatic anxiety and increases in confidence were noted over the course of the treatment regimen.

The authors concluded that their multi-method intervention was successful; they further suggest that such approaches are more likely to be successful if (1) the athlete believes his or her anxiety to be detrimental to performance, (2) the procedures are individually tailored and administered as opposed to being conducted in groups, and (3) the training and testing sessions are conducted in an ecologically valid training environment that approximates the one in which the athlete must actually perform. The Prapavessis et al. article brings into play a number of the topics discussed throughout this chapter.

Sachs, M. L. (1991) Reading list in applied sport psychology: Psychological skills training. *The Sport Psychologist, 5,* 88–91.

In this brief article, Sachs has put together a list of forty-eight readings related to psychological skills training by such authorities as Martens, Nideffer, Orlick, Rotella, Singer, and Suinn, to name only a few. Almost all are books, and citations of pertinent reviews of each are included where applicable. Most of the suggested readings are broad in scope, but several focus on particular sports such as basketball, bodybuilding, golf, and running. Sachs also offers a list of five sources that he regards as the top of the line in the group of forty-eight, and suggests that they would be a good starting point for someone unfamiliar with the area of psychological skills training in sport.

Weinberg, R. S., & Comar, W. (1994) The effectiveness of psychological interventions in competitive sport. *Sports Medicine, 18,* 406–418.

The authors review results of forty-five studies in which educationally based psychological interventions were used to increase sport performance. Thirty-five found positive performance results, though causality could be inferred only in twenty. A four-fold classification system for these intervention techniques was created by the authors: relaxation-based, cognitive, cognitive-behavioral, and behavioral. Suggestions for improving future research efforts are included.

REFERENCES

Anderson, K. J. (1990) Arousal and the inverted-U hypothesis: A critique of Neiss's "reconceptualizing arousal." *Psychological Bulletin, 107,* 96–100.

Benjamin, L. T., Hopkins, R., & Nation, J. R. (1994) *Psychology* (3d ed). New York: Macmillan.

Bird, A. M., & Cripe, B. K. (1986) *Psychology and sport behavior.* St. Louis: Times Mirror/Mosby.

Borkovec, T. D. (1976) Physiological and cognitive processes in the regulation of anxiety. in G. E. Schwartz & D. Shapiro (Eds.), *Consciousness and self-regulation: Advances in research* (pp. 141–180). New York: Plenum.

Brustad, R., & Weiss, M. R. (1987) Competence perceptions and sources of worry in high, medium, and low competitive trait-anxious youth athletes. *Journal of Sport Psychology, 9,* 97–105.

Bunker, L., & Owens, D. (1985) *Golf: Better practice for better play.* West Point, N.Y.: Leisure Press.

Bunker, L., & Rotella, R. (1980) Achievement and stress in sport: Research findings and practical suggestions. In W. F. Straub (Ed.), *Sport psychology: An analysis of athlete behavior.* Ithaca, NY: Mouvement Publications.

Bunker, L., Williams, J. M., & Zinsser, N. (1993) Cognitive techniques for improving performance and building confidence. In J. M. Williams (Ed.), *Applied sport psychology: Personal growth to peak performance* (pp. 225–242). Mountain View, CA: Mayfield.

Burton, D. (1988) Do anxious swimmers swim slower? Reexamining the elusive anxiety-performance relationship. *Journal of Sport and Exercise Psychology, 10,* 45–61.

Carlson, N. R. (1991) *Psychology: The science of behavior.* (2d ed.). Boston: Allyn and Bacon.

Carson, R. C., & Butcher, J. N. (1992) *Abnormal psychology and modern life* (9th ed.). New York: HarperCollins.

Cotman, C. W., & McGaugh, J. L. (1980) *Behavioral neuroscience.* New York: Academic Press.

Cox, R. H. (1990) *Sport psychology: Concepts and applications* (2d ed.). Dubuque, IA: Wm. C. Brown.

Cox, R. H., Qiu, Y., & Liu, Z. (1993) Overview of sport psychology. In R. N. Singer, M. Murphey, and L. K. Tennant (Eds.), *Handbook of research on sport psychology* (pp. 3–31). New York: Macmillan.

Crafts, L. W., Schneirla, T. C., Robinson, E. E., & Gilbert, R. W. (1938) *Recent experiments in psychology.* New York: McGraw-Hill.

Daniels, F. S., & Landers, D. M. (1981) Biofeedback and shooting performance: A test of disregulation and systems theory. *Journal of Sport Psychology, 2,* 288–294.

DeWitt, D. J. (1979) Biofeedback training with university athletes. In *Proceedings of the Biofeedback Society Annual Meeting.* Denver, CO: The Biofeedback Society.

DeWitt, D. (1980) Cognitive and biofeedback training for stress reduction with university athletes. *Journal of Sport Psychology, 2,* 288–294.

Dicara, L. (1970) Learning in the autonomic nervous system. *Scientific American, 22,* 30–39.

Druckman, D., & Swets, J. A. (1987) *Enhancing human performance: Issues, theories, and techniques.* Washington, D.C.: National Academy Press.

Dworkin, B. R., & Miller, N. E. (1986) Failure to replicate visceral learning in the acute curarized rat preparation. *Behavioral Neuroscience, 100,* 299–314.

Emmelkamp, P. M. G., & Wessels, H. (1975) Flooding in imagination vs. flooding in vivo: A comparison with agoraphobics. *Behavior Research and Therapy, 13,* 7–15.

Endler, N. S., Parker, J. D. A., Bagby, R. M., & Cox, B. J. (1991) Multidimensionality of state and trait anxiety: Factor structure of the Endler Multidimensional anxiety scales. *Journal of Personality and Social Psychology, 60,* 919–926.

Fenz, W. D. (1985) Coping mechanisms and performance under stress. In D. M. Landers and R. W. Christina (Eds.), *Psychology of sport and motor behavior II* (pp. 64–84). University Park, PA: College of HPER, The Pennsylvania State University.

Foa, E. B., Grayson, J. B., Steketee, G. S., Doppelt, H. G., Turner, R. M., & Latimar, P. R. (1983) Success and failure in the behavioral treatment of obsessive-compulsives. *Journal of Consulting and Clinical Psychology, 51,* 287–297.

French, S. N. (1978) Electromyographic biofeedback for tension control during gross motor skill acquisition. *Perceptual and Motor Skills, 47,* 883–889.

Gauron, E. F. (1984) *Mental training for peak performance.* Lansing, MI: Sport Science Associates.

Gerson, R., & Deshaies, P. (1978) Competitive trait anxiety and performance as predictors of precompetitive state anxiety. *International Journal of Sport Psychology, 9,* 16–26.

Gould, D., Horn, T., & Spreeman, J. (1983) Perceived anxiety of elite junior wrestlers. *Journal of Sport Psychology, 5,* 58–71.

Gould, D., & Krane, V. (1992) The arousal-performance relationship: Current status and future directions. In T. Horn (Ed.), *Advances in sport psychology* (pp. 119–141). Champaign, IL: Human Kinetics.

Gould, D., Petlichkoff, L., Simons, J., & Vevera, M. (1987) Relationships between Competitive State Anxiety Inventory-2 subscale scores and pistol shooting performance. *Journal of Sport Psychology, 9,* 33–42.

Greer, H., and Engs, R. (1986) Use of progressive relaxation and hypnosis to increase tennis skill learning. *Perceptual and Motor Skills, 63,* 161–162.

Hackfort, D., & Schwenkmezger, P. (1989) Measuring anxiety in sports: Perspectives and problems. In D. Hackfort & C. D. Spielberger (Eds.), *Anxiety in sports.* New York: Hemisphere.

Hardy, L., & Fazey, J. A. (1987) The inverted-U hypothesis—a catastrophe for sport psychology and a statement of a new hypothesis. Paper presented at the Annual Conference of the North American Society for the Psychology of Sport and Physical Activity, Vancouver, Canada.

Hatfield, B. D., & Landers, D. M. (1983) Psychophysiology—A new direction for sport psychology. *Journal of Sport Psychology, 5,* 243–259.

Heyman, S. R. (1987) Research and intervention in sport psychology: Issues encountered in working with an amateur boxer. *The Sport Psychologist, 1,* 208–223.

Huddleston, S., & Gill, D. L. (1981) State anxiety as a function of skill level and proximity to competition. *Research Quarterly for Exercise and Sport, 52,* 31–34.

Hull, C. L. (1943) *Principles of behavior.* New York: Appleton-Century-Crofts.

Jacobson, E. (1938) *Progressive relaxation.* Chicago: University of Chicago Press.

Johnson, W. R. (1961) Hypnosis and muscular performance. *Journal of Sports Medicine and Physical Fitness, 1,* 71–79.

Jones, J. G. (1990) A cognitive perspective on the processes underlying the relationship between stress and performance in sport. In J. G. Jones (Ed.), *Stress and performance in sport* (pp. 16–42). New York: Wiley.

King, M., Stanley, G., & Burrows, G. (1987) *Stress: Theory and practice.* London: Grune and Stratton.

Klavora, P. (1977) An attempt to derive inverted-U curves based on the relationship between anxiety and athletic performance. In D. M. Landers & R. W. Christina (Eds.), *Psychology of motor behavior* (pp. 369–377). Champaign, IL: Human Kinetics.

Krakauer, J. (1985) Hypnosis. *Ultrasport, 2,* 22–27.

Landers, D. M. (1989) The arousal performance relationship revisited. *Research Quarterly for Exercise and Sport, 51,* 77–90.

Landers, D. M., & Boutcher, S. H. (1993) Arousal-performance relationships. In J. M. Williams (Ed.), *Applied sport psychology: Personal growth to peak performance* (2d ed.) (pp. 170–184). Mountain View, CA: Mayfield.

Lehrer, P. M., Carr, R., Sargunaraj, D., & Woolfolk, R. L. (1993) Differential effects of stress management therapies on emotional and behavioral disorders. In P. M. Lehrer & R. L. Woolfolk (Eds.), *Principles and practice of stress management.* New York: Guilford Press.

Lehrer, P. M., & Woolfolk, R. L. (1993) Specific effects of stress management techniques. In P. M. Lehrer and R. L. Woolfolk (Eds.), *Principles and practice of stress management* (2d ed.) (pp. 481–520). New York: Guilford Press.

Leitenberg, H. (1976) Behavioral approaches to treatment of neuroses. In H. Leitenberg (Ed.), *Handbook of behavior modification and behavior therapy* (pp. 41–64). Englewood Cliffs, NJ: Prentice-Hall.

Long, B. C. (1980) Stress management for the athlete: A cognitive behavioral model. In C. H. Nadeau (Ed.), *Psychology of motor behavior and sport* (pp. 111–119). Champaign, IL: Human Kinetics.

Lykken, D. (1968) Neuropsychology and psychophysiology in personality research. In E. F. Borgatta & W. W. Lambert (Eds.), *Handbook of personality theory and research* (pp. 16–41). Chicago: Rand McNally.

Mace, R. D., & Carroll, D. (1986) Stress inoculation training to control anxiety in sport: Two case studies in squash. *British Journal of Sports Medicine, 20,* 115–117.

Mace, R. D., Eastman, C., & Carroll, D. (1986) Stress inoculation training: A case study in gymnastics. *British Journal of Sports Medicine, 20,* 139–141.

Mace, R. D., Eastman, C., & Carroll, D. (1987) The effects of stress inoculation training on gymnastics performance on the pommelled horse: A case study. *Behavioural Psychotherapy, 15,* 272–279.

Mahoney, M. J., & Avener, M. (1977) Psychology of the elite athlete: An exploratory study. *Cognitive Therapy and Research, 7,* 135–141.

Marks, I., Boulougouris, J., & Marset, P. (1971) Flooding versus desensitization in the treatment of phobic patients: A cross over study. *British Journal of Psychiatry, 119,* 353–375.

Martens, R. (1974) Arousal and motor performance. *Exercise and Sport Science Reviews, 2,* 155–188.

Martens, R., Burton, D., Vealey, R. S., Bump, L. A., & Smith, D. E. (1989) The Competitive State Anxiety Inventory-2 (CSAI-2). In D. Burton & R. Vealey (Eds.), *Competitive anxiety.* Champaign, IL: Human Kinetics.

Martens, R., Gill, D., Simon, J., & Scanlan, T. (1975) Competitive anxiety: Theory and research. Proceedings of the seventh Canadian Psycho-Motor Learning and Sport Psychology Symposium, Quebec City (October).

Martens, R., & Landers, D. M. (1970) Motor performance makes stress: A test of the inverted-U hypothesis. *Journal of Personality and Social Psychology, 16,* 29–37.

Martin, G., & Pear, J. (1992) *Behavior modification: What it is and how to do it* (4th ed.). Englewood Cliffs, NJ: Prentice-Hall.

Meichenbaum, D. M. (1977) *Cognitive behavior modification: An integrative approach.* New York: Plenum.

Meichenbaum, D. M. (1993) Stress inoculation training: A 20-year update. In P. M. Lehrer and R. L. Woolfolk (Eds.), *Principles and practice of stress management* (2d ed.) (pp. 373–406). New York: Guilford Press.

Morgan, W. P. (1972) Hypnosis and muscular performance. In W. P. Morgan (Ed.), *Ergogenic aids in muscular performance* (pp. 193–233). New York: Academic Press.

Morgan, W. P., & Brown, D. R. (1983) Hypnosis. In M. H. Williams (Ed.), *Ergogenic aids in sport* (pp. 223–252). Champaign, IL: Human Kinetics.

Mowrer, O. H. (1960) *Learning theory and behavior.* New York: Wiley.

Miller, N. E. (1978) Biofeedback and visual learning. *Annual Review of Psychology, 29,* 373–404.

Neiss, R. (1988) Reconceptualizing arousal: Psychobiological states in motor performance. *Psychological Bulletin, 103,* 345–366.

Nideffer, R. M. (1981) *The ethics and practice of applied sport psychology.* Ithaca, NY: Mouvement Publications.

Passer, M. W. (1983) Fear of failure, fear of evaluation, perceived competence, and self-esteem in competitive-trait anxious children. *Journal of Sport Psychology, 5,* 172–188.

Rotella, R. J. (1985) Strategies for controlling anxiety and arousal. In L. Bunker & R. J. Rotella (Eds.), *Sport psychology* (pp. 185–195). Ann Arbor, MI: McNaughton and Gunn.

Sandweiss, J. H. (1985) Biofeedback and sports science. In J. H. Sandweiss and S. L. Wolf (Eds.), *Biofeedback and sports science* (pp. 1–31). New York: Plenum.

Sandweiss, J. H., and Wolf, S. L. (1985) *Biofeedback and sports science.* New York: Plenum.

Scanlan, T. K., & Passer, M. W. (1979) Factors influencing the competitive performance expectancies of young female athletes. *Journal of Sport Psychology, 1,* 151–159.

Schreiber, E. H. (1991) Using hypnosis to improve performance of collegiate basketball players. *Perceptual and Motor Skills, 72,* 536–538.

Schwartz, G. E. (1993) Foreword: Biofeedback is not relaxation is not hypnosis. In P.M. Lehrer and R.L. Woolfolk (Eds.), *Principles and practice of stress management* (2d ed.) (pp. ix–x). New York: Guilford Press.

Schwartz, G. E., Davidson, R. J., & Goleman, D. J. (1978) Patterning of cognitive and somatic processes in the self-regulation of anxiety: Effects of meditation versus exercise. *Psychosomatic Medicine, 40,* 321–328.

Seligman, M. E. P. (1991) *Learned optimism.* New York: Knopf.

Serling, R. J. (1986) Curing a fear of flying. *USAIR,* 12–19.

Smith, R. E. (1984) Theoretical and treatment approaches to anxiety reduction. In J. M. Silva & R. S. Weinberg (Eds.), *Psychological foundations of sport* (pp. 157–170). Champaign, IL: Human Kinetics.

Smith, R. E. (1980) A cognitive-affective approach to stress management training for athletes. In C. H. Nadeau (Ed.), *Psychology of motor behavior and sport, 1979.* Champaign, IL: Human Kinetics.

Smith, R. E., Smoll, F. L., & Schutz, R. W. (1990) Measurement and correlates of sport-specific cognitive and somatic trait anxiety: The Sport Anxiety Scale. *Anxiety Research, 2,* 263–280.

Sonstroem, R. J. (1984) An overview of anxiety in sport. In J. M. Silva & R. S. Weinberg (Eds.), *Psychological foundations of sport* (pp. 104–117). Champaign, IL: Human Kinetics.

Sonstroem, R. J., & Bernardo, P. (1982) Intraindividual pregame state anxiety and basketball performance: A re-examination of the inverted-U curve. *Journal of Sport Psychology, 4,* 235–245.

Spence, K. W., Farber, I. E., & McFann, H. H. (1956) The relation of anxiety (drive) level to performance in competitional and noncompetitional paired-associated learning. *Journal of Experimental Psychology, 52,* 296–305.

Spielberger, C. D. (1972) *Anxiety: Current trends in theory and research* (Vol. 1). New York: Academic Press.

Stampfl, T. G., & Levis, D. J. (1967). Essentials of implosive therapy: A learning theory based psychodynamic behavioral therapy. *Journal of Abnormal Psychology, 72,* 496–503.

Wankel, L. M. (1980). Social facilitation of motor performance: Perspective and prospective. In C. H. Nadeau, W. R. Halliwell, K. M. Newell, & G. C. Roberts (Eds.), *Psychology of motor behavior and sport—1979* (pp. 41–53). Champaign, IL: Human Kinetics.

Weinberg, R. S., & Genuchi, M. (1980). Relationship between competitive trait anxiety state anxiety and golf performance: A field study. *Journal of Sport Psychology, 2,* 148–154.

Winter, B. (May 1982) Relax and win. *Sports and athletes,* 72–78.

Wolpe, J. (1982) *The practice of behavior therapy.* New York: Pergamon.

Zaichkowsky, L. D., & Fuchs, C. Z. (1989) Biofeedback-assisted self-regulation for stress management in sports. In D. Hackfort and C. D. Spielberger (Eds.), *Anxiety in sports: An international perspective* (pp. 235–245). New York: Hemisphere.

Zajonc, R. B. (1965) Social facilitation. *Science, 149,* 269–274.

Social-Psychological Dimensions

Motivation in Sport

INTRODUCTION

The behavioral perspective, as was noted in the two previous chapters, has intrigued psychologists for quite a period of time. However, interest in what motivates people to behave as they do, separate and apart from the interplay of reinforcement and punishment, has reemerged as a major focus of scientific inquiry. We say *reemerged* to emphasize the fact that theories of motivation were held in some disrepute in the psychology community, most particularly by the behaviorists of the 1960s and 1970s, because of the prevailing fascination with the simplistic stimulus-response (S-R) thinking of that era. Cognitive processes or thoughts were taboo for a period of time in many circles of psychology. However, as it became clear that many human behaviors appear to fall outside a strict S-R interpretation, the role of internal, organismic, or cognitive intervening variables crept back into scientific respectability. Geen, Beatty, and Arkin (1984, p. 11) refer to this reemergence of the acceptability of consciousness and thinking as mediators of behavior as "the cognitive revolution."

In this chapter, motivation will be defined. Two major approaches to motivation, attribution theory and need achievement, and the related nuances of each, will be discussed. In addition, two moderators of motivation—locus of control and self-esteem—will be entertained to flesh out our consideration of this most important topic. At the same time, motivation has been a major focus of research interest in sport psychology for the past fifteen years, and sport-related applications will be made where possible.

WHAT IS MOTIVATION?

There is no doubting the fact that motivation is of interest to us all, whether we are lay persons or scientists. At the international level, we are concerned that the average American student is not measuring up favorably with his or her counterpart in Japan or some of the more industrialized countries of western Europe. Fitness experts, as we will note in chapter 11, have been concerned for the better part of forty-five years about the lack of fitness in young people in this country as compared to European children; much motivational effort (not to mention money) has been expended by the President's Council on Fitness and Sport in an effort to alter this disconcerting picture.

In the American business sector, management is always trying to find ways to inspire employees to produce more and be happy in the process; so-called motivational speakers abound in this area due to the demand for their services. Such speakers abound in religious circles, hopefully inspiring or motivating others to lead more spiritual lives. Teachers at all levels of education are deluged with academic instruction and parental pressures aimed at making them more effective motivators of young people; some might view this as a daunting task.

In the sports world, coaches are fascinated with motivation; they generate motivational slogans, deliver motivational talks to their players, and sometimes even become motivational speakers for a variety of audiences during the off-season. Roberts (1992) asserts that nowhere is motivation less well understood than in sports. He goes on to say that coaches make three fundamentally erroneous assumptions about motivation. Perhaps the biggest mistaken notion is that motivation and arousal are synonymous. Delivering emotional pregame speeches, biting off the heads of chickens or frogs, throwing football helmets against lockers, and heaving chairs through locker room windows are thought to be motivating by some coaches. In all likelihood, such absurdities will cause arousal, but whether or not they will motivate is another question. Athletes are likely to react in a variety of ways to emotional approaches, but not always in the direction coaches would choose. A second mis-understanding is that "positive thinking" is always an answer to motivational problems. Clearly, realistic expectations have to prevail; some difficulties are not overcome by effort or expectancy, and the result is frustration rather than improved performance. Finally, there is a tendency among coaches to view motivation as an innate entity; that is, some people are born with motivation and some are not. This mental error is compounded by the fact that coaches will tend to give up prematurely on some players.

From the point of view of psychologists who make it their work to study motivation, the definition provided by Roberts (1992, p. 5) will serve as this chapter's framework as we try to attain a better understanding of the construct. According to Roberts, "motivation refers to those personality factors, social variables, and/or cognitions that come into play when a person undertakes a task at which he or she is evaluated, enters into competition with others, or attempts to attain some standard of excellence." Roberts goes on to state that in sports we use language like "try harder," "concentrate more," "persist longer," "pay more attention," "perform better," and "practice longer and harder" to describe achievement or motivational behavior.

Given this definition and related elaboration provided by Roberts, it would seem instructive to now move to a discussion of the major motivational models that have been generated to date. Each will be discussed in detail and, where appropriate, sport applications will be made. There are any number of ways of conceptualizing theories of motivation depending on which authority you consult. It appears that there are two major theoretical perspectives that have dominated both psychological research and research in sport psychology; each will be discussed in turn. These perspectives are attribution theory (with its many variants) and need achievement. Major reviews of the motivational litera-ture by Biddle (1993) and Roberts (1992, 1993) will serve as general guides for our discussion.

ATTRIBUTION THEORY

One topic in the motivation area of continuing interest to sport scientists is attribution theory, which was first advanced by Fritz Heider (1944, 1958). Representing a move toward a more cognitive approach to psychology, attribution theory essentially deals with the *"naive psychology"* of the average person and how he or she interprets behavior. According to Heider, behavioral inferences may take two forms, either causal or dispositional attributions. *Causal attributions* are inferences as to why something happened; for example, tennis players playing as a doubles team may attribute their success to their capacity for teamwork. As for *dispositional attributions,* we are dealing with inferences about some quality or trait that an individual may possess. The football player who plays at a level generally above his apparent ability is said to be a "winner" or an "overachiever." Both causal and dispositional attributions represent an attempt on the part of laypersons and professionals alike to explain both their behavior and that of those around them. By engaging in such attributions, a measure of psychological closure is achieved, integrity and self-esteem are maintained, and a degree of order is achieved in the environment. Such is the function of our continuous behavioral attributions.

According to Geen, Beatty, and Arkin (1984), attributions are subject to a number of biases, and these must be taken into account when dealing with related theory, research, or application. One source of error is *informational bias* and this comes about as the result of discrepancies between what we know about ourselves, what we know about others, and what they know about us. As a result, misunderstanding of motives and behavior takes place. A second error source is *perceptual bias*. Briefly stated, we cannot perceive ourselves as others do because we cannot observe ourselves and are more prone than others to make external as opposed to personal attributions about life events. A final source of problems is *motivational bias,* and here we are dealing primarily with defensive attributions. Of particular interest to sport researchers has been the notion of the self-serving attribution bias. In this situation, the person involved assumes too much personal responsibility for success and too little for failure. We are all prone, in our athletic endeavors, to see victory or success as due to ability or effort and defeat or failure as attributable to poor officiating, faulty equipment, unfavorable weather conditions, and bad luck. More will be said on this topic later.

Attribution Theory Models

In general, three models of attribution theory have caught the fancy of theorists and researchers. They are cognitive, social cognitive, and functional models.

The Cognitive Model

The cognitive model is based on an integration by Weiner (1974, 1980) of Heider's work and that of Julian Rotter and his locus of control theory. Weiner's formulation in its simplest form essentially asserts that task outcome (O) in any achievement-related activity is a function of ability (A), effort (E), task difficulty (T), and luck (L):

$$O = f(A, E, T, L)$$

This formula allows for an assessment of success or failure through evaluation of level of ability, amount of effort expended, the difficulty of the task at hand, and the strength and direction of luck or chance factors confronted (Weiner, 1980).

These causal antecedents for behavior suggested by Weiner (i.e., ability, effort, task difficulty, and luck) allow for inferences about achievement outcomes.

Ability Antecedents. According to Weiner (1980), ability antecedents are primarily drawn from past experience with success ("I can") or failure ("I cannot"). High academic achievement often leads to an inference that a person is "smart" or is "a brain" just as general speed and agility may lead to the conclusion that the person possessing these qualities is a "good all-around athlete."

Effort Antecedents. The amount of effort put forth in order to achieve is an important variable though there is not necessarily a one-to-one correspondence between the two. If that were so, the student who studies the most would always make the highest grade. In the athletic realm, as will be discussed later in more detail, the black athlete is often perceived as successful not due to effort but to natural or innate ability, an obviously erroneous but common attribution.

Task Antecedents. If many succeed at a task, it is seen as easy, whereas the opposite is true when few succeed. Running the hurdles without embarrassing or injuring oneself is seen as a major accomplishment by many, and such a task is generally seen as difficult because so few can do it. The same can be said for the pole vault. The role of consensus information in assessing task difficulty is of paramount importance, though objective factors—such as length, complexity, and novelty—also enter into the overall process of judging task antecedents.

Luck Antecedents. The flip of the coin, the luck of the draw, and various weather events in outdoor sports are examples of things that are perceived as chance or luck attributions contributing to success or failure in achievement

Bernard Weiner as a Fifth Grader: The Genesis of a Theory of Attribution

In 1988, the California School of Professional Psychology, Los Angeles (CSPP-LA) hosted a conference dedicated to assessing the state of the art, so to speak, of attribution theory. As part of the proceedings, Bernard Weiner, the major architect of the cognitive approach to attribution theory, was given a plaque as conference honoree. In his acceptance "speech," Weiner gave the audience (and us) a glimpse into his experiences as a fifth grader that provided the germ of an idea that ultimately became the very sophisticated theory of human motivation that has been so instrumental in guiding attributional research inside and external to sport psychology. The following is Weiner's acceptance speech from the 1988 CSPP-LA conference.

The attainment of an award provides the occasion for self-reflection, a time to be self-indulgent, and even perhaps the opportunity to provide guidance to others striving for accomplishment and recognition. Hence, at this time I would like to think back autobiographically and reconstruct some of the past to explain, in my own biased way, what events might have been responsible for the receipt of this award.

I think I am best known for a 2 x 2 taxonomy of causal attributions that was presented in 1971 and for my analysis of the dynamics associated with causal explanations. These related ideas all originated with the same event that happened to me somewhat early in my life — actually, when I was in the fifth grade.

While in the fifth grade, I decided to run for student government. A number of different positions were being contested in our class of twenty-five students. I first considered running for student president. That had the highest utility, but typically the president is the most popular student in class. Hence, I rejected that possibility. Note, then, that already I had decided to embrace Expectancy X Value theory, recognizing that if expectancy of success is zero, then the action should not, and will not be pursued.

Next I considered the possibility of vice president. That also had high utility. Unfortunately, that position is held usually by the second most popular class member. Guided again by Expectancy X Value theory, I therefore dismissed that idea also. Treasurer was next on my hierarchy of desired offices, but that is held by the most trusted class member, and I had to discard that thought. Finally, I considered being class secretary. But that post is held by the person with the best handwriting. Those of you who know me will immediately understand why I gave up on that pursuit.

(Continued next page)

Highlight 5.1 (Continued)

Bernard Weiner as a Fifth Grader:
The Genesis of a Theory of Attribution

There was one possibility left — becoming a member of student council. I reasoned as follows: Each of the offices of president, vice-president, treasurer, and secretary will be pursued by two students. This eliminated eight of the most successful of my peers from seeking to be on the council, leaving seventeen class members. Of these, seven are elected to serve on the council. Quick calculation revealed that my probability was at least .50 of a victory, and being on the council did have some prestige and other perks. I thus threw my hat into the council member ring. Unfortunately, I lost.

Now, the reader may be wondering what on earth does this have to do with taxonomies and classifications, and how does this relate to the dynamics of causal attribution? That is easily answered. At this time I noticed who was elected president, and knew that this person had received numerous other awards and plaudits. I also recognized others in my class who had never been recognized for any of their major or minor accomplishments. And it then dawned on me that there were two kinds of people in the world — those who received honors, awards, social recognition, and the like, and those that do not. This was my very first psychological taxonomy, and it came to be during the fifth grade. It also became clear that, in my classification, I was included with the non-recipients. This taxonomy, like many of the later ones in psychology, basically contrasted the "good guys" or the winners, with the "bad guys" or the losers.

Now, I then asked one of my first attributional questions: "Why did the winners in fact win, and why did the losers lose?" And the first answer was that it was deserved. The president, by virtue of his merits and accomplishments, "should" be president, and similarly for the vice-president, treasurer, secretary, and the members of the student government. Antedating Kelley but not perhaps Hume, I presumed that the covariation between accomplishments and election results would provide a causal explanation. But this proved to be incorrect. Close analysis of the participants revealed that the president indeed deserved his position, but this was not true of the vice-president nor the treasurer. Similarly, about one-half of the members of the student council in my estimation deserved their position, but not the other one-half. That is, deservingness proved to be entirely independent of award winning. In this manner I developed my first 2 x 2 taxonomy, which on

(Continued next page)

Highlight 5.1 (Continued)

Bernard Weiner as a Fifth Grader: The Genesis of a Theory of Attribution

one dimension included winners and losers, and on the other dimension was anchored with deserved and not deserved.

It was clear that I was a loser on one of the dimensions, and another fact was also clear to me—I deserved to be a winner. Now, this might now be called "hedonic bias," and in fact I take credit for discovering the phenomenon while I was in the fifth grade, in the year 1946, well before the Heider book.

This world-view served me well for more than forty years. It explained many facts in my environment; it was a very convenient and useful construct system. And it provided the foundation for my later attributional work related to taxonomy and dynamics.

But now I am thrown into turmoil. With this award, I have to change my position in the 2 x 2 table. I had assumed that being a loser was a trait—it had long-term stability. Now I find that I am no longer a loser, but actually a winner. I have to change my construct system, and those of you who are followers of George Kelly know that any impending change in construct systems produces threat. And, moving from loser to winner has elicited another source of anxiety. Do I really deserve it? Perhaps some of the readers will find out that the most complicated statistic I can do is a Chi-Square; they will be told that I do not know where the computer center is; they will discover that I write with a typewriter; they will read that my latest references are in the 1970s; and they will learn that I do not have plans for a forthcoming research program. That is, I may have gone from a person who did not deserve to lose to a person who did not deserve to win! I fear I may be uncovered as an imposter. As you know, this is labeled "The Imposter Syndrome."

I thus have learned that receiving an award has its costs, as well as its benefits. I have gone from self-righteous indignation to fear and guilt.

But, I must admit that on balance I prefer the latter state. I want to thank Sy Zelen and the California School of Professional Psychology for this award. I feel very happy (an outcome-dependent affect); increased self-esteem (an attribution to sustained effort, which also results in the tendency to bask in my glory); and great gratitude (based on my ascription of success to my many students and colleagues). Thank you so much, Dr. Zelen and the Professional School, for providing me this fine honor.

Source: Weiner (1991).

situations. And we are prone to bring luck attributions to bear on losing efforts. For example, Mann (1974) asked spectators at a football game why the winning team had triumphed over its opponent. Ninety-three percent of the winner's fans cited superior play as the reason for victory, whereas the loser's fans in 50 percent of the cases cited bad luck as the cause of their team's defeat.

An expanded list of reasons for success and failure related to ability, effort, task difficulty, and luck is presented in table 5.1. Carrying this work a step further, we see that Weiner has expanded beyond the elements of ability, effort, task difficulty, and luck to include stability and locus of causality in what becomes a two-dimensional taxonomy, represented in figure 5.1. As can be seen, ability and effort are internal and task difficulty and luck are external. At the same time, ability and task difficulty are seen as stable whereas effort and luck are unstable or changing over time. A number of possible inferences can be drawn. Among them are:

1. The low ability athlete who loses would expect to lose in future events because of his or her perception of ability as stable. Defensiveness could be expected to enter in here, thereby salvaging self-esteem by attributing failure to any of the other three elements of effort, task difficulty, or luck.

2. Winning or losing attributable to changeable elements such as effort or luck offer something for both successful and less successful sport participants in that the latter may view more effort as a means of reversing losing, and the former may see that luck can change things in a negative way so that they, too, may expend more effort in order to neutralize chance events. The latter is typified by the coach who pushes his already successful team to even greater effort with exhortations such as, "The harder I work, the luckier I get," or "I believe in luck and the harder I work, the luckier I get," or "Good

luck is what happens when preparation meets opportunity."

Though Weiner has expanded his model beyond the two-dimensional framework in recent years, it is the most influential in terms of creating research in sport psychology (Biddle, 1993).

In an effort to expand Weiner's work in the sport realm, Roberts and Pascuzzi (1979) have offered a more inclusive model, which is described in figure 5.2. Roberts and Pascuzzi arrived at their formulation through a study they conducted at the University of Illinois using 346 male and female undergraduate students. Subjects were asked to respond to eight stimulus items aimed at determining causal attributions for success or failure as a player and as a spectator.

Table 5.1

Some Cues Utilized for Inferences Concerning the Causes of Success and Failure

Causes	Cues
Ability	Number of successes, percentage of success, pattern of success, maximal performance, task difficulty
Effort	Outcome, pattern of performance, perceived muscular tension, sweating, persistence at the task, covariation of performance with incentive value of the goal
Task difficulty	Objective task characteristics, social norms
Luck	Objective task characteristics, independence of outcomes, randomness of outcomes, uniqueness of event

Source: Weiner (1980).

Figure 5.1: **Dimensions and Elements of Weiner's Original Two-Dimensional Taxonomy (1972)**

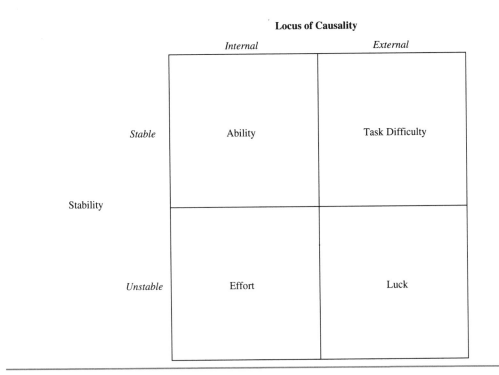

Locus of Causality

	Internal	*External*
Stable	Ability	Task Difficulty
Unstable	Effort	Luck

Stability

Source: Biddle (1993).

Only 45 percent of the subjects' attributions fell into Weiner's four elements of ability, effort, task difficulty, and luck. Frieze (1976), in a study of an academic environment, found that 83 percent of all attributions were within Weiner's four elements, leading Roberts and Pascuzzi to conclude that perhaps the two-dimensional model is more applicable to academic than sport environments.

Though all other factors reported by Roberts and Pascuzzi can be seen in figure 5.2, it is interesting to note that psychological factors (such as motivation, anxiety, and arousal), practice, and unstable ability factors related to day-by-day performance variations were cited so often by the subjects in the study.

Though Roberts and Pascuzzi's work is an extension of the Weiner two-dimensional model and, in general, is characteristic of the kind of research spawned therefrom, Weiner's updated *three-dimensional taxonomy* has not gone unnoticed by sport researchers. The three-dimensional taxonomy (Weiner, 1979, 1980) adds to the stability and locus of causality dimensions a third leg, that of controllability (events are seen as either controllable or uncontrollable). The three-dimensional model can be seen in table 5.2. Consistent with the new addition to the earlier models, antecedents such as effort would be viewed as controllable whereas ability has a strong element of uncontrollability. In terms of

Figure 5.2: Dimensional Categorization of Sport-Relevant Activities

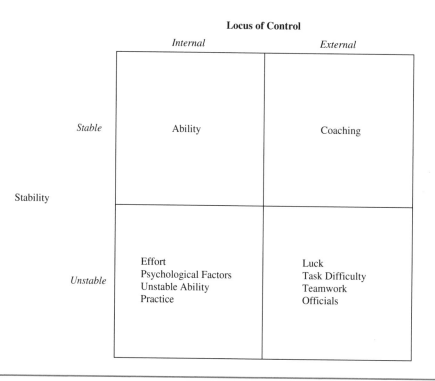

Source: Roberts and Pascuzzi (1979).

Table 5.2
A Three-Dimensional Taxonomy of the Perceived Causes of Success and Failure

| | Controllable | | Uncontrollable | |
	Stable	Unstable	Stable	Unstable
Internal	Stable effort of self	Unstable effort of self	Ability of self	Fatigue, mood, and fluctuations in skill of self
External	Stable effort of others	Unstable effort of others	Ability of others; task difficulty	Fatigue, mood, and fluctuations in skill of others; luck

Source: Weiner (1980).

the originally stated concepts of ability, effort, task difficulty, and luck, a perusal of table 5.2 will yield the following generalizations:

1. Individual ability is internal, stable, and uncontrollable.
2. Individual effort is internal, stable or unstable, and controllable.
3. Task difficulty is external, stable, and uncontrollable.
4. Luck is external, unstable, and uncontrollable.

Generalizations can also be made about the contributions of others (teammates, opponents) with regard to the success-failure dichotomy, and these are also revealed in table 5.2.

Considerable research has been generated in an effort to evaluate the three-dimensional taxonomy. Illustrative of one of the earlier attempts to test the three-dimensional model is the work of Gill, Ruder, and Gross (1982). Using both field and laboratory experiments (two each), Gill and her associates gathered a total of 352 open-ended attributions by simply asking their subjects, once they had completed actual or laboratory competitions, to respond to the question, "What is the most important reason for your team's winning or losing in today's match?" The preponderance of responses indicated an emphasis on internal, unstable, and uncontrollable attributions in team competition. References to teamwork were the most frequent attributions and the traditional attributional elements of ability, effort, task difficulty, and luck were not particularly salient. Partial substantiation of the point made by Gill et al. is provided by Roberts and Pascuzzi (1979); they found that the traditional foursome of ability, effort, task difficulty, and luck accounted for only 45 percent of the attributions made by undergraduate students taking part in their sport attribution experiment. This finding would suggest that a reliance on the basic

four elements in sport attribution research would be overrestrictive (Biddle, 1993).

As a caveat related to their work, Gill and associates suggest that coding difficulties and psychometric weaknesses associated with the open-ended format are problem areas of note. To partially deal with this problem, Gill et al. suggest that the Causal Dimension Scale (CDS) (Russell, 1982) might be useful to researchers with a penchant for more objective measures of attributions. The Causal Dimension Scale is presented in figure 5.3.

Accordingly, McAuley has been at the forefront of the research efforts aimed at validating the CDS (McAuley, 1985; McAuley and Duncan, 1989; McAuley and Gross, 1983). In the latter study, sixty-two male and female undergraduates who were enrolled in a physical education skills class in table tennis served as subjects. Upon completion of matches between same-sex players, thirty-one winners and thirty-one losers of each sex were identified. All subjects were administered the Causal Dimension Scale. Winners and losers alike made attributions that were internal, unstable, and controllable, though winners used more of them than losers. McAuley and Gross also reported high reliability coefficients for the dimensions of locus of causality and stability, but the controllability dimension had lower reliability than expected. Reservations were expressed about the latter scale's applicability to sport research as a result.

The second study by McAuley was conducted with fifty-two women intercollegiate gymnasts as subjects. Each gymnast was judged on the traditional gymnastic events (vault, balance beam, uneven parallel bars, floor exercises). Each was asked how she felt she had done in each event prior to finding out her scores, and all subjects then completed the CDS. Among the more salient findings were that high success gymnasts made more internal, stable, and controllable attributions for their performance; made significantly more stable attributions on all four events; made more internal attributions on two events (vault, balance beam); and made more controllable attributions on all events except the floor exercise. Perceived success was seen as a more powerful predictor of causal attributions than actual performance scores. Impressions of success for all gymnasts were lowest for the balance beam, an event many believe to be the hardest of the group of exercises to accomplish successfully.

In the third study, McAuley and Duncan (1989) tested fifty-five male and female undergraduates on a bicycle ergometer task operating in what they called "expectancy disconfirmation" conditions; that is, one group was high expectancy/failure and the other low expectancy/success. For the success group, no single attribution dimension predicted emotional responses to the experimental treatment conditions; however, all three dimensions predicted feelings of confidence. In the failure group, depressed emotion was related to the stability and locus dimensions. These results are again seen as partially supporting the CDS.

Figure 5.3: The Causal Dimension Scale

Instructions: Think about the reason or reasons you have written above. The items below concern your impression or opinions of this cause or causes of your outcome. Circle one number for each of the following scales.

1. Is the cause(s) something that:
   Reflects an aspect of yourself   9 8 7 6 5 4 3 2 1   Reflects an aspect of the situation

2. Is the cause(s):
   Controllable by you or   9 8 7 6 5 4 3 2 1   Uncontrollable by you or other
   other people   people

3. Is the cause(s) something that is:
   Permanent   9 8 7 6 5 4 3 2 1   Temporary

4. Is the cause(s) something:
   Intended by you or other people   9 8 7 6 5 4 3 2 1   Unintended by you or other people

5. Is the cause(s) something that is:
   Outside of you   1 2 3 4 5 6 7 8 9   Inside of you

6. Is the cause(s) something that is:
   Variable over time   1 2 3 4 5 6 7 8 9   Stable over time

7. Is the cause(s):
   Something about you   9 8 7 6 5 4 3 2 1   Something about others

8. Is the cause(s) something that is:
   Changeable   1 2 3 4 5 6 7 8 9   Unchanging

9. Is the cause(s) something for which:
   No one is responsible   1 2 3 4 5 6 7 8 9   Someone is responsible

---

Note: A total score for each of the three subscales is arrived at by summing the responses to the individual items as follows: (1) locus of causality—items 1, 5, and 7; (2) stability—items 3, 6, and 8; (3) controllability—items 2, 4, and 9. High scores on these subscales indicate that the cause is perceived as internal, stable, and controllable.

Source: Russell (1982).

Other research using the CDS has been conducted using a variety of participants by Grove, Hanrahan, and McInman (1991) with recreational basketball players, coaches, and spectators; Robinson and Howe (1987; 1989) with undergraduate students in the first study and elite male soccer players in the second study; Vallerand (1987) with undergraduate students and high school basketball players; and White (1993) with adolescent and adult softball players. In general, support for the CDS was found in each instance, although a pervasive problem with the scale has consistently been noted, which will be discussed shortly.

A major conclusion drawn from several of the preceding studies demonstrates support for the "intuitive-reflective appraisal model" of attributions (Vallerand, 1987). Essentially, Vallerand's model contains two key concepts: intuitive appraisal (immediate and relatively automatic response to an event) and reflective appraisal (less immediate and more reflective response to an event accompanied by attributional processing). Subsequent support for Vallerand's work has been reported by Biddle and Hill (1992a; 1992b) and Robinson and Howe (1987; 1989).

As stated earlier, support for the CDS has been considerable. However, the CDS is not without its critics, including Russell himself, and they have particularly pointed to problems with reliability and scale orthogonality (Biddle and Hill, 1992a; McAuley, Duncan, and Russell, 1992). In the case of reliability, low internal consistency of the controllability subscale is problematic. Also, the lack of orthogonality seen in the overlap of the controllability subscale and the locus of causality is troublesome. In an attempt to remedy these subscale shortcomings, McAuley et al. have proposed a revised CDS that is called the CDSII. Data generated from four separate studies (introductory psychology students in studies one and two, college students in a gymnastics class in study three, and students volunteering to play one-on-one basketball in

study four) were analyzed through confirmatory factor analysis for the purpose of demonstrating the validity of CDSII. The authors concluded that CDSII is reliable and valid across a spectrum of domains, but make the obligatory and necessary call for more research. The items included on the CDSII can be seen in figure 5.4.

Future research will undoubtedly focus on Weiner's three-dimensional model, and further utilization and refinement of Russell's Causal Dimension Scale can be expected. Also, self versus team attributions will be more intensively scrutinized in an effort to shed light on individual and team dynamics.

Social Cognitive Models of Attribution

In addition to the cognitive model of Weiner and its various updates and extensions to sport, three related approaches have received considerable attention: self-efficacy, perceived competence, and the achievement goal approach.

Self-efficacy. A veritable explosion of interest in self-efficacy has taken place in the sport psychology literature of late, with at least thirty papers emerging between 1989 and 1993.

Self-efficacy theory owes its origins to Albert Bandura (1977). This theory purports that performance will be determined jointly by the strength of the person's conviction that he or she has the competency to execute the skills that are demanded by the situation and the responsiveness of the environment. One determinant of responding, which might be called "self-confidence," is *efficacy expectation.* A second variable is known as *outcome expectation.* The differential effects that these two types of expectancy are likely to have on responding is profiled in figure 5.5. The term *efficacy expectancy* refers to the person's belief about his or her own ability. "Can I even do this? Sure, other people are good at this sort of thing, but what am I capable of doing?" Because efficacy expectancies are integrated with the person's perception of self-worth, they often constitute the target for behavioral change in therapy. It really makes little difference that an individual possesses talent if that person is convinced of his or her inability to succeed. Remediation in this case must take the form of enhancing self-esteem and making patients believe they are winners, not losers. Conversely, with outcome expectancy the person's beliefs relate to predictions about the likelihood that rewards will occur, even when efficacious responses are made. In this

Figure 5.4: Revised Causal Dimension Scale (CDSII)

Instructions: Think about the reason or reasons you have written above. The items below concern your impressions or opinions of this cause or causes of your performance. Circle one number for each of the following questions:

Is the cause(s) something:

1. That reflects an aspect of yourself	9 8 7 6 5 4 3 2 1	reflects an aspect of the situation
2. Manageable by you	9 8 7 6 5 4 3 2 1	not manageable by you
3. Permanent	9 8 7 6 5 4 3 2 1	temporary
4. You can regulate	9 8 7 6 5 4 3 2 1	you cannot regulate
5. Over which others have control	9 8 7 6 5 4 3 2 1	over which others have no control
6. Inside of you	9 8 7 6 5 4 3 2 1	outside of you
7. Stable over time	9 8 7 6 5 4 3 2 1	variable over time
8. Under the power of other people	9 8 7 6 5 4 3 2 1	not under the power of other people
9. Something about you	9 8 7 6 5 4 3 2 1	something about others
10. Over which you have power	9 8 7 6 5 4 3 2 1	over which you have no power
11. Unchangeable	9 8 7 6 5 4 3 2 1	changeable
12. Other people can regulate	9 8 7 6 5 4 3 2 1	other people cannot regulate

Note: The total scores for each dimension are obtained by summing the items, as follows:
1, 6, 9 = locus of causality; 5, 8, 12 = external control; 3, 7, 11 = stability; 2, 4, 10 = personal control.
Source: McAuley, Duncan, and Russell (1992).

Figure 5.5: Relations of Efficacy Expectations and Outcome Expectations to the Individual, the Individual's Behavior, and Behavioral Outcomes

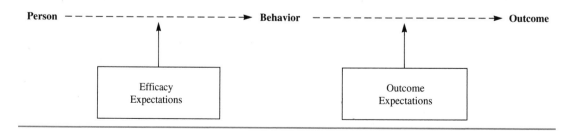

instance, it is not that the individual does not believe in himself or herself; rather, the situation is viewed as harsh and unresponsive: "Why bother with responding if nothing happens?" Obviously, this type of expectancy problem dictates a different intervention approach than that required in the case of efficacy expectation difficulties.

As Feltz (1984) indicates, efficacy expectancies may be of greater importance in the mediation of athletic performances than outcome expectancies. When a player loses confidence, his or her perceptions about the payoff ratio in the environment may be incidental. For example, a golfer may be acutely aware of the need to take the ball from right to left out on the fairway. But questions about his or her ability to accomplish this feat may be intrusive, and may prevent the athlete from executing the swing appropriately. Although a detailed review of the major sources of influence on efficacy expectation is beyond the scope of our coverage, Feltz notes that performance accomplishments (one's own mastery experiences), vicarious experience (information obtained by watching others), verbal persuasion (the opinions of others), and emotional arousal (the person's perception of his or her anxiety status) all contribute to the formation of efficacy expectations.

Much of the experimental literature on self-efficacy has centered on the relation between self-confidence and athletic achievement. Performance in competitive gymnastics, for instance, has been found to vary as a function of one's efficacy expectations (Lee, 1982). In this investigation of fourteen female athletes, individual gymnasts' expectations about how well they thought they could do in competition were determined to be a better predictor of their actual performance than their previous competition scores. Curiously, the athlete's coach made even more accurate predictions about the athlete's ultimate performance score than either the athlete or the past record. This overall pattern was particularly apparent when the participants were more experienced and

of greater natural ability. Similar findings have been reported by Feltz, Landers, and Raeder (1979) in a laboratory study of motor behavior.

In other empirical tests of Bandura's self-efficacy theory, Weinberg, Gould, and Jackson (1979) conducted a study of high or low self-efficacy men and women using a muscular leg-endurance task. A confederate was said to be either a varsity track athlete who exhibited higher performance on a related task (the high self-efficacy condition) or an individual suffering from a knee injury who exhibited lower performance on a related task (the low self-efficacy condition). With the experiment rigged so that subjects lost to the confederates in competitive trials, the findings revealed that subjects in the high self-efficacy manipulation maintained leg extensions for longer periods of time than those in the low self-efficacy manipulation. The results from self-report questionnaires administered after the experiment confirmed that confidence was a major factor in determining individual performance.

More recent experiments relating self-efficacy to performance have been concerned with induction procedures that may change efficacy expectations, thus modulating athletic outcome. Along these lines, Kavanaugh and Hausfeld (1986) have examined the role of mood in optimal sport performance. Elevations in mood may alter what athletes think they can achieve. Accordingly, competitive efficacy should be enhanced when athletes are made happy as compared to cases in which a sad state is induced. Using an audiotape that asked some subjects, but not others, to visualize winning $10,000 from a lottery, performance on handgrip (dynamometer) task was observed to be positively influenced by an elevated mood state. However, the increases in motor performance that paralleled improvements in mood did not appear to be related to changes in efficacy expectations. So, at this point, the proposed mediational link between mood/self-efficacy and athletic performance is uncertain.

Although the relation of self-efficacy to anxiety is often implicitly stated in such basic research projects, serious attempts at documenting the assumed tie between these two phenomena are scant (see Duncan and McAuley, 1987). One report that does pertain directly to this issue comes from a study by Lan and Gill (1984). In this experiment, subjects performed either easy or difficult tasks and cognitive worry, somatic anxiety, self-confidence, and heart rate were measured concurrently. The easy task generated higher self-confidence (self-efficacy) and lower anxiety whereas the opposite pattern was produced by the difficult task. Such findings of an explicit link between anxiety reduction and a self-efficacy intervention forcefully argue for the validity of this cognitive strategy as a treatment device in the sport realm. What is needed, of course, are more systematic field studies in this area.

It has been suggested that self-efficacy theory, for all of its surface appeal, reliably accounts for a modest amount of the variance in athletic achievement (Feltz, 1982; McAuley, 1985; Roberts, 1993). It appears that self-efficacy theory actually fares best in the area of exercise behavior, where it has reliably predicted exercise compliance, exercise adherence, and recovery from cardiac problems (McAuley, 1992). A study by Marcus, Selby, Niaura, and Rossi (1992) is instructive in documenting the exercise/efficacy connection. Marcus and her associates looked at the relationship between stages of fitness and self-efficacy in 1,500 government and hospital employees in Rhode Island. All subjects were placed in one of four categories for analysis purposes: (1) precontemplation (having no interest in exercise and no intent to begin), (2) contemplation (not involved in exercise but thinking about becoming involved), (3) action (participates in occasional exercise), and (4) maintenance (actively participates in regular weekly exercise). A five-item self-efficacy measure was administered to all subjects, and scores on the scale suc-

cessfully differentiated among the employees at most stages. The authors suggest that efficacy-related interventions would be useful at all levels of involvement, but most particularly early in the establishment of exercise behavior.

One interesting contemporary application of self-efficacy theory has to do with collective or team efficacy (Bandura, 1990). As has been noted by Bandura, most self-efficacy research been focused on individual success expectations and little has been done concerning perceived efficacy involving the collective (or team). He feels certain that successful teams are characterized by a strong sense of group efficacy and resiliency, which manifests itself in both times of prosperity and adversity. Conversely, average or inconsistent teams appear to be functioning in an inefficacious fashion, particularly in times of adversity.

Two recent studies, one specifically sport-related, attest to the emerging interest in collective efficacy. In the first instance, Whitney (1994) divided 108 introductory psychology students into thirty-six groups of three each; all were mixed-sex in composition, randomly assigned to one of six experimental treatment conditions, and given a problem-solving task designed to shed light on the interaction of group efficacy, goal setting, and cohesion. Chief among Whitney's results were: (1) groups assigned difficult goals performed better than groups with lower goals, (2) high-efficacy groups outperformed moderate-efficacy groups, and (3) more goal-committed and cohesive groups outperformed less committed and cohesive groups under difficult goal conditions. Whitney concluded that the cognitive and motivational mechanisms by which goals affect performance on a given task may operate similarly for individuals and groups, thereby providing support for the notion of collective efficacy.

In the second study by Hodges and Carron (1992), a muscular endurance task involving 153 male and female high school students was used to test collective efficacy theory. The students were assigned to three-person, mixed-sex groups and assigned to a high- or low-efficacy condition involving bogus feedback on a hand dynamometer task. Irrespective of actual results on the dynamometer task, one group of students was told that its hand strength was greater than it actually was; conversely, the other group was fed bogus information in the opposite direction, thereby setting up the high- and low-efficacy groups. Both groups then participated in a medicine ball task supposedly emphasizing strength (the perception of which had already been manipulated in the dynamometer task). Results of assessing arm strength in both preferred and nonpreferred arms indicated no statistically significant differences in either of the expectancy groups. However, when competing against a confederate supposedly stronger than him or her, subjects in the low-efficacy group consistently handled failure poorly whereas those in the high-efficacy condition responded to failure by improving subsequent performance. These results are seen by Hodges and Carron as demonstrating the transferability of self-efficacy from the individual to the group situation.

Clearly, these two studies are supportive of Bandura's collective efficacy idea, but one was not sport-related and both were essentially laboratory studies. More research in both the laboratory and actual sport settings are needed in the area of collective or team efficacy.

Perceived Competence. A second social cognitive model of attributions is *perceived competence,* which has its roots in the work of Harter (1978; 1980). Harter uses a mastery approach to achievement situations, with much emphasis placed on the role of evaluation on the part of significant others, such as parents, peers, or team leaders. In cases where the evaluation by these significant others is positive, there should be a concomitant increase in feelings of mastery and internal well-being; these positive emotions should

then result in escalations in achievement behavior. In the reverse instance, negative evaluations result in unhealthy attitudes about personal competence or mastery, thus causing anxiety and other mood disturbance accompanied by a concomitant decrease in motivated behavior. A representation of Harter's theory can be seen in figure 5.6.

Most of the sport psychology work with Harter's model has been conducted with children, but little support has been noted. It is likely that children participate in sports for a variety of reasons having little or nothing to do with mastery or competence, as we shall see in chapter 11 when motivation to participate in sports is explored in greater detail. Overall, as Roberts (1993) clearly points out, the applicability of Harter's motivation theory leaves something to be desired in the context of sport.

Achievement Goal Approach. A third and final social cognitive model emphasizes goal achievement, and owes its origins to the work of Dweck (1986) and Maehr and Nicholls (1980). This model examines the interaction between (1) task, learning, and mastery goals; and (2) ego, performance, and ability goals. An understanding of the role of these multiple goals in determining achievement behavior is at the heart of the achievement goal approach. Achievement behavior is viewed as being multidimensionally driven by complex individual goals and interpretations of situations. For example, Roberts (1993) points out that variations in achievement behavior may not be due to high or low motivation; rather they may be reflective of differential perceptions of what is an appropriate goal in any specific situation. To elaborate, Roberts uses the example of children who are motivated to achieve in sports for social approval as opposed to those who strive to excel for mastery or competence reasons. Individual interpretation or perception of goals, then, drives them motivationally.

Goals in this model have been termed the *mastery goal perspective* (task involvement) and the *competitive goal perspective* (ego involvement), according to Roberts. In the first case, the individual engages in motivated behavior for reasons that are largely internal; that is, demonstrating mastery or competence on a task becomes an end in itself. As for the competitive goal perspective, it is more external; that is, the individual demonstrates ability in comparison with others. Perceptions of ability here are other-referenced and depend heavily on social comparisons in the competitive situation. Roberts goes on to say that little is known about the mechanisms that create one orientation versus another, and additional research is called for.

Figure 5.6: **Harter's Theory of Perceived Competence**

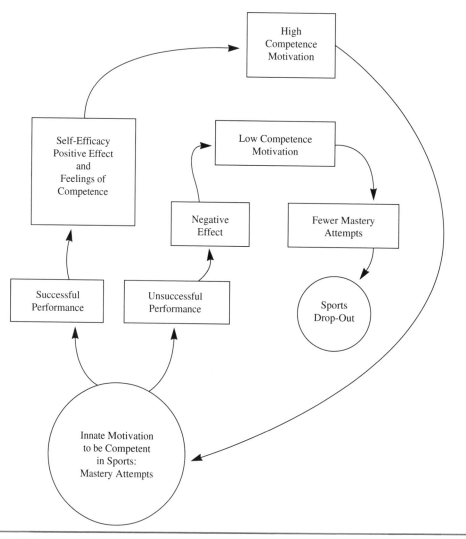

Source: Harter (1978).

Overall, the goal achievement approach to attributions has received good support in the sport psychology literature. Undoubtedly, additional research in this area will be forthcoming over the next several years.

The Functional Model

The functional or motivational model posits that the motivation to maintain or enhance feelings of self-esteem is at the core of attributional

For many athletes defeat or failure is rationalized in such a way as to maintain self-esteem. These Little Leaguers might well offer a variety of explanations as to just how this particular play occurred: one player might credit ability and effort, while another might chalk it up to good luck.

efforts. This is, of course, the *self-serving attributional bias* mentioned earlier, whereby feelings of self-worth are maintained or enhanced through attributing success to internal factors (ability, effort) and failure to external events (task difficulty, luck).

Early studies by Iso-Ahola (1975, 1977) and Roberts (1975) were supportive of the existence of a self-serving attributional bias in Little League baseball players. Essentially all of the preceding three studies indicated that evaluations of self and team are disparate; players from unsuccessful teams tended to be rather critical of team ability and effort but did not view losing as an indictment of their own ability and work output. Conversely, players from successful teams made both self- and team-serving attributions (Bird and Brame, 1978; Roberts, 1975). However, Bird and Brame, in their study of female collegiate basketball players, found consistency between self- and team-serving attributions on effort but not on ability. Winners generally saw the team as possessing more ability than they themselves did individually. In a later study, Bird, Foster, and Maruyama (1980) introduced another variable into the process, namely, team cohesion. Cohesive teams in women's collegiate basketball demonstrated greater agreement on team- and self-attributions than did low cohesive teams. However, there were no differences in either ability or effort attributions between the two groups, though low cohesive teams made greater luck and lesser task attributions for their performance than for that of the team.

Bukowski and Moore (1980), in a disclaimer, found little evidence for the existence of a self-serving bias in their study of seventy-seven Canadian youths attending an overnight camp who participated in a camp "Olympics" made up of a variety of physical activities. Also, luck and task difficulty were not seen as particularly salient by their subjects.

Two days prior to competing in the "Olympics," each contestant was asked to rate how important certain factors would be in terms of succeeding in the upcoming events. Ratings were on a 5-point scale ranging from 1 (important) to 5 (not important). A second rating was made one day after the camp competition was concluded. Results from the two administrations can be seen in table 5.3.

In general, there is agreement between pre- and postcompetition evaluations, though equipment came under careful scrutiny by the competitors in both the attributions for success and failure conditions. Also, the quality of officiating was seen as increasingly critical in the attributes for failure condition.

Overall, trying hard (effort), being good athletes (ability), being interested in competing, and good officiating were seen as very important to success in the post-test condition. On the other hand, having lots of luck (luck) and because the events are easy (task difficulty) were viewed as less important to success.

Another failure to support the existence of the self-serving attributional bias is provided by Mark, Mutrie, Brooks, and Harris (1984). Mark et al. reported results from two studies, one with fifty-nine squash players in a national tournament and the second with twenty-six racquetball players participating in an open tournament in Pennsylvania. In general, winners and losers in both situations did not differ in their attributions on locus of causality dimensions. Winners, as opposed to losers, did make more stable and controllable attributions, however.

An interesting slant on this locus of causality issue has been provided by Biddle (1993). He suggests that statistically significant differences may obscure real differences between winners and losers. Sometimes both winners and losers report internal attributions, but the strength of those reported by winners may simply outstrip those of losers. In short, what we may be seeing

Table 5.3
Mean Ratings of Attributions for Success and Failure

Attributions for Success		Attributions for Failure	
	M		**M**
Trying hard	1.23/1.29	Not trying hard	1.84/1.84
Good officiating	1.61/1.63	Bad officiating	2.07/2.42
Being good athletes	1.61/1.66	Not being interested in competing	2.08/1.98
Being interested in competing	1.67/1.58	Not being interested in winning	2.22/2.07
Being in a good mood	1.80/2.06	Being in a bad mood	2.30/2.55
Having good leaders	1.84/1.91	Having bad leaders	2.32/2.52
Being interested in winning	1.97/2.04	Being poor athletes	2.52/2.27
Having good equipment	2.44/2.76	Having poor equipment	2.77/3.25
Having lots of experience	2.55/2.67	Having no experience	3.30/3.28
Being smart	2.95/2.89	Perceiving the events as hard	3.43/3.27
Perceiving the events as easy	3.68/3.79	Not being smart	3.58/3.29
Having lots of luck	3.66/3.81	Having bad luck	4.00/3.79

The number to the left of the slash is the item's mean rating from the postevents evaluations and the number to the right of the slash is the item's mean rating based on the pre-events evalutions. Sixty-nine subjects provided postevents evaluations, seventy subjects provided pre-events evaluations.

Source: Bukowski and Moore (1980).

What We Know or Think We Know about Sport Attributions and What We Need to Know

Stuart Biddle has written an authoritative review of the literature on attribution theory as it relates to sport. In the process, he has summarized very succinctly some of what we know or think we know about attributions and what we need to know about the area. Students interested in sport attributions should find the section on what we need to know to be particularly informative because it contains suggestions for research that represent the cutting edge of future investigative efforts.

WHAT WE KNOW OR THINK WE KNOW

1. The attribution model developed in educational psychology has provided a useful framework for the study of attributions in sport. However, although the dominant attributions associated with ability, effort, task, and luck have been found in sport, it is thought that sport contexts encourage more diverse attributions to be made than are made in classroom settings. Nevertheless, attributions associated with ability and effort appear to be very important in sport.
2. Winners of sports events tend to make attributions to internal and controllable factors more than losers do.
3. The existence of a self-serving bias has been supported in sport research, although the underlying mechanisms have not been clearly identified.
4. Attributions are more likely to be made when the outcome is unexpected or a goal is not reached.
5. Few gender differences have been found in sport research, often in contradiction to research in other contexts.
6. Age differences are thought to exist in the processing of information concerning attributions, and in particular in the differentiation of ability, effort, and outcome.
7. The achievement goal orientations, identified as "mastery" and "ego" orientations, tend to be associated with attributions to effort and ability, respectively.
8. The stability dimension of attributions is associated with the prediction of expectancy change.
9. Both attribution elements and dimensions are associated with emotional feeling, although the exact nature of these relationships is not known.
10. Perceived (subjective) performance is thought to be a more powerful predictor of emotion in sport than the attributions given for either outcome or performance.

(Continued next page)

Highlight 5.2 (Continued)

What We Know or Think We Know about Sport Attributions and What We Need to Know

11. **Attribution research in sport has adopted a narrow perspective and is in need of research investigating wider issues making use of alternative theories and paradigms.**

WHAT WE NEED TO KNOW

1. **The applicability of alternative theoretical perspectives for sport attribution research.**
2. **The types of attributions used in real sport settings and the difference between attributions for outcome and those for performance.**
3. **The dimensional properties of attributions in sport, without sole reliance on one measuring instrument such as the CDS.**
4. **The role of individual and team attributions within sport team contexts.**
5. **The nature and content of "spontaneous" attributions in sport.**
6. **The nature of actor-observer differences in sport attributions.**
7. **The role of expectancy disconfirmation in sport attributions and emotions.**
8. **The nature of attributional style in sport and the possible consequences of different styles for emotion and behavior.**
9. **Developmental trends of attributions for children playing sport.**
10. **Cultural influences and cross-cultural differences in sport attributions, and the implications for sport behavior.**
11. **The influence of multidimensional self-esteem, and in particular physical self-worth, on sport attributions and behavior.**
12. **The nature, type, and predictability of attribution-emotion relationships in sport.**
13. **The consequences for behavior of links between attributions and emotions.**
14. **The extent to which learned helplessness exists in sport and the role that attributions may play in its development and/or alleviation.**
15. **The utility and effectiveness of attribution retraining techniques in sport.**
16. **The role of attributions in understanding the feelings and behaviors of spectators, officials, and coaches.**
17. **The nature and content of attributional thoughts in health-related exercise contexts.**

Source: Biddle (1993).

is not internal-external differences but differences in degrees of internality.

It would appear that evidence for the existence of a self-serving attributional bias is inconclusive. At a very commonsense level, however, it seems to be a viable concept. In view of the significance of such a bias in terms of its protective role with regard to self-esteem, further research on the issue would seem useful. Mark and his colleagues do suggest that research in the area could profit from more real-life as opposed to contrived, novel test situations in the laboratory; from better measures of attribution, such as Russell's Causal Dimension Scale; and from less emphasis on team as opposed to individual success.

Future Directions

Excellent reviews containing suggestions for future work in the realm of attributions and sport are offered by Brawley and Roberts (1984); Mark, Mutrie, Brooks, and Harris (1984); and Rejeski and Brawley (1983). All parties show common concerns about such research, and their suggestions may be summarized as follows:

1. Let the athlete define the causal attributions, not the experimenter. Seldom has the relevance of subject definition been seen as important (Bukowski and Moore, 1980; Roberts and Pascuzzi, 1979). The biggest step in this direction of subject definition of attributions has been the use of the Causal Dimension Scale mentioned earlier; it clearly lets the subject define the causes of his or her achievement behavior. There appears to be generally universal agreement as to its efficacy in future research.
2. Much emphasis has been placed on winning and losing and they have been equated with success or failure; it is certainly likely that the two pairings are not equivalent. Many an athlete has won and seen his or her performance as a failure, and many losses have been viewed as successes. The win/lose dichotomy is simply too narrow a definition of success or failure.
3. The team versus individual attribution becomes blurred because of team mores, folkways, pressures, and concerns. Attributions for success and failure are complicated greatly by team pressures to present oneself in ways that may or may not represent one's true ascriptions for those matters. The need for further studies of group dynamics on attributional concerns is clearly accentuated here.
4. The role of perceived ability as a moderator of causal ascriptions has been studied fairly thoroughly but has not been exhausted.
5. There seems to be universal agreement that research in the area of youth sport represents a considerable gap in the attributional research. How this deficiency might be rectified in view of the tendency of young people to make few or primitive attributions is quite problematic.
6. The original Weiner model is limited and should be replaced with more updated models emphasizing elements far more broad than ability, effort, task difficulty, and luck.
7. Too heavy a reliance has been placed in past attributional research on the use of college students, and team sports have been studied far more often than have individual sports. More research with individual athletes is called for.

NEED FOR ACHIEVEMENT

Closely related to our discussion of attribution theory is the concept of need for achievement, often expressed as *n ach*.

Murray's Contribution

Inquiry into the need to achieve is generally thought to have begun in the late 1930s with the work of the accomplished Harvard personality theorist Henry Murray. It was Murray's position that people differ in their need "to overcome obstacles, to exercise power, to strive to do something difficult as well and as quickly as possible" (Murray, 1938, pp. 80–81). He called this striving the need for achievement. Murray devised the very popular projective test of personality, the *Thematic Apperception Test (TAT)*, as a means of measuring variations in human motivation. The TAT, over the years, has become one of the most popular projective tests available to psychologists and psychiatrists working in clinical settings. The TAT is made up of twenty stimulus cards into which subjects are asked to project hidden personality themes or dimensions through fantasy stories. These fantasy stories are, in turn, analyzed by specialists in thematic analysis who categorize the various response themes. The TAT has undergone revision over the years and is still used in clinical work and research studies, though its use in the latter has been sparse to nonexistent in sport psychology.

The McClelland-Atkinson Model

Murray's pioneering efforts were further advanced through the efforts of David McClelland and associates in the early 1950s (McClelland, Atkinson, Clark, and Lowell, 1953). McClelland and his associates revised and added considerable sophistication to the scoring procedure of the TAT, and they have greatly extended Murray's original premises. Though they have engaged in several collaborative efforts, much of the work of McClelland and Atkinson has proceeded independent of one another. The net effect of their independent efforts, however, has led Cox (1985) and others to refer to their work as the *McClelland-Atkinson model*.

Basically, the McClelland-Atkinson model takes the position that motivation to achieve is a function of the relative strengths of the motive or tendency to approach success and the motive or tendency to avoid failure. Atkinson (1957) calls these simply hope of success and fear of failure. In any event, goal-directed or achievement behavior is mediated by the joint action of the two motives regardless of the terminology used. Atkinson proposes that quantification can be brought to bear on the issue, and suggests that three factors *must* be considered in making the determination of hope of success. These three determinants are as follows:

1. Motivation to achieve success $= M_s$
2. Perceived probability of success $= P_s$
3. Incentive value of success $(1 - P_s) = In_s$

With the tendency to achieve or hope of success expressed as T_s, the following formula emerges:

$$T_s = M_s \times P_s \times In_s$$

With regard to fear of failure, again three forces are at work:

1. Motive to avoid failure $= M_f$
2. Probability of failure $(1 - P_s) = P_f$
3. Negative incentive value of failure $= In_f$

Again, a formula emerges to help quantify fear of failure where this tendency is expressed as T_f:

$$T_f = M_f \times P_f \times In_f$$

In turn, Atkinson indicates that these two motives, hope of success and fear of failure, are additive, resulting in a formula for total motivation as follows:

$$T_s + T_f = (M_s \times P_s \times In_s) + (M_f \times P_f \times In_f)$$

This total score, which is called resultant achievement motivation (RAM), allows for prediction of individual motivation in a variety of settings, not the least of which is sport.

A view of how the mathematics of the formula work is provided in table 5.4, which calculates the tendency to succeed and the tendency to avoid failure under varying conditions of task difficulty. Several noteworthy points emerge from a thorough reading of table 5.4. Most salient among them are:

1. Maximum motivation occurs when task difficulty is .5 for conditions in which motivation to succeed surpasses fear of failure, even though success and failure are equally likely. Athletic teams made up of highly talented players with a high need for achievement thrive on competition with the better teams. Conversely, there is little to excite them when playing weaker teams; weak task difficulty demands simply do not inspire achievement motivation.

2. In conditions where the tendency to avoid failure (M_f) is greater than the tendency to succeed (M_s), maximum motivation will occur at either the .1 or .9 difficulty level. Accordingly, athletes at each point would select to play either under conditions in which success is a virtual guarantee or, paradoxically, under conditions where failure is likely. In the latter case, because task difficulty is so high, no loss of face or stature is associated with defeat. If you are a duffer on the golf course, losing to the city or course champion in a head-to-head confrontation is not likely to be deflating.

Intrinsic versus Extrinsic Motivation

An important addition to this model was made by Atkinson (1974) when he incorporated

Table 5.4

Calculations of T_s and T_{-f} for Five Levels of Task Difficulty When $M_s > M_F$, When $M_F > M_s$, and When $M_s = M_F$

	Task (P_s)	($M_s \times P_s \times In_s$)	+	($M_F \times P_f \times In_f$)	=	$T_s + T_{-f}$
$M_s > M_F$ where $M_s = 5$ and $M_F = 1$	A (.9)	(5 × .9 × .1)	+	(1 × .1 × −.9)	=	.36
	B (.7)	(5 × .7 × .3)	+	(1 × .3 × −.7)	=	.84
	C (.5)	(5 × .5 × .5)	+	(1 × .5 × −.5)	=	1.00
	D (.3)	(5 × .3 × .7)	+	(1 × .7 × −.3)	=	.84
	E (.1)	(5 × .1 × .9)	+	(1 × .9 × −.1)	=	.36
$M_F > M_s$, where $M_F = 3$ and $M_s = 1$	A (.9)	(1 × .9 × .1)	+	(3 × .1 × −.9)	=	−.18
	B (.7)	(1 × .7 × .3)	+	(3 × .3 × −.7)	=	−.42
	C (.5)	(1 × .5 × .5)	+	(3 × .5 × −.5)	=	−.50
	D (.3)	(1 × .3 × .7)	+	(3 × .7 × −.3)	=	−.42
	E (.1)	(1 × .1 × .9)	+	(3 × .9 × −.1)	=	−.18
$M_s = M_F$, where $M_s = 5$ and $M_F = 5$	A (.9)	(5 × .9 × .1)	+	(5 × .1 × −.9)	=	0
	B (.7)	(5 × .7 × .3)	+	(5 × .3 × −.7)	=	0
	C (.5)	(5 × .5 × .5)	+	(5 × .5 × −.5)	=	0
	D (.3)	(5 × .3 × .7)	+	(5 × .7 × −.3)	=	0
	E (.1)	(5 × .1 × .9)	+	(5 × .9 × −.1)	=	0

Source: Atkinson (1957).

Winning or losing is simply too narrow a definition of success or failure. These track team members, for example, may feel a large measure of success for having performed their best.

the notion of *extrinsic motivation* (M_{ext}) to the motivational prediction formula. Money, verbal praise, pats on the back, medals, trophies, and other awards all constitute sources of extrinsic motivation, and their relevance to performance has not gone unnoticed.

Deci (1975) has suggested that the interplay of intrinsic and extrinsic motivation can be explained through his *cognitive evaluation theory.* Essentially Deci states that intrinsic motivation is a function of the degree of competency, self-determination, and feelings of self-worth that are created by sport competition. In turn, these intrinsic qualities are lessened or greatened by two external reward characteristics: control and information. In the control aspect, we are essentially dealing with a locus of causality artifact; that is, the extent to which the sport participant views his or her rewards as residing internally greatly determines how much an activity is enjoyed. Briefly stated, when a player perceives that a sport is no longer played for the intrinsic enjoyment but rather for a trophy or medal, intrinsic motivation may decrease. How often have the fans and the sports writers decried the performance decrement in the first year after a professional athlete has signed a secure and financially lucrative contract? Though these decrements may vary from performer to performer, they do serve notice that internal motivation can decrease when external rewards become more salient.

Insofar as the informational aspect is concerned, participation that increases feelings of self-worth and self-determination due to the message it transmits to the player is seen as facilitating intrinsic motivation. When these coveted qualities are not created, external rewards decrease intrinsic motivation. A player who is voted Most Valuable Player (MVP) on his team is being afforded information as to his worth and competence; this should lead to considerable intrinsic motivation. On the other hand, a player who wins a trophy as part of a championship team to which he or she frankly contributed little is getting a very different message about worth and competence. Further athletic participation, for this competitor, may greatly be a function of the extrinsic reward associated with the activity.

The controlling and informational aspects of rewards are not mutually exclusive; they do interact to effect intrinsic motivation. For example, the high school athlete who is playing football because it is expected by his father and because of expectancies created by the prevailing football climate but who is also doing well at the task may feel that he is getting positive information about himself though he is primarily playing to please others; it might be expected that his intrinsic motivation would be lessened, thereby giving increased importance to external results.

To put the issue of intrinsic and extrinsic motivation in a succinct manner, Weinberg (1984, p. 182) says: "If the controlling aspect is more salient, rewards will decrease intrinsic motivation whereas if the informational aspect is the more salient aspect and provides positive information about one's competence, rewards can enhance intrinsic motivation."

Two additional concepts that add to our understanding of internal and external motivation are the *overjustification hypothesis* (Lepper, Greene, and Nisbett, 1973) and the *discounting principle* (Kelley, 1972). The following example illustrates the overjustification hypothesis: Jane, a twelve-year-old girl, plays slowpitch softball because, in her words, "It's fun." At the same time, overzealous parents decide that the season would be more successful for everyone if trophies were made available to all players. According to the overjustification hypothesis, Jane is already playing the game because it is enjoyable, and playing for a trophy may actually decrease her enjoyment and intrinsic motivation to compete.

At the same time, the enjoyment of the game for its own sake has been stripped away or discounted, at which point the discounting principle becomes operational in lowering intrinsic motivation. The trophy, rather than the game, becomes the goal of participating in softball. Parents, coaches, and youth league administrators need to be alert to this caveat about external rewards for activities that might well survive as a function of their own internally reinforcing properties. At the minimum, a balanced perspective with regard to the use of external incentives to compete needs to be maintained.

Enjoying sport and physical activity for internal reasons is preferable to liking them for external ones. This is not to denigrate or downplay the role of external rewards; they are real, sometimes very powerful, and likely to be with us as sport motivators for quite some time. Weinberg (1984) offers five ways to enhance intrinsic motivation:

1. Coaches and others involved in physical activity should structure their activities in ways that guarantee a certain amount of success. People are not successful in everything they do every time they do it, and such should and will not be the case in sport. But some success should be assured. Weinberg cites the example of the 10-foot-high basket for youth basketball players. In the case of very young novices, few successes can be achieved with the 10-foot goal; on the other hand, lowering the goal a few feet creates a situation that is conducive to success.

2. Athletes should be allowed more of a role in goal setting and decision making. This granting of responsibility coincides with the locus of causality concern of Deci (1975); athletes who are a part of the decision-making process should feel more in control, which should, in turn, be conducive to the development and maintenance of intrinsic motivation. Using the input of older, more experienced players to guide the development of younger teammates would be an example in which this principle is applicable.

3. Praise is a facilitator of intrinsic motivation. Players whose role is of lesser influence are just as much in need of praise as are the team stars. Role players or substitutes need to feel that they also contribute to overall team goals. Your senior author can recall a high school experience in which this principle was brutalized. A third-team linebacker

named Hall who never played in any of the games made a bone-jarring tackle in a mid-week scrimmage. Excitedly, Hall awaited the expected praise. Once the pile was sorted out and the coach could determine the involved parties, his response was "Oh, hell, it was only Hall!" This, of course, was devastating to the player and was a source of considerable bitterness some six years later when Hall graduated from college. *All* players need periodic reinforcement for desirable behavior!

4. Realistic goals feed the players' feelings of competence, which is translated into intrinsic motivation. Despite what many would mistakenly have us believe, winning is not everything. Playing well, improving on previous skill levels, and further social development are desirable goals and need to be stressed. Everyone cannot win; there will be losers on the scoreboard. But these win/loss statistics are far from the only standards with which to measure success.

5. Variation in content and sequence of practice drills helps generate intrinsic motivation. Boredom is one enemy of sport participation; when it is no fun, people drop out or stay on only for extrinsic rewards. Practices do not need to be repetitious nor do they have to be exercises in stamina or drudgery. The mark of a good practice is not measured by the amount of time, repetition, or drudgery involved. At the extreme, some practices do not even have to be practices.

One highly successful high school football coach in the Gulf Coast region of Texas has been known to take his team fishing once or twice a year in lieu of the usual activities. Everyone fishes, food is cooked on the beach, a spirit of camaraderie is generated, and boredom and drudgery are avoided.

Clearly, a number of ways exist to create, maintain, and even enhance extrinsic motivation. A little creativity coupled with a lot of knowledge of human motivation can be a significant force in creating a positive atmosphere for competition at all levels.

LOCUS OF CONTROL

Closely intertwined with attribution theory and need for achievement is the concept of *locus of control*. Rotter (1966), a social learning theorist with a cognitive bent, gave initial impetus to the notion that has spawned so much research. For example, Throop and MacDonald (1971) put together a bibliography of locus of control research that contained 339 studies for the period 1966 to 1969 alone. Rotter (1975) cited more than six hundred I-E studies prior to 1975. To Rotter, locus of control was conceived as a generalized expectancy to perceive reinforcement as contingent upon one's behavior (internal) or as the result of forces outside one's control and related to luck, chance, fate, or powerful others (external).

The I-E Scale

In order to measure the various dimensions of locus of control, Rotter (1966) developed the *I-E Scale*. The scale itself is made up of twenty-nine items, six of which are used as fillers. Subjects are asked to respond to each of the twenty-nine items by choosing between two alternative statements. Scores range from 0 to 23, with higher scores denoting externality. *Sample items from the Rotter scale are represented below:*

> a. In the case of the well prepared student there is rarely if ever such a thing as an unfair test.
> b. Many times exam questions tend to be so unrelated to course work, that studying is useless.
>
> a. There is too much emphasis on athletics in high school.
> b. Team sports are an excellent way to build character.

The I-E Scale has not gone unnoticed by sport researchers, though findings have been somewhat equivocal.

Perhaps the first locus of control study utilizing the I-E Scale in sport was conducted by Lynn, Phelan, and Kiker (1969). Lynn et al. administered the I-E scale to thirty basketball players (group sport), thirty gymnasts (individual sport), and thirty nonparticipants in sport; all were twelve to fifteen years of age and matched for intelligence. Group sport participants were significantly more internal than were members of the other two groups. Finn and Straub (1977) used the I-E Scale in a study of highly skilled female softball players from the Netherlands (N = 35) and the United States (N = 44). Statistically significant differences (.01) were noted, with the Dutch players being more external than their American counterparts. Further analyses also showed that American pitchers and catchers were significantly more internal than the Dutch battery-mates as well as groups of Dutch infielders and outfielders. Correlational analyses of the relationship of locus of control to height, weight, years of playing experience, playing position, and position in batting order failed to produce significant differences. As a caveat, Finn and Straub point to potential problems related to translating the I-E Scale to the Dutch language. Hall, Church, and Stone (1980) used the Rotter scale with twenty nationally ranked weight lifters. Firstborn lifters were more external than later borns, but all were basically internal when compared to overall norms reported by Rotter.

Other studies involving the I-E Scale have been conducted by Hall (1980) and Scheer and Ansorge (1979). Hall administered the locus of control measure and the Spielberger State-Trait Anxiety Inventory (STAI) to three hundred subjects at the University of Virginia. Two groups of thirty-two subjects were then selected to take part in a motor task based on whether or not they were internal (scores of 0 to 6) or external (scores of 16 to 23). Subsequent analyses re-

vealed, among other things, that externals were significantly higher than internals on trait anxiety. Laboratory manipulations of success and failure revealed that internals made more internal attributions for failure; this finding, of course, is consistent with much of the attributional locus of control literature.

In the Scheer and Ansorge study, ten national- or regional-level female gymnastic judges served as subjects. Based on I-E Scale results, five were designated as internals (M = 5.8) and five as externals (M = 15.4). They were then asked to evaluate videotapes of the 1977 Region VI AIAW Gymnastics Championships in four Olympic events. In all, forty gymnasts were rated by the ten judges. Data analysis revealed that external judges were more susceptible to their own preconceived expectancies for athletic performance than were internal evaluators. Based on their findings, Scheer and Ansorge suggest that the I-E Scale might eventually become a part of the process for selecting the most qualified officials for championship athletic events.

On the other side of the coin, at least four studies have failed to support the validity of the I-E Scale. Celestino, Tapp, and Brumet (1979) found no differences between seventy-four finishers and twenty-three nonfinishers in male marathoners in New York. They did find, however, a small (.28) but significant correlation between internality and order of finish. Di Giuseppe (1973) divided 167 high school freshmen into four groups: team sports, individual sports, intramural sports, and no athletic involvement. No significant differences were noted among the four groups. Gilliland (1974) divided ninety San Jose State University males and females into five groups related to sports involvement. Again, various analyses by sex and by athletic activity or nonactivity revealed no differences in locus of control. Finally, McKelvie and Huband (1980) studied various college-athletes (N = 92) and nonathletes (N = 93) and concluded that no systematic relationship exists between athletic participation and locus of control.

Despite the preceding disclaimers, it would appear that Rotter's I-E Scale remains a useful instrument for future investigations of the locus of control concept.

Levenson's Multidimensional Approach

A more recent and increasingly popular measure of locus of control has been provided by Levenson (1973). Reacting to both personal considerations (Levenson, 1981) and a body of growing research indicating that these were problems associated with Rotter's original conceptualization (e.g., Collins, 1974; Gurin, Gurin, Lao, and Beattie, 1969; and Mirels, 1970), Levenson arrived at a multidimensional locus of control measure that tapped into *internality* and two dimensions of externality, *powerful others* and *chance*. Her feeling was that Rotter's notion of externality was greatly confounded by the fact that one could be external on the I-E Scale and yet arrive at that point through greatly different avenues; that is, the individual who views external causation as a function of chance or luck events may be very different from one who perceives causality as a function of powerful others in the environment. Hence, the creation of what we shall call hereafter the *IPC Scale*.

The refined IPC Scale is made up of twenty-four items, eight of which load respectively on the Internal, Powerful Others, and Chance dimensions. Responses are made based on a 7-point Likert scaling procedure with scores on all three dimensions ranging from 0 to 48. Representative items for each of the dimensions include:

1. *Internal.* "When I make plans, I am almost certain to have them work."
2. *Powerful Others.* "In order to have my plans work I make sure that they fit in with the desires of people who have power over me."

3. *Chance.* "It's not wise for me to plan too far ahead because many things turn out to be a matter of good or bad luck."

According to Levenson (1981, p. 18) the IPC Scale was designed to differ from Rotter's I-E scale in five important ways:

1. The items are presented as a Likert scale instead of in a forced-choice format, so that the three dimensions are more statistically independent of one another than are the two dimensions of Rotter's scale.
2. The I, P, and C subscales make a personal-ideological distinction. All statements are phrased so as to pertain only to the person answering. The subscales measure the degree to which an individual feels he or she has control over what happens, not what the person feels is the case for "people in general."
3. The items in the scales contain no wording that might imply modifiability of the specific issues. The factors of personal versus ideological control and system modifiability were found by Gurin et al. (1969) to be contaminating factors in Rotters' I-E Scale.
4. The I, P, and C scales are constructed in such a way that there is a high degree of parallelism in every three-item set.
5. Correlations between items on the new scales and the Marlowe-Crowne Desirability Scale are negligible and nonsignificant.

Levenson (1981, p. 18) further offers the following interpretive caution:

A word of caution about interpretation is necessary. High scores on each subscale are interpreted as indicating high expectations of control by the source designated. Low scores reflect tendencies not to believe in that locus of control. We cannot interpret a low I Scale score as indicating that a subject believes in chance; we can say only that this subject does not perceive him or herself as determining outcomes. Empirically, one could score high or low on all three scales; that is, a person could say he or she was personally in control yet also say that life is a random series of events controlled by powerful others. Rarely has such a profile been obtained. Before one could interpret such a seemingly inconsistent profile one would have to give serious consideration to the presence of confounding factors (e.g., acquiescence response set or random responding).

Perhaps the first sport studies using the IPC Scale were made by LeUnes, Nation, and Daiss (Daiss, LeUnes, and Nation, 1986; LeUnes and Nation, 1982; Nation and LeUnes, 1983a, 1983b). Summing across these four studies of 108 major university football players and two groups of college students not playing football, the following results were reported:

1. In comparing the traveling squad of this football team (N = 60) with an equal number of college students who had lettered in football in high school but were not playing collegiate football and yet another equal group of college students who had never won an athletic letter ("nonathletes"), the college football players scored significantly higher on the powerful others dimension (.05) than did their two peer groups. This powerful others finding suggests that coaches undoubtedly play a significant role in the lives of collegiate players; their athletic careers literally are in the hands of these "powerful others" coaches.
2. In looking at differences across playing positions, no significant findings were noted.
3. In terms of black/white differences, two findings of statistical significance (.05) were isolated. Black defensive linemen were more internal than white offensive linemen and, more significantly, black players overall were

more chance-oriented than white players. Given the state of racial affairs that currently exists in the United States and given the history of blacks overall, this finding comes as no great surprise.

4. In a five-year follow-up of the thirty-four out of 108 who were freshmen in 1980 when the original data were collected, sixteen had stayed with the football program for either four or five years and eighteen had departed. The chance score of the "stayers" was 19.39 while "leavers" scored 11.65, a difference that is significant at the .001 level. Before they ever played a down of football, players who ultimately stayed appeared to have an early realization of the vagaries of a college football career. Apparently, they were aware of the role of chance factors (coaching decisions, academic difficulties, bad luck in the form of injury, and other unpredictables) in determining their ultimate success.

The most recent utilization of the IPC in sport-related research was reported by Van Raalte, Brewer, Nemeroff, and Linder (1991). Van Raalte et al. were interested in the relationship between Levenson's chance scale and the development of sport-related superstitious behavior. They hypothesized that there would be a significant negative correlation between IPC chance scores and the development of superstitious behavior associated with a putting task. Subjects were introductory psychology students with little or no golfing background. These subjects were chosen so as to control for already developed superstitions so common among experienced golfers (and other athletes). Subjects completed a putting task using golf balls of four different colors, and superstitious behavior was defined as using the same colored ball immediately after a successful putt (i.e., the "lucky ball"). Subjects scoring low on chance orientation chose the lucky ball significantly more often for ensuing putts than did high scorers, thus confirming the original hypothesis. The authors concluded that low-chance subjects believed they could take control of events by use of the so-called "lucky ball."

Despite early promise, research on the IPC scale seems to be in decline, hopefully a temporary state. Levenson's scale has been shown to be psychometrically sound (Blau, 1984; Levenson, 1974), and the locus of control construct itself merits additional exploration in sport psychology.

Locus of Control Measurement with Youth

Nowicki and Strickland (1973) have created a scale for measuring locus of control in children and, though their work has been applied rather widely with children in general, its use in youth sport has been sparse. Anshel (1979), Lufi, Porat, and Tenenbaum (1986), and Morris, Vaccaro, and Clarke (1979) represent three such studies. Anshel used the forty-item Nowicki-Strickland Scale with fifty-seven fifth graders and eighty eighth-grade students in Florida. Based on locus of control scores, thirty-two subjects were assigned by age and internality-externality scores to one of four groups of sixteen each. All subjects took part in a pursuit rotor task in which success and failure conditions were randomly determined. Overall, older subjects, as expected, were superior to the younger ones on the motor task. Also, older subjects were more internal than their younger peers. Thirdly, high internals in both age groups performed better than high externals under positive as opposed to negative feedback conditions; however, negative feedback adversely affected the motor performance of high internals but facilitated that of high externals. In general, Anshel's work supported previous locus control work with youth in other settings of a nonsport nature.

In the Lufi et al. study, fifty-six males ages seven to eleven were selected for a one-year study

of psychological variables and gymnastic potential. Based on results of a battery of tests of physical skills, the boys were divided into two groups of twenty-eight each, one considered high in potential, the other average. After a month of training, a battery of psychological tests, including the Nowicki-Strickland, were administered; briefly put, the high potential boys were significantly more internal than the average ones. The authors suggest that coaches would be well-advised to take into account psychological variables, such as direction of locus of control, in talent identification and selection.

As for Morris et al., they administered the Nowicki-Strickland Scale to twenty competitive swimmers (seven to seventeen years of age). When their scores were compared with norms published for similar aged youth by Nowicki and Strickland (1973), the swimmers were significantly more internal than their nonathletic age mates.

As is the case with the IPC Scale, little of late has been done with the Nowicki-Strickland Scale and with young athletes' attributions in general. More work needs to be done to get a more learned perspective on attribution and locus of control in young athletes.

Current Status of the Locus of Control Construct

As has been noted over the past several pages, there was a burst of activity in the early 1970s to the mid-1980s in sport psychology concerning the locus of control construct. Since then, there has been a mere trickle of activity. Part of the problem may center around questions of interpretation. What does being a high internal or a low chance athlete tell us with regard to adjustment or sport performance? There is some intimation in the literature that being a high internal is the most desired state (i.e., Chalip, 1980; Rotter, 1971). At the same time, there are legitimate instances in which a powerful others orientation is adaptive. It is our suspicion, for example, that an athlete playing basketball for Bobby Knight at Indiana or one who may have played for Paul "Bear" Bryant at Texas A&M or Alabama in his heyday would be best served by a powerful others orientation. Both coaches appear to have used a "my way or the highway" approach to player selection and retention. It is even conceivable that a high-chance orientation is essential to performance excellence, as was noted earlier in the LeUnes and Nation football research. Much remains to be done in determining the best locus of control for sport performance, if such a thing exists at all.

Another obstacle to locus of control research, according to Lefcourt (1992), is that it has been assimilated into the burgeoning literature of related constructs. We have discussed some of these earlier, such as Bandura's self-efficacy, Weiner's causal attribution, and Harter's perceived competence. Other "cousins" to locus of control include perceived control (Langer, 1983), personal causation (deCharms, 1968), and explanatory style (Seligman, 1975). Like locus of control theory, these theories deal with aspects of perceived causality and control. Lefcourt goes on to point out that each of these authors insist on the unique properties of their respective theories, but the overlap is obvious. The end result, says Lefcourt, is "convergent findings obtained with widely divergent methodologies" (p. 413).

It is our suspicion that locus of control theory and research will continue to be important, but will grow at a slower rate than before. The fact that there are eighteen different locus of control scales available (Lefcourt, 1992) and that foreign versions have appeared in places like Argentina (deMinzi, 1991) and Holland (Finn and Straub, 1977) attests to the robustness of the concept and its assessment.

SELF THEORY

After a while you learn the subtle difference between holding a hand and chaining a soul,

And you learn that love doesn't mean leaning and company doesn't mean security,

And you begin to learn that kisses aren't contracts and presents aren't promises,

And you begin to accept your defeats with your head up and your eyes open, with the grace of an adult, not the grief of a child,

And you learn to build all your roads on today because tomorrow's ground is too uncertain for plans.

After a while you learn that even sunshine burns if you get too much.

So plant your own garden and decorate your own soul, instead of waiting for someone to bring you flowers.

And you learn that you really can endure . . . that you really are strong,

And you really do have worth.

—Anonymous

Yet another moderator of attribution, achievement, and locus of control is *self theory*. The self, like each of the preceding terms, is a hypothetical construct used to describe a personality variable. We cannot see the self any more than we can view an electrical current, but we can infer it based on behavioral predispositions and occurrences in the same way that electricity can be defined by its effects. A historical review of self theory would set the stage for an appropriate discussion of the topic.

According to Hamachek (1987), the first awakening of interest in *self theory* can be traced to the works of the French mathematician and philosopher, Rene Descartes. Descartes' notions, in turn, were scrutinized by the likes of Leibnitz, Locke, Hume, and Berkeley. With the turn of the twentieth century, interest in the self was primarily vested in the works of William James, who gives us a flavor of his feelings about the self with the following passage:

I am not often confronted by the necessity of standing by one of my empirical selves and relinquishing the rest. Not that I would not, if I could, be both handsome and fat and well-dressed, and a great athlete, and make a million a year, be a wit, a bon-vivant, and lady-killer, as well as a philosopher, a philanthropist, statesman, warrior, and African explorer, as well as a "tone-poet" and saint. But the thing is simply impossible. The millionaire's work would run counter to the saint's; the bon-vivant and the philanthropist would trip each other up; the philosopher and lady-killer could not keep house in the same tenement of clay . . . to make any one of them actual, the rest must more or less be suppressed. . . . So the seeker of his truest, strongest, deepest self must review the list carefully, and pick out the one on which to stake his salvation. All other selves thereupon become unreal, but the fortunes of this self are real. Its failures are real failures, its triumphs real triumphs, carrying shame and gladness with them. . . .

I, who for the time have staked my all on being a psychologist, am mortified if others know more psychology than I. But I am contented to wallow in the grossest ignorance of Greek. My deficiencies there give me no sense of personal humiliation at all. (1890, p. 91)

With the advent of the behavioral movement in the late 1800s and the early 1900s, it became unfashionable or unscientific to spend one's time studying what might be viewed as mystical imponderables, so self theory became temporarily passé. However, much has been made of the conception in the past forty years. Gordon Allport, one of those most instrumental in furthering the revival, summarized the revolution as follows:

In very recent years the tide has turned. Perhaps without being fully aware of the historical situation, many psychologists have commenced to embrace what two decades ago would have been considered a heresy. They have re-introduced self and ego unashamedly and, as if to make up for lost

time, have employed ancillary concepts such as self-image, striving, and many other hyphenated elaborations which to experimental positivism still have a slight flavor of scientific obscenity. (1955, pp. 104–105)

Since that time, self theory has been greatly promoted by the noted works of Maslow (1954) and Rogers (1961).

As is evidenced from the last sentence in the quote from Allport, many terms have been used to describe essentially the same thing. In an effort to clarify the issue, we shall discuss, in turn, definitions of the self, self-concept, and self-esteem.

The Self

Jersild (1952) tells us that a person's *self* "is the sum of all he can call his. The self includes, among other things, a system of ideas, attitudes, values, and commitments. The self is a person's total subjective environment; it is the distinctive center of experience and significance. The self constitutes a person's inner world as distinguished from the other world consisting of all other people and things." Calhoun and Acocella (1983, p. 38) define the self accordingly: "The *self* may be defined as a hypothetical construct referring to the complex set of physical processes of the individual." These authors go on to describe five aspects of the self:

1. The physical self: the body and its biological processes
2. The self-as-process: the perception, response, problem-solving, and action component of the self
3. The social self: people and roles (father, student, Republican, industrious worker, leader, wife, and so on)
4. The self-concept: what Calhoun and Acocella call the "mental self-portrait"
5. The self-ideal: what the person could be if all barriers were down

It is clear from the preceding that the self-structure is multidimensional.

The Self-Concept

Martens (1975) tells us that the *self-concept* (the "mental self-portrait" of Calhoun and Acocella) has three important components: cognitive, affective, and behavioral. The *cognitive component* refers to self-descriptive terms that we apply to ourselves, words such as bright, attractive, slow, athletic, and so forth. The *affective component* in the formula refers to how we feel about the totality of cognitive ascriptions we have made about ourselves, and it is often referred to as self-esteem. The *behavioral aspect* refers to our tendencies to behave in ways consistent with the other aspects of the self. The

Regular workouts, such as this step-aerobics class, may give the participants healthier self-concepts than those of people who work out little or not at all.

behavioral component was expressed by Jourard (1974, p. 153) when he defined the self-concept as a self-fulfilling prophecy:

> When a person forms a self-concept, thereby defining himself, he is not so much describing his nature as he is making a pledge that he will continue to be the kind of person he believes he is now and has been. One's self-concept is not so much descriptive of experience and action as it is prescriptive. The self-concept is a commitment.

From the perspective of the behaviorist, positive experiences lead to enhanced feelings of worth that lead to positive experiences that lead to enhanced feelings of worth, and so on. Unfortunately, the same is not true if the word "negative" is inserted for "positive" in the formulation. Coaches, particularly but not exclusively in youth sports, should take heed of the implied admonition!

Some mention of one other perspective of self-concept is warranted. Calhoun and Acocella (1983) tell us that the self-concept is made up of knowledge, expectations, and evaluative dimensions. The knowledge dimension translates to what we think we know about ourselves. Expectations are what we aspire to or could be. The evaluative dimension measures what we are (knowledge) against what we could be (expectations) and manifests itself as "what-I-should-be." This determination to be, Calhoun and Acocella call self-esteem.

Self-Esteem

Derlega and Janda (1981) tell us that *self-esteem* is a more specialized concept than self-concept but admit that distinctions are of the hairsplitting variety; Calhoun and Acocella (1983) view self-esteem as the measurement of what we are against what we could and should be; Martens (1975) sees it as an affective evaluation of self; Hamachek (1987) appears to largely agree with Martens. Thus, subtle evaluative distinctions can be made between self-concept and self-esteem, but as Derlega and Janda (1981) point out, terms such as "good self-concept," "favorable self-image," "high self-concept," and "high self-esteem" have much in common in that they all refer to positive self-evaluations. The literature in sport psychology, sparse as it may be, seems to indicate that there is little quarreling with the Derlega and Janda position.

Self-Actualization

Related to our discussion is the *self-actualization motive* of Maslow. It seems only natural that sport and physical activity would be an important part of what Maslow considers self-actualization: "man's desire for self-fulfillment, namely, to the tendency for him to become actualized in what he is potentially" (1970, p. 46). Carrying this definition a step beyond, Maslow (cited in Gundersheim, 1982, p. 187) says:

> We may define it as an episode or a spurt in which the powers of the person come together in a particularly efficient and intensely enjoyable way, and in which he is more integrated and less split, more open for experience, more idiosyncratic, more perfectly expressive or spontaneous, or fully functioning, more creative, more humorous, more ego-transcending, more independent of his lower needs, etc. He becomes in these episodes more truly himself, more perfectly actualizing his potentialities, closer to the core of his Being, more fully human.

Certainly, these self-actualizing feelings and notions have been attributed to sport by players, coaches, and spectators. And it would seem that sport would be a perfect forum for the manifestation of self-actualizing behavior. The available research, however, has shown little relationship between actualization and sport. Gundersheim (1982), in the introduction to a research report,

cited eight references prior to 1980, none of which found any relationship between the two variables. Gundersheim goes on to report on a study he did with 339 male and female university athletes and nonathletes. Numerous cross-sport, cross-sex and sport and nonsport comparisons were made based on results from the *Personal Orientation Inventory (POI)* (Shostrom, 1963), a noted measure of self-actualization. The only significant difference found was between male and female athletes; the females were more actualized. Ibrahim and Morrison (1976), using the POI, found a tendency for male and female high school and college athletes to be average or above on self-actualization. Interestingly, and symptomatic of the confused self-concept literature in sport psychology, the athletes they studied scored significantly lower than their nonathletic peers on eight of the fifteen dimensions of the Tennessee Self-Concept Scale.

Research on Self Theory in Sport Psychology

Sport psychologists have shown little interest in the relationship between the two variables of self and sport and physical activity. A notable exception is found in the self-serving attributional bias in which defeat or failure is rationalized in such a way as to maintain self-esteem.

Early research in self-concept and self-esteem centered around the relationship of esteem and physical appearance or concerned itself with the relationship between physical activity and attitudes about the self (e.g., Hellison, 1970; Ludwig and Maehr, 1967; Read, 1969; Zion, 1965). In general, these various investigations found that physical activity has a facilitative effect on self-esteem, particularly when positive experiences are provided. These generalizations are particularly true for youth sport, which we shall take up in greater detail later.

One of the more consistent efforts in this area has been that of Tucker (1981, 1982a, 1982b,

Maslow's Concept of Self-Actualization

Highlight 5.3

Abraham Maslow devoted most of his professional life to an in-depth analysis of normal personality, undoubtedly in response to a psychology that was fascinated with a far more sensational facet of the human condition, that of psychopathology. His optimistic view of the organism was in sharp contrast to the pessimism of the psychoanalytic model of the Freudians. Among Maslow's major contributions to our understanding of human behavior is the concept of *self-actualization*. To Maslow, the self-actualized person is someone who has achieved a sense of personal harmony or unity and has maximized his or her potentials across a broad spectrum. In order for this actualization of personality to take place, the individual must have come to grips with and mastered a *hierarchy of needs*. This hierarchy is arranged from the more prepotent fundamental needs through the psychological needs to the need for self-actualization. A pictorial representation of the needs hierarchy tells us much about the dynamic, ongoing process of self-actualization.

Clearly, the lowest but most compelling needs in the hierarchy are the *physiological* ones; the need for food, water, and warmth, as examples, is quite powerful. Assuming that these lower level needs are met, the

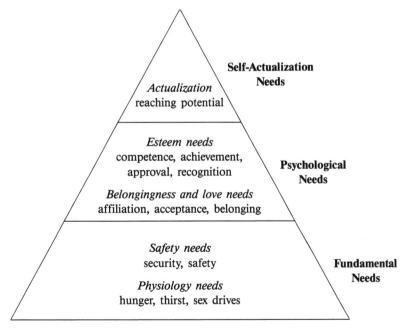

(Continued next page)

Highlight 5.3 (Continued)

Maslow's Concept of Self-Actualization

safety needs come into play. A realization that we are generally safe from harm within normal limits gives us the freedom to pursue the *love and belongingness* needs, or the feeling that we are loved and accepted by whatever individual standards we use to gauge such acceptance. Out of this acceptance grows a feeling of *esteem,* a belief that we are not only accepted or loved but also that we are respected for our capabilities. If all of the preceding levels of needs are in good order, we are free to achieve the maximization of potential called *self-actualization.* It is easy to lapse into a pattern of thinking that would suggest that the various needs in the hierarchy are met in a step-by-step, static progression. Clearly, the process is ongoing and dynamic and is always in a potential state of flux. Sudden regressions in service of the basic or *deficiency* needs can interfere with the achievement of the growth or *meta-needs,* which is Maslow's explanation for the various adjustment difficulties. Although Maslow's work is not without its critics, the emphasis on the positive, on growth, and on the capacity for change has made an indelible and lasting impression on our views of human behavior.

Sources: Hamachek (1987); Suinn (1984).

1982c, 1983a, 1983b, 1983c, 1983d, 1984) with his research on self-concept and weight training. By way of summarizing across these nine reports, the following trends were noted:

1. Standard instrumentation included the Tennessee Self-Concept Scale (Fitts, 1965), the Body Cathexis Scale (Secord and Jourard, 1953), the Eysenck Personality Inventory (Eysenck and Eysenck, 1968), and the Perceived Somatotype Scale (Tucker, 1982a).

2. All subjects were male university undergraduates primarily in beginning weight-training classes as compared to samples of students from a wide variety of major fields of study with little or no involvement with weights.

3. The subjects who participated in regular weight-training activities had healthier self-concepts than did students who worked out little or not at all. Body satisfaction scores also were enhanced by weight training.

4. Evidence for somatotype theory (Sheldon, 1942), particularly the mesomorphic body build, as a moderator of self-concept and body satisfaction was also found. Though Tucker's work has been conducted with similar subjects and measures, generalizing from weight training to all domains of sport and physical activity may be hazardous. Nevertheless, he has added to our knowledge of the relationship of self-concept to at least one sport.

Tucker's research is focused but is subject to criticism because the conclusions are drawn from studies of males who have self-selected into weight programs to improve their strength and physical appearance. What we may be seeing in Tucker's research are positive self-concept changes that have occurred due to a selection times treatment interaction. It would be interesting to see if the same kinds of results would occur under conditions where the selection variable was minimized. Irrespective of this caveat concerning Tucker's work, it does appear that weight training may be an effective mechanism for enhancing self-concept or self-esteem (Brone and Reznikoff, 1989; Brown and Harrison, 1986; and Trujillo, 1983).

Several conclusions are readily deducible concerning the status of self research in sport psychology. First of all, there is precious little of it, and the research that exists may be generously summarized as scattered. Second, there is little or no theory driving the research; the end result of such a state is limited generalizability of results. A third and most important conclusion is that the measurement of self-concept has been a shaky proposition at best. To date, the most commonly used assessment device has been the Tennessee Self-Concept Scale (TSCS); according to McInman (1992), 33 percent of all self-concept studies in the area of aerobic fitness used the TSCS. In the case of weight-training studies, the figure is 80 percent, undoubtedly a partial function of the fact that Tucker's research mentioned earlier is numerically overrepresented in that area of inquiry. Critics of the TSCS are not kind, and deservedly so. Berger and McInman (1993), for example, criticize the TSCS for being too broad, having too much overlap with other psychological constructs, having high subscale intercorrelations, possessing low convergent validity, and being plagued by broad problems of reliability and validity as a function of the other shortcomings. It is the opinion of Berger

and McInman that researchers in the future would be better served by using more recent and psychometrically promising scales such as the Physical Self-Perception Profile (PSPP) (Fox and Corbin, 1989) or the Self-Description Questionnaire series, SDQ, SDQII, and SDQIII (Marsh, 1990a, 1990b, 1990c). In the case of the PSPP, it is strictly a measure of the physical self, with five subscales of body, strength, condition, sport, and global physical self-worth. Each subscale has six Likert-type formatted items. The authors report satisfactory psychometric documentation for their scale.

As for the SDQ series, SDQI is for use with primary school students, SDQII is for early adolescents, and SDQIII is for late adolescents, college students, and young adults. Seven, eleven, and thirteen dimensions of self-concept (corresponding to versions I, II, or III) have been identified by Marsh and various colleagues through the use of factor analysis (Marsh, 1987, 1990a, 1990b, 1990c; Marsh, Parker and Barnes, 1985; Marsh and O'Neill, 1984). There appears to be little subscale overlap and the overall psychometric properties of the SDQ series seem to be most acceptable.

There appears to be a healthy awareness of the methodological and assessment problems that have plagued self-related sport psychology to date. The creation of sounder assessment tools is particularly encouraging, and the future of this line of research in sports and fitness appears to be bright.

THREE FINAL THOUGHTS ON MOTIVATION

No mention has been made to this point concerning three developments that we think are germane to the topic of motivation and sport psychology. They are sport self-confidence, sport motivation, and explanatory style.

Sport Self-Confidence

Vealey (1986) has been at the forefront of research on sport self-confidence. Borrowing from and extending the literature on self-efficacy and perceived competence, Vealey has created a theoretical base for sport self-confidence with three sport self-confidence measures known as the Trait Sport-Confidence Inventory (TSCI), the State Sport-Confidence Inventory (SSCI), and the Competitive Orientation Inventory (COI). To Vealey, SC-Trait refers to the belief or degree of certainty individuals *usually* possess about their ability to succeed in sports; in the case of SC-State, emphasis is placed on a more "right now" orientation that stresses the degree to which an individual believes or expresses certainty *at one particular moment.* The COI was developed to deal with problems inherent in the distinction between performance and outcome orientations to competition. Athletes may publicly endorse an "I'd rather perform well than win" sentiment, and yet engage in behavior of a completely different sort (i.e., "win at all costs") in the heat of battle. The COI forces athletes to choose one or the other approach to competition, thus resulting in either a performance orientation (COI-Performance) or an outcome orientation (COI-Outcome) to competitive situations. In Vealey's initial report in 1986, five separate studies of 666 high school, college, and adult athletes demonstrated that the three scales are psychometrically sound. Additional support for the scales and the theoretical model was reported in a later study by Vealey (1988).

Partial substantiation of Vealey's efforts has been reported from at least two sources. Gayton and Nickless (1987) administered the TSCI and SSCI to thirty-five runners (twenty-five males, ten females) competing in the Casco Bay marathon in Portland, Maine. Both scales correlated significantly with predicted and actual finishing times of the runners. Martin and Gill (1991) administered the Vealey scales to seventy-three male high school

middle- and long-distance runners; these athletes were more performance- than outcome-oriented and were high in trait and state self-confidence.

As is so often the case with new scales, they are not without their detractors. Feltz (1988), for one, has been critical of the inventories, primarily because of the redundancy of the trait and state measures. Feltz indicates that the only thing the trait scale actually predicts well is SC-State, thereby rendering the SC-Trait score redundant and, ultimately, unnecessary. Feltz goes on to say that determining SC-State may be more fruitful than assessing dispositional aspects of self-confidence. Data from the Gayton and Nickless study also raised questions about the necessity for conceptualizing sport self-confidence in terms of a trait-state construct.

Feltz has also criticized the COI, primarily because of the measurement difficulties inherent in assessing something so situationally ephemeral as competitive orientation. This criticism has led Feltz to conclude that a dispositional competitive orientation measure is of little value, a point echoed in the Martin and Gill study.

Despite these criticisms, it appears that Vealey's work is salvageable. Certainly, the trait-state distinction problem and the situational changeability of competitive orientation are troublesome and will undoubtedly undergo changes. However, it seems that additional research into and refinement of these scales could still be fruitful. One thing is certain: there is still much to be learned about sport self-confidence, and Vealey as well as her critics have been instrumental in providing direction for future work in the area.

Sport Motivation

A second line of research offering promise for the future is that of sport motivation from the perspective of Willis (1982; Willis and Layne, 1988). Borrowing from the McClelland-Atkinson model of achievement motivation discussed earlier in this chapter, Willis has created a sport motivation scale designed to measure motive to achieve success (MAS), motive to avoid failure (MAF), and motive to achieve power (MAP). The initial psychometric work on the Willis scale was done in 1982 using 1,017 male and female subjects, all of whom were members of an organized sport team ranging from junior high through college. Seventeen sports and twenty-two schools were represented in the original Willis sample. The end result of this preliminary research was a 45-item scale arranged on a five-point Likert-like format; each of the three subscales (MAS, MAF, MAP) are assessed by fifteen items. Initial psychometric work indicated satisfactory Alpha and test-retest reliability, adequate content, criterion-related, and construct validity, and relative freedom from social desirability bias. In the 1988 paper, additional construct and concurrent validity was demonstrated in a study of eighty-eight high school football players. Recent preliminary and as yet unpublished work involving well over a thousand subjects has convinced us of the utility of the Willis measure. Of particular interest is the consistent relationship noted between the motive to achieve power and positive constructs from other psychological tests; athletes at all levels strongly endorse MAP as a sport motivation. At the same time, these athletes score in the positive direction on psychological constructs thought to be desirable, such as physiological vigor, internal locus of control, and positive traits measured within what is known as the Personality Big Five (to be discussed later in chapter 8).

Based on the early work of Willis and the results that have emerged strongly and consistently in our own work, we are convinced that additional research in sport motivation as conceived by Willis is warranted.

Explanatory Style

Considerable interest has emerged of late with regard to what is known as explanatory style. By way of summary, Seligman, Nolen-Hoeksema, Thornton, and Thornton (1990) suggest that some people habitually explain bad life events by causative factors that are stable in time, global in effect, and internal. Conversely, they explain good happenings by causes that are unstable, specific, and external. Seligman et al. regard this explanatory style as pessimistic, and posit that it results in poor performance in achievement situations, generalizes across behavioral domains and lower performance accordingly, and likely leads to lowered behavioral resiliency in the face of failure. To measure explanatory style, Seligman and his colleagues created the Attributional Style Questionnaire (ASQ) (Peterson, Semmel, von Baeyer, Abramson, Metalsky, and Seligman, 1982; Seligman, Abramson, Semmel, and von Baeyer, 1979). Scores for good and bad explanatory styles are derived from responses to items assessing three causal dimensions: stable versus unstable, global versus specific, and internal versus external. A composite score is derived for bad events by adding scores on the three dimensions for bad events. Good event scores are derived in essentially the same way—by adding responses to good events. A composite score can also be obtained by subtracting good from bad scores.

Seligman et al. (1990) investigated explanatory style and performance in swimmers from two college teams by administering the ASQ to members of the University of California-Berkeley men's and women's swimming teams prior to the start of the 1987–1988 season. Four major findings resulted from the study:

1. Swimmers with a pessimistic explanatory style were more likely to perform poorly during the season than were those with an optimistic style.
2. Pessimistic swimmers rebounded from a simulated defeat situation less well than did optimistic ones.

3. Swimming ability was a less powerful predictor of success than was explanatory style, thereby suggesting that actual performance is jointly determined by an interaction between talent and habitual belief patterns about causes of events.

4. Female swimmers were significantly more negative in explanatory style than were males, though their scores were very similar to those for college women in general. The males, on the other hand, were as optimistic in explanatory style as any group the experienced investigators had ever seen other than life insurance agents.

In a bit of a disclaimer, Hale (1993) administered the ASQ to ninety-two collegiate male and female athletes and found little support for Seligman's theoretical base, but did suggest methodological shortcomings in his study as a possible explanation for the discrepancy. Disclaimer notwithstanding, it is likely that explanatory style will continue to be of interest to sport researchers, and the ASQ should be the assessment tool of choice for the foreseeable future though it has been criticized for low reliability and other psychometric shortcomings (Carver, 1989).

SUMMARY

1. Two major motivational theories have dominated research in psychology over the past fifty years: attribution theory and need achievement theory. Two psychological constructs that exert an effect on motivation are locus of control and self-esteem.

2. The topic of motivation is fascinating to professionals and laypersons alike. According to Glyn Roberts, "motivation refers to those personality factors, social variables, and/or cognitions that come into play when a person undertakes a task at which he or she is evaluated, enters into competition with others, or attempts to attain some standard of excellence." (1992, p. 5).

3. Attribution theory owes a considerable debt to the impetus provided in the 1940s and 1950s by Fritz Heider. Causal attributions are inferences made about why something happened. Dispositional attributions concern inferences about some trait an individual may possess.

4. Three attributional theory models dominate: cognitive, social cognitive, and functional.

5. The cognitive approach to attributions owes much to Julian Rotter, whose work in locus of control theory has been significant. Another key figure has been Bernard Weiner, who initially suggested that causal attributions for behavior could be conceptualized along four dimensions: ability, effort, task difficulty, and luck. Later theorizing by Weiner added stability-instability and controllability-uncontrollability to the formulation.

6. The assessment of attributions of late has centered around Russell's Causal Dimension Scale (CDS) and an updated version, CDSII.

7. Three variants of Weiner's work are in the social cognitive realm: self-efficacy, perceived competence, and the achievement goal approach.

8. Self-efficacy owes its origins to the work of Albert Bandura. Emphasis in the model is placed on efficacy expectations and outcome expectations. The former deals with a person's belief about his or her own ability while the latter involves outcome perceptions as they interact with efficacious responding. A relatively new application of efficacy theory has to do with collective (i.e., team) efficacy.

9. Perceived competence is associated with Harter who emphasized a mastery approach to achievement situations.

10. Dweck, Maehr, and Nicholls have been at the forefront of research in the achievement goal approach. Achievement behavior, according to these theorists, is driven by multidimensionally complex goals and situational interpretations. Much is made of (1) task, learning, and mastery goals; and (2) ego, performance, and ability goals.

11. The functional model takes the position that maintenance of self-esteem is at the heart of attributional efforts. This notion has led to the emergence of what is known as the self-serving attributional bias, whereby success is attributed internally (ability, effort) and failure is attributed externally (task difficulty, luck).

12. Future directions in attribution research in sport should focus on the athlete as the definer of causal attributions, not the researcher. Also, winning and losing have too long served as the only indices of success or failure; future research should look more at performance. Thirdly, team versus individual attributions need to be viewed separately. Fourth, perceived ability as opposed to actual ability as a moderator of attributions bears additional scrutiny. Fifth, youth sport suffers from a dearth of research. Sixth, the original Weiner model seems limited and needs expansion. Finally, basing attributional generalizations on studies largely conducted with college students seems narrow in scope.

13. Henry Murray introduced the concept of the need to achieve to the psychological literature. He also devised a projective test, the Thematic Apperception Test (TAT), to measure the construct.

14. McClelland and Atkinson have advanced a model for need for achievement that has been scrutinized continually in the sport psychology literature. Intrinsic versus extrinsic motivation has, in turn, played a big part in the total picture of unraveling the need for achievement in athletics and physical activity.

15. Locus of control theory continues to be a salient personality variable in sport research. The I-E Scale of Rotter has been a very popular instrument for the measurement of internal or external locus of control. Though the literature is generally supportive of the construct, there is a body of research that does not vindicate the I-E Scale.

16. In response to Rotter's early work, Hanna Levenson developed a multidimensional scale of locus of control. The primary difference in the two scales has to do with the external dimension, which Levenson divides into powerful other and chance.

17. The measurement of locus of control in youth has been largely the province of Nowicki and Strickland. The inability of the young athlete to make a variety of attributions has plagued the locus of control research in youth sport.

18. Interest in the locus of control construct has lessened, but it is an area of interest that will continue to grow but perhaps at a slower rate than was the case in the 1970s and 1980s.

19. The relatively sparse, confused, and atheoretical research in the area of self-esteem and self-concept has generated an image of an overlooked research domain.

20. Significant literature contributions in self-theory have been advanced by James, Maslow, and Rogers, to name only a significant few.

21. Definitions of what constitutes the self are varied. Dimensions such as the physical self, the self-as-process, the social self, the self-concept, and the self-ideal have generally received some degree of universal acceptance.

22. Distinctions in the literature between self-concept and self-esteem are largely ambiguous and confused, hence the general use herein of the two terms as synonymous.

23. Maslow's conceptualization of the self-actualization motive has been most significant in psychology. However, no consistent relationship between sport and physical activity and self-actualization has been noted.
24. Research on self-concept or self-esteem has largely been atheoretical, methodologically flawed, and beset by measurement problems. Much of the research conducted thus far has used the Tennessee Self-Concept Scale, and its use has been called into serious question due to problems of validity, reliability, and subscale overlap. It has been suggested that more promising scales, such as the Physical Self-Perception Scale and the Self-Description Questionnaire series, should be used in future sport psychology research on self theory.
25. Three additional motivational topics of interest include Robin Vealey's work in the area of sport self-confidence; sport motivation measurement as viewed by Joe Willis involving the motive to achieve success, the motive to avoid failure, and the motive to achieve power; and Martin Seligman's explanatory style, which is measured with the Attributional Style Questionnaire.

SUGGESTED READINGS

Duda, J. L., & Nicholls, J. G. (1992) Dimensions of achievement motivation in schoolwork and sport. *Journal of Educational Psychology, 84,* 290–299.

Schoolwork and sport, according to Duda and Nicholls, loom large in the lives of U.S. adolescents. The purpose of this paper is to relate achievement motivation theory to school and sport, with much emphasis on previous work in the area by Nicholls and a variety of collaborators. In general, their study of 207 adolescents indicated conceptually similar achievement goals and beliefs cut across both achievement domains.

Dweck, C. S. (1992) The study of goals in psychology. *Psychological Science, 3,* 165–167.

In this brief article, Dweck discusses the resurgence of interest among psychologists over the past several years concerning motivation. At the same time, she reviews a considerable body of literature in the area. Dweck concludes the article by making a case for her own work in goals and their attendant behavior-cognition-affect patterns as a primary motivating force in human behavior.

Lefcourt, H. M. (1966) Internal versus external control of reinforcement: A review. *Psychological Bulletin, 65,* 206–220.

A summary of the literature concerning the locus of control construct is presented by Lefcourt, one of the leading authorities in the area. Of particular interest is Lefcourt's review of his own early work as well as that of Rotter and Phares. Along with Levenson, these researchers have spearheaded investigative efforts concerning locus of control theory over the past three decades.

Pelletier, L. G., Fortier, M. S., Vallerand, R. J., Tuson, K. M., Briere, N. M., & Blais, M. R. (1995). Toward a new measure of intrinsic motivation, extrinsic motivation, and amotivation in sports: The Sport Motivation Scale (SMS). *Journal of Sport and Exercise Psychology, 17,* 35–53.

The authors of this paper have taken an existing sport motivation scale that was written in French and have attempted to demonstrate the reliability and validity of an English translation. The SMS purports to measure three dimensions of sport motivation: Intrinsic Motivation (IM: IM to Know, IM to Accomplish Things, IM to Experience Stimulation), Extrinsic Motivation (EM: Identified, Introjected, External), and Amotivation. Two studies reported by the authors indicate satisfactory reliability and validity for the English translation. As such, the SMS may offer a new assessment device for sport psychologists interested in motivation.

Roberts, G. C. (Ed.) (1992) *Motivation in sport and exercise.* Champaign, IL: Human Kinetics.

Nine separate articles by authorities in motivation theory in sport psychology such as Duda, Feltz, McAuley, Nicholls, and Roberts, to name a few, are included in this excellent reference. Part one has six readings on definitions, achievement motivation, goal setting, and self-efficacy. The second section has three readings designed to illustrate applications of several theories of motivation. This is an excellent reference for the sport psychology student or professional interested in the latest in motivation.

Sanna, L. J. (1992) Self-efficacy theory: Implications for social facilitation and social loafing. *Journal of Personality and Social Psychology, 62,* 774–786.

Sanna conducted two experiments aimed at linking together self-efficacy theory as it relates to topics we will discuss at length in chapter 6, social facilitation and social loafing. Predictions based on social facilitation and social loafing theory were substantiated through a variety of manipulations of self-efficacy conditions with the experimental subjects.

Smith, H. J., & Dechter, A. (1991) No shift in locus of control among women during the 1970's. *Journal of Personality and Social Psychology, 60,* 638–640.

In this article, Smith and Dechter respond to previous research indicating that U.S. women were becoming more external in locus of control orientation. It is their contention that the move was more apparent than real, and could easily be explained in terms of methodological flaws, particularly coding errors in scoring the data, in previous works. They suggest that "surprising results that are based on miscoded data are not unknown and are perhaps more frequent than we are aware" (p. 640).

Weiner, B. (1990) History of motivational research in education. *Journal of Educational Psychology, 82,* 616–622.

Bernard Weiner traces the history of motivational research in education from 1941 to 1990. Major conclusions arrived at by Weiner are (1) the grand formal theories of the early days, namely drive, psychoanalytic, cognitive, and associationistic theory, have largely faded into obscurity; (2) achievement strivings remain at the center of motivation research, and goal theory is one of the bright stars in this regard; (3) efficacy beliefs, causal cognitions, and learned helplessness are increasingly being used in explaining success and failure in achievement settings; (4) there is a lack of cross-situational generality, unfortunately, with most of the motivation theories; and (5) there is an increasing interest in the interplay of emotions and motivation. Weiner sees a bright future for motivation theory and research, but does suggest that studying motivation primarily in educational settings is limiting.

REFERENCES

Allport, G. (1955) *Becoming.* New Haven: Yale University Press.

Anshel, M. (1979) Effect of age, sex, and type of feedback on performance and locus of control. *Research Quarterly, 50,* 305–317.

Atkinson, J. W. (1957) Motivational determinants of risk-taking behavior. *Psychological Review, 64,* 359–372.

Atkinson, J. W. (1974) Strength of motivation and efficiency of performance. In J. W. Atkinson & J. O. Raynor (Eds.), *Motivation and achievement* (pp. 193–218). Washington, D.C.: V.H. Winston.

Bandura, A. (1977) Self-efficacy: Toward a unifying theory of behavioral change. *Psychological Review, 84,* 191–225.

Bandura, A. (1990) Perceived self-efficacy in the exercise of personal agency. *Journal of Applied Sport Psychology, 2,* 128–163.

Berger, B. G., & McInman, A. (1993) Exercise and the quality of life. In R. N. Singer, M. Murphey, & L. K. Tennant (Eds.), *Handbook of research in sport psychology* (pp. 729–760). New York: Macmillan.

Biddle, S. (1993) Attribution research and sport psychology. In R. N. Singer, M. Murphey, & L. K. Tennant (Eds.), *Handbook of research on sport psychology* (pp. 437–464). New York: Macmillan.

Biddle, S. J. H., & Hill, A. B. (1992a) Attributions for objective outcome and subjective appraisal of performance: Their relationship with emotional reactions in sport. *British Journal of Social Psychology, 31,* 215–226.

Biddle, S. J. H., & Hill, A. B. (1992b) Relationships between attributions and emotions in a laboratory-based sporting contest. *Journal of Sport Sciences, 10,* 65–75.

Bird, A. M., & Brame, J. (1978) Self versus team attributions: A test of the "I'm OK, but the team's so-so" phenomenon. *Research Quarterly, 49,* 260–268.

Bird, A. M., Foster, C., & Maruyama, G. (1980) Convergent and incremental effects of cohesion on attributions for self and team. *Journal of Sport Psychology, 2,* 181–194.

Blau, G. (1984) Brief note comparing the Rotter and Levenson measures of locus of control. *Perceptual and Motor Skills, 58,* 173–174.

Brawley, L. R., & Roberts, G. (1984) Attribution in sport: Research foundations, characteristics, and limitations. In J.M. Silva & R.S. Weinberg (Eds.), *Psychological foundations of sport* (pp. 197–213). Champaign, IL: Human Kinetics.

Brone, R., & Reznikoff, M. (1989) Strength gains, locus of control, and self-description of college football players. *Perceptual and Motor Skills, 69,* 483–493.

Brown, R. D., & Harrison, J. M. (1986) The effects of a strength program on the strength and self-concept of two female age groups. *Research Quarterly for Exercise and Sport, 57,* 315–320.

Bukowski, W., & Moore, D. (1980) Winners' and losers' attributions for success and failure in a series of athletic events. *Journal of Sport Psychology, 2,* 195–210.

Calhoun, J., & Acocella, J. (1983) *Psychology of adjustment and human relationships* (2d ed.). New York: Random House.

Carver, C. S. (1989) How should multifaceted personality constructs be tested? Issues illustrated by self-monitoring, attributional style, and hardiness. *Journal of Personality and Social Psychology, 56,* 577–585.

Celestino, R., Tapp, J., & Brumet, M. (1979) Locus of control correlates with marathon performances. *Perceptual and Motor Skills, 48,* 1249–1250.

Chalip, L. (1980) Social learning theory and sport success. *Journal of Sport Behavior, 3,* 76–85.

Collins, B., (1974) Four components of Rotter internal-external scale. *Journal of Personality and Social Psychology, 29,* 381–391.

Cox, R. (1985) *Sport psychology: Concepts and applications.* Dubuque, IA: Wm. C. Brown.

Daiss, S., LeUnes, A., & Nation, J. R. (1986) Mood and locus of control of a sample of college and professional football players. *Perceptual and Motor Skills, 63,* 733–734.

DeCharms, R. (1968) *Personal causation.* New York: Academic Press.

Deci, E. (1975) *Intrinsic motivation.* New York: Plenum.

DeMinzi, M. C. R. (1991) A new multidimensional children's locus of control scale. *The Journal of Psychology, 125,* 109–118.

Derlega, V., & Janda, L. (1981) *Personal adjustment: The psychology of everyday life* (2d ed.). Glenview, IL: Scott, Foresman.

Di Giuseppe, R. (1973) Internal-external control of reinforcement and participation in team, individual, and intramural sports. *Perceptual and Motor Skills, 36,* 33–34.

Duncan, T., & McAuley, E. (1987) Efficacy expectations and perceptions of causality in motor performance. *Journal of Sport Psychology, 9,* 385–393.

Dweck, C. S. (1986) Motivational processes affecting learning. *American Psychologist, 41,* 1040–1048.

Eysenck, H. J., & Eysenck, S. B. G. (1968) Manual for the *Eysenck Personality Inventory.* San Diego, CA: Educational and Industrial Testing Service.

Feltz, D. L. (1982) Path analysis of the causal elements in Bandura's theory of self-efficacy and an anxiety based model of avoidance behavior. *Journal of Personality and Social Psychology, 42,* 764–781.

Feltz, D. L. (1984) Self-efficacy as a cognitive mediator of athletic performance. In W. F. Straub and J. M. Williams (Eds.), *Cognitive sport psychology: Personal growth to peak experience* (pp. 114–148). Lansing, NY: Sport Science Associates.

Feltz, D. L. (1988) Self-confidence and sports performance. In K. B. Pandolf (Ed.), *Exercise and sport sciences review,* Vol. 16. New York: Macmillan.

Feltz, D. L., Landers, D. M., & Raeder, U. (1979) Enhancing self-efficacy in high avoidance motor tasks: A comparison of modeling techniques. *Journal of Sport Psychology, 1,* 112–122.

Finn, J., & Straub, W. F. (1977) Locus of control among Dutch and American women softball players. *Research Quarterly, 48,* 56–60.

Fitts, W. (1965) Manual: *Tennessee Self-Concept Scale.* Nashville, TN: Counselor Recordings and Tests.

Fox, K. R., & Corbin, C. B. (1989) The Physical Self-Perception Profile: Development and preliminary validation. *Journal of Sport and Exercise Psychology, 11,* 408–430.

Frieze, I. (1976) Causal attributions and information seeking to explain success and failure. *Journal of Research in Personality, 10,* 293–305.

Gayton, W. F., & Nickless, C. J. (1987) An investigation of the validity of the trait and state sport self-confidence inventories in predicting marathon performance. *Perceptual and Motor Skills, 65,* 481–482.

Geen, R., Beatty, W., & Arkin, R. (1984) *Human motivation: Physiological, behavioral, and social approaches.* Boston: Allyn and Bacon.

Gill, D. L., Ruder, M., & Gross, J. (1982) Open-ended attributions in team competition. *Journal of Sport Psychology, 4,* 159–169.

Gilliland, K. (1974) Internal versus external locus of control and the high-level athletic competitor. *Perceptual and Motor Skills, 39,* 38.

Grove, J. R., Hanrahan, S. J., & McInman, A. (1991) Success/failure bias in attributions across involvement categories in sport. *Personality and Social Psychology Bulletin, 17,* 93–97.

Gundersheim, J. (1982) A comparison of male and female athletes and nonathletes on measures of self-actualization. *Journal of Sport Behavior, 5,* 186–201.

Gurin, P., Gurin, G., Lao, R., & Beattie, M. (1969) Internal-external control in the motivational dynamics of Negro youth. *Journal of Social Issues, 25,* 29–53.

Hale, B. D. (1993) Explanatory style as a predictor of academic and athletic achievement in college athletes. *Journal of Sport Behavior, 16,* 63–75.

Hall, E. (1980) Comparison of post performance state anxiety of internals and externals following failure or success in a simple motor task. *Research Quarterly for Exercise and Sport, 51,* 306–314.

Hall, E., Church, G., & Stone, M. (1980) Relationship of birth order to selected personality characteristics of nationally ranked Olympic weight lifters. *Perceptual and Motor Skills, 51,* 971–976.

Hamachek, D. (1987) *Encounters with the self* (3d ed.). New York: Holt, Rinehart and Winston.

Harter, S. (1978) Effectance motivation reconsidered: Toward a developmental model. *Human Development, 21,* 34–64.

Harter, S. (1980) The development of competence motivation in the mastery of cognitive and physical skills: Is there still a place for joy? In G. C. Roberts & D. M. Landers (Eds.), *Psychology of motor behavior and sport* (pp. 3–29). Champaign, IL: Human Kinetics.

Heider, F. (1944) Social perception and phenomenal causality. *Psychological Review, 51,* 358–377.

Heider, F. (1958) *The psychology of interpersonal relations.* New York: Wiley.

Hellison, D. (1970) Physical education and the self-attitude. *Quest, 13,* 41–45.

Hodges, L., & Carron, A. V. (1992) Collective efficacy and group performance. *International Journal of Sport Psychology, 23,* 48–59.

Ibrahim, H., & Morrison, N. (1976) Self-actualization and self-concept among athletes. *Research Quarterly, 47,* 68–79.

Iso-Ahola, S. (1975) A test of attribution theory of success and failure with Little League baseball players. *Mouvement, 7,* 323–327.

Iso-Ahola, S. (1977) Effects of team outcome on children's self-perceptions: Little League baseball. *Scandinavian Journal of Psychology, 18,* 38–42.

James, W. (1890) *Principles of psychology, I.* New York: Henry Holt & Company.

Jersild, A. (1952) *In search of self.* New York: Teachers College Press, Columbia University.

Jourard, S. (1974) *Healthy personality: An approach from the viewpoint of humanistic psychology.* New York: Macmillan.

Kavanaugh, D., & Hausfeld, B. (1986) Physical performance and self-efficacy make happy and sad moods. *Journal of Sport Psychology, 8,* 112–123.

Kelley, H. H. (1972) *Causal schemata and the attribution process.* Morristown, NJ: General Learning Press.

Lan, L. Y., & Gill, D. L. (1984) The relationship among self-efficacy, stress responses, and a cognitive feedback manipulation. *Journal of Sport Psychology, 6,* 227–238.

Langer, E. J. (1983) *The psychology of control.* Newbury Park, CA: Sage.

Lee, C. (1982) Self-efficacy as a predictor of performance in competitive gymnastics. *Journal of Sport Psychology, 4,* 405–409.

Lefcourt, H. M. (1992) Durability and impact of the locus of control construct. *Psychological Bulletin, 112,* 411–414.

Lepper, M. R., Greene, D., & Nisbett, R. E. (1973) Undermining children's intrinsic interest with extrinsic rewards: A test of the "overjustification" hypothesis. *Journal of Personality and Social Psychology, 28,* 129–137.

LeUnes, A., & Nation, J. (1982) Saturday's heroes: A psychological portrait of college football players. *Journal of Sport Behavior, 5,* 139–149.

Levenson, H. (1973) *Reliability and validity of the I, P, and C Scales: A multidimensional view of locus of control.* Paper presented at 81st Annual Convention of the American Psychological Association, Montreal.

Levenson, H. (1974) Activism and powerful others: Distinctions within the concept of internal-external control. *Journal of Personality Assessment, 38,* 377–383.

Levenson, H. (1981) Differentiating among internality, powerful others, and chance. In H. Lefcourt (Ed.), *Research with locus of control construct,* Vol. I (pp. 1–39). New York: Academic Press.

Ludwig, D., & Maehr, M. (1967) Changes in self concept and stated behavioral preferences. *Child Development, 38,* 453–467.

Lufi, D., Porat, J., & Tenenbaum, G. (1986) Psychological predictors of competitive performance in young gymnasts. *Perceptual and Motor Skills, 63,* 59–64.

Lynn, R., Phelan, J., & Kiker, V. (1969) Beliefs in internal-external control of reinforcement and participation in group and individual sports. *Perceptual and Motor Skills, 29,* 551–553.

Maehr, M., & Nicholls, J. (1980) Culture and achievement motivation: A second look. In N. Warren (Ed.), *Studies in cross-cultural psychology,* Vol 2. (pp. 53–75). New York: Academic Press.

Mann, L. (1974) On being a sore loser: How fans react to their team's failure. *Australian Journal of Psychology, 26,* 37–47.

Marcus, B., Selby, V. C., Niaura, R. S., & Rossi, J. S. (1992) Self-efficacy and the stages of exercise behavior change. *Research Quarterly for Exercise and Sport, 63,* 60–66.

Mark, M. M., Mutrie, N., Brooks, D. R., & Harris, D. V. (1984) Causal attributions of winners and losers in individual competitive sports: Toward a reformulation of the self-serving bias. *Journal of Sport Psychology, 6,* 184–196.

Marsh, H. W. (1987) The factorial invariance of responses by males and females to a multidimensional self-concept instrument: Substantive and methodological issues. *Multivariate Behavioral Research, 22,* 457–480.

Marsh, H. W. (1990a) *The Self-Description Questionnaire (SDQ): A theoretical and empirical basis for the measurement of multiple dimensions of late adolescent self-concept: An interim test manual and a research monograph.* San Antonio, TX: The Psychological Corporation.

Marsh, H. W. (1990b) *The Self-Description Questionnaire (SDQ): A theoretical and empirical basis for the measurement of multiple dimensions of late adolescent self-concept: An interim test manual and a research monograph.* San Antonio, TX: The Psychological Corporation.

Marsh, H. W. (1990c) *The Self-Description Questionnaire (SDQ): A theoretical and empirical basis for the measurement of multiple dimensions of late adolescent self-concept: An interim test manual and a research monograph.* San Antonio, TX: The Psychological Corporation.

Marsh, H. W., & O'Neill, R. (1984) Self Description Questionnaire III: The construct validity of multidimensional self-concept ratings by late adolescents. *Journal of Educational Measurement, 21,* 153–174.

Marsh, H. W., Parker, J., & Barnes, J. (1985) Multidimensional adolescent self-concepts: Their relationship to age, sex, and academic measures. *American Educational Research Journal, 22,* 422–444.

Martens, R. (1975) *Social psychology and physical activity.* New York: Harper and Row.

Martin, J. J., & Gill, D. L. (1991) The relationships among competitive orientation, sport-confidence, self-efficacy, anxiety, and performance. *Journal of Sport and Exercise Psychology, 13,* 149–159.

Maslow, A. (1954) *Motivation and behavior.* New York: Harper and Row.

Maslow, A. (1970) *Motivation and behavior* (2d ed.) New York: Harper and Row.

Maslow, A. (1971) *The farthest reaches of human nature.* New York: Viking Press.

McAuley, E. (1985) Success and causality in sport: The influence of perception. *Journal of Sport Psychology, 7,* 13–22.

McAuley, E. (1992) Understanding exercise and achievement behavior: A self-efficacy perspective. In G. C. Roberts (Ed.), *Motivation in sport and exercise* (pp. 107–127). Champaign, IL: Human Kinetics.

McAuley, E., & Duncan, T. E. (1989) Causal attributions and affective reactions to disconfirming outcomes in motor performance. *Journal of Sport and Exercise Psychology, 11,* 187–200.

McAuley, E., Duncan, T. E., & Russell, D. W. (1992) Measuring causal attributions: The revised Causal Dimension Scale (CDSII). *Personality and Social Psychology Bulletin, 18,* 566–573.

McAuley, E., & Gross, J. (1983) Perception of causality in sport: An application of the Causal Dimension Scale. *Journal of Sport Psychology, 5,* 72–76.

McClelland, D., Atkinson, J., Clark, R., & Lowell, E. (1953) *The achievement motive.* New York: Appleton-Century-Crofts.

McInman, A. D. (1992) The effects of weight-training on self-concept. Unpublished master's thesis, University of Western Australia, Nedlands, Australia.

McKelvie, S., & Huband, D. (1980) Locus of control and anxiety in college athletes and non-athletes. *Perceptual and Motor Skills, 50,* 819–822.

Mirels, H. (1970) Dimensions of internal vs. external control. *Journal of Consulting and Clinical Psychology, 34,* 226–228.

Morris, A., Vaccaro, P., & Clarke, D. (1979) Psychological characteristics of age-group competitive swimmers. *Perceptual and Motor Skills, 48,* 1265–1266.

Murray, H. A. (1938) *Explorations in personality.* New York: Oxford Press.

Murray, H. A. (1943) *Thematic Apperception Test.* Cambridge, MA: Harvard University Press.

Nation J. R., & LeUnes, A. (1983a) Personality characteristics of intercollegiate football players as determined by position, classification, and redshirt status. *Journal of Sport Behavior, 6,* 92–102.

Nation, J. R., & LeUnes, A. (1983b) A personality profile of the black athlete in college football. *Psychology, 20* (3/4), 1–3.

Nowicki, S., & Strickland, B. (1973) A locus of control scale for children. *Journal of Consulting and Clinical Psychology, 40,* 148–154.

Peterson, C., Semmel, A., von Baeyer, C., Abramson, L. Y., Metalsky, G. I., & Seligman, M. E. P. (1982) The Attributional Style Questionnaire. *Cognitive Therapy and Research, 6,* 287–299.

Read, D. (1969) *The influence of competitive and non-competitive programs of physical education on body-image and self-concept.* Paper presented at the Association for Health, Physical Education and Recreation National Convention, Boston, Massachusetts.

Rejeski, W. J., & Brawley, L. R. (1983) Attribution theory in sport: Current status and new perspectives. *Journal of Sport Psychology, 5,* 77–99.

Roberts, G. C. (1975) Win-loss causal attributions of Little League players. *Mouvement, 7,* 315–322.

Roberts, G. C. (1992) Motivation in sport and exercise: Conceptual restraints and convergence. In G. C. Roberts (Ed.), *Motivation in sport and exercise.* Champaign, IL: Human Kinetics.

Roberts, G. C. (1993) Motivation in sport: Understanding and enhancing the motivation and achievement of children. In R. N. Singer, M. Murphey, & L. K. Tennant (Eds.), *Handbook of research on sport psychology.* New York: Macmillan.

Roberts, G. C., & Pascuzzi, D. (1979) Causal attributions in sport: Some theoretical implications. *Journal of Sport Psychology, 1,* 203–211.

Robinson, D., & Howe, B. (1987) Causal attributions and mood state relationships of soccer players in a sport achievement setting. *Journal of Sport Behavior, 10,* 137–146.

Robinson, D., & Howe, B. (1989) Appraisal variable/effect relationships in youth sport: A test of Weiner's attributional model. *Journal of Sport and Exercise Psychology, 11,* 431–443.

Rogers, C. (1961) *On becoming a person.* Boston: Houghton Mifflin.

Rotter, J. B. (1966) Generalized expectancies for internal versus external control of reinforcement. *Psychological Monographs, 80,* No. 1 (Whole No. 609).

Rotter, J. B. (1975) Some problems and misconceptions related to the construct of internal versus external control of reinforcement. *Journal of Consulting and Clinical Psychology, 43,* 56–67.

Rotter, J. B. (1971) External control and internal control. *Psychology Today, 5*(1), 37–42, 58–59.

Russell, D. (1982) The Causal Dimension Scale: A measure of how individuals perceive causes. *Journal of Personality and Social Psychology, 42,* 1137–1145.

Scheer, J., & Ansorge, C. (1979) Influence due to expectations of judges: A function of internal-external locus of control. *Journal of Sport Psychology, 1,* 53–58.

Secord, P., & Jourard, S. (1953) The appraisal of body-cathexis: Body-cathexis and the self. *Journal of Consulting Psychology, 17,* 343–347.

Seligman, M. E. P. (1975) *Helplessness: On depression, development, and death.* San Francisco: W. H. Freeman.

Seligman, M. E. P., Abramson, L., Semmel, A., & von Baeyer, C. (1979) Depressive attributional style. *Journal of Abnormal Psychology, 88,* 242–247.

Seligman, M. E. P., Nolen-Hoeksema, S., Thornton, N., & Thornton, K. M. (1990) Explanatory style as a mechanism of disappointing athletic performance. *Psychological Science, 1,* 143–146.

Sheldon, W. H. (1942) *The varieties of human temperament.* New York: Harper.

Shostrom, E. (1963) *Personal Orientation Inventory.* San Diego, CA: Educational and Industrial Testing Service.

Suinn, R. M. (1984) *Fundamentals of abnormal psychology.* Chicago: Nelson-Hall.

Throop, W., & MacDonald, A. (1971) Internal-external locus of control. A bibliography. *Psychological Reports, 28,* 175–190.

Trujillo, C. M. (1983) The effect of weight training and running exercise intervention programs on the self-esteem of college women. *International Journal of Sport Psychology, 14,* 162–173.

Tucker, L. A. (1981) Internal structure, factor satisfaction, and reliability of the Body Cathexis Scale. *Perceptual and Motor Skills, 53,* 891–896.

Tucker, L. A. (1982a) Relationship between perceived somatotype and body cathexis of college males. *Psychological Reports, 50,* 983–989.

Tucker, L. A. (1982b) Effect of a weight-training program on the self-concept of college males. *Perceptual and Motor Skills, 54,* 1055–1061.

Tucker, L. A. (1982c) Weight training experience and psychological well-being. *Perceptual and Motor Skills, 55,* 553–554.

Tucker, L. A. (1983a) Self-concept: A function of self-perceived somatotypes. *Journal of Psychology, 113,* 123–133.

Tucker, L. A. (1983b) Effect of weight-training on self-concept: A profile of those influenced most. *Research Quarterly for Exercise and Sport, 54,* 389–397.

Tucker, L. A. (1983c) Muscular strength: A predictor of personality in males. *The Journal of Sports Medicine and Physical Fitness, 23,* 213–220.

Tucker, L. A. (1983d) Muscular strength and mental health. *Journal of Personality and Social Psychology, 45,* 1355–1360.

Tucker, L. A. (1984) Trait psychology and performance: A credulous viewpoint. *Journal of Human Movement Studies, 10*(1), 53–62.

Vallerand, R. J. (1987) Antecedents of self-related affects in sport: Preliminary evidence on the intuitive-reflective appraisal model. *Journal of Sport Psychology, 9,* 161–182.

Van Raalte, J. L., Brewer, B. W., Nemeroff, C. J., & Linder, D. E. (1991) Chance orientation and superstitious behavior on the putting green. *Journal of Sport Behavior, 14,* 41–50.

Vealey, R. S. (1986) Conceptualization of sport-confidence and competitive orientation: Preliminary investigation and instrument development. *Journal of Sport Psychology, 8,* 221–246.

Vealey, R. S. (1988) Sport-confidence and competitive orientation: An addendum on scoring procedures and gender differences. *Journal of Sport and Exercise Psychology, 10,* 471–478.

Weinberg, R. S. (1984) The relationship between extrinsic rewards and intrinsic motivation in sport. In J. M. Silva & R. S. Weinberg (Eds.), *Psychological foundations of sport* (pp. 177–187). Champaign, IL: Human Kinetics.

Weinberg, R. S., Gould, D., & Jackson, A. (1979) Expectations and performance: An empirical test of Bandura's self-efficacy theory. *Journal of Sport Psychology, 1,* 320–331.

Weiner, B. (Ed.) (1974) *Achievement motivation and attribution theory.* Morristown, NJ: General Learning Press.

Weiner, B. (1979) A theory of motivation for some classroom experiences. *Journal of Educational Psychology, 71,* 3–25.

Weiner, B. (1980) *Human motivation.* New York: Holt, Rinehart and Winston.

Weiner, B. (1991) Self-reflections: The origins of an attribution theorist. In S. L. Zelen (Ed.), *New models, new extensions of attribution theory* (pp. 7–11). New York: Springer-Verlag.

White, S. A. (1993) The effect of gender and age on causal attributions in softball players. *International Journal of Sport Psychology, 24,* 49–58.

Whitney, K. (1994) Improving group-task performance: The role of group goals and group efficacy. *Human Performance, 7,* 55–78.

Willis, J. D. (1982) Three scales to measure competition-related motives in sport. *Journal of Sport Psychology, 4,* 338–353.

Willis, J. D., & Layne, B. H. (1988) A validation study of sport-related motive scales. *Journal of Applied Research in Coaching and Athletics, 3,* 299–307.

Zion, L. (1965) Body concept as it relates to self-concept. *Research Quarterly, 36,* 490–495.

Leadership, Cohesion, and Audience Effects

INTRODUCTION

The sport scientist interested in social psychology will find much to captivate him or her in the area of athletics. Sports teams literally abound with social-psychological components. Leadership is but one of them. No one in sport questions the role of the coach as leader; less scientific interest has been expressed in players as leaders, and this represents an area for future exploration. Also, it is widely believed that cohesive teams are, for whatever reason, successful ones. It is usually the coach (or leader) who is expected to forge these cohesive and successful units. In the process of leading and generating team cohesion, we find that athletic performance is moderated by the effects of being around other participants, being evaluated by significant others, or being cheered by friendly supporters, all of which falls under what might be called audience effects. This three-some from the social psychology literature will be discussed in this chapter.

LEADERSHIP

Psychologists have studied the ubiquitous concept of leadership for more than 90 years. Though much has been learned overall, there are still as many definitions and ideas of what constitutes leadership as there are experts to generate them. Burns (1978, p. 2) states unequivocally that "leadership is one of the most observed and least understood phenomena on earth."

Though leadership has always been recognized as an important part of the sport process, it has been scientifically addressed for only about twenty years (Danielson, 1976; Danielson, Zelhart, and Drake, 1975). All of us are familiar with individuals within the sport context who have established a winning tradition through their leadership capabilities. The football fans of the 1970s can attest to the leadership of Roger Staubach in making the Dallas Cowboys a perennial power. He never believed the Cowboys were

going to lose and the effect on his teammates was obviously highly positive. At one time Staubach's ability to play in the National Football League had been widely questioned inasmuch as he had incurred a five-year military obligation as a function of his enrollment in the U.S. Naval Academy. Near the end of his service obligation, your author (LeUnes) expressed concern about the effects of the long hiatus. An acquaintance who had played with Staubach at the Naval Academy took exception, suggesting that Staubach would become a force in the NFL primarily but not exclusively because of his leadership ability. As the ex-teammate said, "If Roger wanted you to do it, it was simple. You did it! We knew he was right, and we would have done anything he asked. He's the greatest leader I have ever seen." Obviously, Staubach's admirer/ex-teammate knew what he was talking about. Many of us, Cowboy fans or not, thrilled to his last-ditch efforts and exhortations in snatching victory from apparent defeat; Staubach rallied his mates to wins on twenty-three occasions after trailing in the fourth quarter, and fourteen of those comebacks came in the last two minutes of regulation play or in the overtime period. A more contemporary player, John Elway of the Denver Broncos, exemplifies many of the leadership qualities attributed to Hall of Famer Staubach. According to Hoffer (1993), Elway rallied his teams to wins in the fourth quarter on thirty-one occasions in his first ten years in the NFL. Part of this success can undoubtedly be explained by athletic ability, but some of the variance in performance must be explained by leadership. Kip Corrington (1994), an ex-Bronco, says: "John raises his game to another level in pressure situations, and the rest of the team seems to do the same thing. He leads more by example than anything else, but he gets the job done." Whether this ability to perform at a peak level when the outcome of a competition hangs in the balance is really a function of leadership is clearly open to conjecture; however, Corrington strongly suggests that during his years with the Broncos, Elway's leadership in game situations was clearly a major factor in the numerous come-from-behind wins posted by the team.

The annals of sport are filled with similar examples, and this has led to an awakening of interest in the relationship of sport and leadership. Before examining the topic of leadership, however, a review of the more general conceptualizations and research contributions is in order.

A Brief History

According to Bass (1981), discussion of leadership dates back to the time of Plato, Caesar, and Plutarch. Also, the ancient Chinese and Egyptians wrote of leadership. Homer's *Iliad* provides us with an early Greek reference on the topic; Agamemnon represented justice and judgment, Nestor exemplified wisdom and counsel, Odysseus personified shrewdness and cunning, and Achilles was the prototype for valor and action. Most, if not all, of these qualities we expect and admire, now as then, in our leaders.

In a more contemporary vein, leadership studies in this country probably began around the turn of the twentieth century (Bass, 1981). These early efforts have generated theorizing and research that has continued unabated for the better part of ninety years. Though many theories have been advanced, six general theories or models and one approach specific to sport will be discussed. The general theories are as follows: Trait Theory, Behavior Theory, Fiedler's Contingency Model, Path-Goal Theory, Life Cycle Theory, and the Functional Model. The sport-specific approach is Chelladurai's Multidimensional Model.

LEADERSHIP THEORIES

Trait Theory

The earliest theory of leadership is the trait or "great man" theory, which views leadership

totally from the vantage point of the leader. In its simplest form, the theory suggested that a leader in one situation would be a leader in any circumstance because he or she possesses the traits that make for universality in leadership. The typical paradigm for testing trait theory is to select effective and ineffective leaders through some subjective judgment, measure both types of leaders on a variety of demographic and/or personality variables, and apply appropriate statistical procedures to see if there are differences between the two groups on any of the preceding dimensions. Assuming that the theory is correct and all of the preceding conditions have been met satisfactorily, critical traits distinguishing leaders should then emerge.

One variable that has received mild support in the literature on trait theory is intelligence. According to Carron (1980), intelligence is in fact the only trait for which support can be found; Bass (1981) cites twenty-three studies supportive of the position that leaders are intellectually brighter than so-called followers. Bass cites only five references to the contrary, but also mentions five more indicating that large disparities in the intelligence of leaders and others can actually militate against successful leadership. If the latter group of studies are true, too much (or too little) intelligence could be detrimental to the leader-follower relationship.

Even though intelligence does appear to be a consistent trait of leaders, comprehensive literature reviews (e.g., Campbell, Dunnette, Lawler, and Weick, 1970; Mann, 1959) show only modest correlations between intelligence and leadership, relationships sufficiently modest so as to lead Carron (1980) to conclude that less than 10 percent of task performance can be explained by the leader's intellectual ability. Also, Cattell (1946) has pointed out that intelligence taken separately is still a multifaceted trait made up of a lot of other characteristics such as wisdom, maturity, and perseverance, to name only a few.

There appears to be little support for personality variables as they relate to the trait theory of leadership. This was substantiated in literature reviews by Stogdill as early as 1948; a subsequent review by Hollander and Julian (1969) is supportive of Stogdill's position on the issue. Part of the problem, according to Muchinsky (1987, p. 501), is what he calls "shotgun empiricism"; that is, taking the innumerable personality traits available and relating them to leadership minus any sensible rationale for their selection. Other criticisms that can be leveled at the available research linking personality measures to leadership include questions of test validity and reliability, and the fact that no explanation of why these traits might make one a more effective leader has been forth-

coming. In partial summation of the problems inherent in trait theory, perhaps a quote by Brown (1954, p. 219) is as relevant today as it was over forty years ago: "The longer and more comprehensive the list of qualities, the more obvious it must be that their possession would be of no use as a junior leader in industry, for he would inevitably be in demand elsewhere as a Prime Minister, or maybe as an Archangel."

Behavior Theory

A behavioral approach to leadership has much in common with trait theory—both focus

Miami Dolphin quarterback Dan Marino exudes the kind of confidence that brings out the best in himself and his teammates. "Players have to feel that you're the kind of guy who can make it happen when you're called on," he says.

on the leader as opposed to situational variables. The two theories differ considerably in terms of emphasis, however. While trait theory focuses on leader characteristics, behavior theory stresses what the leader actually does. There are three facets to the behavioral approach. First, leaders are studied and their behaviors categorized. Then, a checklist is made based on similarities noted in the first step. Finally, leader effectiveness is evaluated based on the checklist and external criteria such as employee turnover, group productivity, morale, or work absences. The seminal study of behavioral leadership was conducted at Ohio State University in the early 1950s. Two major contributions to the knowledge base on leadership emerged from the Ohio State studies. First of all, several valuable scales for assessing leadership were created. Secondly, the important factors underlying leadership were isolated: consideration and structure. Consideration refers to trust, rapport, concern for subordinates, and an interest in maintaining two-way communication. Structure includes behaviors that relate to planning, production, role assignment, and the relationship of the leader to the group.

With regard to the first point concerning scale development, the Leader Behavior Description Questionnaire (LBDQ) and the Leader Opinion Questionnaire (LOQ) were created by the Ohio State research team. The LOQ is completed by supervisory personnel and deals with methods of supervision. The LBDQ, on the other hand, is completed by subordinates in an attempt to describe how leaders behave in a variety of situations. Early validation studies were supportive of the psychometric soundness of both scales, though more support was found for the LBDQ (Schriesheim and Kerr, 1974; Schriesheim and Stogdill, 1975).

The LBDQ has been used in several sport-related leadership studies. One early effort by Danielson, Zelhart, and Drake (1975) involved a modification of the LBDQ. In their study, Danielson et al. tested 160 adolescent hockey players in an attempt to see how they viewed coaching leadership behavior. In general, coaches in this instance were seen as much more communication oriented and less involved in dominance kinds of behavior. Support for the modified LBDQ was also reported. Neil and Kirby (1985) administered a version of the LBDQ to 205 elite and novice male and female competitive rowers. Statistical analyses indicated, among other things, that younger and lesser skilled rowers exhibited a decided preference for open communication and individual consideration from the coaches to a greater extent than did the older, more experienced ones. Snyder (1990) was able to demonstrate the utility of the LBDQ in a study of 117 collegiate coaches (thirty-six females and eighty-one males) from seventeen colleges and universities in California. Each coach was asked to respond to the consideration and structure components of the LBDQ for purposes of assessing the coaches' perceptions of their respective athletic directors (i.e., leaders). In terms of overall job satisfaction, male coaches were more likely to show a preference for highly considerate athletic directors whereas women preferred ones with a structure orientation. It is not clear why males preferred consideration and females preferred structure, though gender-related socialization practices may partially account for the different responses.

One notable plus with regard to the trait and behavioral theories of leadership has been their impact on the development of competing points of view. One conceptualization that attempts to incorporate both perspectives is that of Hollander (1978), who speaks of a "locus of leadership." As can be seen in figure 6.1, this locus is the point at which there is a convergence of leader, follower, and situational variables. Charming in its simplicity, the Hollander model provides a convenient springboard for discussing variants of this interactive theme.

Fiedler's Contingency Model

Fiedler (1967, 1978) proposed an interactive model that places emphasis on both traits and situational variable as predictors of leadership. Much is made in Fiedler's model of type of leadership; leaders are seen as task oriented and autocratic or interpersonally oriented and democratic. A second key aspect of contingency theory is the favorableness of the group-task situation. This favorableness arises out of three subfactors: leader-member interactions, task structure, and the power position of the leader. Fiedler asserts that the task-oriented or directive leader will be more influential in either of two conditions: (1) when task structure is loose and unfavorable, and (2) when task structure is rigid and favorable. On the other hand, the interpersonally oriented leader will be most effective in situations neither too loose nor too rigid and of intermediate favorableness. A visual representation of the Fiedler model can be seen in figure 6.2.

By way of summarizing points made so far, Carron (1980, p. 115) offers the following:

> The main tenets of the Contingency Theory are that: group-work situations differ in their degree of favorableness; individual leaders

Figure 6.1: Locus of Leadership

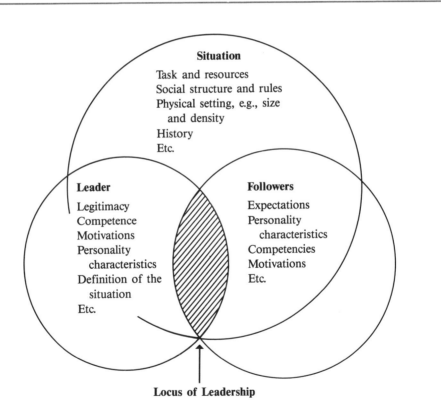

Locus of Leadership

Note: The arrows indicate the social exchange that occurs between leader and followers. The shaded area (locus of leadership) represents the intersection of three elements involved in leadership—the situation, the leader, and the followers. Some relevant attributes of each element are listed.

Source: Hollander (1978).

Figure 6.2: **Proposed Relationship between Situational Favorability and Leader LPC Score as They Affect Group Performance**

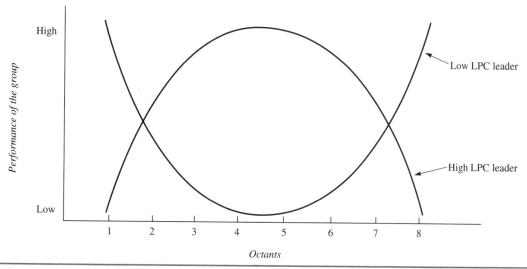

Source: Muchinsky (1987).

vary along a continuum from task to person orientation; and any individual can be an effective leader provided his/her leadership style coincides with a situation of appropriate favorableness.

In his work, Fiedler has made extensive use of a technique known as the Least Preferred Coworker Scale (LPC). Bipolar adjectives, sixteen to twenty in number, are used. Typical items from the LPC include the following:

Friendly   *Unfriendly*

| 8 | 7 | 6 | 5 | 4 | 3 | 2 | 1 |

Efficient   *Inefficient*

| 8 | 7 | 6 | 5 | 4 | 3 | 2 | 1 |

Respondents in this situation are asked to think of one person he or she would least like to work with, i.e., the least preferred coworker. This least preferred coworker is then evaluated on the LPC scale, using the eight-point continuum or "octant." Positive scores (i.e., 8) are indicative of friendliness and efficiency while scores at the other end of the continuum are suggestive of unfriendliness and inefficiency. The total score is called the LPC score; high scores indicate that the leader can separate competence from personality in coworkers. Conversely, low scores indicate an inability to make this discrimination. In the latter instance, a low score would be tantamount to saying: "You are inefficient as a coworker and, in addition, you are an unfriendly person." Respondents who react in a relatively favorable way to the least preferred coworker stimuli are then viewed as interpersonal or people oriented whereas those with more negative responses are seen as task oriented.

In evaluating the contingency model, Muchinsky (1987) has indicated that Fiedler was successful in elevating the importance of situational leadership factors to the same level as had been previously done with trait theory. As a result, it has been the most widely researched and criticized of the modern theories of leadership (Berry and Houston, 1993). Though there may be other problems with contingency theory, Muchinsky is convinced that most of the shortcomings lie within the psychometric shortcomings of the LPC scale. To support his contention, Muchinsky cites evidence from a variety of sources who attack the LPC scale's validity and reliability (e.g., Evans and Dermer, 1974; Rice, 1978; Stinson and Tracy, 1974).

Some attempts have been made to apply the contingency model to sport. The payoff has not been very big in these efforts. Possibly, contingency theory simply has little applicability. Other hypotheses used to account for its lack of applicability include the paucity of studies in the area (Cox, 1990) and the lack of variation in situational favorableness created by applying the theory to teams homogeneous in type of sport and organizational context (Chelladurai, 1984a).

Concerning the shortage of studies aimed at testing the theory in sport, Cox (1990) has stated that only two have been conducted bearing on this point; Chelladurai (1984a) set the figure at seven whereas Carron (1980) cited three studies of contingency theory. Irrespective of the numbers, all of these sources agree that little if any support for the efficacy of Fiedler's model exists within the sport context. All equally agree that the theory has been insufficiently or inadequately tested, and the case should not be closed to additional attempts to link contingency theory to sport.

Three consistently cited sport-related studies of the contingency model, all of which used the LPC as the measure of leadership style, are those of Inciong (1974), Danielson (1976), and Bird (1977). Inciong, in his study of forty-three high school basketball teams, found correlations between performance effectiveness and situation favorableness to be sufficiently low so as to war-

rant rejection of the theory. Danielson, studying forty minor league hockey coaches, concluded that leadership in hockey may have peculiar properties that differ from those in business and industry, where the Fiedler model may have been more applicable. Bird studied female intercollegiate volleyball coaches and players, and she found no support for Fiedler's formulation.

Path-Goal Theory

House (1971) has popularized a situation-specific leadership model known as the path-goal theory. Emphasis in the path-goal theory is placed on the leader as a catalyst for or facilitator of follower success. House and Mitchell (1974) indicated that the basic function of the leader is to provide a "well-lighted path" for subordinates. House and Dessler (1974, p. 31) state: "The motivational function of the leader consists of increasing personal pay-offs to subordinates for work-goal attainment, and making the path to these easier to travel by clarifying it, reducing road blocks and pitfalls, and increasing the opportunities for personal satisfaction en route." A relatively simple representation of this relationship can be seen in figure 6.3.

Figure 6.3: **Path-Goal Model of Leadership**

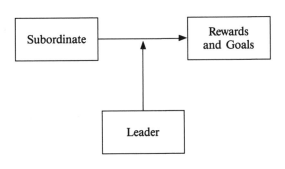

Source: Carron (1980).

Another key aspect of path-goal theory is concerned with the situational nature of leadership; that is, leadership effectiveness should largely be a function of situational variables. Situational variables of significance include: (1) subordinate characteristics (i.e., personality, ability); and (2) environmental demands placed upon subordinates that impinge on their job effectiveness and needs (i.e., the task, formal structure of the organization, and the primary work group). Of particular significance for sport research is the nature of the task at hand. Path-goal theory posits that tasks can be categorized in terms of routineness/variability, dependence/interdependence, and inherent satisfaction/nonsatisfaction (Carron, 1980). Given that these three dimensions do exist, it becomes clear that situational demands on sport leaders (usually coaches) will require much diversity on their part if they are to be effective. The routineness of the usual practice session as opposed to that of game conditions varies greatly. Task interdependence is highly variable; coaching a track sprinter may be very different from molding a sophisticated offensive scheme in football. Also, satisfaction will surely vary from practice to game conditions or from sport to sport.

Although appealing in a commonsense way, path-goal theory has not generated much research in or out of the sport domain. One exception in sport is reported by Chelladurai and Saleh (1978). Their study was conducted with 160 physical education students, and partial support for the theory was gained to the extent that members of team sports had a preference for leaders who would improve their individual performances through training, as well as facilitate improvement through clarification of the relationships among team members.

Another test of path-goal theory has been reported by Vos Strache (1979), who investigated leadership style of coaches as perceived by female basketball players from twenty-nine universities. Players on winning teams perceived their coaches

to be high in the more technical aspects of coaching (e.g., persuasion, production emphasis), but this was not the case with players from losing teams, who viewed their coaches as high on tolerance. Vos Strache interpreted these results as supportive of the path-goal theory notion that the main role of the coach is as a catalyst or facilitator.

Life Cycle Theory

Life cycle theory, or what Carron (1980) prefers to call situational theory, is a situation-specific approach to leadership that places greater emphasis on subordinate behavior than on that of the leader (Hersey and Blanchard, 1969, 1977; Hersey, Blanchard, and Hambleton, 1980).

In the life cycle model, great reliance is placed on three factors: maturity of the group, task behavior, and relationship behavior. Maturity may be viewed in terms of both levels and components. Levels of maturity will vary with the situational demands of the task at hand; as such, there is no such thing as maturity or immaturity in a total sense. As for components of maturity, they may be psychological or job related. Task behavior refers to the extent to which a leader engages in one-way communication by explaining what each follower is to do, when they are to do it, and how tasks are to be accomplished. As for relationship behavior, it is the extent to which the leader engages in two-way communication through social support, psychological "stroking" of followers, and other facilitative behaviors. Thus, the life cycle theory rests on the interplay of the amount of direction (task behavior) provided by the leader, the amount of social-psychological support (relationship behavior) provided, and the maturity level exhibited by followers with regard to group or leader goals.

According to Hersey, Blanchard, and Hambleton (1980), four kinds of leaders will emerge from their model, and their effectiveness will vary according to the variables previously discussed.

The leader types and their corresponding places in the leadership scheme, which are presented in figure 6.4, are as follows:

1. *Low task/high relationship leader behavior (Q1).* In this type of leadership, the term "telling" is applicable. The leader is thus very assertive and one-way in communication style.
2. *High task/high relationship leader behavior (Q2).* In this instance, the leader engages in "selling" behavior. Two-way communication and social-psychological support is of paramount importance here.

3. *High task/low relationship leader behavior (Q3).* "Participating" is the key term here. Shared decision making and two-way communication pervade this leadership style.
4. *Low task/low relationship leader behavior (Q4).* "Delegating" is the trademark of this approach to leadership. Because of follower maturity, much freedom for decision making is left in the hands of followers by this kind of leader.

Applying the model to a sport-related context might best be illustrated by the progression from beginning youth sport to competition at the

Figure 6.4: **Life Cycle Model of Leadership**

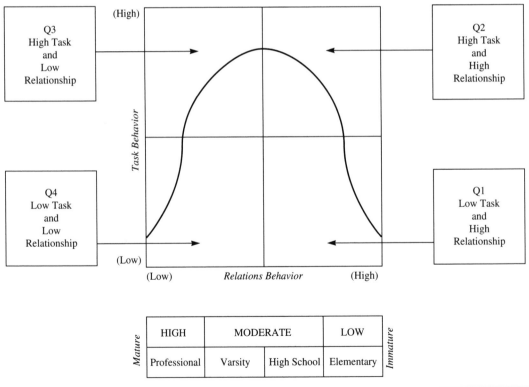

Source: Carron (1980).

elite level. In Q1, athlete immaturity would dictate a lot of high task/high relationship leadership from coaches and other youth leaders. As the athlete progresses to the elite amateur or professional level, the Q4 approach to leadership (that is, low task/low relationship) could be put into operation due to athlete maturity, ability to accomplish tasks independently, and willingness to learn and make progress toward personal and/or group goals.

Partial support for this formulation has been provided by Neil and Kirby (1985). These investigators asked 128 elite and seventy-seven novice Canadians (average age 20.3 years) involved in rowing, canoeing, and kayaking to respond to a leadership questionnaire. Overall, differences indicated that the novices preferred a coach who explained how each athlete fit into the total picture, helped new members adjust, did not place unnecessary barriers between him- or herself and team members, did little things to facilitate player satisfaction, and who could rule in a decisive fashion when necessary. No gender differences were noted.

The Functional Model

Another model of leadership that warrants some elaboration is the *functional model,* as proposed by Behling and Schriesheim (1976). Though tested little in sport, the face validity of the functional model is appealing for future sport applications. Essentially, the functional model posits that any group lives or dies based on the satisfaction of two functions: expressive and instrumental. The *expressive function* has to do with social and emotional aspects whereas the *instrumental function* is task-related. The leader who is trying to meet the expressive needs of subordinates would be concerned with how they interact, or with cohesion, or with morale factors. On the other hand, the leader dealing with the instrumental function would be concerned with task achievement. Cox (1990) cites

a possible application of the functional model to a coaching situation by suggesting that the task-oriented head coach often selects an assistant who is excellent in the expressive function, one who relates well, who takes the psychological pulse of the team and individual players and rounds off the rough edges that are sometimes created in the pursuit of skill acquisition and, ultimately, success in sport. Another example at the player level might involve the selection of team co-captains who in some way strike a balance between the instrumental and expressive functions; certainly some player-leaders are task-oriented while others serve to meet the social-psychological needs of their peers.

One test of the functional model has been made by Rees (1983). Twenty-three collegiate intramural basketball teams answered questionnaires designed to measure leadership development in their respective organizations. In general, Rees found moderate correlations between both functions, thereby failing to lend support to the theory. Rees also found integration of the two roles to be more the norm than was differentiation. These results are further supported by work done by Rees and Segal (1984) and varsity football teams. Though otherwise untested and not particularly supported, the functional model does have an appeal for future research that is intriguing.

The Multidimensional Model

In a series of papers on leadership, Chelladurai proposed a *multidimensional model of leadership* that is at the forefront in sport-related leadership research (Chelladurai, 1984b; Chelladurai and Carron, 1978). An updated version of this model is presented in figure 6.5. As can be seen, the model proposes three states of leader behavior: actual leader behavior, preferred leader behavior, and required leader behavior. *Actual leader behavior* is behavior that is engaged in irrespective of norms or subordinate preferences.

Figure 6.5: **A Multidimensional Model of Leadership**

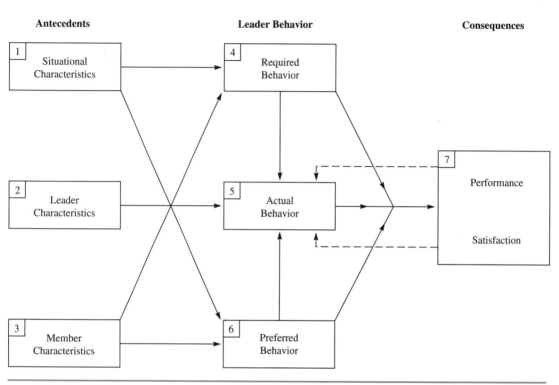

Source: Chelladurai (1990).

Preferred leader behavior is behavior that subordinates would like to see in the leader. Finally, *required leader behavior* is behavior expected of the leader on a more formal basis, such as organizational demands. In any athletic situation, but particularly as it becomes more advanced and formalized, the leader is expected by the organization to behave in certain ways. The leader, usually the coach, is expected to select players, organize practices, create a disciplined atmosphere, meet the press and public, and otherwise engage in a host of other leader-related behaviors. At the same time, the players have expectancies for competence, humaneness, and fairness from the coach. The coach in turn has to lead in a way that is con-sistent with his or her own goals, ability, and personality; these will, of course, dictate much of his or her actual leadership. The antecedents of leader behavior as proposed by Chelladurai will be the leader characteristics, the subordinate characteristics, and the situation. The interaction of these antecedents with the various leader behaviors results in performance and satisfaction at varying levels. According to Chelladurai (1990), the major proposition of the model is that performance and satisfaction will ultimately be determined by the degree of congruence among the three states of leader behavior.

To test the essential proposition just stated, Chelladurai developed the *Leadership Scale for*

Sports (LSS) (Chelladurai and Saleh, 1978; 1980). The 1980 effort resulted in a forty-item scale with five dimensions of coaching behavior. A total of 485 subjects from various Canadian universities (in both studies) responded to the scale; roughly half of the participants were physical education students of both sexes with the other half being male athletes in basketball, rowing, track and field, and wrestling. The physical education students were asked to indicate their respective favorite sports. The athletes responded similarly but were also asked to indicate the actual behavior of their coaches. Appropriate statistical analyses yielded five dimensions of coaching leadership behavior; training and instruction, democratic behavior, autocratic behavior, social support, and positive feedback. Chelladurai and Saleh (1980) further categorized the five dimensions into one direct task factor (training and instruction), two decision-style factors (democratic and autocratic behavior), and two motivational factors (social support and positive feedback). An elaboration on these dimensions is provided in table 6.1.

Efforts aimed at validating the Chelladurai and Saleh measure have been steady, if not numerous. Chelladurai and Carron (1981) have attempted to extend the LSS to youth sport. High school wrestlers (n = 54) and basketball players (n = 193) were administered the LSS and, with the exception of the autocratic behavior subdimension, the applicability of the LSS to high school sport was supported. Incidentally, the autocratic behavior scale was not particularly salient in the 1980 work of Chelladurai and Saleh.

Chelladurai and Carron (1983) had sixty-seven high school midget, sixty-three junior, sixty-three senior, and sixty-nine university basketball players complete the "preferred leader

Table 6.1
The Leadership Scale for Sports (LSS)

Dimension	Description
Training and instruction behavior	Coaching behavior aimed at improving athletes' performance by emphasizing and facilitating hard and strenuous training; instructing athletes in the skills, techniques, and tactics of the sport; clarifying the relationship among the members; and structuring and coordinating the members' activities
Democratic behavior	Coaching behavior that allows greater participation by athletes in decisions pertaining to group goals, practice methods, and game tactics and strategies
Autocratic behavior	Coaching behavior that involves independent decision making and stresses personal authority
Social support behavior	Coaching behavior characterized by a concern for the welfare of individual athletes, positive group atmosphere, and warm interpersonal relations with members
Rewarding (positive feedback) behavior	Coaching behavior that reinforces an athlete by recognizing and rewarding good performance

Source: Chelladurai (1989).

behavior" version of the LSS. The goal of the research was to assess the relationship between maturity as defined by level of competition and preferences for training and instruction (task-oriented) and social support (relationship-oriented) approaches to leadership style. In general, findings with regard to both training and instruction and social support were the opposite of what was predicted; that is, preference for both increased rather than decreased with maturity. Several methodological problems are raised by this study. One has to do with maturity. The definitional range from high school to the university level is quite narrow and may not accurately reflect increases in maturity. A second relates to sport as a mechanism for fostering maturity. Chelladurai and Carron (1983) point out that sport is largely an autocratic enterprise that may run counter to the development of maturity. Sage (1978, p. 225), quoting ex-pro football player George Sauer, offers food for thought on this issue.

> The traditional pattern of training for self-discipline is exposed for the joke that it is by former All-Pro football player George Sauer [see Scott, 1971] who said, "It's interesting to go back and listen to the people on the high school level talk about sport programs and how they develop a kid's self-discipline and responsibility. I think the giveaway, that most of this stuff being preached on the lower levels is a lie, is when you get to college and professional levels, the coaches still treat you as an adolescent. They know damn well that you were never given a chance to become responsible or self-disciplined. Even in the pros you are told when to go to bed, when to turn off your lights, when to wake up, when to eat, and what to eat." It is ironic, but pitifully illustrative of how traditional sports practices, which claim to develop self-discipline, keep those who have been exposed to these methods the longest, the pros, in virtual bondage.

Another effort by Chelladurai (1984b) bears on the issue of congruence mentioned earlier. Canadian university athletes (eighty-seven basketball players from ten teams, and fifty-seven track and field athletes from six teams) took part in the study. The LSS was used to assess leadership behavior by coaches. Both the preferred and the perceived variants of the LSS were used. Briefly, training and instruction and positive feedback were the most prevalent dimensions of leadership behavior that bear on athlete satisfaction. To quote Chelladurai (1984a, pp. 338–339):

> The discrepancy between athletes' perception of coaching behaviors and their preferences for specific behaviors was significantly correlated with their satisfaction with leadership, team performance, and overall involvement. Although the pattern of relationships between the discrepancies in the five dimensions of leader behavior and the satisfaction measures varied in the three sport groups studied (basketball, wrestling, and track and field), the relationship between discrepancy in training and instruction and satisfaction with leadership was similar in all three groups. That athletes' satisfaction with leadership increased as the coach's perceived emphasis on this dimension also increased was considered to be consistent with the task-oriented nature of athletics. Another finding of their study highlights the effects of situational differences. Basketball players were satisfied even when the coach's positive feedback exceeded their preferences (linear relationship), while the wrestlers were dissatisfied with discrepancy in either direction (curvilinear relationship). Such discrepancy did not have any effect in the track and field group.

In another study, Chelladurai (1986) administered the LSS to 229 collegiate and other adult athletes in India in an effort to establish its utility in other countries. Though limited by the fact that only Indian athletes proficient in the English language were able to participate in the study, the reliability of the LSS was demonstrated.

The most recent study by Chelladurai (Chelladurai, Haggerty, and Baxter, 1989) involved ninety-nine male and female university basketball players and twenty-two coaches in Canada. Consistent with theory and previous research, considerable congruence among coaches and players was noted in their decision style choices. Interestingly, both male and female players demonstrated a preference for more autocratic versus participative leadership styles.

Other than work done by Chelladurai and various associates, a number of studies of the LSS have emerged over the past several years. One particularly notable movement has been translation of the LSS into a number of foreign languages to include Finnish (Liukkonnen, Salminen, and Telama, 1989), French (Lacoste and Laurencelle, 1989), Japanese (Chelladurai, Imamura, Yamaguchi, Oinuma, and Miyauchi, 1988), Portuguese (Serpa, Pataco, and Santos, 1991), and Swedish (Isberg and Chelladurai, 1990).

In a review paper, Chelladurai (1990) indicated that the multidimensional theory and the LSS have been successful for the most part. He does, however, indicate that there are problems to be addressed in future research, particularly concerning the relationship between leadership and group performance. Chelladurai suggests that the problem may lie in the scale itself or it could be an artifact of the fragile outcome measures often employed in sports such as win-loss records, which are potentially contaminated by a number of external factors such as the opponents or game officials. In any event, research to date is most positive with regard to the multidimensional model and the LSS, and it is anticipated that Chelladurai's work will be at the forefront of leadership research in sports for the foreseeable future.

Player Leadership

A largely overlooked area of leadership in sports is that generated by the players themselves. Good player leadership may transcend bad coaching and, in turn, add much when the coaching leadership is superb. One effort in this area has been offered by Yukelson, Weinberg, Richardson, and Jackson (1983) in a study of collegiate baseball and soccer teams. Though limited in scope and more correlational than causal, preliminary support is generated for the notion of player leadership. Significant correlations were found between leadership status and coaches' ratings of performance, eligibility, and locus of control. Leaders in both sports were generally viewed as excellent performers by the coaches, were more experienced, and tended to be more internal than external on Rotter's I-E Scale. In a study of collegiate football players, Garland and Barry (1988) found team leaders to be more group dependent, tough-minded, extroverted, and emotionally stable. In research conducted with female soccer athletes, Glenn and Horn (1993) separated the players into central (i.e., center forward, center midfielder, center back, sweeper, and goalkeeper) or non-central (all other player positions), and found self- and coaches' ratings of leadership to be significantly associated with centrality of position. Player leaders also exhibited significantly higher competitive trait anxiety levels than nonleaders on peer evaluations, perhaps indicating highly competitive or highly motivated behavior on the part of leaders, at least in the view of their teammates. Much more work needs to be done in the neglected area of player leadership.

Evaluation of Leadership Research

Despite the fact that leadership has been the subject of much theorizing and research, only "partial truths" (Muchinsky, 1987, p. 525) have emerged. The trait approach is not without its truths, but it fails in its comprehensiveness. Behavioral approaches have their applicability, but a leader in one situation may not be a leader in another. The various contingency-related theories are appealing, but the number of leadership factors to be considered appears to be unlimited. Muchinsky suggests that future research may move away from the content of leadership to a more organizational approach emphasizing practices that produce functional or dysfunctional consequences. This transformation would thus result in leadership becoming more of a means than an end.

In sport psychology, little research of consequence has been conducted related to most of the models borrowed from industrial/organizational psychology. However, the sport-specific adaptation of a number of these models by Chelladurai shows promise as a potentially viable mechanism for sport scientists to conduct leadership research in the foreseeable future.

GROUP COHESION

"All that year, the animals worked like slaves. But they were happy in their work: they grudged no effort or sacrifice, well aware that everything they did was for the benefit of themselves and those of their kind who would come after them."

   George Orwell, *Animal Farm* (1946)

Union gives strength.

   Aesop, *Fable of the Bundle of Sticks*

Shaw (1976, p. 11) defines a group as "two or more persons who are interacting with one another in such a manner that each person influences and is influenced by each other person." Carron (1980, p. 233) states that "a group is not simply a crowd of people—a group is characterized by purposive interaction in goal

directed and/or interpersonal behavior." Carron and Chelladurai (1981) further assert that the factors that most saliently separate the group from the random gathering of individuals is the degree of attraction, commitment, and involvement of the individual members related to the collective totality. This triumvirate—attraction, commitment, and involvement—is the essence of cohesion.

The term cohesion is derived from the Latin word *cohaesus,* which means to cleave or stick together (Carron, 1984), and the theme of sticking together is at the core for most definitions of the term. The resistance of the group to disruptive forces (Gross and Martin, 1952) and the total field of forces causing members to remain within a group (Festinger, Schachter, and Back, 1950) are two early examples from the psychology literature that lend additional attestation to the theme of sticking together. In sport, Carron (1984, p. 341) views cohesion as a "dynamic process that is reflected in the group's tendency to stick together while pursuing its goals and objectives."

In the eyes of coaches and players at all levels of sophistication, team cohesion seems both highly desirable and extremely necessary to ultimate team success. Coaches are expected to forge cohesion among their players through a host of actions, and this expectancy has not gone unnoticed by members of the coaching profession. Silva (1982), in a national survey, found that the issue of how to create and maintain cohesion in sport teams was the most frequently cited concern among coaches he polled. Players also point to cohesion as a necessary condition for excellence. For example, quarterback Danny White, now retired from the Dallas Cowboys, undoubtedly spoke for many an athlete when he said: "This is not a game you can be successful at on nothing but raw talent. Sooner or later, the team that works together and supports each other is going to come out on top" (Stowers, 1985, p. 20).

The issue of team unity also extends to the fans. A particularly noticeable example is seen

A San Francisco high school girl's volleyball team wins the city championship. According to Danny White, retired Dallas Cowboys quarterback, "Sooner or later, the team that works together and supports each other is going to come out on top."

in the baseball World Series championship team of 1979, the Pittsburgh Pirates. Led by the team leader, Willie Stargell, the Pirates generated excitement and unity seldom seen in the annals of sport. To quote Dickey (1982, p. 264):

> The "Family" was the big news in the National League in 1979, and one of the great stories in baseball history.
>
> It started one rainy spring day in Pittsburgh. The Pirates had been in the habit of playing the Sister Sledge record, "We Are Family," in the clubhouse before and after games. During a rain delay that day, the song was played over the public address system and the fans started singing it. The song became the team's anthem and it forged a bond between fans and players.

> No team ever deserved the family nickname more. For years the Pirates had been a close knit team, largely because of Wilver ("Willie") Stargell.

The examples given here notwithstanding, the relationship between cohesion and team success is less than clear. The popular literature is replete with examples of teams who appeared to be disharmonious but successful. The Oakland A's teams of the early 1970s fought among themselves and with their controversial owner, Charles O. Finley, who was no shrinking violet when it came to a fight with those above or below him. Yet the A's won three consecutive World Series in 1972, 1973, and 1974. The New York Yankees of 1978 were reputedly a group of malcontents, and yet they won the World Series that year. Professional basketball superstar Charles Barkley, somewhat cynically perhaps, sums up this view of the cohesion/team success issue as follows: "Harmony isn't important. The only thing that matters is winning and getting paid" ("The Last Word," 1989, p. 6C.).

On a more scientific level, a study by Lenk (1977) is instructive. Lenk worked with a 1960 Olympic champion rowing team from Germany. Though the team was highly successful by most standards, team unity was minimal according to Lenk. In summing up his observations, Lenk (p. 12) says: "The strength of achievement of the crew even increased in the two years in which the crew existed, parallel with the strength of conflict in its increase. The crew was not beaten at all and won the Olympics in 1960. Sports crews can, therefore, perform top athletic achievements in spite of strong internal conflicts." To put it another way, Lenk (p. 38) said: "Even fierce social internal conflicts in top performance rowing crews need not noticeably weaken their achievement strength and capacity if these conflicts do not really blow up the crew."

These examples of both positive and negative reflections on cohesion only serve to illustrate its complex and controversial nature. And the issue of whether or not togetherness is in fact necessary for athletic success only touches the tip of the iceberg insofar as the issue of cohesion is concerned. Let us now address some of the more relevant issues related to team cohesion.

Models of Team Cohesion

Carron (1984) suggests that there are three cohesion models. The first of these is the *pendular model,* which hypothesizes that team cohesion operates in a pendular fashion with the amount of cohesion in a constant state of oscillation. This can be illustrated by an example from high school basketball. During the initial tryout period, a sense of cohesion comes from merely being a part of what all expect will become a well-oiled machine capable of winning most if not all of its games. Also, the mental and physical demands being made on all participants to perform well are a force for cohesion. After a short time, however, athletes will be broken into subgroups for certain parts of the overall workout; that is, the guards become identified, as are the forwards and centers. Drills and skills somewhat unique to each group are stressed, and one's competition for a starting spot on the team is more clearly identified. At this point, team identity and cohesion are lessened. As skills develop, as players are selected, and as the team is put back together to form a whole, cohesion among team members should again increase. This increase in togetherness will be particularly true as actual game competition begins and feelings of "we" are heightened. During the course of the season, events may arise that lessen the team's cohesion and the pendulum may swing in the direction of disunity. These waxings and wanings of cohesion thus continue to resemble a pendulum.

A second proposal by Carron is a *linear model,* and it states that cohesion progresses in a linear fashion as teams go through various developmental phases. These stages have been identified by Tuckman (1965) as *forming, storming, norming,* and *performing.* The basic tenet of Tuckman's formulation is that cohesion progresses in a linear fashion from its most primitive state (forming), proceeding from there to conflict and polarization (storming) to resolution of these problems and the institution of a more cooperative stance (norming) to the final stage in which goal attainment is paramount (performing).

A third model is the *life cycle model,* which emphasizes a "cradle to grave" approach to group formulation. In this model, initial formative efforts or encounters are followed by a period in which limit testing predominates. This testing process is followed by the creation of a system of expected behaviors or norms which, in turn, lead to a phase in which goal attainment is emphasized. Finally, the group will face its eventual death through separation or dissolution.

The similarities in the three models appear to be considerable, and none has emerged as superior to the others. Carron (1984) is quick to point out that, regardless of the model preferred, the element of dynamism that pervades each of them is most noticeable. Cohesion is definitely not a static, lockstep sort of phenomenon.

Factors Affecting Team Cohesion

Inasmuch as cohesion is a dynamic process, a number of forces must be at work in its creation. There are at least four factors of note.

Group Size

One of the correlates of cohesion is group size. As is intuitively obvious, the problems of handling a golf team are very different from those associated with a university football team that is allowed by NCAA rules to award eighty-five scholarships to players. In view of the demands in football, much reliance is placed on individual assistant coaches as catalysts for cohesion within their respective offensive or defensive subdomains.

As a group becomes larger, communications problems will almost certainly arise. Also, it is easy to get lost in the shuffle. Coaches (as well as player-leaders) must be alert to both communication difficulties and feelings of depersonalization. Another negative outgrowth of too much size is the feeling that the individual can slack off because the group will collectively make up the difference. It may be tempting, for instance, to go at half-speed for a few plays in football on the assumption that the other ten players will pick up the slack. Such a mentality, if pervasive, sounds like a prescription for team failure.

Related to slacking off are two social-psychological concepts known as the *Ringel-mann Effect* and *social loafing*. The *Ringelmann Effect* is named after a French agricultural engineer (Hardy, 1990) who observed some fifty years ago that average effort decreases with an increase in group size. To demonstrate this, Ringelmann observed individuals and groups of two, three, and eight persons engaged in a rope-pulling task. Eight-person groups pulled only 49 percent of the average individual force. Three-person groups pulled 85 percent of the average individual force, and two-person groups only 93 percent. Ingham, Levinger, Graves and Peckham (1974) resurrected the work done over a half-century ago and found essentially the same results as Ringelmann. However, one important difference between their findings and those of Ringelmann was noted by Ingham et al. (1974); their research replicated that of Ringelmann in instances where group size increased from one to two and two to three, but the effect diminished with the addition of a fourth, fifth, or sixth member. Nonsignificant performance decrements were noted in the latter three situations. This finding led Ingham et al. to conclude that the Ringelmann Effect is not linear as long supposed, but curvilinear.

Social loafing refers to the decrease in individual effort due to the presence of co-workers (Latané, Williams, and Harkins, 1979). Essentially, what happens in social loafing is a decrease in group motivation as a function of increases in group size. The popularity of the concept of social loafing is attested to by the fact that it has been tested in such diverse situations as shouting and clapping, rowing and hand grip, running, swimming, pumping air, cognitive tasks, brainstorming, maze solving, song writing, evaluation and judgment tasks, signal detection tasks, pulling a tug-of-war rope, and making paper moons (Hardy, 1990; Shepperd, 1993). In addition, social loafing research has been conducted in a variety of countries, including the United States, France, India, Japan, Poland, and Taiwan (Harkins and Syzmanski, 1987). This documentation of interest has led Hardy (1990, p. 312) to conclude, "Social loafing is a robust phenomenon, threatening the actual productivity of a variety of collective endeavors."

An example of social loafing in academic life with which we can all undoubtedly identify has been provided by Williams and Karau (1991): a teacher divides a class into small groups and asks students to work together on an assigned task. At the conclusion of the group effort, a final product is expected to emerge and individual grades are thus determined. Invariably, some members contribute to the group effort, others contribute a little, and others add nothing. In general, this scenario is wide open to social loafing, and resultant hard feelings.

At least two factors moderate social loafing: identifiability of individual effort and evaluation of individual effort (Latané, 1973; Latané, Williams, and Harkins, 1979; Williams, Harkins, and Latané, 1981). When groups are large, evaluation potential drops as each individual's contribution becomes blurred by that of the whole. The origins of glitches in the system are unclear because of the inability to correctly identify the sources of poor group performance. Though Latané et al. have conducted group research in a number of situations, one particularly relevant to our concerns within sport is most intriguing. Latané, Harkins, and Williams (1980), through a creative series of experimental manipulations, were able to deal effectively with the identifiability issue in a study of intercollegiate swimmers. Latané and his colleagues asked sixteen swimmers to take part in both individual and relay swimming events. All swimmers participated in two 100-meter freestyle events as individuals and then swam one lap in each of two 400-meter freestyle relay races. Identifiability was manipulated by announcing or not announcing individual lap times. In the low identifiability condition, individual times were faster (61.34 seconds) than were the corresponding relay times (61.66 seconds), all of which is suggestive

of social loafing. However, under the high identifiability condition, individual times were slower (60.95 seconds) than were the relay times (60.18 seconds). The announcing of individual times evidently does much to eliminate social loafing. Also, the high identifiability condition appears to serve as a social incentive to perform.

Some researchers take the counterposition on the social loafing phenomenon. Research conducted by Worchel, Hart, and Butemeyer (1991) and Zaccaro (1984) indicates that there can actually be increased individual effort in instances where task relevance, intergroup competitiveness, partner effort, and personal involvement are salient. Kerr and Brunn (1981) have labeled this phenomenon *social striving*. Based on data and opinions such as these as well as an analysis of an abundance of other pertinent research and theory, Hardy (1990) has arrived at a set of implications for sport psychologists and coaches based on the social loafing literature. Among Hardy's recommendations are:

1. Keep individual effort and subsequent evaluation identifiable.
2. Increase individual responsibility to the group by increasing group interaction, task commitment, and level of task cohesion.
3. Seek to make tasks personally involving, with an emphasis on collective identity.
4. Employ systematic goal setting procedures for both the team and individual members.
5. Keep lines of communication open to prevent and/or treat emerging social loafing.
6. Allow for uniqueness and creativity in individual contributions to the total team effort.
7. Keep in mind that temporary or situational decrements in motivation may actually be adaptive.
8. Where feasible, rotate athletes to other playing positions; this allows for better assessment of the likelihood of social loafing as well as assessing its impact on the collective.

9. Provide breaks in the intensity of preparation to perform athletically. No one can perform at peak intensity at all times, and breaks provide for balance and regeneration.
10. Finally, somxonx will notice of you don't do your bxst! [sic]

Inasmuch as sport teams are highly susceptible to social loafing, it behooves researchers to continue looking into this phenomenon, which is a potential source of performance decrements within sport.

The Task

The task at hand for the sport teams is another correlate of cohesion. Obviously, all sports do not require the same degree of cooperative effort among and between members. Cox (1990) refers to an *interactive–coactive continuum* to explain this relationship. *Interactive sports* are those in which close teamwork is required for success whereas coactive sports require little individual interaction. In turn, Cox talks of low and high means interdependence, a conceptual framework created by Goldman, Stockbauer, and McAuliffe (1977). *Coactive tasks* exemplify low means interdependence and interactive tasks personify high means interdependence. Sports such as golf or riflery require little team interaction, and interdependence is therefore low. On the other hand, basketball and volleyball require that all players depend on each other for success, and interdependence is high. As is almost always the case, the coaction-interaction dichotomy is not steadfast. Some sports (softball and rowing) involve aspects of both coaction and interaction and involve a moderate amount of interdependence. For a summary of the coaction-interaction and means/interdependence relationship, see table 6.2.

In summary, research in the area of task interaction and cohesion is scant. It has been intimated by Cratty (1989) that sports such as hockey require a positive cohesiveness-performance effect whereas the absence of such a relationship has been noted among successful shooters by Widmeyer et al. (1992). Clearly, much remains to be done in the area of task characteristics as they impinge on group cohesiveness.

Table 6.2
Coaction-Interaction and Means-Interdependence Relationship

Coacting teams	Mixed Coacting-interacting	Interacting teams
Low means–interdependent tasks	*Moderate means–interdependent tasks:*	*High means–interdependent tasks*
Archery	American football	Basketball
Bowling	Baseball/softball	Field hockey
Field events (track)	Figure skating	Ice hockey
Golf	Rowing	Rugby
Riflery	Track events	Soccer
Skiing	Tug-of-war	Team handball
Ski jumping	Swimming	Volleyball
Wrestling		
Degree of task cohesion required:		
Low	Moderate	High

Source: Cox (1990).

Team Tenure

The length of time that a team stays together is an important aspect of cohesion. Donnelly (1975) talks of a *team "half-life"* (Donnelly, Carron, and Chelladurai, 1978). Donnelly analyzed data on six major league baseball teams from 1901 to 1965 and concluded that a half-life of five years was most desirable for success, thereby suggesting that cohesion does not take place instantaneously but requires time and nurturance. In Donnelly's study, a half-life was considered to be the amount of time it took for the starting roster of a particular team to turn over by 50 percent. From this, Donnelly arrived at the five-year figure by studying the win-loss records and the player turnover rates. Though caveats are necessary in terms of how relevant this finding is to other teams and sports, Donnelly's work is suggestive of a temporal force in team cohesion. More work needs to be done in the area of team tenure.

A related phenomenon is team stability. Keeping players together for reasonable periods of time would seem to be a necessary first step in creating a cohesive atmosphere. Some evidence indicates that stability does in fact contribute to performance success. Essing (1970), in a study of eighteen German soccer teams, found that the successful teams made fewer lineup changes than did less successful ones (correlation of .62 between winning and lineup stability). Essing also found that successful teams used their better players more on the average and that newly acquired players were put into action less on winning teams.

Zander (1976, p. 974–975) adds another perspective on the team stability issue in discussing reactions of the management of losing teams: "Poorly performing organizations typically release more members than do organizations that are succeeding—this is demonstrated at the end of a professional sports season when losing teams rid themselves of managers and players, while winning teams leave well enough alone."

None of the preceding opinions and assertions addresses the circular nature of the stability-cohesion issue. Are stable teams more cohesive or are cohesive teams more stable? Perhaps future research efforts will shed light on this issue.

Satisfaction

A decided circularity is seen in cohesion and individual or team satisfaction. Satisfaction could either be a cause or an effect of group cohesion. An important third leg of relevance here is performance success, and there are two noteworthy models for viewing the interaction between satisfaction, success, and cohesion. An early model by Martens and Peterson (1971) posits a circular relationship with performance success leading to satisfaction which, in turn, leads to team cohesion. A second model from Williams and Hacker (1982) hypothesizes that performance success leads to both satisfaction and team cohesion, that team cohesion can lead to satisfaction, but that satisfaction in and of itself leads nowhere in terms of either success or cohesion. A representation of both of these models can be seen in figure 6.6.

In brief, the two models agree on the existence of a relationship between performance success, satisfaction, and team cohesion but the direction of causality constitutes a fundamental point of disagreement between them. Based on the Williams and Hacker model in particular, Cox (1990) urges continuation of efforts aimed toward maintaining team cohesion on the part of coaches. Cox also urges researchers to continue to study this interrelationship, and suggests that the Group Environment Questionnaire (Carron, Widmeyer, and Brawley, 1985) may be the most effective way to measure team cohesion.

Measures of Team Cohesion

Four instruments have emerged to measure cohesion in sport. The first of these measures

Figure 6.6: **Two Models of the Relationship among Performance, Satisfaction, and Cohesion**

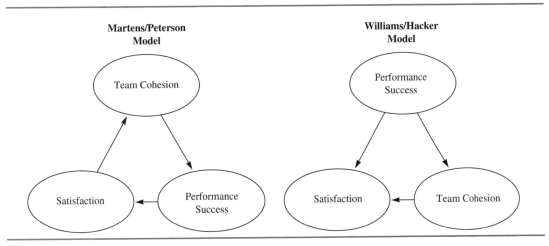

Source: Cox (1990).

was the *Sports Cohesiveness Questionnaire (SCQ)* (Martens and Peterson, 1971). The SCQ has been a popular measure in sport cohesion research, having been a part of at least twelve published studies (Widmeyer, Brawley, and Carron, 1985). The SCQ can be seen in table 6.3, and is made up of seven questions. The first five heavily load on social cohesion whereas the final two are more task related.

Two additional alternatives to the SCQ have been provided in the form of the *Task Cohesiveness Questionnaire (TCQ)* (Gruber and Gray, 1981, 1982) and the previously mentioned *Sport Cohesion Instrument (SCI)* (Yukelson et al., 1984). The TCQ consists of seventeen items and measures six dimensions of team cohesion, whereas the SCI contains twenty-one items loading on four dimensions. Time will tell concerning the efficacy of these two measures, but they appear to be promising due to their emphasis on direct measures of cohesion and the fact that both are relatively equally weighted toward task and social cohesion.

The fourth and most promising sport-related measure of cohesion is the Group Environment Questionnaire (GEQ) (Carron, Widmeyer, and Brawley, 1985; Widmeyer, Brawley, and Carron, 1985). The GEQ represents the soundest integration of cohesion theory and research to date. Widmeyer and his colleagues have been critical of other measures of cohesion, primarily because they are largely atheoretical. Widmeyer et al. also argue that, in addition to theory problems, too little has been done to validate the psychometric properties of cohesion measures used up to this time. Widmeyer and his associates go on to unequivocally state that the lack of conceptual clarity and inadequate measurement procedures add up to equivocal results, which they see as the current status of cohesion research in sport.

The GEQ was thus created in response to the existing inadequacies of other measures. It is an eighteen-item questionnaire responded to along a nine-point continuum from "strongly agree" to "strongly disagree." The GEQ measures

Table 6.3
Sports Cohesiveness Questionnaire

Categories	Items	Questions
Individual-to-individual relationships	Interpersonal attraction	1. On what type of friendship basis are you with each member of your team?
	Personal power or influence	2. How much influence do you believe each of the other members of your team has with the coach and other teammates?
Individual-to-team relationships	Value of membership	3. Compared to other groups that you belong to, how much do you value your membership on this team?
	Sense of belonging	4. How strong a sense of belonging do you believe you have to this team?
	Enjoyment	5. How much do you like competing with this particular team?
The group as a unit	Teamwork	6. How good do you think the teamwork is on your team?
	Closeness	7. How closely knit do you think your team is?

Source: Martens and Peterson (1971).

four dimensions of the group member's perceptions of group cohesiveness:

> group integration–task;
> group integration–social;
> individual attractions to the group–task; and
> individual attractions to the group–social

Group integration is thought to be a category concerning the perceptions of the group as a total unit (or team), while *Individual attractions* to the group concerns each member (or athlete's) attraction to the group. These two basic dimensions are then subdivided into task and social orientations to yield group integration–task (GI-T), group integration–social (GI-S), individual attractions to the group–task (ATG-T), and individual attraction to the group–social (AGT-S). To summarize the GEQ, Brawley (1990, p. 365) says, "The four related dimensions concern-

ing various perceptions of cohesion are likely a product of complex person-environment attraction." Sample items from the GEQ that load on each of the four dimensions are seen in figure 6.7.

Several tests of the utility of the GEQ have been conducted since its creation in 1985 (Brawley, Carron, and Widmeyer 1987; Carron, Widmeyer, and Brawley, 1985). The purpose of the 1985 Carron et al. paper was to introduce the GEQ to the sport psychology literature; in essence, it outlined the conceptual model upon which the GEQ was based. At the same time, various psychometric principles properties of the scale were satisfactorily demonstrated. The conceptual model in its simplest form can be seen in figure 6.8.

From the psychometric viewpoint, the authors generated a 354-item pool from which the final eighteen items were ultimately derived.

Figure 6.7: **Items from the Group Environment Questionnaire**

Individual attraction to the group—social

"I do not enjoy being part of the social activities of this team"

"I am not going to miss the members of this team when the season ends"

"Some of my best friends are on this team"

"I enjoy other parties more than team parties"

"For me this team is one of the most important social groups to which I belong"

Individual attraction to the group—task

"I am not happy with the amount of playing time I get"

"I am unhappy with my team's level of desire to win"

"This team does not give me enough opportunities to improve my personal performance"

"I do not like the style of play on this team"

Group integration—social

"Members of our team would rather go out on their own than get together as a team"

"Our team members rarely party together"

"Our team would like to spend time together in the off season"

"Members of our team do not stick together outside of practices and games"

Group integration—task

"Our team is united in trying to reach its goals for performance"

"We all take responsibility for any loss or poor performance by our team"

"Our team members have conflicting aspirations for the team's performance"

"If members of our team have problems in practice, everyone wants to help them so we can get back together again"

"Our team members do not communicate freely about each athlete's responsibilities during competition or practice"

Sources: Widmeyer and Brawley (1985); Hogg (1992).

Figure 6.8: **Conceptual Model of Group Cohesion**

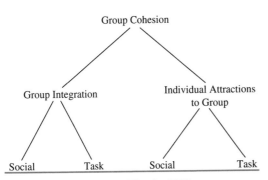

Source: Carron, Widmeyer, and Brawley (1985).

Various statistical procedures were used to satisfactorily demonstrate the reliability and validity of the instrument. At that point in the infancy of the GEQ, the authors issued the customary call for additional research. That is precisely what has taken place over the past decade. The 1987 Brawley et al. paper was actually a summary of three separate validity studies designed to support the utility of the GEQ. Chief among the conclusions from their 1987 work was that the GEQ correlated well with other measures of cohesion (i.e., the Sport Cohesiveness Questionnaire and the Team Climate Questionnaire) while not correlating with other constructs such as affiliation and personal motivation. The second study further demonstrated the validity of the GEQ, as task cohesion scores were predictive of membership in either team or individual sports. Also, team tenure predictions could be made based on social cohesion scores. The final study dealt with attributions of responsibility; the authors concluded that cohesion moderates the self-serving attributional bias in sport outcomes. All of the preceding results were viewed by the research team as supportive of the validity of the GEQ.

Additional confirmatory research has been reported by Spink (Carron and Spink, 1992, 1995; Spink, 1990; Spink and Carron, 1992, 1994). In the 1990 study, the relationship between team cohesion and collective efficacy in elite and recreational Canadian volleyball teams was analyzed. All participants in the study were asked two efficacy questions related to their expectations with regard to personal and team performance in a volleyball tournament. These expectations were then compared statistically with responses to the GEQ. Consistent with previous research, high- and low-efficacy players differed on the ATG-T and GI-S scales. The finding that ATG-T was related to high collective efficacy among the elite players suggests that high task orientation characterizes successful teams. Though it was not predicted by Spink, the GI-S finding indicates that the social factor may also play a significant role in team cohesion.

In the other four studies by Spink and Carron, the GEQ was modified for use in exercise settings. Carron and Spink (1992) reported basic psychometric data supporting the use of the GEQ in exercise settings; Spink and Carron (1992) followed up on this modification, and were able to show differences in measures of exercise adherence. Specifically, they found that exercisers who were absent less often than a comparable group gave a stronger endorsement to the ATG-T and AGT-S dimensions of the GEQ. Additionally, exercisers who were late less often than their counterparts endorsed the ATG-T dimension more strongly.

Results from other studies have been favorable with regard to the GEQ. Rainey and Schweickert (1988) administered the GEQ to thirty-seven collegiate baseball players prior to a ten-day road trip; twenty-two players made the trip and fifteen remained on campus. Players making the trip reported higher social and lower task scores than did the others upon their return home; it would appear that travelling as a team for an extended period created a socially cohesive effect, though it is not clear why the task orientation was less pronounced. In another study, Williams and Widmeyer (1991) looked at cohesion in a coacting sport: golf. Specifically, they administered the GEQ to eighty-three female collegiate golfers from eighteen teams and compared team scores with cohesion responses. Cohesion significantly predicted performance (i.e., golf scores), with task cohesion being the best predictor. Finally, in an international application, Kim and Sugiyama (1992) tested 114 Japanese high school athletic teams with regard to the cohesion/performance relationship; these researchers again found strong support for the GEQ.

On a less supportive note, a recent study calls into question the factor structure of the GEQ (Schutz, Eom, Smoll, and Smith, 1994). Schutz et al. administered the GEQ to 740 high school athletes (426 males, 314 females). A confirmatory factor analysis indicated that the males and females had different factor structures, and neither group conformed to the structure hypothesized to exist by the authors of the GEQ. Also, they were not able to produce a satisfactory four-factor structure said to exist in the scale. The Schutz et al. findings are provocative, and serve as a reminder that there is still work to do in establishing the validity and utility of the GEQ.

Despite this disclaimer by Schutz et al., Widmeyer and his colleagues assert that the GEQ is an improvement over existing measures because it incorporates both existing group cohesion theory from social psychology and sound psychometrics. Whether the authors of the GEQ are correct in their assertion will be answered by research conducted over the next several years, but the instrument looks promising.

Two Final Notes

Two additional issues warrant discussion. One has to do with the *issue of circularity,* particularly as it relates to the cohesion-performance distinction. Perhaps the ultimate question revolves around whether cohesion facilitates performance or whether performance dictates cohesion. Studies within sport by Landers, Wilkinson, Hatfield, and Barber (1982), Ruder and Gill (1982), and Williams and Hacker (1982) all lend support to the notion that the direction of causality is more likely to be from performance to cohesion than vice versa. If the assertion of these researchers is so, team cohesion may well have been traditionally overrated as a cause of success. Nevertheless, coaches should strive for cohesive units, but also maintain an awareness of the significance of task success in shaping the coveted spirit of togetherness.

A final point related to cohesion (and very much related to the issue of circularity) is the negative side of the coin. Cohesion is not altogether a positive; if overdone, it may lead to conformity and lessened task success. Individuality may be suppressed, self-deception may become more likely, and cliques may be formed. The Klein and Christiansen (1969) and Fiedler (1967) studies, which showed that basketball players who are close friends tended to pass more often to each other to the detriment of the collective effort, demonstrate the dangers of cliques within a team. The role of the coach in creating a winning *and* cohesive atmosphere is essential and it will be explored in chapter 12.

AUDIENCE EFFECTS

Anyone who participated in any form of athletics is acutely aware of what it is like to be evaluated by others. We aspire to perform well because of internal forces, such as personal desire to excel, but we are also impelled to success because of pressures generated by those who are interacting at one level or another with us. Our peers serve as one point of evaluative reference; coaches are also formidable forces; and audiences for which we may demonstrate our skills serve as a third evaluative source. Also, as Cratty (1981, p. 191) has pointed out: "Even a solitary workout may be accompanied by an unseen audience, a group of people residing psychologically and socially in the mind of the performer. This audience, the athlete knows, stands ready to judge his or her performance at some future time, harshly or with kindness and praise."

The interaction between internal motivational and external evaluative forces is most complex and intriguing, and a number of theorists and researchers have tried to shed light on the tangled web of audience effects on human performance. This fascination with audience effects owes a great debt to research that has been done over the years in what is known as social facilitation.

Social Facilitation

To Zajonc (1965, p. 269), social facilitation "examines the consequences upon behavior which derive from the sheer presence of other individuals." Zajonc also classifies social facilitation research into two basic paradigms: audience effects and coactive effects. *Audience effects* are those created by observing behavior in front of passive spectators, and *coactive effects* are behavioral effects occurring as a result of the presence of other individuals engaging in the same activity.

Early Research

Social facilitation research dates back to the work of Triplett (1898). In what Allport (1954) calls the first experiment in social psychology, Triplett studied bicycle racers under a variety of conditions and concluded that the presence of others actually facilitated performance. In the same study, Triplett also showed that adolescents could spin a fishing reel-like device more rapidly when working with another individual than when working alone. Allport (1924) was another significant figure in social facilitation research and is, in fact, given credit for coining the term (Cox, 1990; Wankel, 1984). In 1933, the mere presence hypothesis received its first significant challenge as a result of research reported by Pessin (1933). Pessin noted that college students learned nonsense syllables better when alone than in the presence of others. In 1935, Dashiell, a protégé of Allport, added some refinements to his mentor's suggestion that there is no such thing as a pure alone or pure coactive situation because of the intrusion of internal psychological mediators. Also, Dashiell observed that the presence of others tended to speed up performance rate but not accuracy of response. This latter point served as a precursor to the substantial contribution of Zajonc, though thirty years elapsed in the process.

The Work of Zajonc

In 1965, Zajonc published a pivotal paper in which he outlined his approach to social facilitation. Borrowing heavily from Hull-Spence drive theory, Zajonc suggests that the mere presence of an audience heightens physiological arousal, which in turn enhances the likelihood that the individual will emit his or her dominant response in social situations. To quote Zajonc (1965, p. 270), "The emission of these well-learned responses is facilitated by the presence of spectators, while the acquisition of new responses is impaired." This expostulation, according to Zajonc, means that performance is enhanced and learning hindered by the presence of others. Based on these kinds of predictions, it would follow that audiences would have differential effects on sport performance as a function of skill level, with young athletes most adversely affected by audiences and highly skilled ones least affected. A visual representation of this hypothesis can be seen in figure 6.9.

While there has been support for Zajonc's model in the motor learning area (i.e., Hunt and

Figure 6.9: Audience Effects on Athletes at Various Skill Levels

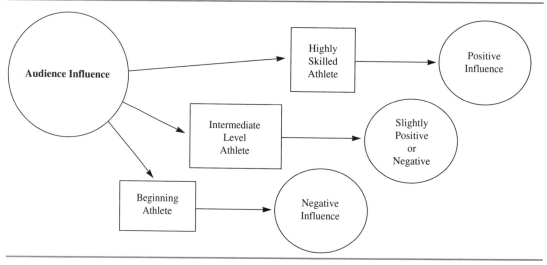

Source: Cox (1990).

Hillery, 1973; Landers, Brawley, and Hale, 1978; Martens, 1969), studies such as those reported by Paulus and associates (Paulus and Cornelius, 1974; Paulus, Shannon, Wilson, and Boone, 1972) present a less rosy view of Zajonc's work. In the two Paulus studies, college gymnasts were used as subjects, and in both instances it was found that spectator presence resulted in findings directly opposite to the Zajonc model's predictions. As Paulus et al. note, it may be that naturalistic performance situations cannot be directly compared with laboratory manipulations of audience effects. This comparability problem, of course, is not unique to this area of scientific inquiry.

As a result of equivocal findings both inside and external to sport-related research, there has been considerable interest in developing competing models to explain audience effects on performance.

Other Drive Theories

Cottrell (1972) has taken exception to Zajonc's mere presence hypothesis, and suggests that drive is facilitated by the presence of someone who can evaluate performance. This presence Cottrell calls *evaluative apprehension*. Through socialization experiences, the individual comes to anticipate positive or negative outcomes as a result of the presence of evaluative others. This emphasis on the critical audience is a point of separation between Cottrell's work and that of Zajonc; Zajonc would suggest that the uncertainty created by the presence of an audience would increase arousal as opposed to Cottrell's emphasis on evaluation effects as the cause of an increased drive state. As is the case with the Zajonc model, some support for the Cottrell approach has been generated in the area of motor behavior (e.g., Haas and Roberts, 1975; Martens and Landers, 1972). All in all, however, the research on the Cottrell model has been equivocal and rather scant of late.

Other drive theories of note include those of Sanders, Baron, and Moore (1978) and Guerin

and Innes (1982). Sanders et al. view *attentional conflict* as the cause of drive; that is, the presence of people who can provide social comparison data that will conflict with attention to the task at hand serves as a source of generalized drive. Guerin and Innes suggest a *social monitoring theory*, which posits that the presence of others who cannot be visually monitored or the presence of others who are unfamiliar, unpredictable, or threatening increases drive. According to Bond and Titus (1983, p. 266), "Drive will not be increased by the mere presence of innocuous others if those others can periodically be monitored. According to this social monitoring theory, the individual should be less affected by the presence of coactors than by the presence of spectators because coactors are more predictable."

An Evaluation of Drive Theory

Wankel (1984) suggests that drive theory has been dominant in social facilitation research partially because of its generally parsimonious nature. On the other hand, Wankel states that the various drive theories are too mechanistic to be of value in trying to explain complex human behavior. Sanders (1981) indicates that the various drive models have much overlap and are generally not comprehensive enough to explain socially facilitated behavior. Cox (1990) raises objections to drive theory on relevancy grounds; although important from a research viewpoint, noninteractive audiences used in drive theory studies are far less relevant to sport than interactive ones. Most athletic situations are characterized by interactions between coaches and athletes and spectators.

Because of the preceding charges, calls for other approaches to explaining social facilitation have been made (Geen and Gange, 1977; Landers, 1980; Wankel, 1984). Each of these authorities has issued a call for more cognitive explanatory models. Several models of recent vintage, however incomplete, have responded to the challenge. We shall take a brief look at three of them.

Alternative Nondrive Theory Models

Duval and Wicklund (1972) have posited a model that stresses *objective self-awareness*. In theory, the performer who is self-aware should be motivated to reduce discrepancies that arise from the disparities between actual and ideal task performance.

Another formulation is that of Bond (1982), who proposes a *self-presentational model*. Bond contends that the motivation to project an image of competence in the presence of others will facilitate performance. Whereas the drive theorists equate drive with physiological arousal, Bond sees possible embarrassment as the source of arousal (Bond and Titus, 1983).

An *arousal-cognitive information processing model* is a third approach. Within sport, Landers (1980) and Wankel (1984) are proponents of the model because it represents a step away from the mechanistic drive theory and places emphasis not only on the energizing effects of social factors but also on the informational or cognitive aspect.

Though intuitively appealing, the cognitive models have, for the most part, been of recent creation and little has been done to test them within sport. Perhaps future efforts will be directed toward confirming or disconfirming these cognitive approaches, thereby shedding light on the complex issue of social facilitation.

Interactive Audience Effects on Sport Performance

As stated earlier, the preponderance of sport interactions are with an active audience as opposed to the passive audience so prominent in social facilitation research. The effects of supportive versus nonsupportive audiences, audience size, and viewer sophistication are only a few of the interactive forces at work in shaping athletic behavior. Of the preceding, far more is known about the supportive audience than the other variables. This supportive audience generally is viewed in athletics as constituting the home advantage, a topic of considerable interest to spectators, athletes, coaches, sport announcers, and sport scientists. The remainder of our discussion will be devoted to this effect and what has come to be known as basking in reflected glory (BIRG).

Table 6.4

Percentage of Games Won by Home Team in Four Sports

Home Team Outcome	Sport				
	Baseball (1971)	Professional Football (1971)	College Football (1971)	Hockey (1971–1972)	Basketball (1952–1966)
Win	53% (989)	55% (100)	59% (532)	53% (286)	82% (290)
Lose	47 (891)	41 (74)	40 (367)	30 (163)	18 (64)
Tie	— —	4 (8)	1 (11)	17 (93)	— —
Total	100% (1,880)	100% (182)	100% (910)	100% (542)	100% (354)

Number of games in parentheses.

Source: Schwartz and Barsky (1977).

The Home Advantage

Much is made in the media of the so-called *home court advantage*. A rule of thumb in basketball, according to some experts, is that the home court is worth 3 to 7 points to the home team. In major league baseball, the goal often seems to be to win big at home and break even on the road. While one can speculate that, for the visitors, the demands of travel, disrupted schedules, and unfamiliar surroundings are causes of the home advantage, fans typically believe that their support of the home team is at the heart of the edge enjoyed by their beloved players.

The first significant study of the home advantage was conducted by Schwartz and Barsky (1977). Their data analysis was made on 1,880 major league baseball games played in 1971, on 182 professional football games played that same year, on 542 National Hockey League games from the 1971–1972 season, and on 1,485 college basketball games played from 1952 through 1966 by the big five in Philadelphia (LaSalle, Pennsylvania, St. Joseph's, Temple, and Villanova). The percentage of games won by the home teams in each of these sports can be seen in table 6.4. Clearly, a home advantage is reflected, with the edge being greatest in basketball. Also, hockey teams profit from playing at home, particularly if tie games are excluded; the winning percentage for the home team in hockey then becomes 64. All things considered, Schwartz and Barsky concluded that the source of this advantage was social support from a friendly audience.

In another significant study, Varca (1980) lends support to the idea of the home advantage. Varca used game statistics for all men's basketball games in the Southeastern Conference for the 1977–1978 season in arriving at his conclusions as to why the home advantage exists. Varca's main hypothesis was that differences in aggressive play between the home team and visitors could account for the advantage. Simply

Studied closely since 1971 home advantage has been shown to have significant effects on the visiting team. The combined efforts of travel demands, disrupted schedules, and unfamiliar surroundings add to this advantage.

stated, *functionally aggressive play* by the home team and *dysfunctionally aggressive play* by the visitors accounts for the edge afforded the home team. *Functionally aggressive play* to Varca includes skill in rebounding, stealing the ball from opponents, and blocking shots, whereas *dysfunctionally aggressive play* was limited to personal fouls, a generally detrimental force in basketball. As predicted, the home team was superior in all three of the functional behaviors, and the visitors were guilty of more fouls (dysfunctional aggression) than were the home teams. Varca gave the credit to arousal states generated by the friendly, supportive audiences at the various home courts, with the arousal being channeled positively by the home team and negatively by the visitors.

Yet a third study of the home advantage, and one similar to that of Varca, was conducted by Silva, Andrew, and Richey (1983). In their study of the home and away performance of the North Carolina Tarheels and their Atlantic Coast Conference basketball opposition over a ten-year period, Silva et al. arrived at the conclusion that performance decrements by visiting teams were more influential than performance increments by home teams in explaining the home court edge.

Based on the results of the three preceding pieces of research, it seems that a home advantage in a number of fairly advanced sport settings is a reality. Major league baseball, football, and hockey teams and collegiate basketball teams do indeed seem to profit from playing at home. However, a study by Baumeister and Steinhilber (1984) adds a most provocative caveat to this conclusion. These researchers looked at baseball's World Series for the years 1924 through 1982 and the National Basketball Association championship playoffs games from 1967 through 1982 in an effort to see if the home audience is in fact a positive force in the final or deciding games. In both instances, they found the home field or court advantage to be valid for early games in the playoffs but not for the games that actually determined the ultimate winner. Of particular interest to Baumeister and Steinhilber was the source of this effect; was the home team choking or were the visitors merely playing unusually well? In baseball, they chose fielding errors to analyze because their low mutual determinacy makes them a relatively pure measure of choking. In the first two games of the series, the visiting team made the most errors; in the seventh game, it is reversed, with the home team committing the most errors. The difference in errors

noted in the seventh game is significant at the .01 level of confidence. These data are reflected in table 6.5.

In basketball, free throw shooting was chosen for analysis, and the results follow those of baseball. In games one through four of a seven-game playoff, the home team shot about the same as the visitors but the tables again turned in game seven, with the visitors having an edge that was statistically significant. These data are available in table 6.6.

Yet another analysis made by Baumeister and Steinhilber was of the NBA semifinal and championship series, again from 1967 through 1982. In games one through four, the home team won 70.1 percent of the contests; in series decided in the seventh game, the home court advantage dropped to 38.5 percent. Clearly, the home team advantage does not appear to exist in critical games at the highest levels of professional basketball.

Baumeister and Steinhilber feel that the presence of supportive others may actually be more harmful than helpful in some situations. This performance decrement is seen as choking on the part of the home team. Further support for this idea is offered by Baumeister, Hamilton, and Tice (1985) in a laboratory experiment with college students.

Table 6.5

Fielding Errors in World Series Games, 1924–1982

Games	Errors per game		Errorless games	
	Home	*Visitor*	*Home*	*Visitor*
1 and 2	0.65	1.04	33	18
7	1.31	0.81*	6	12**

*p = <.01

**p = <.02

Source: Baumeister and Steinhilber (1984).

Table 6.6
Free Throw Performance in NBA
Playoffs, 1967–1982

Performance	Home	Visitor
Games 1–4:		
Success (scored)	3368	3412
Failure (missed)	1303	1266
Scoring percentage	.72	.73*
Last (7th) game:		
Success	873	937
Failure	391	328
Scoring percentage	.69	.74**

*p. = not significant

**p. = <.01

Source: Baumeister and Steinhilber (1984).

Gayton, Matthews, and Nickless (1987) have taken the work of Baumeister and Steinhilber to the Stanley Cup playoffs in the National Hockey League (NHL) for the years 1960 through 1985 and obtained very different results. They found no support for a significant home court disadvantage at any level in the NHL playoffs. Additionally, the choking phenomenon alluded to by Baumeister and Steinhilber did not occur in those series that went to a seventh game. In the twelve playoffs that went to a seventh and deciding game, the home team won seven.

Attesting to the continuing popularity of research concerning the home advantage are ten additional studies conducted in the late 1980s and early 1990s. Most are supportive of the early research but they do represent attempts to broaden our knowledge base in a significant area of sports; a summary of these articles appears in table 6.7.

Considering the provocative nature of the findings of nearly two dozen studies over the past twenty years, more research needs to be done to shed additional light on a fascinating facet of audience effects, namely, the home advantage.

A Final Note

The home advantage is perhaps more clearly understood than other facets of audience effects. Audience size, audience sophistication, gender effects, team identification factor, and audience density are also important aspects of the overall audience issue. Much work remains to be done in clarifying these and other parameters that impinge on the audience effects issue.

Basking in Reflected Glory (BIRG)

Everyone likes to be associated with a winner, and a 1976 report of three studies conducted by Robert Cialdini and his associates (Cialdini, Borden, Thorne, Walker, Freeman, and Sloan, 1976) has added an element of scientific verification to the notion. In the first of the three studies, Cialdini and associates sought support for the existence of a phenomenon known as "basking in reflected glory" (BIRG) by covertly observing the apparel worn to introductory psychology classes by students from seven universities with major football programs. Essentially what the observers did was look for the wearing of various paraphernalia (buttons, T-shirts, jackets, sweatshirts) that displayed the school name, team nickname or mascot, or university insignia on Mondays after football games. Students clearly tended to wear more school-related paraphernalia on Mondays after wins than after losses, a finding that was interpreted as lending support to BIRG.

In the second experiment, an examination of pronoun usage served as the mechanism for studying BIRG. Simply stated, it was hypothesized that students would respond to wins with increased use of the pronoun *we* and to losses with greater use of the pronoun *they*. In order to more covertly test this hunch, students were contacted by telephone and the investigators identified themselves as employees of a "Regional

Table 6.7
Recent Studies of Home Advantage in Sports

Author(s)	Participants	Results
Courneya and Carron (1990)	360 slow-pitch teams	No win-loss advantage to batting first or last by gender, playing ability, or time of season
Courneya and Carron (1991)	26 Double-A Professional baseball teams	Significant home advantage (55.1 percent) wins by home team; length of home stand or road trip not related to home advantage
Gayton and Langevin (1992)	Wrestlers in 792 matches	61 percent of home matches won (statistically significant difference)
Glamser (1990)	49 soccer matches in England	Significant home advantage; rule violations increased in away matches; black players charged with significantly more violations away from home
Irving and Goldstein (1990)	No-hitters in major league baseball since 1900	111 of 175 no-hitters (63 percent) and seven of nine perfect games (78 percent) pitched at home
Leonard (1989)	Summer Olympics 1896–1988 and Winter Olympics 1924–1988	Host teams win more medals than they do at previous or following games
McAndrew (1992)	4,172 high school wrestlers	Home wrestlers won 1,422 matches; visitors won 964
Nelson and Carron (1991)	Four men's and four women's Division I teams in five sports	68.6 percent of home games won over five-year period; 48 percent games won by same teams when on the road
Wright, Jackson, Christie, McGuire, and Wright (1991)	British Open Golf Championship	British golfers in contention achieved progressively worse scores in comparison with foreign players over four rounds of play
Wright, Voyer, Wright, and Roney (1995)	National Hockey League Stanley Cup Playoffs	Substantial home disadvantage noted in decisive games

Choking Under Pressure: An Athlete's Worst Nightmare

A constant fear of athletes, and an equally compelling topic of conversation among fans and sport talk-show hosts, is the phenomenon known as choking. It is one of the greatest fears that athletes have in the performance arena. How many times have we, as sports competitors, seen an opponent grab his or her neck and make the all-too-familiar choking noise? Perhaps a quote from professional golfer Scott Hoch, known at one time as a choker because he missed a two-foot putt that would have won the 1989 Master's, best exemplifies the role choking plays in sport: "It will always be Hoch as in choke until I do otherwise" (Hershey, 1989).

Baumeister has defined choking as "performance decrements under pressure circumstances" and pressure as "any factor or combination of factors that increases the importance of performing well on a particular occasion" (1984, p. 610). In his 1984 paper, Baumeister reported the results of six separate studies; particular emphasis was placed on the role of self-consciousness as a cause of choking. Baumeister suggests that increases in self-consciousness are accompanied by deteriorations in the lawfulness or predictability of behavior. Counterintuitively, individuals who are habitually self-conscious should handle pressure situations that engender self-consciousness because they are so accustomed to dealing with it on a daily basis. On the other hand, low self-conscious individuals may suffer incremental escalations in self-consciousness under pressure that may in turn interfere with performance. Greater choking may then be expected from low as opposed to high self-conscious individuals under pressure. Baumeister's results confirmed just such an expectancy. Essentially, the model emphasizes attentional shifts as crucial to the choking process; that is, attention shifts to internal processes to the detriment of attending to the external demands of the task that may be critical to success and the avoidance of choking. Heaton and Sigall (1991), in a study of introductory psychology students, also found choking to be associated with low self-consciousness.

In a most interesting interchange that brings together both the home field advantage/disadvantage and research on choking, Baumeister and Steinhilber (1984) have been taken to task by Schlenker, Phillips, Boniecki, and Schlenker (1995a; 1995b); in turn, Baumeister (1995) was afforded the opportunity to respond to the critics. All three papers were published as a package in volume 68, number 4, of *Journal of Personality and Social Psychology*; Schlenker et al. (1995a) presented their disagreements with the 1984 Baumeister and Steinhilber research, followed by a rebuttal by Baumeister and concluding with a rejoinder by Schlenker and associates

(Continued next page)

Highlight 6.1 (Continued)

Choking Under Pressure: An Athlete's Worst Nightmare

(1995b) (hereafter referred to merely as Schlenker for purposes of brevity and avoidance of repetition).

Schlenker suggests that Baumeister and Steinhilber have taken a kind view as opposed to a dark view of the mechanism at work in choking. Baumeister and Steinhilber advocate that choking arises due to poorer-than-usual task performance produced by anticipation of success in front of a supportive audience—the kinder view. It is Schlenker's contention that self-doubt, self-consciousness, and unwanted and aversive self-attention are at the heart of choking under pressure, which represents a more negative or darker view of the process. Schlenker also found fault with the data-gathering process used by Baumeister and Steinhilber, suggesting a failure to properly sample the archival data used for analyzing the "home" choke. Like Baumeister and Steinhilber, Schlenker used all baseball World Series since the institution of the seven-game series in 1924, excluding four-game sweeps (Schlenker did have an additional eleven World Series to consider beyond Baumeister and Steinhilber's stopping point of 1982). Unlike Baumeister and Steinhilber, Schlenker chose to exclude the years 1943-1945 because of the significant changes in baseball brought about by World War II. Another difference between the two pieces of research was that Schlenker analyzed all divisional playoffs since the start of the seven-game format in 1985, using this as a moderator for some of his subsequent analyses. Other points of departure included analyzing *when* fielding errors occurred and choking across eras (three eras were identified; 1924 through 1949, 1950 through 1968, and 1969 through 1993).

Through clever methodological controls and statistical analyses, elaborate and compelling arguments are made by Schlenker et al. that there is not a disadvantage to playing at home in the decisive seventh game of a series. It was important to note that the era from 1950 through 1968 did in fact show a huge home field disadvantage, whereas the effect was not there for the other two time periods. Eleven series went to seven games in the 1950-1968 era, and the visiting team won nine of the eleven. Schlenker contends that any analysis of the home field advantage/disadvantage that makes major use of the period 1950–1968 is going to yield biased results indicating a home field choke. Otherwise, there was little evidence for the home choke. Fielding errors were used in the original work as a validation of the home field disadvantage; this relationship was shown earlier in table 6.5.

(Continued next page)

Highlight 6.1 (Continued)

Choking Under Pressure: An Athlete's Worst Nightmare

Schlenker found those errors to be salient only when the home team falls behind in the decisive seventh game. Perhaps anxiety, self-consciousness, and pressing too hard become operational at that point, thereby creating a favorable environment for failure, or choking.

Based on the preceding analyses and others too numerous and complex to mention here, Schlenker concludes that Baumeister and Steinhilber were simply wrong, theoretically, methodologically, and interpretively.

The rebuttal by Baumeister points out a variety of problems with the Schlenker work. He also points to the larger issue of social psychology research employing archival data. It is Baumeister's contention that science proceeds best by controlled research under laboratory controls not present in "real world" archival data. Baumeister does admit, however, that the Schlenker finding concerning the timing of fielding errors represents a breakthrough in the refinement of choking theory within and external to the sport world.

The preceding interchange makes it abundantly clear that choking is a real phenomenon that bears additional investigation, particularly with regard to the mechanisms and conditions bearing on its creation and maintenance. It is also clear that the home advantage/disadvantage research area will remain a hot one, particularly in light of the challenges offered by Schlenker and his colleagues.

An alternative view of choking which departs considerably from the Baumeister and Steinhilber and Schlenker et al. variety has been proposed by Brant (1988). Brant has linked the problem to physiological processes centered around the interplay of the sympathetic and parasympathetic nervous systems. He asserts "the choking response itself begins in the middle of the brain, at the hypothalamus, the so-called governor of the autonomic nervous and endocrine systems" (p. 23). In short, we choke because of bodily sabotage. Again, Brant says, "our circuitry and chemistry couldn't give a fig how we perform in the clutch; they want us (and thereby themselves) to survive" (p. 24). Undoubtedly, the Brant view is a bit too simplistic, but it does bring into play the role of physiological processes in choking that more psychosocial models tend to ignore or downplay.

Sources: Baumeister (1984, 1995); Brant (1988); Heaton and Sigall (1991); Hershey (1989); Schlenker, Phillips, Boniecki, and Schlenker (1995a, 1995b).

Survey Center"; the subjects were asked to respond to six questions about campus life in general. Students were then given feedback that placed them in success or failure groups irrespective of how well they actually did on the six questions. They were then asked to respond to questions about their teams' recent football games, half of which had been won and half lost. Two hypotheses were generated by the experimental manipulations just described; one was that team wins would result in more *we's* than would losses. The second hypothesis was that the effect of the first hypothesis would be greater for those who had "failed" the test from the so-called Regional Survey Center. The latter supposition was based on the idea that those who had "failed" the campus events test would want to enhance themselves in the eyes of the investigators by associating themselves with positive entities, such as a team victory the previous Saturday. Clear support for BIRG was found in both instances. There was strong support for the use of the pronoun *we* and an even stronger relationship was noted when the respondents' public prestige was in jeopardy.

The third experiment arose out of the results of the previous manipulations of BIRG. Specifically, the investigators were curious as to how the students would respond when they were told that the phone calls were from either a University Survey Center or a Regional Survey Center. The idea here was that the students would demonstrate a stronger BIRG response to the regional than to the local center. The rationale for this hypothesis rested in the supposition that BIRG would be stronger when the respondent had a stronger link to the prestigious object than did the observer. The likelihood that a local caller would have a reasonably similar degree of identification was thought to be quite high; on the other hand, an outsider would not be so likely to have the same emotional investment in the admired object, and identifying with the source of prestige would enhance their perception in the

eyes of the more geographically and presumably emotionally remote caller. By way of paraphrasing the authors, little prestige is to be gained from bragging about the virtues of California weather to another Californian; however, relating the same message to someone from states with more severe weather conditions might be more image enhancing. As expected, confirmation for BIRG was again demonstrated.

Overall, support for BIRG in all three studies was most evident, and the results were viewed as providing support for the importance of perceived esteem of others. Alternatively, however, an explanation for the results that is couched in terms of enhancing the self-concept might also be a viable one. Cialdini and his associates contend that BIRG is best explained in terms of its enhancing effects on social image, but the interplay between social image and self-image cannot be ignored.

Additional support for the BIRG phenomenon has been provided by other sources (i.e., Hirt, Zillman, Erickson, and Kennedy, 1992; Murrell and Dietz, 1992; Wann and Branscombe, 1990). Of particular salience is the Hirt et al. research in which a series of studies was conducted with university students with the intent of assessing the interplay of social and self identity and mood as they relate to BIRG. Strong support was found for the role of self-esteem in image maintenance, while mood appeared to be of less explanatory value in terms of the results of their study. Hirt and his associates concluded, "BIRGing is a strategic impression management technique whereby individuals raise their esteem in the eyes of others" (p. 724). The authors were also quick to point out that BIRGing is not confined to fanship at athletic events; they are convinced that it would also manifest itself in any social situation (i.e., national identity, political party, ethnic group) involving strong personal allegiances.

A phenomenon related to BIRGing that has received considerably less attention but is nevertheless of interest is CORFing, or cutting off reflected failure (Snyder, Higgins, and Stucky, 1983). CORFing is an image protection tactic that allows individuals to avoid negative evaluation from others by distancing themselves psychologically from unsuccessful people, teams, or other entities (Hirt et al., 1992; Wann, 1993). As such, BIRGing represents an image enhancement technique and CORFing is an image protection mechanism, a subtle but important difference (Hirt et al., 1992).

Given the tremendous importance of spectators at athletic events in terms of economics and social-psychological dynamics, research such as that represented by BIRGing and CORFing is likely to continue for the foreseeable future in an attempt to better understand this important aspect of audience effects.

SUMMARY

1. Leadership, cohesion, and audience effects represent three variables within social psychology that have intrigued sport and other social scientists.
2. The discussion of leadership dates back to the time of Plato, Caesar, and Plutarch. Early Chinese and Egyptian writings also reflect an interest in leadership. Leadership studies have been pursued in this country for about ninety years.
3. The trait theory of leadership (the great-man theory) takes the position that leaders are leaders by nature, and would be leaders in most if not all situations. Support for the great-man perspective is equivocal.
4. The behavioral approach to leadership emphasizes what a leader does as opposed to what he or she is. Major work on this model was conducted at Ohio State University in the 1950s. A major outgrowth from the Ohio State study was the development of the Leader Behavior Description Ques-

tionnaire (LBDQ) and the Leader Opinion Questionnaire (LOQ). The LBDQ has been used in several sport-related studies of leadership. Along with the trait model, the behavioral approach has served as an impetus for the creation of models that stress interactional leadership styles.

5. Fiedler's contingency model incorporates both traits and situational variables into the leadership formula. Much is made in Fiedler's theory of type of leadership and situational favorableness as predictors of leadership. Research within sport has been sparse and not especially supportive of Fiedler's approach.
6. Path-goal theory suggests that the leader is a catalyst for group success and satisfaction. Again, research within sport has been scant but the issue of the efficacy of path-goal theory has not been determined.
7. Life cycle theory places much reliance on the motivational and maturity level of subordinates to attain group goals. There is some support within the sport literature for the life cycle formulation.
8. A model with little research support so far, but one of intuitive appeal, is the functional approach of Behling and Schriesheim. Instrumental and expressive functions are emphasized, with the former referring to task-related aspects and the latter to social and emotional needs of the group members.
9. The multidimensional model is currently at the forefront of sport leadership research and has been advanced by Chelladurai, Carron, and Saleh in a series of studies. Quite a bit of interest has been generated by the multidimensional model, and research and refinement are continuing.
10. Despite its obvious importance to team success, player leadership is a largely neglected area of inquiry in sport psychology. Additional research is badly needed in this area.

11. It appears that the study of leadership is an evolving enterprise, and much speculation exists with regard to exactly where the field is going. The multidimensional model of Chelladurai looks promising from the perspective of leadership researchers in sport psychology.

12. Group cohesion is generally but not universally considered to be essential to success in sport. The term itself comes to us from the Latin word *cohaesus* and refers to a group organized around purposeful behavior.

13. Three models—the pendular, the linear, and the life-cycle—are suggested by Carron as representative of current thinking about group cohesion.

14. Group size is a correlate of cohesion, and cohesion is generally lessened as groups increase in size. The Ringelmann Effect and social loafing are two key terms here, both referring to performance decrements associated with increases in group size. The literature in social loafing is quite rich and varied. Two crucial moderators of social loafing include identifiability and evaluation of individual effort. Based on the available literature, Hardy has recommended ten things coaches and sport psychologists can do to deal with social loafing.

15. The task at hand greatly affects group cohesion. Cox talks of an interactive-coactive dichotomy to partially explain differences in task demands across sport. Coactive activities include such sports as archery and golf, whereas examples of interactive sports include soccer and volleyball. Mixed coactive-interactive activities include baseball, football, and rowing.

16. The length of time that a team stays together affects cohesion. Research by Donnelly suggests that there is indeed an optimal length of time for cohesion to develop and subsequently dissipate.

17. Two models, one by Martens and Peterson and the other by Williams and Hacker, are used to illustrate the relationship between task performance, cohesion, and satisfaction.

18. Four measures of team cohesion have emerged. They are the Sport Cohesiveness Questionnaire, the Task Cohesiveness Questionnaire, the Sport Cohesiveness Instrument, and the Group Environment Questionnaire. The GEQ has been used widely in sport studies, and there is some suggestion that it may supplant the other three instruments. The GEQ is derived from Chelladurai's multidimensional model of leadership, and places emphasis on social and task aspects of group behavior.

19. The circularity of the cohesion-performance relationship is troublesome, but the available evidence supports a performance success to cohesion sequence rather than vice versa. Also, cohesion does have some potentially negative aspects, and an awareness of them is important to all involved in team cohesion.

20. Audience effects on athletic performance represent an area of considerable scientific interest, getting its impetus from early social facilitation research.

21. Triplett, in 1898, was the first to study social facilitation, though the term was coined in 1924 by Allport.

22. A reawakening of interest in social facilitation took place in 1965, prompted by a pivotal paper in *Science* by Zajonc. To Zajonc, the mere presence of others increases arousal that facilitates well-learned responses and hinders the acquisition of new ones. Zajonc's mere presence theory has sparked much controversy and resultant research and theory.

23. Cottrell, while agreeing with Zajonc on several issues, disagreed with the mere presence formulation and suggested that evaluative apprehension generated by others

viewing behavior is at the heart of the issue. Other recent theories have been advanced by Sanders, Baron, and Moore and by Guerin and Innes.

24. Critics of the various drive theories indicate that they are too mechanistic to explain complex human behavior. Also, the typical research in the drive theory area deals with noninteractive audiences whereas the typical sport situation involves an interactive one, thereby rendering much of the drive theory research inapplicable to sport psychology.

25. Alternate and more current theories take a more cognitive approach to the topic of social facilitation. Though little used so far, these newer approaches are appealing to sport scientists.

26. Research is supportive of the existence of a home advantage, though the studies so far have been either with professional hockey, baseball, and basketball teams or with collegiate basketball teams. Research by Baumeister and Steinhilber suggests that this advantage does not extend to championship games in the baseball World Series or the National Basketball Association (NBA) playoffs.

27. Fans are susceptible to the effects of BIRGing (basking in reflected glory) and CORFing (cutting off reflected failure), because both mechanisms cut right to the core of individual and group esteem. We like to be associated with a winner to build esteem (BIRG) and choose to distance ourselves psychologically from losers in order to preserve our sense of well-being (CORF).

SUGGESTED READINGS

Carron, A. V. (1990) Group size in sport and physical activity: Social psychological and performance consequences. *International Journal of Sport Psychology, 21,* 286–304.

Carron summarizes the literature on group size, including several of his own (see the *Journal of Sport and Exercise Psychology,* 1990, pp. 177–190 and 376–387 for two excellent articles on group size in both sport and exercise settings written by Carron, Widmeyer, and Brawley). The importance of group size in relationship to productivity and a positive psychosocial climate cannot be emphasized enough, according to Carron. Determining optimal group size has significance for sports teams, but it is equally applicable to successful functioning in military, business, and industrial settings.

Cota, A. A., Evans, C. R., Dion, K. L., Kilik, L., & Longman, R. S. (1995) The structure of group cohesion. *Personality and Social Psychology Bulletin, 21,* 572–580.

A review of the literature on group cohesion is provided, and an alternate way of conceptualizing cohesion is suggested by the authors. Both unidimensional and multidimensional models are discussed. The authors conclude that cohesion is a multidimensional concept with primary and secondary dimensions. In the case of primary dimensions, applicability to describing virtually all groups is implied. As for secondary dimensions, applicability to specific groups is intended. The group cohesion literature within sport psychology, particularly the work of Carron and his colleagues, is discussed at length.

Courneya, K. S., & Carron, A. V. (1992) The home advantage in sport competitions: A literature review. *Journal of Sport and Exercise Psychology, 14,* 13–27.

These authors review the home advantage in sport competition literature beginning with what is generally thought to be the first work in the area by Schwartz and Barsky (1977) on professional sports. They indicate that explanations for the effect range from biological (territoriality and circadian rhythm changes) to psychological (social facilitation and self presentation) to sociological (ritual integration). They propose a model for explaining the home advantage that emphasizes game location, game location factors, critical psychological states, critical behavioral states, and performance outcomes. They also organize their literature review around the "what," "when," and "why" of the home advantage; as such, this article is helpful in understanding the many facets of this interesting sports phenomenon.

Eagly, A. H., Makhijani, M. G., & Klonsky, B. G. (1992) Gender and the evaluation of leaders: A meta-analysis. *Psychological Bulletin, 111,* 3–22.

Eagly and her co-authors review literature relevant to gender and leadership using the statistical technique known as meta-analysis. Surprisingly, there has been quite a number of studies of women in leadership roles despite the limited number of leadership positions traditionally open to them. Sixty-one studies from the years 1966–1988 were analyzed by the authors. Results of the meta-analysis indicated that women in leadership positions were not viewed particularly negatively in comparison with males in similar positions. However, female leaders who carried out their duties in a more stereotypically male style were devalued, as were women in male-dominated situations in which they were being evaluated by men.

Evans, C. R., & Dion, K. L. (1991) Group cohesion and performance: A meta-analysis. *Small Group Research, 22,* 175–186.

A computer search of the Educational Research Information System (ERIC) and the Psychological Abstracts data bases produced 317 published and unpublished studies on group cohesion, twenty-seven of which addressed the issue of cohesion and performance. Meta-analytic procedures indicated a relatively strong and positive correlation of .419 between group cohesion and performance. This supports the contention that cohesive groups are more productive than non-cohesive ones. Caveats to the study and research in cohesion and performance were also discussed.

Hogg, M. A. (1992) *The social psychology of group cohesiveness: From attraction to social identity.* New York: New York University Press.

Hogg has put together a readable and brief (185 pages) treatise on a variety of aspects of group cohesion. Definitions, a brief history of theory and research, models of cohesion, measurement techniques, social identity and attraction, groupthink, and social loafing are some of the more critical topics discussed in this informative book.

Hogan, R., Curphy, G. J., & Hogan, J. (1994) What we know about leadership: Effectiveness and personality. *American Psychologist, 49,* 493–504.

Hogan et al. review the literature on leadership, assess the current state of the art, and examine where leadership theory, research, and practice are going in the near future. They ask and provide answers to such relevant questions as "Does leadership matter?" "How are leaders chosen?" "How should leaders be evaluated?" "Why do we choose so many flawed leaders?" "How do we forecast leadership?" "Why do leaders fail?" "How do leaders build teams?" and "How about leadership in workforce 2000?" They end their intriguing review by making recommendations for the future, including preparing for an economy that will shift from manufacturing to service and a workforce that will be older, more diverse, less well-trained, and female. Managers or leaders will have to do a better job; their performance will be more scrutinized; they will have to cope with the diversity issue more capably; they will have to learn to identify, nurture, and respect creativity; and they will have to make better use of psychological tests in screening for both "bright side" and "dark side" traits in potential and existing employees.

Moore, J. C., & Brylinsky, J. A. (1993) Spectator effect on team performance in college basketball. *Journal of Sport Behavior, 16,* 77–83.

This brief paper deals with an interesting slant on the audience effects literature. A measles epidemic during the 1988–1989 basketball season dictated that Siena and Hartford play eleven games without spectators. This afforded the authors a unique opportunity to investigate crowd effects in the natural setting. Analyses of Siena involved away games and Hartford home games, and each played a number of games with and without spectators during the season. The performance of both teams improved in the no-spectator condition as measured by total points scored, field goal percentage, and free throw percentage. The results, while very interesting, are not easily explained in terms of the usual social facilitation, audience arousal, or audience evaluation theories.

Weese, W. J. (1994) A leadership discussion with Dr. Bernard Bass. *Journal of Sport Management, 8,* 179–189.

This report is a synopsis of an interview with Bernard Bass, Distinguished Professor Emeritus of Management and director of the Center for Leadership Studies at State University of New York—Binghamton, who Weese calls "arguably the most prolific writer in the leadership field" (p. 180). The paper gives glimpses of the current perspectives of one of the pioneers in the area of leadership theory and research. Weese also attempts to relate information gathered through the interview with Dr. Bass to the field of sport management.

REFERENCES

Allport, F. H. (1924) *Social Psychology.* Boston: Houghton Mifflin.

Allport, G. (1954) The historical background of modern social psychology. In G. Lindzey & E. Aronson (Eds.), *Handbook of social psychology* (pp. 3–56). Reading, MA: Addison-Wesley

Bass, B. (1981) *Stogdill's handbook of leadership.* New York: Free Press.

Baumeister, R. F. (1984) Choking under pressure: Self-consciousness and paradoxical effects of incentives on skillful performance. *Journal of Personality and Social Psychology, 46,* 610–620.

Baumeister, R. F. (1995) Disputing the effects of championship pressures and home audiences. *Journal of Personality and Social Psychology, 68,* 644–648.

Baumeister, R. F., Hamilton, J., & Tice, D. (1985) Public versus private expectancy of success: Confi-dence booster or performance pressure? *Journal of Personality and Social Psychology, 48,* 1447–1457.

Baumeister, R. F., & Steinhilber, A. (1984) Paradoxical effects of supportive audiences on performance under pressure: The home field disadvantage in sports championships. *Journal of Personality and Social Psychology, 47,* 85–93.

Behling, O., & Schriesheim, C. (1976) *Organizational behavior theory, research, and application.* Boston: Allyn and Bacon.

Berry, L. M., & Houston, J. P. (1993) *Psychology at work: An introduction to industrial and organizational psychology.* Dubuque, IA: Brown & Benchmark.

Bird, A. M. (1977) Development of a model for predicting team performance. *Research Quarterly, 48,* 24–32.

Bond, C. F. (1982) Social facilitation: A self-presentational view. *Journal of Personality and Social Psychology, 42,* 1042–1050.

Bond, C. F., & Titus, L. J. (1983) Social facilitation: A meta-analysis of 241 studies. *Psychological Bulletin, 94,* 265–292.

Brant, J. (1988) The choke: Lament for a species of overreactors. *Outside,* February, 23–26.

Brawley, L. R., Carron, A. V., & Widmeyer, W. N. (1987) Assessing the cohesion of teams: Validity of the Group Environment Questionnaire. *Journal of Sport Psychology, 9,* 275–294.

Brawley, L. R. (1990) Group cohesion: Status, problems, and future directions. *International Journal of Sport Psychology, 21,* 355–379.

Brown, J. A. (1954) *The social psychology of industry.* New York: Penguin Books.

Burns, J. M. (1978) *Leadership.* New York: Harper & Row.

Campbell, J., Dunnette, M., Lawler, E., & Weick, K. (1970) *Managerial behavior, performance, and effectiveness.* New York: McGraw-Hill.

Carron, A. V. (1980) *Social psychology of sport.* Ithaca, NY: Mouvement.

Carron, A. V. (1984) Cohesion in sport teams. In J. M. Silva and R. S. Weinberg (Eds.), *Psychological foundations of sport* (pp. 340–351). Champaign, IL: Human Kinetics.

Carron, A. V. & Chelladurai, P. (1981) The dynamics of group cohesion in sport. *Journal of Sport Psychology, 3,* 123–139.

Carron, A. V., & Spink, K. S. (1992) Internal consistency of the Group Environment Questionnaire modified for an exercise setting. *Perceptual and Motor Skills, 74,* 304–306.

Carron, A. V., & Spink, K. S. (1995) The group-cohesion relationship in minimal groups. *Small Group Research, 26,* 86–105.

Carron, A. V., Widmeyer, W. N., & Brawley, L. R. (1985) The development of an instrument to assess cohesion in sport teams: The Group Environment Questionnaire. *Journal of Sport Psychology, 7,* 244–266.

Cattell, R. (1946) *Description and measurement of personality.* New York: World Book.

Chelladurai, P. (1984a) Leadership in sports. In J. M. Silva & R. S. Weinberg (Eds.), *Psychological foundations of sport* (pp. 329–339). Champaign, IL: Human Kinetics.

Chelladurai, P. (1984b) Discrepancy between preferences and perceptions of leadership behavior and satisfaction of athletes in varying sports. *Journal of Sport Psychology, 6,* 27–41.

Chelladurai, P. (1986) Applicability of the Leadership Scale for Sports to the Indian context. In J. Watkins, T. Reilly, & L. Burwitz (Eds.), *Sport science* (pp. 291–296). New York: E. & F. N. Spon Ltd.

Chelladurai, P. (1989) Decision style choices of university basketball coaches and players. *Journal of Sport and Exercise Psychology, 11,* 201–215.

Chelladurai, P. (1990) Leadership in sports: A review. *International Journal of Sport Psychology, 21,* 328–354.

Chelladurai, P., & Carron, A. V. (1978) *Leadership* (Monograph). Ottawa: Canadian Association of Health, Physical Education and Recreation.

Chelladurai, P., & Carron, A. V. (1981) Applicability to youth sport of the Leadership Scale for Sports. *Perceptual and Motor Skills, 53,* 361–362.

Chelladurai, P., & Carron, A. V. (1983) Athletic maturity and preferred leadership. *Journal of Sport Psychology, 5,* 371–380.

Chelladurai, P., Haggerty, T. R., & Baxter, P. R. (1989) Decision style choices of university basketball coaches and players. *Journal of Sport and Exercise Psychology, 11,* 201–215.

Chelladurai, P., Imamura, H., Yamaguchi, H., Oinuma, Y., & Miyauchi, T. (1988) Sport leadership in a cross-national setting: The case of the Japanese and Canadian university athletes. *Journal of Sport and Exercise Psychology, 10,* 374–389.

Chelladurai, P., & Saleh, S. (1978) Preferred leadership in sports. *Canadian Journal of Applied Sport Sciences, 3,* 85–92.

Chelladurai, P., & Saleh, S. (1980) Dimensions of leader behavior in sports: Development of a leadership scale. *Journal of Sport Psychology, 2,* 24–35.

Cialdini, R. B., Borden, R. J., Thorne, A., Walker, M. R., Freeman, S., & Sloan, L. R. (1976) Basking in reflected glory: Three (football) field studies. *Journal of Personality and Social Psychology, 34,* 366–375.

Corrington, K. (1994, July) Personal communication, College Station, Texas.

Cottrell, N. B. (1972) Social facilitation. In C. G. McClintock (Ed.), *Experimental social psychology* (pp. 185–236). New York: Holt, Rinehart and Winston.

Courneya, K. S., & Carron, A. V. (1990) Batting first versus last: Implications for the home advantage. *Journal of Sport and Exercise Psychology, 12,* 312–316.

Courneya, K. S., & Carron, A. V. (1991) Effects of travel and length of home stand/road trip on the home advantage. *Journal of Sport and Exercise Psychology, 13,* 42–49.

Cox, R. H. (1990) *Sport psychology: Concepts and applications* (2d ed.) Dubuque, IA: Wm. C. Brown.

Cratty, B. J. (1981) *Social psychology in athletics.* Englewood Cliffs, NJ: Prentice-Hall.

Cratty, B. J. (1989) *Psychology in contemporary sport* (3d ed.). Englewood Cliffs, NJ: Prentice Hall.

Danielson, R. R. (1976) Leadership motivation and coaching classification as related to success in minor league hockey. In R. Christina and D. Landers (Eds.), *Psychology of motor behavior and sport,* Vol. II (pp. 183–189). Champaign, IL: Human Kinetics.

Danielson, R. R., Zelhart, P. F., & Drake, C. J. (1975) Multidimensional scaling and factor analysis of coaching behavior as perceived by high school hockey players. *Research Quarterly, 46,* 323–334.

Dashiell, J. F. (1935) Experimental studies of the influence of social situations of the behavior of individual human adults. In C. Murchison (Ed.), *A handbook of social psychology* (pp. 1097–1158). Worcester, MA: Clark University Press.

Dickey, G. (1982) *The history of National League baseball since 1876.* New York: Stein & Day.

Donnelly, P. (1975) *An analysis of the relationship between organizational half-life and organizational effectiveness.* Paper completed for an advanced topics course, Department of Sport Studies, University of Massachusetts, Amherst.

Donnelly, P., Carron, A. V., & Chelladurai, P. (1978) *Group cohesion and sport* (Sociology of Sport Monograph Series). Ottawa, Ontario: Canadian Association for Health, Physical Education, and Recreation.

Duval, S., & Wicklund, R. (1972) *A theory of objective self-awareness.* New York: Academic.

Essing, W. (1970) Team line-up and team achievement in European football. In G. Kenyon (Ed.), *Contemporary psychology of sport* (pp. 349–354). Chicago: Athletic Institute.

Evans, M. G., & Dermer, J. (1974) What does the Least Preferred Co-worker scale really measure? A cognitive interpretation. *Journal of Applied Psychology, 59,* 202–206.

Festinger, L., Schachter, S., & Back, K. (1950) *Social pressures in informal groups.* New York: Harper.

Fiedler, F. (1967) *A theory of leadership effectiveness.* New York: McGraw-Hill.

Fiedler, F. E. (1978) The contingency model and the dynamics of the leadership process. In L. Berkowitz (ed.), *Advances in experimental social psychology,* Vol. 11. New York: Academic Press.

Garland, D. J., & Barry, J. R. (1988) The effects of personality and perceived leader behaviors on performance in collegiate football. *The Psychological Record, 38,* 237–247.

Gayton, W. F., & Langevin, G. (1992) Home advantage: Does it exist in individual sports? *Perceptual and Motor Skills, 74,* 706.

Gayton, W. F., Matthews, G. R., & Nickless, C. J. (1987) The home field advantage in sports championships: Does it exist in hockey? *Journal of Sport Psychology, 9,* 183–185.

Geen, R., & Gange, J. (1977) Drive theory of social facilitation: Twelve years of theory and research. *Psychological Bulletin, 84,* 1267–1288.

Glamser, F. D. (1990) Contest location, player misconduct, and race: A case from English soccer. *Journal of Sport Behavior, 13,* 41–49.

Glenn, S. D., & Horn, T. S. (1993) Psychological and personal predictors of leadership behavior in female soccer athletes. *Journal of Applied Sport Psychology, 5,* 17–34.

Goldman, M., Stockbauer, J., & McAuliffe, T. (1977) Intergroup and intragroup competition and cooperation. *Journal of Experimental Social Psychology, 13,* 81–88.

Gross, N., & Martin, W. (1952) On group effectiveness. *American Journal of Sociology, 57,* 533–546.

Gruber, J., & Gray, G. (1981) Factors patterns of variables influencing cohesiveness at various levels of basketball competition. *Research Quarterly for Exercise and Sport, 52,* 19–30.

Gruber, J., & Gray, G. (1982) Responses to forces influencing cohesion as a function of player status and level of male basketball competition. *Research Quarterly for Exercise and Sport, 53,* 27–36.

Guerin, B., & Innes, J. (1982) Social facilitation and social monitoring: A new look at Zajonc's mere presence hypothesis. *British Journal of Social Psychology, 21,* 7–18.

Haas, J., & Roberts, G. (1975) Effects of evaluative others upon learning and performance of a complex motor task. *Journal of Motor Behavior, 7,* 81–90.

Hardy, C. J. (1990) Social loafing: Motivational losses in collective performance. *International Journal of Sport Psychology, 21,* 305–327.

Harkins, S. G., & Syzmanski, K. (1987) Social loafing and social facilitation: New wine in old bottles. In C. Hendrick (Ed.), *Review of personality and social psychology,* Vol. 9 (pp. 167–188). Beverly Hills, CA: Sage.

Heaton, A. W., & Sigall, H. (1991) Self-consciousness, self-presentation, and performance under pressure. *Journal of Applied Social Psychology, 21,* 175–188.

Hersey, P., & Blanchard, K. (1969) *Management of organizational behavior.* Englewood Cliffs, NJ: Prentice-Hall.

Hersey, P., & Blanchard, K. (1977) *Management of organizational behavior: Utilizing human resources.* Englewood Cliffs, NJ: Prentice-Hall.

Hersey, P., Blanchard, K. L., & Hambleton, R. K. (1980) Contracting for leadership style: A process and instrumentation for building effective work relationships. In P. Hersey and J. Stinson (Eds.), *Perspectives in leader effectiveness* (pp. 95–119). Center for Leadership Studies: Ohio University, Athens.

Hershey, S. (1989) Hoch responds to pressure, wins with 8-foot birdie putt. *USA Today,* May 1, 10C.

Hirt, E. R., Zillman, D., Erickson, G. A., & Kennedy, C. (1992) Costs and benefits of allegiance: Changes in fans' self-ascribed competencies after team victory versus defeat. *Journal of Personality and Social Psychology, 63,* 724–738.

Hoffer, R. (1993) Happy days. *Sports Illustrated,* August 2, 20–23.

Hogg, M. A. (1992) *The social psychology of group cohesiveness.* New York: New York University Press.

Hollander, E. P., & Julian, J. W. (1969) Contemporary trends in the analysis of leadership processes. *Psychological Bulletin, 71,* 387–391.

House, R. (1971) A path-goal theory of leader effectiveness. *Administrative Science Quarterly, 16,* 321–338.

House, R., & Dessler, G. (1974) The path-goal theory of leadership: Some post hoc and a priori tests. In J. Hunt & L. Larson (Eds.), *Contingency approaches to leadership* (pp. 29–62). Carbondale, IL: Southern Illinois University Press.

House, R. J., & Mitchell, T. R. (1974, Autumn) Path-goal theory of leadership. *Journal of Contemporary Business,* 81–97.

Hunt, P., & Hillery, J. (1973) Social facilitation in a coaction setting. An examination of the effects over learning trials. *Journal of Experimental Social Psychology, 9,* 563–571.

Inciong, P. (1974) Leadership style and team success. Unpublished doctoral dissertation, University of Utah.

Ingham, A., Levinger, G., Graves, J., & Peckham, V. (1974) The Ringelmann effect: Studies of group size and group performances. *Journal of Experimental Social Psychology, 10,* 371–384.

Irving, P. G., & Goldstein, S. R. (1990) Effect of home-field advantage on peak performance of baseball pitchers. *Journal of Sport Behavior, 13,* 23–27.

Isberg, L., & Chelladurai, P. (1990) *The Leadership Scale for Sports: Its applicability in the Swedish context.* Unpublished manuscript, University College of Falun/Borlange, Sweden.

Kerr, N. L., & Bruun, S. E. (1983) Ringelmann revisited: Alternative explanations for the social loafing effect. *Personality and Social Psychology Bulletin, 7,* 224–231.

Kim, M., & Sugiyama, Y. (1992) The relation of performance norms and cohesiveness for Japanese athletic teams. *Perceptual and Motor Skills, 74,* 1096–1098.

Klein, M., & Christiansen, G. (1969) Group composition, group structure and group effectiveness of basketball teams. In J. W. Loy and G. S. Kenyon (Eds.), *Sport, culture, and society* (pp. 397–408). London: Macmillan.

Lacoste, P. L., & Laurencelle, L. (1989) *The French validation of the Leadership Scale for Sports.* Unpublished abstract, Universite de Quebec a Trois Rivieres, Canada.

Landers, D. M. (1980) The arousal-performance relationship revisited. *Research Quarterly for Exercise and Sport, 51,* 77–90.

Landers, D. M., Brawley, L., & Hale, B. (1978) Habit strength differences in motor behavior. The effects of social facilitation paradigms and subject sex. In D. M. Landers and R. W. Christina (Eds.), *Psychology of motor behavior and sport, 1977* (pp. 420–433). Champaign, IL: Human Kinetics.

Landers, D. M., Wilkinson, M., Hatfield, B., & Barber, H. (1982) Causality and the cohesion–performance relationship. *Journal of Sport Psychology, 4,* 170–183.

Last word, The. (1989) *The Houston Chronicle,* Dec. 26, 6C.

Latané, B. (1973) *A theory of social impact.* St. Louis, MO: Psychonomic Society.

Latané, B., Harkins, S., & Williams, K. (1980) *Many hands make light the work: Social loafing as a social disease.* Unpublished manuscript, The Ohio State University.

Latané, B., Williams, K., & Harkins, S. (1979) Many hands make light the work: The causes and consequences of social loafing. *Journal of Personality and Social Psychology, 37,* 823–832.

Lenk, H. (1977) *Team dynamics.* Champaign, IL: Stipes.

Leonard, W. M. (1989) The "home advantage": The case of the modern olympiads. *Journal of Sport Behavior, 12,* 227–241.

Luikkonen, J., Salminen, S., & Telama, R. (1989) The psychological climate of training sessions in Finnish youth sports. Paper presented at Seventh World Congress in Sport Psychology, Singapore, August 7–12.

Mann, R. D. (1959) A review of the relationship between personality and performance in small groups. *Psychological Bulletin, 56,* 241–270.

Martens, R. (1969) Effects of an audience on learning and performance of a complex motor skill. *Journal of Personality and Social Psychology, 12,* 252–260.

Martens, R., & Landers, D. M. (1972) Evaluation potential as a determinant of coaction effects. *Journal of Experimental Social Psychology, 8,* 347–359.

Martens, R., & Peterson, J. (1971) Group cohesiveness as a determinant of success and member satisfaction in team performance. *International Review of Sport Sociology, 6,* 49–61.

McAndrew, F. T. (1992) The home advantage in individual sports. *The Journal of Social Psychology, 133,* 401–403.

Muchinsky, P. M. (1987) *Psychology applied to work: An introduction to industrial and organizational psychology* (2d ed.). Chicago: Dorsey Press.

Murrell, A. J., & Dietz, B. (1992) Fan support of sport teams: The effect of common group identity. *Journal of Sport and Exercise Psychology, 14,* 28–39.

Neil, G., & Kirby, S. (1985) Coaching styles and preferred leadership among rowers and paddlers. *Journal of Sport Behavior, 8,* 3–17.

Nelson, B., & Carron, M. (1991) Home court advantage as perceived by coaches and players in selected division I college sports. In W. K. Simpson, A. LeUnes, & J. S. Picou (Eds.), *Applied Research in Coaching and Athletics Annual.* Boston: American Press.

Orwell, G. (1946) *Animal farm.* New York: Harcourt, Brace.

Paulus, P. B., & Cornelius, W. L. (1974) An analysis of gymnastic performance under conditions of practice and spectator observation. *Research Quarterly, 45,* 56–63.

Paulus, P. B., Shannon, J. C., Wilson, D. L., & Boone, T. D. (1972) The effects of spectator presence on gymnastic performance in a field situation. *Psychonomic Science, 29,* 88–90.

Pessin, J. (1933) The comparative effects of social and mechanical simulation on memorizing. *American Journal of Psychology, 45,* 263–281.

Rainey, D. W., & Schweickert, G. J. (1988) An exploratory study of team cohesion before and after a spring trip. *The Sport Psychologist, 2,* 314–317.

Rees, C. R. (1983) Instrumental and expressive leadership in team sports: A test of leadership role differentiation theory. *Journal of Sport Behavior, 6,* 17–27.

Rees, C. R., & Segal, M. (1984) Role differentiation in groups: The relationship between instrumental and expressive leadership. *Small Group Behavior, 15,* 109–123.

Rice, R. W. (1978) Construct validity of the Least Preferred Co-worker (LPC) score. *Psychological Bulletin, 85,* 1199–1237.

Ruder, M. K., & Gill, D. L. (1982) Immediate effects of win-loss on perceptions of cohesion in intramural and intercollegiate volleyball teams. *Journal of Sport Psychology, 4,* 227–234.

Sage, G. H. (1978) Humanistic psychology and coaching. In W. Straub (Ed.), *Sport psychology: An analysis of athlete behavior* (pp. 148–161). Ithaca, NY: Mouvement.

Sanders, G. (1981) Driven by distraction: An integrative review of social facilitation theory and research. *Journal of Experimental Social Psychology, 17,* 227–251.

Sanders, G., Baron, R., & Moore, D. (1978) Distraction and social comparison as mediators of social facilitation effects. *Journal of Experimental Social Psychology, 14,* 291–303.

Schlenker, B. R., Phillips, S. T., Boniecki, K. A., & Schlenker, D. R. (1995a) Championship pressures: Choking or triumphing in one's own territory? *Journal of Personality and Social Psychology, 68,* 632–643.

Schlenker, B. R., Phillips, S. T., Boniecki, K. A., & Schlenker, D. R. (1995b) Where is the home choke? *Journal of Personality and Social Psychology, 68,* 649–652.

Schriesheim, C. A., & Kerr, S. (1974) Psychometric properties of the Ohio State leadership scales. *Psychological Bulletin, 81,* 756–765.

Schriesheim, C. A., & Stogdill, R. M. (1975) Differences in factor structure across three versions of the Ohio State leadership scales. *Personnel Psychology, 28,* 189–206.

Schutz, R. W., Eom, H. J., Smoll, F. L., & Smith, R. E. (1994) Examination of the factorial validity of the Group Environment Questionnaire. *Research Quarterly for Exercise and Sport, 65,* 226–236.

Schwartz, B., & Barsky, S. F. (1977) The home advantage. *Social Forces, 55,* 641–661.

Scott, J. (1971) *The athletic revolution.* New York: Macmillan.

Serpa, S., Pataco, V., & Santos, F. (1991) Leadership patterns in handball international competition. *International Journal of Sport Psychology, 22,* 78–89.

Shaw, M. (1976) *Group dynamics: The psychology of small group behavior* (2d ed.) New York: McGraw-Hill.

Shepperd, J. A. (1993) Productivity loss in performance groups: A motivation analysis. *Psychological Bulletin, 113,* 67–81.

Silva, J. M. (1982) *The current status of applied sport psychology: A national survey.* Paper presented at American Alliance for Health, Physical Education, Recreation, and Dance Convention, Houston.

Silva, J. M., Andrew, A., & Richey, S. (1983) *Game location and basketball performance variation.* Paper presented at the North American Society for the Psychology of Sport and Physical Activity Annual Convention, Michigan State University, East Lansing, Michigan.

Snyder, C. J. (1990) The effects of leader behavior and organizational climate on intercollegiate coaches' job satisfaction. *Journal of Sport Management, 4,* 59–70.

Snyder, C. R., Higgins, R. L., & Stucky, R. J. (1983) *Excuses: Masquerades in search of grace.* New York: Wiley-Interscience.

Spink, K. S. (1990) Group cohesion and collective efficacy of volleyball teams. *Journal of Sport and Exercise Psychology, 12,* 301–311.

Spink, K. S., & Carron, A. V. (1992) Group cohesion and adherence to exercise classes. *Journal of Sport and Exercise Psychology, 14,* 78–86.

Spink, K. S., & Carron, A. V. (1994) Group cohesion effects in exercise classes. *Small Group Research, 25,* 26–42.

Stinson, J. E., & Tracy, L. (1974) Some disturbing characteristics of the LPC score. *Personnel Psychology, 27,* 477–485.

Stowers, C. (1985) Danny White: Back in the saddle again. *Inside Sports,* October, 18–23.

Triplett, N. (1898) The dynamogenic factors in pace-making and competition. *American Journal of Psychology, 9,* 507–533.

Tuckman, B. (1965) Developmental sequence in small groups. *Psychological Bulletin, 63,* 384–399.

Varca, P. (1980) An analysis of home and away game performance of male college basketball teams. *Journal of Sport Psychology, 2,* 245–257.

Vos Strache, C. (1979) Players' perceptions of leadership qualities for coaches. *Research Quarterly, 50,* 679–686.

Wankel, L. M. (1984) Audience effects in sport. In J. M. Silva and R. S. Weinberg (Eds.), *Psychological foundations of sport* (pp. 293–314). Champaign, IL: Human Kinetics.

Wann, D. L. (1993) Aggression among highly identified spectators as a function of their need to maintain positive social identity. *Journal of Sport and Social Issues, 17,* 134–143.

Wann, D. L., & Branscombe, N. R. (1990) Die-hard and fair-weather fans: Effects of identification on BIRGing and CORFing tendencies. *Journal of Sport and Social Issues, 14,* 103–118.

Widmeyer, W. N., Brawley, L. R., & Carron, A. V. (1985) *The measurement of cohesion in sports teams: The Group Environment Questionnaire.* London, Ontario: Sports Dynamics.

Widmeyer, W. N., Brawley, L. R., & Carron, A. V. (1992) Group dynamics in sport. In T. S. Horn (Ed.), *Advances in sport psychology* (pp. 124–139). Champaign, IL: Human Kinetics.

Williams, J. M., & Hacker, C. (1982) Causal relationships among cohesion, satisfaction, and performance in women's intercollegiate field hockey teams. *Journal of Sport Psychology, 4,* 324–337.

Williams, J. M., & Widmeyer, W. N. (1991) The cohesion-performance outcome relationship in a coacting sport. *Journal of Sport and Exercise Psychology, 13,* 364–371.

Williams, K., Harkins, S., & Latané, B. (1981) Identifiability and social loafing: Two cheering experiments. *Journal of Personality and Social Psychology, 40,* 303–311.

Williams, K. D., & Karau, S. J. (1991) Social loafing and social compensation: The effects of expectations and co-worker performance. *Journal of Personality and Social Psychology, 61,* 570–581.

Worchel, S., Hart, D., & Butemeyer, J. (1991) Is social loafing a group phenomenon? The effect of membership and interdependence on work output. Unpublished manuscript, Texas A&M University.

Wright, E. F., Jackson, W., Christie, S. D., McGuire, G. R., & Wright, R. D. (1991) The home-course disadvantage in golf championships: Further evidence for the undermining effect of supportive audiences under pressure. *Journal of Sport Behavior, 14,* 51–60.

Wright, E. F., Voyer, D., Wright, R. D., & Roney, C. (1995) Supporting audiences and performance under pressure: The home-ice disadvantage in hockey championships. *Journal of Sport Behavior, 18,* 21–28.

Yukelson, D., Weinberg, R. S., & Jackson, A. V. (1984) A multidimensional group cohesion instrument for intercollegiate basketball teams. *Journal of Sport Psychology, 6,* 103–117.

Yukelson, D., Weinberg, R. S., Richardson, P., & Jackson, A. V. (1983) Interpersonal attraction and leadership within collegiate sport teams. *Journal of Sport Behavior, 6,* 28–36.

Zaccaro, S. J. (1984) "Social loafing: The role of task attractiveness." *Personality and Social Psychology Bulletin, 10,* 99–106.

Zajonc, R. B. (1965) Social facilitation. *Science, 149,* 269–274.

Zander, A. (1976) The psychology of removing group members and recruiting new ones. *Human Relations, 10,* 969–987.

Aggression and Violence in Sport

Man isn't a noble savage; he's an ignoble savage. He is irrational, brutal, weak, silly, unable to be objective about anything where his own interests are involved—that about sums it up. Any attempt to create social institutions on a false view of the nature of man is doomed to failure.

  Stanley Kubrick, director, *A Clockwork Orange*

People are basically bad, corrupt. I always sense that man has not progressed one inch, morally, since the Greeks.

  Malcolm McDowell, actor, *A Clockwork Orange*

The myth of the noble savage is bull. People are born to survive. They have instincts that go back millions of years. Unfortunately some of these instincts are based on violence in every human being.

  Sam Peckinpah, director, *Straw Dogs*

Violence ends by defeating itself. It creates bitterness in the survivors and brutality in the destroyers.

  Martin Luther King, Jr.

I speared him, I pole-axed him, and I cut him close to the eye. Things like that happen in the heat of the game.

  Hockey player

A defensive lineman can do just about anything. He can damn near haul an axe out of his jock and slash around with it before he'll be called for anything.

  Football player

Dancing is a contact sport. Football is a collision sport.

  Vince Lombardi, football coaching great

I'll tell you Dreamer Tatum is a stud sumbitch on the football field . . . Dreamer Tatum is what we call a pisser. I mean that sumbitch will make your helmet ring when he puts it on you.

  Dan Jenkins, author, describing a "fictional" character in his novel, *Semi-Tough*

A nice quiet person who lifts weights and sometimes separates people's heads from their shoulders.

  Sports Illustrated, 1977, description of Kermit Washington of the Los Angeles Lakers shortly before he did exactly that to Rudy Tomjanovich of the Houston Rockets

Violence is as American as apple pie.

  Eldridge Cleaver, *Soul on Ice*

INTRODUCTION

We most certainly live in a world filled with acts of violence. Violent events occurred in the 1990s in such places as Bosnia, Rwanda, and Somalia, just to name a few. Here in the United States, there are numerous reminders of man's inhumanity to man. According to statistics from the Federal Bureau of Investigation (1993), a crime is committed every two seconds in the United States; more specifically, there is a property crime every three seconds and a violent crime every twenty-one seconds. For a more detailed look at the overall crime picture, refer to the "time clock" in figure 7.1.

  A particularly unwholesome aspect of the crime statistics is found in domestic violence, including child and spousal abuse. With regard to child abuse, Corby (1993) reports that as many as 652,000 instances occur annually in the United States. Whitcomb (1992) reports statistics indicating that this figure could be as high as 6.9 million if one is willing to allow an expanded definition that includes hitting with a belt or stick. A particularly abhorrent child abuse variant, child sexual abuse committed by parents or care givers, endangers the welfare of 155,000 young people annually (Whitcomb, 1992). In the case of spousal abuse, or what Zawitz (1994, p. 1) calls "violence between intimates," statistics from the National Crime Victimization Survey of the U.S. Department of Justice for the years 1987–1991 indicate that intimates committed over 621,000 rapes, robberies, or assaults. Of this number, 90 percent

Figure 7.1: **Crime Time Clock**

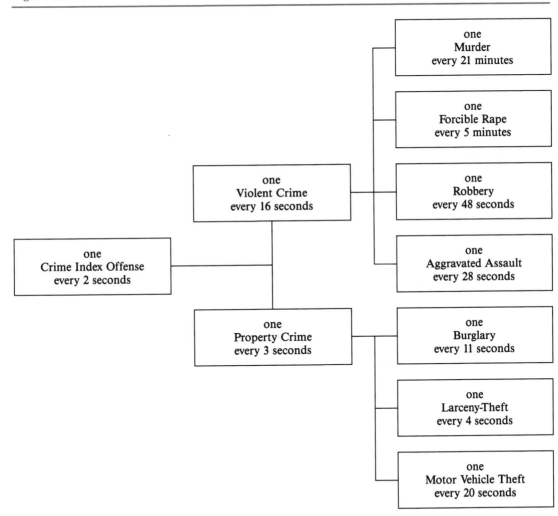

Source: Federal Bureau of Investigation, *Crime in the United States: Uniform Crime Reports, 1993* (Washington, DC: U.S. Government Printing Office), p. 4.

were committed against females by spouses, ex-spouses, or boyfriends. White and black females were abused at the same rates; this ratio was maintained when Hispanic females were compared with non-Hispanics. There was an inverse relationship between abuse and educational attainment; women who had earned college degrees reported the lowest abuse rates. The same relationship existed with regard to income; women earning less than $9,999 were abused at a rate of 11 per 10,000, while women earning over $30,000 were abused at a rate of 2 per 10,000. Divorced or separated women were ten times more likely to be a victim of violence by an intimate than were their married counterparts (Bachman, 1994; Zawitz, 1994). By any measure, it appears that domestic violence is an unfortunate reality of American life.

As mentioned above, wars on other continents seem to be a dime a dozen. This sort of violence is driven by class conflicts, tribal rivalries, religious conviction, racial or ethnic hatred, and/or dreams of geographical expansionism. In addition to these more serious manifestations of aggressive or violent acts, our ears are constantly besieged by the sounds of everyday discontent or disagreement. Angry lovers having a verbal spat, teenage gangs verbally jousting with their rivals, harried taxi drivers shouting among themselves over traffic snarls, and angry sports enthusiasts filling the air with epithets hurled in the direction of a player or coach are constant reminders that violence is never far away.

Unfortunately, the sports world is not exempt from the effects of aggression gone awry, and the brief chronology of recent violent events in sports listed in figure 7.2 serves to remind us that fan and player behavior can be volatile, unpredictable, unmanageable, and violent.

AGGRESSION DEFINED

To put it mildly, the term *aggression* is a ubiquitous one. On the one hand, aggression is an admired trait in our society. The person from the ghetto who works hard to become a success or the highly motivated young business executive with lofty ambitions is thought to be aggressive. The general belief is that they would not be where they are without some aggressiveness. Captains of American industry are widely held in esteem for their aggressive qualities.

On the other side of the coin are the people whose aggressions result in much pain and suffering for others, aggression gone awry. This tawdry end of the aggression continuum is of much interest to social scientists of all persuasions because of the emotional and monetary toll involved. This type of aggression is known as *antisocial.*

Somewhere generally but not exclusively in the middle of the scale is aggression in sport. Most of the examples of aggression in the athletic world are not criminal acts, but they are of concern because people do get hurt in the process. In the case of the occasional deaths associated with sport violence, most of these involve unruly fans rather than the players, and we shall address this issue shortly. But first let us proceed with a definition of aggression.

According to *Webster's New Twentieth Century Dictionary* (1984), aggression is derived from the Latin *ad* and *gradi* (to step, go) or from *aggredi* (to attack, to go toward). Taking these etymological roots and putting them into a psychological context, we define aggression in terms of several properties to include aversiveness, intent, and victim unwillingness (Geen, Beatty, and Arkin, 1984). The first step in an aggressive act is the delivery of an aversive stimulus to another person. This aggressive stimulus might take the form of a verbal insult, a punch in the nose, or a bullet in the back. A second property of aggression has to do with *intent.* The person who is being aggressive must intend to do harm to the victim. The thief who hits you over the head in order to steal the contents of your wallet or handbag is being aggressive; his intent is to do you harm. On the other hand, physicians often inflict pain upon their clients, but the intent is to cure or heal rather than harm. Thirdly, aggression involves an *unwilling victim*. Few of us have any desire to be hit over the head for a few dollars. However, there are masochists who willingly accept the infliction of pain from others; again, as in the case of the physician, this would not constitute aggression.

Cox (1990) adds a fourth dimension to the previous three, namely *expectancy of success*. Little aggression would likely take place in the absence of some reasonable assurance that the act would be successful in some way.

All things considered, it appears that aggression is defined as the infliction of an aversive stimulus upon one person by another, an act committed with intent to harm, one perpetrated against an unwilling victim, and done

Figure 7.2: **A Recent Chronology of Sports Violence**

1968	A riot at a soccer match in Buenos Aires, Argentina, kills seventy-four and injures at least 150 more.
1971	Celebration over the World Series triumph of the Pittsburgh Pirates leaves two dead. An additional dozen rapes are linked to the "celebration."
1971	Soccer rioting in Kayseri, Turkey, kills four hundred and injures six hundred.
1971	Soccer riot in Glasgow, Scotland, kills sixty-six and injures 140.
1973	Paul Smithers, a seventeen-year-old hockey player, is convicted of manslaughter after killing an opposing player in a Toronto, Canada, parking lot following a hockey game.
1975	David Forbes of the NHL Boston Bruins is charged with aggravated assault by use of a dangerous weapon after attacking an opponent during a hockey match. After more than a week of testimony and eighteen hours of jury deliberation, Forbes is acquitted.
1975	*Nabozny v. Barnhill* lawsuit is lodged when a youth soccer goalie is kicked in the head by an opponent.
1976	*Bourque v. Duplechin* lawsuit is filed when a twenty-year-old baseball infielder suffers a broken jaw and eight loosened teeth after being taken out on a double play by an opponent.
1976	*Hogensen v. Williamson* lawsuit is filed when a junior high football player suffers a neck injury when assaulted by his coach at practice.
1977	Rudy Tomjanovich of the NBA Houston Rockets suffers critical facial and skull injuries during a brawl when attacked by Kermit Washington of the Los Angeles Lakers.
1978	Daryl Stingley of the NFL New England Patriots is left quadriplegic after sustaining a crippling blow from Jack Tatum of the Oakland Raiders.
1982	Twenty-five policemen are hospitalized in Tallahassee, Florida, after fights erupted at the end of the Florida-Florida State college football game.
1984	Celebrations over the World Series triumph by the Detroit Tigers fans leave sixteen injured and much related property damage to stores, businesses, and police cars.
1985	Soccer rioting in Brussels, Belgium, kills thirty-eight and injures 437 others.
1989	Soccer rioting in Sheffield, England, kills ninety-four and injures 170 fans of Liverpool soccer club.
1991	Soccer rioting in Orkney, South Africa, kills forty and injures fifty others.
1994	Andres Escobar, soccer star from Colombia, is gunned down in his home town of Medellin for accidentally scoring a goal for the United States in the 1994 World Cup.

with the expectancy that the behavior will be successful.

Dimensions of Aggression

Now that we have arrived at a definition of aggression, a brief look at some related dimensions is in order. Accordingly, let us consider five such aspects of aggression.

Provoked versus Unprovoked

Hakeem Olajuwon of the Houston Rockets and Mitch Kupchak of the Los Angeles Lakers were ejected from their 1986 National Basketball Association playoff game for exchanging punches, a fracas that led to both benches coming to the aid of their respective teammates. To quote Olajuwon: "He threw the first punch and I could not help it" ("Sampson Answers a Prayer," 1986, p. 3B). If we assume that Hakeem has the facts of the matter straight, we can say that his aggressive act was generated by the actions of his opponent. This, then, would be an example of *provoked aggression.* On the other hand, had a vandal randomly selected either of these two athletes' automobiles in the parking lot for an act of vandalism, the aggression would be considered unprovoked aggression. This random sort of aggression is less likely to affect the sport world than is the provoked variety. Many acts of aggression in sport take place as a result of some sort of verbal or physical provocation.

Direct versus Indirect

Had our vandal broken the windshield, snapped off the radio antenna, or slashed the tires of Olajuwon's automobile while he was playing against the Lakers because of frustration with his or her overall life situation, the aggression would have been indirect. This variety of aggression is commonly referred to as *displaced aggression;* that is, the aggression is directed at a source other than the one that created the need

to aggress. However, had our villain been at the Rockets–Lakers game and become incensed because Olajuwon attacked his or her favorite player, left the arena early, and sought out Olajuwon's car based on prior knowledge as to its type and whereabouts, then we have a clearcut case of *direct aggression.*

Physical versus Verbal

Singling out Olajuwon and Kupchak for further analysis, we note that their altercation obviously attained physical proportions. In all likelihood, there had been a fair number of verbal exchanges between the two prior to the outbreak of physical aggression. More of the verbal than the physical type of aggression probably occurs in sport. Fortunately, we tend to talk more than we fight.

Adaptive versus Maladaptive

In some cases aggression in sport may be adaptive. Our suspicion is that a certain amount of aggression is adaptive due to the physical nature of such activities as basketball, football, or hockey. An athlete in these sports probably cannot function without establishing the fact that he (or she in some cases) will not be pushed around and intimidated. This is not to condone the kinds of borderline sportsmanship and rules infractions that take place, but to merely point out that, given the way the games are played and officiated today, an athlete simply must be aggressive. However, blatant high-sticking in hockey or fistfights on the basketball court have little adaptive value and should be considered counter to the spirit of sport.

Hostile versus Instrumental

Aggression may also be viewed in terms of the reinforcement that is sought through its use. For example, it is generally known by those who play high-level slowpitch softball that the pitcher is inordinately vulnerable to being hit by the batted

A Longitudinal Study of Prosocial and Aggressive Behavior

In 1987, Leonard Eron reported results of a twenty-two-year study of prosocial and aggressive behavior that began in 1960 when more than six hundred third graders (ages seven to nine) from one county in New York were interviewed and tested along with 75 percent of their parents. Aggression was assessed through peer nominations by asking such questions as "Who pushes or shoves children?" Prosocial behaviors were gathered in the same way with questions such as "Who says 'excuse me' even if they have not done anything bad?" and "Who will never fight even when picked on?" Three salient correlates of aggression that were picked up through the testing and parent interviews were: (1) the less nurturant and accepting the parents were, the higher the levels of aggression displayed; (2) the more the child was punished for aggression, the more aggressive he or she was at school; and (3) the less the child identified with the parents, the higher the aggression displayed.

At the end of ten years, a follow-up was conducted through interviewing 427 of the original subjects. The most salient conclusion reached at that juncture was that those who were aggressive in the third grade were three times more likely to have police records at age nineteen than were those not so rated.

Twenty-two years after the original study, 414 of the original subjects were again interviewed. The correlation between aggression in the third grade and aggression displayed in the intervening twenty-two years was .46, a hefty figure. On the other hand, prosocial third graders strongly tended to be prosocial adults as exemplified by educational and occupational attainment, low levels of antisocial acts, and overall good mental health. Aggression at age eight, unfortunately, predicted social failure, psychopathology, aggression, and low educational and occupational attainment.

Clearly, Eron's results add to the literature that points to early childhood antecedents of both prosocial behavior and aggression in adults.

Source: Eron (1987); "A 22-Year Longitudinal Study of Aggression and Prosocial Behavior" (1988).

ball due to the sheer physical proximity to home plate and the ample force applied to the ball by a strong and skilled hitter. Some players try to take advantage of this vulnerability by hitting the ball directly at or near the pitcher. To truly enjoy hitting the pitcher for the sake of it would be *hostile aggression;* that is, the reward here is seeing the person in physical pain. In the case of *instrumental aggression,* it would be perfectly acceptable to hit the pitcher not so much as to inflict pain or injury but more to promote a winning effort. Winning in instrumental aggression, simply stated, is a more important goal than infliction of harm or injury. In both hostile and instrumental aggression, the deviance is rewarded, which of course increases the likelihood of its subsequent occurrence.

Hostile Aggression, Instrumental Aggression, and Sport Assertiveness

A fine line separates the various types of aggression and assertiveness in the sport situation, and these differences are reflected in figure 7.3. As can be seen, both types of aggression involve the intent to harm; such is not the case in sport assertion. The three concepts can further be separated on the dimension of winning versus harming: in *hostile aggression,* the goal is to harm; in *instrumental aggression,* it is to win; and in *assertiveness,* it is to play with as much enthusiasm, force, and skill as possible. Finally, the hostile assertive athlete is characterized by much anger whereas the athlete using instrumental force does so without anger; in sport assertion, anger is not an issue. Unusual force and energy expenditure are, however. The constitutive or formal rules (Silva, 1981) of the game matter in assertion, whereas they are violated, at least in spirit, by acts of aggression, regardless of type.

To illustrate how assertiveness might differ from the two types of aggression, let us return to our slowpitch softball example. A batter who

Figure 7.3: **Relationship among Hostile Aggression, Instrumental Aggression, and Sport Assertiveness**

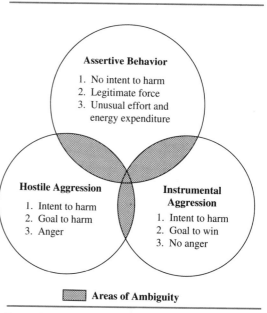

Source: Cox (1990); Silva (1979).

is being assertive rather than aggressive realizes when he enters the batter's box that there are several distinct advantages well within the rules and the spirit of the game that are available by hitting at or near the pitcher. For one thing, the pitcher is very close to home plate. For another, he or she is often the poorest fielder in the infield. Also, a relatively vast expanse of territory must be covered by all fielders in the middle of the diamond. This would indicate that a well-hit drive in the area of the pitcher would be an intelligent decision. Should the pitcher take a shot or two off the body, those are the breaks of the game.

This illustration serves to indicate that there are arguable or ambiguous areas of overlap among hostile and instrumental aggression and assertiveness. The three are not completely distinct entities. For example, the forceful but clean and legal tackle in football can be viewed as assertive in that no intent to harm was involved. In view of the generally violent nature of the game of football, it may be argued that all tackles are acts of aggression. Equally plausible, however, is the hypothesis that all of them are merely examples of assertiveness. As for the goals sought, it is probably a truism that most if not all football players hold winning in higher regard than hurting their opponents. As for the third area of overlap, the anger as seen in aggression and the force and expenditure of energy in assertion are hard to separate. Collision sports, such as football, are possessed of a certain amount of controlled anger, something Kiester (1984) says can be put to constructive use. He cites the example of Conrad Dobler, the now retired offensive lineman for the St. Louis Cardinals, who achieved a great deal of notoriety through his brinksmanship exploitation of the rules and constructive use of anger. He attributed much of his success to being able to do things verbally and physically that greatly angered his opponents, thereby distracting them from the task at hand, namely, playing their positions as well as they were expected to perform. John McEnroe, the tennis great of the 1980s, was also a master at turning anger to his advantage through distraction of the opposition.

Inferring whether aggressiveness or assertiveness has taken place in any particular event is a judgment call all the way. Collision sports, such as football, offer many legitimate opportunities to injure and yet stay within the rules. Certain kinds of blocks, such as the crackback, can be applied legally and yet be intended to injure; a number of serious knee injuries owe their genesis to the crackback block. In baseball, the legal brushback pitch and the illegal and potentially life-threatening beanball are very difficult to distinguish. Often, these examples from two sports are labeled as aggressive or assertive based not on the behaviors themselves but on more subtle cues. For instance, stares,

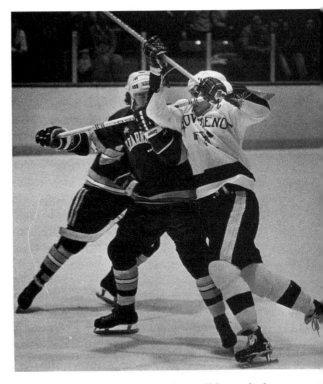

Hockey players recognize that they will be pushed around and intimidated. But blatant high-sticking is clearly counter to the spirit of the sport.

glares, hand gestures, and verbal exchanges in temporal proximity to the crackback block or the brushback pitch could be used to determine whether the behavior was aggressive or assertive.

Aggression and Violence: One and the Same?

In defining aggression, it is appropriate to look at the relationship between aggression and violence. There is a reasonable continuum (with obvious overlap) ranging from sport assertiveness to instrumental aggression to hostile aggression and, finally, to sports violence. The similarities between the latter two states is considerable, and they may easily be equated.

Adding to the confusion is the eternal use of the term *aggressive* by players, coaches, the media, and sports fans when they are most likely referring to assertive behavior, not aggression. Rebounding aggressively in basketball is not really an example of aggression at all.

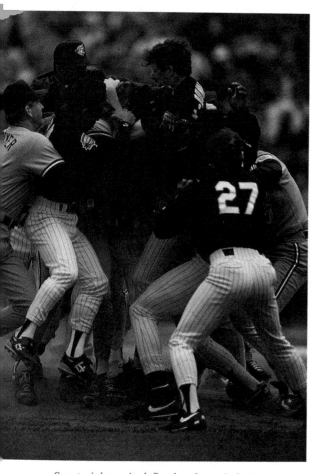

Sport violence is defined as harm-inducing behavior bearing no direct relationship to the competitive goals of sport, and relates, therefore, to incidents of uncontrolled aggression outside the rules of sport, rather than highly competitive behavior within the rule boundaries.

Silva asserts that the failure to properly deal with the definition of aggression in sports has created disarray, leading him to suggest that "confusion will be the epitaph of this research area" (Silva, 1979, p. 200). What we would like to propose, then, is that the aforementioned continuum serve as a guide for future discussion, keeping in mind that hostile aggression and violence have many characteristics in common. Terry and Jackson (1985, p. 27) provide a good working definition of sport violence: "Violence is defined as harm-inducing behavior bearing no direct relationship to the competitive goals of sport, and relates, therefore, to incidents of uncontrolled aggression outside the rules of sport, rather than highly competitive behavior within the rule boundaries." Because of the definitional overlap between certain aspects of sport aggression and that of violence, and despite the admonition of Silva, from this point on, we shall grant a certain degree of interchangeability between the two terms as they apply to sport.

THEORIES OF AGGRESSION

Biological Bases

Efforts at arriving at an understanding of our aggressive nature have taken many forms. One emphasizes the role of *genetics*. Though there is some evidence from the animal world in terms of the breeding of fighting cocks or fighting dogs, little substantiation for a genetic hypothesis exists in the human domain. Perhaps the closest example in humans is the XYY chromosomal theory of aggression and criminality. In the 1960s it was hypothesized that many examples of male criminality could be explained on the basis of such a chromosomal abnormality, the theory being that males with this abnormality were predisposed to a life of crime by chromosomal factors over which they had little or no control. Evidence gathered since then has cast

Bredemeier's Conceptualization of Aggression and Its Measurement in Sport

Brenda Jo Light Bredemeier has an interesting way of looking at aggression in the sporting context. She takes the position that any definition of sport aggression arises out of an implicit or explicit moral judgment, and her research has been driven by this view. One by-product of her theorizing and research on aggression is a sport-specific measure known as the Bredemeier Athletic Aggression Inventory (BAAGI). The BAAGI is composed of one hundred items that purport to measure instrumental (goal-related) and reactive (injurious, harmful, or violent) aggression. Early investigations using the BAAGI by Wall and Gruber (1986) and Worrell and Harris (1986) have been equivocal; subsequent attempts to validate the BAAGI have been sparse to nonexistent. More recent efforts by Bredemeier (1994) have maintained the same general position of linking aggression to moral judgments, and are outgrowths of work by Deluty (1979). Deluty created an instrument called the Children's Action Tendency Scale (CATS), a thirty-item measure of submissiveness, aggressiveness (subdivided into physical and nonphysical), and assertiveness in children. Bredemeier has created a similar scale that is adapted to sports known as the Scale of Children's Action Tendencies in Sport (SCATS). The SCATS and the CATS are similar in every respect except for the use of sport-related items on the SCATS. A typical item from the SCATS would look as follows:

You're running in a long distance race, and one of the other runners comes up from behind, trips you, and runs on ahead.

What would you do?

Circle *a* or *b*   a) Forget about it.
Or
b) Report that runner to the race official.

Circle *a* or *b*   a) Try to catch up and get that runner back.
Or
b) Forget about it.

Circle *a* or *b*   a) Report that runner to the race official.
Or
b) Try to catch up and get that runner back.

(Continued next page)

Highlight 7.2 (Continued)

Bredemeier's Conceptualization of Aggression and Its Measurement in Sport

In the one study conducted to date, Bredemeier administered the SCATS to 106 fourth- to seventh-grade children. Chief among her findings: support for the proposition that behavioral tendencies are indeed linked to interactional morality; general support for the reliability and validity of the SCATS; sex differences in aggression, with males being more aggressive and less submissive than females across both the CATS and the SCATS; and age-related increases in physical aggression across both the sport and daily life contexts.

Sources: Bredemeier (1975, 1983, 1994); Bredemeier and Shields (1986); Deluty (1979); Wall and Gruber (1986); Worrell and Harris (1986).

much doubt on such a simplistic explanation for complex human behavior.

Among females, Meyer-Bahlburg (1981) has looked at XO and XXX chromosomal composition. If the X-chromosome hypothesis concerning aggression is correct, we would expect more aggression from XO females; conversely, we would anticipate less from the XXX females. Meyer-Bahlburg found the XO females to be relatively nonaggressive. As for the XXX females, they appeared to be overrepresented in institutional settings, but for reasons having little or nothing to do with aggressive behavior. It may be that the X-chromosome has little bearing on the instigation or mediation of aggression.

A second approach to understanding aggression has been to look at the role of various *neurological structures,* such as the hypothalamus, the limbic system, and temporal lobe pathology. A morbid but fascinating case of temporal lobe pathology is represented by Charles Whitman. In 1966, Whitman killed his wife and his mother in separate stabbings and then killed fourteen people and injured twenty-four others while

perched atop the tower of the administrative building at the University of Texas (Austin). His lack of a history of violence coupled with a postmortem autopsy finding of what appeared to be a brain tumor led authorities to suspect temporal lobe pathology as a likely etiological factor in his aggressive acts. All things considered, however, there is no conclusive support for neurological processes as a major cause of aggression.

Yet a third viewpoint is that certain hormonal agents are involved in an interactive fashion with learned and/or cognitive factors in producing aggressive acts. Chief among the suspected hormonal culprits is testosterone, the male sex hormone (which is ten times higher in males than females). A particularly interesting investigation of the testosterone/aggression relationship was conducted by Dabbs and Morris (1990). They studied over four thousand male military veterans by comparing the top 10 percent with the remaining 90 percent on blood testosterone levels. The males with high testosterone levels reported more trouble with authority and peers, more frequent assaultive behavior, more absent without leave (AWOL) violations, and more frequent abuse of drugs than did the lower group. Because of the size of their sample, Dabbs and Morris feel that their study has produced compelling evidence for the testosterone/aggression relationship.

In the case of females, the estrogen/progesterone ratio has been a focus of some research. Imbalances in the ratio have been known to cause irritability or hostility, particularly around the menstrual period. Dalton (1961, 1964) has linked this hormonal imbalance to criminal acts outside and behavior problems inside the prison environment among incarcerated females.

A final point about hormonal influences on aggression bears mentioning. Baron and Richardson (1994) suggest that the relationship between testosterone and aggression is most likely a bidirectional one; that is, high levels of testosterone may produce aggression and, conversely, aggressive acts may increase the production of testosterone. The potentially bidirectional nature of the testosterone/aggression relationship gives some indication of just how complicated things are in the area of hormonal influences on behavior.

Baron and Richardson (1994, p. 253), in addressing the necessarily interdisciplinary approaches to the study of hormones and behavior, succinctly summarize the issue: "Regardless of the research approach or the disciplinary affiliation of the investigator, the results are similar—and inconclusive."

Psychosocial Approaches

The notion of reducing aggression through allowing its expression is neither novel nor unappealing. All of us at times have probably subscribed to the idea that "letting off steam" or "getting it off of our chest" is a constructive way of dealing with pent-up emotion. The release felt at these times is often referred to as catharsis, which comes from the Greek *kathairein,* meaning "to cleanse." As used in the ensuing discussion, *catharsis* will refer to the release of aggressive tendencies through their expression. A number of theorists—including Freud, Lorenz, Ardrey, and Dollard and Miller and their associates—have generated scholarly explanations that are in line with the catharsis hypothesis.

Instinct Theory

Instinct theory has its origin in the expostulations of Sigmund Freud. Freud hypothesized that we are all possessed of a powerful life wish (Eros) and a potent death wish (Thanatos), with the former manifested in the sex drive and the latter in the need to aggress. Because the death wish involved self-destructiveness, the avoidance of harm to oneself could be avoided by aggressing against others. Freud viewed these tendencies toward self-destruction and harm avoidance as instinctual. Given Freud's hypothesis, it should come as no surprise that we live in such a stressful and war-torn world. Out of all of this, aggression is seen as being dissipated by its expression.

Alternative instinctive theories have been proposed by such contemporary ethologists as Ardrey (1966) and Lorenz (1966). Both authorities posit that man is like any other animal with the same need to aggress. For Lorenz, aggression is an instinctive behavior that persists because it facilitates the survival of the species. Because of its innate nature, it does not have to be learned. Ardrey talks in terms of *territoriality,* or the tendency of all animals to drive intruders out of their chosen territory. Territoriality is clearly seen in the behavior of animals, but is more nebulous in humans. However, the way we construct our dwellings, our locks, our fences, and our "beware of dog" or "no solicitors allowed" signs all point to defense of our territory. Vigilance with our young children and the increasing freedom granted them as they mature are reminiscent of the ways animals treat their young.

Frustration–Aggression Hypothesis

Another approach with cathartic leanings is the *frustration–aggression model,* first proposed by Dollard, Doob, Miller, Mowrer, and Sears (1939). Though having similarities with previous models, the theory of Dollard et al. differs in that learned experiences rather than instinctive tendencies are emphasized. Their hypothesis is that frustration, or the blocking of motivated or goal-directed behavior, leads to aggression. Conversely, aggression is always preceded by frustration. Though this provocative hypothesis has served as the spark for a great deal of research over the past fifty years, it has fallen on rather hard times. For one thing, it greatly oversimplifies the issue by stating that frustration always leads to aggression, and vice versa. Secondly, in view of the rich abundance of other possible explanations, to assume that frustration is the primary or only cause of aggression is too simplistic.

The Social Learning Approach

A point of view that seriously calls into question the basic tenets of the various cathartic theories is *social learning theory,* of which Bandura (1973) is a prime architect. A brief description of the social learning position can be seen in figure 7.4.

Essentially, this theoretical stance asserts that aggression is reinforced rather than alleviated or lessened by aggression. Two primary mechanisms are at work here, namely, *reinforcement* and *modeling.* Instances in which unacceptable or aggressive behavior are reinforced increase rather than reduce the likelihood of their future occurrence, which is consistent with everything the behaviorists have validated in their theorizing, research, and application. Aggressive acts on the part of players that are reinforced by either tacit approval or by failure to punish on the part of a coach or parent may be seen as acceptable and therefore are reinforced. As for modeling, parents are usually the first sources

Figure 7.4: Bandura's Social Learning Theory

Aggression is *Acquired* through:
Biological factors (e.g., hormones, neural systems)
Learning (e.g., direct experience, observation)

Aggression is *Instigated* by
Influence of models (e.g., arousal, attention)
Aversive treatment (e.g., attack, frustration)
Incentives (e.g., money, admiration)
Instructions (e.g., orders)
Bizarre beliefs (e.g., delusions of paranoia)

Aggression is *Regulated* by:
External rewards and punishments (e.g., tangible rewards, negative consequences)
Vicarious reinforcement (e.g., observing others' rewards and punishments)
Self-regulatory mechanisms (e.g., pride, guilt)

Note: This theory explains the acquisition, instigation, and regulation of aggressive behavior.
Source: Baron and Richardson (1994).

of identification that a child has. A parent who displays aggression serves as a model for aggressive acts on the part of the child. The Little League coach who verbally attacks the umpires is likely to have the same effect on his young charges. Also, the aggressive athlete serves as a negative model for youthful admirers. As will be discussed in chapter 11, reinforcement and modeling of aggression are not to be glorified by people involved with young athletes in particular.

Catharsis or Social Learning?

The issue of cathartic versus enhancing effects of aggression is a complex one, and no easy answers are at hand. Perhaps the complexity of the whole issue is best illustrated by the furor generated over violence in television, whether in sport or otherwise. If the cathartic school of thought is correct, viewing television violence should decrease its incidence in the real world; if Bandura and his followers are correct, aggression as seen on television should promote rather than discourage aggression. No doubt the issue is far from resolved, and heated debate over both the theories and their application to sport and television violence will continue for quite a long while. Russell (1993), in a comprehensive review of the literature, has concluded that there is little support for a cathartic view and substantial evidence for the social learning position.

Our personal stance is that the role of learning in the development of human behavior cannot be dismissed, and its relationship to aggression and violence is no exception. Perhaps our viewpoint is best expressed by Montagu (1975, pp. 438, 449):

> No matter who or what was responsible for making us into what we have become, that does not for a moment relieve us of the responsibility of endeavoring to make ourselves over into what we ought to be. . . . To suggest that man is born ineradicably aggressive, warlike, and violent is to do violence to the facts. To maintain that he is innately already "wired" or "programmed" for aggression is to render confusion worse confounded, to exhibit a failure to understand the pivotally most consequential fact about the nature of man. That fact is not that man becomes what he is predetermined to become, but that he becomes, as a human being, whatever—within his genetic limitations—he learns to be.

Sociological Explanations

From the vantage point of the sport sociologist, violence in sports can be looked at in a number of ways. According to Snyder and Spreitzer (1983; 1989) there are four perspectives: the contagion theory, the convergence theory, the emergent norm theory, and the value-added theory.

Contagion Theory

Critical to an understanding of this viewpoint is "milling," the process whereby tension, uneasiness, and excitation are manifested by fans or players. As tensions mount, the tendency to react in impulsive or counterproductive ways escalates. At this point, a psychological contagion may emerge that can manifest itself in active participation in collective violence. Inherent in all of this is a tendency toward circularity of response, that is, the restlessness and irritability serve to influence others through what amounts to modeling. As Snyder and Spreitzer (1989, p. 242) put it: "The mutual interstimulation results in a circular spiral of feelings and action."

Convergence Theory

As opposed to psychological contagion, the convergence model emphasizes commonality of interests and goals in a highly divergent group of people whose emotions are brought to a fever pitch by the sporting event. The behavior of soccer hooligans in Britain (to be discussed later in the chapter) serves as an exemplar for the convergent model. The soccer matches become a forum for ruffians and ne'er-do-wells to engage in intense, ritualistic misbehavior that is fueled by the sport and the fever pitch of the action.

The Emergent Norm Theory

The "oneness" and the contagion of the previous models is in contrast to the emergent norm idea, which posits that group interaction creates a situation-specific set of standards that emerge over time among spectators at a sports event. The emphasis here is on the collective response that emerges as a function of the crowd interaction that is situation-specific. It may be that the politeness of the typical golf gallery or of tennis fans is an emergent norm with a long history, one in stark contrast to the behavior often seen at hockey games or soccer matches.

Value-Added Theory

This approach owes its genesis to Smelser (1962); it is inclusive of aspects of the other three models and more comprehensive in scope. Crowd behavior, to Smelser, can escalate in healthy or unhealthy ways as a function of six steps; they are:

1. *Structural conduciveness,* which is a function of fan and player personal and social characteristics, avenues, or lack of avenues for expression of emotion, proximity of targets for verbal or physical attack, and physical setting characteristics.
2. *Structural strain,* which represents a dissonance between what fans want to happen and what actually transpires; the larger the gap, the more unpredictable behavior becomes.
3. *Dissonance reduction,* which dictates that there must be some attempt to deal with the dissonance created in step two. Poor officiating, an antagonistic fan for the opposition, or a dirty player may serve as a source of resolution of the dissonance state. At this point, there may be an escalation in psychological contagion.
4. *A specific precipitator* of violence must present itself, such as a particularly rough play or a decidedly bad officiating decision.
5. *Mobilization for action* characterizes the next step in the process. The interaction between the crowd, the physical surroundings of the sports facility, and the emergence of a leader to force the action are at work here.
6. *A breakdown in the physical and/or psychological mechanisms for social control* to keep behavior within reasonable bounds further contributes to the problem.

In summary, each stage adds its respective value to the totality, thus increasing the likelihood of collective violence in sports fans.

THE MEASUREMENT OF AGGRESSION

The measurement of aggression has been carried out from a variety of angles. One method is naturalistic observation, such as might be the case with violence in such sports as hockey or soccer. Another procedure would be to look at aggression in the laboratory. Manipulation of aggression variables under laboratory conditions has much appeal, though its critics argue that much may be lost in translating laboratory findings to the so-called real world. Another interesting approach is archival research, which involves the collection of data from public sources, such as police files or crime statistics. Another method is to rely on self reports, which might include the use of questionnaires and psychological tests. Questionnaires that ask people to engage in self-disclosure with regard to their own use of aggression have been used with some degree of success. As for personality measures, they have typically been dichotomized as projective and objective. The success of projective tests lies in the assumption that people will project hidden personality traits into ambiguous stimuli such as those provided by the Rorschach Inkblot Test, the Thematic Apperception Test (TAT), or a variety of sentence completion techniques. In the case of the Rorschach, the subject is presented with ten inkblots; assuming that the person being tested will generate enough responses to the ten cards to have a scorable protocol, inferences about personality can then be made. If one were engaged in aggression research, it would be possible to deduce the trait from Rorschach responses. In the case of the TAT, subjects are presented with a series or real pictures from which they are to tell detailed stories; emerging themes (i.e., aggression) are then ascertained and analyzed. Much the same can be said for the various sentence completion tests. Subjects are presented with incomplete sentence stems, and it is anticipated that personality traits, such as aggression, will emerge.

As for objective tests of personality, they employ a variety of forced choice formats (i.e., true-false, choose between A and B) to assess personality. Examples in the broader field of psychology include the Overcontrolled Hostility Scale (Megargee, Cook, and Mendelsohn, 1967), which is derived from the MMPI (to be discussed in some detail in chapter 8); the Buss-Durkee Hostility Scale (Buss and Durkee, 1957); and the Aggression Questionnaire (Buss and Perry, 1992). Of particular interest is the latter scale, which is really an outgrowth or extension of the Buss and Durkee work of some thirty-five years ago. Building on the popularity of the Buss-Durkee Scale, which has been cited 242 times in the Social Science Citation Index (Bushman, Cooper, and Lemke, 1991), Buss and Perry have created a twenty-nine-item scale that measures Physical Aggression, Verbal Aggression, Anger, and Hostility. Preliminary psychometric work by Buss and Perry was supportive of the scale's efficacy. Subsequent study by Bourgeois, Biffle, and LeUnes (1994) has lent further credibility to the scale. Bourgeois et al. administered the Aggression Questionnaire, the Profile of Mood States (POMS), the Sports Inventory for Pain (SIP), the Willis Sports Attitude Inventory (SAI), and the NEO Personality Scale to seventy-four college students in an abnormal psychology class. Chief among their results was fifty-eight significant correlations between Aggression Questionnaire scores and those from the other inventories. While not sport-specific, it is likely that the Buss-Perry scale will have relevancy for sport researchers in the area of aggression.

Little has been done in sport-specific measures of aggression. Bredemeier's BAAGI (Bredemeier, 1978) has met with only modest acceptance to date, and her Scale of Children's Action Tendencies in Sport (SCATS) (see highlight 7.2) is quite new and relatively unexplored at this point. The SCATS does show promise in future research on aggression in youth sports. Overall, however, with all the fascination we share with regard to sports violence, little has been done in sport psychology to unravel its many nuances.

FACTORS PROMOTING AGGRESSION

A virtually unlimited number of factors may cause or facilitate aggression. Some are of a physical nature: temperature, noise, and crowding. Others, such as modeling, reinforcement, and deindividuation, are psychological forces. At the sociological level, one of the more interesting phenomena is hooliganism. Also, no discussion of aggression and violence would be complete without a look at the role of the various media in promoting such misbehavior.

Physical Factors

Three physical factors that contribute in a complex fashion to create or promote aggressive acts are temperature, noise, and crowding.

Temperature
As has been so eloquently pointed out by William Shakespeare, in *Romeo and Juliet,* temperature, most particularly excessive heat, has a significant and negative effect on behavior:

> I pray thee, good Mercutio, let's retire;
> The day is hot, the Capulets abroad,
> And, if we meet, we shall not 'scape a brawl,
> For now, these hot days, is the mad blood
> stirring. (III, 1, 1-4)

There has been considerable research substantiation for the temperature and aggression relationship, and the preponderance indicates that there is a linear relationship between the two

Figure 7.5: **Relationship between Temperature and Aggression**

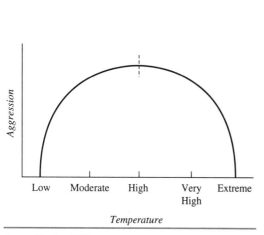

Source: Franken (1982).

variables; that is, there will be concomitant increases in aggression as temperature rises. However, research by Baron (1977) has cast some doubt on this linear explanation; he suggests that be readily seen, aggressive episodes are low in frequency at the temperature extremes; too high or too low temperature actually serves to limit the kinds of arousal and human interaction that lead to violence. Clearly, there may be an optimal temperature in which aggression flourishes. Further substantiation for this curvilinear explanation was offered by Baron and Ransberger (1978) when they demonstrated its existence in a study of temperature and the incidence of riots in large U.S. cities. This relationship between temperature and riots is presented in figure 7.6. Obviously, riots are linked to temperature in a curvilinear fashion. Riots are infrequent below

Figure 7.6: **Relationship between Ambient Temperature and Riots**

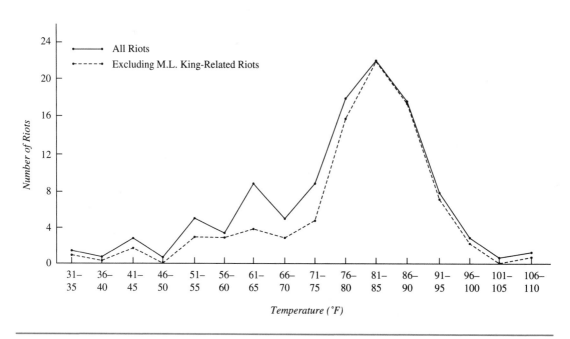

Source: Baron and Ransberger (1978).

temperatures of 55° and above 95°F. How all this relates to sport violence is unclear because of a paucity of research on temperature and sport behavior. However, those hot baseball or soccer stadia or those steamy, sweaty basketball arenas must in some way contribute to instances of player or fan aggression that occur from time to time.

One sport-related test of the temperature/ violence relationship has been conducted by Reifman, Larrick, and Fein (1991). In their research, Reifman et al. looked at archival data from the 1986, 1987, and 1988 major league baseball seasons. Their methodology was to relate game temperature to number of batters hit by the pitchers in 826 games over those three seasons. A positive and significant relationship was found between game temperature and number of hit batters. However, as opposed to the cur- vilinearity proposed by Baron and Ransberger, the relationship between hit batters and temper- ature in this study was a linear one. This linear- ity can be readily seen in figure 7.7.

Two additional points merit mention. First, methodological controls over potential con- founding variables having nothing to do with aggression per se were factored into the study. For example, walks, wild pitches, passed balls, errors, home runs, attendance, and home versus visiting ballpark were analyzed statistically and deemed to be of minimal influence in their effects on the overall results. Secondly, as a check on their results for 1986–1988, Reifman et al. found a similar linearity effect when they ana- lyzed archival data from the 1962 season.

Noise

Though there is little research in the area of noise and sport violence, the roar of the crowd is likely to be a factor in increasing arousal. Con- comitantly, the likelihood of aggression is greater in heightened states of arousal. Part of the home advantage so well documented in sport and dis- cussed in chapter 6 is the noise factor. Basket-

Figure 7.7: **Number of Batters Hit by Pitchers as a Function of Game Temperature**

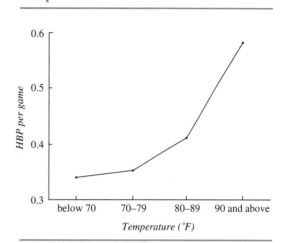

Note: Mean number of players hit by a pitch (HBPs) in games played below 70°F ($n = 176$), between 70°F and 79°F ($n = 315$), between 80°F and 89°F ($n = 224$), and at 90°F and above ($n = 111$).

Source: Reifman, Larrick, and Fein (1991).

ball coaches intentionally place the visitors' bench behind the home team's band, and foot- ball cheerleaders exhort the home crowd to drown out the opponent's signals. Although the intent in these instances is not to create aggres- sion, noisy outbursts such as these can promote already existing hostile feelings or emotions.

Donnerstein and Wilson (1976) have demon- strated a link between noise and aggression, though not in a sport setting. They exposed stu- dents to either 55- or 95-decibel bursts of noise while the students were administering electric shocks to a confederate of the researchers. Stu- dents exposed to the higher noise level delivered more shock to the confederate than did the low noise intensity group. If we can extrapolate from the results of this research to the world of ath- letics, we can infer a possible relationship between noise and aggression. Perhaps Franken (1982, p. 290) says it best: "Noise does not seem to evoke aggression by itself. Rather, noise simply facilitates this behavior if it has already been evoked." Obviously, more sport-related research linking noise and aggression needs to be conducted.

Crowding

Information arising from the 1994 International Conference on Population and Development held in Cairo, Egypt, indicated that it took well over one hundred years for the world population to grow from 1 billion to 2 billion, but only thirteen years to grow from 4 to 5 billion. Left unchecked, the world population is projected to become 12.5 billion by the middle of the twenty-first century (Ambah, 1995). In and of itself, this does not represent a problem of crowding according to Berkowitz (1986), but more one of density. Density is thought of as the actual amount of physical space and the people filling it whereas crowding is the psychological stress response created by the problems of density. How all of this relates to aggression is not clear. Freedman (1975), after reviewing the available research, concluded that crowding itself is not a causative factor in aggression, but is most definitely a facilitator when the propensity for hostility already exists.

What emerges from the research in temperature, noise, and crowding is the conclusion that they are more facilitators than causes of aggression; that is, they interact with other variables to produce aggression in situations in which the propensity for hostile action already exists. One does not have to look far in the world of sport to find applications for this generalization. The heat generated by the sun and/or lots of warm bodies coupled with the roar of the crowd and accentuated by a moving, shoving mass of people has contributed to more than one act of sport violence.

Psychological Factors

A number of psychological variables are related to the expression of aggression. Though

modeling and reinforcement were discussed briefly earlier in this chapter, a more detailed elaboration on them will be made. Also, the role of external rewards will be discussed. Finally, the effects of deindividuation and becoming inured to violence will be accorded proper mention.

Vicarious Reinforcement and Modeling

According to Silva (1984, p. 268), one of the main promoters and maintainers of aggressive behavior in sport is *vicarious reinforcement* or what he calls "the tendency to repeat behaviors that we observe others rewarded for performing." A related concept is vicarious punishment. In defining the term, Silva says: "We are less likely to perform a behavior that we have seen another individual being punished for doing."

To Bandura (1973), the acquisition of behavior through either vicarious reinforcement or vicarious punishment is greatly mediated by model and observer similarity, by reward and punishment intensity, by setting similarity, and by the status of the model being observed. As might be expected, the greater the similarity between the model and the observer, the greater is the likelihood of any given behavior being repeated. Reward value is rather obvious in this context; something meaningful to an individual is likely to be pursued with vigor. Also, if the setting in which a behavior is to be performed is similar to that in which it was originally observed and vicariously reinforced, the greater the transfer will be. Finally, the status of the model for the observer is critical; young aspiring athletes emulate their heroes, which of course is one of the reasons why positive role models should be promoted and negative ones downplayed.

The relationship of these variables advanced by Bandura to aggression in sport is reasonably obvious. Youngsters viewing aggressive models with whom they strongly identify and whose sport they themselves play are prone to believe that aggression is an acceptable behavior.

Direct External Rewards

Bandura (1973) has identified four forms of external reward that are operative in human interactions, and their applicability to sport is undeniable. One is *tangible reward*. Perhaps the most powerful of these tangible rewards is money. If being aggressive means more money in the personal coffers, then aggression it shall be. In a highly publicized incident from the football world in the 1970s, some members of the coaching staff at a major university in the Southwest offered various amounts of money to players on the specialty teams for tackles, breaking up wedges, kicks into the end zone, and so forth. Being particularly assertive (if not aggressive) was highly prized and rewarded accordingly. As the reader may suspect, this external reward system was met with disfavor among the various organizations that govern the conduct of intercollegiate athletics.

A second external reward is *status reward;* being aggressive in many sports carries with it a certain amount of respect and recognition among peers. Also, the use of nicknames connoting and reinforcing aggression (The Hammer, Assassin, Dr. Death, Enforcer) are liberally applied from a variety of sources to those who characterize higher levels of aggressive demeanor. This somewhat deviant form of recognition only furthers aggression in these athletes as their nicknames become a sort of self-fulfilling prophecy. You cannot be an "assassin" without working hard at it!

A third external reward, one whose relation to sport is less clear, is *expression of injury*. It is possible that hurting an opponent may actually promote aggression; it seems equally plausible that injury infliction may act to inhibit displays of aggression. Research in and outside of sport has not sufficiently established just what the effects are. For some athletes, hopefully a minority, the sight of blood from an opponent is probably reinforcing because it is evidence that the aggressive act worked. A sport such as boxing, in which intent to hurt is so manifest, would seem to be a prime example of the reinforcing properties of injury infliction.

A fourth and final reinforcer cited by Bandura is *alleviation of aversive treatment*. Aggression that reduces aggression on the part of the opponent is reinforcing. Establishing one's territory is inherent in this consideration, and failure to be aggressive in defending what one has is likely to be frowned upon by all involved parties, including the opposition. Loss of self-esteem and status with others is at stake here. We are reminded of the case of Paul Mulvey, a National Hockey League player who refused his coaches' order to take part in a brawl between his team, the Los Angeles Kings, and that of the opposition, the Vancouver Canucks. Mulvey's reticence to fight was poorly received by his peers and the team management, and because of his violation of the eye-for-an-eye norms of hockey, he soon found himself out of the league altogether. Such violations of the aggressive norm simply are not to be tolerated in contact sports.

Deindividuation

Another contributor to aggression, and one unstudied but not unrelated to sport, is *deindividuation*. The concept of deindividuation was introduced by Festinger, Pepitone, and Newcomb in 1952 and highlighted by research conducted by Zimbardo (1969). Deindividuation refers to the notion that, as density increases, personal identity and evaluation decreases and conformity to group dictates increases. The loss of identity or sense of belonging, in turn, promotes the incidence of aggressive acts. When the individual can no longer be separated from the mass and, concomitantly, individual responsibility for proper behavior is diluted, then deindividuation has taken place. Unfortunately, no research has attempted to relate deindividuation to aggression in sport. Also, the issue has not been satisfactorily resolved in research with nonsport groups.

As has been the case with so many other variables, to make a case for singular causation is difficult when most human behavior is dictated in a complex fashion. In any event, loss of personal responsibility for behavior would appear to be explanatory in at least some cases of sport aggression.

Inurement to Violence

According to a widely held supposition, we have become so accustomed to violence in our daily lives that it no longer exerts a negative effect on us. The media report incredible numbers of acts of individual and group violence every day, and incidents of sport aggression are often highlighted. This exposure to violence on a continual basis tends to inure us to aggressive acts, thereby raising our tolerance for such behaviors.

Sociological Considerations

One of the more interesting phenomena associated with sport is soccer violence, something that has come to be known as *hooliganism*. From all appearances, it is a social class-related behavior and merits further attention. The *role of the various media* in fostering and promoting aggression is also a significant sociological consideration and will be addressed at length.

Hooliganism

According to *Webster's New Twentieth Century Dictionary*, a *hooligan* is "a young ruffian, especially a member of a street gang; hoodlum." The same source defines hooliganism as "the behavior or character of a hooligan; rowdiness; vandalism." Accordingly, the term hooliganism has been used extensively to refer to the behavior or soccer fans in Britain (Dunning, 1983; Dunning, Maguire, Murphy, and Williams, 1982; Marsh, Rosser, and Harre, 1978). Dunning indicates that hooliganism, in the eyes of those who engage in it, has become an accepted, almost normal part of professional soccer. Hooliganism's most central feature, the thing that marks

it most, is physical violence. Sometimes hooligan violence is directed toward the players, at other times the officials and, more often than not, at rival fan groups. The violence may take the form of close hand-to-hand combat, the use of weaponry, or aerial bombardment from a distance. The fact that darts, coins, beer cans, and petrol bombs have been used as weapons is indicative of the intent to harm that is so integral a part of our definition of aggression. In an effort to curb some of these hostilities, officials have resorted to segregating various fan groups by penning them together in separate areas within the stadium.

Dunning's opinion is that the behavior of football (soccer) hooligans is dominated by a misplaced attempt to demonstrate masculinity, with an exaggerated emphasis on toughness and ability and willingness to fight. He further asserts that the rival groups are recruited principally from the rougher segments of the working class populace. Dunning also feels that the soccer games themselves may merely serve as a forum for rival gangs to conduct their longstanding feuds; that is, fighting appears to be more important than watching the soccer match. Curry and Jiobu (1984, p. 250) sum it up as follows: "For the soccer hooligan, the soccer stadium is a battlefield, not a sports field." A final noteworthy observation by Dunning concerns the conformity to group dictates that characterizes the various hooligan gangs. Hooligans tolerate little individuality from gang members, and they reinforce group identification and conformity through ritualized songs and chants that they engage in at the matches. One of the more benign of these chants is provided by Marsh, Rosser, and Harre (1978, p. 66):

In their slums,
In their Nottingham slums,
They look in the dust bin for something to
    eat,
They find a dead cat and think it's a treat,
In their Nottingham slums.

Hooliganism has become an almost accepted part of professional soccer. Perhaps the ultimate act of hooliganism occurred in 1985 in Brussels, when drunken Britishers attacked rival Italian fans. A collapsing safety barrier killed nearly forty people and injured over four hundred.

Incidentally, the theme of most of these incantations is enhancement of masculinity.

A major instance of hooliganism occurred in 1985 in Brussels, Belgium, when 38 people were killed and 437 injured by a group of young Britishers. Severe sanctions were sought against these people; 26 British participants were prosecuted for manslaughter ("Soccer," 1988). Some ways of controlling these hooligans will be entertained later in this chapter as a part of the overall recommendations for controlling aggression or sport violence.

The Media
Much ado has been made concerning the role of the media in the glorification of violence.

Of particular concern has been the sex and violence issue as it relates to young, impressionable children, but the role of the media in promoting violence through their handling of sport has most certainly not gone unnoticed. Bryant and Zillman (1983, p. 197) have summarized part of our inconsistent feelings with regard to media portrayals of violence in sport with the following questions: "Why does the public *tolerate* such extensive violence in its favorite spectator sports? Or is it the wrong question? Better, perhaps, why do people *desire,* why do they *demand* so much violence in their spectator sports?"

In answer to their own query, Bryant and Zillman offer three theories as to why people enjoy aggression in sports. One possible clue has to do with the *catharsis hypothesis.* Though the scientific support for the catharsis view is not strong, its popular appeal to the wider society is considerable. Its acceptance by the media has been largely with open arms. From cathartic theory it follows that engaging in or viewing aggression lessens aggression; if this is the case, then the more violence we observe, the more cathartic the effect will be. The media therefore provide us with as much blood and gore as we can tolerate, all the while assuring us that our aggressive needs will be ameliorated by these megadoses of violence.

A second explanation for our enjoyment of violence in sports has to do with *assertive dominance* over others, a viewpoint popularized in the psychological literature by Adler (1927). The need to be assertive and to dominate others, according to this theory, is among the strongest of human motivations. Opportunities for the expression of these strivings for assertion and dominance abound in such sports as basketball, football, hockey, and soccer, and the vicarious viewing of these dominance moves should account for some of our enjoyment of sport aggression. And, as we noted earlier in the cathartic approach, the greater the dominance displayed within the rules, the greater the enjoyment should be for the fans.

A final theory focuses on competition, or the *enjoyment of drama*. As Bryant and Zillman say, the catch phrase "The human drama of athletic competition" captures the essence of this theory. In this context of human drama, aggression is seen as exemplifying the ultimate in competition. The athlete who aggresses is only trying to win, and aggression is proof positive of that fact. Part of our fascination with thrill or high risk sports in which the contestants actively risk serious injury or death may lie not in our perversity but in the high drama realm. Participants who are willing to tempt the fates so severely may represent the ultimate in intensity (i.e., competitiveness) for the spectators. An alternate and probably more widely accepted view is that people enjoy the high risk sports because of the likelihood of serious injury or death to the participants. It is hoped that this unproven perspective sells the human organism short.

No consensus is apparent as to which of the three theories is most valid, but general agreement exists with regard to the notion that sports violence has entertainment value. Three studies by Jennings Bryant and various colleagues have lent credibility to the supposition that spectators like violence in sports. In the first study, Comisky, Bryant, and Zillman (1977) looked at the sport of ice hockey because of its rough and tumble nature. In the Comisky et al. research, the effect of color commentary was studied in terms of its relationship to viewer enjoyment. As can be seen in figure 7.8, enjoyment of play was not a function of actual roughness but rather one of perceived roughness; that is, color commentary emphasizing how rough play was when it actually was not and the downplaying of very rough play greatly affected spectator enjoyment.

In the second study (Bryant, Comisky, and Zillman, 1981), professional football served as the sport under scrutiny. Male and female viewers were asked to rate their enjoyment of preselected plays from National Football League (NFL) games. As can be seen in figure 7.9 enjoy-

ment increased as a function of concomitant increases in rough play. This was true for both sexes but was statistically significant for males only. Apparently, football fans like aggressive play from their warriors.

Figure 7.8: **Viewers' Perceptions of Roughness of Play in Ice Hockey as a Function of Broadcast Commentary**

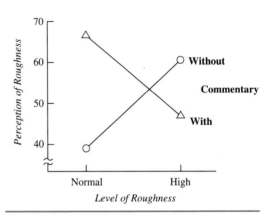

Source: Bryant and Zillman (1983).

Figure 7.9: **Viewers' Enjoyment of Plays of Televised Football as a Function of Degree of Roughness and Violence Involved**

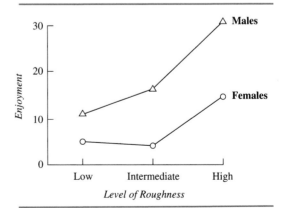

Source: Bryant, Comisky, and Zillman (1981).

The third study (Bryant, Brown, Comisky, and Zillman, 1982) was done with the less violent sport of tennis as target, and the variable manipulated was how much or how little tennis players were perceived to like each other. Enjoyment of a tennis match was clearly a function of perceived enmity; when players were perceived as intensely disliking each other, enjoyment was high. Such was not the case when the tennis adversaries were thought to be friends. Competitiveness was also seen as much more intense when supposed enemies were playing each other. This material is presented in figure 7.10.

Collectively, these three studies suggest that fans really do like violence in their sports fare. How far this enjoyment of violence extends is unclear, however. Within limits, aggression is seen as acceptable and enhances spectator enjoyment. However, there must be a limit to this affinity for aggression. Russell (1986) suggests that the acceptance of violence is curvilinear; that is, fans enjoy aggression within limits but are not willing to endure excessive violence. Perhaps future research will answer this question,

though obvious logistical and ethical problems are associated with such an undertaking. Manufacturing violence under laboratory conditions to see how far people would go before they would draw the line is impractical. Also, it is hoped that sport violence would not escalate to the point that we would have a real-world laboratory for the study of injurious or sadistic acts in sports.

Bryant and Zillman (1983) suggest that the media exploit violence in three ways. One is in the *coverage of violent plays.* How many times can you recall seeing replays of a bone-jarring and injurious tackle in football or a savage knockout in boxing? One encouraging development in this area, however, is the general policy of the various television networks not to give coverage to fights and other misbehaviors by players or fans at sporting events.

A second media exploitation method is to give articles the status of *features.* Many of our print media articles focus on violence; it is difficult to pick up a newspaper or any of the popular sport magazines without encountering a featured article on sport violence per se or one glorifying it in some form or fashion.

Finally, *promotions,* or promos, in television programming are exploitative. The filming of deaths in various high risk sports, such as automobile or power boat racing, and using the footage later to promote upcoming events in those sports appears to be pandering, as Bryant and Zillman so aptly put it, to some rather base human emotions.

Figure 7.10: **Viewers' Enjoyment of Identical Play in Tennis as a Function of Perceived Affect between the Players**

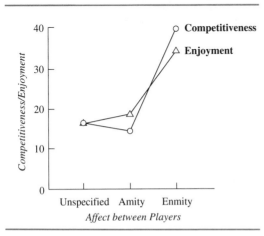

Source: Bryant et al. (1982).

CRITICAL SPORT-RELATED SITUATIONS AFFECTING AGGRESSION

A number of game-related variables have an impact on the expression of aggression. Summing across a number of studies, Bird and Cripe

(1986) and Cox (1990) have provided us with five critical situations that affect aggression in sport.

Point Spread

When the score is close, aggressive acts will be in relative abeyance because a penalty suffered at a critical juncture in a game can be decisive in determining the eventual winner. Also, when there is a substantial disparity in the score, aggression tends to be less because arousal is not so salient. Aggression is most likely to occur at a point midway between the two extremes.

Home/Away Factor

As was discussed in chapter 6, a general home advantage apparently exists in most sports. One of the more provocative hypotheses used to account for this supposed edge has been advanced by Varca (1980), who found that home basketball teams were more assertive in terms of rebounds, blocked shots, and steals, whereas the visitors were charged with more fouls. These results from Varca's work suggest some sort of dysfunctional use of assertion (if not aggression).

Outcome

Winning or losing makes a difference in frustration level, needless to say. Winners tend to display less aggression than losers. Temperamental outbursts on the part of losing players are reasonably common occurrences. They lend some support to the frustration–aggression hypothesis discussed earlier if one can assume that losing is in fact frustrating, an assumption that is probably a safe one in most instances.

League Standing

Though there are some conflicting data concerning this issue, concensus exists on the point that first place teams commit fewer aggressive acts than do their competitors. The real point of contention in this area concerns the other teams. For example, Volkamer (1971) found in a study of soccer teams that the lower a team was in the standings, the more likely it would engage in aggression. Russell and Drewry (1976), studying Canadian hockey teams, found that the teams trailing the league leader most closely were actually the most aggressive. Again, however, the two studies are in agreement as to lower levels of aggression on the part of the first place teams.

Period of Play

In a study of hockey players, Cullen and Cullen (1975) found that aggression increased in a linear function for winning teams and in a curvilinear mode for losing units; that is, losing teams were lowest in aggression at the beginning and end of play, with most of the aggression occurring in the middle of the match. Winning teams, on the other hand, displayed more aggression as the game went on. This latter finding has drawn support from Russell and Drewry (1976) in their study of hockey teams.

Clearly, critical events and junctures in various sports partially determine the frequency and intensity of aggression. However, their relationship to sport aggression is far from understood and more research in these situational variables is needed. Also, broadening the data base beyond hockey and soccer, which have dominated so far, would be most illuminating.

VIOLENCE IN SELECTED SPORTS

Though many athletic events possess much propensity for violence on the part of players and/or spectators, three that have captured our imaginations—boxing, football, and hockey—will be discussed in the next several pages.

Boxing

Virtually no other sport besides boxing has as its avowed purpose the infliction of harm on the opposition; the clear intent in boxing is to render the other person in the ring unconscious if at all possible. Very little pretense is made about boxing skill, artistry, and outpointing the opponent.

Dr. George Lundberg, editor of the *Journal of the American Medical Association*, sums up the state of the art of boxing as follows: "The intention in professional boxing is to damage your opponent's brain. What counts is a knock-out, a blow to the head" (Gavzer, 1990, p. 5.).

Boxing has been, continues to be, and will probably always be the subject of much controversy and public outcry. The sport is besieged on virtually every front; powerful lobbying directed toward cleaning up or abolishing boxing is being conducted by the powerful American Medical Association, and their protestations have not fallen on deaf ears at the national level of politics. Given that boxing has long been viewed as a brutal, barbarian spectacle, and given also that calls have been made for its abolition for several thousand years, the present brouhaha is unlikely to change much of anything.

As was noted in chapter 2, ancient Greek and Roman pugilists went to great lengths to subdue the enemy, including such machinations as wrapping their hands in rawhide and adding lead weight or metal spikes to their gloves. One legendary figure, Theagenes of Thasos, reputedly won 1,400 championships and killed as many as eight hundred of his opponents in the process over a twenty-year career.

The modern era of boxing began in the 1800s in Great Britain and the United States, and it initially took the form of bare-knuckled brawls. Fights generally lasted until someone quit or was beaten into bloody submission. Though the contemporary version is slightly more humane, boxing remains a brutal sport. Perhaps the violence is best summarized by a quote from an anonymous boxer: "I don't want to knock him out. I want to hit him, step away, and watch him hurt. I want his heart" (Yeager, 1979, p. 124).

Interestingly, psychologists know very little about the psychological makeup of boxers. Virtually no psychological data exist on this intriguing group of athletes. Armchair speculation abounds but very little substantial data are available.

One attempt to bring applied sport psychology to the understanding of boxing is provided by Butler, Smith, and Irwin (1993). In their work, Butler et al. applied the Performance Profile (Butler, 1989, 1991; Butler and Hardy, 1992) to an analysis of three amateur boxers. Briefly, Butler and his colleagues asked the boxers to produce the attributes of an elite boxer on the assumption that these attributions will lend insights into the performance needs of the athlete in question. In the case of one amateur boxer, twenty-two attributes were identified that were then subsumed by the authors under six major headings; Physical, Defense, Punches, Technical Work, Attitude, and Psychological. A variety of needs within each of the six headings were expressed, and served as focal points to work on for the athlete and his coach. Butler concludes by asserting that Performance Profiling has utility as a means of exploring and assessing an athlete's perception of his or her performance needs. Though interesting, Butler et al. shed little light on the personality makeup of boxers, however.

Football

Just bring along the ambulance.
And call the Red Cross nurse,
Then ring the undertaker up,
And make him bring a hearse:
Have all the surgeons ready there,
For they'll have work today,
Oh, can't you see the football teams
Are lining up to play.
    J. R. Betts

This description by Betts (1974, p. 244) aptly describes the nature of the game of football. Although football is not as controversial as boxing, it is not without its detractors, and there is undoubtedly some validity to the criticisms. Take, for example, injury statistics from high schools and colleges. According to Mueller and Schindler (1984), there were 893 deaths between 1931 and 1983 that were directly attributable to football (that is, due to head injury); of that total, 572 occurred at the high school level. An additional 465 deaths during that same time period were attributable to indirect causation; that is, systemic failure due to coronary problems or heat stroke. In another study involving data analysis for the years 1977–1987, Mueller, Blyth, and Cantu (1989) indicated that there were 105 catastrophic cervical cord injuries; of these, eighty-six were in the high schools, fourteen in college, and the remaining five in semi-pro or sandlot football. Of the total, nearly three-fourths were suffered by defensive players, most commonly defensive backs (33 percent). Fortunately, there has been a continuous diminution in the number of these catastrophic injuries each year; in the first five years beginning with 1977, there were fifty-eight such injuries. In the four-year period of 1984–1987, there were twenty-four cervical cord injuries. More recently, Gorman (1992) indicates that permanent cervical cord injuries have plummeted from thirty-four reported in 1976 to just one in 1991. Improvements in football headgear and changes in tackling techniques have undoubtedly contributed to this improving injury picture. Also, advances in the treatment of spinal cord injuries, especially in the first hours and days after their occurrence, have greatly improved the treatment picture for all victims of spinal cord injury, football or otherwise (Gorman, 1992).

As for minor head injuries, Wilberger (1993) estimates that there are a quarter of a million such occurrences annually in all contact sports including football. In a bit of a disclaimer, Clarke and Braslow (1978) put together a response to critics of football in which they showed that deaths attributable to football in the year 1964 among high school and college players occurred at about the same rate as nonfootball-related fatalities in the age group under consideration. Nevertheless, it seems safe to say that football is a violent sport.

In all likelihood, most of these football fatalities and injuries were inflicted within the limits of the rules and spirit of the game; that is, they were tragic responses to assertive rather than aggressive actions though, as indicated previously, a fine line exists between the two behaviors. All of these injury data underscore just how rough the game of football really is. No one knows how many injuries were the result of aggressive acts.

The National Football League (NFL) personifies the worst in the area of football violence, though catastrophic injuries are rare. The NFL projects its injury rate each year at 100 percent. In other words, it is anticipated that all 1,200 players will be injured to some degree during each season. To arrive at some understanding of the magnitude of the injury problem in professional football, the following statistics are also revealing (King, 1992):

- Twenty-seven quarterbacks and forty-seven running backs, players the fans most often want to see in action, missed from one to twelve games during the first twelve weeks of the 1992 season. Five quarterbacks and eight running backs missed all twelve games.
- Eleven weeks into the 1992 season, 213 players were on the injured reserve list, down from 219 for the same time period in 1991.
- By the first week in December, 1992, 482 pro players had missed at least one game. This represents seventeen players per team.
- Based on the above, and given that the average player salary is $480,000, a total of nearly three thousand games were missed at a loss of nearly $84 million.

Joe Jacobi, upon retirement from the Washington Redskins at the age of thirty-five, summed up his feelings in the following manner: "You just get tired of hurting . . . and I'm not even talking about the major injuries . . . my body can't do it anymore" (Bell, 1994, p. 7c). In line with Jacobi's sentiments about the injury situation in professional football, table 7.1 illustrates the nagging injuries from a recently retired professional defensive back.

Table 7.1
Injuries Sustained by a Professional Defensive Back over Two Seasons

1989	07/25/89	Right hip flexor strain
	08/03/89	Right hand first metacarpal contusion
	08/12/89	Right thumb thenar laceration
	09/18/89	Right knee patella contusion
	09/24/89	Right posterior lateral ankle sprain and contusion
	10/01/89	Left hip contusion
	11/26/89	Mild acute cerebral concussion
	11/26/89	Right brachial plexus compression
	11/26/89	Left shoulder glenohumerous joint subluxation
	12/16/89	Right superior knee contusion, quadricep tendon
	01/07/90	Right upper arm contusion; biceps brachii
	01/14/90	Right quadriceps contusion
1990	09/17/90	Right knee pre-patellar bursae contusion
	09/23/90	Right shoulder posterior rotator cuff irritation
	11/18/90	Left wrist sprain

Source: K. A. Corrington, Personal communication, Nov. 15, 1994, College Station, TX.

Some of this grim injury projection is undoubtedly related to aggression. Perhaps the following quote from Dave Peurifory of the Green Bay Packers says it all:

It's vicious and barbaric. They try to make it safe, but they can't. It's like playing tag on a highway. You can try to make it safe, but sooner or later, it's going to get you. They draft the biggest, meanest, nastiest players they can find and line them up. Nice guys can't play this game. There is no way a nice guy can make it. Smart guys can't play this game. You have to be on a low mentality. It's like butting your head into a brick wall. . . . I'm no different. I'm just as bad as the rest. I'm on a different level during the season as opposed to the off-season. Football is not conducive to a good vocabulary and being articulate. I'm a degenerate, just like the rest. ("Page Three," 1985)

Similar quotes abound on the violent mentality so pervasive among professional football players. One of the all-time greats, Jerry Kramer, also of the Green Bay Packers, was quoted as follows in his autobiography:

Forrest Gregg tackled Andrie just as he crossed the goal line, and I was only a step or two behind Forrest, and I suddenly felt the greatest desire to put both my cleats right on Andrie's spinal cord and break it. We had been victimized by these stupid plays—scooped up fumbles, deflected passes, blocked kicks, high school tricks—so many times during the season that I felt murderous. I'd never in my career deliberately step on a guy, but I was so tempted to destroy Andrie, to take everything out on him, that I almost did it. A bunch of thoughts raced through my mind—I'd met Andrie off the field a few times and I kind of liked him—and, at the last moment, I let up and stepped over him. (Kramer and Schaap, 1969, p. 257)

These expressions of aggressive tendencies are indicative of just how violent the game of football can be, and little is being done about the precarious situation. Football, like boxing, runs along with many critics and few restraints on its violent ways.

Hockey

Headlines from popular newspapers and magazines (i.e., *USA Today, Sports Illustrated*) continue to document violence in hockey, and frequently express concern about its effect on the future of the sport:

"Some Fans Rate Fisticuffs Integral Part of Big Picture"
"Probert, Wilson at Top of Heap in Scrapping"
"Hockey's Top Ice Warriors"
"Fighters Aren't Always Winners"
"Gretzky has Good Hands—Not Fists"
"Horror Show: Galloping Goons and Gratuitous Gore Marred the Dramatic Opening Round of the NHL Playoffs"
"Players Join Game's Furor over Fighting"
"Gretzky: We Have to Stop the Fights"

It is widely accepted that ice hockey is a violent sport. Perhaps Rodney Dangerfield, the stand-up comedian with the never-ending supply of one-liners, says it best: "I went to a fight the other night and a hockey game broke out." To the casual observer, the sport looks unusually rough. The players look rather haggard, few are in possession of their front teeth, speed of movement is breathtaking, sticks seem to be flying everywhere, and bodies are sacrificed with reckless abandon. The resulting perception is one of institutionally condoned mayhem. Penalty calls would seem to support this perception; penalties for the 1989–1990 season were up by 1,330 near the end of the season. In the 1991 NHL Playoffs, the Detroit and St. Louis teams were assessed a total of 298 minutes of violence-related penalties in Game 5 alone (Greenberg, 1991).

Smith's Violence Typology

Smith (1986) provides a typology with which to analyze sport violence. Smith's typology is based largely on material drawn from the legal area and has relevance to hockey. The first type of violence he refers to as *body contact*. In this instance, the body blocks, checks, and blows are inherent in the sport and the risks involved are accepted as part of the game by the participants. In legal terms, the players are consenting to receive such blows. Hockey, of course, is filled with a variety of physical acts that fall under the game rules but border on violence.

A second category of misbehavior is *borderline violence*. The frequent fistfights that break out in hockey would be an example. Potentially, serious injuries could result from these altercations, but they seldom do. And if such an eventuality were to occur, it would be regarded as "part of the game" in all likelihood. Smith (1982, p. 294) quotes an unidentified NHL player as follows on this issue: "I don't see any violence in two players dropping their gloves and letting a little steam escape. I think that's a lot better than spearing somebody. I think it's an escape valve because you know yourself pressure builds up and there's no other way to release it and if fighting is not allowed then another violent act will occur." Players involved might be fined, but legal involvement is unlikely. The legal community tends to stay away from acts of this type within sport because the public mandate to do anything about it is not present.

The third leg in Smith's typology is *quasi-criminal violence,* which involves both the formal rules and the informal norms of the game. Serious injury is apt to be involved and the legal authorities are likely to step in and impose penalties beyond what the league structure might levy. The most notable case of this type of violence in hockey involved David Forbes of the Boston Bruins and Henry Boucha of the Minnesota North Stars. Both players were sent to their respective penalty boxes simultaneously during a particularly heated match, and they exchanged verbal unpleasantries while in exile. Upon reentering the ice, Forbes assaulted Boucha with his hockey stick, causing extensive damage to Boucha's vision in one eye. Forbes was fined and barred from play for a short period, but was later charged by a Minnesota grand jury with assault with a deadly weapon. After much testimony and eighteen hours of jury deliberation, a mistrial was declared. As an interesting postscript, Boucha filed a civil suit against the Boston Bruins and the NHL, and an undisclosed amount of money was awarded to him in an out-of-court settlement (Smith, 1986).

The final category suggested by Smith is *criminal violence.* Here, the violation is such that the league sanctions will generally be transcended and the courts become involved from the outset. A case reported by Runfola (1974) is still regarded as a legal classic in sport violence. Paul Smithers, a seventeen-year-old youth league player, became so upset with game-related events that he carried the hostilities with him to a Toronto parking lot after a game. An opposing player was killed and young Smithers was convicted of manslaughter as a result of the melee.

It is apparent that there are gradations of violence as indicated in Smith's typology. What is less clear is why these various kinds of behavior have become such an integral part of hockey. A number of possible explanations have been advanced by various authorities, one of which implicates the already beleaguered *mass media.* Without beating previously stated points to death, the media tend to promote violence in hockey. A prominent example is an article by O'Malley (1977), in which he perhaps unwittingly extols violent actions in a tribute to one of the all-time greats, Gordie Howe, on the occasion of his fiftieth birthday. O'Malley (p. 40) writes:

> It's not as if he played some Caspar Milquetoast game, shying away from the corners, relying on speed and finesse. He is of the

generation that disdains the now accepted protection of helmets and he never was one to skate from a fight. After he was nearly killed from a check into the boards by Ted Kennedy of Toronto Maple Leafs—a skull operation saved his life—he returned as one who knows it is better to give than to receive, that retribution is best administered quickly and decisively. With Lou Fontinato of New York Rangers he participated in what many regard as the greatest hockey fight in the history of the NHL. Fontinato was the terror of the league then, intimidating everyone, pulverizing even the mighty Rocket Richard, but Howe destroyed him in that fight. He broke his nose, splattered Fontinato's blood over his face and jersey, and Fontinato never was as terrifying again.

Perhaps more troublesome than this sort of gratuitous glorification of violence involving adults is its impact on children, who are supposedly learning sport skills and sportsmanship. Research from a number of sources indicates that youth players admire aggressive players and learn much from these role models in terms of illegal or violent play. Smith (1982) reports a list of things young players learn from watching violent behavior by their role models who are playing on television. They are summarized in figure 7.11.

A second substantive explanatory mechanism for learning of violence is the role of *significant others.* Parents, coaches, and peers are generally significant others in the lives of children. Parents are often intensely involved in the activities of their children, and their approval of violence, tacit or otherwise, is positively related to the incidence of violent behaviors in their children (Clark, Vaz, Vetere, and Ward, 1978; Smith, 1979). Players also translate coaches' approval into aggression. Vaz and Thomas (1974) found a statistically significant relationship between insistence by coaches on being rough and aggressive and subsequent willingness to resort to unusual aggression on the part of youth participants. As for peer influence, youth hockey

Figure 7.11: **Illegal Actions Young Players Learn from Watching Professional Hockey**

I learned spearing and butt-ending.

You sort of go on your side like turning a corner and trip him with a skate.

Charging. You skate towards another guy who doesn't have the puck and knock him down. Or coming up from behind and knocking him down.

Sneaky elbows, little choppy slashes Bobby Clarke style.

Hitting at weak points with the stick, say at the back of the legs.

Coming up from behind and using your stick to hit the back of his skates and trip him.

Butt-end, spearing, slashing, high sticking, elbow in the head.

Put the elbow just a bit up and get him in the gut with your stick.

Along the boards, if a player is coming along you angle him off by starting with your shoulder then bring up your elbow.

The way you "bug" in front of the net.

Clipping. Taking the guy's feet out by sliding underneath.

Sticking the stick between their legs. Tripping as they go into the boards.

I've seen it and use it: when you check a guy, elbow him. If you get in a corner you can hook or spear him without getting caught.

Giving him a shot in the face as he's coming up to you. The ref can't see the butt-ends.

How to trip properly.

Like Gordie Howe, butt-ends when the ref isn't looking.

Source: Smith (1982).

players live in an increasingly aggressive subculture in which masculinity and defense of territory are valued highly. To demonstrate this point, Smith (1979) reported the extent to which players agree with violent statements as a function of increasing age. These data are presented in table 7.2. It is apparent that the approval of violence in this instance is linear, with an increase in acceptance as a function of increasing age. Magnify these data considerably because of the stakes involved and you get an index of what the NHL represents in terms of violent norms and resulting misbehavior. Terry and Jackson (1985) report that more than thirty-one player minutes per game over a ten-year period in professional hockey were spent in the penalty box as a result of rule violations. The figure for the years 1981 through 1983 averaged nearly thirty-five minutes. This sort of violation of the rules is reinforced by findings of Widmeyer and Birch (1984) in a study of 1,176 professional hockey games over a four-year period; among other things; they found a correlation of .48 between games won and penalties in the first period of play. Setting an aggressive tone early appears to be a productive strategy. Also, results from Russell (1974), in which a correlation of .43 was found between hockey assists and acts of hostile aggression, further add fuel to the fire associated with hockey violence.

Two final points are worthy of mention. First, there is actually some evidence that hockey violence may, in fact, be counterproductive. In analysis of data from the 1989–1990 NHL season in which league standing was correlated with fighting penalties, a negative correlation of .05 was found; that is, fighting and winning were actually at odds with each other ("Fighters Aren't Always Winners," 1990). Perhaps information such as this can be used with management to stem the tide of violence in the NHL. Secondly, the economics of violence are compelling and provide some interesting food for thought. Jones, Ferguson, and Stewart (1993) compared NHL

Table 7.2
Acceptance of Violence as a Function of Age

	Minor Midget through Juvenile (N = 169)	PeeWee through Bantam (N = 313)	Junior B and Junior A (N = 122)
If you want to get personal recognition in hockey it helps to play rough. People in hockey look for this.	52	70	88
Roughing up the other team might mean getting a few penalties, but in the long run it often helps you win.	51	64	74
Most people in hockey don't respect a player who will not fight when he is picked on.	31	42	59
To be successful, most hockey teams need at least one or two tough guys who are always ready to fight.	43	57	84

Source: Smith (1982).

attendance figures with a variety of violence indicators and found that violence is positively related to attendance; in short, violence sells. In the words of Jones et al.: ". . . hockey is show biz, hockey is blood sport" (p. 74). Jones and his colleagues, all economics professors, also reported that American fans have an even greater appreciation for violence than do their Canadian counterparts if attendance figures are used as the indicator. In Canada, attendance is actually negatively related to the more extreme acts of violence whereas the relationship is a positive one for American fans.

RECOMMENDATIONS FOR CURBING VIOLENCE IN SPORT

Many recommendations have been made aimed at curtailing aggression in athletic events. The ensuing discussion will integrate the suggestions of a number of authorities to include Bird and Cripe (1986), Coakley (1994), Cox (1990), Mark, Bryant, and Lehman (1983), and Snyder and Spreitzer (1989). These recommendations will cover a broad front because the solution to the problem of sport violence must be a systems approach involving all interested parties. Accordingly, things that can be accomplished by management, the media, game officials, coaches, and players will be addressed.

Management

At the highest level of intervention is the management structure of sport. There are at least five innovations that management can implement in an effort to slow down the apparent escalating pace of violence.

1. *Abolish or control the use of alcoholic beverages at sporting events.* Abuse of alcohol interferes with good judgment. Most of us have attended a sporting event at which

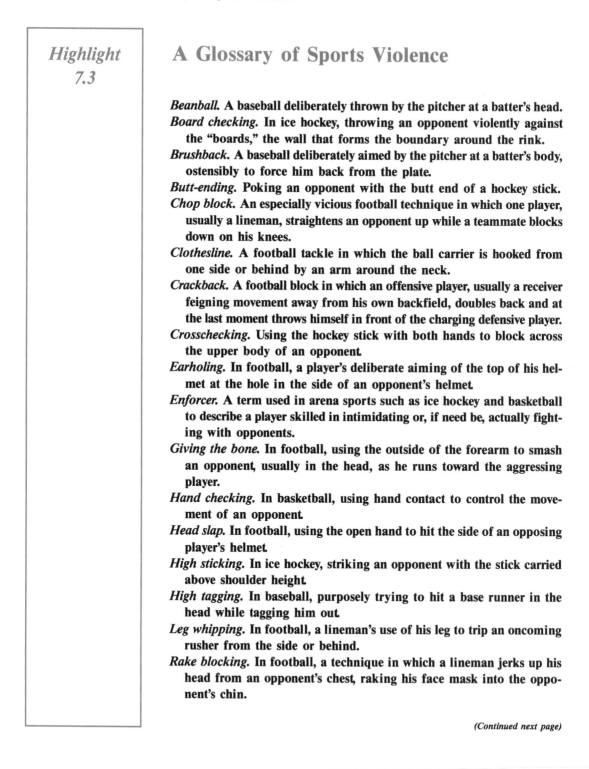

*Highlight
7.3*

A Glossary of Sports Violence

Beanball. A baseball deliberately thrown by the pitcher at a batter's head.

Board checking. In ice hockey, throwing an opponent violently against the "boards," the wall that forms the boundary around the rink.

Brushback. A baseball deliberately aimed by the pitcher at a batter's body, ostensibly to force him back from the plate.

Butt-ending. Poking an opponent with the butt end of a hockey stick.

Chop block. An especially vicious football technique in which one player, usually a lineman, straightens an opponent up while a teammate blocks down on his knees.

Clothesline. A football tackle in which the ball carrier is hooked from one side or behind by an arm around the neck.

Crackback. A football block in which an offensive player, usually a receiver feigning movement away from his own backfield, doubles back and at the last moment throws himself in front of the charging defensive player.

Crosschecking. Using the hockey stick with both hands to block across the upper body of an opponent.

Earholing. In football, a player's deliberate aiming of the top of his helmet at the hole in the side of an opponent's helmet.

Enforcer. A term used in arena sports such as ice hockey and basketball to describe a player skilled in intimidating or, if need be, actually fighting with opponents.

Giving the bone. In football, using the outside of the forearm to smash an opponent, usually in the head, as he runs toward the aggressing player.

Hand checking. In basketball, using hand contact to control the movement of an opponent.

Head slap. In football, using the open hand to hit the side of an opposing player's helmet.

High sticking. In ice hockey, striking an opponent with the stick carried above shoulder height.

High tagging. In baseball, purposely trying to hit a base runner in the head while tagging him out.

Leg whipping. In football, a lineman's use of his leg to trip an oncoming rusher from the side or behind.

Rake blocking. In football, a technique in which a lineman jerks up his head from an opponent's chest, raking his face mask into the opponent's chin.

(Continued next page)

Highlight 7.3 (Continued)

A Glossary of Sports Violence

Raking. **In rugby, deliberately running over a fallen opponent with cleated rugby shoes.**

Rip-up. **In football, a forearm uppercut, usually administered by either an offensive or a defensive lineman with the intent of catching an opponent under the chin.**

Spearing. **In ice hockey, poking an opponent with the point of the stick; in football, driving the top of the helmet into a player who is down.**

Spikes high. **In baseball, trying to avoid being tagged out by aiming the spikes high while sliding into a base.**

Source: Yeager (1979).

our enjoyment was lessened by one or several persons misbehaving while under the influence of alcohol. Alcohol abuse has been repeatedly linked with acts of sport-related vandalism in this country and hooliganism in Europe.

American baseball represents a case in point. Dewar (1979) analyzed factors associated with fights among spectators at professional baseball games. Dewar's analysis of forty games included thirty-nine fights that occurred in nineteen of the forty games. Chief among the findings were that thirty-three of the thirty-nine fights took place on weekends, primarily at night, mostly in the cheaper seats, usually when attendance was above 80 percent of capacity, most often in the hottest months of the year, usually late in the game, particularly when the home team was making a rally. Dewar had no data on alcohol sales and fights, but surmised that the late innings effect was probably related to alcohol consumption. Gammon (1985), in analyzing fights at major league baseball games, arrived at conclusions virtually identical to those of Dewar.

Major League owners have responded in an effort to combat this problem by creating nondrinking sections in ten of the stadiums ("Alcohol-Free," 1987). Certainly, this move is in line with results of a poll conducted by *USA Today* in which 42 percent of the respondents voted for the creation of nondrinking sections ("Yes beer," 1987). In a later survey by *USA Today,* 28 percent of their respondents were for banning alcohol sales at sporting events ("Fans Say," 1991).

2. *Deal swiftly and firmly with acts of spectator aggression.* Management should take a very firm stand. Players and nonaggressive fans should be protected from those who would interfere with their right to participate in or watch sport. Cox (1990) has suggested that barring the flagrant first-time or chronic offender would not be a bad course of action for those having the power to do so.

3. *Make sports more of a family affair.* Perhaps professional baseball has done as much in this area as anyone with its sponsorship of family nights, cap or travel bag nights for children, and similar promotions. Certainly, bringing more of a family orientation to

baseball and other sports should reduce aggressive behavior. This idea might be facilitated by reducing the price of tickets for families and by offering creative promotions that would be attractive to adults and children alike.

4. *Monitor the behavior of coaches.* Management should hold coaches accountable for their actions (or inaction) when they encourage or fail to penalize their players for aggressive acts. Athletes who are convinced that aggression on their part will meet with censure from the coaches are less likely to engage in aggressive acts. Coaches are powerful others in the eyes of players and they should act the part insofar as acceptance of sport violence is concerned.

5. *Monitor the behavior of players.* Managers should make players aware of the fact that violence will not be condoned at the upper levels of the organization, whether peewee or professional. Penalties for violating institutional policy should fit the crime; a $1,000 fine for a professional player who makes $3 million per year hardly serves as a deterrent to future misbehavior.

The Media

As stated earlier, the role of the media in promoting sports violence is a continuing source of interest for social and behavioral scientists. Though its effects are subject to argument, the media could collectively assist in at least three ways in defusing potentially violent episodes in sports.

1. *Do not glorify aggressive athletes for children and, conversely, provide as much coverage of counter examples to aggression as is possible.* There are many sensitive and humane athletes in the sports world, and every attempt should be made to present them in as favorable a light as possible to young people. Conversely, athletes who openly espouse aggression should be given as little media visibility as possible. Watching some oversized professional football player threatening to break someone's head if he does not purchase a certain product or subscribe to a particular sports magazine serves no healthy purpose that we can see. Such unadulterated nonsense provides a poor example for young players (as well as for those of us a bit older).

2. *Refrain from glamorizing violence.* Progress has been made, particularly in refusing to give airtime or print to fan misbehavior. The same restraint should apply in cases of player aggression against each other. The 1994 World Cup soccer match between the United States and Brazil, in which an American player got his skull fractured by an intentionally errant elbow from a Brazilian opponent, serves as a case in point. The celebrated altercation was replayed over and over on television and rehashed for days. Little of value is accomplished by such media sensationalism.

3. *Do not attempt to promote hostility between teams.* There is already plenty of healthy rivalry in sports, and more than enough ego and money riding on the outcome, so that the media need not feed into the system. Sport is not war but it can be made to appear that way with a little assistance from the various media.

Game Officials

Umpires, referees, and line judges are an important part of various sport events. They are charged with the responsibility for making important split-second decisions and rule interpretations that can greatly affect game outcomes. As a result, they can be a catalyst for arousing emotions conducive to player or spectator violence. Two procedures for improving officiating are suggested.

1. *Eliminate perceived officiating injustices.* Mark and his associates (1983) indicate that officials get themselves into hot water with players or spectators because they are perceived as having committed an injustice either in terms of applying a rule inaccurately or unfairly or as a result of a perception that the game itself is unfair, irrespective of officiating excellence. In the first case, judgment calls and decisions as to rule infractions are predominant. Certainly, blown calls or misapplied rule interpretations can trigger violence. In the second case, judgments and interpretations are secondary to the fact that the rules of the game themselves are seen as unfair. Sometimes an official can be dead right about a call and still inflame the players or audience because they perceive the overall situation as unfair.

   Mark and his colleagues suggest that the incidence of rules infractions can be reduced and the resultant violence lessened through proper implementation of two types of penalties, equity based and deterrent based. *Equity-based punishment* is an "eye for an eye"; for example, a basketball player fouled while in the act of shooting will be awarded not one but two shots. This is equity. As for *deterrent-based penalties,* the probation for illegal recruiting in intercollegiate sports is an increasingly prominent example; the hope is that these penalties will deter further excesses. With the proper use of both equity- and deterrent-based penalties, perhaps violence in sports can be brought within acceptable limits.

2. *Take part in workshops on aggression and violence in sport.* Obviously, clinics would be most useful for people who officiate the sports in which aggression is likely. Intuitively, it is recognized that some officials exercise more control over games than others; however, this is not to say that these same control measures cannot be taught. There will always be gradations of control over the way games are played, but all officials can be schooled better in the anticipation, recognition, and control of potentially explosive situations.

Coaches

Coaches are important determinants of the course of violence in sports. Coaches who espouse notions such as that expressed by a prominent college basketball coach ("Defeat in sports is worse than death because you have to live with defeat") or that of an equally esteemed professional football coach ("To play this game you must have fire in you, and there is nothing that stokes the fire like hate") are partially to blame for setting a tone for violence in sport. However, ways exist to improve on the current situation.

1. *Encourage athletes to engage in prosocial behavior.* There is much to be said for the athlete who treats the opponent with respect. A verbal give and take or a friendly handshake before and after a game can only serve to reduce violence. The coach should reinforce nonviolence, as when an athlete takes a very assertive blow without resorting to very aggressive types of retaliation. As Cox (1990, p. 295) says: "Acts of great self-control *must* be identified and strongly reinforced."

2. *Participate in workshops on aggression and violence.* Like officials, coaches should acquire an awareness of the counterproductive nature of sport violence, not only in their own immediate situations but also in terms of society as a whole. As the proponents of social learning theory would say, "Violence begets violence."

Sports Officials

What do we know about the men and women who officiate sports? What is their actual role in causing, preventing, or remedying sports violence? The answers are not clear to these questions, but there is a growing body of literature about these important sports figures. Umpires and referees can make a big difference in how much and in what ways crowd behavior is manifested. In a discussion of factors that facilitate the expression of fan violence, Snyder and Spreitzer (1989) suggest that one of the key precipitators is crowd perception of lax, biased, or incompetent officiating.

Demographically, we have learned that officials will most likely be young, well-educated, first-born, politically conservative males who are involved in professional or managerial occupations (Furst, 1989; Purdy and Snyder, 1985; Quain and Purdy, 1988). In terms of personality, they have variously been reported as gregarious, outgoing, and practical (Spurgeon, Blair, Keith, and McGinn, 1978), as authoritarian (Aresu, Bucarelli, and Marongiu, 1979), and as self-sufficient, self-assured, self-reliant, and socially sensitive (Fratzke, 1975). In terms of attitudinal variables, professional baseball and hockey officials have been shown to be very suspicious of fans, view their job as challenging and rewarding, see themselves as a major and integral part of their sport, and not terribly fond of the travel and the diminished family life associated with their profession (Mitchell, Leonard, and Schmitt, 1982).

Psychologically, little is known about sports officials. One line of preliminary research has focused on sources of stress that affect these individuals. Anshel and Weinberg (1995) studied 132 basketball referees, 70 from the southwestern United States and 62 from Australia. As part of their study, the authors created an assessment scale arranged on a 10-point continuum known as the Basketball Official's Sources of Stress Inventory (BOSSI). The top five sources of stress for these basketball officials were, in order of importance, making a wrong call, verbal abuse by coaches, threats of physical abuse, being in the wrong place when making a call, and experiencing injury. Easily the least stressful of the fifteen stress situations on the BOSSI was the presence of media. With regard to cross-cultural comparisons, there were more similarities than differences noted.

In a related study, Rainey (1995) adapted a scale used in measuring stress in Canadian soccer officials and mailed it to 1,500 baseball and softball umpires in one state; 782 properly completed the scale and served as subjects for subsequent scrutiny. Exploratory and confirmatory factor

(Continued next page)

Highlight 7.4 (Continued)

Sports Officials

analyses yielded four factors of note: Fear of Failure, Fear of Physical Harm, Time Pressure, and Interpersonal Conflict (i.e., personality clashes with players, coaches, or fans, dealing with abusive players, and so forth). It is important to note, however, that while these perceived stressors were the most salient for this sample of umpires, they were viewed as only "mildly" contributing to their officiating stress. Also, these results are in line with previous research by Goldsmith and Williams (1992) with football and volleyball officials and by Taylor and Daniel (1987) with soccer officials.

Stress, then, appears to be a fact of life for sports officials, but its effects are viewed as manageable by the majority. For those officials for whom the stress is more severe, the stress management strategies discussed in chapter 4 may have considerable utility.

In terms of actual skills related to officiating, David Rainey has conducted several studies of baseball umpires. Rainey, in conjunction with a number of associates, has looked at such baseball umpiring phenomena as the "phantom tag" at second base (Rainey, Larsen, Stephenson, and Olson, 1991), first base calls (Larsen and Rainey, 1991), ball and strike calls (Rainey and Larsen, 1988; Rainey, Larsen, and Stephenson, 1989; Rainey, Larsen, and Williard, 1987), and fan evaluations of umpires (Rainey and Schweickert, 1991; Rainey and Schweickert, Granito, and Pullella, 1990). A major and consistent finding that runs throughout the Rainey efforts is the fact that normative rules of officiating seem to dictate umpire behavior more than do the actual rules. Perhaps this normative effect is most salient with the "phantom tag," the situation in which an infielder is given the benefit of the doubt on tagging the bag on force plays at second base; umpires made significantly fewer correct calls when the ball beat the runner but the fielder never came into contact with the second base bag. The existence of a normative rule that may be more salient than the actual rule also exists in Rainey's research on close or tie calls at first base and with regard to ball and strike calls behind home plate. With regard to the latter case, it is interesting to note that umpires were more prone to call marginal pitches strikes for so-called wild pitchers than they were for those pitchers with a reputation for extremely fine pitching control, probably due to normative rules. In theory, marginal pitches for throwers of either reputation should get the same treatment from the umpires; such does not appear to be the case.

(Continued next page)

Highlight 7.4 (Continued)

Sports Officials

Finally, in the case of fan evaluations of umpires, responses were interesting. In the Rainey and Schweickert study, players and coaches believe that umpires perform below acceptable and expected standards. For example, players and coaches in their study believe that umpires miss sixteen calls per two hundred in a seven-inning game (mostly on balls and strikes), for an error rate of 8 percent for all calls. Conversely, umpire certainty about their calls was quite high, an expected finding. In the Rainey et al. study, fans rated perceived performance of umpires on the "phantom tag," first base calls, and balls and strikes calls lower than expected performance; fans generally believe that umpires fail to live up to expected standards, and this effect was especially true for female fans. In terms of how umpires should be treated by players or coaches, the most popular response chosen was "Question Politely." "Argue Heatedly" got some support but little endorsement was given to "Do Nothing" and "Yell and Swear." Ninety-eight percent of the sample of 159 men chose "Never" or "Rarely" with regard to "Physically Attack"; ninety-six percent of the fifty-two women chose those two alternatives. Apparently the old refrain "Kill the ump" is endorsed by fans in a figurative as opposed to a literal way. A final note: in several of the studies, matched samples of males with no officiating experience were as good as, or in some cases better than, the baseball officials at making the various calls described here. It is only fair to say, however, that most of the Rainey studies did employ laboratory manipulations as opposed to real-life ones, and the results may not be generalizable to an actual baseball game. Also, generalizations about officials in other sports based on a study of baseball umpires can only be made with extreme caution. Nevertheless, the emerging literature on the sports official is intriguing and offers much food for thought with regard to future research efforts in the area.

Sources: Anshel and Weinberg (1995); Aresu, Bucarelli, and Marongiu (1979); Fratzke (1975); Furst (1989); Goldsmith and Williams (1992); Larsen and Rainey (1991); Mitchell, Leonard, and Schmitt (1982); Purdy and Snyder (1985); Quain and Purdy (1988); Rainey (1995); Rainey and Larsen (1988); Rainey and Schweickert (1991); Rainey, Larsen, and Stephenson (1989); Rainey, Larsen, and Williard (1987); Rainey, Larsen, Stephenson, and Olson (1991); Rainey, Schweickert, Granito, and Pullella (1990); Spurgeon, Blair, Keith, and McGinn (1978); Taylor and Daniel (1987).

Players

Ultimately the individual player must assume most of the responsibility for reducing aggressive behavior. Individual initiative in controlling aggressive urges must not be sold short. It is the responsibility of each player to remain under control. To try to sell anything less than that is to abrogate each person's responsibility for emotional self-governance. We are all too quick to project the blame on our provocateurs, but such projections should in no way be accepted or reinforced. Accordingly, each player should volunteer to take part in programs aimed at helping them cope with aggressive feelings and actions. Visual imagery and mental practice are two techniques that should be valuable in learning greater emotional control.

Overall, if a carefully orchestrated effort is generated by management, the media, spectators, coaches, and players, a substantial reduction in sport violence could be effected. However, so long as social conditions that transcend sport are in effect, the task will be difficult; sport cannot do it alone. Nevertheless, we in sport should willingly do our part. We can have an impact on violence in sport and hope that our efforts generalize to the society as a whole.

VIOLENCE IN FEMALE ATHLETES

The general psychology literature strongly indicates that women are less prone than men to

resort to the use of physical aggression when provoked. The literature in sport psychology relevant to this issue is virtually nonexistent. Female involvement in the sports most likely to evoke aggression is either nonexistent (e.g., professional football or boxing) or limited (e.g., soccer or hockey). As a consequence, female athletes are spared being involved in activities in which spectators or players are most apt to lose control over their emotions. Generalizations about female athletes and aggression are therefore difficult to make; simply put, if they are not confronted with the stimuli most likely to evoke aggression, they will not display it. As women move more and more into the competitive realm, perhaps we shall see an increase in aggression on their part. The issue remains unresolved at this time.

SUMMARY

1. We live in a violent world with numerous examples of man's inhumanity to man.
2. Aggression is defined as the infliction of an aversive stimulus upon one person by another, an act committed with intent to harm, one perpetrated against an unwilling victim, and done with the expectancy that the behavior will be successful.
3. Aggression may be viewed from a number of perspectives to include provoked versus unprovoked, direct versus indirect, physical versus verbal, adaptive versus maladaptive, and hostile versus instrumental.
4. Hostile aggression, instrumental aggression, and sport aggression are differentiated by intent or lack of intent to harm, by the nature of the goal that is valued, and by the presence or absence of anger or unusual effort and energy expenditure. Nevertheless, the distinctions among the three behaviors can be quite blurred in many sport situations.
5. Though there are differences in the eyes of some, we shall use the terms aggression and

violence interchangeably because of the overlap in their definitional properties.
6. Biological theories of aggression have been advanced that emphasize certain physical predispositions to include genetics, neurological structures, and hormonal influences.
7. Psychosocial models of aggression include instinct theory, the frustration-aggression hypothesis, and the social learning approach.
8. Cathartic approaches to explaining aggression emphasize the release of aggressive tendencies through their expression. Various instinctive theories, such as those advanced by Freud, Lorenz, and Ardrey as well as the frustration–aggression hypothesis of Dollard and Miller are examples of cathartic theories.
9. Bandura has challenged the cathartic theory with his social learning approach, in which reinforcement and modeling are emphasized. The social learning approach stresses the fact that aggression is made more likely by its expression as opposed to the cathartic notion of reduction through expression.
10. Our shared opinion is that the social learning approach has the most to offer in terms of understanding aggression.
11. Sociological explanations of aggression include contagion theory, convergence theory, the emergent norm theory, and the value-added theory.
12. The measurement of aggression has been conducted in a variety of ways, to include laboratory research, archival analysis, questionnaires, and self-report measures. In the latter case, projective and objective tests of personality have been employed. One of the more promising scales is the Aggression Questionnaire of Buss and Perry. Little of note is taking place in terms of sport-specific measures of aggression.
13. Factors promoting aggression include physical, psychological, and sociological forces.
14. Heat, noise, and crowding are three physical factors affecting aggression. Though

there is much research in the general application of these variables to the human condition, little has been done in the sport realm and their respective roles are poorly understood.

15. Vicarious reinforcement and modeling, external rewards, deindividuation, and becoming inured to violence are four psychological variables that have been studied as they relate to aggression.

16. The person who has been reinforced for aggression or who has seen it work for others, particularly in role models, is more prone to try it to see if it works for him or her.

17. External rewards of significance include tangibles (money, intimidation), status rewards (aggressive nickname), expression of injury, and alleviation of aversive treatment (evading coaches' wrath by being aggressive), and each is likely to facilitate aggression.

18. Deindividuation is a process whereby individual conformity to group dictates increases as personal identity and evaluation decreases.

19. Becoming inured to violence may be occurring because we are so inundated with violence through the media. The ramifications for sport are considerable.

20. Significant sociological forces at work in creating and promoting violence are hooliganism and the media.

21. Hooliganism is a term used for the misbehavior of British fans at soccer matches. Displays of masculinity underscore much of the fan violence there; the participants are in actuality working-class gangs more intent on fighting than watching soccer. A major incident of hooliganism occurred in Belgium in 1985 in a riot in which 38 people were killed and 437 injured.

22. The media have not been spared criticism when it comes to sport violence. Why the American sports fan appears to thrive on a steady diet of descriptions of violence remains unanswered. Theories include catharsis, the assertion of dominance, and the enjoyment of the drama.

23. The media have been described as encouraging violence in three ways, namely, giving excess coverage to violent plays, featuring stories that glorify violence, and using promos depicting violence as a way of selling future sporting events.

24. Five sport-related variables influence the way violence is expressed. Point spread, the home/away factor, outcome, league standing, and period of play all are pertinent to an understanding of the way in which violence works in sport.

25. Three sports have been singled out for further elaboration because of their violent properties: boxing, football, and hockey.

26. Boxing is clearly the best example of a sport in which the avowed purpose is to inflict intentional harm on the opponent. In other sports, that intent is at least hidden behind sport assertiveness. Little is known of the psychological makeup of boxers.

27. Injury data suggests that football is, if not violent, a very dangerous sport at the high school and intercollegiate levels. At the professional level, manifestations of hostile thoughts and violent actions abound.

28. A sport that has been researched more than others, thanks primarily to the Canadian sport psychologists, is ice hockey.

29. Using a typology suggested by Smith (1986), hockey can be analyzed for violence in four ways. One is body contact in which aggressive acts are consented to by those who play the game. Borderline violence exists in the form of fistfights, and this is seen as "part of the game." In quasi-criminal violence, serious injury is involved and so are the courts in most cases. Finally, criminal violence, such as the Smithers case in which a youth player killed an opponent in the parking lot

after a game, is the fourth leg in the Smith typology.

30. The media and the encouragement from significant others are viewed as prime contributors to violence in hockey.

31. Recommendations for curbing violence in sport involve changes in the way the games are viewed by management, the media, the officials, the coaches, and the players themselves.

32. Management needs to curb alcohol abuse at sports events, deal swiftly and firmly with fan violence, try to make sports more of a family affair, more effectively monitor coaching behavior with regard to the encouragement of aggression, and monitor players better to reduce aggressive acts.

33. The media needs to be sure that it is not glorifying violence, particularly where children are involved. Children need to see more prosocial and less antisocial behavior from their sport heroes. Player and fan violence should never be played up, and trying to stoke the fires of hostility between players or teams is to be discouraged.

34. Sport officials are important in the controlling of sport violence. Useful goals include making the rules fairer and clearer to reduce perceived injustices; training officials in rule interpretation and application; and having officials attend clinics on the anticipation, recognition, and control of violence.

35. Coaches should encourage prosocial behaviors on the part of their athletes, and exceptional cases of emotional control in adverse circumstances should be reinforced. Also, coaches should attend clinics on violence management.

36. Ultimately, individual players must assume much of the responsibility for aggressive behavior. Taking part in emotional control exercises, such as visual imagery and mental practice, are strongly encouraged.

37. Little is known about aggressive sport behavior on the part of female athletes.

SUGGESTED READINGS

Berkowitz, L. (1989) Frustration-aggression hypothesis: Examination and reformulation. *Psychological Bulletin, 106,* 59–73.

Berkowitz has examined the literature related to the original 1939 hypothesis by Dollard and his colleagues related to frustration and aggression. His opinion is that there is still much to be said for the basic propositions of the frustration-aggression hypothesis, but feels that his own cognitive-neoassociationistic reformulation adds sophistication to the original work by Dollard et al.

Bushman, B., & Bertilson, H. (1985) Psychology of the scientist: Frequently cited research on human aggression. *Psychological Reports, 56,* 55–59.

Seven major journals in social psychology and personality were reviewed over a three-year period (1980–1982) to determine books and articles that authors most often cited when writing about aggression. Bushman and Bertilson selected thirty-five references for discussion in their paper on the basis of the frequency with which they were cited. Most often cited in books was Baron's 1977 text, *Human aggression,* followed by Bandura's *Aggression: A social learning analysis,* and *The physiology of aggression* by Buss. Berkowitz (40), Baron (37), Zillman (32), and Bandura (31) were the most frequently cited authorities in all types of publications. This paper would be a good reference for those interested in aggression.

DiLalla, L. F., & Gottesman, I. (1991) Biological and genetic contributors to violence—Widom's untold tale. *Psychological Bulletin, 109,* 125–129.

DiLalla and Gottesman have put together a rejoinder to the 1989 article by Widom. The theme of their response strongly suggests that Widom failed to take into account biological and genetic influences on violence in her treatise on intergenerational transmission of violence. The authors make a good case for the role of biological and genetic factors in criminality and violence.

Frank, M. G., & Gilovich, T. (1988) The dark side of self- and social perception: Black uniforms and aggression in professional sports. *Journal of Personality and Social Psychology, 54,* 74–85.

> This experiment examined whether professional football and hockey teams that wear black uniforms are more aggressive than those wearing other colors. In general, teams wearing black uniforms appear to be more aggressive. Also, they are apparently perceived as more aggressive by the game officials, which may contribute to their being penalized more often than other teams.

Goldstein, J. (Ed.). (1983) *Sports violence.* New York: Springer-Verlag.

> Though several of the contributions to Goldstein's volume were cited frequently in the text of this chapter, a number of other important readings should appeal to the serious student of sports violence. This reader represents the starting point for any discussion of the topic because of the depth and breadth of coverage it gives to violence in sports.

Rainey, D. (1986) A gender difference in acceptance of sport aggression: A classroom activity. *Teaching of Psychology, 13,* 138–140.

> The author gave three psychology classes examples of six sport competition situations and asked the students to rate the acceptability or unacceptability of each. Substantial sex differences were noted, with males endorsing nearly twice as many of the aggressive acts depicted. This exercise can easily serve as a springboard for discussing aggression in sport and in society as a whole.

Widom, C. S. (1989) Does violence beget violence? A critical examination of the literature. *Psychological Bulletin, 106,* 3–28.

> The author takes a protracted look at seven aspects of the idea that violence breeds violence. Areas explored include child abuse, delinquency, violent and homicidal offenders, aggression in small children, and the effects of viewing aggression. Widom concludes that much is yet to be learned about abusive home environments and subsequent violence.

REFERENCES

Adler, A. (1927) *The theory and practice of individual psychology.* New York: Harcourt Brace.

Alcohol-free seating not solution to some. (1987) *USA Today,* June 29, 7C.

Ambah, F. (1994) World population conference. *Houston Chronicle,* September 4, 24A.

Anderson, C. A. (1989) Temperature and aggression: Ubiquitous effects of heat on occurrence of human violence. *Psychological Bulletin, 106,* 74–96.

Anshel, M. H., & Weinberg, R. S. (1995) Sources of stress in American and Australian basketball referees. *Journal of Applied Sport Psychology, 7,* 11–22.

Ardrey, R. (1966) *The territorial imperative: A personal inquiry into the animal origins of property and nations.* New York: Atheneum.

Bachman, R. (1994) *Violence against women.* Washington, DC: U. S. Department of Justice.

Bandura, A. (1973) *Aggression: A social learning analysis.* Englewood Cliffs, NJ: Prentice-Hall.

Baron, R. (1977) *Human aggression.* New York: Plenum.

Baron, R., & Ransberger, V. (1978) Ambient temperature and the occurrence of collective violence. The "long hot summer" revisited. *Journal of Personality and Social Psychology, 36,* 351–360.

Baron, R. A., & Richardson, D. R. (1994) *Human aggression.* (2d ed.). New York: Plenum.

Baumeister, R. F. (1984) Choking under pressure: Self-consciousness and paradoxical effects of incentives on skillful performance. *Journal of Personality and Social Psychology, 46,* 610–620.

Baumeister, R. F. (1995) Disputing the effects of championship pressures and home audiences. *Journal of Personality and Social Psychology, 68,* 644–648.

Bell, J. (1994) Bears' Anderson decides to retire. *USA Today,* July 8, 7C.

Berkowitz, L. (1986) *A survey of social psychology.* New York: Holt, Rinehart and Winston.

Betts, J. R. (1974) *America's sporting heritage, 1850–1950.* Reading, MA: Addison-Wesley.

Bird, A. M., & Cripe, B. (1986) *Psychology and sport behavior.* St. Louis, MO: C. V. Mosby.

Bourgeois, A. E., Biffle, T., & LeUnes, A. (1994) A psychometric study of the Aggression Questionnaire. Unpublished manuscript.

Brant, J. (1988) The choke: Lament for a species of overreactors. *Outside,* February, 23–26.

Bredemeier, B. (1978) Applications and implications of aggression research. In W. F. Straub (Ed.), *Sport psychology: An analysis of athlete behavior.* Ithaca, NY: Mouvement.

Bryant, J., Brown, D., Comisky, P. W., & Zillman, D. (1982) Sports and spectators: Commentary and appreciation. *Journal of Communication, 32,* 109–119.

Bryant, J., Comisky, P., & Zillman, D. (1977) Drama in sports commentary. *Journal of Communication, 27,* 140–149.

Bryant, J., Comisky, P., & Zillman, D. (1981) The appeal of rough-and-tumble play in televised football. *Communication Quarterly, 29,* 256–262.

Bryant, J., & Zillman, D. (1983) Sports violence and the media. In J. Goldstein (Ed.), *Sports violence* (pp. 195–211). New York: Springer-Verlag.

Bushman, B.J., Cooper, H. M., & Lemke, K. M. (1991) Meta-analysis of factor analyses: An illustration using the Buss-Durkee hostility inventory. *Personality and Social Psychology Bulletin, 17,* 344–349.

Buss, A. H., & Durkee, A. (1957) An inventory for assessing different kinds of hostility. *Journal of Consulting Psychology, 21,* 343–348.

Buss, A. H., & Perry, M. (1992) The Aggression Questionnaire. *Journal of Personality and Social Psychology, 63,* 452–459.

Butler, R. J. (1989) Psychological preparation of Olympic boxers. In J. Kramer & W. Crawford (Eds.), *The psychology of sport: Theory and practice* (pp. 74–84). BPS Northern Ireland Branch: Occasional Paper.

Butler, R. J. (1991) Amateur boxing and sports science II: Psychology. *Coaching Focus, 18,* 14–15.

Butler, R. J., & Hardy, L. (1992) The performance profile: Theory and application. *The Sport Psychologist, 6,* 253–264.

Butler, R. J., Smith, M., & Irwin, I. (1993) The performance profile in practice. *Journal of Applied Sport Psychology, 5,* 48–63.

Carron, A. V., & Spink, K. S. (1995) The group-cohesion relationship in minimal groups. *Small Group Research, 26,* 86–105.

Clark, W. J., Vaz, E., Vetere, V., & Ward, T. A. (1978) Illegal aggression in minor league hockey: A causal model. In F. Landry and W. A. R. Orban (Eds.), *Ice hockey: Research, development and new concepts* (pp. 81–88). Miami, FL: Symposium Specialists.

Clarke, K., & Braslow, A. (1978) Football fatalities in actuarial perspective. *Medicine and Science in Sports, 10*(2), 94–96.

Coakley, J. J. (1994) *Sport in society: Issues and controversies* (5th ed.). St. Louis, MO: Mosby.

Comisky, P., Bryant, J., & Zillman, D. (1977) Commentary as a substitute for action. *Journal of Communication, 27,* 150–153.

Corby, B. (1993) *Child abuse.* Philadelphia: Open University Press.

Corrington, K. A. Personal communication, November 15, 1994, College Station, Texas.

Cox, R. H. (1990) *Sport psychology: Concepts and applications* (2d ed.). Dubuque, IA: Wm. C. Brown.

Cullen, J., & Cullen, F. (1975) The structural and contextual conditions of group norm violation: Some implications from the game of ice hockey. *International Review of Sport Sociology, 10,* 69–78.

Curry, T. J., & Jiobu, R. (1984) *Sports: A social perspective.* Englewood Cliffs, NJ: Prentice-Hall.

Dabbs, J. M., & Morris, R. (1990) Testosterone, social class, and antisocial behavior in a sample of 4462 men. *Psychological Science, 1,* 209–211.

Dalton, K. (1961) Menstruation and crime. *British Medical Journal, 3,* 1752–1753.

Dalton, K. (1964) *The pre-menstrual syndrome.* Springfield, IL: Charles C. Thomas.

Deluty, R. H. (1979) Children's Action Tendency Scale: A self-report measure of aggressiveness, assertiveness, and submissiveness in children. *Journal of Consulting and Clinical Psychology, 47,* 1061–1071.

Dewar, C. (1979) Spectator fights at professional baseball games. *Review of Sport and Leisure, 4,* 14–25.

Dollard, J., Doob, L., Miller, N., Mowrer, O., & Sears, R. (1939) *Frustration and aggression.* New Haven, CN: Yale University Press.

Donnerstein, E., & Wilson, D. (1976) Effects of noise and perceived control on ongoing and subsequent aggressive behavior. *Journal of Personality and Social Psychology, 34,* 774–781.

Dunning, E. (1983) Social bonding and violence in sport: A theoretical-empirical analysis. In J. H. Goldstein (Ed.), *Sports violence* (pp. 129–146). New York: Springer-Verlag.

Dunning, E., Maguire, J., Murphy, P., & Williams, J. (1982) The social roots of football hooligan violence. *Leisure Studies, 1,* 139–156.

Fans say alcohol sponsorship and sports mix. (1991) *USA Today,* February 19, 10C.

Festinger, L., Pepitone, A., & Newcomb, T. (1952) Some consequences of de-individuation in a group. *Journal of Abnormal and Social Psychology, 47,* 382–389.

Fighters aren't always winners. (1990) *USA Today,* March 1, 3C.

Franken, R. E. (1982) *Human motivation.* Belmont, CA: Wadsworth.

Freedman, J. (1975) *Crowding and behavior.* San Francisco, CA: W. H. Freeman.

Gammon, C. (1985) A day of horror and shame. *Sports Illustrated,* June 10, 20–35.

Gavzer, B. (1990) Is it time to investigate boxing? *Parade Magazine,* October 21, 3–7.

Geen, R., Beatty, W., & Arkin, R. (1984) *Human motivation: Physiological, behavioral, and social approaches.* Boston, MA: Allyn and Bacon.

Goldsmith, P. A., & Williams, J. M. (1995) Perceived stressors for football and volleyball officials from three rating levels. *Journal of Sport Behavior, 15,* 106–118.

Gorman, C. (1992) Tackling spinal trauma. *Time,* December, 14, 57.

Greenberg, J. (1991) Horror show. *Sports Illustrated,* April 22, 40–44.

Heaton, A. W., & Sigall, H. (1991) Self-consciousness, self-presentation, and performance under pressure. *Journal of Applied Social Psychology, 21,* 175–188.

Hershey, S. (1989) Hoch responds to pressure, wins with 8-foot birdie putt. *USA Today,* May 1, 10C.

Hollander, E. P., & Julian, J. W. (1969) Contemporary trends in the analysis of leadership processes. *Psychological Bulletin, 71,* 387–391.

Jones, J. C. H., Ferguson, D. G., & Stewart, K. G. (1993) Blood sports and apple pie: Some economics of violence in the National Hockey League. *American Journal of Economics and Sociology, 52,* 63–77.

Kiester, E. (1984) The uses of anger. *Psychology Today, 18*(7), 26.

King, P. (1992) The unfortunate 500. *Sports Illustrated, 77*(24), 20–29.

Kramer, J., & Schaap, D. (1969) *Instant replay.* New York: Signet.

Lorenz, K. (1966) *On aggression.* New York: Harcourt, Brace & World.

Mark, M. M., Bryant, F. B., & Lehman, D. R. (1983) Perceived injustice and sports violence. In J. Goldstein (Ed.), *Sports violence.* New York: Springer-Verlag.

Marsh, P. Rosser, E., & Harre, R. (1978) *The rules of disorder.* London: Routledge and Kegan Paul.

Megargee, E. I., Cook, P. E., & Mendelsohn, G. A. (1967) Development and validation of an MMPI scale of assaultiveness in overcontrolled individuals. *Journal of Abnormal Psychology, 72,* 519–528.

Meyer-Bahlburg, H. F. L. (1981) Sex chromosomes and aggression in humans. In P. F. Brain & D. Benton (Eds.), *The biology of aggression* (pp. 109–123). Rockville, MD.: Sythoff and Noordhoff.

Mitchell, J. S., Leonard, W. M., & Schmitt, R. L. (1982) Sport officials' perceptions of fans, players, and their occupations: A comparative study of baseball and hockey. *Journal of Sport Behavior, 5,* 83–95.

Montagu, A. (1975) Is man innately aggressive? In W. Fields and W. Sweet (Eds.), *Neurological symposium on neural bases of violence and aggression* (pp. 431–451). St. Louis, MO: Warren H. Green.

Mueller, F. O., Blyth, C. S., & Cantu, R. C. (1989) Catastrophic spine injuries in football. *Physician and Sportsmedicine, 17*(10), 51–53.

Mueller, F., & Schindler, R. (1984) Annual survey of football injury research, 1931-1983. *Athletic Training, 19,* 189–192, 208.

Nash, O. (1980) Confessions of a born spectator. In R. Dodge (Ed.), *A literature of sports.* Lexington, MA: D. C. Heath.

O'Malley, M. (1977) Some day they'll retire Gordie Howe's sweater—If, of course, he takes it off. *Macleans, 90* (26), 40.

Page three. (1985) *Houston Chronicle,* July 12, 3.

Rainey, D. (1995) Sources of stress among baseball and softball umpires. *Journal of Applied Sport Psychology, 7,* 1–10.

Rainey, D. W., & Larsen, J. D. (1988) Balls, strikes, and norms: Rule violations and normative rules among baseball umpires. *Journal of Sport and Exercise Psychology, 10,* 75–80.

Rainey, D. W., Larsen, J. D., & Stephenson, A. (1989) The effects of a pitcher's reputation on umpires' calls of balls and strikes. *Journal of Sport Behavior, 12,* 139–150.

Rainey, D. W., Larsen, J. D., Stephenson, A., & Olson, T. (1991) Normative rules among umpires: The "phantom tag" at second base. *Journal of Sport Behavior, 14,* 147–155.

Rainey, D. W., Larsen, J. D., & Williard, M. J. (1987) A computer simulation of sport officiating behavior. *Journal of Sport Behavior, 10,* 183–191.

Rainey, D. W., & Schweickert, G. (1991) Evaluations of umpire performance and perceptions of appropriate behavior toward umpires. *International Journal of Sport Psychology, 22,* 66–77.

Rainey, D. W., Schweickert, G., Granito, V., & Pullella, J. (1990) Fans' evaluations of major league baseball umpires' performances and perceptions of appropriate behavior toward umpires. *Journal of Sport Behavior, 13,* 122–129.

Reifman, A. S., Larrick, R. P., & Fein, S. (1991). Temper and temperature on the diamond: Heat-aggression relationships in major league baseball. *Personality and Social Psychology Bulletin, 17,* 580–585.

Runfola, R. (1974) He is a hockey player, 17, black and convicted of manslaughter. *New York Times,* Oct. 17, 2–3.

Russell, G. W. (1974) Machiavellianism, locus of control, aggression, performance, and precautionary behaviour in ice hockey. *Human Relations, 27,* 825–837.

Russell, G. W. (1986) Does sports violence increase box office receipts? *International Journal of Sport Psychology, 17,* 173–183.

Russell, G. W. (1993) Violent sports entertainment and the promise of catharsis. *Medienpsychologie: Zeitschrift fur Individual- & Massenkommunikation, 5,* 101–105.

Russell, G. W., & Drewry, B. R. (1976) Crowd size and competitive aspects of aggression in ice hockey: An archival study. *Human Relations, 29,* 723–735.

Sampson answers a prayer. (1986) *Bryan-College Station (TX) Eagle,* May 23, 3B.

Schlenker, B. R., Phillips, S. T., Boniecki, K. A., & Schlenker, D. R. (1995a) Championship pressures: Choking or triumphing in one's own territory? *Journal of Personality and Social Psychology, 68,* 632–643.

Schlenker, B. R., Phillips, S. T., Boniecki, K. A., & Schlenker, D. R. (1995b) Where is the home choke? *Journal of Personality and Social Psychology, 68,* 649–652.

Silva, J. M. (1979) Assertive and aggressive behavior in sport: A definitional clarification. In C. H. Nadeau, W. R. Halliwell, K. M. Newell, and G. C. Roberts (Eds.), *Psychology of motor behavior and sport—1979* (pp. 199–208). Champaign, IL: Human Kinetics.

Silva, J. M. (1981) Normative compliance and rule violating behavior in sport. *International Journal of Sport Psychology, 12,* 10–18.

Silva, J. M. (1984) Factors related to the acquisition and expression of aggressive sport behavior. In J. M. Silva and R. S. Weinberg (Eds.), *Psychological foundations of sport* (pp. 261–273). Champaign, IL: Human Kinetics.

Smelser, N. J. (1962) *Theory of collective behavior.* New York: The Free Press.

Smith, M. (1979) Towards an explanation of hockey violence: A reference-other approach. *Canadian Journal of Sociology, 4*(2), 105–124.

Smith, M. (1982) Social determinants of violence in hockey: A review. In R. Magill, M. Ash, & F. Smoll (Eds.), *Children in sport* (pp. 294–309). Champaign, IL: Human Kinetics.

Smith, M. (1986) Sports violence: A definition. In R. Lapchick (Ed.), *Fractured focus: Sport as a reflection of society* (pp. 221–227) Lexington, MA: D. C. Heath.

Snyder, E. E., & Spreitzer, E. A. (1983) *Social aspects of sport* (2d ed.). Englewood Cliffs, NJ: Prentice-Hall.

Snyder, E. E., & Spreitzer, E. A. (1989) *Social aspects of sport* (3rd ed.). Englewood Cliffs, NJ: Prentice-Hall.

Soccer. (1988) *Bryan College Station (TX) Eagle,* January 9, 2B.

Steinmetz, S. K. (1978) The battered husband syndrome. *Victimology, 2,* 507.

Spink, K. S., & Carron, A. V. (1994) Group cohesion effects in exercise classes. *Small Group Research, 25,* 26–42.

Spurgeon, J. H., Blair, S. V., Keith, J. A., & McGinn, C. J. (1978) Characteristics of successful and probationary football officials. *Physician and Sportsmedicine, 6*(5), 106–112.

Taylor, A. H., & Daniel, J. V. (1987) Sources of stress in soccer officiating: An empirical study. *First world congress on science and football* (pp. 538–544). Liverpool, England: E. & F. N. Spon.

Terry, P. C., & Jackson, J. J. (1985) The determinants and control of violence in sport. *Quest, 37,* 27–37.

Varca, P. (1980) An analysis of home and away performance of male college basketball teams. *Journal of Sport Psychology, 2,* 245–257.

Vaz, E., & Thomas, D. (1974) What price victory? An analysis of minor hockey league players' attitudes toward winning. *International Review of Sport Sociology, 2*(9), 33–53.

Volkamer, N. (1971) Investigations into the aggressiveness in competitive social system. *Sportswissenschaft, 1,* 33–64.

Whitcomb, D. (1992) *When the victim is a child* (2d. ed.). Washington, DC: U.S. Department of Justice.

Widmeyer, W. N., & Birch, J. S. (1984) Aggression in professional ice hockey: A strategy for success or a reaction to failure? *Journal of Psychology, 117,* 77–84.

Wilberger, J. E. (1993) Minor head injuries in American football. *Sports Medicine, 15,* 338–343.

Wright, E. F., Voyer, D., Wright, R. D., & Roney, C. (1995) Supporting audiences and performance under pressure: The home-ice disadvantage in hockey championships. *Journal of Sport Behavior, 18,* 21–28.

Yeager, R. (1979) *Seasons of shame: The new violence in sports.* New York: McGraw-Hill.

Yes beer or no beer? (1987) *USA Today,* Oct. 1, 9C.

Zawitz, M. W. (1994) *Violence between intimates.* Washington, DC: U.S. Department of Justice.

Zimbardo, P. (1969) The human choice: Individuation, reason, and order versus deindividuation, impulse, and chaos. In W. Arnold & D. Levin (Eds.), *Nebraska Symposium on Motivation,* Vol. 17 (pp. 237–307). Lincoln: University of Nebraska Press.

Personality and Assessment

Part Three

Chapter Eight

Personality and Psychological Assessment

INTRODUCTION TO PERSONALITY

The study of personality has intrigued psychologists for most of the twentieth century. Sport psychologists have been no exception; according to Ruffer (1975, 1976a, 1976b), almost six hundred original studies of the relationship of personality to sport performance had been conducted by the mid-1970s alone. By way of update, Fisher (1984) set the figure at well over one thousand. More recent estimates are not available, but it is certain that the number is substantially larger at this date.

Though considerable skepticism has been expressed about the type and quality of inquiry done in many of those investigations, the quest for the link between sport and personality continues unabated. This interest arises out of a desire to find better answers to questions of importance to sport scientists, questions such as:

1. What personality variables are at work in producing the choking response in the face of competitive pressure?
2. What personality variables may contribute to good leadership from coaches and players?
3. Can personality tests be used to identify elite youth athletes at an early age so that they can be given the best of training for future athletic development?
4. Does sex role orientation relate in any way to performance among female athletes?
5. What unique features, if any, compel people to seek new experiences by jumping out of airplanes or diving beneath the oceans, seas, bays, and lakes?
6. Are there personality predictors that might be of use in promoting fitness and exercise adherence?

These questions represent a scant few of the multitude that might be asked with regard to the personality–sport performance relationship. Before attempting to answer some of them, we would like to anchor the chapter discussion to a definition of personality, a discussion of various theories of personality that have guided thought and research, some reflections on argumentative issues, and suggestions for improving research in sport. We will then discuss what is presently known about psychological assessment and personality variables.

PERSONALITY DEFINED

Lazarus and Monat (1979, p. 1) define personality as "the underlying, relatively stable, psychological structure and processes that organize human experience and shape a person's activities and reactions to the environment." Essentially, what Lazarus and Monat refer to is the notion that a *core* personality exists and is more or less "the real you." In other words, there are core components of personality by which you know yourself and are known by others, and these are generally quite stable and unchanging. For the most part a healthy self-concept is stable and unchanging, just as is being aggressive. Similarly, being warm and friendly and trusting of others are core traits. They may be buffeted by life events, but generally will withstand these trials and tribulations with little alteration. The core you, simply put, does not change much once it is set. Think of your parents or grandparents as examples; how much are they changing or likely to change their basic patterns of reacting to life? Not much, we suspect!

Looking at only the personality core as a means of explaining behavior clearly has limitations; there is much more to each of us than a set psychological core. Allport (1937, p. 48) provides us with a way of incorporating more into the personality than the static core traits by offering the following definitional stance: "Personality is the dynamic organization within the individual of those psychophysical systems that determine his unique adjustments to the environment." Though laced with sexist language, Allport's time-tested work in the area of personality theory and research provides us with an additional facet or component of the personality, that of *peripheral states.* This is not to deny the considerable influence of the psychological core, but Allport's emphasis on dynamism allows for more changeable peripheral states to exert an influence on behavior. Some aspects of our personalities are always in a state of flux. For example, our responses to religious, political, or racial issues are often subject to variability. Also, daily events take their toll in such areas as depression, anxiety, and other related mood states. The dynamic interaction between the core (trait) and peripheral (state) portions of each of us composes the essence of what is known as personality.

Hollander (1967) has taken the discussion a step further by talking about a psychological core, typical responses, and role-related behaviors (see the schematic representation in figure 8.1). Hollander has maintained the core as conceptualized earlier in this discussion and broken the peripheral portion into *typical responses* and *role-related behaviors.* We respond to typical daily events with fairly predictable behaviors, but in ways that are more amenable to change than are the core traits. In other words, typical responses operate at a level slightly less entrenched than the core. Role-related behaviors are the most superficial, therefore malleable, aspect of the personality. Each of us is called upon daily to fulfill a number of different roles, and we accomplish them in ways that get us by but are not always representative of our true core predispositions. How many times have you had to refrain from stating your true opinion about a life event because role expectations did not allow for honest expression?

One final point about Hollander's model merits attention. The social environment is a constant source of pressure on adjustment. Role-

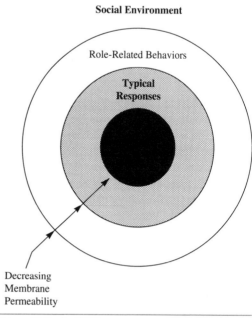

Figure 8.1: Hollander's Model of Personality Structure

Source: Hollander (1967).

related behaviors are the most susceptible to the influence of the social environment, whereas typical responses and the psychological core are increasingly less affected. This relationship can also be seen in figure 8.1.

THEORIES OF PERSONALITY

Theories concerning the nature of personality are numerous, all striving to explain why the human organism behaves as it does. These various theories have guided further theorizing and research about personality, and we will examine six of them.

Biological Theories

One theory advanced to account for behavior is the *constitutional theory* of William Sheldon

(Sheldon, 1940, 1942). Sheldon's theory takes the position that there are basic *somatotypes*, or body types, that are predictive of personality. For instance, Sheldon's *ectomorph* is characterized by leanness and angularity of build, and responds behaviorally with a high level of activity, tension, and introversion. The classic *mesomorph* is likely to be very muscular and athletic, and responds to environmental stimuli with aggression, risk taking, and leadership. It follows logically that team leaders would emerge from such a somatotype. Finally, the *endomorph* has a more round body type and reacts behaviorally with joviality, generosity, affection, and sociability. Jolly Old Saint Nick most closely serves as the prototype for the endomorphic individual. Clearly, the three somatotypes are stereotypes and, as such, they suffer from all of the shortcomings and criticisms of such a conceptualization. The reader is referred to Eysenck, Nias, and Cox (1982) for a review of Sheldon's theory as it relates to sport.

More closely related to sport is Dishman's *psychobiological theory* (Dishman, 1984), which is gaining acceptance as a means of predicting exercise adherence. Dishman's contention is that biological factors, such as body composition, interact with psychological variables, such as motivation, to produce an index of exercise compliance. More elaboration on Dishman's work will be made in chapter 13.

Psychodynamic Theory

One of the more well-developed, complex, and controversial theories about human behavior is the *psychoanalytic theory* of Sigmund Freud. The cornerstone of Freud's theory is that humans are inherently bad and, if left to their own devices, will self-destruct. This pessimism has fueled Freudian thought since its formative days in the late 1800s and early 1900s. The psychoanalytic model is an *intrapsychic* one; that is, the *psyche* is made up of an id, an ego, and a superego, with the id and the superego in a con-

stant state of conflict over control of the psyche. The arbiter of this eternal dispute is the ego, and its strength is a prime determinant of adjustment. Should the id win the intrapsychic conflict, a hedonistic thrill seeker in constant search of pleasure is produced. Should the superego become dominant, a dogmatic moralist is the end result. When the ego is able to arbitrate a healthy rapprochement between the pleasure-seeking id and the moralistic superego, a healthy, well-adjusted person is produced.

Unfortunately, the psychoanalytic model has focused almost exclusively on pessimism and pathology, and this preoccupation with abnormality has served to limit its applicability to the more normal manifestations of behavior. Inasmuch as sport participants, on the whole, appear to have no more and no fewer psychological problems than do nonparticipants, the Freudian model has limited utility for the sport psychologist. On a broader scale, however, psychoanalytic thought has served as an impetus for a mammoth amount of research and a number of competing theories.

Humanistic Theory

A view counter to the Freudian model is that of the *humanists*. Beginning in the eighteenth century with the writings of the French philosopher, Jean Jacques Rousseau, all the way to the recent works of Abraham Maslow and Carl Rogers, humanists have adopted a stance that is diametrically opposite to that of the psychoanalysts. To the humanist, the nature of man is basically good and behavior, rather than being determined by deep, dark psychic forces, is free. The capacity for growth and change is at the heart of this personal freedom. In the analytic model, badness must be kept in check by laws, rules, mores, and folkways if the person is to adjust properly. Thus, when a person turns out bad, it is because society has failed. To the humanist, society with all its strictures is seen as a potential corruptive force; when a person turns out bad, it is because society interfered in some way with this natural expression of goodness.

Rogers accounts for the ultimate in adjustment with his concept of the *fully functioning person*. In Maslow's terminology, the person who maximizes his or her potentials across a broad spectrum of human endeavors has achieved *self-actualization*. Recall the discussion of self-actualization in chapter 5.

The Behavioral Model

A view counter to the previous models is that of the *behaviorists*. Behaviorism owes its origins to the work of Pavlov in Russia in the late 1800s and of Watson in the United States in the early 1900s. Modern behaviorists believe that behavior is inherently neither good nor bad; rather, it is the product of an interaction between genetic endowment and learned experience. This stance relegates the goodness-badness issue to its proper place in the eyes of the behaviorist, namely, in the realm of philosophy. With regard to the issue of freedom versus determinism, behaviorists are somewhat like the analysts in that they feel that behavior is determined. However, they differ on the mechanism by which behavior is stamped in. Traumatic childhood events are crucial to the analyst; to the behaviorist, reinforced early experiences are critical. Behaviorists also differ from analysts in their views of the extent to which these childhood experiences are changeable at a later point in time. In the view of the behaviorist, if a behavior can be learned, it can be unlearned, though not necessarily easily.

The behavioral approach has been warmly embraced by sport psychology. The behavioral coaching procedures discussed earlier represent one contribution from the behaviorists. The emphasis on modeling and social reinforcement as espoused by Bandura represents a second

major offering. Most certainly, the performance enhancement and anxiety reduction strategies so integral to improving sport performance have had considerable impact on sport psychology practice and research. Finally, the use of reinforcement principles as a means of facilitating exercise adherence is another valuable contribution. In brief, the behavioral model, with its emphasis on learning new productive behaviors and unlearning old counterproductive ones, has been a bright beacon of light for sport psychology and the field of psychology as a whole.

Trait Theory

Much research in sport has been triggered by the trait (or factor) approach to personality as advanced by such psychologists as Gordon Allport, Raymond Cattell, and Hans Eysenck. Trait theorists contend that personality is best understood in terms of enduring traits or predispositions to respond in similar ways across a variety of situations. This is not to say that behavior is invariable; however, a strong tendency exists to respond in persistent, predictable, and measurable ways. Out of this belief has arisen a host of psychometric instruments that have purported to assess these various traits. Much sport research (and controversy) has been generated by trait psychology.

The Interactional Perspective

In an attempt to bring some clarity to the issue of personality within sport, an interactional model has emerged. The interactional perspective suggests that behavior is, in fact, an interaction of the person and the environment. The interactive model is summed up by a single formula advanced more than sixty years ago by Kurt Lewin (1935), as follows: $B = f(P,E)$. A significant point here is that traits are still viewed as pertinent determinants of behavior, but not nearly so salient as the purists in trait psychology would

The Big Five Personality Traits

One of the more exciting events in the study of personality to come along in years is the big five personality traits proposed by Costa and McCrae (1985). Summarizing a substantial number of studies of personality and many different methodologies for doing so, McCrae and Costa have concluded that personality can essentially be reduced to their "big five": Extraversion, Agreeableness, Neuroticism, Conscientiousness, and Openness to Experience. In the case of *Extraversion,* such elements as sociability, activity, and the tendency to experience positive emotional states are part and parcel of this trait. There is evidence in the sport personology literature to suggest that athletes as a group would score higher on the Extraversion dimension. As for *Agreeableness,* it relates to interpersonal style; high-A individuals are cooperative and easy to establish rapport with. On the other hand, low-A people tend to be negative and more unapproachable. In the sport realm, it might be hypothesized that coachable athletes would be high-A people. Concerning *Neuroticism,* the authors are talking of a more clinically-related scale pertaining to poor coping mechanisms and resulting psychological distress. Where athletes might fall on this trait is speculative; our hunch is that they would be no more or less represented on this trait than would the population at large. The fourth trait composite, *Conscientiousness,* contrasts well-organized, scrupulous, and diligent people with those who are lax, disorganized, and lackadaisical. The application of this trait to sport research is unclear, though the argument could be made that successful athletes may differ from less successful ones in terms of their organizational skills. The final big five trait, *Openness to Experience,* relates to creativity, sensitivity, and behavioral flexibility. Costa and McCrae (1992) do stress that clinical psychologists would probably regard this trait as an indicator of good mental health, but they are not so confident that such is always the case. They suggest that conformity and conventionality are also viable paths to good adjustment. In terms of sport, it could be argued that conformity and conventionality would be more productive avenues for expression than creativity and imagination. Admittedly, each of the hypotheses advanced concerning sport research are nothing more than speculation. Obviously, research is needed to see if the big five can breathe some new life into trait psychology as related to sport.

In this connection, Costa and McCrae have created an assessment device, the NEO Personality Inventory (NEO-PI), to measure the big five personality traits (Costa and McCrae, 1985, 1992). Fifteen years of research

(Continued next page)

Highlight 8.1 (Continued)

The Big Five Personality Traits

and development by Costa and McCrae has resulted in the current 181-item version of the NEO-PI, which has two forms: S for self-reports and R for observer ratings. All items are arranged on a five-point Likert scale from strongly agree to strongly disagree, and the scales are balanced to control for acquiescent response patterns. Reliability and validity studies

Some sport psychologists speculate that conformity and conventionality are more productive personality traits for an athlete than openness to experience. Speed skater Bonnie Blair, world champion and Olympic gold medalist, seemed to combine both kinds of traits. Like most athletes, she conformed to rigorous training conventions—in her case, two 2-3 hour sessions per day, six days per week. But she was also open to the unexpected. "Sometimes strange things happen in competition," she said. "I try to approach every race like it is the Olympics, so when I get there, I'm prepared."

(Continued next page)

Highlight 8.1 (Continued)

The Big Five Personality Traits

conducted to date are supportive of the NEO-PI (Hogan, 1989; Mount, Barrick, and Strauss, 1994). The authors have developed a number of features to assist the test user, one of which is a sixty-item abbreviated scale known as the NEO Five Factor Inventory (NEO-FFI).

The utility of both the big five trait theory and the scale derived from it remains to be demonstrated, both external to and within the sport realm. It is hoped that this challenge will be accepted in what could prove to be a very interesting chapter in personality theory and research as well as in the area of sport personology.

Sources: Costa and McCrae (1985, 1992); Hogan (1989); Mount, Barrick, and Strauss (1994).

suggest. Another important issue is the emphasis on environmental variables and their interaction with traits.

A major elaboration on the interactional perspective has been made by Endler and Hunt (1966). These investigators studied the responses of nearly three hundred college students from three universities to the S-R Inventory of Anxiousness (Endler, Hunt, and Rosenstein, 1962). After considerable statistical manipulations of the data as well as in-depth interpretive effort, Endler and Hunt concluded the question of whether individual traits or situational differences explain behavior is a pseudo-issue. By way of elaboration, their statistical analyses indicated that only 13 percent of response tendencies to the S-R Inventory of Anxiousness could be explained by traits (i.e., the person) and situations. The remaining 87 percent was accounted for with other combinations and permutations of the person times situation equation. By way of elaboration, there are seven different sources of behavioral variance suggested by the Endler and Hunt model: Person (P); Situation (S); Modes of Response (M-R); P × S; P × M-R; S × M-R; and Residual, which is a function of

a three-way interaction involving P × S × M-R. A visual representation of these relationships can be seen in figure 8.2.

Similar results have been reported by Fisher, Horsfall, and Morris (1977) in a study of male collegiate basketball players using a sport-specific variant of the S-R Inventory of Anxiousness. These investigators were able to link 19 percent of the performance variation in their sample of 147 athletes to Person (P) and Situation (S).

As a final note on the interactional model and its relationship to trait and/or situational explanations of behavior, Endler and Hunt (1966, pp. 344–345) conclude:

Human behavior is complex. In order to describe it, one must take into account not only the main sources of variance (subjects, situations, and modes of response) but also the various simple interactions (Subjects with Situations, Subjects with Modes of Response, and Situations with Modes of Response) and, where feasible, the triple interaction (Subject with Situations and Modes of Response). Behavior is a function of all these factors in combination.

Figure 8.2: **Endler and Hunt Interactional Model of Behavior**

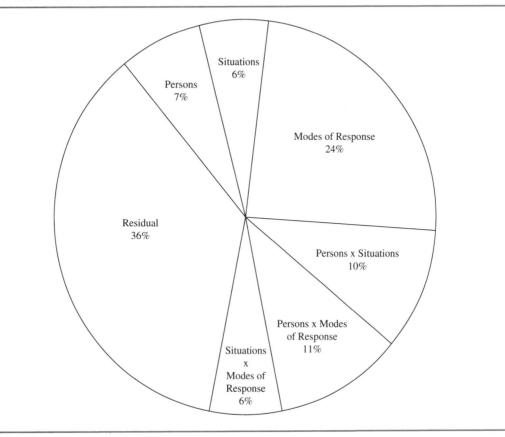

Source: Endler and Hunt (1966).

PROBLEMS IN SPORT PERSONALITY RESEARCH

The utility of personality measures in sport personality research, or what Martens (1975, 1981) refers to as *sport personology*, has been limited by a number of factors that may be viewed as conceptual, methodological, and interpretive.

Conceptual Problems

The failure to think in conceptual terms when devising investigations has led to a variety of difficulties that impinge on the quality of sport personology research and the reliance that can be placed on resulting findings.

Theoretical versus Atheoretical Research
Much of the research in sport personology has proceeded in the absence of any driving theoretical framework. All too frequently, psychological assessment devices have been selected for a variety of sometimes sound but more often unsound reasons and administered to the most available captive audience of athletes. From this shaky research design have emerged published

studies purporting to be descriptions of the personality of the athlete. The problems inherent in such a shotgun approach to data collection, analysis, and reporting are numerous. Ryan (1968, p.71) characterized this chaotic situation very well more than twenty-five years ago:

> The research in this area has largely been of the "shotgun" variety. By this I mean the investigators grabbed the nearest and most convenient personality test, and the closest sport group, and with little or no theoretical basis for their selection fired into the air to see what they could bring down. It isn't surprising that firing into the air at different times and different places, and using different ammunition, should result in different findings. In fact, it would be surprising if the results weren't contradictory and somewhat contrary.

Cox (1985, p. 20) sums up the situation this way:

> A large percentage of the sports personality research has been conducted atheoretically. That is, the researchers had no particular theoretical reason for conducting the research in the first place. They just arbitrarily selected a personality inventory, tested a group of athletes, and proceeded to "snoop" through the data for "significant" findings.

That so few answers about sport personology have emerged from so many studies is therefore not surprising. Gill (1986, p. 34) says: "If researchers do not ask meaningful questions, their efforts cannot produce meaningful answers." If sport personology is to advance our understanding of this significant aspect of sport, future research must be driven by meaningful questions that are byproducts of sound theoretical underpinnings.

Failure to Operationalize

One reason for the conflicting results within sport personology studies undoubtedly has to do with the inconsistency with which terms are defined from study to study. For example, what does the term "elite athlete" mean? It could easily be argued that only professional athletes are elite. On the other hand, this would eliminate the so-called amateur Russian hockey players participating in the Olympic Games. If one wanted to broaden the definition of elite athlete, all Olympians might be a useful standard. The inclusion of substandard Olympic performers such as Eddie "The Eagle" Edwards, the ski jumper from Great Britain who participated in the 1988 Winter Olympics in Calgary, would cast serious doubt on such a definitional stance. This issue will resurface later in the chapter, when the elite athlete is discussed more fully; the elite athlete serves here as a point of departure for illustrating the difficulties in operationalizing sport-related terms. Equally problematic in the research have been terms like athlete, nonathlete, nonparticipant, youth athlete, sportsman, and so forth. The need for proper definition of terms does indeed warrant greater attention in the design of future studies.

Methodological Problems

Above and beyond the conceptual problems just discussed, a host of methodological shortcomings have plagued the sport personology research, not the least of which has been *sampling* inconsistencies. For example, many studies have used college athletes and nonathletes from the United States as subjects for a variety of comparisons. The problems of defining the terms athlete and nonathlete notwithstanding, there is little assurance that college athletes and nonathletes from different universities going to school in different geographic locations are similar in personality makeup. The probability that the varsity athlete and nonathlete from Stanford (or Slippery Rock), for instance, is representative of all college students is low. Limits in generalizing results in these situations are present; we shall examine the implications of the generalization problem shortly.

A second methodological problem has to do with *data analysis*. Too much reliance has been placed on *univariate analysis* of results and too little on *multivariate approaches*. Essentially, univariate approaches to data analysis compare two or more groups on one variable and, as such, are useful. However, they provide what Silva (1984, p. 65) calls a "snapshot" of the subject being studied without capturing the interactions that take place between or among the variables being studied. Consequently, a fuller picture of

the relationship between or among events is portrayed through multivariate methods.

Response distortion represents a third methodological problem in sport personology research. A number of issues must be addressed when administering psychological assessment devices to sport participants, not the least of which is response distortion. Sports participants, like other groups of people, respond to psychological assessment in a variety of ways. It would be naive to think that all responses to psychological inventories are completely honest and void of distortion. Careless responding, faking

---

The Credulous-Skeptical Argument

Highlight 8.2

William Morgan published a pivotal paper in 1980 in which he elaborated on what he considered to be a crucial problem in sport personology, that of the call by a number of authorities in the field to abandon the trait approach. Morgan contended that to do so would be to throw the baby out with the bathwater, so to speak. He suggested that the problem was not so much with the trait approach as with the way it had been applied in sport research. Out of this scholarly exchange emerged the *credulous-skeptical argument*. Morgan intimated that the *skeptical* camp was made up of "knowledge brokers," authorities such as Fisher (1977), Kroll (1976), Martens (1975), Rushall (1975), and Singer and associates (1977), all of whom were calling for the abandonment of the trait approach within sport psychology. Morgan used the term "knowledge brokers" because of their tendency to cite only studies disconfirming trait studies in their own research. At the other extreme were those who took the *credulous* position, spokespersons such as Ogilvie and Tutko (1966), who were willing to accept the power of the trait approach in predicting sport accomplishment.

Morgan has since suggested that the skeptical/credulous dichotomy is in fact a pseudo-argument, one that needs to be set aside in favor of a more interactional position incorporating traits, states, and situations into the predictive formula for sport behavior. Important in this position is awareness that it is still too early to abandon the trait approach in sport personology.

Sources: Fisher (1977); Kroll (1976); Martens (1975); Ogilvie and Tutko (1966); Rushall (1975); Singer, Harris, Kroll, Martens, and Sechrest (1977).

bad, and faking good are but a few of the possible ways in which a subject may distort data gathered from trait, state, or sport-specific inventories. The serious researcher should employ, wherever possible, measures to detect these various response distortions. Trait, state, and sport-specific assessment techniques, as well as one of the possible sources of response distortion, will be discussed later.

Too few studies have been made of the *interactional model* that incorporates traits, states, and situations, and this omission represents a fourth methodological difficulty. As the earlier discussion of the various models of personality indicated, the interactional approach offers the most in terms of long-term return in sport personology.

A fifth methodological consideration is the absence of virtually any *longitudinal research* in sport psychology. The problem is bad enough in psychology generally, though the recent work of Eron (1987) on aggression mentioned in chapter 7 represents a most heartening exception. Unfortunately, sport psychology is virtually devoid of research looking at sport populations over extended periods of time. Youth sport and the sport for all movement, just to name two areas of inquiry, lend themselves beautifully to such an approach.

Finally, the *"one-shot method"* of data collection merits mentioning. At times, collecting data on a one-time basis may be useful. However, conducting intensive investigations of sport samples is advocated in most cases. The benefits to the discipline, the investigator(s), and the sport participants being sampled are undoubtedly going to be greater in most cases with the in-depth approach.

Interpretive Problems

Two prime areas of concern that interfere with proper communication of research findings in the area of interpretation include *faulty generalizations* and *inferring causation from correlation.*

Faulty Generalizations

As mentioned earlier, generalizing from one study to another has been problematical in sport personology. For example, generalizing about sport participants taking part in team activities based on data collected from those involved in individual sports is treacherous at best; the same can be said for generalizing from the reverse situation. Equally shaky are generalizations made between various age groups, different sexes, and participants from different countries, just to name a few. Another of the more common sources of error in sport personology research has to do with generalizations made among the various assessment devices. Tests, such as the Eysenck Personality Inventory (EPI) (Eysenck and Eysenck, 1963) and the Minnesota Multiphasic Personality Inventory (MMPI) (Hathaway and McKinley, 1943), have little in common philosophically and yet are often used for comparative purposes.

Inferring Causation from Correlation

A persistent problem in all of psychology (and life in general) is inferring causation from correlated things. A high correlation between events does not per se infer a cause and effect relationship between them. Eating pickles and death are correlated. Almost everyone eats pickles and everyone eventually dies, and this implies a high correlation; to infer that the eating of pickles causes death would be to misinterpret the data. To infer that the existence of a personality trait causes sport performance of a certain level of sophistication is also fraught with danger. The cause of sport performance is determined by many factors. To attribute too much to a certain personality trait may be stretching the data too far. This is not to say that traits are not important; rather, it is an admonition to beware of attributing too much to a given trait. The earlier call for more multivariate procedures in sport research is underscored here.

INTRODUCTION TO PSYCHOLOGICAL ASSESSMENT

Psychological testing is big business in the United States; the role of testing in athletics is also substantial. Tests may be administered to individuals or groups and cover such diverse aspects of human behavior as intelligence, aptitude, achievement, personality, and interests. One type of testing academic aptitude involves well over 2 million people annually (Kaplan and Sacuzzo, 1989). Of that number, 1.8 million take the Scholastic Aptitude Test (SAT), another 120,000 the Law School Admission Test (LSAT), and 75,000 a special test for admission to business school. Coupled with the considerable use of various other aptitude and interest tests in the public high schools and colleges, and the use of personality tests in our employment/clinical psychology/criminal justice networks, psychological testing represents a multibillion dollar enterprise of considerable significance.

Important, sometimes critical, decisions are made about people based on test results. Children with intellectual deficits are assigned to special education classes or schools for the mentally retarded; other children are placed in gifted and talented classes in order to capitalize on their mental abilities; individuals are classified as schizophrenic or psychopathic because of test results that substantiate their behavioral idiosyncrasies. Tests have been with us for most of the twentieth century and will continue to play an important role, despite their controversial status, in events of the foreseeable future.

A BRIEF HISTORY

Testing is, by and large, an American enterprise. However, Kaplan and Sacuzzo (1989) tell us that the Chinese four thousand years ago had a reasonably sophisticated system of testing that was used in work evaluation and job promotion decisions. Subsequent developments extended into many facets of Chinese life to include examinations to determine who was qualified to serve in public office, a precursor of our civil service testing program in this country. Kaplan and Sacuzzo point out that the Western world probably learned about testing through interactions with the Chinese in the nineteenth century.

Though rudimentary attempts were made at testing in the late 1800s, and considerable theorizing about individual differences was starting to emerge, the first major breakthrough came at the turn of the twentieth century through the work of two Frenchmen, A. Binet and T. Simon. Initially, Binet was commissioned by the French ministry of education to design a paper-and-pencil test to separate the mentally fit from the intellectually subnormal. Out of this initial effort the two men developed the Binet-Simon Scale, which was published in 1905, revised in 1908, and again in 1911. A Stanford psychologist, Lewis Terman, adapted the scale for use in the United States in 1916, and the testing movement as a major force in psychology was under way. World Wars I and II intensified interest in testing, and led to many important improvements.

On another front, personality testing was given its initial impetus by events surrounding World War I. These first efforts led to a proliferation of paper and pencil instruments designed to measure both global and isolated traits of personality. Of these tests, none has achieved the stature of the Minnesota Multiphasic Personality Inventory (MMPI). Its impact across a number of areas of personality research and application extends to sport psychology, as we shall see shortly. A brief history of the testing movement is provided in table 8.1.

Psychological tests remain one of the most salient aspects of psychology. They have not been without critics, however, and some of the criticisms are justified. Tests have many uses and, as a consequence, are susceptible to abuse. Proper selection, use, and reporting of tests is a challenge for all psychologists, sport psychologists among them.

WHAT IS A TEST?

To Cronbach (1970, p. 26) a *test* is "a systematic procedure for observing a person's behavior and describing it with the aid of a numerical scale or a category-system." The emphasis here is on avoiding unsystematic, spur-of-the-moment procedures for evaluation, such as casual conversation. To Anastasi (1988, p. 23), a psychological test is "essentially an objective and

Table 8.1

Selected Events in the History of Psychological and Educational Measurement

2200 B.C.	Mandarins set up civil-service testing program in China.	1919	L. Thurstone's Psychological Examination for College Freshmen published.
1219 A.D.	First formal oral examination in law held at University of Bologna.	1920	H. Rorschach's Inkblot Test first published.
1575	J. Huarte publishes book, *Examen de Ingenios,* concerned with individual differences in mental abilities.	1921	Psychological Corporation, first major test publishing company, founded by Cattell, Thorndike, and Woodworth.
1869	Scientific study of individual differences begins with publication of Galton's "Classification of Men According to Their Natural Gifts."	1923	First achievement test battery, Stanford Achievement Tests, published.
		1936	Soviet Union bans psychological tests.
1879	Founding of first psychological laboratory in the world by Wilhelm Wundt at Leipzig, Germany.	1938	Buros publishes first *Mental Measurements Yearbook.*
		1939	Wechsler-Bellevue Intelligence Scale published.
1888	J. M. Cattell opens testing laboratory at the University of Pennsylvania.	1942	Minnesota Multiphasic Personality Inventory (MMPI) published.
1904	C. Spearman describes his two-factor theory of mental abilities.	1949	Wechsler Intelligence Scale for Children published.
1905	First Binet-Simon Intelligence Scale published.	1974	Wechsler Intelligence Scale for Children Revised.
1916	Stanford-Binet Intelligence Scale published by L. Terman.	1981	Wechsler Adult Intelligence Scale (Revised) published.
1917	Army Alpha and Army Beta, first group intelligence tests, constructed and administered to U.S. army recruits; R. Woodworth's Personal Data Sheet, the first standardized personality inventory, used in military selection.	1985	*Standards for Educational and Psychological Testing* published.
		1986	Ninth edition of *Mental Measurements Yearbook* published.
		1989	MMPI-2 published.

Source: Aiken (1987).

standardized measure of a sample of behavior." Emphasis in this case is placed on the use of objective measurement and on the important notion that test responses are merely a sample of a person's overall behavior. It is hoped, of course, that the sample will be representative of the totality; this is the essence of creating a valid testing instrument. A third definitional stance is taken by Kaplan and Sacuzzo (1989, p. 4): "A psychological test is a device for measuring characteristics of human beings that pertain to behavior." Kaplan and Sacuzzo add that these behaviors include both the overt, or observable, and the covert, or internal and unobservable (feelings and thoughts). They also point to the fact that tests can be used to measure past, present, and future behaviors. For example, a test over this text material might be representative. How much you have studied (i.e., the past) is tapped, your level of current functioning is measured, and some predictions for future performance can be made. We suspect your professor will be concurrently doing all three of these things with his or her tests! In any event, the emphasis on the objective study of behavior that is implied in all three definitions will serve as our guide for the rest of the material in this chapter.

VALIDITY, RELIABILITY, AND NORMS

Three critical dimensions of any psychological test are validity, reliability, and norms; that is, does a test measure what it is designed to do, does it do so in a consistent fashion, and is it based on an appropriate reference group? If these three conditions are met, it is likely that we have a useful psychological assessment device at our disposal.

Validity

The generally accepted definition of *validity* is couched in terms of the degree to which

a test measures what it is created to measure. This definition, according to Aiken (1982), assumes that validity is rather unidimensional, which is not the case at all. Aiken says:

> Among the methods for studying the validity of a test are analyzing its content, relating scores on the test to scores on a criterion of interest, and investigating the particular psychological characteristics or constructs measured by the test. All of these procedures for assessing validity are useful to the extent that they increase understanding of what a test is measuring so that the scores will represent more accurate information on which to base decisions. (P. 80)

This broadened definition sets the stage for a discussion of the three dimensions of validity: content, criterion, and predictive. Guion (1980) has referred to these dimensions as the "trinitarian" view.

Before undertaking our discussion of the trinitarian view, however, there is an important aspect of validity that is relevant to any discussion of psychological assessment: face validity.

Face Validity

Face validity is the extent to which an assessment device *appears* to measure what it is intended to assess. In other words, does the test look valid to the person conducting an experiment or assessment or the person being evaluated? This issue is at the heart of the call for more sport-specific tests, ones that athletes can readily identify with because they seem to make sense as they respond to them. The abstractness of some of the traditional personality measures to be discussed later have been criticized by athletes because they do not seem relevant. To put it another way, how many of you have taken a classroom exam that seemed to get right to the heart of the subject matter at hand, while another exam seemed to have been pulled from thin air by the professor? The former probably possesses face validity, the latter does not. All in all, it is important in sport psychology and elsewhere that a test have face validity because of its facilitative effect on motivation to undertake the task at hand in a serious manner.

Content Validity

Content validity refers to a judgment about the degree to which a group of test items are representative of the totality or universe of items that could be asked. Obviously, there is a practical limit to how many questions we might ask an athlete at any point in time, so we settle for a sample that we hope is representative; that is, one with content validity. For instance, your professor in sport psychology will not be able to test you over every question that could possibly be asked because of time and other practical matters. Therefore, he or she will settle for a sample of fifty, seventy-five, or one hundred representative items from the hypothetical pool of all possible questions related to the course content. The extent to which these items are representative of the course content will determine the content validity of the examination.

Criterion Validity

A criterion is a standard upon which a judgment or decision can be based. Operationally, a criterion can be just about anything: success at selling insurance, facility at flying an airplane, time in the 100-meter dash, or score on a sport psychology examination. Subtypes of criterion validity are *concurrent* and *predictive*. In concurrent validity, statements or inferences about an individual's present standing on a criterion are made. An example is found in psychodiagnostic work where scores or classifications made by an individual based on test scores are validated against a criterion of already diagnosed clients. In the case of predictive validity, test scores may be obtained at one time and criterion scores at a later juncture. The classic example, and one that is well-known to college students,

is the use of Scholastic Aptitude Test (SAT) scores and high school grades to predict college achievement. Fortunately for many, the relationship of the test scores or grades to the criterion of grades in college is far from a perfect positive one. In sport psychology, as will be pointed out later, Morgan's work with successful and "unsuccessful" Olympic athletes represents an example of predictive validity; that is, scores on the Profile of Mood States (POMS) differentiated between the two groups of athletes, thereby allowing for some predictions about athletic performance based on psychometric results.

Construct Validity

A construct is a mechanism for inferring the existence of something that is essentially hypothetical or unobservable. For example, intelligence and locus of control are two of innumerable constructs common to psychology; a number of assessment devices have been generated to validate their existence. If three measures of intelligence or locus of control yield similar results and these relate to some external criterion of behavior, construct validity of the two concepts is established, at least partially.

Reliability

A *reliable test* is one that yields consistent results, or to quote Aiken (1982):

> To be useful, psychological and educational tests, and other measuring instruments, must be fairly consistent or reliable in what they measure. The concept of the reliability of a test refers to its relative freedom from unsystematic errors of measurement. A test is reliable if it measures consistently under varying conditions that can produce measurement errors. Unsystematic errors affecting test scores vary in a random, unpredictable manner from situation to situation; hence, they lower test reliability. On the other hand, systematic (constant) errors may inflate or

deflate test scores, but they do so in a fixed way and hence do not affect test reliability. Some of the variables on which unsystematic error depends are the particular sample of questions on the test, the conditions of administration, and the internal state of the examinee at testing time. (P. 72)

Psychologists generally use three methods of determining reliability, namely, *test-retest, parallel forms,* and *internal consistency.* Simply stated, the test-retest format requires the same group of examinees to respond to a given test on two separate occasions. In parallel forms, two equivalent forms in terms of content and difficulty are administered to the same subjects. The internal consistency method is achieved through several statistically-based procedures in which the inter-

nal properties of tests are scrutinized. These procedures are known as the split-half method, Kuder-Richardson reliability, and coefficient alpha. The nuances of each procedure are beyond the scope of the present discussion, but the serious student can find readable discussions of them in a number of standard reference works on psychological assessment. A summary of these respective methods of assessing reliability and some caveats or problems associated with their usage are presented in table 8.2.

Norms

Most tests provide a good summary of the individuals that make up the sample for which the test was normed and is therefore intended. Any speculation beyond this is suspect until

Table 8.2
Methods of Assessing Reliability and Some Related Caveats

Method	Procedure	Caveats/Problems
1. Test-Retest	Same test is administered at two points in time	Length of time between tests and effects of memory and/or practice effects must be taken into account
2. Parallel Forms	Two forms of same test are administered to same subjects	Difficult to construct equivalent forms; potentially expensive procedure; virtually unheard of in sport psychology
3. Internal Consistency		
a. Split-Half	Correlations between odd and even or first and last half of items computed	Yields reliability of half the test; requires further statistical analysis to get reliability of full test
b. Kuder-Richardson	Statistical formula applied to test responses	Useful when responses are dichotomous; that is, yes or no, true or false
c. Coefficient Alpha	Statistical formula applied to test responses	Applicable when multiple responses are used, such as in Likert scaling

research indicates that further applications are justified. The original MMPI, normed on mental patients, has been used with graduate students, medical students, law enforcement officers, and athletes, and the violation of the norms that is inherent here has not gone unnoticed or uncontested. As shall be noted later, the publication of an updated version of the MMPI, with a new normative group, represents an attempt to remedy this criticism. In any event, the applicability of either form of the MMPI to sport remains suspect.

Selecting valid, reliable, and applicable psychological tests remains a trying task for psychologists in all fields of the discipline; the sport psychologist is not at all exempt from this challenge.

SOURCES OF ERROR IN TESTING

An implicit assumption generally made with regard to the various tests is that the subjects involved are cooperative and honest respondents. Sport psychologists tend to compound this error by assuming that athletes will be even more cooperative and honest than other test populations; no evidence supports this notion. Therefore, each of us in testing situations must be aware of possible sources of error that are subject-related.

In and of itself, no test is perfect; compounding the problem is the tendency of subjects to try to enhance themselves through their responses to the test or, conversely, to look as bad as possible. Other problems are conservative response style, defensiveness, fear, ignorance, and misinformation about testing in general. An exploration of three of these problems—faking good, faking bad, and conservative response style—seems appropriate.

Faking Good

We all are prone to project self-enhancing images in social situations, and this phenome-

non is not unusual in psychological assessment. Athletes are no exception. They may try to outguess the test, and one way to do this is always to answer troublesome questions in a manner that will project the most positive image. Tests vary considerably in their transparency, so any response set on the part of a respondent is guesswork. This transparency, of course, accentuates measurement error.

Faking Bad

Obviously, faking bad is an aberrant response pattern; why anyone would want to project a poor or maladjusted image is hard to comprehend. In reality, the sport psychologist is probably not nearly as likely to see this pattern as is the psychologist working in a clinical setting. When faking bad does occur, Nideffer (1981) suggests that it should be interpreted as a cry for help. Another interpretation might be that an improper testing climate has been created by the sport psychologist. Obviously, care should be exercised to insure that an atmosphere of rapport or cooperation is generated so that fake bad protocols are avoided or, if they do occur, are not a function of hostility or rejection on the part of the athlete.

Conservative Response Style

Nideffer suggests that the tendency to respond to tests in the most conservative, middle-of-the-road, pedestrian way is largely a function of rejection of the situation, the coach, the sport psychologist, or a combination thereof. Obviously, scores that cluster near the mean for the test are going to render decisions based on the results inconclusive or useless.

TEST ETHICS AND SPORT PSYCHOLOGY

With regard to psychologist testing with sport populations, the NASPSPA guidelines are aimed at maintaining quality control on these assessment devices. The guidelines are applicable to test development, test utilization, and the use of results obtained from such sources. They address such issues as validity, reliability, proper test manual development in the case of new instruments, user qualifications, conditions of administration, and the use of proper norms. Sport psychologists who are conducting psychological assessment with athletes or others involved in physical ability must be familiar with the guidelines. Many errors in the past could have been prevented by a greater awareness of the strengths and weaknesses of psychological tests and their ethical usage both within and outside the domain of sport psychology.

Nideffer (1981) indicates that sport psychologists are generally called upon for their expertise in psychological assessment to accomplish two basic tasks, selection and/or screening decisions and program development and/or counseling. He further suggests that test users within sport psychology should be alert to the following considerations:

1. Determining the relevance of a test to the assigned task at hand should be well within the sport psychologist's capabilities.
2. Evaluation of test validity and reliability is a critical skill.
3. Being aware of ethical considerations related to testing is essential.
4. Test interpretation skills are most important, and this process can be aided by the use of other available information, such as the case history.
5. Proper establishment of a testing climate that fosters cooperation is an invaluable asset.
6. Care must be exercised in the reporting of test results to individuals or organizations so as to minimize misunderstanding and maximize effective usage of the communicated information.

USES OF TESTS IN SPORT: AN INTRODUCTION

In the broadest sense, testing can include structured interviews, systematic behavioral observations, and a host of other techniques. However, for the purposes of our discussion, testing will unless otherwise indicated be restricted largely to paper-and-pencil measures, and primarily but not exclusively to those dealing with personality traits and states.

At this juncture, a look at several specific types of tests that are used in sport research and counseling would seem appropriate. Primary emphasis will be placed on the measurement of personality variables, both enduring and temporary. Secondary emphasis will be assigned to sport-specific tests, an area of increasing interest to sport psychologists. Finally, a brief mention will be made of attitude measures used in sport.

TESTS OF ENDURING PERSONALITY TRAITS

Three standardized measures of enduring traits have dominated research in sport for the past fifty years, beginning with the *Minnesota Multiphasic Personality Inventory (MMPI)* in 1943 (Hathaway and McKinley). Two other instruments of somewhat more recent vintage that have been utilized often are the *16 Personality Factor Questionnaire (16PF)* (Cattell, 1949) and the *Eysenck Personality Inventory (EPI)* (Eysenck and Eysenck, 1963). Each will be discussed in terms of its origin and its application to sport.

Minnesota Multiphasic Personality Inventory (MMPI)

The MMPI, 550 items long and answered "yes," "no," or "cannot say," was created by S.R. Hathaway, a psychologist, and J. C. McKinley, a physician, in 1943. The original purpose of the test was to differentiate among various psychiatric categories. No particular theoretical approach characterizes the MMPI; rather, it represents an example of criterion keying. The criterion groups (N = 50 per group) used in the development of the MMPI were psychiatric inpatients at the University of Minnesota Hospital.

The eight clinical scales resulting from the original research, according to Cohen, Swerdlik, and Smith (1992, p. 419) were:

1. Hypochondriasis—patients with exaggerated concerns about their physical health.
2. Depression—unhappy, depressed, and pessimistic patients.
3. Hysteria—patients tending to convert psychological stress into physical symptomatology.
4. Psychopathic deviate—patients with histories of antisocial behavior.
5. Paranoia—suspicious, grandiose, persecuted patients.
6. Psychasthenia—anxious, obsessive-compulsive, guilt-ridden patients.
7. Schizophrenia—patients with severe thought disturbances.
8. Hypomania—patients displaying mood elevation, excessive activity, and unusual distractibility.

The four hundred criterion individuals were then compared to approximately seven hundred control subjects consisting (unfortunately) of relatives and friends of the criterion cases. Critics of the MMPI have not let this point go unnoticed.

In addition to the eight so-called clinical scales derived from and labeled according to the types of patients, two others were subsequently added: the masculinity-femininity (MF) scale and the social-introversion (SI) scale. The MF was designed to assess male-female differences, the SI to assess the tendency to be (or not to be) outgoing. Finally, scales to measure test-taking abil-

ities, honesty in test taking, carelessness, misunderstanding, malingering, or the operation of special response sets were created; these were called the L (Lie), F (Frequency or Infrequency), and K (Correction) scales.

The MMPI is easily the most used personality test, having been the subject of approximately six thousand research studies (Kaplan and Sacuzzo, 1989); in addition, it has been translated into all European languages (Blaser and Schilling, 1976), the only personality instrument having that distinction.

Predictably, the MMPI is not without its shortcomings. Charges have been leveled that the size and representativeness of the normative sample is questionable. Other criticisms include item overlap among the various scales, imbalance in true-false keying, high scale intercorrelations, relatively weak reliability, and generalizability problems across demographic variables (Kaplan and Sacuzzo, 1989). Despite these weaknesses, the MMPI enjoys immense popularity in clinical psychology.

Perhaps the first sport study in which the MMPI was utilized was conducted by LaPlace (1954). In this instance, the MMPI was administered to forty-nine major league baseball players and sixty-four of their minor league counterparts. The major league players, as predicted, demonstrated a generally healthier profile with significantly lower scores on the schizophrenia and psychopathic deviate scales. A subsequent study by Booth in 1958 gave further credibility to the MMPI. Booth, using freshman and varsity athletes, team and individual sport participants, and athletes rated as good or poor performers, found several differences. Chief among these differences was the finding that varsity athletes who participated in individual sports scored significantly higher on the depression (D) scale and that varsity athletes competing in individual sports scored significantly higher than athletes competing in both team and individual sports on the psychasthenia (Pt) variable. Twenty-two items that discriminated good from poor athletes were identified from among the total item pool of 550 items. Booth (p. 136) concludes: "The MMPI has demonstrated merit as an instrument of measurement of personality traits of participants in programs of physical education and athletics." Booth's 22-item scale and the MMPI came under criticism by Rasch, Hunt, and Robertson (1960) when they failed to replicate Booth's findings using varsity wrestlers from the University of California at Los Angeles and the University of Oklahoma. Booth (1961) rebutted the contention of Rasch and associates by pointing to critical methodological and sampling differences between his work and theirs. Finally, Slusher (1964) showed that high school athletes and nonathletes respond quite differently to the MMPI. In his study, the two groups were different on all MMPI clinical scales except hypomania. Also, a difference was noted on the validity scale. The important thing here is that the MMPI did in fact differentiate clearly between the two groups.

Studies continued into the 1970s with a variety of athletes. Williams and Youssef (1972), in looking at the relationship of personality variables to personality stereotypes based on position played, administered the MMPI to 251 football players from four different colleges in Michigan. No differences were found across thirteen positions that the authors used to categorize football players. In a series of studies of gifted athletes, William Morgan and various associates demonstrated the efficacy of a trait approach to personality assessment in athletics, and one of the tests used was the MMPI. Beginning with a study of collegiate wrestlers over a five-year period, Morgan (1968) found that successful wrestlers (those who entered as freshmen and went on to win two or three letters) demonstrated superior adjustment when compared with their less successful peers (freshmen going on to win one or no letters). Morgan and Johnson (1978), in a similar vein, followed up on fifty college

Psychological testing in sports focuses extensively on personal variables. Studies of Olympic wrestlers, for example, show that successful participants are lower in anger, tension, depression, and fatigue than their less successful counterparts.

oarsmen after four years of competition and found, again, that the successful competitors (two or three varsity letters) had a more favorable MMPI profile than the less successful oarsmen (one or no letters). All eight clinical subscales yielded a more desirable profile for the successful oarsmen.

A rather interesting comparison was made by Johnsgard, Ogilvie, and Merritt (1975) in their study of elite sports parachutists, race drivers, and football players. In order to be a part of the research, all parachutists (N = 43) must have made at least one thousand free fall jumps; the race drivers were considered to be the top thirty participants in the world at that time; the football players (N = 50) were all professionals with five or more years of experience and at least one selection as an All-Pro performer. MMPI differ-

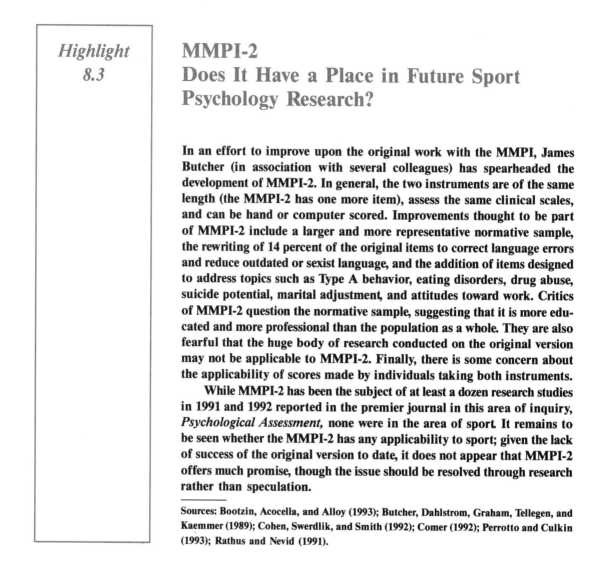

*Highlight
8.3*

MMPI-2
Does It Have a Place in Future Sport Psychology Research?

In an effort to improve upon the original work with the MMPI, James Butcher (in association with several colleagues) has spearheaded the development of MMPI-2. In general, the two instruments are of the same length (the MMPI-2 has one more item), assess the same clinical scales, and can be hand or computer scored. Improvements thought to be part of MMPI-2 include a larger and more representative normative sample, the rewriting of 14 percent of the original items to correct language errors and reduce outdated or sexist language, and the addition of items designed to address topics such as Type A behavior, eating disorders, drug abuse, suicide potential, marital adjustment, and attitudes toward work. Critics of MMPI-2 question the normative sample, suggesting that it is more educated and more professional than the population as a whole. They are also fearful that the huge body of research conducted on the original version may not be applicable to MMPI-2. Finally, there is some concern about the applicability of scores made by individuals taking both instruments.

While MMPI-2 has been the subject of at least a dozen research studies in 1991 and 1992 reported in the premier journal in this area of inquiry, *Psychological Assessment,* none were in the area of sport. It remains to be seen whether the MMPI-2 has any applicability to sport; given the lack of success of the original version to date, it does not appear that MMPI-2 offers much promise, though the issue should be resolved through research rather than speculation.

Sources: Bootzin, Acocella, and Alloy (1993); Butcher, Dahlstrom, Graham, Tellegen, and Kaemmer (1989); Cohen, Swerdlik, and Smith (1992); Comer (1992); Perrotto and Culkin (1993); Rathus and Nevid (1991).

ences among the three groups were relatively small. According to Johnsgard and his associates, there were no differences between parachutists and race drivers on any of the scales. Football players did score significantly higher on the psychasthenia (Pt) scale than either of the other two groups suggesting, along with the hypochondriasis (Hs) differences between them and parachutists, that football players are more concerned with physical health and body functions. The difference between football players and race drivers on the psychopathic deviate (Pd) scale is interesting, suggesting authority concerns among footballers. Finally, the paranoia (Pa) difference between football players and parachutists may be suggestive of greater social awareness on the part of the first group. More recently, Geron, Furst, and Rotstein (1986) administered the MMPI to 273 male athletes and 379 male nonathletes. In general, the utility of the MMPI in discriminating among various groups of athletes was upheld by the Geron et al. research.

All in all, the MMPI has an interesting history within sport research. Though it has had its moments, there is no ground swell of movement at this time to suggest that it is *the* instrument for sport research. The broad issue of validity, the usefulness of nonsport normed tests for sport research, and the highly clinical nature of the instrument are all problematical.

Sixteen Personality Factor Questionnaire (16PF)

As opposed to the criterion-based approach found in the MMPI, the 16PF (Cattell, 1949)

represents an attempt to develop a personality test through the use of the sophisticated statistical technique known as factor analysis. Cattell began his work with nearly 18,000 adjectives found in the dictionary by Allport and Odbert (1936). By consistent refinement, Cattell arrived at 180 items that measure sixteen factors assumed to be descriptive of personality. These original factors are listed in table 8.3.

Though not as popular a research instrument overall as the MMPI, the 16PF has had many advocates and users in sport circles. An early study using the 16PF was conducted by Heusner (1952), who looked at the personality of forty-one Olympic athletes as part of his master's degree requirements at the University of Illinois. For an extensive review of subsequent studies through the next fifteen years, consult

Table 8.3
Sixteen Personality Factor Questionnaire (16PF) Traits

Trait	Low Score	High Score
Sociability	Reserved, detached	Outgoing, cooperative
Intelligence	Low in intelligence	Bright
Ego Strength	Changeable, less stable	Calm, stable, mature
Dominance	Obedient, easily led	Assertive, aggressive
Cheerfulness	Sober, taciturn	Enthusiastic, cheery
Superego	Disregards rules	Conscientious
Adventurousness	Sensitive to threat	Daring, venturesome
Mindedness	Tender-minded	Tough, self-reliant
Suspiciousness	Suspicious, untrusting	Trusting, accepting
Imaginative	Practical, conventional	Imaginative, bohemian
Shrewdness	Naive, socially clumsy	Astute, polished
Security	Timid, guilt-prone	Secure, self-assured
Radicalness	Conservative	Experimenting, liberal
Self-sufficiency	Follower, joiner	Leader, resourceful
Control	Undisciplined	Controlled
Tension	Tense, frustrated	Composed, tranquil

Hardman (1973), who amassed the results of forty-two studies through 1969 involving sports such as cross country, swimming, gymnastics, climbing, tennis, riflery, golf, judo, wrestling, karate, association football, rugby football, American football, and basketball. Hardman found a great deal of variability in the results of these works.

Interest in the 16PF continued unabated into the 1970s. For example, Williams, Hoepner, Moody, and Ogilvie (1970) studied thirty national-level female fencers using the 16PF. In general, the subjects could be described, when compared with national collegiate norms, as intelligent, experimenting, self-sufficient, independent, and creative. Straub and Davis (1971), in a study of football athletes playing at four different levels of competition (Ivy League, small private school, small state-supported college, Big Ten university), found considerable differences within their samples. These investigators concluded that football players involved in major college football are very different from those taking part in football at a lower level. In a somewhat similar vein, Rushall (1972) studied the 1966, 1967, and 1968 football teams at Indiana University using the 16PF. Rushall isolated few differences among the squads from those three years even though performance varied considerably over time (1966 team was 1–8–1, 1967 team 9–1, and 1968 team 6–4). In a separate study reported in the same article, Rushall administered the 16PF to five college and six high school football squads. Upon analysis, he again found few personality differences and concluded that no football player personality exists. A third study, again included in the same 1972 report, generally supported Rushall's previous conclusions.

Studies from the mid-1970s include King and Chi (1974) and Foster (1977). In general, King and Chi found track athletes to be most similar to nonathletes, football players to be least similar to nonathletes, with swimmers and basketball players generally falling in between the extremes. Foster studied athletes from four sports — football, baseball, basketball, and track. His six-part groupings of athletes (successful-unsuccessful athletes, outstanding-other, successful-unsuccessful football, successful-unsuccessful baseball, successful-unsuccessful basketball, and successful-unsuccessful track) yielded few significant differences on the 16PF. Factor F, surgency, and Factor H, adventurousness, differentiated between the two football groups, and Factor G, imaginativeness, separated the two track groups.

As testimony to the continuing popularity of the 16PF, a spate of studies from the late 1970s are available. In a study of outstanding Indian table tennis and badminton players, Bhushan and Agarwal (1978) found considerable differences between outstanding international competitors and low achieving participants; also, they found substantial differences between outstanding male and female participants. In a study of physical education majors and nonmajors, Gruber and Perkins (1978) concluded that the 16PF was not effective in discriminating among various categories that they had created. In a 1979 report, Renfrow and Bolton (1979a) compared 16PF responses of twenty-three adult male exercisers with an equal number of nonexercisers. Differences were found on six primary and four secondary factors. The exercisers were found to be more reserved, expedient, suspicious, forthright, liberal, and self-sufficient on the primary traits and more alert, more independent, less discreet, and showed lower superego strength on the secondary patterns. In a related study, the same authors (1979b) report data in which they compared twenty-seven adult female joggers with twenty-five female nonexercisers. In contrast to their study of males, only two primary factors and one secondary dimension achieved statistical significance. The authors defend these differences with the arguable point that "there appears to be a substantial divergence between males and females in the motivational factors that lead to the adoption of an aerobic jogging program" (p. 507).

Use of the 16PF as a research tool continued in the 1980s. For example, Williams and Parkin (1980) studied eighty-five male field hockey players in New Zealand and found the 16PF to be useful in discriminating among three groups of varying ability and experience. In India, Pestonjee, Singh, Singh, and Singh (1981) compared male and female athletes with nonathletes and found consistent personality differences. Also in India, Thakur and Ojha (1981) administered the 16PF to thirty table tennis, thirty badminton, and thirty football players, and found the footballers to be different from the other two groups, who were rather similar in personality. Finally, Evans and Quarterman (1983) compared successful black female basketball players (N = 20) with forty unsuccessful basketball players and an equal number of nonathletes. Evans and Quarterman found only two significant differences among all comparisons.

All things considered, the 16PF has been a most popular psychometric device for sport psychology researchers. However, the literature generates a picture of somewhat inconsistent results due to a multiplicity of reasons involving statistical treatments, widely varying athletic groups, cultural inconsistencies, interpretative error, and a host of more subtle problems. Also, critics of the 16PF point out that it is easily faked (Irvine and Gendreau, 1974; O'Dell, 1971; Winder, O'Dell, and Karson, 1975).

Though there appears to be little activity in the 1990s with regard to the 16PF, perhaps a resurgence of interest is in the offing. The publishers of the test have come out with a fifth edition, which incorporates the best features of the original and subsequent work while streamlining and updating the 185 items now in use (WPS 1995–96 catalog, 1995). The scales found on the most current version include: Warmth, Dominance, Social Boldness, Abstractedness, Tension, Openness to Change, Reasoning, Liveliness, Sensitivity, Privateness, Self-Reliance, Emotional Stability, Rule-Consciousness,

Vigilance, Apprehension, and Perfectionism. These sixteen scales can be subsumed under five global factors: Extraversion, Anxiety, Tough-Mindedness, Independence, and Self-Control. It may that this updated and streamlined version will bring sport psychology researchers back into the 16PF fold.

All things considered, the 16PF has had a good run in sport-related research and represents a success story for trait psychology in general.

Eysenck Personality Inventory (EPI)

The EPI, made up of fifty-seven yes-no items, emerged in 1963 as a product of many years of work by the Eysencks, and while similar in etiology to the 16PF, it is considerably more parsimonious. The EPI purports to measure only two personality dimensions, neuroticism and introversion-extroversion. As a validity check, a third scale made up of eight MMPI Lie items is included. To give the reader an idea of what might constitute a Lie item, the following examples are representative:

1. Have you ever been late for an appointment or work?
2. Do you sometimes gossip?
3. Do you sometimes talk about things you know nothing about?
4. Are all your habits good and desirable ones?

The transparency of these questions is obvious, but it much less so when they are embedded in the other items designed to measure neuroticism or extroversion. Scores of four or above on the eight Lie items are considered suspect on the EPI.

The EPI has not been as popular a research instrument as the MMPI or the 16PF, but sport researchers have made some use of it. Morgan's research with wrestlers at the 1966 World Tournament (Morgan, 1968) was perhaps the first usage of the EPI in athletics. Morgan found a significant corrlation (r = .50) between extroversion and success at that event. Though a correlation of .50 only accounts for 25 percent of the variance, Morgan (1980) asserts that the coupling of this data with other sources of psychological or physical data can make a significant contribution to the prediction of sport performance. Support for this finding is given by Brichin and Kochian (1970), who studied accomplished female athletes in Czechoslovakia. Brichin and Kochian found a significant difference between their accomplished athletes (N = 81) and eighty-six female performers of lesser interest and accomplishment on the extroversion dimension. Delk (1973) found a significant difference between forty-one experienced male skydivers and the norms reported in the manual on extroversion. Kirkcaldy (1980) found similar results in a study of German sportsmen. On the other hand, researchers such as Reid and Hay (1979) and Fuchs and Zaichkowsky (1983) failed to find this difference in their respective studies. Nevertheless, Eysenck, Nias, and Cox (1982) conclude that sportsmen and sportswomen, regardless of level of expertise, do tend to be characterized by an extroverted temperament. They do emphasize that the relationship is a tendency and not an incontrovertible fact. Eysenck and his associates also point to a tendency for athletes, particularly outstanding ones, to be low on the EPI neuroticism measure.

In summary, the EPI offers the measurement of two traits, extroversion and neuroticism, that are predictive of athletic participation and success in cases where the former is high and the latter is low. It is anticipated that the EPI has utility in psychological and sport research and application, but its use of late admittedly has been sparse.

STATE MEASURES USED IN SPORT PSYCHOLOGY

As opposed to enduring traits, there are other measures of a more transient or temporary nature. Foremost among them are the *State-Trait Anxiety Inventory (STAI)* (Spielberger, Gorsuch and Lushene, 1970) and the *Profile of Mood States (POMS)* (McNair, Lorr, and Droppleman, 1971).

State-Trait Anxiety Inventory (STAI)

Spielberger and his associates make a distinction between anxiety that is relatively enduring (trait) and that which is more a function of recent events (state). Spielberger et al. attempt to measure each dimension of anxiety through responses to brief statements, twenty for state and twenty for trait.

Attesting to the overall popularity of the STAI is the fact that it has been the subject of more than two thousand archival publications (Spielberger, 1983). Also, Spielberger, Gorsuch, Lushene, Vagg, and Jacobs (1983) report research on such diverse populations as the learning disabled, psychiatric patients, psychosomatic sufferers, coronary patients, and neurotics.

In the realm of sport, Klavora (1975) reported results from a study of high school football and basketball players. In response to competitive stress, all subjects showed significant increases in state anxiety. High trait subjects exhibited significantly higher elevations than did low trait competitors. The STAI also discriminated between practice and game conditions and, overall, lent support to Spielberger's theory. Sanderson and Ashton (1981), in a study of the top eighteen- to twenty-one-year-old badminton players in England (what they call "colts"), concluded that the efficacy of the STAI lies in individual as opposed to group applications. Other applications of the STAI to sport research that are generally supportive include Gemar and Bynum (1990) with university students in exercise classes; Griffiths, Steel and Vaccaro (1978, 1979, 1982) and Griffiths, Steel, Vaccaro, and Karpman (1981) with scuba divers; Powell and Verner (1982) with first time parachutists; Williams, Tonymon, and Andersen (1991) with recreational athletes; and research in the area of motor performance (Hall, 1980; Pemberton and Cox, 1981; Weinberg, 1979).

Profile of Mood States (POMS)

Another test that purports to measure transient states is the *Profile of Mood States (POMS)* (McNair, Lorr, and Droppleman, 1971). The POMS, made up of sixty-five words or phrases, measures six mood states: Tension-Anxiety, Depression-Dejection, Anger-Hostility, Vigor-Activity, Fatigue-Inertia, and Confusion-Bewilderment. By subtracting the Vigor-Activity score from the sum of the other five subscale totals, a Total Mood Disturbance (TMD) score can be computed. The authors of the test caution that the TMD score is highly tentative at this time, however.

The original intent of the POMS was to provide a tool for assessing mood states and mood changes in psychiatric outpatients, and its usefulness in that area has been demonstrated (McNair, Lorr, and Droppleman, 1971). Further testimony as to its utility is found in sport psychology.

William Morgan has been at the forefront in demonstrating the validity of the POMS in sport research. Morgan served as a consultant to the U.S. Olympic Committee in 1972 and 1976 and was able to test fifty-six contenders for positions on the Olympic wrestling team. From the results, he was able to differentiate successful from nonsuccessful team candidates; individuals who made the team were lower in tension, depression, anger, confusion, and fatigue and higher on vigor (Morgan, 1968, 1980). This configuration of scores represents the Iceberg Profile, discussed at length later. Further efforts by Morgan have shown that Olympic oarsmen and top marathoners have the same Iceberg configuration (Morgan, 1978; Morgan and Pollock, 1977).

Based on the success of Morgan and other researchers, a study of college football players

---

Short Forms of the POMS

Highlight 8.4

While the original POMS contains only sixty-five items, there are occasions in which an abbreviated form of the scale may be useful. Examples include the assessment of mood states in athletes nearing competition, people in pain who are candidates for pain reduction procedures, or those who for whatever reason are unwilling to undertake the longer version.

THE SHACHAM VERSION

The first attempt to abbreviate the POMS was made by Shacham (1983), who deleted anywhere from two to seven items for each of the subscales, thereby creating a thirty-seven-item POMS. The correlations between the original and shortened scales ranged from .951 on Tension-Anxiety to .979 on Fatigue-Inertia. Also, Shacham found that his subjects, terminal cancer patients, reduced the time needed to complete the POMS from fifteen to twenty minutes to three to seven minutes.

(Continued next page)

Highlight 8.4 (Continued)

Short Forms of the POMS

THE EDITS VERSION

The Educational and Industrial Testing Service (EDITS), the original and current publisher of the POMS, created its own shortened version of the instrument in 1990. Their abbreviated POMS consists of thirty items distributed equally across each of the six subscales. Preliminary data reported from EDITS indicates that the reliability coefficients range from .75 on Confusion-Bewilderment to .95 on Fatigue-Inertia.

Only one study assessing the psychometric properties of the EDITS scale has been conducted, by Fleming, Bourgeois, LeUnes, and Meyers (1992). Fleming et al. tested 665 subjects from a variety of sport and non-sport samples and report correlations between each POMS subscale and its abbreviated equivalent ranging from .901 on the Anger-Hostility subscale to .980 on the Fatigue-Inertia scale. Fleming et al. also report that the EDITS abbreviated version is less susceptible to social desirability effects than is the original POMS, a definite plus.

THE GROVE AND PRAPAVESSIS VERSION

Grove and Prapavessis (1992) adopted the basic format of Shacham in creating their shortened POMS; they modified Shacham's work to the extent that they dropped two items of the thirty-seven in that scale and added five new items aimed at assessing self-esteem. This modification resulted in a forty-item scale that was administered to forty-five netball players in Australia. Reliability coefficients for the subscales ranged from .664 on Depression-Dejection to .954 on Fatigue-Inertia. Some evidence of subscale validity was demonstrated through differences between winning and losing teams, all in the expected direction with the exception of fatigue.

These three scales suggest that abbreviated forms of the POMS could have utility in sport research with little or no decrement in psychometric soundness. In general, it seems to make sense from the standpoint of parsimony to use thirty-five or forty items if they will yield results that are as dependable as those garnered from a sixty-five-item version. It remains to be seen if such will be the case. Clearly, more research is needed.

Sources: Fleming, Bourgeois, LeUnes, and Meyers (1992); Grove and Prapavessis (1992); Revised Edition of the Manual for the POMS (1990); Shacham (1983).

was initiated to see if the POMS and the Iceberg Profile would hold up in exceptional university-level athletes (LeUnes and Nation, 1982). Sixty varsity football players at Texas A&M University were compared with sixty individuals from the same university who had lettered in football in high school, and sixty peers who had never won a high school letter in any sport. In general, support was lent to the POMS and Morgan's concept; the college athletes exhibited significantly less depression, fatigue, and confusion while scoring significantly lower on total mood disturbance. Additionally, the athletes had a significantly higher vigor score than the other two groups.

An interesting outgrowth of the LeUnes and Nation football study was isolated some five years after the original data were collected; these results were reported by LeUnes, Daiss, and Nation (1986). As most of you know, the regulations of the National Collegiate Athletic Association (NCAA) allow college athletes five years to complete their four years of eligibility. We returned to the original data base when the freshmen in our sample had completed their athletic eligibility. There were thirty-three freshmen in the sample; sixteen stayed with the program to the end of their eligibility ("stayers"), and seventeen dropped out at some point in the five-year span in question ("leavers"). Analysis of the data from the POMS and Levenson's locus of control scale discussed at length in chapter 5 was revealing. Using a statistical technique known as multiple discriminant analysis, we were able to accurately place 86.7 percent of the football players in the correct group; that is, stayer or leaver. In other words, the administration of two brief psychometric instruments, one a trait measure and the other a state one, prior to the *beginning* of the athletic careers of these players, allowed us to predict with considerable accuracy which of these athletes ultimately stayed with the program and which did not. If our research were to be replicated and substantiated, this informa-

tion could have important implications for the recruitment and retention of college athletes. In addition, the validity of the POMS as a research tool was again enhanced through this research.

Overall, the POMS has proven to be an effective state measure with considerable utility in sport research. Egeberg and LeUnes (1988), for instance, cite sixty-six publications between 1975 and 1990 encompassing twenty different sports in which the POMS has been used. Further testimony to the broader appeal of the POMS is found in a bibliography amassed by the publisher that has 1,994 citations (Updated POMS Bibliography, 1995).

SPORT-SPECIFIC TESTS

Global tests of personality that measure relatively stable traits may have problems of applicability to athletes due to the situational nature of sport performance (Carron, 1980). None of the commonly used test batteries in psychology discussed earlier (MMPI, EPI, 16PF, POMS, STAI) were standardized on or intended for use with athletes, and the results when these tests have been used in sport have been mixed. Because of this, a call has been put out for assessment devices that are developed with and for athletes, or what are known as sport-specific tests (e.g., Carron, 1980; Kroll, 1970; Nideffer, 1981).

Athletic Motivation Inventory (AMI)

Though the call for sport-specific assessment devices is relatively recent, Tutko, Lyon, and Ogilvie actually developed the first major sport-specific test in 1969, the *Athletic Motivation Inventory (AMI)*. The sport-specific nature of the AMI is accentuated by the test authors in the preliminary technical manual:

> The inventory assesses *only* athletic behavior and attitudes. Its use should be confined to

those directly involved in athletics, and its results should not be generalized to other areas of the athlete's life. (P. 3)

The initial AMI reference groups were professional athletes (4,003 males and 1,026 females), college athletes (10,286 males and 1,843 females), and high school athletes (23,305 males and 1,855 females). The AMI, 190 items long, is answered in a basic "true," "in between," "false" or "often," "sometimes," "never" format. Sample questions include such items as:

1. When I was young, I thought about breaking a sports record.
2. Sometimes I feel like I just don't give a damn about anybody.
3. I try to think about unexpected things that might come up during competition.
4. I rarely think that training rules inhibit my personal freedom.
5. Hustle is important, but it can't compensate for lack of talent.
6. One problem with athletics is that the individual athlete has so little to say in what happens.
7. I am sometimes hurt more by how the coach says things than by what he says.
8. If asked to follow a rigid off-season training schedule, I would stick to it religiously.
9. I need the encouragement of the coach.
10. I seldom stay after practice to work out.

The 190 items fall into three categories (Ogilvie, Tutko, and Lyon, 1973):

1. Desire to be successful in athletics
2. Ability to withstand the emotional stress of competition
3. Dedication to the coach and sport

Early reliability and validity data are presented by Lyon (1972). Lyon indicated that college athletes and nonathletes differed significantly on all subtests of the AMI. Fosdick (1972), in a study of twenty-six collegiate swimmers, found two significant correlations between the AMI and the 16PF; Factor E-Assertiveness and Leadership (.50) and Factor Q-Tense and Emotional Control (−.72). In research comparing starting athletes with substitutes, Hammer and Tutko (1974), Hightower (1973), Hirst (1972), and Stewart (1970) all found consistent differences between the two groups. In a similar vein, Ogilvie (1974) and Tombor (1970) both found differences among professional, college, and high school athletes. Morris (1975), in a study of highly skilled female field hockey players in Canada, found them to be significantly more aggressive, more seeking of the role of leadership, and mentally tougher than their counterparts not selected to represent their country in international play.

Despite this early burst of enthusiasm about the AMI, it had many critics and it lapsed into a long period of disuse. Ogilvie responded to a decade-long period in which few, if any, published papers on the AMI were generated by calling for its resurrection (Straub, 1986). Two recent papers have emerged in response to this call. Davis (1991) studied 649 ice hockey players who were eligible for the National Hockey League (NHL) draft. Hockey scouts were asked to generate a global estimate of the psychological strength of each of these competitors. Subsequent comparison of the AMI scores with the scout ratings of psychological strength revealed that 4 percent of the variance in scout ratings of these hockey players was accounted for by AMI scores, leading Davis to conclude that the AMI has limited utility in predicting on-ice hockey behaviors regarded by scouts as representing psychological strength. Davis' data do little to support the validity of the test, but the AMI remains the psychometric instrument of choice with the NHL.

A second study by Klonsky (1991) reports data from 135 male baseball and 129 female softball players in which high school coaches rated their athletes on a number of variables using an adaptation of the AMI. Though Klonsky's adaptation met with some success, little can actually be inferred concerning the utility of the AMI itself in view of the nature of this study other than to indicate that interest in the instrument still exists.

Sport Competition Anxiety Test (SCAT)

A more well-received sport-specific instrument is the *Sport Competition Anxiety Test* (SCAT) of Martens (Martens, 1977; Martens, Vealey, and Burton, 1990). Based on the more general work of Spielberger and his associates, the SCAT is an attempt to measure competitive A-Trait or what Rupnow and Ludwig (1981, p. 35) call "the tendency to perceive competitive situations as threatening and to respond to the situations with feelings of apprehension or tension." Martens would add to this definition the point that some degree of state anxiety would accompany the response to whatever threat was being confronted.

The Sport Competition Anxiety Test (SCAT) is frequently used in current research. A well-supported conclusion drawn from the SCAT is that individuals with high competitive anxiety, or A-trait, perceive greater threat in competitive situations than do low competitive A-trait participants. From analyzing this photograph of runners awaiting the start of their event, can you distinguish between the high and low competitive A-trait athletes?

Martens bases his SCAT on four factors:

1. An awareness that an interactive paradigm for studying personality is superior to trait or situational explanations
2. The recognition that situation-specific instruments are superior to general A-trait measures
3. The distinction between A-trait and A-state in the trait-state theory of anxiety
4. The desirability of developing a conceptual model for studying the social process of competition

The original work on the SCAT was begun by modifying items from the *Manifest Anxiety Scale* (Taylor, 1953), the *State-Trait Anxiety Inventory for Children* (Spielberger, 1973) and the *General Anxiety Scales* of Sarason, Davidson, Lighthall, Waite, and Ruebush (1960). After considerable refinement, which was guided by the *Standards for Educational and Psychological Tests and Manuals* of the American Psychological Association ("Standards," 1974), two forms of the instrument have emerged. One, for use with children from ten to fourteen years, is the SCAT-C, and the other is the adult form for fifteen years and up, the SCAT-A. Each is made up of fifteen brief statements that are answered "hardly ever," "sometimes," or "often." Items from the SCAT-A are represented in figure 8.3.

There has been no shortage of interest in the SCAT, and this is reflected in the frequency with which it is used in research. For example, Martens et al. (1990) report that the SCAT was cited 217 times between its original publication date and 1990; included in this figure are eighty-eight published papers and thirty-five doctoral dissertations. Martens and his associates have arrived at a number of what they feel are well-supported conclusions about the SCAT as a result of the preceding research:

1. Research does support the reliability and concurrent, predictive, and construct valid-

Figure 8.3: **Sport Competition Anxiety Test (SCAT) Items**

---

1. Competing against others is socially enjoyable.
2. Before I compete I feel uneasy.
3. Before I compete I worry about not performing well.
4. I am a good sportsman when I compete.
5. When I compete I worry about making mistakes.
6. Before I compete I am calm.
7. Setting a goal is important when competing.
8. Before I compete I get a queasy feeling in my stomach.
9. Just before competing I notice my heart beats faster than usual.
10. I like to compete in games that demand considerable physical energy.
11. Before I compete I feel relaxed.
12. Before I compete I am nervous.
13. Team sports are more exciting than individual sports.
14. I get nervous wanting to start the game.
15. Before I compete I usually get uptight.

Source: Martens (1977).

ity of the SCAT as a measure of competitive trait anxiety.
2. Gender differences on the SCAT have proven to be equivocal; regardless of sex, however, it appears that the feminine gender role is associated with higher levels of competitive A-trait and the masculine gender role is linked to lower competitive A-trait.
3. A-trait research looking at age differences is equivocal; there is a trend, however, toward younger athletes being lower than older ones in A-trait. In all likelihood, this difference is related to increasing pressure placed upon winning as a function of age.
4. High competitive A-trait individuals perceive greater threat in competitive situations than do low competitive A-trait participants.
5. Situational and interpersonal factors mediate the influence of competitive A-trait on perception of threat.

6. The SCAT is a significant predictor of competitive A-state.

7. The SCAT is a much better predictor of competitive A-state in athletes than are coaches. The same is generally true with A-trait, though the effects are mediated by coaching experience (older coaches are better predictors) and sex of athletes (competitive anxiety is easier to predict in female athletes).

8. The SCAT has been used in a variety of international settings as a research tool. Included are SCAT translations in France, Germany, Hungary, Japan, Russia, and Spain as well as English-speaking countries such as Canada, Great Britain, and Australia.

Additional research using the SCAT has been generally supportive; examples include an investigation of non-elite runners by Donzelli, Dugoni, and Johnson (1990) and another with rodeo athletes by Rainey, Amunategui, Agocs, and Larick (1992).

Competitive State Anxiety Inventory (CSAI)

A relative of the SCAT is another creation of Martens, the *Competitive State Anxiety Inventory (CSAI)* (Martens, 1977). As with the SCAT, the CSAI has been adapted from Spielberger's work in an effort to have a measure of state anxiety related specifically to sport.

Representative pieces of research with the CSAI include that of Gruber and Beauchamp (1979) and Martens, Burton, Rivkin, and Simon (1980). The first study concluded that the CSAI is most suitable for repeated assessment of athletes in competitive settings. Gruber and Beauchamp based their conclusion on results with twelve University of Kentucky female basketball players who were administered the CSAI on sixteen separate occasions. Gruber and Beauchamp found high internal consistency on the instrument, noted changes before and after competi-

tion, revealed that state anxiety was significantly reduced after wins but remained high after losses, and found differences in state anxiety among games varying in importance. In the second study, Martens et al. reported reliability coefficients ranging between .76 and .97 for both the adult and children's forms. Concurrent validity was established for the CSAI by correlating it with the *Activation-Deactivation Adjective Checklist (AD-ACL)* of Thayer (1967). Similarities were such that confidence in the CSAI was furthered.

Competitive State Anxiety Inventory – II (CSAI-II)

Unlike the CSAI, which is a unidimensional measure of state anxiety associated with competition, the *CSAI-II* (Martens, Burton, Vealey, Bump, and Smith, 1982; Martens, Vealey, and Burton, 1990) is a multidimensional scale that purports to assess somatic anxiety, cognitive anxiety, and state self-confidence. The CSAI-II is composed of twenty-seven items (three nine-item subscales) arranged on a four-point Likert scale, and these items are shown in Figure 8.4.

The CSAI-II has held up well under research scrutiny; for example, Burton (1988) reports strong support for the instrument in a study of two samples of swimmers at the national caliber and intercollegiate levels.

Similar support has been provided by Bird and Horn (1990) with high school softball players, by Jones, Swain, and Cale (1990, 1991) with elite intercollegiate distance runners and a sample of male university athletes from England and Wales, by Swain and Jones (1992) with collegiate track and field competitors, by Hammermeister and Burton (1995) with triathletes, and Maynard, Hemmings, and Warwick-Evans (1995) with semiprofessional soccer players. A Spanish version of the CSAI-II has been shown to have validity and reliability in a study conducted with Uruguayan soccer players, ages eighteen to fifty-one (Rodrigo, Lusiardo, and Pereira, 1990).

Figure 8.4: **Competitive State Anxiety Inventory (CSAI-II) Items**

The CSAI-II lists a number of statements that people have used to describe themselves. Subjects are asked to read each statement and then indicate how they feel at the moment. All responses are arranged on a four-point Likert scale ranging from "not at all" to "very much so." The list of items is given below.

1. I am concerned about this competition.
2. I feel nervous.
3. I feel at ease.
4. I have self-doubts.
5. I feel jittery.
6. I feel comfortable.
7. I am concerned that I may not do as well in this competition as I could.
8. My body feels tense.
9. I feel self-confident.
10. I am concerned about losing.
11. I feel tense in my stomach.
12. I feel secure.
13. I am concerned about choking under pressure.
14. My body feels relaxed.
15. I'm confident I can meet the challenge.
16. I'm concerned about performing poorly.
17. My heart is racing.
18. I'm confident about performing well.
19. I'm concerned about reaching my goal.
20. I feel my stomach sinking.
21. I feel mentally relaxed.
22. I'm concerned that others will be disappointed with my performance.
23. My hands are clammy.
24. I'm confident because I mentally picture myself reaching my goal.
25. I'm concerned that I won't be able to concentrate.
26. My body feels tight.
27. I'm confident of coming through under pressure.

Source: Martens, Burton, Vealey, Bump, and Smith (1990).

Test of Attentional and Interpersonal Style (TAIS)

Yet another test that has come to be sport-related is the *Test of Attentional and Interpersonal Style (TAIS)* (Nideffer, 1976). Nideffer's contention is that athletic performance is closely related to attentional style or focus and, once this is isolated, predicting athletic performance in a variety of situations becomes possible. Nideffer suggests that attention can be viewed in terms of both width and direction. Width, in turn, exists on a broad to narrow continuum; athletes with a broad focus will probably be quarterbacks, linebackers, or point guards, positions all requiring a wide perspective. Narrow focus, on the other hand, is required for driving a golf ball or hitting a baseball; here the athlete must be able to shut out distractions and focus narrowly on the task at hand. As for directionality,

Nideffer talks of internal and external focus. Internals are thought to be wrapped up in their own thought processes, such as world class distance runners (see Morgan, 1978). Externals, of course, would be more tuned in to forces outside themselves. Nideffer suggests that a balance between internality and externality is the optimum; flexibility is important in Nideffer's approach. A visual representation of Nideffer's model with examples from sport can be seen in figure 8.5.

The TAIS is a 144-item self-report that requires approximately twenty-five minutes to complete. It purports to measure the seventeen attentional and interpersonal factors described in table 8.4.

De Palma and Nideffer (1977) demonstrated the versatility of the TAIS in an early study of seventy-eight psychiatric patients who were compared with thirty control subjects. In general, the

Figure 8.5: Nideffer's Model of Attentional Focus

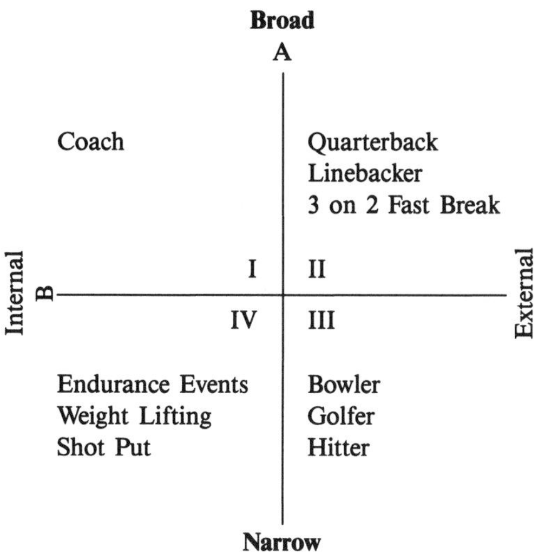

Broad

A

Coach	Quarterback Linebacker 3 on 2 Fast Break
I	II
IV	III
Endurance Events Weight Lifting Shot Put	Bowler Golfer Hitter

Internal ← B → External

Narrow

Source: Nideffer (1976).

TAIS was acquitted quite nicely. In the area of sport, Richards and Landers (1981), in testing 159 elite and subelite shooters of various types, found that the TAIS was capable of discriminating among a number of conditions involving types of shooters (pistol, rifle, trap, skeet), sex (male and female), and experience (experienced and inexperienced). Van Schoyck and Grasha (1981), in an interesting variant, devised a tennis-specific version of the TAIS, and they found the T-TAIS, as they called their instrument, to be more related to tennis performance than the parent TAIS. Van Schoyck and Grasha concluded that their test supported the notion that sport-specific instruments are superior for sport research to more general instruments (though the TAIS lies somewhere between the two points). In a similar vein, Albrecht and Feltz (1987) developed a baseball/softball batting version known as the B-TAIS. Like Van Schoyck and Grasha, Albrecht and Feltz found their more sport-specific variant of the TAIS to be more psychometrically sound. A

basketball-specific version of the TAIS has been generated by Bergandi, Shryock, and Titus (1990).

However, the TAIS is not without its critics. For example, Vallerand (1983) related the TAIS to decision-making processes. Using fifty-nine male basketball players as subjects (mean age 18.62 years) who were either junior college or university competitors, Vallerand asked judges to place them in three groups based on their ability to properly decide what to do on a decision-making task, in this case repeated three-on-two or two-on-one fast breaks. The players were placed in good, average, or poor decision-making groups. It was hypothesized that good decision makers, as compared to the other groups, would display a more positive scan factor (higher BET, BIT, INFP) and a more adequate focus factor (low OET, OIT, high NAR). Analysis of variance results showed no differences. A later analysis of good and poor decision makers using discriminant analysis also yielded no clear results. Vallerand believes that the TAIS may not be sensitive enough to pick up attentional differences in athletic situations, but does feel that a number of problems must be unraveled through research before the TAIS can be abandoned.

Vallerand's reservations are shared by Dewey, Brawley, and Allard (1989) and Summers and Ford (1990). Dewey and her colleagues have raised serious questions concerning both the predictive and factorial validity of the TAIS. These researchers related a visual detection task administered to undergraduate kinesiology majors to TAIS scores, and were not able to substantiate the overall validity of the instrument. Similar results were reported by Summers and Ford in their study of cricket, fencing, and basketball performers in Australia; they suggest that the utility of the TAIS as a measure of attentional style is questionable.

In an in-depth rejoinder, Nideffer (1990) points to methodological and interpretive errors that were made by his critics. Nideffer also cites

Table 8.4
Scales on the Test of Attentional and Interpersonal Style (TAIS)

Scale	Scale description
BET	*Broad External Attention:* High scores indicate good environmental awareness and assessment skills ("street sense")
OET	*Overloaded by External Information:* High scores are associated with errors because attention is inappropriately focused on irrelevant external stimuli
BIT	*Broad-Internal Attention:* High scores indicate good analytical planning skills
OIT	*Overloaded by Internal Information:* High scores are associated with errors due to distractions from irrelevant internal sources (e.g., thoughts and feelings)
NAR	*Narrow-Focused Attention:* High scores indicate the ability to remain task oriented, to avoid distractions, and to stay focused on a single job
RED	*Reduced Attention:* High scores are associated with errors due to a failure to shift attention from an external focus to an internal one, or vice-versa
INFP	*Information Processing:* High scores are associated with a desire for, and enjoyment of, a diversity of activity
BCON	*Behavior Control:* High scores are associated with an increased likelihood of "acting out" in impulsive ways and/or a tendency to establish one's own rules rather than strictly adhering to the rules of others
CON	*Interpersonal Control:* High scores are associated with both needing to be in control in interpersonal situations and with actually being in control
SES	*Self-Esteem:* High scores are associated with feelings of self-worth and self-confidence
P/O	*Physical Orientation:* High scores are associated with having been physically competitive and with the enjoyment of competitive activities
OBS	*Obsessive:* This scale reflects speed of decision making, worry, and anxiety; high scores are associated with increased worry and difficulty making decisions
EXT	*Extroversion:* High scores indicate an enjoyment of social involvements and a tendency to assume leadership in social situations
INT	*Introversion:* High scores indicate a need for personal space and privacy
IEX	*Intellectual Expression:* High scores indicate a willingness to express thoughts and ideas in front of others
NAE	*Negative Affect Expression:* High scores indicate a willingness to confront issues, to set limits on others, and to express anger
PAE	*Positive Affect Expression:* High scores indicate a willingness to express support and encouragement to others
DEP	*Depression:* A high score is associated with situational (transient) depression

Source: Nideffer (1990).

evidence gathered since 1983 from 1,799 athletes at the Australian Institute for Sport (AIS), that country's training site for elite athletes, as further testimony to the validity of his creation (Nideffer and Bond, 1989). In general, the TAIS differentiated among athletes by type of sport with that large and elite sample.

It is clear that the verdict as to the utility of the TAIS remains to be seen; future research will undoubtedly provide answers to this empirical question.

Nideffer (1986), of course, is sold on the utility of the TAIS, and has developed a set of training procedures based on his model known as attentional control training. These are shown in figure 8.6.

The utility of attentional control training has been demonstrated in a study by Ziegler (1994) with four collegiate soccer players. Subjects for the study were selected based on multiple criteria, one of which was a low score on Martens' (1989) test of attentional shift. Two of the subjects scored at the low end of the average range set by Martens, and the other two were below average. A series of attentional shift drills spaced over twenty-four sessions were used with the four players, and all players were able to significantly improve their attentional focus.

Other Sport-Specific Measures

A number of relatively recent sport-specific measures show promise in assessing various aspects of personality as they relate to performance.

Psychological Skills Inventory for Sports (PSIS)

An instrument with considerable face validity in the sporting context is the *Psychological Skills Inventory for Sports* (PSIS) (Mahoney, Gabriel, and Perkins, 1987). Originally composed of fifty-one true or false type items, the PSIS has undergone refinement and is now a forty-five

Figure 8.6: **Training Procedures for Attentional Control Training**

1. Athletes need to be able to engage in at least four different types of attention.

2. Different sport situations will make different attentional demands on an athlete. Accordingly, it is incumbent upon the athlete to be able to shift to different types of concentration to match changing attentional demands.

3. Under optimal conditions, the average person can meet the attentional demands of most sport situations.

4. There are individual differences in attentional abilities. Some of the differences are learned, some are biological, and some are genetic. Thus different athletes have different attentional strengths and weaknesses.

5. As physiological arousal begins to increase beyond an athlete's own optimal level, there is an initial tendency for the athlete to rely too heavily on the most highly developed attentional ability.

6. The phenomenon of "choking," of having performance progressively deteriorate, occurs as physiological arousal continues to increase to the point of causing an involuntary narrowing of an athlete's concentration and to the point of causing attention to become more internally focused.

7. Alterations in physiological arousal affect concentration. Thus, the systematic manipulation of physiological arousal is one way of gaining some control over concentration.

8. Alterations in the focus of attention will affect physiological arousal. Thus, the systematic manipulation of concentration is one way to gain some control over arousal (e.g., muscle tension levels, heart rate, respiration rate).

Source: Nideffer (1990).

item test with a five-item Likert format ranging from strongly agree to strongly disagree (PSIS = R5) (Mahoney, 1989). The original psychometric work on the PSIS involved administering the scale to 126 elite athletes, 141 pre-elite athletes, 446 non-elite collegiate athletes, and 16 sport psychologists who were asked to respond as an elite athlete might. From this original data base came the PSIS and its six subscales of concentration, anxiety management, self-confidence, mental preparation, motivation, and team emphasis. PSIS R-5, in turn, also purports to measure these same aspects of performance. Measuring these six components of athletic performance in language that is pertinent to athletes hopefully will motivate them to respond in an honest, straightforward fashion.

In his 1989 study alluded to earlier, Mahoney introduced the PSIS R-5 in a study of competitive weightlifters. Mahoney cautiously endorses the PSIS R-5 based on data gathered from this sample. Others have not been quite so enthusiastic about the PSIS R-5; for example, Tammen, Murphy, and Jowdy (1990) conducted various psychometric analyses of the responses of nearly 1,000 athletes ranging from elite to recreational and concluded that the factor structure of the PSIS R-5 is suspect. They assert that the subscales are not measured very well by the instrument, that the possibility exists that there are actually subscale domains being tapped other than the six originally proposed by Mahoney. In a later study, Chartrand, Jowdy, and Danish (1992) report serious psychometric problems with the PSIS R-5, including poor internal consistency of the items and questionable factor structure involving the six subscales. It is the contention of Chartrand et al. that additional research be conducted before the PSIS R-5 is used for either research or applied purposes. The Chartrand et al. position is one that we also advocate; the face validity of the PSIS R-5 and its potential applicability to sport psychology practice and research constitute an eloquent plea for its continuance at this point in time.

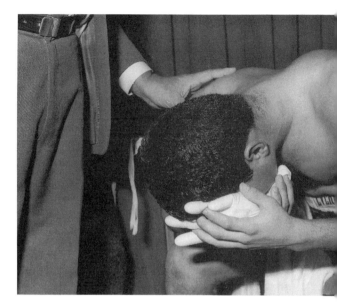

Which Coping Strategies from the Sports Inventory for Pain (SIP) might this boxer be employing?

Sports Inventory for Pain

Much has been made of the role of pain in everyday living, and none of us are immune to periodic bouts of it. Pioneering work in the area of pain has been conducted by Melzack (1975, 1987), who created the McGill Pain Questionnaire (MPQ). This instrument was designed to assess pain along a number of dimensions he labeled sensory-discriminative, affective-motivational, and cognitive-evaluative. Melzack's work has spawned much research in psychology and medicine, but precious little in sport psychology. Athletics and fitness are seldom pain-free, and there is a price attached to participation from time to time in terms of physical discomfort, which may range from mild strains to excruciating knee injuries. The popular press makes frequent reference to athletes who can play through pain, pain that other athletes could not tolerate. What, then, are the mechanisms at work in this situation that allow some to cope better than others? To arrive at a partial answer to this pertinent question, Meyers and his colleagues (Meyers, Bourgeois, Stewart, and LeUnes, 1992) created the Sports Inventory for Pain (SIP), a sport-specific attempt to unravel how different athletes respond *psychologically* when in pain. It seems reasonable to assume that if we can accurately assess these various coping strategies, we ought to be able to eventually move to the next level and assist athletes in the development of more effective coping strategies for dealing with pain.

Beginning with a number of items from general pain inventories such as the MPQ of Melzack, the Coping Strategies Questionnaire (CSQ) (Rosenstiel and Keefe, 1983), the Pain and Impairment Relationship Scale (PAIRS) (Riley, Ahern, and Follick, 1988), and the Controlled Repression-Sensitization Scale (CRS) (Handal, 1973), the SIP was administered over time and at various phases in the research design to injured athletes and college students with athletic backgrounds ranging from none to very extensive. The final SIP is composed of twenty-five items arranged in a five-point Likert format designed to assess which psychological strategy (coping, cognitive, avoidance, catastrophizing, body awareness) an athlete might choose in an effort to cope psychologically with pain (see figure 8.7). Preliminary psychometric analyses indicate satisfactory reliability, both in terms of test-retest and internal consistency measures, as well as promising predictive and factorial validity. Also, the SIP seems to be largely immune to the effects of social desirability as measured by the Marlowe-Crowne Social Desirability Scale (Crowne and Marlowe, 1964). As an aside, one of the more interesting preliminary findings from Meyers et al. is that males scored significantly higher (i.e.,

Figure 8.7: **Sports Inventory for Pain**

1. I see pain as a challenge and don't let it bother me.
2. I owe it to myself and those around me to compete even when my pain is bad.
3. When in pain, I tell myself it doesn't hurt.
4. When injured, I pray for the pain to stop.
5. If I feel pain during an athletic activity, it's probably a sign that I'm doing damage to my body.
6. I have little or no trouble with my muscles twitching or jumping.
7. At this point, I am more interested in returning to athletic competition than in trying to stop this pain.
8. When in pain, I imagine that the pain is outside of my body.
9. My pain is terrible and I feel it's never going to get better.
10. I could perform as well as ever if my pain would go away.
11. I do not worry about being injured.
12. Pain is just a part of competition.
13. When hurt, I play mental games with myself to keep my mind off the pain.
14. When in pain, I worry all the time about whether it will end.
15. I have to be careful not to make my pain worse.
16. I seldom or never have dizzy spells or headaches.
17. When I am hurt, I just go on as if nothing happened.
18. When in pain, I replay in my mind pleasant athletic experiences from my past.
19. If in pain, I often feel I can't stand it anymore.
20. The worst thing that could happen to me is to injure/reinjure myself.
21. I seldom notice minor injuries.
22. When injured, I tell myself to be tough and carry on despite the pain.
23. When hurt, I do anything to get my mind off the pain.
24. When hurt, I tell myself I can't let the pain stand in the way of what I want to do.
25. No matter how bad pain gets, I know I can handle it.

Source: Meyers, Bourgeois, Stewart, and LeUnes (1992).

One-Item Rating Scale

How much do you like jogging for exercise?

not at all ___ ___ ___ ___ ___ ___ ___ very much
　　　　　(1)　(2)　(3)　(4)　(5)　(6)　(7)

Thurstone Scale

(The scale values in parentheses are contrived for this example.)

Check the statements with which you agree.

_____ 1. Jogging is the best way to start a day. (10.7)

_____ 2. Jogging helps a person stay fit and healthy. (7.3)

_____ 3. Jogging is unnecessary and a waste of time for most people. (3.4)

_____ 4. Jogging is distasteful and unpleasant. (2.3)

Likert Scale

For each statement, check the extent to which you agree.

1. Jogging is a good activity for most people.

_____ strongly agree (+2)

_____ moderately agree (+1)

_____ neutral (0)

_____ moderately disagree (−1)

_____ strongly disagree (−2)

2. Jogging is boring.

_____ strongly agree (−2)

_____ moderately agree (−1)

_____ neutral (0)

_____ moderately disagree (+1)

_____ strongly disagree (+2)

Semantic Differential Scale

Rate how you feel about jogging for exercise on each of the scales below:

foolish ___ ___ ___ ___ ___ ___ ___ wise
　　　　(−3) (−2) (−1) (0) (+1) (+2) (+3)

good ___ ___ ___ ___ ___ ___ ___ bad
　　　(+3) (+2) (+1) (0) (−1) (−2) (−3)

beneficial ___ ___ ___ ___ ___ ___ ___ harmful
　　　　　(+3) (+2) (+1) (0) (−1) (−2) (−3)

unpleasant ___ ___ ___ ___ ___ ___ ___ pleasant
　　　　　(−3) (−2) (−1) (0) (+1) (+2) (+3)

valuable ___ ___ ___ ___ ___ ___ ___ worthless
　　　　(+3) (+2) (+1) (0) (−1) (−2) (−3)

Source: Gill (1986).

---

more desirably) on coping and cognitive strategies for dealing with pain, while females scored significantly higher on the catastrophizing scale. Of course, whether or not female athletes are more prone than males to engage in catastrophizing when in pain should be studied further. Certainly, the present finding is most preliminary.

All things considered, it is believed that the Meyers et al. work will result in more research into a fascinating and relatively untapped area in sport psychology, that of dealing with pain from a psychological perspective.

ATTITUDE MEASUREMENT IN SPORT

In addition to personality assessment, there has been a fair amount of interest in measuring various attitudes in sport. Some of the more prominent examples include the Attitudes Toward Physical Activity Scale (ATPA) (Kenyon, 1968) and the Physical Estimation and Attraction Scales (PEAS) (Sonstroem, 1978).

A major conceptual framework for looking at attitudes has been proposed by Triandis (1971), who believes that attitudes can be viewed as having three dimensions, *cognitive, affective,* and *behavioral.* The cognitive dimension deals with beliefs, the affective with feelings, and the behavioral with intended behavior toward the attitude object. Though not without its critics, the Triandis conceptualization serves to illustrate the multidimensional nature of attitudes. Attitude measurement in sport psychology has taken three paths, drawn from the works of Thurstone (1928), Likert (1932), and Osgood, Suci, and Tannenbaum (1957). A sport-related summary of these assessment procedures may be seen in figure 8.8.

Thurstone Scaling

In Thurstone scaling, ratings provided by judges are at the heart of the procedure. Initially, the judges are provided with a large pool of items about an issue from which the ultimate scale will be forged. Once the pool of items is shrunk through these judgments, the remaining statements are assigned numerical weights that are reflective of various attitudinal dispositions along a continuum from favorable to unfavorable. It is hoped that the numerical weights assigned to each of the possible responses will be reasonably equally distributed along the favorable-unfavorable continuum. In general, the Thurstone ✓ procedure is cumbersome to carry out.

Likert Scales

In response to the difficulties associated with the Thurstone method, Likert (1932) created a somewhat similar but simpler procedure that bears his name. In the Likert scheme, judges are not necessary and the determination of scale item values is not made. Basically, subjects are asked to respond to a pool of items along a five-point scale, and those that discriminate most effectively between subjects scoring high or low are retained as the final Likert Scale.

Semantic Differential Scales

Osgood and his associates (1957) have developed a most popular technique in the Semantic Differential Scale. The ATPA of Kenyon, mentioned earlier, is a prominent scale in sport based on the semantic differential method. Subjects in this procedure are asked to respond to a series of bipolar adjectives on a five- or seven-point scale. To Osgood et al., attitudes have evaluative (good-bad), potency (strong-weak), and activity (active-passive) components. In practice, only the evaluative component is used in much of the existing attitude research.

Despite the sophisticated nature of the attitude measurement techniques, their popularity of late has been greater in the larger area of psychology than with sport psychology. In view of

the multitude of attitudinal issues surrounding the sport realm, we should see greater use of Thurstone's, Likert's, and Osgood's procedures in the future.

SUMMARY

1. The study of the relationship between personality and sport performance has generated much interest within sport psychology.
2. Personality is composed of core traits and peripheral states (what Hollander further breaks down into typical responses and role-related behaviors). Constantly exerting pressure on each of these facets of the personality is the social environment.
3. A number of competing theories attempt to explain human behavior.
4. Biological theories include the somatotype theory of Sheldon, who classifies people according to body type and temperament, and the psychobiological model of Dishman, which is used to account for exercise adherence.
5. The psychodynamic or psychoanalytic model of Sigmund Freud represents a detailed though pessimistic model for explaining human behavior. An emphasis on intrapsychic conflict, inherent badness, and determined behavior permeates the Freudian model.
6. Counter to the psychoanalytic approach is the humanistic model most closely identified with Carl Rogers and Abraham Maslow. Key concepts in the humanistic model include inherent goodness of the organism and freedom of choice. The fully functioning person of Rogers and the self-actualized individual of Maslow are key conceptualizations used to account for superior adjustment.
7. The behavioral model suggests that the goodness/badness issue is best left to the philosopher; however, behaviorists are some-

what in consonance with the analysts on the determined nature of behavior though they would suggest a very different explanation for how behavior becomes entrenched. The behavioral approach has been warmly embraced by sport psychologists due to its utility in improving sport performance.

8. Trait theory has been popular in sport psychology because many researchers have felt

that sport performance can be explained by trait dispositions. The model has spawned much research and controversy.

9. The interactional perspective that posits that behavior is a function of both personality and the environment is increasingly popular within sport psychology.

10. Limitations in applying the results of sport personology research have centered around

---

Highlight 8.5

Test Information Sources

Though testing is a dynamic and ever-changing area, the inquisitive user can consult a number of resources with a considerable degree of confidence. Foremost among them is the series of *Mental Measurement Yearbooks (MMY)*, a compendium of information compiled by Buros beginning in 1938 and continuing up to the most recent volume in 1992. Included in the MMY are such mundane things as price, forms, and age of persons for whom each test is intended, as well as expert reviews and a list of studies of each. The emphasis in the MMY is on commercially produced tests.

Another significant source of test information has been compiled by Robinson, Shaver, and Wrightsman (1991). The intent of their work is to provide a source of test information in the social sciences that is not only useful to psychologists but to sociologists and political scientists. Included in the Robinson et al. work are separate chapters on the measurement of self-esteem and related constructs, locus of control, alienation and anomie, authoritarianism and dogmatism, sociopolitical attitudes, values, general attitudes toward people, religious attitudes, and several scales of a methodological nature (e.g., social desirability).

A third significant source of information about tests is the individual test manual. Test usage, norms, relevant studies, reliability and validity data, and other information are included in any good test manual. Prospective users are strongly urged to make considerable use of this most useful source.

Many of the tests in these various sources are not relevant to sport. However, many are, and the test user in sport research and application would be wise to keep open access to as many of them as possible. As time goes by, an increasing number of global and sport-specific tests of demonstrated validity and reliability may find their way into these volumes.

Source: Robinson, Shaver, and Wrightsman (1991).

conceptual, methodological, and interpretive shortcomings.

11. Conceptual problems in sport research include the tendency to conduct too much atheoretical as opposed to theoretical investigation and the failure to properly and consistently define terms, such as the elite athlete.

12. Sampling inconsistencies, an over-reliance on univariate analysis at the expense of multivariate techniques, failure to control for response distortion, too little use of the interactional model, and the use of "one-shot" studies have all served as methodological limitations to sport research.

13. Interpretive problems include making faulty generalizations and inferring causation from correlational data.

14. Testing in the United States is big business, involving millions of people and billions of dollars.

15. Our history of testing is apparently traceable to China some 4,000 years ago. The two world wars served as potent forces in test development.

16. Definitions of what constitutes a test vary, but emphasis is placed on systematic, objective observations of behavior.

17. Reliability, validity, and norms are three critical components of a good psychological test. A test must measure what it is designed to measure, it must do it consistently, and it must be based on sound standardization procedures. There are three major types of validity: content, criterion, and construct. In addition, test instruments should possess face validity; that is, they should look like they measure what it is that they are meant to assess. Reliability can be established through test-retest, parallel forms, and internal consistency procedures. Norms are useful when they are pertinent to the sample being surveyed in a testing situation.

18. Honesty in responding to test situations is often assumed. However, there are a number of sources of error in testing having to do with response styles. Three of these sources of error include faking good, faking bad, and conservative response style.

19. Psychological tests in sport are generally used for two purposes: for selection and/or screening decisions and for program development. The sport psychologist should therefore be alert to a variety of concerns having to do with test selection, reporting of results, and ethics in general.

20. Tests of enduring traits have been an integral part of sport psychology research. Chief among them have been the *Minnesota Multiphasic Personality Inventory (MMPI)*, the *Sixteen Personality Factor Questionnaire (16PF)*, and the *Eysenck Personality Inventory (EPI)*.

21. Personality traits of a more temporary or transient nature also have a rich if recent heritage in sport psychology. Chief among these are the *State-Trait Anxiety Inventory (STAI)* of Spielberger and associates and the *Profile of Mood States (POMS)*.

22. A call has been made for a move away from enduring traits or broadly conceived tests of temporary states to assessment techniques that are sport-specific. The first of these was created in 1969 by Tutko, Lyon, and Ogilvie and was called the *Athletic Motivation Inventory (AMI)*. Subsequent efforts of this sort include the *Sport Competition Anxiety Test (SCAT)*, the *Competitive State Anxiety Inventory (CSAI)*, and the *CSAI-II*, all sport-related modifications by Martens of the work of Spielberger. A fourth effort of some acclaim is the *Test of Attentional and Interpersonal Style (TAIS)* of Nideffer. Also, a number of more recent sport-specific instruments offer promise to sport psychology.

23. Attitude measurement in sport has given rise to such instruments as Kenyon's Attitude Toward Physical Activity Scale (ATPA) and Sonstroem's Physical Estimation and Attraction Scales. According to Triandis, attitudes

have cognitive, affective, and behavioral components.

24. Thurstone scaling, Likert scaling, and the semantic differential technique of Osgood and associates represent three different methods for the assessment of attitudes.

SUGGESTED READINGS

Cronbach, L. J., & Meehl, P. E. (1955) Construct validity in psychological tests. *Psychological Bulletin, 52,* 281–302.

In the November 1992 edition of *Psychological Bulletin,* Robert J. Sternberg reports on the top ten most frequently cited articles over the past forty years of publication of that premier journal in the field of psychology. Frequency of citation was determined through counts made from the *Science Citation Index* and the *Social Sciences Citation Index,* two reputable sources for determining the impact of any particular article in science or the social sciences. The Cronbach and Meehl piece on construct validity of psychological tests was the second most frequently cited article in Sternberg's collection, amassing some nine hundred citations by other authors. Given that the two indexes mentioned above cite many but not all of the journals in science and the social sciences, it is clear that the 900 figure is an underestimate. It is also interesting to note that Cronbach's name appears on four of the top ten articles cited by Sternberg. The historical impact of this article is considerable, and its current utility of no lesser stature. The reader interested in psychometrics would be well-advised to seek out the Cronbach and Meehl article.

Eysenck, H. J., Nias, D. K. B., & Cox, D. N. (1982) Sport and personality. *Behavior Research and Therapy, 4,* 1–56.

Eysenck and his associates have taken an in-depth look at nearly three hundred studies related to sport personology. Topics discussed include measurement of personality in sport, antecedents of personality, the relationship of personality to sport, differences between athletes in various sports, the state-trait distinction, sexuality, exercise and personality, somatotype theory, and strategies for learning physical skills. An excellent summary of the article is provided on pages 47 to 49.

Jensen, M. P., & Karoly, P. (1991) Control beliefs, coping efforts, and adjustment to chronic pain. *Journal of Consulting and Clinical Psychology, 59,* 431–438.

Jensen and Karoly assessed various aspects of pain based on responses of 118 patients, average age of near fifty, who self-report of being in pain for an average of nearly eleven years; most suffered from lower back pain, headaches, or cervical pain. The battery of tests administered to this group included a pain coping scale, a depression scale, a measure of satisfaction with life, a health assessment questionnaire, and the Marlowe-Crowne Social Desirability Scale. In general, these researchers found that personal beliefs about management of pain and the coping strategies subjects used when in pain were positively related to the amount of physical activity they engaged in as well as their appraisal of their overall psychological well-being. In the latter case, three coping strategies—ignoring pain, using coping self-statements, and increasing activity when in pain—were predictors of psychological functioning. The authors of this paper also note that too few studies have taken into account magnitude of pain as a moderator variable, a fact they view as a glaring weakness in this important area of research.

Moreland, K. L., Eyde, L. D., Robertson, G. J., Primoff, E. S., & Most, R. B. (1995) Assessment of test user qualifications. *American Psychologist, 50,* 14–23.

In 1950, the American Psychological Association (APA) instituted guidelines for the ethical distribution of psychological tests. APA arrived at a three-level classification system based on the complexity of the test and the qualifications of the test administrator. Level A tests (e.g., educational achievement tests) could be administered by public school or business personnel, whereas Level C tests (projective tests of personality) would require that the user have credentials as a psychologist.

While the three-level system is no longer formally used, it serves today as a rule-of-thumb for guiding the ethical distribution of tests. The authors of this article suggest that the three-level system is antiquated and difficult to apply and have created what they believe to be a more workable system for governing test distribution. Essentially, the system combines assessing test user competencies, identifying factors related to potential misuse of tests, and characteristics of the tests themselves. The authors suggest that their system has relevance for future ethical selection, use, and distribution of psychological tests.

Osipow, A. C. (1990) *Directory of psychological tests in the sport and exercise sciences.* Morgantown, WV: Fitness Information Technology, Inc.

Osipow has compiled a thorough listing of over 175 tests that have been developed by various sport researchers that are specific to sport and exercise situations, and a brief description of each is provided. Areas covered by Osipow include achievement orientation, aggression, anxiety, attention, attitudes toward fitness and exercise, attitudes toward sport, attributions, body image, cognitive strategies, cohesion, confidence, imagery, leadership, life adjustment, locus of control, exercise motivation, sport motivation, sex roles, and two sets of miscellaneous tests. Also included is a code of ethics section on test usage. One of the real redeeming features of Osipow's work is the fact that virtually none of the tests he mentions are discussed anywhere else in this text, thereby providing the reader with a much more complete listing of possible tests he or she might employ in a sport or exercise context.

Pargman, D. (Ed.). (1993) *Psychological bases of sport injuries.* Morgantown, WV: Fitness Information Technology, Inc.

This edited collection is broken down into four major subareas: conceptual and practical approaches to sport injuries, psychological perspectives, counseling injured athletes, and counseling athletes with permanent disabilities. Within this four-fold framework, discussion centers around such topics as the prevention and treatment responsibilities of the athletic trainer, ethics,

injury assessment, malingering athletes, mental strategies used in treatment, and considerations when dealing with permanently injured or disabled competitors. All fifteen of the readings are written by sport psychologists and other mental health professionals with expertise in athletic injuries or by experienced athletic trainers. This reader has much to offer the person interested in psychological aspects of athletic injury.

Pope, K. S. (1992) Responsibilities in providing psychological test feedback to clients. *Psychological Assessment, 4,* 268–271.

This article is actually an introduction to an entire volume of *Psychological Assessment* devoted to test feedback. As such, the entire set of articles should be valuable in providing the latest on views by psychologists concerning test feedback. In any case, Pope sets the stage for longer discussions of such issues as assessment and feedback as a dynamic as opposed to a *pro forma* process, clarification of test feedback goals, the possibility of crisis intervention as a function of the testing procedure, informed consent and test results feedback, the language of reporting feedback, the acknowledgment of test (and test administrator) fallibility, the misuse of test results, the place of records and documentation in the feedback process, ensuring that the person being given feedback really understands what has been said, and a look at the future of testing. This article and series reveals state of the art perspectives from a variety of experts on psychological testing.

REFERENCES

Aiken, L. (1982) *Psychological testing and assessment.* Boston, MA: Allyn & Bacon.

Aiken, L. (1987) *Psychological testing and assessment* (2nd ed.) Boston, MA: Allyn & Bacon.

Albrecht, R. R., & Feltz, D. L. (1987) Generality and specificity of attention related to competitive anxiety and sport performance. *Journal of Sport Psychology, 9,* 231–248.

Allport, G. W. (1937) *Personality—A psychological interpretation.* New York: Holt and Company.

Allport, G. W., & Odbert, H. S. (1936) Trait names: A psycho-lexical study. *Psychological Monographs, 47*(211), 1–171.

Anastasi, A. (1988) *Psychological testing* (6th ed.). New York: Macmillan.

Bergandi, T. A., Shryock, M. G., & Titus, T. G. (1990) The basketball concentration survey: Preliminary development and validation. *The Sport Psychologist, 4,* 119–129.

Bhushan, S., & Agarwal, V. (1978) Personality characteristics of high and low achieving Indian sports persons. *International Journal of Sport Psychology, 9,* 191–198.

Bird, A. M., & Horn, M. E. (1990) Cognitive anxiety and mental errors in sport. *Journal of Sport and Exercise Psychology, 12,* 217–222.

Blaser, P., & Schilling, G. (1976) Personality tests in sport. *International Journal of Sport Psychology, 7,* 22–35.

Booth, E. (1958) Personality traits of athletes as measured by the MMPI. *Research Quarterly, 29,* 127–138.

Booth, E. (1961) Personality traits of athletes as measured by the MMPI: A rebuttal. *Research Quarterly, 32,* 421–423.

Bootzin, R. R., Acocella, J. R., & Alloy, L. B. (1993) *Abnormal psychology: Current perspectives* (6th ed.). New York: McGraw-Hill.

Brichin, M., & Kochian, M. (1970) Comparison of some personality traits of women participating and not participating in sports. *Ceskoslovenska Psychologie, 14,* 309–321.

Buros, O. K. (1986) *Ninth mental measurements yearbook.* Highland Park, NJ: Gryphon Press.

Burton, D. (1988) Do anxious swimmers swim slower? Reexamining the elusive anxiety-performance relationship. *Journal of Sport and Exercise Psychology, 10,* 45–61.

Butcher, J. N., Dahlstrom, W. G., Graham, J. R., Tellegen, A., & Kaemmer, B. (1989) *Minnesota Multiphasic Personality Inventory: MMPI-2.* Minneapolis: University of Minnesota Press.

Carron, A. V. (1980) *Social psychology of sport.* Ithaca, NY: Mouvement.

Cattell, R. B. (1949) Manual for the *Sixteen Personality Factor Questionnaire.* Champaign, IL: The Institute for Personality and Ability Testing.

Chartrand, J. M., Jowdy, D. P., & Danish, S. J. (1992) The Psychological Skills Inventory for Sports: Psychometric characteristics and applied implications. *Journal of Sport and Exercise Psychology, 14,* 405–413.

Cohen, R. J., Swerdlik, M. E., & Smith, D. L. (1992) *Psychological testing and assessment* (2d ed.). Mountain View, CA: Mayfield.

Comer, R. J. (1992) *Abnormal psychology.* New York: W. H. Freeman.

Costa, P. T., & McCrae, R. R. (1985) *The NEO Personality Inventory* Manual. Odessa, FL: Psychological Assessment Resources.

Costa, P. T., & McCrae, R. R. (1992) Normal personality assessment in clinical practice. *Psychological Assessment, 4,* 5–13.

Cox, R. H. (1985) *Sport psychology: Concepts and applications.* Dubuque, IA: Wm. C. Brown.

Cronbach, L. J. (1970) *Essentials of psychological testing* (3d ed.). New York: Harper and Row.

Crowne, D. P., & Marlowe, D. (1964) *The approval motive: Studies in evaluative independence.* New York: Wiley.

Davis, H. (1991) Criterion validity of the Athletic Motivation Inventory: Issues in professional sport. *Journal of Applied Sport Psychology, 3,* 176–182.

Delk, J. (1973) Some personality characteristics of skydivers. *Life Threatening Behavior, 3*(1), 51–57.

DePalma, D., & Nideffer, R. (1977) Relationships between the Test of Attentional and Interpersonal Style and psychiatric subclassification. *Journal of Personality Assessment, 41,* 622–631.

Dewey, D., Brawley, L. R., & Allard, F. (1989) Do the TAIS attentional-style scales predict how visual information is processed? *Journal of Sport and Exercise Psychology, 11,* 171–186.

Dishman, R. K. (1984) Motivation and exercise adherence. In J. M. Silva & R. S. Weinberg (Eds.), *Psychological foundations of sport* (pp. 420–434). Champaign, IL: Human Kinetics.

Donzelli, G. J., Dugoni, B. L., & Johnson, J. E. (1990) Competitive state and competitive trait anxiety differences in non-elite runners. *Journal of Sport Behavior, 13,* 255–266.

Egeberg, A., & LeUnes, A. (1988) Bibliography in the Profile of Mood States in Sport, 1975–1990. *Social and Behavioral Sciences Documents, 18*(2), 63–64.

Endler, N. S., & Hunt, J. McV. (1966) Source of behavioral variance as measured by the S-R

Inventory of Anxiousness. *Psychological Bulletin, 65,* 336–346.

Endler, N. S., Hunt, J. McV., & Rosenstein, A. J. (1962) An S-R Inventory of Anxiousness. *Psychological Monographs, 76,* (17, Whole No. 536).

Eron, L. (1987) The development of aggressive behavior from the perspective of a developing behaviorism. *American Psychologist, 42,* 435–442.

Evans, V., & Quarterman, J. (1983) Personality characteristics of successful and unsuccessful black female basketball players. *International Journal of Sport Psychology, 14,* 105–115.

Eysenck, H. J., & Eysenck, S. B. G. (1963) *The Eysenck Personality Inventory.* San Diego, CA: Educational and Industrial Testing Service.

Eysenck, H. J., Nias, D. K. B., & Cox, D. N. (1982) Sport and personality. *Behavior Research and Therapy, 4*(1), 1–56.

Feltz, D. L. (1988) Self-confidence and sports performance. In K. B. Pandolf (Ed.), *Exercise and sport sciences review, Volume 16.* New York: Macmillan.

Fisher, A. C. (1977) Sport personality assessment: Fact, fiction, and methodological re-examination. In R. E. Stadulis, C. O. Dotson, V. L. Katch, & J. Schick, (Eds.), *Research and practice in physical education* (pp. 188–204). Champaign, IL: Human Kinetics.

Fisher, A. C. (1984) New directions in sport personology research. In J. M. Silva & R. S. Weinberg (Eds.), *Psychological foundations of sport* (pp. 70–80). Champaign, IL: Human Kinetics.

Fisher, A. C., Horsfall, J. S., & Morris, H. H. (1977) Sport personality assessment: A methodological re-examination. *International Journal of Sport Psychology, 8,* 92–102.

Fleming, S. L., Bourgeois, A. E., LeUnes, A., & Meyers, M. C. (1992) A psychometric comparison of the full scale Profile of Mood States with other abbreviated POMS scales with selected athletic populations. Paper presented to the Association for the Advancement of Applied Sport Psychology, Colorado Springs, CO.

Fosdick, D. (1972) The relationship of the *Athletic Motivational Inventory* and the *16 Personality Factor Questionnaire* as measures of the personality characteristics of college varsity swimmers. Unpublished master's thesis, San Jose State University.

Foster, W. (1977) A discriminant analysis of selected personality variables among successful and unsuccessful male high school athletes. *International Journal of Sport Psychology, 8,* 119–127.

Fuchs, C., & Zaichkowsky, L. (1983) Psychological characteristics of male and female body-builders. *Journal of Sport Behavior, 6,* 136–145.

Gayton, W. F., & Nickless, C. J. (1987) An investigation of the validity of the Trait and State Sport-Confidence Inventories in predicting marathon performance. *Perceptual and Motor Skills, 65,* 481–482.

Gemar, J. A., & Bynum, R. F. (1990) The effect of weight training and jogging on trait anxiety. *Wellness perspectives: Research, theory and practice, 7,* 13–20.

Geron, E., Furst, D., & Rotstein, P. (1986) Personality of athletes participating in various sports. *International Journal of Sport Psychology, 17,* 120–135.

Gill, D. L. (1986) *Psychological dynamics of sport.* Champaign, IL: Human Kinetics.

Griffiths, T., Steel, D., & Vaccaro, P. (1978) Anxiety levels of beginning SCUBA students. *Perceptual and Motor Skills, 47,* 312–314.

Griffiths, T., Steel, D., & Vaccaro, P. (1979) Relationship between anxiety and performance in SCUBA diving. *Perceptual and Motor Skills, 48,* 1009–1010.

Griffiths, T., Steel, D., & Vaccaro, P. (1982) Anxiety of SCUBA divers: A multidimensional approach. *Perceptual and Motor Skills, 55,* 611–614.

Griffiths, T., Steel, D., Vaccaro, P., & Karpman, M. (1981) The effects of relaxation techniques on anxiety and underwater performance. *International Journal of Sport Psychology, 12,* 176–182.

Grove, J. R., & Prapavessis, H. (1992) Reliability and validity data for an abbreviated version of the Profile of Mood States. *International Journal of Sport Psychology, 23,* 93–109.

Gruber, J., & Beauchamp, D. (1979) Relevancy of the Competitive State Anxiety Inventory in a sport environment. *Research Quarterly, 50,* 207–214.

Gruber, J., & Perkins, S. (1978) Personality traits of women physical education majors and nonmajors at various levels of athletic competition. *International Journal of Sport Psychology, 9,* 40–52.

Guion, R. M. (1980) On trinitarian doctrines of validity. *Professional Psychology, 11,* 385–398.

Hale, R. (1987) Don't ban steroids; athletes need them. *USA Today,* Jan. 5, 10A.

Hall, E. (1980) Comparison of postperformance state anxiety of internals and externals following failure or success on a simple motor task. *Research Quarterly for Exercise and Sport, 51,* 306–314.

Hammer, W., & Tutko, T. (1974) Validation of the Athletic Motivation Inventory. *International Journal of Sport Psychology, 5,* 3–12.

Hammermeister, J., & Burton, D. (1995) Anxiety and the Ironman: Investigating the antecedents and consequences of endurance athletes' state anxiety. *The Sport Psychologist, 9,* 29–40.

Handal, P. J. (1973) Development of a social desirability and acquiescence Controlled Repression-Sensitization Scale and some preliminary validity data. *Journal of Clinical Psychology, 39,* 486–487.

Hardman, K. (1973) A dual approach to the study of personality and performance in sport. In H. T. Whiting, K. Hardman, L. B. Hendry, and M. G. Jones (Eds.), *Personality and performance in physical education and sport (pp. 77–122).* London: Henry Kimpton.

Hathaway, S., & McKinley, J. (1943) *MMPI Manual.* New York: Psychological Corporation.

Heusner, W. (1952) Personality traits of champion and former champion athletes. Unpublished master's thesis, University of Illinois.

Hightower, J. (1973) A comparison of competitive and recreational baseball players on motivation. Unpublished master's thesis, Louisiana State University.

Hirst, J. (1972) Differences in motivation between successful and unsuccessful high school basketball teams. Unpublished master's thesis, San Jose State University.

Hogan, R. (1989) Review of the NEO Personality Inventory. In J. C. Conoley and J. J. Kramer, eds, *The tenth mental measurements yearbook.* Lincoln, NE: Buros Institute of Mental Measurements.

Hollander, E. P. (1967) *Principles and methods of social psychology.* New York: Oxford University Press.

Irvine, M., & Gendreau, P. (1974) Detection of the fake "good" and "bad" response on the Sixteen Personality Factor Inventory in prisoners and college students. *Journal of Consulting and Clinical Psychology, 42,* 465–466.

Johnsgard, K., Ogilvie, B. C., & Merritt, K. (1975) The stress seekers: A psychological study of sports parachutists, racing drivers, and football players. *Journal of Sports Medicine, 15,* 158–169.

Jones, J. G., Swain, A., & Cale, A. (1990) Antecedents of multidimensional competitive state anxiety and self-confidence in elite intercollegiate middle-distance runners. *The Sport Psychologist, 4,* 107–118.

Jones, J. G., Swain, A., & Cale, A. (1991) Gender differences in precompetition temporal patterning and antecedents of anxiety and self-confidence. *Journal of Sport and Exercise Psychology, 13,* 1–15.

Kaplan, R., & Sacuzzo, D. (1989) *Psychological testing: Principles, applications, and issues.* (2nd ed.). Monterey, CA: Brooks/Cole.

Kenyon, G. (1968) Six scales for assessing attitudes toward physical activity. *Research Quarterly, 39,* 566–574.

King, J., & Chi, P. (1974) Personality and the athletic social structure: A case study. *Human Relations, 27,* 179–193.

Kirkcaldy, B. (1980) An analysis of the relationship between psychophysiological variables connected to human performance and the personality variables extraversion and neuroticism. *International Journal of Sport Psychology, 11,* 276–289.

Klavora, P. (1975) Application of the Spielberger trait-state theory and STAI in pre-competition anxiety research. Paper presented to the North American Society for the Psychology of Sport and Physical Activity, State College, Pennsylvania.

Klonsky, B. (1991) Leaders' characteristics in same-sex sport groups: A study of interscholastic baseball and softball teams. *Perceptual and Motor Skills, 92,* 943–946.

Kroll, W. (1970) Current strategies and problems in personality assessment of athletes. In L. Smith (Ed.), *Psychology of motor learning* (pp. 349–367). Chicago, IL: Athletic Institute.

Kroll, W. (1976) Reaction to Morgan's paper: Psychological consequences of vigorous physical activity and sport. In M. G. Scott, ed., *The academy papers* (pp. 30–35). Iowa City, IA: American Academy of Physical Education.

LaPlace, J. (1954) Personality and its relationship to success in professional baseball. *Research Quarterly, 25,* 313–319.

Lazarus, R. S., & Monat, A. (1979) *Personality* (3d ed.). Englewood Cliffs, NJ: Prentice-Hall.

LeUnes, A., Daiss, S., & Nation, J. R. (1986) Some psychological predictors of continuation in a collegiate football program. *Journal of Applied Research in Coaching and Athletics, 1,* 1986.

LeUnes, A., & Nation, J. R. (1982) Saturday's heroes: A psychological portrait of college football players. *Journal of Sport Behavior, 5,* 139–149.

Lewin, K. (1935) *A dynamic theory of personality.* New York: McGraw-Hill.

Likert, R. A. (1932) A technique for the measurement of attitudes. *Archives of Psychology, 140,* 1–55.

Lyon, L. (1972) A method for assessing personality characteristics in athletes: The *Athletic Motivational Inventory.* Unpublished master's thesis, San Jose State University.

Mahoney, M. J. (1989) Psychological predictors of elite and non-elite performance in weightlifting. *International Journal of Sport Psychology, 20,* 1–12.

Mahoney, M. J., Gabriel, T. J., & Perkins, T. S. (1987) Psychological skills and exceptional athletic performance. *The Sport Psychologist, 1,* 181–199.

Martens, R. (1975) The paradigmatic crisis in American sport personology. *Sportswissenschaft, 5,* 9–24.

Martens, R. (1977) *Sport Competition Anxiety Test.* Champaign, IL: Human Kinetics.

Martens, R. (1981) Sport personology. In G. R. F. Luschen & G. F. Sage (Eds.), *Handbook of social science of sport* (pp. 492–508). Champaign, IL: Stipes.

Martens, R., Burton, D., Rivkin, F., & Simon, J. (1980) Reliability and validity of the Competitive State Anxiety Inventory CSAI: A modification of Spielberger's state anxiety inventory. In C. H. Nadeau, W. R. Halliwell, K. M. Newell, and G. C. Roberts (Eds.), *Psychology of motor behavior and sport—1979* (pp. 91–99). Champaign, IL: Human Kinetics.

Martens, R., Burton, D., Vealey, R. S., Bump, L. A., & Smith, D. (1982) Cognitive and somatic dimensions of competitive anxiety. Paper presented to the North American Society for the Psychology of Sport and Physical Activity, University of Maryland, College Park.

Martens, R., Burton, D., Vealey, R. S., Bump, L. A., & Smith, D. E. (1990) Development and validation of the Competitive State Anxiety Inventory-2 (CSAI-2). In R. Martens, R. S. Vealey, & D. Burton, eds., *Competitive anxiety in sport* (pp. 117–123). Champaign, IL: Human Kinetics.

Martens, R., Vealey, R. S., & Burton, D. (1990) *Competitive anxiety in sport.* Champaign, IL: Human Kinetics.

Martin, J. J., & Gill, D. L. (1991) The relationship among competitive orientation, sport-confidence, self-efficacy, anxiety, and performance. *Journal of Sport and Exercise Psychology, 13,* 149–159.

Maynard, I. W., Hemmings, B., & Warwick-Evans, L. (1995) The effects of a somatic intervention strategy on competitive state anxiety and performance in semiprofessional soccer players. *The Sport Psychologist, 9,* 51–64.

McNair, D., Lorr, M., & Droppleman, L. (1971) *Profile of Mood States Manual.* San Diego: Educational and Industrial Testing Service.

Melzack, R. (1975) The McGill Pain Questionnaire: Major properties and scoring methods. *Pain, 1,* 277–299.

Melzack, R. (1987) The short-form McGill Pain Questionnaire. *Pain, 30,* 191–197.

Meyers, M. C., Bourgeois, A. E., Stewart, S., & LeUnes, A. (1992) Predicting pain response in athletes: Development and assessment of the Sport Inventory for Pain. *Journal of Sport and Exercise Psychology, 14,* 249–261.

Morgan, W. P. (1968) Personality characteristics of wrestlers participating in the world championships. *Journal of Sports Medicine, 8,* 212–216.

Morgan, W. P. (1978) The mind of the marathoner. *Psychology Today,* April, 38–49.

Morgan, W. P. (1980) Test of champions. *Psychology Today,* July, 92–108.

Morgan, W. P., & Johnson, R. (1978) Personality characteristics of successful and unsuccessful oarsmen. *International Journal of Sport Psychology, 9,* 119–133.

Morgan, W. P., & Pollock, M. (1977) Psychologic characterization of the elite distance runner. *Annals of the New York Academy of Sciences, 301,* 382–403.

Morris, L. D. (1975) A socio-psychological study of highly skilled women field hockey players. *International Journal of Sport Psychology, 6,* 134–147.

Mount, M. K., Barrick, M. R., & Strauss, J. P. (1994) Validity of the big five personality factors. *Journal of Applied Psychology, 79,* 272–280.

Nideffer, R. M. (1976a) *The inner athlete.* New York: Crowell.

Nideffer, R. M. (1976b) *Test of Attentional and Interpersonal Style. Journal of Personality and Social Psychology, 34,* 394–404.

Nideffer, R. M. (1981) *The ethics and practice of applied sport psychology.* Ithaca, NY: Mouvement.

Nideffer, R. M. (1986) Concentration and attention control training. In J. M. Williams (Ed.), *Applied sport psychology: Personal growth to peak experience* (pp. 257–269). Palo Alto, CA: Mayfield.

Nideffer, R. M. (1990) Use of the Test of Attentional and Interpersonal Style (TAIS) in sport. *The Sport Psychologist, 4,* 285–300.

Nideffer, R. M., & Bond, J. (1989) *Test of Attentional and Interpersonal Style—Cultural and sexual differences.* Banff, Canada: Proceedings of the XXI Banff International Conference on Psychology, Sport and Health Promotion.

O'Dell, J. (1971) Method for detecting random answers on personality questionnaires. *Journal of Applied Psychology, 55,* 380–383.

Ogilvie, B. C. (1974) Relationship of AMI traits to three levels of baseball competitors. Unpublished research paper, San Jose State University.

Ogilvie, B. C., & Tutko, T. A. (1966) *Problem athletes and how to handle them.* London: Pelham Books.

Ogilvie, B. C., Tutko, T. A., & Lyon, L. (1973) *The Motivational Inventory. Scholastic Coach, 43,* 130–134.

Osgood, C. D., Suci, G. J., & Tannenbaum, P. H. (1957) *The measurement of meaning.* Urbana, IL: University of Illinois Press.

Pemberton, C., & Cox, R. H. (1981) Consolidation theory and the effects of stress and anxiety on motor behavior. *International Journal of Sport Psychology, 12,* 131–139.

Perrotto, R. S., & Culkin, J. (1993) *Abnormal psychology.* New York: HarperCollins.

Pestonjee, D., Singh, R., Singh, A., & Singh, U. (1981) Personality and physical abilities: An empirical investigation. *International Journal of Sport Psychology, 12,* 39–51.

Powell, F., & Verner, J. (1982) Anxiety and performance in first time parachutists. *Journal of Sport Psychology, 4,* 184–188.

Rainey, D. W., Amunategui, F., Agocs, H., & Larick, J. (1992) Sensation seeking and competitive trait anxiety among college rodeo athletes. *Journal of Sport Behavior, 15,* 307–317.

Rasch, P. J., Hunt, M. B., & Robertson, P. G. (1960) The Booth Scale as a predictor of competitive behavior of college wrestlers. *Research Quarterly, 31,* 117.

Rathus, S. A., & Nevid, J. S. (1991) *Abnormal psychology.* Englewood Cliffs, NJ: Prentice Hall.

Reid, R., & Hay, D. (1979) Some behavioral characteristics of rugby and association footballers. *International Journal of Sport Psychology, 10,* 239–251.

Renfrow, N., & Bolton, B. (1979a) Personality characteristics associated with aerobic exercise in adult males. *Journal of Personality Assessment, 43,* 261–266.

Renfrow, N., & Bolton, B. (1979b) Personality characteristics associated with aerobic exercise in adult females. *Journal of Personality Assessment, 43,* 504–508.

Revised edition of the manual for the POMS. (1990) *EDITS Research and Developments.* San Diego, CA: Educational and Industrial Testing Service.

Richards, D., & Landers, D. M. (1980) Test of Attentional and Interpersonal Style scores of shooters. In G. C. Roberts & D. M. Landers (Eds.), *Psychology of motor behavior and sport—1980* (p. 94). Champaign, IL: Human Kinetics.

Riley, J. F., Ahern, D. K., & Follick, M. J. (1988) Chronic pain and functional impairment: Assessing beliefs about their relationships. *Archives of Physical Medicine and Rehabilitation, 69,* 579–582.

Robinson, J., Shaver, P., & Wrightsman, L. S. (1991) *Measures of personality and social psychological attitudes.* San Diego, CA: Academic Press.

Rodrigo, G., Lusiardo, M., & Pereira, G. (1990) Relationship between anxiety and performance in soccer players. *International Journal of Sport Psychology, 21,* 112–120.

Rosenstiel, A. K., & Keefe, F. J. (1983) The use of coping strategies in lower back pain patients: Relationship to patient characteristics and current adjustment. *Pain, 17,* 33–44.

Ruffer, W. A. (1975) Personality traits in athletes. *Physical Educator, 32,* 105–109.

Ruffer, W. A. (1976a) Personality traits in athletes. *Physical Educator, 33,* 50–55.

Ruffer, W. A. (1976b) Personality traits in athletes. *Physical Educator, 33,* 211–214.

Rupnow, A., & Ludwig, D. (1981) Psychometric note on the reliability of the Sport Competition Anxiety Test: Form C. *Research Quarterly for Exercise and Sport, 52,* 35–37.

Rushall, B. S. (1972) Three studies relating personality variables to football performance. *International Journal of Sport Psychology, 3,* 12–24.

Rushall, B. (1975) Alternative dependent variables for the study of behavior in sport. In D. M. Landers (Ed.), *Psychology of sport and motor behavior II* (pp. 49–59). College Park, PA: The Pennsylvania State University.

Ryan, E. D. (1968) Reaction to "sport and personality dynamics." In *Proceedings* (pp. 70–75). Minneapolis, MN: National College Physical Education Association for Men.

Sanderson, F., & Ashton, M. (1981) Analysis of anxiety levels before and after badminton competition. *International Journal of Sport Psychology, 12,* 23–28.

Sarason, I., Davidson, K. Lighthall, F., Waite, R., & Ruebush, B. (1960) *Anxiety in elementary school children.* New York: Wiley.

Shacham, S. (1983) A shortened version of the Profile of Mood States. *Journal of Personality Assessment, 47,* 305–306.

Sheldon, W. H. (1940) *The varieties of human physique.* New York: Harper.

Sheldon, W. H. (1942) *The varieties of human temperament.* New York: Harper.

Silva, J. M. (1984) Personality and sport performance: Controversy and challenge. In J. M. Silva & R. S. Weinberg (Eds.), *Psychological foundations of sport* (pp. 59–69). Champaign, IL: Human Kinetics.

Singer, R. N., Harris, D., Kroll, W., & Sechrest, L. J. (1977) Psychological testing of athletes. *Journal of Physical Education, 48,* 30–32.

Slusher, H. (1964) Personality and intelligence characteristics of selected high school athletes and nonathletes. *Research Quarterly, 35,* 539–545.

Sonstroem, R. J. (1978) Physical estimation and attraction scales: Rationale and research. *Medicine and Science in Sports, 10,* 97–102.

Spielberger, C. (1973) *State-Trait Anxiety Inventory for Children:* Preliminary manual. Palo Alto, CA: Consulting Psychologists Press.

Spielberger, C. (1983) *State-Trait Anxiety Inventory:* A comprehensive bibliography, Palo Alto, CA: Consulting Psychologists Press.

Spielberger, C., Gorsuch, R., & Lushene, R. (1970) Manual for the *State-Trait Anxiety Inventory.* Palo Alto, CA: Consulting Psychologists Press.

Spielberger, C., Gorsuch, R., Lushene, R., Vagg, P., & Jacobs, G. (1983) Manual for the *State-Trait Anxiety Inventory* (form Y). Palo Alto, CA: Consulting Psychologists Press.

Standards for educational and psychological tests and manuals. (1974) Washington, DC: American Psychological Association.

Stewart, L. (1970) A comparative study measuring the psychological makeup among groups of basketball players and coaches. Unpublished master's thesis, Western Washington State College.

Straub, W. F. (1986) Conversation with Bruce Ogilvie. *AAASP Newsletter 1*(2), 4–5.

Straub, W. F., & Davis, S. (1971) Personality traits of college football players who participated at different levels of competition. *Medicine and Science in Sports, 3,* 39–43.

Summers, J. J., & Ford, S. K. (1990) The Test of Attentional and Interpersonal Style: An evaluation. *International Journal of Sport Psychology, 21,* 102–111.

Swain, A., & Jones, G. (1992) Relationships between sport achievement orientation and competitive state anxiety. *The Sport Psychologist, 6,* 42–54.

Tammen, V. V., Murphy, S. M., & Jowdy, D. (1990) Reevaluating the Psychological Skills Inventory for Sports: Factor analysis and implications. Paper presented to North American Society for the Psychology of Sport and Physical Activity, Asilomar, CA.

Taylor, J. (1953) A personality scale of manifest anxiety. *Journal of Abnormal and Social Psychology, 48,* 285–290.

Thakur, G., & Ojha, M. (1981) Personality differences of Indian table-tennis, badminton, and football players on primary source traits of the 16PF. *International Journal of Sport Psychology, 12,* 196–203.

Thayer, R. E. (1967) Measurement of activation through self report. *Psychological Reports, 20,* 663–678.

Thurstone, L. L. (1928) Attitudes can be measured. *American Journal of Sociology, 33,* 529–554.

Tombor, F. (1970) Personality correlates of football and basketball performances. Unpublished master's thesis, San Jose University.

Triandis, H. C. (1971) *Attitude and attitude change.* New York: Wiley.

Tutko, T. A., Lyon, L. & Ogilvie, B. C. (1969) *Athletic Motivation Inventory.* San Jose, CA: Institute for the Study of Athletic Motivation.

Updated POMS bibliography now available. (1995) *EDITS Research and Developments,* Spring/Summer, 4.

Vallerand, R. (1983) Attention and decision-making: A test of the predictive validity of the Test of Attentional and Interpersonal Style in a sport setting. *Journal of Sport Psychology, 5,* 449–459.

Van Schoyck, R., & Grasha, A. (1981) Attentional style variations and athletic ability: The advantage of a sports-specific test. *Journal of Sport Psychology, 3,* 9–18.

Weinberg, R. S. (1979) Anxiety and motor performance: Drive theory vs. cognitive theory. *International Journal of Sport Psychology, 10,* 112–121.

Williams, J., Hoepner, B., Moody, D., & Ogilvie, B. C. (1970) Personality traits of champion level female fencers. *Research Quarterly, 41,* 446–453.

Williams, J. M., Tonymon, P., & Andersen, M. B. (1991) The effects of stressors and coping resources on anxiety and peripheral narrowing. *Journal of Applied Sport Psychology, 3,* 126–141.

Williams, L. R. T., & Parkin, W. A. (1980) Personality factor profiles of three hockey groups. *International Journal of Sport Psychology, 11,* 113–120.

Williams, R., & Youssef, Z. (1972) Consistency of football coaches in stereotyping the personality of each position's player. *International Journal of Sport Psychology, 3,* 3–11.

Winder, P., O'Dell, J., & Karson, S. (1975) New motivational distortion scales for the 16PF. *Journal of Personality Assessment, 39,* 532–537.

WPS 1995–1996 Catalog. (1995) Los Angeles, CA: Western Psychological Services.

Ziegler, S. G. (1994) The effects of attentional shift training on the execution of soccer skills: A preliminary investigation. *Journal of Applied Behavioral Analysis, 27,* 545–552.

Selected Athletic Populations

INTRODUCTION

As opposed to the broad focus on theory and measurement of personality entertained in the previous chapter, we will now look at four athletic groups in the hope of grasping a better understanding of their psychological makeup: the black athlete, the high risk sport participant, the athlete who performs at the elite level, and those athletes who choose to try to gain the competitive edge through the use of a variety of supposed performance-enhancing practices, including drugs. The degree to which scientists have investigated these diverse (and obviously overlapping) groups varies considerably, and much remains to be done in this area of inquiry in sport psychology. Nevertheless, an attempt will be made to summarize what we think we know at this time about these athletic groups.

THE BLACK ATHLETE

The overrepresentation of black athletes in many sports (e.g., football, basketball, track, boxing) has generated a great deal of interest on the part of professionals and laypersons alike. What factors seem to account for this seeming black dominance in some sports? Is it true that the black athlete is physically superior to the white competitor or are the answers to be found in sociocultural and/or psychological explanations? We will attempt to answer these and other questions in our treatment of this provocative area.

A Brief History

Blacks were first brought to the New World from Africa; the first contingent arrived in 1619 at the English colony of Jamestown, Virginia. Initially, they were brought not as slaves but as indentured servants who were theoretically free at the end of their agreed upon period of servitude. In practice, however, most were made slaves, initially on a more-or-less informal basis, and later, through legislation. This formal enslavement began in the mid-1600s and continued until the Emancipation Proclamation of 1862. The value of these people to the economy of the United States, and particularly states located in the South, was a significant force in the creation and maintenance of slavery.

An extensive literature review of recreation engaged in by blacks living on southern plantations prior to 1860 is provided by Wiggins (1977). The form and substance of the recreation varied greatly depending on the personality and philosophy of the individual plantation owners. Wrestling, boxing, footraces, cockfights, hunting, fishing, boat races, and dancing were all popular pastimes. Related to dancing and music was an activity described by Wiggins as *"patting juba,"* a rhythmic patting or clapping of the hands as a substitute for musical instruments when none were available. All in all, much of the sport and recreation of the pre-Civil War period was tied to the rural life and the work circumstances that prevailed.

After the Civil War, the black athlete began to emerge through the sports of baseball, horse racing, and boxing. Chu (1982) states that the first black to play professional baseball was John (Bud) Fowler, who played for New Castle, Pennsylvania, in 1872. Following the lead of Fowler was Moses Fleetwood Walker, who played for the Toledo (Ohio) Mudhens in 1883 and was the first black to play in the major leagues. Eitzen and Sage (1978) note that Fleetwood was joined by his brother, Weldy (also cited as Weldey) Wilberforce Walker, and together they were the first to play major league baseball. Rader (1983) indicates, by way of elaboration, that Moses preceded his brother Weldy by several months, with Weldy joining the team very late in the season. As one might suspect, the presence of the Walkers did not go unnoticed. Members of the Richmond, Virginia, team sent the following message to the Toledo, Ohio, manager prior to a game between the two teams:

We, the undersigned, do hereby warn you not to play Walker, the negro catcher, the evening that you play in Richmond, as we could mention the names of 75 determined men who have sworn to mob Walker if he comes on the grounds in a suit. We hope you will listen to our words of warning, so that there will be no trouble; but, if you do not, there certainly will be. We only write to prevent much bloodshed, as you alone can prevent. (Peterson, 1970, p. 23)

Peterson provides us with additional insight into the difficulties faced by black ballplayers with another quote from a white player in 1888:

While I myself am prejudiced against playing on a team with colored players, I still could not help pitying some of the poor black fellows that play in the International League. Fowler used to play second base with the lower part of his legs encased in wooden guards. He knew that every player that came down to second base on a steal would head for him and would, if possible, throw the spikes into him. . . . About half the pitchers try their best to hit these colored players when at bat. (p. 41)

Though these vignettes suggest that much remained to be done in race relations and sport, baseball stayed integrated, however troubled, until the 1890s, at which time it became totally segregated and remained so until 1945, when Jackie Robinson joined the Montreal Royales, a farm club of the parent Brooklyn Dodgers.

Curry and Jiobu (1984) indicate that perhaps twenty to thirty blacks formed an elite cadre of post–Civil War jockeys, with one of them riding in the first Kentucky Derby in 1876. Another, Willey Sims, eventually won both the Belmont Stakes and the Kentucky Derby. Another prominent name of the era was Pike Simms, a winner of the Futurity. Coakley (1982) cites a number of factors that led to the demise of the black jockey toward the end of the nine-

teenth century; among them were the discriminatory Jim Crow laws that supposedly guaranteed separate but equal rights or protections, a white jockeys' union, a racist press, and assignment to slower horses. Over a short period of time the black jockey found himself relegated to less prestigious positions such as trainer or stable boy. By 1900, the elite black jockey was a historical relic.

Boxing was, and remains, a somewhat different story. Beginning with Tom Molineaux in 1800, blacks have fared relatively well, at least when compared with other sports. Though blacks have been discriminated against, they have competed on a relatively continuous basis in boxing.

The controversial Jack Johnson won the heavyweight championship of the world in 1908 by defeating the white champion, Tom Burns. Refusing to fit into the white man's preselected mold for blacks, Johnson lived life in the fast lane. He had a penchant for flashy clothes and flashy women, had a succession of girlfriends, generally white, and married two different white women. These interracial relationships created many difficulties for Johnson, and he eventually fled the United States. Following Johnson as a great black boxer was the legendary Joe Louis, blessed with great ability and a more acceptable (to the white establishment) lifestyle. Louis has been succeeded by a series of black champions who have reigned for the better part of four decades.

With the integration of Jackie Robinson into the baseball major leagues in 1947, blacks became more and more a part of the athletic scene. Blacks were allowed in the National Basketball Association in 1950; Althea Gibson embarked on the professional tennis circuit in 1959; Bill Russell became the first black head coach in professional basketball in 1966; in 1968, professional baseball hired its first black major league umpire in Emmit Ashford; and Frank Robinson became the first black manager in the major leagues in 1975.

Despite the presence of figures such as baseball's Jackie Robinson and boxing's Joe Louis, it has only been recently that blacks have been proportionately overrepresented in a few professional sports.

According to Eitzen and Sage (1978), blacks represent 12 percent of the American population. Blacks reached that same figure in professional baseball in 1957, basketball in 1958, and football in 1960. Since that time, blacks have been proportionately overrepresented to the point that by 1992 they held 77 percent of the professional basketball positions, while their numbers in football and baseball were 68 percent and 16 percent respectively (Lapchick and Benedict, 1993).

The Success of Black Athletes

In trying to account for the increasing numerical superiority and performance dominance of blacks in the more visible sports, at least three possible explanations exist. They are *genetic, social/cultural,* and *psychological.* Each in turn will be examined.

Genetic or Other Biological Explanations

It has long been suggested that apparent black superiority in sport is due to genetic or other biological influences. Coakley (1982, p. 265) offers an excellent summary of these differences. They are generally as follows:

1. Compared to whites, blacks have longer legs and arms, shorter trunk, less body fat, more slender hips, more tendon and less muscle, a different heel structure, wider calf bones, more slender calf muscles, greater arm circumference, and more of the muscle fibers needed for speed and power and fewer of those needed for endurance.

2. Compared to whites, blacks mature more rapidly, their lung capacity is lower, they are more likely to have hyperextensibility (be "double jointed"), they dissipate heat more efficiently (they sweat more), they tend to become chilled more easily in cold weather, and they have superior rhythmic abilities.

As is pointed out by Coakley, as well as Chu (1982) and Leonard (1984), a number of problems are associated with these conclusions. First of all, most of what we have learned about black athletes has been gathered from studies, both controlled and anecdotal, of relatively superior athletes; seldom are blacks with average, limited, or no athletic ability taken into account. Second, what the designation *black* means scientifically is subject to interpretation. It is likely that a fair number of blacks have white ancestors, particularly in light of some of the practices that apparently transpired on the plantations of pre–Civil War America (and a number of people labeled as white undoubtedly have black ancestors). While the concept of black has relatively clear-cut political overtones, its scientific validity is suspect. As Coakley so saliently states: "The notion that 'a black is a black is a black' has created enough problems on the street without letting it guide scientific research in the laboratory" (p. 265).

A third problem has to do with the unexplained relevance of many of these supposed superiorities to sport performance. If the first proposition offered by Coakley were true, it would be most troublesome to explain how two prominent white sprinters of the late 1950s and early 1960s (and college teammates at Abilene Christian University in Abilene, Texas), Bobby Morrow and Bill Woodhouse, were world class caliber. Morrow was relatively tall and lean, almost leonine in grace. Woodhouse, perhaps aptly named, was short, stocky, and very powerful. How could these two diverse body types be so closely paired in terms of excellence? How could Curtis Dickey and Rod Richardson, both black sprinters at Texas A&M University during the late 1970s, have claimed so many indoor NCAA sprint titles between them, given their physical diversity? Dickey, at 6 feet, 2 inches and 215 pounds, and Richardson, at 5 feet, 8 inches and 150 pounds, had relatively little in common except skin color and speed. Carrying this reasoning a step beyond, how could Jimmy Howard, for years the American record holder in the high jump (white, 6 feet, 5½ inches, 175 pounds), and Franklin Jacobs (black, 5 feet, 8 inches, 150 pounds), have had so much in common as world class high jumpers? Interestingly, blacks are known as "leapers" and whites are thought to be afflicted with "white man's disease," and yet of the top ten high jumpers in the world in 1985, nine were white, and the other one was an oriental ("High Jump," 1985).

A fourth problem concerns generalizations made about all sports that are based on a select few. The disproportionate representation of blacks in football, basketball, track, and boxing obscures the fact that many sports are dominated by other groups of athletes. For instance, Japanese-Americans, who constitute less than 1 percent of our total population, comprise in excess of twenty percent of the top AAU judo

---

*Highlight
9.1*

Proportional Racial Representation Across Different Sports

Although considerable evidence supports the numerical and performance superiority of black athletes in several of the more visible sports, the picture is not so distorted if one takes the larger perspective. Snyder and Spreitzer (1989) have given us a schematic representation of black involvement across a number of types and levels of sports. However, in the past five to ten years there have been changing demographics with regard to black involvement in sports. The following figure is borrowed from the earlier Snyder and Spreitzer work, but is amended by data presented by Lapchick and Benedict (1993) and Yetman and Berghorn (1993).

Skewed groups are those in which black or white domination is at or near 100 percent; gymnastics and golf for whites and boxing and track sprints for blacks are representative. The ratio for tilted groups is about 65:35, with professional baseball loading in favor of whites and professional basketball for blacks. Interestingly, there is a subtle but continual trend over time showing these two sports potentially moving from tilted to skewed. Professional football is a good example of another sport on the move in terms of the present conceptualization; it has actually gone from balanced to tilted over the past decade. College basketball offers an interesting picture. According to data from 1985–1990 presented by Yetman and Berghorn, 47 percent of men's collegiate basketball teams are black (balanced) whereas the figure is 22 percent (tilted) for women's teams. In summary, the Snyder and Spreitzer formulation captures the essence of black domination of sport, which is quite situational. The visibility of certain sports such as football, basketball, boxing, and the sprints in track tends to give a distorted image of black domination of sport.

Sources: Lapchick and Benedict (1993); Snyder and Spreitzer (1989); Yetman and Berghorn (1993).

competitors (Phillips, 1976). No one has really come forth with a genetic explanation for this overrepresentation. As has been so beautifully stated by Robertson (1981, p. 91):

> Nobody proposes genetic factors, for example, to explain why East Germany has produced so many excellent swimmers, why Canadians do well at hockey, why Japanese Americans are disproportionately represented in judo—or, for that matter, why the British are hopeless at baseball, while white Americans are equally inept at cricket. In each case, it is easy to see cultural factors, not genetic ones, are at work.

Coakley (1994) carries this line of thought a step beyond by suggesting that the Swiss, with a population one-thirtieth the size of that of the United States, have won ten times as many World Cup Championships in skiing and therefore should undergo screening for a skiing gene. He states:

> Similarly, there have been no studies looking for a weight-lifting gene among Bulgarian men, or a swimming gene among East German women, or a cross-country skiing gene among Scandinavians, or a volleyball jumping gene among Californians who hang out on beaches. There have been no claims that Canadians owe their success in hockey to naturally strong ankle joints, or instinctive eye-hand-foot coordination, or an innate tendency not to sweat so they can retain body heat in cold weather. Nobody has looked for or used genetic explanations for the successes of athletes packaged in white skin.
>
> But as soon as athletes with black skin excel or fail at a certain sport, regardless of where they come from in the world, many people start looking for "race-based" genetic explanations. They want to explain the successes and failures of black athletes in terms of "natural" or "instinctive" qualities or

weaknesses. They assume white skinned athletes succeed because of tradition, training opportunities, dedication, and personal sacrifice, not the genetic heritage of the entire white population of a region, a country, or the world. (Pp. 245–246)

A final and most interesting genetic/biological explanation for black superiority states that survival of the fittest and selective breeding among slaves both while en route to this country and subsequent to entry is the real cause. This Darwinian hypothesis presupposes that the survivors of the admittedly brutal trip from Africa to America were physically stronger than those who died, thereby creating a superior gene pool among the survivors, a superiority, of course, that has been transmitted generationally. This rather myopic survival of the fittest notion does not take into account the fact that intelligence and cunning may have been critical contributors to survival and also greatly exaggerates the significance of speed and physical quickness as significant influences. Given the many problems associated with a genetic or biological explanation, perhaps other avenues of exploration should be traversed. Accordingly, let us look at social/cultural influences.

Social/Cultural Influences

Black superiority in sports (or more appropriately, some sports) appears to be best explained in terms of social influences. Among them are discrimination in its various manifestations and what has been termed the *"sport opportunity structure"* (Eitzen and Sage, 1978). This discrimination has its roots in indentured servitude, slavery, and Jim Crow laws; Moses Fleetwood Walker felt it, Jackie Robinson felt it, and athletes of today are not exempt from its effects. In the world of sports, discrimination is manifested in the form of stacking, a phenomenon whereby blacks are relegated to certain peripheral positions in sports such as football

The Disappearance of the White Male Sprinter in the United States

George (1994) has written a provocative article on what he calls the disappearance of the white male track sprinter in the United States (he chose not to deal with white female sprinters primarily because there has not been one of any consequence in this country since the late 1930s). In the process of making his point, he provides a historical review of sprinting from the 1930s up to the present. Most of his conclusions were arrived at after interviewing forty knowledgeable individuals, a veritable *Who's Who* of track and field for the last half century. Chief among his findings were:

- Top black sprinters first emerged in the 1930s, and included Eddie Tolan, Ralph Metcalfe, Jesse Owens, and Mack Robinson (brother of baseball great Jackie Robinson).
- White sprinters such as Hal Davis, Grover Klemmer, Hubie Kerns, and Mel Patton set the standards in the 1940s. Patton ran one 100-yard dash in 1949 in which he was timed at 9.1, 9.1, and 9.0 seconds by the three timers.
- Whites continued to dominate in the 1950s, led by runners such as Bobby Morrow, Dave Sime, Glenn Davis, Eddie Southern, J. W. Mashburn, and Thane Baker. Interestingly, Baker continued to compete well into his fifties, setting world records at all age levels in the process.
- Dave Sime competed in the 1960 Olympics, winning a silver medal in the 100-meter race. He was the last white sprinter to represent the United States in an Olympics or World Championships in the 100 meters. Mike Larrabee won the 400-meter event in the 1964 Olympics and tied the world record in the event when he was past thirty years of age (44.90 seconds). No white American has come close to his time in the intervening thirty-plus years.
- There were some world class white sprinters outside the United States in the 1970s and 1980s, most notably Russian athlete Valery Borzov and Italian sprinter Pietro Mennea, who still holds the world record for 200 meters at 19.72. Marion Woronin of Poland ran 10.0 during the 1980s, and Alan Wells of the United Kingdom became the only man to run 10.30 in the 100 meters past age thirty-five.
- Explanations for the decline/disappearance of the white sprinter in the United States vary. Only two of the forty experts interviewed thought the shift to be a function of black physical superiority. The

(Continued next page)

Highlight 9.2 (Continued)

The Disappearance of the White Male Sprinter in the United States

phenomenon might be better explained in terms of the decline in importance of track in the white teenage subculture; coaches, parents, and peers overtly and covertly pushing blacks toward the shorter distances and whites to the longer ones; and the seeming willingness of young blacks to "pay the price" in terms of training. The latter point appears to fly in the face of racial stereotypes that have long held that black runners are naturally fast and do not have to train hard in order to excel.

- Two other asides of interest: (1) Rick Wolhuter ran 800 meters in 1:43.4 in 1971. The fastest time for an American in that event in 1990 was 1:46.39, or 3 seconds slower. In view of advances in training, diet, equipment, and quality of track surfaces, this discrepancy is hard to explain. (2) No one is able to adequately explain why African countries such as Kenya and Ethiopia produce great distance runners but few if any sprinters whereas Ghana, Gold Coast, and Nigeria have produced only accomplished sprinters. Certainly, these observations do little to support a broad assertion of racial sprinting superiority among blacks.

Source: George (1994).

and baseball, whereas white players are seen in abundance in the more central positions. For example, most quarterbacks are white, but most flankers or wide receivers are black. Yet another example is seen in baseball, where pitchers are predominantly white, whereas outfielders are often black.

Pioneers in this area of research were Loy and McElvogue (1970), who found that 83 percent of major league infielders (central) in 1967 were white whereas 49 percent of the outfielders (peripheral) were black; 96 percent of all catchers and 94 percent of pitchers were white. A reexamination of stacking in 1975 found few changes (Eitzen and Sage, 1978). Ninety-six percent of pitchers and 95 percent catchers were white, data

almost identical to the 1967 findings; 49 percent of the outfielders were black and 76 percent of infielders were white, the latter being the only area of change but still overwhelmingly white. In a recent update using statistics from 1983 and 1993, Lapchick and Benedict (1993) indicate that there are indeed some slight shifts away from stacking. For instance, 86 percent of pitchers were white in 1983 as opposed to 82 percent in 1993. In the case of catchers, 93 percent were white in 1983 as opposed to 87 percent in 1993. The largest changes are among infielders and outfielders. Infielders (excluding first basemen) were 73 percent white in 1983 and 58 percent in 1993. With regard to outfielders, the figures over time read 45 percent white in 1983 and 33 percent ten years later.

In football, the data look amazingly similar to baseball. Central positions, despite the influx of blacks since 1960, remained largely white in 1975. According to Eitzen and Sage (1978), 84 of 87 quarterbacks in professional football, 69 of 70 punters, and 26 of 26 placement holders were white in 1975. Best (1987), using data from the 1982 season, found a similar effect: 78 of 80 quarterbacks, 56 of 56 kickers, and 45 of 47 offensive centers were white. As late as 1991, Lapchick and Brown (1992) found that 92 percent of quarterbacks, 88 percent of kickers, and 89 percent of centers were white. These data are reflective of 7, 10, and 8 percent changes in the direction of fewer whites from 1983 to 1991 with regard to these three central positions.

The suggestion appears to be that blacks, for a host of unverified reasons, are just not suited for these varied duties. On the other hand, running back, wide receiver, and defensive back are particularly suited to the black athlete; 55 percent of running backs, 65 percent of wide receivers and 67 percent of defensive backs in the NFL in 1975 were black. By 1991, these figures were 90, 89, and 94 percent, respectively (Lapchick and Brown, 1992).

The sport of professional basketball, in which 77 percent of the players are black, also has a form of stacking with regard to the center or post position; 55 percent of National Basketball Association (NBA) centers are black, an underrepresentation in terms of the total picture. This point is accentuated when you consider that 83 percent of the guards and 80 percent of the forwards are black.

Unsubstantiated biases have indeed become fact, causing coaches to select athletes for some positions and discouraging athletes from even aspiring to others. How many white track athletes in this country have been charmed (coerced?) into middle distance or field events because the sprints belong to the blacks? Conversely, how many blacks have been discouraged from running distances because of the perception that blacks are sprinters, not distance runners? Evidence from Africa suggests that blacks in fact can excel at distance running. Why is it that we have no great black pole vaulters? Surely speed, upper body strength, and gymnastic ability are not restricted to white athletes. Our own biases have led us into a self-fulfilling prophecy stance that validates them. If we don't have blacks running distances and if they continue to excel in the sprints, there will always be ample reason to suspect that they are not good at longer distances. Perhaps Harry Edwards (1973, p. 322) sums it up best: "The white athletes who do participate in sports operate at a psychological disadvantage because they believe blacks to be inherently superior as athletes. Thus, the white man has become the chief victim of his own lie."

An interesting by-product of this tendency to stack and to stereotype is that few black athletes are being groomed for positions of leadership, such as coaching or administration, when their playing days are over. Another by-product of the sport opportunity structure is lowered earnings for the black athlete due to shorter careers when compared to those of whites. Shorter careers also mean that many do not qualify for the relatively lucrative retirement benefits associated with professional sports. This latter point has been substantiated by results from research on professional football by Best (1987).

Also at work is the belief that sport is the ticket to success for the black in America. Blacks are generally underrepresented in most vocational areas, and role models for young blacks in the broad work arena are quite limited. On the other hand, black role models in sport are abundant. However, job opportunities in sport are quite limited. In sports to which blacks have traditionally gravitated — namely, football, baseball and basketball — jobs are scarce. Football at the professional level employs fifteen hundred people per year, basketball three hundred, and major league baseball approximately six hundred, yielding a total of about twenty-four hundred available jobs. Given that white athletes will fill nearly 50 percent of these slots, job opportunities in professional sport are few. According to Gates (1991) there are twelve hundred black athletes in all of professional sport. He further points out that there are fifteen times as many black physicians and twelve times more black attorneys than there are black professional athletes. By way of elaboration, Harry Edwards has suggested that the likelihood that a black youth will be struck by lightning while walking down the street is greater than his or her chances of being a part of the glamor of profes-

sional sport. To put it another way, Lapchick (quoted in "Bulletin Board," 1985) says that the odds of a high school athlete, black or white, playing in professional sport are 12,000 to 1. Phillips (1988) indicates that this figure may be more like 25,000 to 1. Leonard and Reyman (1988) place the odds at 14,000 to 1 for males and 250,000 to 1 for females. Professional sports are for the chosen few, black, white, or otherwise.

The rather paradoxical result of discrimination, stacking, and the expectancy that sport can serve as a mechanism for black mobility is that a large number of exceptional black athletes have emerged. This excellence has been labeled as black superiority but in no way addresses the

The Likelihood of Being a Professional Athlete in Selected Sports

Highlight 9.3

Sport sociologists Wilbert Leonard and Jonathan Reyman have calculated the chances that white, black, and hispanic males and females have of making it to the top level of selected sports, that is, being a professional athlete. They based their calculations of the various odds on the 1980 census figures for the United States, 1986 and 1987 professional team rosters, and 1986 lists of money winners. In general, the picture is not terribly promising for members of either sex in any of the racial/ethnic groups. All numbers which follow represent the odds per million that an athlete will be a professional in his or her chosen sport.

	White Females	White Males	Black Females	Black Males	Hispanic Males
All Sports	4	16	.04	2	3
Football	x	16	x	21	.4
Baseball	x	12	x	3	2
Basketball	x	2.8	x	6.5	x
Golf	1.9	3.2	x	.008	.003
Tennis	2.3	3.5	.005	.5	.3

Source: Leonard and Reyman (1988).

problem of what happens to those who do not excel and are left in the lurch with no sport career and few vocational opportunities elsewhere.

Psychological Explanations

Precious few investigations have dealt with the black athlete or black/white differences in psychological functioning. However, an excellent summary of a study conducted by Tutko in the early 1970s reported by Chu (1982) is most interesting. According to Chu, three hundred coaches were asked to rate black and white athletes on five dimensions: orderliness, exhibitionism, impulsivity, understanding, and abasement or humility. Most coaches indicated that they expected the blacks to be low on orderliness, understanding, and abasement and high on exhibitionism and impulsivity. Subsequent results reported by Edwards (1973) indicated that the reverse was true in every case. In the same vein, Williams and Youssef (1975) found that college football coaches stereotyped blacks as possessing physical speed and quickness and being high in achievement motivation, whereas white players were viewed as more reliable, more mentally facile, and possessing superior thinking ability. Because these stereotypes are held by college coaches, it is not surprising that practices such as stacking have been so well documented.

Worthy and Markle (1970) have provided an interesting slant on the issue of psychological differences with their study of self-paced versus reactive activities within sport. They theorized that whites would excel at *self-paced activities,* such as golf or bowling or pitching a baseball, and blacks would star at *reactive tasks* such as boxing, tackling in football, or hitting a baseball. Using athletes from college basketball and professional football, baseball, and basketball, Worthy and Markle concluded that blacks indeed do excel at reactive tasks and whites at self-paced tasks. Dunn and Lupfer (1974), studying young soccer players, are supportive of Worthy and Markle. However, Jones and Hochner

(1973) have criticized Worthy and Markle on methodological grounds. Also, Leonard (1984) has suggested that if there is no validity to the Worthy and Markle position, then they must account for the underrepresentation of blacks in clearly reactive activities, such as tennis, squash, fencing, auto racing, and skiing.

Other than the works reported earlier, one of the few studies aimed at black-white differences was conducted by Nation and LeUnes (1983). In a study of fifty-five college football players, significant differences were found on several dimensions. Among them were:

1. As measured by the Profile of Mood State (POMS), white players were significantly higher in vigor (<.05).
2. On the California F-Scale, blacks tended to be more authoritarian than whites, though differences were not particularly pronounced.
3. As for locus of control, black football players scored higher on the chance dimension (<.05). In view of racism in both society and sport, this finding should not be particularly surprising. Blacks, athlete or nonathlete, may well be justified in their belief that life is a chance event.
4. Black football players as seen from the perspective of the Sport Mental Attitude Survey (SMAS) tend to impute responsibility for mental preparation to the coaching staff (<.05), feel confident about performing well even when depressed (<.01), are able to overlook poor past performances (<.05), and view physical not psychological factors as paramount in explaining athletic performance (<.05). Given the lack of data concerning the validity of the SMAS, these findings must be regarded as tentative. In any event, it does appear that there may be psychological differences between white and black football players. How these possible differences translate into performance, however, remains an unanswered question.

Summary

The black athlete is apparently only minimally understood, psychologically. The stark paucity of research in this area is most noticeable. From the sociocultural view, it does appear that much of the superior performance of black athletes in selected sports can be attributed to the job opportunity structure and, often but not always, subtle discrimination that forces them into certain roles that have largely been preselected for them by the long-term effects of racism. Success in these predetermined roles then leads to reinforcement on the part of both blacks and whites that, indeed, the black athlete is superior to the white.

As for genetic or biological theories, we are all too quick to point out that excellence in sport on the part of blacks is "in the genes" but we never explain Nordic skiing superiority or Japanese gymnastics excellence in terms of a particular race-related gene. The overall effect of the perpetuation of this notion is to create a form of discrimination that places blacks in the position of never having their achievements viewed as the product of intelligence, dedication to excellence, and long hours of arduous practice. Much remains to be done in sport and in the society as a whole in completely integrating black athletes and blacks in general into the mainstream of everyday American life.

THE HIGH RISK SPORT PARTICIPANT

Another fascinating area of sport competition, in which high risks of injury or death are an integral part, includes sport parachuting (skydiving), hang gliding, rock climbing, and scuba diving. Some would argue that football and boxing should be included as high risk sports in view of the injuries and deaths associated with them. Granting that any classification system is arbitrary, we shall confine our discussion to the four activities: sky diving, hang gliding, rock climbing, and scuba diving.

One way of conceptualizing high risk activities is provided by Tangen-Foster and Lathen (1983). These investigators sent a questionnaire to chairpersons of 120 physical education departments, primarily in large universities, asking a number of questions about their respective involvements in courses that would be considered a part of the "risk revolution" going on in America; 73 responses were returned and analyzed. Ninety-six percent of the respondents viewed parachuting as "high" or "extraordinary risk," followed by 92 percent for hang gliding, and 64 percent for rock climbing. Scuba diving was viewed in this capacity by 32 percent of the respondents. In any event, we have isolated a few activities that have been viewed as dangerous or high risk to varying degrees. Their selection is based on two factors, their relative dangerousness and the availability of related literature.

Sport Parachuting

USPA Secretary Killed While Making Stunt Jump

On Friday, Jan. 14, Joe Svec, 35, secretary of the United States Parachute Association, was killed in a tragic skydiving accident during filming of a stunt sequence for "The Right Stuff," a film version of Tom Wolfe's best-selling novel about test pilots and astronauts.

Skydiving cameraman Rande Deluca of Big Sky Films was jumping with Svec at the time, and reported seeing no problems. Deluca quit filming at approximately 3500 feet and turned and tracked away to open a distance away from and above where Svec planned to open. Svec was seen by Doc Johnson, an experienced jumper, to turn face-to-earth (he had been facing upward, flying on his back during the filming sequence) and fall flat and stable until impact. Despite very careful analysis and medical tests, no explanation has been found for the accident.

The sequence being filmed depicts famed test pilot Chuck Yeager (first man to break the sound barrier) ejecting from an experimental aircraft. During the fatal jump, however, Svec was wearing no particularly cumbersome or otherwise "odd" gear (except perhaps his helmet) which might have inhibited his movements or reactions.

Svec had achieved meteoric success during his six years as a skydiver and USPA Board member. He began as a well-known figure in the Houston area, at the Spaceland Center and other Texas drop zones. He was elected as a write-in candidate for Conference Director in 1978 and published the very popular Southwest Swooper newsletter, which featured "Don DePloy" who had an opinion about almost every subject in the skydiving world, cleverly drawn and cleverly written. Svec became a National Director in 1980 (when Eric Pehrson succeeded him in the Conference Director slot) and was elected USPA's secretary that same year.

RW meet director of the National Championships in 1980, Svec also competed on various teams and served as Leader of the U.S. National Skydiving Team which won gold medals "across the board" at the World Meet in Zephyrhills in 1981.

As his friends would tell you, Joe Svec was truly a "Renaissance man," with a tremendous collection of skills and achievements. Little known, for example, was his generosity: he funded other people's skydiving teams when they ran out of money in order to permit them to compete in the Nationals and in world competitions. He was a true hero—he held some sort of record as Vietnam's luckiest combat veteran, having returned to combat repeatedly (with and without the Army's permission) after having acquired seven Purple Hearts that the government knew about and a total of more than 20 battle wounds. He served with the Special Forces in their most secret and difficult assignments, where he operated almost exclusively behind the enemy lines for months at a time.

When finally his wounds got to him, he was MED-EVAC'ed to Tripler General Hospital in Honolulu, where he stayed after his recovery and became a successful political cartoonist for the Honolulu Star Bulletin. His interest in politics and his wry humor combined to help him create a series of memorable cartoons and satirical articles, some of which appeared in the pages of PARACHUTIST.

Joe was principally involved in making El Capitan jumping legal (briefly, in 1980) and led the first Park Service-approved jump off the famed cliff. Perhaps one of his greatest disappointments was when a short time later actions by others caused Yosemite's policy to declare cliff jumping out of bounds. More recently Svec became a stunt jumper for the "Fall Guy" television show and this led directly to his commitment to "stand in" for one of the actors in the dangerous sequences to be filmed for the cinema version of Wolfe's best-seller.

Joe was buried by family and friends in a somber ceremony on a wind-swept afternoon on Tuesday, Jan. 18 in Houston, TX. USPA President Larry Bagley led a delegation of USPA officials who joined with hundreds of friends at the ceremony in the cemetery chapel. "This is one of the biggest services we've ever had," was the comment of one of the officials present. (Ottley, 1983, p. 35)

The preceding account points out the perils of parachuting. If an experienced jumper like Joe Svec is at risk, what do the statistics tell us about the novice in the sport? Data from *Parachutist*, the official publication of the United States Parachute Association (USPA), for the years 1973 through 1990, are presented in figure 9.1. Of the twenty-three 1990 fatalities, four died because they did not pull their ripcord or pulled too low, lending support to the advocates of

Figure 9.1: **U.S. Skydiver Deaths, 1973–1990**

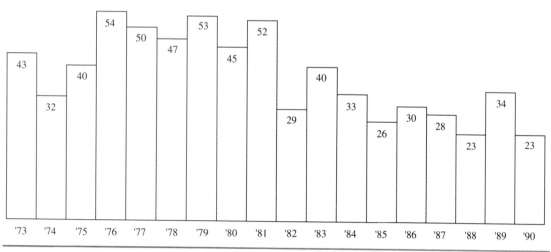

Source: Sitter (1991).

automatic activation devices (AADs). One fatality in 1982 involved a jumper with 5,300 jumps (Correll, 1983), showing the need for vigilance on the part of all participants. A breakdown of 1990 fatalities by experience level can be seen in figure 9.2. Given the considerable dangerousness of sport parachuting, why is it so attractive to so many people of all ages and walks of life? The ensuing discussion will perhaps shed some light on this perplexing and difficult question.

Physiologically, there is no question that the jumper is in a state of arousal. Fenz and Epstein (1967), Fenz and Jones (1972), Hammerton and Tickner (1968), and Powell and Verner (1982) have variously reported elevations in heart rate (HR), galvanic skin response (GSR), respiration rate, anxiety, and self-reports of fear responses in both novice and experienced parachutists. In the Powell and Verner research, twenty naive college-level parachutists were studied. Using the State-Trait Anxiety Inventory (STAI) as a means of measuring anxiety, Powell and Verner found a correlation of .78 between performance as first-

Figure 9.2: **Skydiving Fatalities by Experience Level, 1990**

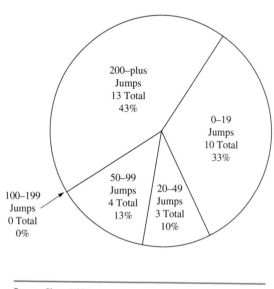

Source: Sitter (1991).

time parachutists and fear rating, heart rate change, and state and trait anxiety, thereby accounting for 61 percent of the variance in performance. These novice parachutists were well below the mean on trait anxiety when compared with 484 undergraduate students reported on in the test manual. Heart rate change between control and jump conditions rose 81 percent, similar to the 96 percent increase reported by Fenz and Epstein. Additionally, Powell and Verner found that low state anxiety is associated with better performance than is high anxiety. Finally, they make a case for good training methods as a means of reducing both competitive anxiety and, more importantly, injuries and deaths.

Beaumaster, Knowles, and MacLean (1978), in a study of the sleep patterns of twenty-seven skydivers, found differences in anxiety of experienced versus novice jumpers, with the latter scoring higher on an anxiety measure. No differences between the two groups on the Neuroticism and Extraversion scales of the Eysenck Personality Inventory (EPI) were found, nor were either of the groups dissimilar to student sample norms reported in the test manual.

Continuing the psychological theme, parachutists are viewed variously as sensation seekers (Zuckerman, 1971; Zuckerman, Kolin, Price, and Zoob, 1964), as "spontaneous dissociaters" (Cancio, 1991), or as stress seekers (Johnsgard, Ogilvie, and Merritt, 1975). A study by Hymbaugh and Garrett (1974) lends support to the sensation seeking notion. Twenty-one skydivers were compared with twenty-one nondivers on the Zuckerman Sensation Seeking Scale (SSS); the divers scored significantly higher than did the nondivers. In a similar vein, Johnsgard et al. studied forty-three male members of the USPA, all of whom had made at least one thousand jumps. Data gathered from the Edwards Personal Preference Schedule (EPPS), the Minnesota Multiphasic Personality Inventory (MMPI), and the Sixteen Personality Factor Questionnaire (16PF) were analyzed. On the

EPPS, parachutists demonstrated high needs for achievement, dominance, exhibition, courage, and heterosexual expression. Conversely, they had little need for deference or order. This psychometric composite gives us a picture of the parachutist as achievement oriented, desirous of being the center of attention, needing change with little concern for orderliness, and being independent and unconventional. MMPI results showed mild elevations on the Mania and Psychopathic Deviate Scales, findings similar to those of Fenz and Brown (1958). These MMPI elevations would suggest that parachutists are highly motivated and unconventional individuals, both of which also came out in the EPPS data. 16PF results showed the USPA members tested to be quite intelligent, happy-go-lucky, expedient, and not particularly influenced by group dictates.

Overall, Johnsgard et al. create an image of the parachutist as an intelligent, independent, achievement-oriented, and generally well-adjusted individual, an image contrary to that provided but not advocated by Ogilvie (1974), who summarizes some psychologically unhealthy stereotypes of skydivers and other stress seekers. According to these stereotypes, sensation seekers do the things they do as a means of fear displacement, as supermasculinity ploys, or because of an unconscious death wish. The available data simply do not support such assertions.

Hang Gliding

The exhilaration of hang gliding is captured in the words of one devotee as quoted in Dedera (1975, pp. 10, 14):

> Forcing an aluminum and Dacron wing that's twenty feet wide into a stiff breeze is work. I heave my body weight into the shoulder harness, and trot heavily toward the cliff edge. Two, three . . . four. The sharp red point of the kite that forms my protective

awning dips with my final lunge. I stagger over the cliff, carrying my glider awkwardly.

And suddenly, without warning, I materialize as a graceful swan. I rotate my hips back on the swing seat, stretch my arms forward and attempt to trim the kite. Up comes the nose, centers on the horizon and stays there. Fifty feet off the ground, and like a fledgling sparrow, I'm flying. Me. An uncoordinated humanoid, blessed with only a rudimentary aptitude the dumbest pelican takes for granted. I'm flying. Leonardo da Vinci would be proud of me. So would Kent Fraunenberger who lived on my block and broke his hand when we were twelve by jumping off the garage roof with a yellow Hi-Flier tied under each arm. Like every other kid who ever dreamed of escaping the mundane by just flying away from it all, I'm serenely gliding over the Southern California landscape, lost in euphoria. A twist of the hips rolls me right. A twitch of the arms, and I yaw left slightly. Pull back, and we dive alarmingly for the earth, sacrificing height for necessary speed. Arms forward, nose up, and we climb into a stall condition . . .

To fly, with no protective layer between you and the elements. To fly, really, like a bird. Dependent solely upon your own instincts, your own reflexes, your own skills

Research has shown that the risk of death in hang-gliding may exceed the Canadian suicide rate and the death by automobile rate for young American males. Despite these dire statistics, no data supports the stereotype that these "stress seekers" harbor an unconscious death wish.

to sustain effervescent flight. It's something you can't ever give up . . . natural, innocent, cleansing flight. You, and the kite, the wind and the sun, and the soft gray hills. And far away down the valley floor, Lake Elsinore, beckoning for you to fly to her once more.

At the same time, it is important to be aware of the element of risk associated with hang gliding. The following account is illustrative:

Obituary—Ian Middleton Pryde

Ian Pryde died as the result of a Gliding accident on the Dunstan Mountains range, 24th January, 1984, whilst competing in the New Zealand National Championships.

Ian was an achiever, and only recently expressed the opinion that one must live each day as if it were a bonus. That is exactly how he lived his life.

Dedicated to Gliding from the early sixties, Ian in his younger days was an Olympic yachtsman of world renown.

His extreme competitiveness, developed in yachting, was carried on into Gliding. He flew for New Zealand in the 1972 and 1976 World Championships, was New Zealand Open Champion in 1976 and winner of the N.Z. 15 Metre class in 1981.

He first crewed for a New Zealand pilot at a World Championship in Poland in 1968, and was a consistent supporter for New Zealand at almost every World event since.

An extremely successful businessman, Ian was a Papakura City Councillor for 20 years, was Chairman of the St. Stephens Maori Boys' and Victoria Maori Girls Colleges for 12 years. A Rotarian and a member of the Masonic Lodge.

One of the instigators of the Matamata Soaring Centre, he steered that Gliding Organisation into a very strong position. As President of the Auckland Gliding Club, and by his very inspiration in land and other deals, he directed the club into its own debt free airfield, almost in the middle of the city. He lifted the morale of the club to the point where it is now the strongest in New Zealand, and the Drury airfield will always be a living tribute to his drive, energy, ability and dedication.

Many a New Zealand Sailplane owner has Ian to thank for rebuilds to accident damaged sailplanes. His ability with his hands and his knowledge of fibre-glass construction will truly be missed. He was always very willing to help an owner in trouble. At his own time and expense he went to Germany to learn how to do it. Many who now have the skills in New Zealand have been taught by Ian.

Always outspoken, always making reasoned sense, he had a failing in not dotting all the "i's" and crossing the "t's" but we all accepted this, a small price for the magnificent "plus's" he scored for New Zealand and its Gliding fraternity.

He would achieve most things. I think he had vague dreams of sailing off into the sunset in a great ocean racer, but that was not to be. His great ambition was for a New Zealander to turn in an exceptional performance at a World Gliding Championship.

The whole New Zealand movement extends their sympathy to his wife Ruth and to Philip and Annette. We all share your loss. (Finlayson, 1984, p. 21)

This obituary notice, taken in 1984 from the *New Zealand Gliding Kiwi,* the official publication of that country's hang-gliding association, serves as a reminder of the dangers inherent in the sport. Further substantiation of this point is seen in the fact that *Kiwi,* in addition to its periodical obituary section, also routinely contains sections known as "Safety Officers Column" and "Sailplane Accident Briefs." The most prominent American publication for gliding enthusiasts, *US Hang-Glider,* is very similar to *Kiwi* in many respects but has discontinued the routine reporting of accidents and deaths for fear of alienating or scaring potential enthusiasts. Such items are now reported only annually.

Brannigan and McDougall (1983) paint a relatively grim picture of the hazards involved in hang gliding, pointing out that the risk of death in sport probably exceeds the suicide rate for all ages in Canada and the death by automobile rate of young American males. Brannigan and McDougall also point to a death rate in hang gliding of 65 per 100,000, and also are of the opinion that the statistics in hang gliding are undoubtedly understated.

As is true for sport parachuting, a strong positive correlation exists between experience and accident rates. Even so, some notable participants feel that hang gliding is misrepresented in terms of risk. For example, Willard (1978, p. 26) quotes Dr. G. M. Yuill, a neurologist and a member of the British Hanggliding Association, as follows: "I believe this sport is no more dangerous than horse riding, rock climbing, potholing, or motorcycle racing, and with training may probably be rendered less hazardous than any of these sports."

Outside of the rather observational data reported by Brannigan and McDougall, little of a psychological nature has been done with hang gliders. Brannigan and his associate observed seven groups of hang gliders from southern Ontario and upper New York and Pennsylvania in an effort to better understand what it is that makes the hang glider tick. Several observational and tentative conclusions were drawn. Among them were:

1. Hang gliders tend to be single male Caucasians in their mid-twenties.
2. They tend to come from every walk of life, though students seem to be most frequent participants.
3. Most get into the activity through a friend.
4. Being a member of the subculture is a powerful force in maintaining their involvement.
5. Most believe that hang gliding is not without risk but they don't view it as a dangerous activity.

6. A "rush," a "blast," "visceral pleasure," and "a high" are often used to describe the experience.
7. A number of participants are able to turn their interest into a vocation as manufacturer, teacher, dealer, designer, test pilot, photographer, or writer.
8. People who give up the sport do so primarily because of accidents and secondarily due to job demands or marital considerations.

Rock Climbing

A true test of the limits to which the human body and spirit can be pushed is found among those who have tried to conquer Mount Everest, the world's tallest peak. In searching for the universal reason for such a risky undertaking, the most usual response is, "Because it's there." Though this quote has been variously attributed to sources ranging from presidents to philosophers, Rowell (1983) asserts that the true source was a disgruntled British mountaineer, George Leigh Mallory. It is said that Mallory was in Philadelphia some sixty years ago attempting to raise funds for another try at Mount Everest (from which he never returned), and his oft-quoted response was uttered sarcastically at a journalist who asked him why once too often. Though perhaps unrepresentative of the totality of rock climbers, those who have been on Everest can give us insights into the thrill and the dangers of such an undertaking. Accounts from elite rockclimbers, or mountaineers as they sometimes refer to themselves, remind us of both the awe and wonderment as well as the dangers of a very perilous enterprise:

> A climber's memory is a golden sieve through which harsh realities slip away. Today, five months later, I vividly recall beautiful sunrises, but stormy days seem as distant as my childhood. (Rowell, 1983, p. 102)

I was on Mount Everest for 50 days before I felt real fear. It came suddenly while climbing a stretch I'd already been up and down eight times. Blood rushed through my head as I looked between my legs down a white wall that dropped thousands of feet to a glacier.

Looking down in itself didn't bother me. Twenty-seven seasons of mountaineering has conditioned me against freaking out simply because I am in the middle of a sheer wall. Just under my skin, however, I have the instinctive fear that all humans share: not a direct fear of heights as many of us wrongly suppose, but it is a more basic fear of being out of control in any potentially dangerous place. Confidence in technique and equipment assuages my fear on Everest, just as confidence in pilot and craft calms most people's fears in a 747 at an altitude even higher than the mountain's 29,028 feet. (Rowell, 1983, p. 90)

I came face to face with Everest three times in four years. I saw the sun rise from the gates of heaven, and I survived. I feel good about my future and glad for the camaraderie I experienced on Everest with my friends. Even the sunrise pictures turned out beautifully. As Anderson recently wrote, "I never knew footsteps or a friendship meant so much." (Webster, 1989, p. 74)

Mountaineers say that descending a mountain is harder and more dangerous than going up. Nowhere is this more true than on Everest. We stumbled back down to our tents at South Col. Even here there was absolutely no chance of our being rescued; our support team was too far away to reach us, we had no radio and rescue helicopters cannot function above 21,000 feet. Nor did we have Sherpas to make tea and soup, carry our packs or otherwise assist us. We were utterly exhausted and very much alone. We had existed for two days in what climbers call the Death Zone—any elevation above 26,200 feet.

For the first time I wasn't sure I would survive the climb. Oxygen deprivation, tiredness and the lack of food, water and sleep made us feel incredibly lethargic. We began to live in slow motion . . . We were ready to head for home. The question was, Could we still get there? (Webster, 1989, p. 71)

Rowell (1983), in an article in *Sports Illustrated,* has suggested that the popular conception of mountain climbers is that they are often loners: he indicates, however, that the team with which he ascended Mount Everest in 1983 was made up of rather gifted athletes. Rowell (p. 99) goes on to say:

Either the aura that surrounds the world's highest mountain attracts competitive types, or in our selection process we unconsciously looked for the strong drive inherent in athletes . . . Craig had been a nationally ranked skier until he shattered a leg. Graber, who played tailback in college for Claremont-Mudd, was the team's most valuable player as a senior in 1973. Momb had been a top freestyle skier and a nationally ranked motocross racer. Harold Knutson had won masters-class marathons. Tackle had been an all-state football player. Jon Reveal had been a nationally ranked ski racer at thirteen. Steve McKinney had held the world's speed record on skis for seven of the last nine years.

Psychological studies of rock climbers have focused largely but not exclusively on the idea that they are sensation seekers, and we shall examine this supposition in more detail in the section on correlates of risk taking. Suffice it to say that it is likely that mountain athletes, amateur or professional, unskilled or skilled, are indeed sensation seekers. According to Robinson (1985), experienced rock climbers are lower in trait anxiety than are the subjects in the normative sample in the manual for the State Trait Anxiety Inventory (STAI). His subjects did not differ from the normative sample, however, on either the need for achievement or affiliative needs. Demographically, climbers in one study were predominantly Anglo, male, and professionals in terms of vocation (Freischlag and Freischlag, 1993); the latter was also supported in a study of elite climbers by Levenson (1990). Interestingly, Freischlag and Freischlag found their subjects, 102 climbers from California, to be unremarkable in terms of physical attributes. Their climbers were 70 inches tall, weighed 163 pounds, and had 15.8 percent body fat, all measurements well within the average for males in general.

Scuba Diving

The following accounts from *Undercurrent,* a publication for serious divers, serve to underscore the risky nature of scuba diving, a sport that has averaged seventy-eight deaths in the United States during the 1990s. It is only fair to point out, however, that the sport averaged 130 deaths per year during the 1970s. Clearly, better training and improvements in diving equipment have been instrumental in making scuba less dangerous.

> A U.S. Navy cruiser, the *San Diego,* sunk by the German Navy during World War I off Fire Island, New York, is one of the most popular wreck diving sites in the Northeast. A double fatality occurred there in October of 1989. The two male victims were both twenty-nine years of age. One was a diving instructor with many hours of wreck diving experience, and the second had a considerable amount of diving experience on wrecks in shallower water. Their bodies were found deep within the wreck in separate compartments and it can only be guessed that they were the victims of silt obscuring their vision and preventing them from finding the way out of the ship. Two more deaths occurred in 1990, bringing the number of deaths on this wreck since 1975 to seven.

> In Jamaica, two U.S. citizens died while scuba diving with their Jamaican divemaster

and six other Americans. The group intended to go no deeper than 70 feet on a drift dive. Missing the intended ledge, the entire dive party reached a depth of 160 feet. Inexperience and nitrogen narcosis resulted in three divers continuing to well over 200 feet. An experienced member of the dive group rescued one diver who had lost consciousness. The other two divers apparently continued to sink and were never recovered. The Jamaican divemaster died, as well.

Again, as we noted in parachuting, hang gliding, and rock climbing, the dangers of high risk sport participants are ever present. Much of the research on scuba diving, a sport involving some 2 million enthusiasts, has centered on the relationship between anxiety and various aspects of scuba training and performance. Griffiths and his associates (Griffiths, Steel, and Vaccaro, 1978, 1979, 1982; Griffiths, Steel, Vaccaro, and Karpman, 1981) have provided us with a fair amount of information. Summing across all four of the Griffiths et al. studies, the following conclusions seem warranted:

1. The subjects were college students or YMCA divers, and all were novices.
2. The State-Trait Anxiety Inventory (STAI) was used in every case.

In the 1978 work, twenty-nine beginning divers (college students) had resting trait and state anxiety scores significantly below college norms for the scale, but moderate increases in state anxiety were noted during the testing phase. The authors did note that anxiety levels were not sufficiently elevated to yield a meaningful indicator of stress that could ultimately prove to be life threatening in an underwater crisis situation. Related to this, Egstrom and Bachrach (1971) indicate that most underwater deaths are due to panic. In their second study, Griffiths and associates used sixty-two beginning scuba divers from the YMCA training program. Four performance indicators were used, and no relationship was found between performance and anxiety on simple tasks, but such was not the case on more complex tasks, thereby indicating that anxiety does in fact interfere with satisfactory performance of complex activities.

The 1981 study was conducted with fifty college scuba divers who were subsequently broken into three groups, one receiving biofeedback (N= 19), one receiving meditation (N = 14), and a control group (N = 17). Each group was asked after receiving the treatment condition to undertake an underwater assembly task borrowed from the U.S. Navy. Neither treatment group performed better than the control group, but state and trait anxiety as measured by the STAI were both significantly related to performance. In the 1982 research, the investigators chose to use the S-R Inventory of General Trait Anxiousness (Endler and Okada, 1975) and the STAI. Subjects were beginning scuba students. Based on results obtained, the authors concluded that the S-R Inventory is more useful than the STAI trait measure in predicting anxiousness prior to underwater testing. Other than this, it was determined that respiration rate is an effective measure of underwater stress in beginning divers, something also suggested by Bachrach (1970).

Two other studies have attempted to look at personality variables other than anxiety. One, by Weltman and Egstrom (1969), looked at personal autonomy as measured by the Pensacola Z-scale in 147 scuba trainees at the University of California at Los Angeles. The Z-scale failed to differentiate among trainees and two other campus groups (engineering students and Peace Corps volunteers) nor did it separate successful trainees and dropouts.

In the second study by Heyman and Rose (1979), twenty-nine male and sixteen female college divers were administered the STAI, the Sensation-Seeking Scale, Rotter's I-E Scale and the Bem Sex Role Inventory (BSRI) (Bem, 1974). Overall, scuba participants were lower on trait anxiety, more adventurous, more internal, and more masculine in sex role orientation than student norms for these dimensions. Also, state and trait anxiety was not related to performance, internals made more dives than externals, and surprisingly, there was an inverse relationship between sensation seeking and depth of dives. Intuitively, one might expect sensation seekers to dive deeper but such was not the case.

Correlates of High Risk Sport Participation

Beyond the various correlates mentioned in specific association with the four high risk activities of parachuting, hang gliding, rock climbing, and scuba diving, at least two others deserve special attention. One is sensation seeking, the other birth order effects.

Sensation seeking is a construct first advanced by Zuckerman and associates (Zuckerman, Kolin, Price, and Zoob, 1964). Their notion was that psychological theories proposing that the human organism is basically a drive or tension reducer were limited; rather, they posit the notion of "optimal stimulation," which takes into account large individual variations in the need for stimulus reduction. Hence, the concept of sensation seeking.

The fifth revision of Zuckerman's test came out in 1984 (Zuckerman, 1984). The various editions of the *Sensation Seeking Scale (SSS)* seek to measure four subdimensions of sensation-seeking. They are:

1. *Thrill and Adventure Seeking (TAS)*—The desire to engage in thrill seeking, risk, adventurous activities such as parachuting, hang gliding, mountain climbing, and so forth.
2. *Experience Seeking (ES)*—Seeking arousal through mind and sense and nonconforming lifestyle.
3. *Disinhibition (Dis)*—Release through partying, drinking, gambling, and sex, generally

regarded as more traditional sensation seeking outlets.

4. *Boredom Susceptibility (BS)*—Aversion for repetition, routine, and dull and boring people; restlessness when escape from tedium not possible.

The SSS has been linked to any number of psychological constructs outside sport (Zuckerman, 1971), and it has generally been a valid assessment tool within the sporting context, particularly in studies of high risk athletes. As stated earlier, Hymbaugh and Garrett (1974) found skydivers to be significantly higher in sensation seeking than matched sample of nondivers. Straub (1982) studied 80 male athletes who participated in hang gliding (N = 25), automobile racing (N = 22), and bowling (N = 25). As might be expected, the bowlers scored significantly lower (.01 level) on the total score and two of the four subdimensions when compared with the other two groups. Table 9.1 reflects these data in their entirety. In response to the question, "Do you consider your sport to be a high-risk activity?" 67 percent of the hang gliders, 50 percent of the auto racers, and none of the bowlers said yes, though 63 percent of the hang gliders

and 41 percent of the auto racers reported having been injured at some point in their careers.

Several studies have been conducted of late with rock climbers. Robinson (1985) contrasted sensation seeking scores of thirty elite rock climbers (ERCs) with SSS normative data reported by Zuckerman; the ERCs were significantly higher in total Sensation Seeking (SS), Thrill and Adventure Seeking (TAS), and Experience Seeking (ES) than were the normative subjects. Similarly, Rossi and Cereatti (1993) compared four kinds of mountain athletes (free-climbers, alpinists, speleologists, and ski jumpers) with control samples of nonathletes and high school physical education students. Significant differences in the predicted direction were found between mountain athletes and controls on all SSS scales except Boredom Susceptibility (BS). Interestingly, all mountain athlete groups scored significantly higher than rock climbers on TAS. A third and novel approach to studying sensation seekers was undertaken by Levenson (1990). He studied antisocial risk takers (drug offenders), adventurous risk takers (rock climbers), and prosocial risk takers (policemen and firemen). The rock climbers scored significantly higher on TAS than did the other two groups. Levenson

Table 9.1

Sensation Seeking Data on Hang Gliders, Automobile Racers, and Bowlers

Test components	Hang gliders (n = 33)		Auto racers (n = 22)		Bowlers (n = 25)		F
	M	**SD**	**M**	**SD**	**M**	**SD**	**F**
TAS	8.12	1.92	7.41	2.56	6.28	2.68	4.35*
ES	5.42	2.26	5.18	1.84	3.56	2.27	5.83**
Dis	5.06	3.04	5.73	2.19	4.40	2.16	1.56
BS	2.67	1.95	4.32	1.89	3.16	1.77	5.17**
Total	21.27	2.29	22.64	2.12	17.40	2.22	3.79*

*p<.05.

**p<.01.

Source: Straub (1982).

further concluded that the SSS results along with other measures used seem to suggest that the three groups studied are characterized by different psychological composition and differing approaches to risk taking.

Another correlate of high risk sport is *birth order effects*. The relationship of birth order to a variety of human behaviors has been a popular area of investigation, and sport has not been exempt from this research. Nisbett (1968) asked a group of judges to rank the most dangerous sports offered at Columbia University; football, soccer, and rugby were so designated. He then asked nearly three thousand undergraduates from Columbia, Yale, and Penn State (about twenty-four hundred were from Columbia) and a sample of professional athletes from the New York Mets (baseball) and the New York Giants (football) to respond to a questionnaire on birth order. Firstborns were overrepresented in all cases, but they were less likely to have participated in high risk sports. Nisbett (p. 352) says: "The underrepresentation of firstborns in the dangerous sports is not a pronounced effect but it is a consistent one. In high school, college, and professional athletics, firstborns are less likely to play the high-risk sports."

In a similar vein, Longstreth (1970) asked students enrolled in two semesters of child development to respond to a seven-point continuum question in which Response 1 was "Physically very conservative at age 12; tended to avoid dangerous activities and rough games; preferred sedentary activities" and Response 7 was "Physically very daring at age 12; never turned down a physical challenge; always ready for rough and tumble with plenty of bruises and cuts to show for it." Like Nisbett, Longstreth found firstborns overrepresented in his classes but underrepresented at the "rough and tumble" end of the continuum; 59 percent of firstborns rated themselves at the conservative end of the scale. Sex differences were noticeable, with 62 percent of the males and 41 percent of the females scoring a 5, 6, or 7 on Longstreth's question.

Yiannakis (1976) compared sixty-seven first-born college students with ninety-nine laterborns concerning their preference for such sports as judo, football, lacrosse, skydiving, ski jumping, and motorcycle racing. In general, firstborns tended to avoid the high-risk activities. Casher (1977), in a study of 127 Ivy League varsity athletes, lends strong support to previous findings with her observation that participation in dangerous sports is significantly related to birth order. In addition to the general underrepresentation of firstborns, Casher found a statistically significant number of third-borns in dangerous sports. Nixon (1981, p. 12), in a study of Vermont collegians, found a "weak tendency for male firstborns to be less attracted than male laterborns to playing risky sports." Nixon also found that males showed a pronounced preference over females for participating in or watching risky sports.

Though not much research has been reported lately on this issue, birth-order effects appear to be relevant to our understanding of high risk sports; firstborns consistently appear to be underrepresented. Most of the writers mentioned here account for this apparent underrepresentation in terms of child-rearing practices, the consensus being that firstborns are often treated differently from subsequent children within the family. Firstborns may have their needs met in more conventional ways whereas later-born children might be forced to resort to nontraditional activities in order to achieve a measure of success and parental and peer approval. Though speculative, this seems to be the gist of the most accepted explanation.

THE ELITE ATHLETE

Research on elite athletes has been unfocused at best. Access to elite populations in which much is at stake for the athlete is understandably limited. Nevertheless, some information about top-flight performers is available.

Kroll's Personality-Performance Pyramid

One way of conceptualizing the relationship between personality and performance is provided by Kroll (1970). His formulation is summarized by Silva (1984) in terms of the *personality-performance pyramid,* which can be seen in figure 9.3. Kroll's model would predict a great deal of heterogeneity among athletes at the entry level and considerable homogeneity at the elite level, though differences would still exist at any and all levels. Part of his similarity could be attributable to preselection variables for sport, and some would certainly be a function of the demands of proceeding from the entry to the elite level. Kroll calls this later phenomenon the *modification and attrition explanation* for personality similarity in top level athletes; that is, their own behaviors and personality have been modified by experience. Athletes who for whatever reason drop out of the process at some point only accentuate this homogeneity of personality. In effect, their attrition takes variability out of the formula.

Morgan's Iceberg Profile

The most creative, continuing, and collected conceptualization of elite sport performance is provided by Morgan and his various associates (Morgan, 1978a, 1978b, 1980; Morgan and Johnson, 1976; Morgan and Pollock, 1977). They conducted a series of studies of elite performers, and from these efforts the Iceberg Profile shown in figure 9.4 emerged. Morgan compared scores on a variety of psychometric inventories administered to American Olympians in rowing, wrestling, and distance running. All athletes invited to the Olympic training camp in 1972 and 1976 completed a battery of physiological and psychological tests; subsequently, the athletes making the

Figure 9.3: **The Personality-Performance Pyramid**

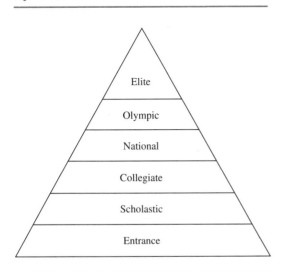

Source: Kroll (1970).

Figure 9.4: **Morgan's Iceberg Profile**

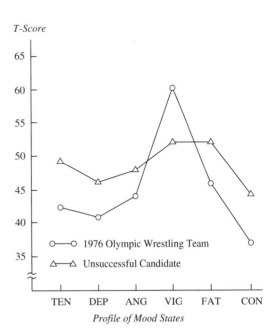

Source: Morgan (1980).

various teams were compared with those invited to camp but not selected to participate in the upcoming Olympics. The "unsuccessful" candidates were higher in tension, depression, anger, fatigue, and confusion on the Profile of Mood States (POMS) (McNair, Lorr, and Droppleman, 1971) and lower on the positive mood dimension of vigor than were the "successful" competitors. The spike effect on the vigor dimension that clearly differentiates between the successful and unsuccessful athletes constitutes the Iceberg Profile.

Morgan and his associates concluded that their sample of elite runners was remarkably similar, affectively, to Olympic wrestlers and oarsmen studied earlier by Morgan (1968) and Morgan and Johnson (1976). National and Olympic class cyclists studied by Hagberg, Mullin, Bahrke, and Limburg (1979) also looked much like profiles isolated by Morgan and his associates for the groups they studied. In view of observed similarities between these elite and

normative samples on other psychological tests of a more enduring nature, it was concluded that these affective differences drawn from the POMS are consequences of competition at a high level as opposed to an antecedent or selection factor.

Research from track, and most particularly from the distance events, has lent further substantiation to the Morgan conceptualization. Morgan and Pollock (1977) made comparisons between and among nineteen world class runners (eleven middle and long distance and eight marathoners) and eight college middle-distance runners. Among the inventories used were the STAI, EPI, POMS, and the Depression Adjective Checklist (DACL) (Lubin, 1967). No differences were found among the three groups on any of these measures. Group means can be seen in table 9.2. All things considered, the groups are remarkably similar. However, when all runners in the study were compared with college norms reported in the test manual for the POMS, substantial differences in favor of the runners were

Table 9.2

Raw Score Means of Three Groups of Runners on Selected Psychological Variables*

Variable	World class runners		College runners (n = 8)	F
	Middle-long distance (n = 11)	Marathon (n = 8)		
State anxiety	33.82	32.75	33.75	0.06
Trait anxiety	34.91	26.63	33.00	2.04
Tension	10.91	9.75	10.88	0.11
Depression (POMS)	9.18	3.88	6.88	1.01
Anger	8.73	6.75	8.13	0.23
Vigor	19.00	22.75	21.25	1.14
Fatigue	6.81	6.38	7.88	0.16
Confusion	8.82	5.63	7.63	1.40
Extraversion	13.27	12.75	14.88	0.44
Neuroticism	10.27	11.00	6.50	1.66
Depression (DACL)	4.73	4.13	3.13	0.81

*Differences between groups were found not to be significant ($p > 0.05$).

Source: Morgan and Pollock (1977).

Dissociative Strategies in Distance Running

In 1977, Morgan and Pollock described elite runners in considerable detail on dimensions other than those generated from psychometric sources. Morgan had originally hypothesized that runners used *dissociative strategies* while competing in order to cope with the painful demands inherent in long distance running. Some of these so-called dissociative strategies are recounted by Morgan and Pollock:

> Prior work conducted by the senior author revealed that marathon runners characteristically attempt to "dissociate" sensory input during competition. Previous interviews with twenty marathoners, as well as more recent interview data from long distance runners, revealed that these athletes are "cognitively active" during competition, but this cognitive activity seldom, if ever, relates to the actual running. Also, this general finding has since been observed for long distance swimmers and cyclists as well. The cognitive strategy employed by these athletes can best be regarded as "dissociative cognitive rehearsal." Many runners reconstruct images of past events throughout the 42.2 km run. For example, one of the first marathoners interviewed by the senior author routinely rehearsed or reconstructed his entire educational experience during each marathon. During the run he would age regress himself to first grade and attempt to recall as much as possible about the experience (e.g., the teacher's name and face, the names and faces of other boys and girls in the class, various experiences such as learning to read, print, work with crayons, and paste, playing an instrument in the rhythm band, recess, and so on). After a while he would proceed to second grade, recall salient "chunks" of information, and then proceed to third grade. This continued throughout grade school, high school, college, his oral defense, receipt of the Ph.D., as well as his current postdoctoral experiences. This marathoner always reconstructed his educational experience during the marathon; it was always somewhat unique, however, in that he would remember different people, events, and activities each time. In other words, the theme was always the same, but the content varied. Other runners have described remarkably similar approaches, and it would be redundant to proceed with a review of these case studies. Suffice it to say that another runner always builds a house when he marathons; another writes letters to everyone he owes a letter to; another listens to a stack of Beethoven records; another participates in extremely complex mathematical exercises; another steps on the imaginary faces of two co-workers she detests throughout the marathon; another repeatedly sings the Star Spangled Banner in crescendo fashion; another age regresses and becomes a steam locomotive at the base of heartbreak hill; and so on. The various rehearsal themes are rather different, but they all seem to be directed toward the same end — dissociating the painful sensory input. As a matter of fact, most of these runners have reported that

(Continued next page)

Highlight 9.4 (Continued)
Dissociative Strategies in Distance Running

use of these techniques helps them negotiate various pain zones and particularly the proverbial (or mythical?) wall. (Pp. 390–391)

Morgan and Pollock had to recant the dissociative notion because of their work with the elite runners. They found that they used associated strategies as follows:

> Dissociation of sensory input did not represent the principal "cognitive strategy," but rather, these elite marathon runners were found to utilize an associative strategy. These runners reported that (1) they paid very close attention to bodily input such as feelings and sensations arising in their feet, calves, and thighs, as well as their respiration; (2) whereas they paid attention to time ("the clock"), pace was largely governed by "reading their bodies"; (3) they identified certain runners they would like to stay with during a given run if possible, but they did not typically employ a "leeching" strategy; (4) during any given marathon they constantly reminded or told themselves to "relax," "stay loose," and so forth; and (5) they typically did not encounter "pain zones" during the marathon, and most of these elite runners dismissed the phenomenon referred to as "the wall" as simply a myth—that is, they did not "come up against the wall" during the marathon run. (P. 390)

More recent research by Morgan and his associates (Morgan, Ellickson, O'Connor, and Bradley, 1992; Morgan, O'Connor, Sparling, and Pate, 1992) has added yet a third interpretation with regard to cognitive strategies used by elite distance runners. These two studies by Morgan and his associates involved fourteen male and fifteen female elite runners as defined by very stringent standards. It was noted that runners of both sexes relied heavily on dissociative strategies during training but shifted to pure associative strategies or a mix of the two when competing. For example, 43 percent of the males used dissociative strategies when training; another 36 percent used both approaches. However, when it came time to compete, 72 percent used association only and the remaining 28 percent used a mixture. Obviously, highly competitive male runners dissociate little when competing. Results for the elite females were generally consistent with those of the elite male runners.

Perhaps the best conclusion to be drawn at this juncture with regard to associative and dissociative strategies is that they are both training tools for use by elite runners. The dissociative approach may help ease the pain of sometimes monotonous training, but seems to be of limited utility to runners during competition.

Sources: Morgan, Ellickson, O'Connor, and Bradley (1992); Morgan (1978); Morgan and Pollock (1977); Morgan, O'Connor, Sparling, and Pate (1992).

noted. Even though the instruments failed to discriminate between world class and collegiate runners, they did discriminate between runners and a general college sample.

Subsequent studies of elite male distance runners by Morgan, Ellickson, O'Connor, and Bradley (1992) and their female equivalents by Morgan, O'Connor, Sparling, and Pate (1992) have further substantiated the existence of the Iceberg Profile. The males in the first study were recruited from the Elite Distance Runner Project of the United States Olympic Training Center (USOTC); in order to qualify, they had to have run 3:37 for 1,500 meters, 8:26 for the steeplechase, 13:42 for 5,000 meters, 28:14 for 10,000 meters, or 2.15 for the marathon. The final number of subjects meeting these stringent requirements were fourteen. The runners were observed by Morgan et al. to possess the Iceberg Profile. In the case of the elite female runners, there were 27 subjects subdivided into elite (n = 15) and near-elite (n = 12) based on previous performances. Both groups in this instance possessed the Iceberg Profile; this finding is somewhat discrepant from results from the original Olympians upon whom the Iceberg Profile idea was based. However, it may well be that the distinction between elite and near-elite runners in this case is an artificial one. In any event, the twenty-seven runners in this study differed from the normative group reported in the POMS manual in the expected direction; that is, lower on the negative mood states and significantly higher on psychic vigor.

An interesting variant on the track and field theme has been provided by Patten, Harris, and Leatherman (1994). These researchers isolated the Iceberg Profile in a sample of elite wheelchair track and field athletes (one female, thirteen males) who had been invited to a special camp sponsored by the U.S. Olympic Training Center in Colorado Springs.

Further testimony to the popularity of the POMS in sport research is documented by Snow and LeUnes (1994) who found seventy-four published studies from 1971 through 1990 in which the scale was used; forty-one of these studies were published in the time period 1986–1990. Twenty-eight different sport and fitness groups were represented in the seventy-four studies, with runners, track and field athletes, and marathoners serving as subjects for nineteen studies and exercise and fitness groups for an additional fourteen. Though no up-to-date bibliography exists at this time, there is every reason to believe that the use of the POMS as a research instrument in sport will continue at a lively pace.

Other Research on Elite Performers

Wrestlers

In addition to Morgan's work with the Iceberg Profile, a number of studies have looked at wrestlers of high quality. Highlen and Bennett (1979) gave a questionnaire to forty elite wrestlers competing for three national-level Canadian teams. Twenty-four of the forty made one of the three teams, and comparisons were made between qualifiers and nonqualifiers. Twelve factors were isolated for study: self-confidence, thoughts under various wrestling conditions, factors affecting performance, dreams, role performance, self-talk, imagery, anxiety associated with major competitions, distraction, negative self-thoughts, blocking, and coping. The largest difference between the two groups was that the qualifiers felt that they were closer to reaching their maximum potential than were nonqualifiers and the former reported much more self-confidence than did the latter. This confidence factor was regarded by the researchers as their strongest finding.

In a separate study, Highlen and Bennett (1983) compared elite divers and wrestlers. The forty-four divers were competing for a place on the Canadian Pan American Games team; eight ultimately qualified. Self-confidence and concentration most saliently discriminated between the qualifiers and the nonqualifiers. Imagery was also a significant difference between the two groups. As for the wrestlers (N = 39), they were competing for positions on either the Canadian teams entered in the Pan American Games or the World Championships. Fifteen qualified for one or the other of the two teams. As with the divers, self-confidence and concentration differentiated between successful and unsuccessful candidates. Imagery did not differentiate between the two groups, however, although it did with the divers.

Gould, Weiss, and Weinberg (1981) have lent support to the previous findings in their study of forty-nine wrestlers competing in the 1980 Big Ten conference tournament. Nineteen place winners (first, second, third, or fourth in various weight classes) were compared with thirty wrestlers who did not place in the competition. The factors of self-confidence, proximity to reaching maximum potential, and focusing attention on match-related thoughts clearly differentiated placers from nonplacers.

Gould and his collaborators conducted intensive interviews with the twenty wrestlers (ten freestyle, ten Greco-Roman) who represented the United States in the 1988 Olympic Games in an effort to ascertain just how these athletes prepared themselves mentally for competition (Eklund, Gould, and Jackson, 1993; Gould, Eklund, and Jackson, 1992a, 1992b, 1993). Of special interest were the differences in preparation that characterized winning and losing performances. In the case of winning, wrestlers followed a mental game plan routinely, were extremely confident and focused, and were optimally aroused. In losing matches, wrestlers deviated from their mental preparation strategies, were less confident, entertained negative thoughts, and were less attentive to the task at hand. With regard to mental preparation, a number of strategies were employed as opposed to one particular approach. In a more detailed look at the six wrestlers who eventually won medals

in the 1988 Games, it was noted that there all used mental preparation strategies, but the content and focus of these approaches varied considerably among the medalists.

The studies described here clearly illustrate the importance of self-confidence, performing at a near maximum capacity, and attention to the task at hand in determining elite wrestling performance.

Olympic Gymnasts

Mahoney and Avener (1977) administered a broad-based questionnaire to American men gymnasts at the 1976 Olympic trials. Subsequent comparisons between those who made the team and those who did not revealed that the better gymnasts tended to be more self-confident (r = .57), reported a higher frequency of gymnastic dreams (r = .45), thought more about gymnastics in everyday situations (r = .78), tended to downplay the role of officiating in influencing their performance (r = .59), and did not rate mental attitude as greatly influencing their success (r = −.59). Also, the more successful participants reported slightly more anxiety prior to competition though the pattern reversed itself when competition actually commenced.

Pan American Athletes

Eighty-one males and fifty-five female Canadian athletes from ten different sports responded to Kenyon's scale for assessing attitudes toward physical activity (Kenyon, 1968). The Kenyon measure looks at six dimensions of physical activity. They are reported by Alderman (1970) as follows:

1. *Physical activity as a social experience.* A characterization of those activities, whose primary purpose is to provide a medium for social intercourse, i.e., to meet new people and to perpetuate existing relationships.
2. *Physical activity for health and fitness.* A characterization of those activities in which

participation is designed to improve one's health and physical fitness.

3. *Physical activity as the pursuit of vertigo.* A characterization of those activities or experiences providing, at some risk to the participant, an element of thrill and excitement through the mediums of speed, acceleration, sudden change of direction, or exposure to dangerous situations, with the participant remaining in control.

4. *Physical activity as an aesthetic experience.* A characterization of those activities that are thought of as possessing beauty or certain artistic qualities such as ballet, gymnastics, or figure skating.

5. *Physical activity as catharsis.* A characterization of those activities that provide, through some vicarious means, a release of tension precipitated by frustration.

6. *Physical activity as an ascetic experience.* A characterization of those activities that are conceived of as requiring long, strenuous, and often painful training and still competition, and which demand a deferment of many other gratifications. (P. 21)

In general, males and females had quite similar attitudes about physical activity. Additionally, male athletes had a strikingly high evaluation of physical activity as an aesthetic experience. Finally, neither group endorsed physical activity as an ascetic experience. Though many arduous hours of training are inherent in most sports at such a competitive level, few athletes appear to enjoy the pain and privation associated with asceticism.

Youth Oarsmen

New Zealand Colts (under age twenty-three) Rowing Team finalists (n = 33) participated in a variety of tests conducted by Williams (1978). In addition to several physical measures, five psychological scales appeared to be related to rowing success and were drawn from the 16PF.

Toughmindedness, emotional stability, self-sufficiency, trustfulness, and imaginativeness emerged as predictors. Trustfulness, however, was in the direction of suspiciousness, a rather unexpected finding.

Collegiate Racquetball Players

Nine members of the Memphis State University racquetball team competing in the Tennessee State Racquetball Championships were questioned by Meyers, Cooke, Cullen, and Liles (1979), generally in an attempt to replicate the work of Mahoney and Avener with the Olympic gymnasts. Two of the nine team members had won individual national championships, two others had won the national doubles championship, and the remaining five performed but had not won anything of national consequence. Comparisons were made between the top two individual players and the other seven players. Consistent with the findings of Mahoney on the Olympic gymnasts, Meyers et al. (1979) found that the top racquetball players tended to be more self-confident, performed more successfully in their sport-related dreams, reported more racquetball-related thoughts in everyday events, downplayed the role of officiating in their performance, reported a more structured lifestyle, and perceived themselves to be performing at nearer their own potential.

Young Skiers

Rotella, Gansneder, Ojala, and Billing (1980) studied twenty-six male and twenty-one female skiers ages twelve to nineteen who were enrolled in a school oriented toward producing World and Olympic caliber athletes. Again, these researchers were attempting to replicate the Mahoney and Avener approach. Only two of fifty-four items on their first inventory modeled after Mahoney and Avener correlated significantly with skiing ability as assessed by the National Ski List Ranking for 1978–1979, and they were operating close to potential and blaming inadequate training for poor performance. The better skiers saw themselves as performing nearer their maximum ability and did not believe that poor performance could be blamed on training inadequacies. The second instrument used by Rotella et al. showed that the better skiers focused much effort on remediation of weaknesses in designing training programs and thought more about actual race course strategy than did their less successful counterparts.

Olympic Weight Lifters

Hall, Church, and Stone (1980) were primarily interested in birth-order effects, though Hall and her collaborators did take into consideration achievement motives, locus of control, and anxiety in elite weight lifters. Overall, they found a very strong relationship between birth order effects and achievement motivation as measured by the Mehrabian Need Achievement Scale (Mehrabian, 1969). Firstborns had a very strong need to approach success whereas laterborns had a tendency to avoid failure. On Rotter's locus of control measure, firstborns and others were generally internal, though the firstborns were more external than later-borns. Both comparison groups were relatively low on trait anxiety as measured by the STAI. Mahoney (1989) compared nationally ranked lifters with a sample of non-elite competitors, and found the elites to be more psychologically healthy as measured by several psychometric instruments. The elite lifters were also more motivated to compete as indicated by self-report.

Figure Skaters

A fair literature has emerged over the past several years concerning elite figure skaters, primarily through the efforts of Gould and Scanlan and their respective associates (Gould, Finch, and Jackson, 1993; Gould, Jackson, and Finch, 1993a, 1993b; Scanlan, Stein, and Ravizza, 1989, 1991). Scanlan et al. have focused their research on sources of enjoyment and sources of stress

among elite skaters. Interviews were conducted with twenty-six former national championship competitors in the United States; from these interviews, a large number of quotes emerged that were subsequently analyzed for sources of both fun and stress. In the case of sources of enjoyment, skaters' quotes focused on four categories, which were summarized by the research team as follows: Social and Life Opportunities (friendship opportunities, broadening experiences afforded by competition, family/coach relationships); Perceived Competence (mastery, competitive achievement, demonstration of athletic ability); Social Recognition of Competence (peer recognition, recognition from fans and others); and Act of Skating (movement and sensory stimulation, self-expression, athleticism expression, flow or peak experience). Sources of stress, on the other hand, were placed in five categories: Negative Aspects of Competition (worries, failure, preparation, importance of competing); Negative Significant-Other Relationships (skating politics, psychological warfare, interpersonal conflict); Demands or Costs of Skating (financial, time, personal costs); Personal Struggles (physical and mental difficulties, self-doubt, perfectionism, dealing with fears of becoming gay); and Traumatic Experiences (family problems, death fears involving the 1961 plane crash that killed the entire U.S. national team). Gould and his colleagues found similar sources of stress in their study of seventeen elite skaters who had won a U.S. national championship between 1985 and 1990. Specifically, they identified dominant sources of stress to be (1) competitive anxiety and self-doubt; (2) financing, media, and time constraints and demands; (3) high performance expectations/standards; and (4) significant-other relationship issues. While categorized somewhat differently, there appears to be quite a bit of overlap in Gould's work and that of Scanlan with regard to stress sources.

By way of summation, a synthesis across sports indicates that elite athletes believe self-confidence to be a big factor in determining success. Also, the ability of elite competitors to perform at a level that is consistent with their view of their potential appears to be a solid discriminator. The role of skill-related dreams is unclear but provocative. Everyday events that are intruded upon by thoughts of competition seem relevant as well. Top-flight competitors are not prone to blame poor performance on practice inadequacies or officiating foibles; they tend to see themselves as the source and focus of success. Finally, elite athletes are not exempt from the effects of stress inherent in intense competition; they do, however, appear to find constructive ways of dealing with stress while maintaining a high level of competitive performance.

Our understanding of elite performers is, to quote Silva, Shultz, Haslam, and Murray (1981), "embryonic." Methodological shortcomings have been considerable; the definition of who is elite is highly variable, sample sizes are quite small in most cases, inconsistencies created by the use of a diversity of instruments are frequent, and variability in data analyses has contributed to the cloudy picture that exists. It is hoped that increasing sophistication can be brought to bear on this important area in the future so that identification and development of excellence can continue worldwide.

THE ATHLETE WHO USES/ABUSES DRUGS

Ours is a drug-oriented society; prescription drugs, over-the-counter medications, and illegal substances are commonplace aspects of our daily lives. We often endorse "a better life through chemistry" orientation to personal well-being, and athletes are no exception. Efforts to improve performance are made at all levels of competition, but the elite athlete is especially prone to look for any competitive edge, and the various drugs available to them are all too often viewed as providing that coveted advantage. Athletes also function at times in the presence of considerable pain or discomfort, and they may seek relief in the form of drugs. Finally, the pressures of competition, particularly at the elite amateur or professional levels, are such that drugs, including alcohol, are seen as tension-reducing and their use and abuse is not at all unusual. Len Bias of the University of Maryland (basketball) and Don Rogers of the Cleveland Browns (football) represent celebrated examples; abuse of the supposed recreational drug of cocaine was clearly implicated as the cause of their very premature deaths in 1986.

Curry and Jiobu (1984) classify the various drugs alluded to in the preceding paragraph as *recreational, restorative,* and *additive.*

Recreational Drugs

Recreational drugs are meant to be pleasurable in general, though many tragic stories involving their use have been documented both in and out of sport. Alcohol, marijuana, and cocaine are three such drugs.

Much has been made about the abuse of marijuana and cocaine in our society, while alcohol gets off lightly at times despite its incredible popularity and potential for abuse. Such is also the case in sport. Studies conducted by Blood (1990) and Evans, Weinberg, and Jackson (1992) are supportive of this position. In both reports, alcohol was a runaway first place finisher in terms of use by athletes. In the Blood study at a small liberal arts college, 81 percent of a group of athletes (n = 85) and a group nonathletes (n = 154) had used alcohol during the semester in which Blood administered his questionnaire. Marijuana use during the same time period was approximately 12 percent for both groups, while cocaine use was reported by no athletes and two of the 154 nonathletes. In a more ambitious survey, Evans et al. sent a questionnaire to 377 male and 167 female athletes from Division 1 athletic programs. Alcohol users in their study numbered 88 percent; marijuana, 15 percent; and cocaine slightly over 4 percent. Interestingly, 34.5 percent of the alcohol group were considered to be high users based on frequency, intensity, and duration of usage. High users also scored significantly higher on the Profile of Mood States subscales of Anger and Fatigue than did the low users in the study. Data such as these reinforce the notion that the real abused drug in sport probably is alcohol.

Restorative Drugs

Muscle relaxants, anti-inflammatories, and painkillers are examples of drugs ostensibly serving a restorative function. A particularly well-known and controversial drug available legally only through prescription is the anti-inflammatory phenylbutazone, known as "bute." Phenylbutazone was brought to greater public awareness in a 1985 *Sports Illustrated* special report on drugs when it was implicated circumstantially in the death of Augustinius Jaspers, a twenty-three-year-old world class distance runner at Clemson University (Brubaker, 1985). Though all parties involved were ultimately exonerated in Jaspers' death, the phenylbutazone found in his system upon autopsy triggered a series of events that blew the lid off an illegal drug delivery ring involving coaches and athletic trainers at Clemson and Vanderbilt as well as suppliers outside the two universities.

One troubling aspect of the anti-inflammatory medications is that they do not treat pain, they merely mask it. In that sense, they are not really restorative at all. At any rate, athletes with musculoskeletal aches and pains tend to play with physical discomfort, thereby placing themselves at risk for greater injury. We sense pain for very good self-preservative reasons and masking it can lead to serious injury. Certainly, the ethics involved in deciding to use anti-inflammatory drugs are dubious at best. The same can be said for painkilling medications and injections, not an uncommon practice in keeping top-flight athletes performing. Novels such as *Semi-Tough* by Dan Jenkins and *North Dallas Forty* by Pete Gent, in part, have poignantly captured the world of pain and the abuse of painkillers to control the hurt associated with professional football.

Additive Drugs

The additive drugs are aimed at performance enhancement and are often called ergogenic aids. Pate, Rotella, and McClenaghan (1984, p. 268) define an ergogenic aid as "any substance or treatment that improves, or is thought to improve, physical performance." The "thought to improve" phrase highlights the fact that the performance-enhancing effects of these various drugs may rest more in the psychology of the individual than in the chemical properties of the various ergogenics. Chief among the ergogenic aids are the amphetamines and the anabolic steroids.

Pate and his associates suggest that the various *amphetamines*, particularly Dexedrine and Benzedrine, are among the most commonly used ergogenics by athletes. Their use has been documented in professional baseball (Kirschenbaum, 1980), professional football (Mandell, 1975), and track (Leonard, 1984). Leonard also reports that nine of twelve medalists in the 1970 world weight lifting championships were disqualified after urinalysis revealed the presence of amphetamines. In football, Mandell found their use to be widespread in the professional ranks, and he cited data to suggest that approximately 50 percent of NFL players were using amphetamines. The stimulating and concurrent analgesic effects of the amphetamines are perhaps best summed up by the comment made by one professional football player: "I'm not about to go out there one-on-one against a guy who is grunting and drooling and coming at me with big dilated pupils unless I'm in the same condition" (Mandell, 1975, p. 43). Jim Bouton, in his best-seller *Ball Four,* suggests that amphetamine use was widespread in major league baseball during his playing days. One player poignantly describes the amphetamine

problem in baseball as follows: "At first they might take them before a big game. Then it was before every game. Then they had to take them to practice. As the players get older, they forget about how to get energy naturally and start getting it through amphetamine pills" (Oliver, 1971,

Highlight 9.5

Blood Boosting

Blood boosting, **or what is more commonly known as blood doping (Rostaing and Sullivan, 1985), was all but unheard of until 1972, when Dr. Bjorn Ekblom of Sweden announced that his research revealed significant increases in endurance through a procedure he had developed in his laboratory. In his original study, Ekblom withdrew approximately a quart of blood from four subjects, removed the red blood cells, and put the samples in cold storage for a month. Upon reinfusion of the red blood cells, all subjects were able to run on a treadmill to exhaustion for a much longer time than had been the case before. The theory behind blood boosting is that the red blood cells will carry more oxygen so essential to the muscle tissue involved in endurance sports. Though tests of the efficiency of blood boosting have been equivocal, its use has continued, culminating in the revelation that seven of the twenty-four-member 1984 U.S. Olympic cycling team had engaged in blood boosting prior to competition. The resulting furor over the doping disclosure and others involving additive drugs led to sanctions against blood boosting in April 1985 by the International Olympic Committee (IOC) and the United States Olympic Committee (USOC) ("Ethics of Blood Doping," 1985). Prior to 1985, blood boosting was against USOC policy but not the organization's rules. As a consequence, blood boosting was a matter of individual physician, coach, or athlete conscience, and abuses such as the one involving the Olympic cycling team have occurred.**

The advantages of blood boosting have not been satisfactorily demonstrated, but the dangers inherent in the practice (risks of infection, possibility of disease transmission) are well documented, thereby bringing the practice under fire from a number of sources ("Ethics of Blood Doping," 1985; Gledhill, 1982; Rostaing and Sullivan, 1985). As a result, testing has been instituted to detect blood boosting, though many problems remain in the area of test accuracy ("New Techniques," 1986).

Sources: "Ethics of Blood Doping" (1985); Gledhill (1982); "New Techniques May Catch Blood Dopers" (1986); Rostaing and Sullivan (1985).

Anabolic-androgenic steroids (AAS), which are analogues or derivatives of testosterone, have anabolic effects such as bone growth, increases in muscle development and strength, greater blood cell production and protein synthesis, and decreases in body fat. Any of these may improve athletic performance and give the user an advantage over his or her competitors. Use of performance-enhancing drugs has been declared illegal in international competition, so all participating athletes are given a drug test. Occasionally, some fail the test and are eliminated from competition. Such was the case of China's Yang Aihua, shown here swimming her way to a gold medal during the 400 meter freestyle final at the World Swimming Championships in Rome, in September of 1994. In November, she tested positive for testosterone and was disqualified.

p. 65). In addition to the dependency problem mentioned by Oliver, the amphetamines may produce rage, unwarranted fearlessness, and irrational feelings of omnipotence, all of which can be potential health detriments to the athlete both on and off the field.

As for the anabolic-androgenic steroids (AAS), there are more than one hundred synthetic compounds that are analogues or derivatives of the male sex hormone, testosterone (Riem and Hursey, 1993). According to Strauss and Yesalis (1991), the AAS have been around since 1935; initially, they were prescribed for medical reasons, but were introduced to sports by Soviet weightlifters in the 1950s. Results of a survey by Buckley, Yesalis, Friedl, Anderson, Streit, and Wright (1988) placed usage at that time among high school students, athletes and nonathletes, at 6.6 percent among males and 1.3 percent among females. As expected, high school athletes were more likely to use AAS than were the nonathletes. The data from Buckley et al. are essentially in agreement with rates reported by Dreyfuss (1990), Evans, Weinberg, and Jackson (1992), and Gannon (1989). Among competitive weightlifters and what Cook (1992) calls "weight-room junkies," AAS use may be more prevalent. Frankle, Cicero, and Payne (1984), in a study of recreational lifters, found 44 percent were users. In a study of competitive weightlifters, Tricker, O'Neill, and Cook (1989) found 54 percent of their sample to be regular AAS users.

The AAS get their name from their masculinizing (androgenic) effects and tissue-building (anabolic) properties. Androgenic effects, in brief, refer to growth and maintenance of the male reproductive system and the development of secondary sex characteristics whereas anabolic effects have to do with bone growth, increases in muscle development and strength, deepening of the voice, increases in red blood cell production and protein synthesis, and a decrease in body fat. Steroid users talk in terms of "dirty" and "clean" drugs; in these instances, they are referring to the androgenic-anabolic ratio (Riem and Hursey, 1993). An example of a "dirty" steroid would be testosterone cypionate with its 1:1 ratio; a "clean" steroid would be Anavar with its 13:1 composition. The fact that AAS vary so much in androgenic-anabolic ratio should serve as a reminder that when we talk of AAS we are really referring to a range of drugs with very different effects and side effects. Lombardo, Longcope, and Voy (1985) have provided us with a representational view of various AAS plotted by androgenic to anabolic ratio, shown in figure 9.5.

It is easy to see the appeal of the AAS in view of the obvious gains to be made in size, strength, and outward manifestations of masculinity. On the other hand, there are drawbacks to the AAS, including negative effects on endocrinal and reproductive functioning, virilization and feminization, cardiovascular and hematologic functioning, hepatic disturbances, musculoskeletal development, dermatological conditions, risk of AIDS and other infections, and behavioral disturbances. Among the latter are withdrawal effects, depression, escalations in aggressive behavior, and rage responses ("roid rages"). Attesting to the latter points concerning violent behavior, former Houston Oiler football player Dean Steinkuhler, a steroid user in college and in the earliest years in the National Football League (NFL), said his drug regimen "made me real moody, violent, I wanted to kill somebody" ("A Former Husker," 1987, p. 24). Darren A. Chamberlain, a young ex-user for so-called aesthetic purposes, said: "I was doing everything from being obnoxious to getting out of the car and provoking fights at intersections . . . I couldn't handle any kind of stress. I'd just blow. You can walk in my parents' house today and see the signs—holes in doors I stuck my fist through, indentations in walls I kicked" (Toufexis, 1989, p. 78).

AAS use appears to be rising among both athletes and young people interested in what Toufexis (1989) calls the "Rambo Look." Toufexis further cites statistics indicating that a half-million adolescents nationwide have used steroids, many in search of a Mr. Universe or Hulk Hogan appearance. One quote from the article by Toufexis captures the spirit of this misguided search for the body beautiful: "His mind is so warped that he said he doesn't care if he dies, so long as he looks big in his coffin" (p. 78).

At the heart of the misuse of the various performance-enhancing drugs, and most particularly the AAS, is the willingness of the athlete to do almost anything to gain the proverbial competitive edge; this win-at-all-costs mentality is called the Faustian philosophy of the athlete by Dr. James Puffer, a sports medicine specialist ("Drug Testing in Sports," 1985). Responses to a question posed by *USA Today* in 1990 are telling: 14 percent of the respondents to a "Speak Out Poll" by that publication indicated that they would still take a pill that would make them a world-class athlete knowing that the medication would kill them in ten years. Perhaps more gratifying, only 3 percent responded positively to the same question when the proposed time line was five years ("Speak Out on Sports," 1990).

Figure 9.5: **Anabolic-Androgenic Steroids Plotted by Anabolic to Androgenic Ratio**

Anabolic
/
Anavar (13:1 oral)
/
Maxibolin (8:1 oral)
/
Winstrol (6:1 IM, oral)
/
Durabolin (6:1 IM)
/
Deca-Durabolin (4:1 IM)
/
Dianabol (3:1 oral)
/
Anadrol (3:1 oral)
/
Halotestin (2:1 oral)
/
Susanon-250 (1:1 IM)
Testosterone cypionate (1:1 IM)
/
Androgenic

Source: Lombardo, Longcope, and Voy (1985).

In a related note, Steve Courson, an eight-year veteran of the NFL and an admitted hard-core AAS user, upon finding out that he was in need of a heart transplant due to dilated cardiomyopathy (a weakening of the heart muscle), said, "There's no glory dying for a sport" (Telander, 1989). We suspect that Courson would agree that his abuse of AAS was driven by Puffer's Faustian mentality notion. The death from brain lymphoma of ex-pro football star Lyle Alzado has been attributed to his more than twenty years of AAS abuse (Alzado, 1991). Again, some would say that the win-at-all-costs mentality claimed another victim (though the relationship between AAS and cancer is far from proven).

Ethical Concerns

The ethical issues associated with steroid abuse (as well as other drugs and performance enhancement techniques) are complex, and there are contrasting points of view on the whole matter. A highly controversial sports personality of the mid-1980s was Brian Bosworth, an All-American linebacker for the Oklahoma Sooners and later a player with the NFL Seattle Seahawks. He was banned from the 1987 Orange Bowl for alleged steroid abuse, and the often flamboyant Bosworth protested his dismissal. Bosworth stated that the National Collegiate Athletic Association (what he called "The National Communists Against Athletes") had engaged in persecutory acts against him for a behavior that was not illegal. Bill Walsh, then the coach of the NFL San Francisco 49ers, sided with Bosworth on his ban: "It's like giving someone a six-year sentence for taking money out of a phone booth" (Walsh, 1987). Ron Hale (1987), a former U.S. powerlifting champion, said that steroids should not be banned because athletes need them to compete at the elite level. Another outspoken advocate for steroid use is Tony Millar, an Australian physician who sees no moral, ethical, or legal problems whatsoever with open-minded and carefully supervised usage among athletes.

Many disagree with the advocates of AAS usage. Ken Fitch, an Australian contemporary of Millar, strongly suggested that Millar has done athletics a disservice by encouraging athletes to cheat (Millar, 1986). The NCAA has continually taken a strong stance against AAS use, and has created a screening program that appears to have reduced the number of athletes using the drugs. *USA Today* ("Revised NCAA Testing," 1991) has indicated that the number of football players reporting to NFL combines for evaluation at the end of their collegiate careers has dropped from thirty-eight in 1987 to four or five in each of the past few years, ostensibly due to the screening efforts. However, the screening programs are not without critics. Yesalis (1990) tells us that the NCAA has budgeted between $1.6 and $3.2 million to catch perhaps a dozen AAS violators, a monetary expenditure that Albrecht, Anderson, and McKeag (1992) suggest may be exorbitant in terms of return on the dollar.

Many states have taken up the gauntlet with regard to the dispensation of AAS by physicians ("Sounding Board," 1989). Also, Congress has undertaken steps to curb AAS distribution through the mail, thereby cutting into one important supplier of AAS ("Congress Considers," 1989). Also, the Anabolic Steroids Control Act (ASCA) of 1990 has instituted penalties for illegal steroid distribution of up to five years' imprisonment and fines of up to $250,000 ("Getting Tougher on Steroids," 1991). Professional organizations within sports such as the American College of Sports Medicine (ACSM) and the International Society for Sport Psychology (ISSP), have taken firm stances against AAS utilization by athletes. The ISSP position is as follows:

> The use of AAS is potentially dangerous, both psychologically and physically, and should not be a part of sport and physical

activity. An emerging body of medical literature suggests that the prolonged AAS intake may reduce the quality and longevity of life. Therefore, the ISSP recommends that all possible preventive measures be taken to eliminate AAS use in sport and physical activity around the world. ("A Position Statement," 1993, p. 76)

Similarly, the ACSM takes a dim view of AAS use; their position is summarized by their position statement in figure 9.6.

Two final issues merit our attention. One point of concern is raised by both Yesalis (1990) and Albrecht, Anderson, and McKeag (1992), who separately suggest that our aforementioned Faustian emphasis on winning is at the heart of AAS and other abuses of performance enhancers, and perhaps we should look into our misguided values with regard to winning and losing as a partial solution to the problem. Secondly, Riem and Hursey (1993), among many, have suggested that much of what is known about the effects of AAS is reasonable supposition as opposed to demonstrated fact. Anecdotal evidence, questionable case histories, subject credibility, subject unwillingness to participate in studies, inappropriate sampling strategies, inadequate control groups, failure to control dose type and length of administration, and other experimental errors have plagued research on AAS. These sorts of lingering problems have made it difficult to make confident generalizations about the effects of AAS.

SUMMARY

1. The black athlete, the high risk sport participant, the athlete who excels at the national or world level, and the athlete who uses steroids or other performance-enhancing procedures are of considerable interest to professional researchers and theorists.

2. Blacks were brought to America as indentured servants in 1619 and were enslaved until the Emancipation Proclamation of 1862. After the Civil War, they became involved extensively in baseball, boxing, and as jockeys in horse racing. Moses Fleetwood

Figure 9.6: **The American College of Sports Medicine (ACSM) Position Statement on Steroid Use: The Use of Anabolic-Androgenic Steroids in Sports**

Based on a comprehensive literature and a careful analysis of the claims concerning the ergogenic effects and the adverse effects of anabolic-androgenic steroids, it is the position of the American College of Sports Medicine that:

1. The anabolic-androgenic steroids in the presence of an adequate diet can contribute to increases in body weight, often in the lean mass compartment.
2. The gain in muscular strength achieved through high-intensity exercise and proper diet can be increased by the use of anabolic-androgenic steroids in some individuals.
3. Anabolic-androgenic steroids do not increase aerobic power or capacity for muscular exercise.
4. Anabolic-androgenic steroids have been associated with adverse effects on the liver, cardiovascular system, reproductive system, and psychological status in therapeutic trials and in limited research on athletes. Until further research is completed, the potential hazards of the use of the anabolic-androgenic steroids in athletes must include those found in therapeutic trials.
5. The use of anabolic-androgenic steroids by athletes is contrary to the rules and ethical principles of athletic competition as set forth by many of the sports governing bodies. The American College of Sports Medicine supports these ethical principles and deplores the use of anabolic-androgenic steroids by athletes.

Source: "The Use of Anabolic-Androgenic Steroids in Sports" (1987).

Walker and his brother Weldy Wilberforce Walker were prominent baseball players of the late 1800s, though their acceptance by whites was very poor. Tom Molineaux was the first black heavyweight boxing champion of the world, and black dominance of boxing continues largely unabated. Willey Sims was an early leader in jockey circles, and blacks dominated the sport of horse racing until 1900, at which time they were relegated to lesser roles in favor in white jockeys.

3. The success of black athletes in certain sports — mainly football, basketball, baseball, track, and boxing — is difficult to explain. Genetic or biological superiority theories abound but are hard to substantiate. Social/cultural influences that arise out of bias, prejudice, misguided preconceptions, and superstition probably constitute a more viable hypothesis for explaining black superiority in certain sports. Psychological explanations are sparse and shed very little light on the issue.

4. Sport parachuting, hang gliding, scuba diving, and rock climbing are popular components of the modern "risk revolution" and the psychological makeup of the participants has been intriguing to sport psychologists.

5. Twenty-three U.S. sport parachutists died while participating in their sport in 1990, a decrease of eleven deaths from 1989. Deaths in sport parachuting are strongly related to inexperience. Physiologically, parachutists experience heightened arousal as well as elevated anxiety and self-reports of fear associated with jumping, but are generally low in state and trait anxiety when compared with reported test norms. Also, parachutists are above average in intelligence and are unconforming sensation seekers with a low need for order and rigidity.

6. Hang gliding is a highly dangerous activity with a death rate exceeding that of suicide for people of all ages in Canada and automobile fatalities among youth in the United States. Based on highly preliminary observational data, hang gliding participants are likely to be single, Caucasian college students who are "tuned in" to the hang gliding lifestyle. They are not unrealistic about the dangers of their sport but do not see it as overly hazardous. Reasons for leaving the sport generally center around injuries, family concerns, or career issues.

7. Rock climbers, like other high risk athletes, are generally conventional sensation-seekers.

8. Scuba diving, while hazardous, appears to be a relatively safe activity when conducted properly. Overall, scuba participants appear to be rather unremarkable in personality makeup when compared with others except in the area of anxiety, where they appear to be generally low. Some evidence exists that these participants are also more internal and more masculine in sex role orientation.

9. Two correlates of risk taking have spawned a fair amount of research: sensation seeking and birth order effects. Clearly, high risk sport participants are sensation seekers; they are unconventional, bored by routine, and seekers of stress through more unconventional means. As for birth effects, high risk sport participants are more likely to be laterborns than firstborn children. Apparently firstborns have their needs met in such a way that "proving" behavior through more unconventional means is not necessary for them.

10. Kroll's conceptualization of the personality performance pyramid is an intriguing way of viewing the elite athlete. Generally, however, the model is hard to support to the extent that research in the area is sparse and disconnected.

11. Morgan's notion of the Iceberg Profile as produced by the Profile of Mood States (POMS) has generated much research, and

substantiation for the idea is considerable. Olympic wrestlers, oarsmen, distance runners, and cyclists all share commonalities in terms of the Iceberg Profile.

12. Wrestlers have been a fertile source of data on elite performers. In general, elite wrestlers when compared with their slightly less elite peers are most commonly differentiated by self-confidence and concentration on the task at hand. Performing at a level that is close to what they regard as their maximum potential is also a salient discriminator between the two groups of wrestlers.

13. Other studies of elite athletes from such diverse populations as Olympic weight lifters, Olympic gymnasts, Canadian Pan American Games participants from ten sports, elite New Zealand youth rowers, elite youth skiers in the United States, national level racquetball players, and figure skaters further substantiate the notion that elite performers are self-confident, task oriented, and actualized performers in terms of ability.

14. Studies of elite athletes are hampered by a host of methodological shortcomings such as sample availability, sample size, definitional problems centering around what elite actually is, instrumentation selection, and data analysis variations. Nevertheless, research will continue in the hopes of shedding more light on the identification and training of elite athletes.

15. The drug-oriented society in which we live has influenced the world of sport, and the abuse of a wide variety of drugs is a major ethical problem for sport psychologists, physicians, and others with a stake in the future of athletics.

16. One type of abuse involves drugs considered to be recreational, such as alcohol, marijuana, and cocaine.

17. Restorative drugs represent another category of concern and include muscle relaxants, anti-inflammatories, and painkillers.

18. Additive drugs purport to enhance performance and are generally referred to as ergogenic aids. Stimulant drugs and anabolic steroids are two significant ergogenic aids. The use of amphetamines, such as Dexedrine and Benzedrine, was widespread in professional sports in the 1970s but is thought to be less of a problem today. Steroids use is widespread among athletes, particularly elite amateur and professional performers. Because the steroids have been shown to have a number of adverse side effects for both male and female athletes, there is an increasing outcry from many sources for a ban on their future use.

SUGGESTED READINGS

Berglund, B., & Safstrom, H. (1994) Psychological monitoring and modulation of training load of world-class canoeists. *Medicine and Science in Sports and Exercise, 26,* 1036–1040.

> In an interesting variation in the use of the *Profile of Mood States,* the authors were able to monitor nine male and five female world-class canoeists in Sweden for purposes of detecting staleness occurring during training for the Olympics. The POMS was useful, based on the total mood disturbance (TMD) score, in monitoring staleness in these athletes. Athlete acceptance of the POMS itself was assessed, and athlete response to the scale was quite favorable. The authors concluded that the POMS has utility in monitoring training of elite canoeists.

Chalk, O. (1975) *Pioneers of black sport.* New York: Dodd, Mead.

> Chalk takes a look at the history of black athletes in four sports—baseball, basketball, boxing, and football. Pictures, historical chronicles, and game records of the early days of black sport serve as useful mechanisms to promote interest. This book is a must for the sport historian.

Davenport, J. (1994) A double-edge sword: Drugs in sport. In P. J. Graham, ed., *Sport business: Opera-*

tional and theoretical aspects (212–222). Dubuque, IA: Brown & Benchmark.

> A particularly nice feature of this brief article is its focus on the history of steroid abuse in sports, beginning with the isolation of the male hormone, testosterone, in 1935. The abuse of steroids at the various Olympic Games since 1952 also receives thorough coverage. Statistics and prominent case histories are featured. This is a highly readable article on an interesting topic.

Dedera, D. (1975) *Hang gliding: The flyingest flying.* Flagstaff, AR: Northland Press.

> This book attempts to capture the essence of the sport of hang gliding through prose and a large number of color pictures. The beauty, the lifestyle, and the danger are all chronicled for the reader in a highly readable way. The photography is particularly compelling, with many of the pictures provided by the author.

Duda, M. (1986) Female athletes: Targets for drug abuse. *Physician and Sportsmedicine, 14*(6), 142–146.

> Increasingly, female athletes are becoming caught up in the win-at-all-cost Faustian mentality so prevalent among male performers, and they are convincing themselves or being encouraged by overzealous coaches to attempt to increase their performance through chemical means. Perhaps this better-life-through-chemistry mentality has its roots in the 1973 World Championships in swimming, which were dominated by East German women just one year after the Americans had handily defeated them in the 1972 Olympics. In that one year East German competitors had grown much bigger and stronger, a change attributable to steroid use. Discussion throughout this article centers on the increasing temptation to gain the athletic advantage through steroids. Dr. Robert Voy, chief medical officer for the USOC says: "In men, steroids offer an unfair advantage. But in women, that advantage is probably magnified ten times" (p. 146).
>
> The importance of this problem in women's sports has been accentuated by the two-year suspension of a number of Chinese swimmers, track and field competitors, and weight lifters for steroid violations at a variety of world competi-

tions in the early and mid-1990s. Many athletes, coaches, and administrators have issued urgent pleas for even greater penalties for steroid abuse in the future (Whitten, 1995).

Fair, J. D. (1993) Isometrics or steroids? Exploring new frontiers of strength in the early 1960s. *Journal of Sport History, 20,* 1–24.

> This article provides a historical perspective on the use of steroids to enhance physical performance. In the fall of 1961, a new technique was introduced to weightlifting called functional isometric contraction. At the same time, early experimentation was being conducted on the pairing of steroids with vigorous isometric workouts. Gains in performance were thus variously attributed to the new technique of isometrics, the steroids, and a host of mental preparation techniques to include hypnosis. By the end of the 1960s, it was clear that the use of steroids was efficacious in boosting weightlifting performance.

Johnson, B. D., & Johnson, N. R. (1995) Stacking and "stoppers": A test of the outcome control hypothesis. *Sociology of Sport Journal, 12,* 105–112.

> In an effort to further test the stacking hypothesis, these researchers divided major league pitchers for the years 1992 and 1993 into three groups—starters, stoppers, and others. Starters were categorized based on having started in 80 percent of the games in which they appeared. Stoppers, or "closers," were assigned based on number of saves and games finished. Others were pitchers who did not meet the definitions of the other two groups. A total of 465 pitchers were used in the study. Though 85 percent of the pitchers were Anglo, the authors concluded that stacking *within* the pitching position in major league baseball did not appear to exist.

Lapchick, R. E. (1991) *Five minutes to midnight: Race and sport in the 1990s.* New York: Madison Books.

> Richard Lapchick, outspoken critic of racism in sport (and the broader societal context), has followed up on his very successful book, *Broken promises: Racism in American sports,* with another outstanding effort. In actuality, the first

eleven chapters of *Five Minutes* are extracted from the previous book; there are, however, six completely new chapters. The end result is a most readable and cogent discourse on racial relations in sport and society. It is Lapchick's position that sport can and should serve as a model for better human relations in all facets of society.

Tricker, R., & Cook, D. L. (1990) *Athletes at risk: Drugs and sport.* Dubuque, IA: Wm. C. Brown.
    Tricker and Cook have compiled an informative collection of edited readings on drugs and sport, drawing from authorities in sports medicine, sport psychology, and pharmacology. Issues addressed include why athletes use drugs, the history of drug use in sport, ethical issues associated with drugs, the steroids, psychological factors associated with drug use, drug use in intercollegiate athletics, drug testing, and the role of the sport psychologist in providing alternatives to drugs for athletes.

REFERENCES

Albrecht, R. R., Anderson, W. A., & McKeag, D. B. (1992) Drug testing of college athletes. *Sports Medicine, 14,* 349–352.

Alderman, R. (1970) A sociopsychological assessment of attitude toward physical activity in champion athletes. *Research Quarterly, 14,* 1–9.

Alzado, L. (1991) I'm sick and I'm scared. *Sports Illustrated,* July 8, 20–27.

Bachrach, A. (1970) Diver behavior. *Human Performance and SCUBA Diving, 11,* 9–13.

Beaumaster, E. J., Knowles, J. B., & MacLean, A. W. (1978) The sleep of skydivers: A study of stress. *Psychophysiology, 15,* 209–213.

Bem, S. (1974) The measurement of psychological androgyny. *Journal of Consulting and Clinical Psychology, 42,* 155–162.

Best, C. (1987) Experience and career length in professional football: The effect of positional segregation. *Sociology of Sport Journal, 4,* 410–420.

Blood, K. J. (1990) Non-medical substance use among athletes at a small liberal arts college. *Athletic Training, 25,* 335–339.

Brannigan, A., & McDougall, A. A. (1983) Peril and pleasure in the maintenance of a high risk sport: A study of hang-gliding. *Journal of Sport Behavior, 6,* 37–51.

Brubaker, B. (1985) A pipeline full of drugs. *Sports Illustrated,* Jan. 21, 18–21.

Buckley, W. E., Yesalis, C. E., Friedl, K. E., Anderson, W. A., Streit, A. L., & Wright, J. E. (1988) Estimated prevalence of anabolic-androgenic steroid use among male high school seniors. *Journal of the American Medical Association, 260,* 3441–3445.

Bulletin board. (1985) *NEA Now, 5*(10), 1–4.

Cancio, L. C. (1991) Stress and trance in freefall parachuting: A pilot study. *American Journal of Clinical Hypnosis, 33,* 225–234.

Casher, B. (1977) Relationship between birth order and participation in dangerous sports. *Research Quarterly, 48,* 33–40.

Chu, D. (1982) *Dimensions of sport studies.* New York: Wiley.

Coakley, J. (1982) *Sport in society: Issues and controversies* (2d ed.). St. Louis, MO: C. V. Mosby.

Coakley, J. J. (1994) *Sport in society: Issues and controversies* (5th ed.). St. Louis, MO: Mosby.

Congress considers ban on mail order steroids. (1989) *Physician and Sportsmedicine, 17*(5), 34.

Cook, D. L. (1992) Steroids in sport: Where has honor gone? *Track and Field Quarterly, 92,* 15–16.

Correll, J. (1983) 1982 fatalities reflect best record since 1971. *Parachutist, 24*(4), 27–30.

Curry, T., & Jiobu, R. (1984) *Sports: A social perspective.* Englewood Cliffs, NJ: Prentice-Hall.

Dedera, D. (1975) *Hang gliding: The flyingest flying.* Flagstaff, AZ: Northland Press.

Dreyfuss, I. (1989) Federal agency to prove anabolic steroid abuse. *Physician and Sportsmedicine, 17*(7), 16.

Drug testing in sports. (1985) *Physician and Sportsmedicine, 13*(12), 69–82.

Dunn, J., & Lupfer, M. (1974) A comparison of black and white boys' performance in self-paced and reactive sports activities. *Journal of Applied Social Psychology, 4,* 24–35.

Edwards, H. (1973) *Sociology of sport.* Homewood, IL: Dorsey.

Egstrom, G., & Bachrach, A. (1971) Diver panic. *Skin Diver, 20*(11), 36–37, 54–55, 57.

Eitzen, S., & Sage, G. (1978) *Sociology of American sport.* Dubuque, IA: Wm. C. Brown.

Eklund, R. C., Gould, D., & Jackson, S. A. (1993) Psychological foundations of Olympic wrestling excellence: Reconciling individual differences and nomothetic characterization. *Journal of Applied Sport Psychology, 5,* 35–47.

Endler, N., & Okada, M. (1975) Multidimensional measure of trait anxiety: The S-R Inventory of General Trait Anxiousness. *Journal of Consulting and Clinical Psychology, 43,* 319–329.

Evans, M., Weinberg, R., & Jackson, A. (1992) Psychological factors related to drug use in college athletes. *The Sport Psychologist, 6,* 24–41.

Ethics of blood doping. (1985) *Physician and Sportsmedicine, 13*(8), 151.

Fenz, W. D., & Brown, M. (1958) Betting preferences and personality characteristics of sports parachutists. *Aerospace Medicine, 29,* 175–176.

Fenz, W. D., & Epstein, S. (1967) Changes in gradients of skin conductance, heart rate and respiration rate as a function of experience. *Psychosomatic Medicine, 29,* 33–51.

Fenz, W. D., & Jones, G. B. (1972) Individual differences in physiological arousal and performance in sport parachutists. *Psychosomatic Medicine, 34,* 1–8.

Finlayson, I. (1984) Obituary. *New Zealand Gliding Kiwi, 16*(1), 21.

A former Husker fesses up. (1987) *Sports Illustrated,* Jan. 5, p. 24.

Frankle, M. A., Cicero, G. J., & Payne, J. (1984) Use of androgenic-anabolic steroids by athletes (letter). *Journal of the American Medical Association, 252,* 482.

Freischlag, J., & Freischlag, T. (1993) Selected psychosocial, physical, and technical factors among rock climbers: A test of the flow paradigm. In W. K. Simpson, A. D. LeUnes, & J. S. Picou (Eds.), *Applied Research in Coaching and Athletics Annual 1993.* Boston: American Press.

Gannon, K. (1989) Pharmacists need to caution athletes about steroid use. *Drug Topics, 133*(12), 25.

Gates, H. L. (1991) Delusions of grandeur, *Sports Illustrated,* Aug. 19, 78.

George, J. (1994) The virtual disappearance of the white male sprinter in the United States: A speculative essay. *Sociology of Sport Journal, 11,* 70–78.

Getting tougher on steroid abuse. (1991) *Physician and Sportsmedicine, 19*(2), 46.

Gledhill, N. (1982) Blood doping and related issues: A brief review. *Medicine and Science in Sports and Exercise, 14*(3), 183–189.

Gould, D., Eklund, R. C., & Jackson, S. A. (1992a) 1988 U. S. Olympic wrestling excellence: I. Mental preparation, precompetitive cognition, and affect. *The Sport Psychologist, 6,* 358–382.

Gould, D., Eklund, R. C., & Jackson, S. A. (1992b) 1988 U. S. Olympic wrestling excellence: II. Thoughts and affect occurring during competition. *The Sport Psychologist, 6,* 383–402.

Gould, D., Eklund, E. C., & Jackson, S. A. (1993) Coping strategies used by U. S. Olympic wrestlers. *Research Quarterly for Exercise and Sport, 64,* 83–93.

Gould, D., Finch, L. M., & Jackson, S. A. (1993) Coping strategies used by national champion figure skaters, *Research Quarterly for Exercise and Sport, 64,* 453–468.

Gould, D., Jackson, S. A., & Finch, L. M. (1993a) Life at the top: The experiences of U. S. national champion figure skaters. *The Sport Psychologist, 7,* 354–374.

Gould, D., Jackson, S., & Finch, L. (1993b) Sources of stress in national champion figure skaters. *Journal of Sport and Exercise Psychology, 15,* 134–159.

Gould, D., Weiss, M., & Weinberg, R. S. (1981) Psychological characteristics of successful and nonsuccessful Big Ten wrestlers. *Journal of Sport Psychology, 3,* 69–81.

Griffiths, T. J., Steel, D. H., & Vaccaro, P. (1978) Anxiety levels of beginning SCUBA students. *Perceptual and Motor Skills, 47,* 312–314.

Griffiths, T. J., Steel, D. H., & Vaccaro, P. (1979) Relationship between anxiety and performance in scuba diving. *Perceptual and Motor Skills, 48,* 1009–1010.

Griffiths, T. J., Steel, D. H., & Vaccaro, P. (1982) Anxiety of scuba divers: A multidimensional approach. *Perceptual and Motor Skills, 55,* 611–614.

Griffiths, T. J., Steel, D. H., Vaccaro, P., & Karpman, M. (1981) The effects of relaxation techniques on anxiety and underwater performance. *International Journal of Sport Psychology, 12,* 176–182.

Hagberg, J., Mullin, J., Bahrke, M., & Limburg, J. (1979) Physiological profiles and selected physiological characteristics of national class American cyclists. *Journal of Sports Medicine, 19,* 341–346.

Hale, R. (1987) Don't ban steroids: Athletes need them. *USA Today,* Jan. 5, 10A.

Hall, E., Church, G., & Stone, M. (1980) Relationship of birth order to selected personality characteristics of nationally ranked Olympic weight lifters. *Perceptual and Motor Skills, 51,* 971–976.

Hammerton, M., & Tickner, A. (1968) An investigation into the effects of stress upon skilled performance. *Ergonomics, 12,* 851–855.

Heyman, S. R., & Rose, K. G. (1979) Psychological variables affecting scuba performance. In C. H. Naudeau, W. R. Halliwell, K. M. Newell, & G. C. Roberts (Eds.), *Psychology of motor behavior and sport—1979* (pp. 180–188). Champaign, IL: Human Kinetics.

High jump. (1985) *Track and Field News, 37*(12), 38.

Highlen, P., & Bennett, B. (1979) Psychological characteristics of successful and nonsuccessful elite wrestlers: An exploratory study. *Journal of Sport Psychology, 1,* 123–137.

Highlen, P., & Bennett, B. (1983) Elite divers and wrestlers: A comparison between open- and closed-skill athletes. *Journal of Sport Psychology, 5,* 390–409.

Hymbaugh, K., & Garrett, J. (1974) Sensation seeking among skydivers. *Perceptual and Motor Skills, 38,* 118.

Johnsgard, K. W., Ogilvie, B. C., & Merritt, K. (1975) The stress seekers: A psychological study of sports parachutists, racing drivers, and football players. *Journal of Sports Medicine, 15,* 158–169.

Jones, J., & Hochner, A. (1973) Racial differences in sports activities: A look at the self-paced versus reactive hypothesis. *Journal of Personality and Social Psychology, 27,* 86–95.

Kenyon, G. (1968) A conceptual model for characterizing physical activity. *Research Quarterly, 39,* 96–105.

Kirschenbaum, J. (1980) Uppers in baseball. *Sports Illustrated,* July 21, 11.

Kroll, W. (1970) Current strategies and problems in personality assessment of athletes. In L. E. Smith (Ed.), *Psychology of motor learning* (pp. 349–367). Chicago, IL: Athletic Institute.

Lapchick, R. E., & Benedict, J. R. (1993) 1993 racial report card. *CSSS Digest 5*(1), 1–13.

Lapchick, R. E., & Brown, J. P. (1992) 1992 racial report card: Do professional sports provide opportunities for all races? *CSSS Digest,* Summer, 1–8.

Leonard, W. M. (1984) *A sociological perspective of sport* (2d ed). Minneapolis, MN: Burgess.

Leonard, W. M., & Reyman, J. E. (1988) The odds of attaining professional athlete status: Refining the computation. *Sociology of Sport Journal, 5,* 162–169.

Levenson, M. R. (1990) Risk taking and personality. *Journal of Personality and Social Psychology, 58,* 1073–1080.

Lombardo, J. A., Longcope, C., & Voy, R. O. (1985) Recognizing anabolic steroid abuse. *Patient Care, 19,* 28–47.

Longstreth, L. (1970) Birth order and avoidance of dangerous activities. *Developmental Psychology, 2,* 154.

Loy, J., & McElvogue, J. (1970) Racial segregation in American sport. *International Review of Sport Sociology, 5,* 5–24.

Lubin, B. (1967) Manual for the *Depression Adjective Checklist.* San Diego, CA: Educational and Industrial Testing Service.

Mahoney, M. J. (1989) Psychological predictors of elite and non-elite performance in Olympic weightlifting. *International Journal of Sport Psychology, 20,* 1–12.

Mahoney, M. J., & Avener, M. (1977) Psychology of the elite athlete. *Cognitive Therapy and Research, 1,* 135–141.

Mandell, A. (1975) Pro football fumbles the drug scandal. *Psychology Today,* June, 39–47.

McNair, D. M., Lorr, M., & Droppleman, L. F. (1971) *Profile of Mood States Manual.* San Diego, CA: Educational and Industrial Testing Service.

Mehrabian, A. (1969) Measures of achieving tendency. *Educational and Psychological Measurement, 29,* 445–451.

Meyers, A., Cooke, C., Cullen, J., & Liles, L. (1979) Psychological aspects of athletic competitors: A replication across sports. *Cognitive Therapy and Research, 3,* 361–366.

Millar, C. (1986) Anabolic steroids: An Australian sports physician goes public. *Physician and Sportsmedicine, 14*(11), 167–170.

Morgan, W. P. (1968) Personality characteristics of wrestlers participating in the world championships. *Journal of Sports Medicine, 8,* 212–216.

Morgan, W. P. (1978a) Sport personology: The credulous–skeptical argument in perspective. In W. F. Straub (Ed.), *An analysis of athletic behavior* (pp. 218–227). Ithaca, NY: Mouvement.

Morgan, W. P. (1978b) Mind of the marathoner. *Sports Illustrated,* April, 38–49.

Morgan, W. P. (1980) Test of champions: The iceberg profile. *Psychology Today, 14*(2), 92–102, 108.

Morgan, W. P., Ellickson, K. A., O'Connor, P. J., & Bradley, P. W. (1992) Elite male distance runners: Personality structure, mood states and performance. *Track and Field Quarterly, 92,* 59–62.

Morgan, W. P., & Johnson, R. (1976) Personality characteristics of successful and unsuccessful oarsmen. *International Journal of Sport Psychology, 9,* 119–133.

Morgan, W. P., O'Connor, P. J., Sparling, P. B., & Pate, R. R. (1992) The elite female distance runner: Psychological characterization. *Track and Field Quarterly, 92,* 63–67.

Morgan, W. P., & Pollock, M. L. (1977) Psychological characteristics of the elite distance runner. *Annals of the New York Academy of Sciences, 301,* 382–403.

Nation, J. R., & LeUnes, A. (1983) A personality profile of the black athlete in college football. *Psychology, 20,* 1–3.

New techniques may catch blood dopers. (1986) *Physician and Sportsmedicine, 14*(2), 36.

Nisbett, R. E. (1968) Birth order and participation in dangerous sports. *Journal of Personality and Social Psychology, 8,* 351–353.

Nixon, H. L. (1981) Birth order and preference for risky sports among college students. *Journal of Sport Behavior, 4,* 12–23.

Ogilvie, B. C. (1974) The sweet psychic jolt of danger. *Psychology Today,* Oct., 8–91.

Oliver, C. (1971) *High for the game.* New York: Morrow.

Ottley, W. (1983) USPA secretary killed while making stunt jump. *Parachutist, 24*(3), 35.

Pate, R., Rotella, R., & McClenaghan, B. (1984) *Scientific foundations of coaching.* Philadelphia, PA: Saunders.

Patten, C. A., Harris, W., & Leatherman, D. (1994) Psychological characteristics of elite wheelchair athletes: The Iceberg Profile. *Perceptual and Motor Skills, 79,* 1390.

Peterson, R. (1970) *Only the ball was white.* Englewood Cliffs, NJ: Prentice-Hall.

Phillips, J. C. (1976) Toward an explanation of racial variations in top-level sports participation. *International Review of Sport Sociology, 11*(3), 39–55.

Phillips, J. C. (1988) A further comment on the 'economic hypothesis' of positional segregation in baseball. *Sociology of Sport Journal, 5,* 63–65.

Position statement—The use of anabolic-androgenic steroids (AAS) in sport and physical activity. (1993) *International Journal of Sport Psychology, 24,* 74–78.

Powell, F. M., & Verner, J. P. (1982) Anxiety and performance relationships in first time parachutists. *Journal of Sport Psychology, 4,* 184–188.

Rader, B. (1983) *American sports from the age of folk games to the age of spectators.* Englewood Cliffs, NJ: Prentice-Hall.

Revised NCAA testing cuts steroid use. (1991) *USA Today,* May 22, 1C.

Riem, K., & Hursey, K. (1993) Effects of anabolic-androgenic steroid use in athletes: A coaches guide. In W. K. Simpson, A. D. LeUnes, & J. S. Picou (Eds.) *Applied Research in Coaching and Athletics Annual 1993.* Boston: American Press.

Robertson, I. (1981) *Sociology* (2d ed.) New York: Worth.

Robinson, D. W. (1985) Stress seeking: Selected behavioral characteristics of elite rock climbers. *Journal of Sport Psychology, 7,* 400–404.

Rossi, B., & Cereatti, L. (1993) The sensation seeking in mountain athletes as assessed by Zuckerman's Sensation Seeking Scale. *International Journal of Sport Psychology, 24,* 417–431.

Rostaing, B., & Sullivan, R. (1985) Triumphs tainted with blood. *Sports Illustrated,* January 21, 12–17.

Rotella, R., Gansneder, B., Ojala, D., & Billing, J. (1980) Cognitions and coping strategies of elite skiers: An exploratory study of young developing athletes. *Journal of Sport Psychology, 2,* 350–354.

Rowell, G. (1983) Mount Everest: Pure and simple. *Sports Illustrated,* Nov. 14, 88–102.

Scanlan, T. K., Stein, G. L., & Ravizza, K. (1989) An in-depth study of former elite figure skaters: II. Sources of enjoyment. *Journal of Sport and Exercise Psychology, 11,* 65–83.

Scanlan, T. K., Stein, G. L., & Ravizza, K. (1991) An in-depth study of former elite figure skaters: III. Sources of stress. *Journal of Sport and Exercise Psychology, 13,* 103–120.

Silva, J. M., Shultz, B., Haslam, R., & Murray, D. (1981) A psychophysiological assessment of elite wrestlers. *Research Quarterly for Exercise and Sport, 52,* 348–358.

Sitter, P. (1991) 1991 fatalities: General observations. *Parachutist, 32*(7), 39–45.

Snow, A., & LeUnes, A. (1994) Characteristics of sports research using the Profile of Mood States. *Journal of Sport Behavior, 17,* 207–211.

Snyder, E. E., & Spreitzer, E. A. (1989) *Social aspects of sport* (3d ed.) (p. 205). Englewood Cliffs, NJ: Prentice-Hall.

Sounding board—Anabolic-androgenic steroid use by athletes (1989) *New England Journal of Medicine,* October 12, 1042–1045.

Speak out on sports. (1990) *USA Today,* Feb. 5, 1C.

Straub, W. F. (1982) Sensation seeking among high and low-risk athletes. *Journal of Sport Psychology, 4,* 246–253.

Strauss, R. H., & Yesalis, C. E. (1991) Anabolic steroids in the athlete. *Annual Review of Medicine, 42,* 449–457.

Tangen-Foster, J. W., & Lathen, C. W. (1983) Risk sports in basic instruction programs: A status assessment. *Research Quarterly for Exercise and Sport, 54,* 305–308.

Telander, R. (1989) In the aftermath of steroids. *Sports Illustrated,* April 3, 34.

Toufexis, A. (1989) Shortcut to the Rambo look. *Time,* Jan. 30, 78.

Tricker, R., O'Neill, M. R., & Cook, D. (1989) The incidence of anabolic steroid use among competitive bodybuilders. *Journal of Drug Education, 19,* 313–325.

The use of anabolic-androgenic steroids in sports. (1987) *Medicine and Science in Sports and Exercise, 19,* 102.

Walsh, B. (1987) Quotelines. *USA Today,* Jan. 5, 10A.

Webster, E. (1989) Cold courage. *Sports Illustrated,* Jan. 16, 62–74.

Weltman, G., & Egstrom, G. H. (1969) Personal autonomy of scuba diver trainees. *Research Quarterly, 40,* 613–618.

Whitten, P. (1995) No news is bad news. *Swimming World and Junior Swimmer,* February, 37–38.

Wiggins, D. (1977) Good times on the old plantation: Popular recreations of the black slave in Antebellum South, 1810–1860. *Journal of Sport History, 4,* 260–281.

Willard, N. (1978) Testing the limits. *World Health,* Nov., 22–26.

Williams, L. (1978) Prediction of high-level rowing ability. *Journal of Sports Medicine, 18,* 11–17.

Williams, R., & Youssef, A. (1975) Division of labor in college football along racial lines. *International Journal of Sport Psychology, 6,* 1–13.

Worthy, M., & Markle, A. (1970) Racial differences in reactive versus self-paced sports activities. *Journal of Personality and Social Psychology, 16,* 439–443.

Yesalis, C. E. (1990) Winning and performance-enhancing drugs—our dual addiction. *Physician and Sportsmedicine, 18,* 161–163, 167.

Yetman, N. R., & Berghorn, F. J. (1993) Racial participation and integration in intercollegiate basketball: A longitudinal perspective. *Sociology of Sport Journal, 10,* 310–314.

Yiannakis, A. (1976) Birth order and preference for dangerous sports among males. *Research Quarterly, 47,* 62–67.

Zuckerman, M. (1971) Dimensions of sensation-seeking. *Journal of Consulting and Clinical Psychology, 36,* 45–52.

Zuckerman, M. (1984) Experience and desire: A new format for Sensation Seeking Scales. *Journal of Behavioral Assessment, 6,* 101–114.

Zuckerman, M., Kolin, E. A., Price, L., & Zoob, I. (1964) Development of a Sensation-seeking Scale. *Journal of Consulting Psychology, 28,* 477–482.

A Wider Perspective

The Female Athlete

I am strong. I am invincible. I am woman.

  Helen Reddy, *I Am Woman* (1972)

They are women; they are getting strong; and they feel damn near invincible.

  Sally B. Donnelly, *Time* magazine writer (1990)

What are little boys made of?
Frogs and snails and puppy dog tails;
That's what little boys are made of.
What are little girls made of?
Sugar and spice and everything nice;
That's what little girls are made of.

  Anonymous

INTRODUCTION

The prevailing view of women as the so-called weaker sex and, as such, subservient to men has a long history, the ancient Olympic Games notwithstanding. The French philosopher Jean-Jacques Rousseau (1712–1778) said, "Woman was made especially to please man. . . . If woman is formed to please and live in subjugation, she must render herself agreeable to man instead of provoking his wrath; her strength lies in her charms" (quoted in Spears, 1978, p. 7).

Further testimony to woman's frailty was noted in the most unlikely of settings, the 1933 meeting of the American Physical Education Association, where its president, Agnes Wayman, stated: "External stimuli such as cheering audiences, bands, lights, etc., cause a great response in girls and are apt to upset the endocrine balance. Under emotional stress a girl may easily overdo. There is widespread agreement that girls should not be exposed to extremes of fatigue or strain either emotional or physical" (cited in Loggia, 1973, p. 64).

Accompanying the passage of the Title IX legislation in 1972, which opened the doors for women to enter the mainstream of all walks of American life including sports, was widespread gender bias bordering on paranoia. Coaches, in many instances, were at the forefront in this battle, using sexist statements to either spur their players to greater effort or to affront their manhood. How many times has the chant "You throw like a girl" been used to impugn the masculinity of a young baseball player?

Perhaps the ultimate sexist putdown was offered up by Woody Hayes, the legendary Ohio State University football coach, who was quoted as follows: "I hear they're even letting w-o-m-e-n in their sports programs now [referring to Oberlin College]. That's your Women's Liberation, boy—bunch of goddam Lesbians. . . . You can bet your ass that if you have women around— and I've talked to psychiatrists about this—you aren't gonna be worth a damn. No sir! Man has to dominate . . . the best way to treat a woman . . . is to knock her up and hide her shoes" (cited in Vare, 1974, p. 38).

The view of a contemporary of Woody Hayes, a high school athletic director, is not terribly different: "We tried to organize a girls' sports program but it hasn't worked out very well. . . . Unfortunately, the girls didn't show a lot of interest. Only twelve came out for the team. There were two big tomboyish girls who remained quite enthused, but the others have not been faithful about practice. I'm not blaming them because I think a normal girl at that age is going to be more interested in catching a boy than catching a basketball" (cited in Gilbert and Williamson, 1973, p. 47).

A similar quote from a woman in South Carolina in the mid-1970s when women's sports were struggling for recognition, is as follows: "There is hardly a real mother in this nation who would not prefer to see her daughter dressed in a cute outfit, attracting boys and getting voted the most popular girl in her class and maybe marrying a football star after she graduates, rather than growing big muscles and looking like a man in some sport" (cited by Michener, 1976, p. 182).

In the Olympics, long the province of males, the gold medalist discus thrower Olga Connolly was nominated to be the flag bearer in the 1972 Munich Olympic Games parade, a fact that led observer Russell Knipp to respond: "The flag bearer ought to be a man, a strong man, a warrior. A woman's place is in the home" (cited in Leonard, 1984, p. 190). Perhaps the ultimate put-down in gender bias and the emergence of women in sports in the 1970s and 1980s was offered up by an anonymous source quoted in Lipsyte (1975, p. 217): "Sports is a male sanctuary; therefore any woman who tries to invade it is not really a woman."

As we shall see in the ensuing discussion, women in sport have indeed come a long way; much progress has been made in carving out a genuine niche in sport and society. There is also much more work to be done to achieve total integration of women into the fabric of sport and everyday life. But before tackling some of these substantive issues in detail, a brief look at some historical antecedents of women's participation in sport is in order.

A BRIEF HISTORY

The history of female involvement in sport and physical activity is almost nonexistent. Female involvement in sport is relatively recent.

Ancient Greece

Women did take part in some activities in early Greece, but they were barred from participating in Olympic events and even faced a death penalty for being so bold as to try to view

---

The Heraean Games

The Heraean Games represented a formalized outlet for athletic skills among young women in ancient Greece. However, evidence suggests that the games were actually limited to a footrace. Pausanias describes the games as follows:

> The games consist of footraces for maidens. These are not all of the same age. The first to run are the youngest; after them come the next in age, and the last to run are the oldest of the maidens. They run in the following way: Their hair hangs down, a tunic reaches to a little above the knee, and they bare a right shoulder as far as the breast. These too have the Olympic stadium reserved for their games, but the course of the stadium is shortened for them by about one-sixth of its length. To the winning maidens they give crowns of olive and a portion of the cow sacrificed to Hera. They may also dedicate statues with their names inscribed upon them. (Robinson, 1955, p. 9)

There is some evidence that the Heraean Games actually predated the Olympic Games and continued well into the first century A.D. (Spears and Swanson, 1983).

Source: Robinson (1955); Spears and Swanson (1983).

Highlight 10.1

Two milestones in the history of women in baseball: the Resolutes, Vassar College's first baseball team, and members of the Racine Belles (right), who from 1943 to 1954 played in the only professional women's baseball league in the United States.

them. Nevertheless, they had an outlet for their athletic energies in the form of the Heraean Games, named in honor of Hera, the wife of Zeus. Like the Olympics, these Heraean Games were held every four years and consisted of races for unmarried girls (Mouratidis, 1984). The games were held in Olympus beginning in what Spears (1984) calls the Archaic Period (800 B.C.–500 B.C.). In summarizing the overall influence of sports on early Greek women, Spears has written: "The history of women's sport in ancient Greece must be viewed in the perspective of men's sport of the same period. Throughout the ancient literature *any* suggestion of sport-like activity for women becomes evidence because of its rarity" (p. 44).

Little of significance took place in women's athletics until the inclusion of females in the Olympic Games in 1900. Prior to that time, little, if any, involvement in physical activity was expected or condoned. However, participation in the modern Olympics ushered in a new era in women's athletics.

The Modern Olympics

The founder of the modern Olympics, Baron Pierre de Coubertin, reinstituted the games in 1896. Women began to participate in 1900, though Coubertin was vehemently opposed to women taking part in the competition (Emery, 1984; Gerber, Felshin, Berlin, and Wyrick, 1974). Over his considerable protests, two events for women, tennis and golf, were added to the 1900 games. Archery followed in 1904, though it had unofficial status at that time. In 1908, figure skating was made an official event, and unofficial competition was staged in gymnastics, swim-

Ice hockey, a traditionally male-dominated sport, has recently acquired outstanding female participants. Pictured here is goalie Manon Rheaume at Hockey International's 1994 All-Star Game in Vancouver, Canada.

ming, and diving. Track and field events were added in 1928, though the debut was inauspicious. Emery (1984) reports that several runners fell upon completing the 800-meter run, thereby leading the opponents of female participation to conclude that women were indeed not up to the challenge of strenuous athletics. The extent of the setback created here is reflected by the fact that the event was discontinued until the 1960 Olympics. Perhaps the ultimate in strenuousness, the marathon, was not added to the female events until 1984.

Female competitors are now an integral part of the Olympic process, and this is reflected not only in the relatively wide variety of sports in which they participate but also by their numbers. According to Pensinger (1992), 7,555 men and 3,008 women (29 percent of the total) participated in the 1992 Olympic Games; twenty-three events were offered for females. A further attestation of the continuing development of women in the Olympics is provided by Eitzen and Sage (1982), who noted that in 1976 the time of a fifteen-year-old East German girl in the 400-meter freestyle swimming event was a full 3 seconds better than American Olympian Don Schollander's winning time in the same event for men only twelve years earlier. The Olympic Games have clearly served as a vehicle for promoting feminism in general and female sport involvement in particular.

Title IX Legislation

Another significant landmark in the development of women's athletics in this country was the passage of the Higher Education Act of 1972 and its Title IX provision. Title IX essentially prohibited sex discrimination in educational institutions receiving federal funds, thereby creating an atmosphere of sex equity in a spectrum of activities to include sports. Though its effects were not immediately felt, some equalization of opportunity in sport at the high school

A Modern Time Line of Historic Moments in Women's Sports

Highlight 10.2

1884   **Women are allowed to participate at Wimbledon, the premier tennis event in the world. According to Hargreaves (1990, p. 17), the first all-female match was described as "a leisurely affair, all the more so as the distinguished charmers participating were weighed down by heavy dresses over multi-petticoats, and were permitted to simper, to take a rest if their service broke down — in a final which provided more titters than jitters."**

1896   **The Olympic Games are reinstituted, but participation by women is not considered. Melpomene, a female runner from Greece, is an unofficial entrant in the marathon.**

1900   **Tennis and golf, each with six entries, are the first Olympic events for women.**

1912   **Tennis and swimming are the only two Olympic events for women. However, the American women are not allowed to take part because of the scanty nature of the swimwear; the American tennis players boycott their event in a sympathy gesture to the swimmers.**

1920   **Twenty countries send 136 women to the Olympic events of archery, figure skating, swimming, tennis, and yachting.**

1928   **Sonja Henie, arguably the best female figure skater of all time, wins the first of her three Olympic medals.**

1930   **A Czech, Zdena Koublova, wins the 800-meter run at the Third World Women's Games. Czech officials later admit that Koublova is male, and this admission eventually leads to the institution of gender testing for females in sports.**

1948   **Fannie Blankers-Koen, a Dutch woman and mother of two, wins four Olympic gold medals in track.**

1956   **College rodeo nationals feature a women's event, the barrel race, for the first time.**

1964   **The first team sport for women, volleyball, is added to the Olympic Games in Tokyo.**

(Continued next page)

Highlight 10.2 (Continued)

A Modern Time Line of Historic Moments in Women's Sports

1968   Enriquetta Basilio becomes the first woman to carry the Olympic torch into a stadium during the Mexico City games.

Gender testing is implemented at the Olympic Games.

1971   Billie Jean King, of professional tennis fame, wins $117,000 during the year, marking the first time a woman has earned a six-figure income in any sport.

1972   Olga Connolly, a five-time Olympian in track and field, is named captain of the United States team, a fact that did not merit mentioning in the Olympic Games book of 1972.

1976   Margaret Murdock outshoots numerous males to win a silver medal in riflery at the Olympic Games.

The East German women win twenty of twenty-eight possible gold medals in swimming and track and field, raising the specter of illegal use of banned substances in competition.

1977   Janet Guthrie becomes the first woman to drive in the Indianapolis 500, qualifying with a four-lap average of 188 miles per hour.

1982   Judy Mahle Lutter founds the Melpomene Institute, named in honor of the Greek marathon runner in the 1896 Olympic Games. The institute is created to foster a greater awareness of women's issues both inside and external to athletics.

1984   The marathon is added for women at the Los Angeles Olympics.

1988   Dorothy Harris is the first woman to receive a Fulbright Fellowship specifically for the purpose of conducting research in sports.

1990   Rick Pitino of the University of Kentucky appoints Bernadette Locke as the first female assistant coach of a Division 1-A men's basketball team. Locke took over as head coach of the Kentucky women's basketball team in 1995.

1991   Rebecca Andreas makes the all-league team in California eight-man football.

(Continued next page)

Highlight 10.2 (Continued)

A Modern Time Line of Historic Moments in Women's Sports

Judy Sweet, Athletic Director at San Diego State University, becomes the first female President of the National College Athletic Association (NCAA).

Eleanor Keeling, a fifty-nine-year-old undergraduate student at California State University-Sacramento, files an age discrimination suit against the NCAA for blocking her efforts to make the university tennis team.

Sanna Neilson, twenty-two, becomes the first female rider to win both the Virginia and Maryland Gold Cup events in the same year.

Lyn St. James and Desire Wilson of the United States and Tomiko Yoshikawa of Japan form the first all-female driving team for the twenty-four hours of LeMans automobile race.

Vojai Reed of Oklahoma is the first woman to fish in a nationally sanctioned tournament sponsored by the Bass Anglers Sportsman Society (BASS).

Susan O'Malley is named president of the Washington Bullets of the National Basketball Association, a first for the NBA.

Sandra Ortiz-Del Valle, forty, becomes the first woman to officiate a men's professional basketball game (United States Basketball League); Basketball Hall of Fame asked for her jersey and whistle to commemorate the occasion.

1992   **Terry Taylor, forty, is named sports editor for the Associated Press, a rarity in sports writing.**

1994   **The twenty-four-member Colorado Silver Bullets become the first female baseball team to compete against males; 1,700 women tried out for the team, which played a forty-five-game schedule against a variety of male teams. They were managed by Phil Niekro and supported by $2.6 million from Coors Brewing Company.**

1995   **Kendra Wecker becomes the first female to qualify for the national finals in the National Football League Punt, Pass, and Kick Competition**

Sources: *Houston Chronicle; Inside Sports; Sports Illustrated, Time, USA Today.*

and college level has come about through the provision of separate but equal women's teams, athletic scholarship opportunity, and other perquisites previously available only to male athletes. As Coakley (1982) says, the question of what constitutes equal opportunity has been and will continue to be a hot debate topic, but the net effect of Title IX legislation so far is that women have not been shortchanged in terms of access to facilities, coaching, fair scheduling, equipment, and selection of sports.

Contemporary Forces in Women's Athletics

In addition to the historical antecedents, a few contemporary forces have been at work in propelling women's efforts to the athletic forefront. Over and above the Title IX legislation, Coakley (1982) cites four reasons why there has been a demonstrable increase in female participation in sport. One is simply an increase in *opportunity.* Greater numbers of teams in a broader array of sports are highly noticeable today. Also, the fallout created by what might be called the *women's movement* has most certainly touched women's sport. Yet a third force is the *fitness boom* of the past decade. It has become fashionable for women to work out, strive for fitness, and take part in the fitness revolution. Finally, the *presence of role models* for aspiring young female athletes is a refreshing addition. Young girls are increasingly being afforded worthy role models in track and field, golf, tennis, swimming, marathoning, and other sports. As Coakley points out, professional athletes are important role models, but they are surpassed in impact by "real life" neighborhood or school athletes with whom younger girls can identify in a sporting capacity.

Now that we have a historical and contemporary perspective on women's sports, our attention can be turned to other dimensions of female sport participation.

THE PHYSIOLOGICAL DIMENSION IN WOMEN'S ATHLETICS

The scientific community has questioned the ability of women to compete because of a variety of psychological concerns including menstrual function, reproduction, and the breasts and genitals. Some members would propose that involvement in strenuous physical activity is quite damaging to these various structures and/or functions.

Menstrual Functioning

There has been an ongoing debate concerning the issue of physical activity and the menstrual cycle. Arnold (1924), a prominent physical educator of the early 1900s, discouraged female involvement in sport because the deleterious effects of physical exertion on the frequency and extent of menstruation, a situation that ostensibly endangered the reproductive capabilities of female participants. Another prominent physical educator of that era, Mabel Lee, conducted surveys in 1923 and 1930 in which 60 percent of her respondents echoed Arnold's concern with the dangers of disrupting the menstrual process (Lee, 1924, 1931). Incidentally, Ms. Lee was the first woman president of the American Alliance for Health, Physical Education, Recreation and Dance (AAHPERD) and, at age ninety-six, wrote a book on the history of sport and physical activity (Lee, 1983).

Early Studies

Despite early skepticism, evidence began to surface that countered the prevailing pessimism about the interactive effects of exercise on menstruation and reproduction. Landmark studies by Erdelyi (1962) and Zaharieva (1965) did much to demonstrate that strenuous exercise did not negatively affect the menstrual cycle nor did menstruation significantly affect physical performance in a negative way. Erdelyi conducted an

The Unintended Consequences of Title IX

While the overall effect of the Title IX legislation has been an extremely positive one with regard to women's sports, there have been a number of unintended and potentially harmful outgrowths. Though not a complete list, some of the more salient side effects are:

1. Of the 1,025 complaints made to the federal government in which violations of Title IX have been alleged, not one has resulted in the withdrawal of federal funding to sports or other institutional programs.
2. Coaching salaries have become increasingly disproportionate. For example, in Division 1-A collegiate basketball, a male coach makes almost twice as much in salary as does his female counterpart. Data from the Women's Basketball Coaches Association reveal that 32 percent of Division I women's coaches make over $60,000, compared to 88 percent of men's coaches ("Survey," 1995).
3. Only 24 percent of all expenditures in Division 1-A sports were allocated to the women's side of the ledger; as of 1993–1994, the average Division 1-A school was 50.8 percent female, yet only 35.7 percent of scholarship money was earmarked for females.
4. Males have taken over the administration of women's sports. In 1972, 90 percent of all women's programs (all divisions) were administered by women; in 1992, that figure was 16.8 percent. In addition, only 15 percent of all women's programs in Division 1-A had at least one woman involved in athletic administration; Division 2 had 39 percent and Division III had 32 percent.
5. Perhaps the so-called bottom line is best represented by the fact that in Division 1-A athletic programs, 70 percent of the scholarship money, 77 percent of the operating expenses, and 83 percent of recruiting dollars were spent on men's programs in 1990.
6. At another level of involvement, intramural sports, Tharp (1994) surveyed sixty-five directors of intramural programs and found that participation by women had noticeably increased since the passage of Title IX. However, sixteen of the sixty-five directors responding to Tharp's survey reported reductions in the number of activities offered for women. The money saved from program reductions was then used to fund intercollegiate sports for women attending these sixteen universities. Also

(Continued next page)

Highlight 10.3 (Continued)

The Unintended Consequences of Title IX

noted was a decrease over time in the number of women intramural directors, obviously an unintended consequence. Concerning this point, survey data from Pufahl (1987) indicates that 81 percent of all intramural program directors are male.

7. All is not lost, however. Recent evidence from Berg (1995) points to an ever-so-slight reversal of the unintended consequences theme and offers a note of optimism for the future. R. Vivian Acosta and Linda Jean Carpenter at Brooklyn College have observed women's collegiate sports since 1978, serving as monitors of the progress (or, at times, the lack thereof) of the Title IX legislation. Data from their 1994 report, *Women in Intercollegiate Sport: A Seventeen-Year Update,* are encouraging. Chief among the findings: (1) the percentage of female coaches has edged closer to 50 percent than it has in eight years; (2) the number of athletic programs with no female administrator dropped below 25 percent for the first time in ten years; (3) 49.4 percent of women's teams in 1994 were coached by females, up from the 48.1 percent figure in 1993; (4) NCAA schools offered 7.22 sports for women in 1994, up from 7.02 in 1993 and 5.61 in 1978; (5) there were 6,371 head-coaching jobs with women's teams, a gain of 653 since 1990; the number of jobs held by women has grown by 411 since 1990; (6) there were 2,533 athletic administration jobs in women's sports programs, a gain of 659 since 1990; (7) 21 percent of women's programs were headed by women, up from 16.8 percent in 1992.

By way of summary, Acosta and Carpenter say: "This year's summary brings with it good news on several fronts. Participation rates are up. The percentage of females serving as head coaches is up. The number of programs administered by women is up, and the number of schools including a woman's voice somewhere within their athletic administrative structure is up" (Berg, 1995, p. 9). It is clear that much work remains to be done in bringing about the equity of participation and money allocations that was the intent of the creators of the Title IX legislation. Perhaps the same thing can be said for the broader issue of women's rights across the societal spectrum.

Sources: Abney (1991); Babb (1992); Berg (1995); Brown (1994); "Gender Equity Survey" (1992); "Many Women Fear Stalling of Title IX" (1992); Pastore (1991); Pufahl (1987); Sullivan (1992); "Survey" (1995); Tharp (1994); van Keuren (1992); Wieberg (1992).

intensive study of 729 Hungarian female athletes whereas Zaharieva's work was with sixty-six female Olympians from ten different countries taking part in four different sports (gymnastics, swimming, track and field, and volleyball). Much of the early scientific data bearing on the exercise-menstruation issue has come from their combined works. Major conclusions drawn from their efforts are as follows:

1. Some athletes do in fact suffer a performance decrement during the menses, but the majority of their subjects reported similar or improved performance as the norm.
2. Of Zaharieva's subjects, 46 percent reported that they felt no differently during the menses; 32 percent reported feeling weaker at the time.
3. Ninety-two percent of Zaharieva's subjects were rhythmic with regard to the menstrual period. Length of menses was not adversely affected, and blood flow was generally normal. Among those who were irregular (6.1 percent), most were young enough for their irregularity to be more likely a function of youth than of sport participation. Erdelyi found similar results with his Hungarian athletes, with 83.8 percent reporting no change in menstrual cycle throughout training and competition. Eleven percent reported irregularly. Further elaboration on these results is offered by Astrand, Eriksson, Nylander, Engstrom, Karlberg, Saltin, and Thoren (1963) and Ingman (1952). Astrand et al. studied eighty-four Swedish swimmers and found that 15.5 percent reported menstrual problems while training, though the complaints ceased upon cessation of competition. Ingman, in a study of 107 top Finnish athletes, reported unfavorable changes in 18 percent of his subjects.

Overall, it would appear that these papers from the 1960s did much to dispel misconceptions about menstruation and performance. Efforts of late have centered around the third of the three conclusions mentioned earlier. Considerable argument concerns whether the picture is as good as was portrayed by some of the early researchers. The emphasis of late has been on the cessation of menses (amenorrhea) and on irregular menstrual functioning (oligomenorrhea).

Later Studies

Given that some research (Webb, Millan, and Stolz, 1979) has shown higher rates of menstrual disturbance than reported by earlier authorities, as well as concern with menstrual difficulties associated with overtraining (Erdelyi, 1976), the furor over the exercise-menstruation issue continues unabated. For instance, Webb et al. reported a 59 percent rate in menstrual difficulties in a group of fifty-six Olympic athletes (basketball, gymnastics, track and field, swimming, and rowing). Primary among the complaints were "missing my period" (n = 17) and "delay in onset of period" (n = 16). Foreman (see Bloomberg, 1977), in a study of the woman's AAU cross-country championships in 1971 and 1973, found 43 percent of the runners to be either irregular or very irregular in menstrual functioning. Lutter and Cushman (1982) found, in a study of thirty-five distance runners, that 19.3 percent of these women reported irregular menstrual periods and 3.4 percent reported having no period for the previous year.

A link seems to exist between strenuous physical activity and disruptions in the menstrual cycle. Why this relationship exists and what the consequences are in terms of the total health picture of the participants are the subjects of considerable speculation.

Causes of Menstrual Difficulties

A number of theories have been advanced as to why sport participation causes menstrual difficulties. One advanced by Frisch (Frisch, 1976; Frisch and McArthur, 1974) involves the relationship between body mass and percentage of body fat. She suggests that once body fat percentage drops below a certain point, a chain reaction of biochemical changes takes place that causes a cessation of menstrual periods.

Though her argument has a certain amount of surface appeal, evidence is not universally supportive of Frisch's hypothesis. For example, Plowman (1989) cites three areas of criticism that can be leveled against Frisch's work. The first area of criticism relates to methodological concerns, namely a failure to use standard methods for assessing percentage of body fat. Second, Plowman points to additional problems in the area of statistical interpretation. Third, Plowman cites experimental evidence from a dozen pieces of research in which the conclusions run counter to those of Frisch. It appears that Plowman is correct in her assertion that there are methodological, statistical, and evidentiary concerns that call the Frisch hypothesis into serious question.

Another possible source of menstrual difficulties has been advanced from an endocrinological perspective, pointing to hormonal changes within female athletes (Dale, Gerlach, and Wilhite, 1979; Loucks, 1990). Also implicated as possible etiological agents have been heavy exercise training, most particularly in runners who log many miles per week (Dale, Gerlach, Martin, and Alexander, 1979; Feicht, Johnson, Martin, Sparkles, and Wagner, 1978); stress (Feicht et al., 1978; Galle, Freeman, Galle, Huggins, and Sondheimer, 1983; Sasiene, 1983); diet (Sanborn, 1986); and becoming involved in strenuous physical activity prior to menarche (Frisch, Gotz-Welbergen, McArthur, Albright, Witschi, Bullen, Birnholz, Reed, and Hermann, 1981; Wakat and Sweeney, 1979).

Consequences of Menstrual Difficulties

Several sources point to disruption of the normal menstrual cycle and the effects of strenuous training as possible causes of difficulties associated with pregnancy. However, the prepon-

derance of the data bearing on this issue are not supportive of such a stance. Erdelyi (1962) and Zaharieva (1965), in a combined study of more than 740 female athletes, showed that the athletes had shorter labor periods, fewer instances of toxemia, fewer premature deliveries, and a lower rate of Caesarean sections than did a comparable nonathletic sample. Astrand et al. (1963) found similar results in their study of eighty-four elite swimmers. Gerber, Felshin, Berlin, and Wyrick (1974) attribute this finding to superior conditioning in fit females.

The fitness associated with athletics does in fact appear to be conducive to a good pregnancy and delivery. However, is pregnancy a handicap when one is trying to perform? Anecdotal reports would have us believe that the answer is no. Juno Stover Irwin won an Olympic medal in diving (10-meter board) when she was in her fourth month of pregnancy (Kaplan, 1979); Sue Pirtle Hays successfully competed in world championship rodeo as a bareback bronco rider when she was eight months pregnant (Kaplan, 1979); three medal winning divers in the 1952 Olympics were pregnant at the time they competed (Dyer, 1982); ten of twenty Russian medal winners in the 1956 Olympics were pregnant at the time (Dyer, 1982). Reports such as these certainly give the impression that pregnancy and top-level performance are not incompatible. Evidence from Erdelyi is most supportive of the various anecdotal observations; she found that two-thirds of 172 Hungarian athletes with children continued normal sport functioning in the early phases of pregnancy, though performance decrements were typically visible beyond the third or fourth month, at which time most of these athletes stopped serious competition.

Athletes appear to return to top form rather quickly after childbirth. Zaharieva and Sigler (1963), in a combined effort involving 207 Spanish and Hungarian athletes, found that all had between one and four children and over 75 percent of them bettered their Olympic results within two years after delivery, most in the first year. Bloom (1986) interviewed the world class American distance runner, Mary Decker Slaney, and reported that she was back on the track six days after giving birth, and was running almost normally at one month. Brownlee (1988) cites personal records achieved following childbirth in such world-class athletes as Valerie Brisco, Ingrid Kristiansen, and Tatyana Kazankina (track); Nancy Lopez (golf); Karen Kania (speed skating); Pat McCormick (diving); and Steffi Martin Walter (luge). Gwen Torrance won the 1992 Olympics 200-meter dash three years after giving birth to son Manley Waller, Jr.; she continued to be the top 200-meter runner in the world through 1994 (Patrick, 1994).

With regard to exercising during pregnancy, recent research by Sternfeld, Quesenberry, Eskenazi, and Newman (1995) demonstrates that there are many similarities with the findings related to elite athletes. Sternfeld et al. studied 388 pregnant women, mean age 31.7, and found that participation in a regular program of aerobics did not adversely affect birth weight or other maternal or infant outcomes and was associated with fewer perceived pregnancy-related discomforts. The position statement of the American College of Obstetricians and Gynecologists (ACOG) as presented by Pivarnik (1994) lends additional support. Based on the results of eighty-five published studies since 1985 and input based on clinical experience, the ACOG recommendation encourages a proactive consultative partnership between a woman and her obstetrician concerning an individualized program of exercise during pregnancy.

All things considered, fears of menstrual problems and pregnancy complications as a function of sport participation and/or exercise may be largely unfounded. Perhaps Gerber et al. (1974, pp. 514–515) summarize the research best: "On the whole, female athletes can look forward to a normal, vigorous and robust life, for the most part free of menstrual disorders and complications with marriage, pregnancy, and childbirth."

Other Problems

Coakley (1982) discusses at length a number of myths that serve as means for excluding women from total participation in sport. Three that Coakley cites have already been discussed; others include *damage to the breasts and reproductive organs,* a more *fragile bone structure* in females, and the notion that *sport participation creates bulging muscles* in females. All, according to Coakley, are myths. No convincing evidence exists that either the breasts or the reproductive organs are at risk. The breasts are spared risk for the early years due to maturation and can readily be protected when potential harm is a factor. In a study of 361 colleges and universities, Gillette (1975) indicated that breast injuries associated with sport were the least common among nine areas of injury. Similarly, Hunter and Torgan (1982) found no instance of injury to any University of Washington female athlete during the period 1976 through 1981. As for the uterus, Dunkle (1974) and Eitzen and Sage (1982) both indicate that it is a most shock-resistant organ. In terms of actual risk, males are much more susceptible in that the sexual organs are external from the earliest age and thus are highly vulnerable to trauma.

As for bone structure, women are indeed smaller but not more fragile. According to Gerber et al. (1974), the average male is 20 percent stronger than the average female, has a 25 percent faster reaction time, and has a cardiovascular capacity advantage of 25 to 50 percent. These sex differences translate into more power, speed, quickness, and strength for males, according to Curry and Jiobu (1984). These same factors also contribute to what appears to be high injury rates among males. Coakley indicates that the injury rates are actually about as high for females as males, but these equal rates are more attributable to poor coaching, training, and general carelessness in the case of female competitors than to any inherent "fragile" structures.

Bulging muscles simply are not going to happen to any great extent in the absence of male sex hormones. Normal exercise has a facilitative effect on muscle tone, and females should not shy away from exertion out of fear of becoming mannish. In a study of 116 American elite female athletes from seven different sports, May, Veach, Daily-McKee, and Furman (1985) indicated that the majority of them did not feel that vigorous training resulted in a masculine appearance. Moreover, even among those who believed that their training was conducive to muscle development, the consensus was that the effects were largely positive. Count all-time tennis great Martina Navratilova among the enthusiasts of muscle development, though such was not always the case. When she defected to the United States from Czechoslovakia in 1975, Martina was embarrassed by her powerful build and did her best to hide her muscular physique. As time wore on, it became apparent to her that muscles were acceptable, largely as a function of the growing fitness movement among women. At that point of realization, Martina felt more free to dress as she pleased (Donnelly, 1990).

PSYCHOLOGICAL VARIABLES

Though an unlimited number of psychological variables deserve mention here, only a few have a sufficient literature to justify elaboration. Chief among them are *attribution theory, fear of success,* and *psychological androgyny.*

Attribution Theory

Some overlap between the discussions here and in chapter 5 will permit us to fully develop issues related to attribution theory and female participation in sport. One significant area of research has been concerned with *gender differences.* Deaux and Emswiller (1974) have suggested that sex role stereotypes are conducive to the distortion of one's cognitive processes, particularly in the area of attributions. Deaux and Farris (1977) indicated that adult males are likely to make internal attributions (e.g., ability) for success whereas females are likely to view their successes as less attributable to ability and more a function of situational factors such as luck. For example, Iso-Ahola (1979) studied the motor performance of equal numbers (n = 80) of male and female fourth graders from physical education classes and found, among other things, that boys are less likely to admit to ability deficiencies when they fail in competitive situations involving girls than in situations where they are surpassed by other boys. Also, girls tended to see the ability of boys as a more significant factor in losses to boys than in defeats by other girls. Applying generalizations generated from the preceding studies to sport led McHugh, Duquin, and Frieze (1978) to conclude the following:

1. Based on women's internalization of beliefs in their own physical inferiority, female athletes attribute success to external factors such as luck, and failure to low ability. This pattern may be found in young girl athletes or women in general, but the female that makes this type of attribution probably would not be found in advanced athletic programs.
2. Alternatively, the societal attitudes that allude to females' natural inability in sports may produce a pattern of external attributions. Thus, the female athlete that reports playing just for fun, and winning by luck or task ease conforms more to society's view than the female who admittedly tries hard.
3. A third prediction of female athletes' attributional patterns could be based on the fact that female athletes have been found to

Sex-role stereotypes in sports start early. The consensus of players in this soccer game is likely to be that boys win because of ability and effort; if girls win, it's a function of luck.

be generally self-confident, autonomous, persevering, and achievement oriented. Preliminary studies have suggested that highly motivated women imply more effort attributions for both success and failure than low achievement oriented women. (Pp. 182–183).

As a result of observations such as these, a fair amount of related research has been generated, though it is not universally supportive of the McHugh et al. position. Bird and Williams (1980) studied 192 males and an equal number of females divided into four age groups (seven to nine, ten to twelve, thirteen to fifteen, sixteen to eighteen). Subjects were asked to respond to stories about various athletic events in which failure or success themes were programmed. Based on in-depth analysis of the results, Bird and Williams concluded that by late adolescence sex role stereotypes in sport do exist and that the directional bias is positive for males and negative for females. They further concluded that by age thirteen male success was explained by effort whereas by age sixteen female success was viewed as a function of luck.

Two additional studies with adults lend further credence to sex differences in attribution. One, by Reiss and Taylor (1984), involved an analysis of 141 male and 116 female alpine ski racers of various skill levels. A second, by Riordan, Thomas, and James (1985), included fifty-four male and twenty-five female racquetball players. Both studies concluded that females were more likely to make external attributions than were males.

A second area of interest in attribution theory research with females involves the *self-serving attributional bias*. Research on the self-serving bias has been equivocal, as was pointed out in chapter 5. Recent studies related to female athletes do little to clarify the picture. Riordan et al. (1985) found partial support for the notion in their study of racquetball players whereas Reiss and Taylor (1984), in their study of alpine skiers, interpreted their findings as not supportive of the self-serving bias. In general, so many inconsistencies occur along methodological and sampling lines that, as stated earlier, it would seem premature to stop researching the topic.

A third thrust in attributions has to do with *self versus team responses*. Bird and Brame (1978), Bird, Foster, and Maruyama (1980), and Scanlan and Passer (1980a) have all taken a look at self versus team attributions. In the first of these three studies, Bird and Brame selected subjects from several collegiate basketball conferences and found that winners perceived themselves as having less ability than they were perceived to have by their teammates. Also, winners viewed their teams as having more ability than did losers. Effort was seen to play a greater role with winners. Winners also saw their own individual task assignments as more difficult than that of the team. Finally, losers viewed luck as playing a greater role in team success than did winners. Overall, their most salient finding was that the team-ability attribution most powerfully separated winners from losers.

Bird and her associates also looked at female basketball players, but added the dimension of team cohesion into the formula. In general, cohesive teams made more convergent attributions for both self and team at the end of the season. Players from less cohesive teams saw luck as more significant than did their winning counterparts. Players from cohesive teams, in the face of occasional adversity, behaved in ways that preserved the team's integrity. In general, the Bird et al. study was also supportive of the notion that the team-self distinction is an important one in sport.

Scanlan and Passer studied young female soccer players, and their overall conclusions were generally in agreement with those of Bird and her various associates. Based on the findings of the preceding study and those of three others (Scanlan and Passer, 1978, 1979, 1980b), these researchers posit that sex differences in attributional styles are more similar than dissimilar. This position, of course, runs counter to much of our earlier discussion but does point to the

need for continuing research on athletes of both sexes and their attributional efforts.

Fear of Success

One aspect of the need achievement literature that has drawn a lot of recent attention has been the concept of *fear of success (FOS)* as formulated by Matina Horner (1968, 1972). Blucker and Hershberger (1983, pp. 353–354) summarize Horner's 1968 basic premises as follows:

1. The motive to avoid success is a stable characteristic of the personality acquired early in life in conjunction with sex-role standards. It is conceived as a disposition: (a) to feel uncomfortable when successful in competitive achievement situations because such behavior is inconsistent with one's femininity (an internal standard), and (b) to expect to become concerned about social rejection following success in such situations.
2. The motive is much more common in women than in men.
3. It is probably not equally important for all women. Fear of success should be more strongly aroused in women who are highly motivated to achieve and/or who are highly able (e.g., who aspire to and/or are readily capable of achieving success).
4. It is more strongly aroused in competitive achievement situations than where competition is directed against an impersonal standard.

Horner apparently viewed FOS as a highly feminine characteristic that would be manifested most noticeably in competitive situations.

In her original work, Horner asked women to respond to the following verbal lead: "After first-term finals, Anne finds herself at the top of her medical school class." For men, John was substituted for Anne. In their responses, the females wrote many more negative responses to their cues than did the males; 65 percent of the women wrote fear of success themes whereas only 9 percent of the men did. For a variety of reasons subsequent research on FOS has not yielded such clear-cut results, but the construct has caught the attention of sport researchers.

One of the first efforts in this area was generated by McElroy and Willis (1979). Female varsity athletes (n = 262) in five different sports attending three large East Coast universities responded to a series of yes-no statements related to sport-specific situations, and no evidence of FOS was noted in these participants. McElroy and Willis concluded that perhaps FOS is not generalized to athletic situations, that changing women's roles may be at work, or that women have legitimized their athletic participation and feel no need for rationalizing or justifying it. The authors summarize their results as follows: "The absence of fear of success suggested that the female athlete does not seem to be bothered by role conflicts surrounding achievement activities" (p. 246).

Silva (1982), using the Objective Fear of Success Scale (FOSS) created by Zuckerman and Allison (1976), studied 193 undergraduate athletes and nonathletes of both sexes. As was the case with Zuckerman and Allison, Silva's females (when grouped together) scored higher on the FOSS than did the males. However, because the mean scores of the female athletes were lower than both the male and female nonathletes and also those reported by Zuckerman and Allison, it does not appear that women in sport are particularly fearful of succeeding.

In view of the works of McElroy and Willis and of Silva, it seems safe to conclude that female athletes do not appear to have fear of success problems. Perhaps the following anecdote from a twenty-four-year-old woman cited by Loverock (1991, p. 85) summarizes the FOS transition from the days of the original work by Horner and a more common view of achievement in competitive situations today:

As a kid I played a lot of tennis. I signed up for lessons when I was ten and I became pretty good at the game. When I met my first "serious" boyfriend, around age sixteen, he saw the tennis racquets in our garage and suggested we go out to the courts at a nearby school and play a game. After a few serves it was obvious to me I was better at tennis than he was. He was really frustrated because I was winning the game. I hate to say this, but I was afraid he wouldn't like me as much if I beat him, so I played a lousy game and let him win. Of course, young love didn't last and we broke up anyway! Now I'm married to a man who plays tennis badly, but he doesn't mind when I beat him.

Psychological Androgyny

The measurement of sex differences in personality is not new. A number of instruments of the 1940s and 1950s (i.e., the Minnesota Multiphasic Personality Inventory, the Guilford-Zimmerman Temperament Survey, and the California Psychological Inventory) included subscales concerned with sex differences. More recent efforts from the 1970s have been oriented toward the measurement of *psychological androgyny* (Bem, 1974; Spence, Helmreich, and Stapp, 1974).

Expressive and Instrumental Components

Androgyny is generally viewed as a mixture of the best of both sexes, that is, "combining assertiveness and competence with compassion, warmth, and emotional expressiveness" (Anastasi, 1982, p. 557). Duquin (1978) differentiates among these various traits by talking of *expressive* and *instrumental* behaviors. Expressive behaviors are associated with women, who may be seen as understanding, sympathetic, affectionate, compassionate, tender, sensitive, warm, and shy. On the other hand, males are expected to act instrumentally by being independent, ambitious, assertive, aggressive, competitive, and risk-taking. Duquin further states that, while society generally attributes instrumentality to males and expressiveness to females, the validity and desirability of the ascriptions are questionable. This ambiguity is at the heart of the role conflict female athletes face in the traditionally male proving ground of sport.

Bem (1974) asserts that masculinity and femininity have long been viewed as bipolar ends of a single continuum, or as dichotomous variables. Bem's contention is that the manifestation of both is entirely possible in males and females. To put it another way, Bem feels that people with healthy self-concepts will be capable of freely engaging in both "masculine" and "feminine" behaviors and will not be restrained by traditional sex role definitions. This perception is shared by Spence, Helmreich, and Stapp (1974). As a result of their combined speculations, both Bem and Spence and her associates have devised scales aimed at measuring this propensity toward expressing both the masculine and feminine aspects of the self, or what is popularly known as psychological androgyny.

Measures of Androgyny

The two most notable of the measures of androgyny are the *Bem Sex-Role Inventory (BSRI)* (Bem, 1974) and the *Personal Attributes Questionnaire (PAQ)* (Spence, Helmreich, and Stapp, 1974). Of the two measures, the BSRI has been used more often in sport. Before looking at the BSRI, however, research involving the PAQ should be mentioned.

Spence, Helmreich, and Stapp (1974) developed the PAQ in response to what they perceived to be a need for an instrument that would add to our understanding of masculinity, femininity, and androgyny. The PAQ is a fifteen-item five-choice response format instrument yielding a male valued (MV) score and a female valued (FV) score. In turn, the MV and FV can be subdivided through a four-way median split into the following categories: (1) *androgynous*, operation-

ally defined as scores above the median on both MV and FV; (2) stereotypically *masculine*, consisting of a score at or above the median on MV and below the median on FV; (3) stereotypically *feminine*, defined as a median score or above on FV and below median on MV; and (4) *undifferentiated*, defined as scores below the median on both MV and FV.

In a study using the PAQ, Del Rey and Sheppard (1981) administered the instrument to 119 female athletes from three universities covering ten sports. Collapsing across the three universities, 33 percent of the athletes were androgynous, 23 percent masculine, 22 percent feminine, and 23 percent undifferentiated (100 percent is surpassed here due to rounding errors). Of more importance, a highly significant relationship was seen between the androgynous description and athlete self-esteem as measured by the Texas Social Behavior Instrument (TSBI) (Helmreich, Stapp, and Ervin, 1974).

Another investigation involving the PAQ was conducted by Hochstetler, Rejeski, and Best (1985). Their subjects were 149 undergraduate students, all of whom were moderate to low in cardiovascular fitness and not participating in intercollegiate sport. Thirty-three of the original 149 females were then randomly selected for further testing, eleven in each of the androgynous, masculine, and feminine conditions. The exertion tasks used in the experiment involved a treadmill task and a 30-minute job, and the subjects were asked to rate their perceptions of the exertion involved therein. Feminine women perceived the rate of physical exertion higher than did masculine and androgynous subjects though all subjects worked at the same intensity. Interestingly, the feminine subjects were also the least fit of the three groups. Hochstetler et al. suggest that feminine-type women who enter fitness or rehabilitation programs may be at high risk for noncompliance.

Both studies cited here lend validity to the use of the PAQ in sport-related research. They further suggest that androgyny and related issues are important ones within the female sport domain. Bem's work in the area lends even more substantiation to the findings.

The *Bem Sex-Role Inventory (BSRI)* (Bem, 1974) is a sixty-item scale made up of twenty masculine, twenty feminine, and twenty neutral statements requiring responses based on a seven-point continuum from "Never or almost never true" to "Always or almost always true." Scoring is essentially similar to that of the PAQ in that one's position above or below the median determines classification as masculine, feminine, androgynous, or undifferentiated. Sample items from the BSRI include:

Masculine	Feminine
____ self-reliant	____ yielding
____ defends own beliefs	____ cheerful
____ independent	____ sly
____ athletic	____ affectionate
____ assertive	____ flatterable

Neutral
____ helpful
____ moody
____ conscientious
____ theatrical
____ happy

Research in female sport in which the BSRI has been used is considerable, and a summary of relevant studies can be seen in table 10.1. A number of conclusions can be drawn from this literature. One is that female athletes do not express a feminine sex role orientation. Rates such as 17 percent of elite racquetball players (Myers and Lips, 1978), 13 percent of elite field hockey players in New Zealand (Chalip, Villiger, and Duignan, 1980), 22 percent of gymnasts taking part in the NCAA championships (Edwards, Gordin, and Henschen, 1984), and 17 percent of individual sport participants (Colley, Roberts, and Chipps, 1985) lend credence to such a notion.

Myers and Lips did find a 43 percent femininity rate in a group of Canadian badminton, handball, and squash players, thereby suggesting that the issue is not totally conclusive. Nevertheless, a strong trend exists toward a less feminine sex role orientation among widely diverse female athletes.

A second conclusion is that a masculine sex role orientation is indeed an integral part of female participation in sport. Gackenbach (1982) reported that collegiate swimmers view themselves as significantly more masculine in sex role orientation than do nonathletes. Kane (1982) reported 39 percent of junior college athletes in three sports score masculine on the BSRI. Twenty-five percent of eighty-four gymnasts reported a masculine orientation in the study of Edwards, Gordin, and Henschen (1984). Again, these rates of masculine sex role endorsement were not without exceptions. Colley et al. report only a 17 percent rate among individual sport participants in their study. Henschen, Edwards, and Mathinos (1982) found no differences between rates of femininity and masculinity in their study of high school track athletes and nonathletes, though masculinity was significantly related to the need to achieve.

A third conclusion is that the picture related to androgyny as measured by the BSRI is mixed. The range of androgynous responses in female athletes is from 65 percent reported by Chalip and associates (1980) to 17 percent of the individual sport subjects studied by Colley et al. (1985). In between are percentages of 25 percent (Edwards et al.), 42 percent (team sport participants, Chalip et al.), 43 percent (Henschen et al.), and 44 percent (Myers and Lips). Given the substantial heterogeneity of these various samples, these discrepancies are possibly to be expected.

The sex role orientation of female athletes would appear to be substantially more androgynous or masculine than feminine or undifferentiated. Holding athletic ability constant, this

Table 10.1
Summary of BSRI Studies in Female Sport

Myers and Lips (1978)	Study 1: 25 males and 23 females in Canadian National Racquetball Championships	44% of females androgynous, 24% of males; 40% of males masculine, 17% of females feminine
	Study 2: 27 females and 24 males in badminton, squash, and handball tournaments in Winnipeg	26% of females androgynous, 20% of males; 44% of males masculine, 43% of females feminine
Wark and Wittig (1979)	61 introductory psychology students; 32 males endorsing masculine sex-role, 29 females endorsing feminine role—all administered the Sport Competition Anxiety Test (SCAT)	Masculine males significantly less anxious than feminine females
Chalip, Villiger, and Duignan (1980)	23 elite field hockey players registered with New Zealand Women's Hockey Association	65% androgynous, 13% feminine, 13% masculine, 9% undifferentiated
Gackenbach (1982)	13 females, 14 males involved in intercollegiate swimming—all administered the Multiple Affect Adjective Checklist (MAACL); also compared with 50 male and female nonathletes	Swimmers of both sexes saw themselves as more masculine than did nonathletes, females significantly so; male swimmers significantly less anxious and hostile than female swimmers
Henschen, Edwards, and Mathinos (1982)	67 high school track and field athletes and 67 nonathletes—also admininistered Mehrabian's Scale of Achieving Tendency	43% of athletes androgynous, 30% of nonathletes; virtually no differences in masculinity or femininity dimensions; female athletes significantly higher in achievement motivation; androgyny and masculinity associated with high achievement, femininity with low achievement
Kane (1982)	33 junior college athletes in volleyball, softball, and basketball and 65 nonathletes—also administered Webb's Socialization of Play Scale	39% of athletes scored masculine; 49% of nonathletes were androgynous and 47% feminine; masculine women scored significantly higher on professional end of Webb Scale than did feminine women
Edwards, Gordin, and Henschen (1984)	84 gymnasts from NCAA Championships	25% androgynous, 25% masculine, 22% feminine

Table 10.1 *(continued)*

Segal and Weinberg (1984)	166 female and 125 male undergraduates; also administered SCAT	19% of males and 34% of females androgynous; 38% of males and 10% of females masculine; 10% of males and 34% of females feminine; males significantly lower on competitive trait anxiety regardless of sex role orientation
Butcher (1985)	213 adolescent girls observed from grade 6 through grade 10; complete data after five years on 66% of the original sample	Significant increase over five-year period in both independent and expressive descriptors
Colley, Roberts, and Chipps (1985)	48 male and female undergraduates participating in individual sports, 48 team sport athletes, and 48 nonathletes; and 12 females in noncompetitive individual sports also administered SCAT, Eysenck Personality Questionnaire, and Rotter's I-E Scale	42% of team sport females androgynous, 38% feminine; 17% of individual sport females androgynous, 33% feminine, 17% masculine; 13% of female nonathletes androgynous, 71% feminine; 33% of male team sport athletes androgynous, 46% masculine, 4% feminine; 25% of individual sport participants androgynous, 58% masculine, 4% feminine; 13% of nonathletes androgynous, 42% masculine, 17% feminine
Wittig, Duncan, and Schurr (1987)	151 female and 119 male university undergraduates; also administered the SCAT and the Physical Self-Efficacy Scale (Ryckman, Robbins, Thornton, and Cantrell, 1982)	Males and females endorsing a masculine role showed more physical satisfaction than did other groups, with males higher than females on satisfaction index.
Friedman and Berger (1991)	387 college students in introductory health science course assigned to stress reduction group or control group; also administered Profile of Mood States (POMS)	High masculinity associated with mood benefits from jogging and relaxation training; students high in femininity had less desirable mood profiles on POMS
Swain and Jones (1991)	37 female and 60 male track and field athletes from club in England; also given CSAI-2 and SCAT	Masculine males lower in competitive trait anxiety than other three groups; feminine females highest in competitive state anxiety

Sources: Butcher (1985); Chalip, Villiger, and Duignan (1980); Colley, Roberts, and Chipps (1985); Edwards, Gordin, and Henschen (1984); Friedman and Berger (1991); Gackenbach (1982); Henschen, Edwards, and Mathinos (1982); Kane (1982); Myers and Lips (1978); Segal and Weinberg (1984); Swain and Jones (1991); Wark and Wittig (1979); Wittig, Duncan, and Schurr (1987).

would suggest that the androgynous or masculine female should succeed in sport without experiencing the sex role conflict that the feminine scorer would feel. Duquin (1978, p. 271) sums the issue up: "Sport, when perceived as an instrumental, cross sex-typed activity has little overall appeal to women and has a low appeal to the feminine female who, in fact, has the greatest need for experiencing such instrumental activities." Duquin further suggests that, in the best of all possible worlds, sport would be regarded not as masculine or feminine, but as androgynous. In this ideal setting, androgynous and masculine females would find sport to be a great outlet for their expressive and instrumental energies. Best of all, perhaps, is the fact that in Duquin's view feminine females would also find reinforcement in physical activity and competition. Sport perceived as an androgynous activity is portrayed in table 10.2.

SOCIALIZATION INTO SPORT

Rees and Andres (1980) found no significant grip strength differences in four- to six-year-old boys and girls; however, 72 percent of their respondents reported that boys are stronger. Csikszentmihalyi and Bennett (1971) have suggested that game complexity and skill levels demanded for various activities favor young males. These writers suggest that the "ceiling" on boys' games

Table 10.2
Sport Perceived as an Androgynous Activity

Females Classified on the BSRI	Expected Performance	Expected Attraction
Masculine	moderate-high	moderate-high
Androgynous	high	high
Feminine	moderate	moderate

Source: Duquin (1978).

is higher than that of girls. For example, tee ball baseball may be most captivating for six- or seven-year-olds. Athletes who stick with the sport for the next several years and who acquire the necessary skills will continue to find the game of baseball intriguing. On the other hand, games that first grade girls enjoy, such as jumping rope or playing tag, will still be played four or five years later, but with little enjoyment. In effect, the girls reached their ceiling of skill long ago. These sorts of differences are at the heart of the issue of sex role socialization and sport. Males are rewarded for competing whereas females are seen as sacrificing femininity if they throw themselves into competitive situations, such as sport. In an effort to explain some of the more relevant findings in women's sports participation, we shall, in turn, look at four dimensions that appear to be salient, namely, role conflict, agents of socialization, the acceptability of various sports, and why females compete.

Role Conflict

Oglesby (1984) cites various sources of evidence indicating that parents consistently perceive sex differences between their male and female children even though no objective differences exist. Oglesby further indicates that bipolar trait definitions of the two sexes imply that males are active, aggressive, public, cultural, rule-governed, instrumental, goal oriented, organized, dominating, competitive, and controlled. On the other hand, females are viewed as passive, submissive, private, natural, idiosyncratic, expressive, chaotic, disorganized, subordinate, cooperative, and uncontrolled. This sort of thinking has dominated sex differences in general and female sport participation in particular.

One of the earliest investigations in this area of role conflict was conducted by Brown (1965). Using the semantic differential technique (Osgood, Suci, and Tannenbaum, 1957) in which concepts are evaluated through responses to words arranged in a bipolar fashion (e.g., weak-

Babe Didrikson Zaharias

*Highlight
10.4*

In 1950, the Associated Press (AP) named Mildred Ella Didrikson Zaharias, or "the Babe," the top female athlete of the first half of the twentieth century. There is every reason to believe that she will also be named the athlete of the entire century at some point in the near future. There have been, and continue to be, many outstanding female athletes in the world, but most were exceptional within a narrow range of activity. Not so the Babe; her awe-inspiring list of accomplishments cross a variety of athletic endeavors.

GOLF

Amateur

First to win United States Women's Amateur title
First to win British Women's Amateur title
Won seventeen Amateur Tournaments in succession in 1946–1947

Professional

Leading money winner on Ladies Professional Golf Association (LPGA) tour in 1948, 1949, 1950, 1951
Won world championship 1948, 1949, 1950, 1951
Won U. S. Women's Open championship 1948, 1950, 1954, the latter by twelve strokes

TRACK AND FIELD

Amateur Athletic Union (AAU) National Championships

First Place, Javelin (1930)
First Place, 80-Meter Hurdles (1931)
First Place, Long Jump (1931)
First Place, Eight-Pound Shot Put (1932)
First Place, Baseball Throw (1930, 1931, 1932)

The Olympic Games (1932)

Gold Medal, Javelin
Gold Medal, 80-Meter Hurdles
Silver Medal, High Jump

(Continued next page)

Highlight 10.4 (Continued)

Babe Didrikson Zaharias

MISCELLANEOUS SPORTS

Baseball
 Pitched and Played Infield for touring House of David men's team
 Pitched spring training for major league men's teams. It was reported
 that she once struck out Joe DiMaggio.

Basketball
 Three-Time All-American (1930, 1931, 1932)

Softball
 Played on two city championship teams in Dallas

Babe Didrikson Zaharias drives the ball from the tenth tee in the first round of the U.S. Women's Open golf championship at Peabody, Massachusetts, July 1, 1954.

(Continued next page)

Highlight 10.4 (Continued)

Babe Didrikson Zaharias

HONORS

Woman Athlete of the Half Century by Associated Press
AP Female Athlete of the Year (1932, 1945, 1946, 1947, 1950, 1954)
Elected to LPGA Hall of Fame (1951)
Elected to National Track and Field Hall of Fame (1974)
Elected to the International Women's Sports Hall of Fame (1980)
Elected to the United States Olympic Hall of Fame (1983)

In addition to the preceding accomplishments, Babe Didrikson Zaharias was an accomplished seamstress, gourmet cook, interior decorator, harmonica player, and pool player. Throughout all of these competitions, Babe

In the Olympic Games, August 3, 1932, Mildred Didrikson (second from left) *winner of the javelin throw, came back with her second world record performance, winning the first heat of the 80-meter hurdles.*

(Continued next page)

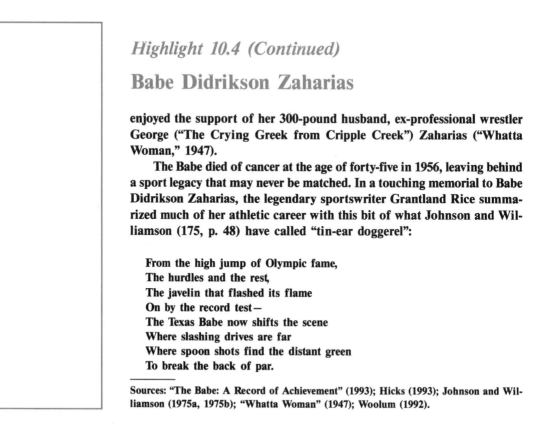

Highlight 10.4 (Continued)

Babe Didrikson Zaharias

enjoyed the support of her 300-pound husband, ex-professional wrestler George ("The Crying Greek from Cripple Creek") Zaharias ("Whatta Woman," 1947).

The Babe died of cancer at the age of forty-five in 1956, leaving behind a sport legacy that may never be matched. In a touching memorial to Babe Didrikson Zaharias, the legendary sportswriter Grantland Rice summarized much of her athletic career with this bit of what Johnson and Williamson (175, p. 48) have called "tin-ear doggerel":

From the high jump of Olympic fame,
The hurdles and the rest,
The javelin that flashed its flame
On by the record test—
The Texas Babe now shifts the scene
Where slashing drives are far
Where spoon shots find the distant green
To break the back of par.

Sources: "The Babe: A Record of Achievement" (1993); Hicks (1993); Johnson and Williamson (1975a, 1975b); "Whatta Woman" (1947); Woolum (1992).

strong, hot-cold, beautiful-ugly), Brown investigated attitudes toward such female roles as cheerleader, sexy girl, twirler, tennis player, feminine girl, swimmer, and basketball player. The female athletic roles were consistently viewed by both college males and females as less desirable. Griffin (1973), in summarizing results of her 1972 master's thesis, reported that semantic differential responses to the concepts of ideal woman, girlfriend, mother, housewife, woman professor, and woman athlete indicated that the latter two concepts were least favorably viewed by 279 undergraduate students (128 males, 151 females). A model representing the semantic distance between these six roles is reported in figure 10.1. Griffin viewed these results as indicative of no shift in attitudes toward nontraditional roles for women.

Snyder, Kivlin, and Spreitzer (1975) found that 65 percent of college women respondents reported feeling that a stigma is attached to female participation in sport. Sage and Loudermilk (1979), in a study of 268 college female athletes, reported that 26 percent of these women reported great or very great role conflict.

Subsequent reports have been more encouraging. For instance, Snyder and Spreitzer (1978), in a comparison of the attitudes of 500 high school girls participating in sports or music, found no real stigma attached to female participation in sports. Female athletes were as well-adjusted as the female nonathletes in this study. Kingsley, Brown, and Seibert (1977) compared college students' (120 athletes and 120 nonathletes) attitudes toward the concepts of dancer with high and low success aspirations with soft-

Figure 10.1: **A Model Representing the Semantic Distance between Six Women's Roles**

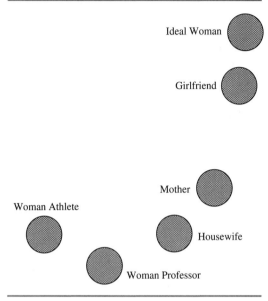

Source: Griffin (1973).

ball player with high and low success aspirations. Results indicated that athletes, regardless of sport, rated the softball player as more acceptable than the dancer; nonathletes did not rate the dancer significantly higher than the softball player concept; and, for all subjects, the softball player was rated significantly higher than the dancer. Vickers, Lashuk, and Taerum (1980) used a semantic differential technique to evaluate four concepts: male, male athlete, female, and female athlete. Subjects were 264 students from the seventh grade, tenth grade, and college classes, and all subjects were positive toward both male and female athletes. In fact, female athlete was the highest rated of the four concepts. Michael, Gilroy, and Sherman (1984) asked equal numbers of male and female athletes and nonathletes to evalute hypothetical female athletes and nonathletes. Athletes and nonathletes of both sexes found the athletic stimulus person to be more attractive than the nonathletic figure.

Brown (1988), in summarizing a survey conducted under the auspices of the Women's Sport Foundation and Wilson Sporting Goods, found that as girls get older, they view girls who play sports as either very popular (55 percent) or a little popular (41 percent). Seventy-eight percent of the respondents did not think that boys made fun of girls who play sports. Apparently, female involvement in sports is increasingly being accepted by both sexes and may actually be positively related to popularity in high-school-age girls. Overall there have been positive changes toward female involvement in athletics. However, much remains to be done to insure that women are accorded proper respect for sport participation.

Agents of Socialization

The family is the primary socialization force in the early years. In the area of women's athletics, this is certainly true. Malumphy (1970) has indicated that the family is the primary source of socialization into sport, not only for females but also for males. Greendorfer (1977) states that the family is most influential in childhood, but this influence becomes weaker in adolescence and adulthood. Snyder and Spreitzer (1978) support this notion, indicating that parental interest is a big factor in sport involvement by females. Weiss and Knoppers (1982), in a study of collegiate volleyball players, found that parents, peers, and teachers/coaches were most influential in childhood, but the influence of brothers was most salient in college. The latter finding, as might be expected, has not been corroborated by prior or subsequent research. Finally, Higginson (1985), in a study of 587 participants in the Empire State Games in Syracuse, New York, found that parents were the most influential socialization forces prior to age thirteen, being replaced in adolescence by coaches and physical education teachers.

Parents are very important in the early sport socialization of females. When children reach adolescence, coaches and physical educators take on increased significance. Beyond adolescence, the socialization agents become nebulous and more research here is warranted.

Acceptability of Various Sports

Early studies indicated that individual sports were more acceptable than team sport insofar as women were concerned (DeBacy, Spaeth, and Busch, 1970; Harres, 1968; Layman, 1968). Support for this conclusion of sport acceptance was suggested by Snyder and Kivlin (1975). They asked 328 college female athletes, "Do you feel that there is a stigma attached to women who participate in the sport you specialize in?" Fifty-eight percent of basketball players said yes, followed by 47 percent of track and field athletes, 38 percent of swimmers, and 27 percent of gymnasts. Following up on the notion that some sports are more acceptable for females than others, Snyder and Spreitzer (1973) asked a random sample of the citizens of Toledo, Ohio, the question, "In your opinion, would participation in any of the following sports enhance a girl's/woman's feminine qualities?" Responses indicated that 67 percent felt that swimming would, followed by 57 percent for tennis, 54 percent for gymnastics, 14 percent for softball and basketball, and 13 percent for track and field. Sage and Loudermilk (1979) reported that female athletes in what they called the less approved sports (softball, basketball, volleyball, field hockey, and track and field) experienced significantly more role conflict than those in more accepted sports (tennis, golf, swimming, gymnastics). Ostrow, Jones, and Spiker (1981), in a study of ninety-three undergraduate nursing majors, isolated a number of sex appropriate sports. For example, figure skating and ballet were rated as significantly feminine; no significant differences were noted for swimming, bicycling, and bowling;

marathon running, the shot put, basketball, archery, tennis, racquetball, and jogging were seen as masculine activities.

Hoferek and Hanick (1985) asked people in a town in Iowa to respond to a questionnaire related to women and sports and compared their results with those from Ohio reported by Snyder and Spreitzer (1973). A summary of the major findings of both studies can be seen in tables 10.3 and 10.4. Hoferek and Hanick concluded that, in general, sport participation by females was seen as neither enhancing nor detracting in terms of image. Another interesting finding was that basketball was not seen in the Iowa study as enhancing or detracting but nevertheless was the sport of choice with the Iowa sample insofar as the responses went to the question, "If you had a daughter, what sports would you prefer that she participate in?" Fifty-three percent of the respondents cited basketball; no other sport was cited in more than 9 percent of the cases. In summation, the authors concluded that the comparison of the Ohio and Iowa results suggests that traditional, rigid sex role stereotypes were transcended and the opportunity set was dominant.

Comparing responses in Toledo, Ohio, in 1973 with those from a small Iowa town in the early 1980s may be a bit like the proverbial comparison of oranges and apples. Also, the finding that basketball was so popular may very easily be attributed to the long-term popularity of the sport in Iowa. For most of its interscholastic sport history, Iowa played a brand of six-on-six basketball in which each team had three offensive and three defensive players. Thus, there were six players at each end of the court, and at no time were any of them allowed to cross the midcourt line. The typical offense in this format was built around a tall, high-scoring center and two quick ball-handlers. Iowa abandoned this format in 1994, leaving Oklahoma as the last state to play six-on-six basketball. Each district actually voted whether to play full-court five-on-five or half-court six-on-six basketball. Oklahoma

Table 10.3
Percent Responding That Participation Enhances Feminine Qualities

"In your opinion, would participation in any of the following sports enhance a girl's/woman's feminine qualities?"

| Sport | Percent Saying Yes | | |
	Ohio city	Iowa town	x^2*
Gymnastics	54	48	—
Swimming	67	42	***
Tennis	57	35	***
Basketball	14	24	**
Track	13	23	**
Softball	14	20	—

*x^2 based on 2 (Ohio vs. Iowa) × 2 (yes vs. no) analysis with df = 1.

**$p < .05$.

***$p < .01$.

Source: Hoferek and Hanick (1985).

Table 10.4
Percent Responding That Participation Detracts from Feminine Qualities

"In your opinion, would participation in any of the following sports detract from a girl's/woman's feminine qualities?"

| Sport | Percent Saying Yes | | |
	Ohio city	Iowa town	x^2*
Gymnastics	6	0	**
Swimming	2	0	—
Tennis	2	0	—
Basketball	21	7	***
Track	30	7	***
Softball	20	9	**

*x^2 based on 2 (Ohio vs. Iowa) × 2 (yes vs. no) analysis with df = 1.

**$p < .05$.

***$p < .01$.

Source: Hoferek and Hanick (1985).

finally did away with the six-on-six format in 1995 ("The End," 1995). Undoubtedly, six-on-six basketball serves as a reminder of the time when endurance sports were viewed as excessively demanding for females, physically and psychologically. In any event, a healthy change seems to be under way in the way female participation in sport is perceived. Snyder and Spreitzer (1983, p. 7) sum up their response to the Ohio and Iowa data: "From 1972 to 1981, the popular conception of femininity vis-à-vis the athletic role has become more flexible; this openness was more evident in the relatively rural Iowa sample than in the urban Ohio sample."

Why Women Compete

Kidd and Woodman (1975) created a tripartite notion as to why females compete in sports, with "have fun," "play well," and "to win" serving as the respective parts of the formula. Nicholson (1979) used the same conditions in a study of 502 athletes and nonathletes in the eighth and ninth grades in Michigan. Generally speaking, Nicholson found few differences between the two groups concerning "having fun" and "winning"; however, sport participants placed much more emphasis on "playing well." Nicholson's results were corroborated by Siegel and Newhof (1984). Siegel and Newhof studied basketball players in Divisions I, II, and III of the Association for Intercollegiate Athletics for Women (AIAW) and found no statistically significant differences across divisions concerning participation satisfaction. Personal satisfaction was viewed most positively, followed by winning and pressures to participate.

An interesting development that bears on the issue of female competitiveness concerns the ability of women to respond to what is considered to be a standard "gut-check" in sport, coming from behind to win. Weinberg and various associates (Weinberg, Richardson, and Jackson, 1981; Weinberg, Richardson, Jackson, and Yukelson, 1983;

Ransom and Weinberg, 1985) have been at the forefront in studying this dimension. In the 1983 study, twenty-four hundred collegiate and professional men's and women's basketball games and nineteen-hundred collegiate and open men's and women's volleyball matches for 1980–1981 were dissected for sex differences in the ability to come from behind. Being behind in basketball was determined by halftime scores, whereas in volleyball, the loss of the first set was considered to be the critical point for this determination. In professional basketball, men's teams came from behind to win 30 percent of the time; only 7 percent of the women's teams did. At the collegiate level, these figures were 37 percent and 24 percent, respectively. No significant sex differences in volleyball were noted.

In the 1981 and 1985 works, coming from behind on the part of tennis players of both sexes was studied. The 1981 study found that male tennis players at both the amateur and professional levels came from behind (i.e., they lost the first set) more often than did female players. The more recent of the two studies was along the same lines. The top twenty male and female players in the 1980 United States Tennis Association yearbook were studied, and particularly the 242 matches in which they dropped the first set. No sex differences in ability to come back were noted, thereby indicating that elite players of both sexes appear to possess equal ability in overcoming adversity. This equality notion is further substantiated when these top twenty athletes are compared with the ability to come from behind of the top five hundred players. In this situation, 39 percent of males and 37 percent of females in the top twenty came from behind to win; in the case of the top five hundred, the figures drop rather precipitously to 15 percent for males and 9 percent for the females.

This come from behind phenomenon represents an interesting aspect of competitiveness in females. Preliminary evidence from Weinberg and associates indicates that elite females

Besides being a sports reporter for KGO-TV (ABC) in San Francisco, Bonnie Warner is a top-ranked luge competitor. In summer, Bonnie practices pushing away from the starting line.

are as capable of responding positively to potential defeat, at least in tennis. Males at a lower level of competitiveness show a slight superiority to equal ability females, but both groups are inferior to the top-flight females in coming from behind to win.

OTHER ISSUES INVOLVING WOMEN IN SPORT

Currently, research is being conducted that focuses on other issues related to women's sports. One issue is the way in which female athletes are portrayed in the media. Another concerns an emerging literature on homophobia, particularly aimed at females in sport; it appears that there is a widespread perception of rampant lesbianism among women athletes. Finally, eating disorders will be discussed, as there appears to be a problem in this area among female athletes. Let us begin with media portrayals of female athletes.

The Media

According to McGregor (1989), the term *hegemony* is synonymous with authority and leadership and pertains to systems that go unquestioned. One such system is the "good old boy" network in sports, just one manifestation of male dominance at all levels. This hegemonic tendency is highly noticeable in media coverage of sports and fitness. Three recent studies exemplify this point, one dealing with sports publications, another with sports photography, and the final one with the naming of athletic teams. In the first instance, Lumpkin and Williams (1991) conducted a content analysis of nearly four thousand feature articles in *Sports Illustrated* from 1954 through 1987. Chief among their findings were that males were featured in nearly 91 percent of these articles, nearly 92 percent were written by male authors, most dealt with exclusively male sports, more white males were featured than were blacks or females, the articles on the white males were longer, and the descriptors in articles on females were blatantly sexist in content. In a similar vein, Shifflett and Revelle (1994) analyzed articles and pictures chosen from the *NCAA News* for the years 1988–1991 and found that twice the number of paragraphs and pictures were allocated to male sports, players, and coaches than those afforded the females. These sorts of findings are supportive of earlier work along these general lines conducted by Gilbert and Williamson (1973a) and Rintala and Burrell (1984). Interestingly, this general picture has also been reported from Aus-

tralia (McKay and Rowe, 1987) and Canada (Theberge, 1991). In the case of Australia, McKay and Rowe report an overwhelming male bias in their media. As for Canada, Theberge analyzed print media accounts of sports in four major Canadian newspapers over a six-month period; she found little emphasis on female sports and physical activity and equally little effort devoted to changing stereotypes of females who engage in these activities.

Insofar as sports photography is concerned, a study by Duncan (1990) is instructive. Duncan looked at the portrayal of women in the 1984 and 1988 Olympic Games by analyzing photographs from such popular magazines as *Life, Sports Illustrated, Newsweek, Time, Maclean's* and *Ms.* Chief among Duncan's findings were that the more attractive females such as Katarina Witt and Florence Griffith Joyner, received a disproportionate amount of photographic attention. Many references to their sexiness accompanied the photography. Another point made was that the poses and camera angles employed in the photographs often bordered on the soft porn variety. Yet another conclusion was that women are often photographed crying, thereby promoting an image of female athletes, and females in general, as incapable of controlling their emotions. The net effect of these kinds of photographic nuances, contends Duncan, is that women are placed in a position of weakness through a deliberate political strategy that has such subjugation as its objective.

Speaking of photography and prominent sports publications, it would be difficult to discuss the area without at least a cursory reference to the controversial but immensely profitable swimsuit editions published annually by *Sports Illustrated* and *Inside Sports.* Norman Jacobs, the publisher of *Inside Sports,* refers to the annual exercise as a "little fun" while Twiss Butler, in a letter to *USA Today,* calls it "an annual exercise for hit and run sexual harassment" (1991, p. 10C). Undoubtedly, swimsuit editions will be around for a while, and much indignation will accompany their publication. It is not likely, however, that they do much for the women's movement in and external to sport.

A third discriminatory mechanism, according to Eitzen and Zinn (1989), exists in the form of the naming and gender marking of sports teams. They looked at data from 1,185 four-year schools and found that over half of American universities and colleges employ team names, mascots, or logos that are demeaning to women. Examples cited by Eitzen and Zinn (p. 367) which, in their words, "de-athleticize" women's teams include physical markers (Belles, Rambelles), girl or gal (Green Gals), feminine suffix (Tigerettes, Duchesses), lady (Lady Aggies, Lady Eagles), male as a false generic (Cowboys, Hokies, Tomcats), male name with a female modifier (Lady Rams, Lady Dons), double gender marking (Choctaws/Lady Chocs, Jaguars/Lady Jags) and male/female paired polarity (Panthers/Pink Panthers, Bears/Teddy Bears). This tendency was strongest in the South, thought by some to be the last bastion of male domination in the United States. From these data (and others not reported here), Eitzen and Zinn conclude that "institutional sexism is deeply entrenched in college sports" (p. 369).

Homophobia

Yet another concern for the female athletes is the common perception that women's sport is filled with lesbians. The term *homophobia* connotes a fear and/or hatred of individuals who engage in homosexual behavior or behavior that is deemed to be outside the boundaries of traditional gender role expectations (Griffin, 1989). This broader stance proposed by Griffin is at the heart of the issue in that women athletes who are not lesbians may still, in some sense and to varying degrees, violate the expectancies held for women in general.

Cahn (1993) traces the societal and sport roots of homophobia in a most informative historical article. It is Cahn's contention that the emergence in the early to middle part of this century of women's athletics, sport heroines like Babe Didrikson Zaharias, and professional physical education departments opened up a veritable fire storm insofar as the way society viewed females. Much talk was made of "mannish" females who participated in sport, and athletic teams and physical education departments were eternally vigilant in promoting the most effeminate image possible. Sports, most particularly softball, offered an opportunity for lesbians to gather in socially acceptable surroundings. At the same time, the prevailing societal attitudes about lesbianism and homosexuality were such that it was best to keep one's sexual preference a secret. Out of this suspicion and secrecy, homophobia was born.

Homophobia has taken on considerable political baggage as a result of the continuing furor within our society with regard to gay and lesbian issues. Undoubtedly, there are individuals within and external to sport who are homosexual, others who are supportive of the behavior, yet others who are tolerant, some who are opposed, and a segment who are actively homophobic. The degree to which each of these groups might see homosexuality in the world of sport and fitness is conjectural, with the exception of homophobes, who are probably predisposed to seeing it everywhere. These are probably the same 15 percent Baumann (1991) found in his *USA Today* survey of sports fans who would ban homosexuals from all competition. Incidentally, in the same survey, 59 percent of all respondents considered homosexual behavior to be morally wrong.

Gays are not unknown in the sports world. Professional football player Dave Kopay, major league baseball umpire Dave Pallone, Olympic champion diver Greg Louganis (an AIDS victim), Olympic decathlete Tom Waddell, and major league baseball player Glenn Burke (who died of AIDS in 1995) are just a few of the male athletes who have come out of the closet in the past several years. Among females, professional tennis stars Billie Jean King and Martina Navratilova are admitted lesbians. It is interesting that so few examples of lesbianism have been uncovered, given the widely held assumption that lesbianism in sport is so common. For example, Carson (1987) conducted a survey of 250 introductory psychology students in which they were asked to estimate the percentage of female athletes who are lesbians; the mean response was 47 percent.

"Sweaty lesbians," "dyke," "butch," "lezzies," and "jock" are just a few of the pejorative epithets female athletes hear bandied about as a function of homophobia. To combat this image problem, some coaches have instituted a "no lesbian" policy insofar as such a stricture can be enforced. Other coaches remove players from the team if lesbianism is discovered. Still others have started hair-style and make-up seminars to give their female players a more acceptable image. As an aside, some coaches have engaged in quasi-ethical behavior by telling parents of prospective athletes undergoing the recruitment process not to send their daughter to School X because lesbianism is widespread there (Griffin, 1993; Thorngren, 1990).

Several authorities have recently suggested ways to combat homophobia in women's sports (Griffin, 1993; Lenskyj, 1991). Chief among their suggestions include attacking homophobia through education, continuing to seriously address the problem within the organizational structure of the various sports sciences professional societies, and being aware of our own homophobic tendencies and those of others.

Eating Disorders

The American Psychiatric Association has published the *Diagnostic and Statistical Manual* (4th ed.) in an effort to enhance the reliability of psychiatric diagnoses. The DSM-IV is the "bible" for all practicing psychologists and psychiatrists; it represents the collective wisdom of both groups of practitioners with regard to the diagnostic process. One inclusion in DSM-IV involves two interrelated eating disorders known as anorexia and bulimia. The distinction between these two disorders essentially has to do with restricted food intake, anorexia, or excessive food intake, bulimia (Suinn, 1988). Of primary concern in our discussion is anorexia. According to Carson and Butcher (1992) and Suinn (1988), anorexia occurs almost exclusively in adolescence or young adulthood, the preponderance of the victims are females (15–20 to 1 ratio), and has a mortality rate of around 5 percent. Side effects include menstrual cessation; a morbid fear of obesity; a distorted body image; brief binges of overeating (a link with bulimia), followed by self-induced vomiting or excessive use of laxatives; and marked overactivity. In many instances, the overactivity is calculated to the nth degree as a means of keeping weight to a minimum and as a method of exerting control over what may seem to the victim to be an uncontrollable world.

Anorexia is quite well-known among female athletes, particularly in sports where, to quote Yates, Leehey, and Shisslak (1983), "grim asceticism" is required. By way of documenting the problem in women's sport, estimates from Halliburton and Sanford (1989) indicate that 10 percent of all female athletes at the University of Texas were diagnosed as having an eating disorder within an eighteen-month period; overall statistics indicate an incidence of 4 to 5 percent among female nonathletes at the same university. Walberg and Johnston (1991) report that 42 percent of a sample of competitive female body builders they studied had been anorexic at some point in their lives; 67 percent reported being terrified of becoming fat and an additional 58 percent were obsessed with food. Perhaps most inclusive in terms of statistics, Dick (1991) asked senior female administrators at 803 NCAA institutions to respond to a question aimed at ascertaining the prevalance of anorexia or bulimia in their respective programs during the period 1988–1990. Nearly five hundred administrators responded; 40 percent of them reported at least one case during the specified time frame. Wrestling for males and gymnastics, cross country, swimming, and the running events in track (in that order) for females had the highest prevalence of eating disorders by sport. As might be predicted, 93 percent of the cases involved females. Based on Dick's survey, it seems safe to conclude that eating disorders are in fact a serious problem in big-time intercollegiate sports, and particularly in those where women are involved. Other data suggest that the problem is not restricted to collegiate competitors.

A poignant reminder of the effects of an eating disorder, anorexia, was the premature and tragic death of gymnast Christy Henrich, a member of the United States national team for several years. At the peak of her competitive run, Christy, who was 4 feet, 10 inches tall, weighed 95 pounds; when she died in July of 1994, her weight had dropped below 50 pounds. Christy was a perfectionist possessed of an incredible work ethic. However, like many anorexics, she had a poor self-image and low self-esteem; she fought these twin problems with obsessions about eating and exercise. At one point during her most competitive phase, she had reduced her dietary intake to an apple a day. The crash diet ended her career as a gymnast and, ultimately, her life (IG Staff, 1994).

To date, little has been proffered in the sport psychology and sport medicine literature with regard to what might be done to combat the eating disorders problem in female athletes, though Sundgot-Borgen (1994) has delineated some risk factors and treatment strategies worthy of consideration. For the most part, however, other than early detection, prolonged psychotherapy, and medical intervention, the larger medical/psychological community has not really come up with anything that might be regarded as definitive in terms of treating eating disorders in nonathletes or athletes. Clearly, much remains to be done in this problematic area of eating disorders.

SUMMARY

1. Because of past biases and the current developmental status of women's sport, a separate chapter has been devoted to the female athlete.
2. Though women in ancient Greece were generally oppressed athletically, they did have their own analogue to the Olympics, the Heraean Games, named after Hera, the wife of Zeus.
3. Not until 1896, with the founding of the modern Olympic Games, were women really accorded much of a place in sport. With each successive Olympics since then, the athletic menu for women has gradually expanded. Over three thousand women took part in the 1992 Games.
4. Title IX of the Higher Education Act of 1972 has served as another landmark in women's sports. Its main effect has been to set the stage for equal opportunity in sport.
5. Contemporary factors such as increased opportunity, fallout produced by the women's movement, the recent fitness boom, and the presence of female role models have all served as additional forces in enhancement of sport involvement on the part of women.
6. Physiological issues of relevance within sport include menstrual functioning, pregnancy, and childbirth, and myths related to female participation in sport.
7. Menstrual functioning has attracted much interest among sport scientists. Early speculation was that menstruation and physical exertion did not mix, thereby creating a host of problems for the involved females.
8. Early 1960s research by Erdelyi with Hungarian female athletes and by Zaharieva with Olympic athletes from ten different countries did much to dispel the earlier skepticism about menstrual function and athletic participation.

9. Recent studies have complicated our understanding of the relationship between menstruation and sport. Though not as negative as the earliest speculations, they are not quite as positive as Erdelyi and Zaharieva.

10. Causes of menstrual difficulties in athletes are numerous. Frisch has advanced a theory suggesting that these problems are reactions to a disturbed body mass to percentage of body fat ratio. Other authorities point to an endocrinological explanation, excessively strenuous training, and heavy training prior to menarche as possible etiological agents.

11. The consequences of these menstrual cycle disruptions appear to be minimal or nonexistent in terms of pregnancy or childbirth. Female athletes compete well in the early stages of pregnancy, appear to have easy, uncomplicated deliveries, and compete even more effectively in some cases after childbirth.

12. The myth that sport participation by women endangers their breasts and internal sexual structures has not been supported. Further myths lacking support include the notion that women are structurally less able to compete and the idea that sport produces bulging, unattractive muscles.

13. Three psychological variables of considerable interest to sport psychologists include attribution theory, fear of success, and psychological androgyny.

14. Research in the late 1970s showed that young females attributed success to external things, such as luck. They, like males, also attributed male success to ability, an internal attribute. Further research indicates that by age thirteen, sex role stereotypes are in effect. These stereotypes attribute male success to effort, female success to luck. A more recent area of interest, self versus team attribution, has emerged and bears more investigation.

15. Horner suggested in 1972 that females manifest a fear of success (FOS) in a variety of competitive situations. Subsequent research has not been supportive of the Horner position.

16. The concept of psychological androgyny was introduced to the literature in 1974. Androgyny is viewed as an optimal amalgamation of the best of what have been viewed as bipolar traits, masculinity and femininity. Research using both the Personal Attributes Questionnaire (PAQ) and the Bem Sex-Role Inventory (BSRI) have been provocative. In general, female athletes who are successful are either androgynous or masculine on these measures. Feminine females do not find the athletic realm particularly rewarding, though they may need its benefits most. Overall, it appears that females feel little sex role conflict in their sport involvement.

17. Socialization into sport is a most complex issue. Some of the more relevant subaspects of socialization into sport include role conflict, socialization agents, sport acceptance, and why females compete.

18. Traditional definitions of the concepts of male and female have generated much research interest within psychology. Research from the mid-1960s showed a preference for traditional female roles and a rejection of the female athlete. Even as late as 1975, 65 percent of college women saw a stigma attached to women's participation in sport. Recent research is indicative of healthy changes in the perception of the female athlete.

19. Parents are the prime source of early socialization into sport. In adolescence, coaches and physical educators replace the parents. Beyond adolescence, little is known of socialization forces.

20. The acceptability of the broad array of sport for females varies. In general, the more feminine sports carry slightly more acceptance. Sports such as basketball, volleyball, and softball appear to be regarded more unfavor-

ably. Research in Iowa is suggestive of positive changes concerning the acceptance of a greater number of sport activities.

21. Though the evidence is sparse, female athletes appear to place more importance on having fun and playing well than on winning. In another facet of competition, women participating in some sports seem to be less likely than men to come from behind to win. Males at lower levels of skill in tennis appear to be better than females of similar skill level at coming from behind, but this diminishes somewhat at the elite level. In professional basketball, substantial differences favor the male players; though not as pronounced, male collegiate players also come from behind to win more often. Volleyball studies show no sex differences in the ability to come from behind to win.

22. Over the past two decades, new issues of concern to women athletes have emerged. Among these new concerns are the portrayal of women in the media, homophobia, and eating disorders.

23. In terms of the coverage accorded females in the major sports periodicals, sports photography, and the naming and marketing of athletic teams, it is clear that women are portrayed in a less than optimal fashion.

23. There is a widespread perception that women in sports are violating traditional gender role expectations, one manifestation of which is lesbianism. The admission of their lesbianism by athletes such as Martina Navratilova and Billie Jean King has reinforced the notion in the minds of many that female athletes are gay.

24. Eating disorders, such as anorexia, are particularly prominent in sports where thinness is rewarded such as gymnastics, running, and swimming. The incidence of anorexia appears to be higher among women athletes than among females in general. Specific guidelines for dealing with anorexic athletes are not well-developed at this point in time.

SUGGESTED READINGS

Birrell, S., & Cole, C. L. (Eds). (1994) *Women, sport, and culture.* Champaign, IL: Human Kinetics.

This reader includes twenty-four different entries dealing broadly with such topics as: women, sport, and ideology; gender and the organization of sport; women in the male preserve of sport; media, sport, and gender; and sport and the politics of sexuality. Subtopics such as the African-American athlete, Title IX, coaching, cheerleaders, the male hegemony in sport, gender stereotyping in the media, homophobia, and feminist bodybuilding are addressed in a readable manner. This collection of readings offers much to those interested in the female sport experience.

Cahn, S. K. (1994) *Coming on strong: Gender and sexuality in twentieth-century women's sport.* New York: Free Press.

Cahn approaches the gender and sexuality issues from both a historical and contemporary viewpoint, taking on such issues as sexual sensation in the Flapper Era, black women in track and field, the All-American Girls Baseball League, the lesbian threat, and homophobia.

Creedon, P. J. (1994) (Ed.). *Women, media, and sport: Challenging values.* Thousand Oaks, CA: Sage.

Thirteen readings written by authorities on women's issues in sport such as Mary Jo Kane, Susan Greendorfer, Susan Birrell, and the editor herself, to name a few, are included in this edited volume. Particular emphasis is placed on several readings that deal with the image of women athletes in the various media.

Leon, G. R. (1990) Bulimia and athletics—The need to maintain a low body weight. In G. R. Leon (Ed.), *Case histories of psychopathology* (4th ed.). Needham Heights, MA: Allyn & Bacon.

Leon describes a case history of a twenty-one-year-old collegiate gymnast, Ginny N., who had an eating disorder in which she was binging and purging. Her MMPI and other psychological test results indicated a good deal of anxiety, depression, and feelings of alienation. The therapy provided was a ten-week program of a cognitive-behavioral nature, with specific emphasis on the irrational beliefs she held with regard to her eating behavior. Progress was made over the ten weeks of counseling, though her case required periodic monitoring beyond that point. The author concludes the case history with a description of bulimia as described in DSM-III-R, and its causes from the standpoint of available research on the topic.

Lovett, D. J., & Lowry, C. D. (1994) "Good old boys" and "good old girls" clubs: Myth or reality? *Journal of Sport Management, 8,* 27–35.

Lovett and Lowry analyzed over 1,100 secondary schools in Texas in an attempt to link administrative structure, policies, and practices to the selection, assignment, and retention of coaches in interscholastic sports. In general, the existence of a "good old boy" network was confirmed; however, a viable "good old girl" network was not operative in the administrative structures and functions studied.

Messner, M. A., & Sabo, D. F. (Eds.) (1990) *Sport, men, and the gender order.* Champaign, IL: Human Kinetics.

The authors have amassed research, theory, and speculation about a variety of issues bearing on the issue of male and female involvement in sport. Several chapters deal with the historical foundations, others with masculinity, gay issues, and black concerns. Chapter 17 is a discussion of homophobia in physical education, and an epilogue is provided by Carole Oglesby, a sport psychologist concerned with women's issues in society and sport.

Nelson, M. B. (1991) *Are we winning yet?* New York: Random House.

Nelson, herself a prominent athlete at the collegiate and national levels, addresses some issues of concern that have arisen as a function of the ascent of women's sport in the United States. She deals with such issues as coed sports, lesbianism, and the potential for dehumanization of women in sport in a male-dominated society.

Pearl, A. J. (Ed.) (1993) *The athletic female.* Champaign, IL: Human Kinetics.

Pearl takes an in-depth look at a variety of issues related to females in sport through a series of edited readings. Such topics as history, Title IX, gender role orientation, osteoporosis, diet, menstrual status, exercise and pregnancy, the use of oral contraceptives, substance abuse, eating disorders, strength training, and injury are addressed by various authorities chosen by Pearl as contributors. This book is comprehensive and offers much to the reader interested in the female sport experience.

Spence, J. T. (1991) Do the BSRI and PAQ measure the same or different concepts? *Psychology of Women Quarterly, 15,* 141–165.

Janet Spence, a past president of the American Psychological Association and an author of the PAQ, deliberates at length about the merits of the BSRI and her own instrument, discussing issues such as reliability, validity, and comparability of the masculinity and femininity scales. She concludes that both measures are valid in terms of the potential for assessing instrumental and expressive traits so pivotal to an understanding of gender issues and the concept of psychological androgyny.

The SIRLS sport and leisure database. (1990) Gender and the media. *Sociology of Sport Journal, 7,* 412–421.

Thirty annotated references dealing with media issues and women's sport are listed for the period 1980–1989. These citations provide the interested researcher or reader with a starting point for understanding the problems associated with the portrayal of female athletes in the media.

REFERENCES

Abney, R. (1991) Recruiting and mentoring sports leaders. *Journal of Physical Education, Recreation and Dance, 62*(3), 48–50.

Anastasi, A. (1982) *Psychological testing* (5th ed.). New York: Macmillan.

Arnold, E. H. (1924) Athletics for women. *American Physical Education Review,* October, 452–457.

Astrand, P. O., Eriksson, B. O., Nylander, I., Engstrom, I., Karlberg, P., Saltin, B., & Thoren, C. (1963) Girl swimmers with special reference to respiratory and circulatory adaptation and gynaecological and psychiatric aspects. *Acta Paediatrica Scandinavica,* Supplement 147.

Babb, R. A. (1992) An issue of fair play. *Balls and Strikes,* August-September, 8–9.

Baumann, M. (1991) Mixed feelings on gay athletes. *USA Today,* September 18, 10C.

Bem, S. (1974) The measurement of psychological androgyny. *Journal of Consulting and Clinical Psychology, 42,* 155–162.

Berg, R. (1995) A gain of inches: in women's college sports, good news comes in small packages. *Perspective, 18*(10), 9.

Bird, A. M., & Brame, J. (1978) Self versus team attributions: A test of the "I'm OK, but the team's so-so" phenomenon. *Research Quarterly, 49,* 260–267.

Bird, A. M., Foster, C., & Maruyama, G. (1980) Convergent and incremental effects of cohesion on attributions for self and team. *Journal of Sport Psychology, 2,* 181–194.

Bird, A. M., & Williams, J. M. (1980) A developmental–attributional analysis of sex role stereotypes for sport performance. *Developmental Psychology, 16,* 319–322.

Bloom, M. (1986) You've come a long way, baby. *The Runner,* Dec., 26–36.

Bloomberg, R. (1977) Coach says running affects menstruation. *Physician and Sportsmedicine, 5*(9), 15.

Blucker, J., & Hershberger, E. (1983). Causal attribution theory and the female athlete: What conclusions can we draw? *Journal of Sport Psychology, 5,* 353–360.

Brewington, P. (1990) Iowa schools refuse to let popular six-on-six game die. *USA Today,* March 8, 10C.

Brown, B. (1988) Study: Girls find activities for a lifetime. *USA Today,* June 8, 9C.

Brown, B. (1994) Gender equity study shows slow change. *USA Today,* October 24, 2C.

Brown, R. (1965) A use of the semantic differential to study the image of girls who participate in competitive sports and certain other school related activities. Unpublished doctoral dissertation, Florida State University.

Brownlee, S. (1988) Moms in the fast lane. *Sports Illustrated,* May, 56–60.

Butcher, J. (1985) Longitudinal analysis of adolescent girls' participation in physical activity. *Sociology of Sport Journal, 2,* 130–143.

Butler, T. (1991) Media unwittingly protecting sexual harassers. *USA Today,* February 19, 10C.

Cahn, S. K. (1993) From the "muscle moll" to the "butch" ballplayer: Mannishness, lesbianism, and homophobia in U.S. women's sport. *Feminist Studies, 19,* 343–368.

Carson, K. (1987) The effects of sex-role orientation and fear of success on attitudes toward women in sport. Unpublished master's thesis, Texas A&M University.

Carson, R. C., & Butcher, J. N. (1992) *Abnormal psychology and modern life* (9th ed.). New York: Harper Collins.

Chalip, L., Villiger, J., & Duignan, P. (1980) Sex-role identity in a selected sample of women field hockey players. *International Journal of Sport Psychology, 11,* 240–248.

Coakley, J. (1982) *Sports in society: Issues and controversies* (2d ed.). St. Louis, MO: C. V. Mosby.

Colley, A., Roberts, N., & Chipps, A. (1985) Sex-role identity, personality, and participation in team and individual sports by males and females. *International Journal of Sport Psychology, 16,* 103–112.

Cook, K. (1989) The Iowa girl stands tall. *Sports Illustrated, 70*(7), 76–84.

Csikszentmihalyi, M., & Bennett, S. (1971) An exploratory model of play. *American Anthropologist, 73,* 45–58.

Curry, T., & Jiobu, R. (1984) *Sports: A social perspective.* Englewood Cliffs, NJ: Prentice-Hall.

Dale, E., Gerlach, D., Martin, D., & Alexander, C. (1979) Physical fitness profiles and reproductive physiology of the female distance runner. *Physician and Sportsmedicine, 7*(1), 83–95.

Dale, E., Gerlach, D. H., & Wilhite, A. L. (1979) Menstrual dysfunction in distance runners. *Obstetrics and Gynecology, 54,* 47–53.

Deaux, K., & Emswiller, T. (1974) Explanations of successful performance on sex-linked tasks: What is skill for the male is luck for the female. *Journal of Personality and Social Psychology, 29,* 80–85.

Deaux, K., & Farris, E. (1977) Attributing causes for one's own performance: The effects of sex, norms, and outcome. *Journal of Research in Personality, 11,* 59–72.

DeBacy, D., Spaeth, R., & Busch, R. (1970) What do men really think about athletic competition for women? *Journal of Health, Physical Education, and Recreation, 41,* 28–29.

Del Rey, P., & Sheppard, S. (1981) Relationship of psychological androgyny in female athletes to self-esteem. *International Journal of Sport Psychology, 12,* 165–175.

Dick, R. W. (1991) Eating disorders in NCAA athletic programs. *Athletic Training, 26,* 136–140.

Donnelly, S. B. (1990) Work that body! *Time,* Fall Special Issue, 68.

Duncan, M. C. (1990) Sports photographs and sexual difference: Images of women and men in the 1984 and 1988 Olympic Games. *Sociology of Sport Journal, 7,* 22–43.

Dunkle, M. (1974) Equal opportunity for women in sport. In B. Hoepner (Ed.), *Women's athletics: Coping with controversy.* Washington, DC: American Association for Health, Physical Education, and Recreation.

Duquin, M. E. (1978) The androgynous advantage. In C. A. Oglesby (Ed.), *Women and sport: From myth to reality* (pp. 89–106). Philadelphia, PA: Lea and Febiger.

Dyer, K. (1982) *Challenging the men: The social biology of female sporting achievement.* St. Lucia, Queensland, Australia: University of Queensland Press.

Edwards, S. W., Gordin, R. D., & Henschen, K. P. (1984) Sex-role orientations of female NCAA championship gymnasts. *Perceptual and Motor Skills, 58,* 625–626.

Eitzen, D. S., & Sage, J. (1982). *Sociology of American sport* (2d ed.). Dubuque, IA: Wm. C. Brown.

Eitzen, D. S., & Zinn, M. B. (1989) The de-athleticization of women: The naming and gender marking of collegiate sport teams. *Sociology of Sport Journal, 6,* 362–370.

Emery, L. (1984) Women's participation in the Olympic Games. *Journal of Physical Education, Recreation and Dance, 55*(5), 62–63, 72.

Erdelyi, G. (1962) Gynecological survey of female athletes. *Journal of Sports Medicine and Physical Fitness, 2,* 174–179.

Erdelyi, G. (1976) Effects of exercise on the menstrual cycle. *Physician and Sportsmedicine, 4*(3), 79–81.

Feicht, C., Johnson, T., Martin, B., Sparkles, K., & Wagner, W. (1978). Secondary amenorrhea in athletes. *Lancet,* Nov. 25, 1145–1146.

Female athletes will participate in record numbers at Atlanta. (1995) *USA Today,* May 4, 16C.

Friedman, E., & Berger, B. G. (1991) Influence of gender, masculinity, and femininity on the effectiveness of three stress reduction techniques: Jogging, relaxation response, and group interaction. *Journal of Applied Sport Psychology, 3,* 61–86.

Frisch, R. (1976) Fatness of girls from menarche to age 18 years, with a nomogram. *Human Biology, 48,* 353–359.

Frisch, R., & McArthur, J. (1974) Menstrual cycles: Fatness as a determinant of minimal weight for height necessary for their maintenance or onset. *Science, 185,* 949–951.

Frisch, R., Gotz-Welbergen, A., McArthur, J., Albright, T., Witschi, J., Bullen, B., Birnholz, J., Reed, R., & Hermann, H. (1981) Delayed menarche and amenorrhea of college athletes in relation to age of onset of training. *Journal of American Mental Association, 246,* 1559–1563.

Gackenbach, J. (1982) Collegiate swimmers: Sex differences in self-reports and indices of physiological stress. *Perceptual and Motor Skills, 55,* 555–558.

Galle, P. C., Freeman, E. W., Galle, M. G., Huggins, G. R., & Sondheimer, J. J. (1983) Physiologic and psychologic profile in a survey of women runners. *Fertility and Sterility, 39,* 633–639.

Gendel, E. (1976) Psychological factors and menstrual extraction. *Physician and Sportsmedicine, 4*(3), 72–75.

Gender equity survey numbers. (1992) *USA Today,* March 12, 7C.

Gerber, E., Felshin, J., Berlin, P., & Wyrick, W. (Eds.). (1974) *The American woman in sport.* Reading, MA: Addison-Wesley.

Gilbert, B., & Williamson, N. (1973a) Sport is unfair to women. *Sports Illustrated,* May 28, 88–98.

Gilbert, B., & Williamson, N. (1973b) Are you being two-faced? *Sports Illustrated,* June 4, 45–54.

Gillette, J. (1975) When and where women are injured in sport. *Physician and Sportsmedicine, 3*(5), 61–63.

Greendorfer, S. (1977) Role of socializing agents in female sport involvement. *Research Quarterly, 48,* 304–310.

Griffin, P. (1973) What's a nice girl like you doing in a profession like this? *Quest, 19,* 96–101.

Griffin, P. (1989) Homophobia in physical education: *Canadian Association for Health, Physical Education and Recreation Journal, 55*(2), 27–31.

Griffin, P. (1993) Homophobia in women's sports: The fear that divides us. In G. L. Cohen, ed., *Women in sport: Issues and controversies* (pp. 193–203). Newbury Park, CA: Sage.

Halliburton, S., & Sanford, S. (1989) Making weight becomes torture for UT swimmers. *Austin American Statesman,* July 31, D1, D7.

Hargreaves, J. (1990) Changing images of the sporting female. *Sport and Leisure, 31*(3), 14–17.

Harres, R. (1968) Attitudes of students toward women's athletic competition. *Research Quarterly, 39,* 278–284.

Helmreich, R., Stapp, J., & Ervin, C. (1974) The Texas Social Behavior Inventory (TSBI). *Journal Supplement Abstract Service Catalog of Selected Documents in Psychology, 4,* 79. (Ms. No. 681)

Henschen, K., Edwards, S., & Mathinos, L. (1982) Achievement motivation and sex-role orientation of high school female track and field athletes versus nonathletes. *Perceptual and Motor Skills, 55,* 183–187.

Hicks, B. (1993) The legendary Babe Didrikson Zaharias. In G. L. Cohen (ed.), *Women in sport* (pp. 38–48). Newbury Park, CA: Sage.

Higginson, D. (1985) The influence of socializing agents in the female sport-participation process. *Adolescence, 20,* 73–82.

Hochstetler, S., Rejeski, W. J., & Best, D. (1985) The influence of sex-role orientation on ratings of perceived exertion. *Sex Roles, 12,* 825–835.

Hoferek, M., & Hanick, P. (1985) Woman and athlete: Toward role consistency. *Sex Roles, 12,* 687–695.

Horner, M. (1968) Sex differences in achievement motivation and performance in competitive and noncompetitive situations. Unpublished doctoral dissertation, University of Michigan.

Horner, M. (1972) Toward an understanding of achievement-related conflicts in women. *Journal of Social Issues, 28,* 157–175.

Hunter, L. Y., & Torgan, C. (1982) The bra controversy: Are sports bras a necessity? *Physician and Sportsmedicine, 10*(11), 75–76.

IG Staff. (1994) Christy Henrich: 1972–1994. *International Gymnast, 36*(10), 49.

Ingman, O. (1952) Menstruation in Finnish top class sportswomen. International symposium of the medicine and physiology of sports and athletes. Finnish Association of Sports Medicine.

Iso-Ahola, S. (1979) Sex-role stereotypes and causal attributions for success and failure in motor performance. *Research Quarterly, 50,* 630–640.

Johnson, W. O., & Williamson, N. (1975a). Babe. *Sports Illustrated,* October 6, 113–127.

Johnson, W. O., & Williamson, N. (1975b). Babe: Part three. *Sports Illustrated,* October 20, 48–62.

Kane, M. (1982) The influence of level of sport participation and sex-role orientation on female professionalization of attitudes toward play. *Journal of Sport Psychology, 4,* 290–294.

Kaplan, J. (1979) *Women and sports.* New York: Viking Press.

Kidd, T. R., & Woodman, W. F. (1975) Sex and orientations toward winning in sport. *Research Quarterly, 46,* 476–483.

Kingsley, J., Brown, F., & Seibert, M. (1977) Social acceptance of female athletes by college women. *Research Quarterly, 48,* 727–733.

Layman, E. (1968) Attitudes towards sports for girls and women in relation to masculinity-femininity stereotypes of women athletes. Paper presented at Symposium of American Association for the Advancement of Science, Dallas, Texas.

Lee, M. (1924) The case for and against intercollegiate athletics for women and the situation as it stands today. *American Physical Education Review, 29,* 13–19.

Lee, M. (1931) The case for and against intercollegiate athletics for women and the situation since 1923. *Research Quarterly, 2,* 93–127.

Lee, M. (1983) *A history of physical education and sports in the U.S.A.* New York: Wiley.

Lenskyj, H. (1991) Combating homophobia in sport and physical education. *Sociology of Sport Journal, 8,* 61–69.

Leonard, W. (1984) *A sociological perspective of sport* (2d ed.). Minneapolis, MN: Burgess.

Lipsyte, R. (1975) *Sports world: An American dreamland*. New York: Quadrangle Books.

Loggia, M. (1973) On the playing fields of history. *Ms.,* July, 62–65.

Loucks, A. B. (1990) Effects of exercise training on the menstrual cycle: Existence and mechanisms. *Medicine and Science in Sports and Exercise, 22,* 275–280.

Loverock, P. (1991) On your mark get set go. *Shape,* May, 83–87.

Lumpkin, A., & Williams, L. D. (1991) An analysis of *Sports Illustrated* feature articles, 1954–1987. *Sociology of Sport Journal, 8,* 16–32.

Lutter, J., & Cushman, S. (1982) Menstrual patterns in female runners. *Physician and Sportsmedicine, 10*(9), 60–72.

Malumphy, T. (1970) The college woman athlete — questions and tentative answers. *Quest, 14,* 18–27.

Many women fear stalling of Title IX. (1992) *USA Today,* June 8, 1–2C.

May, J. R., Veach, T. L., Daily-McKee, D., & Furman, G. (1985) A preliminary study of elite adolescent women athletes and their attitudes toward training and femininity. In N. K. Butts, T. T. Gushiken, & B. Zarins (Eds.), *The elite athlete* (pp. 163–169). New York: Spectrum Pub.

McElroy, M., & Willis, J. (1979) Women and the achievement conflict in sport: A preliminary study. *Journal of Sport Psychology, 1,* 241–247.

McGregor, E. (1989) Mass media and sport: Influences on the public. *The Physical Educator, 46*(1), 52–55.

McHugh, M. C., Duquin, M. E., & Frieze, I. H. (1978) Beliefs about success and failure: Attribution and the female athlete. In C. A. Oglesby (Ed.), *Women and sport: From myth to reality* (pp. 173–191). Philadelphia, PA: Lea and Febiger.

McKay, J., & Rowe, D. (1987) Ideology, the media and Australian sport. *Sociology of Sport Journal, 4,* 258–273.

Michael, M., Gilroy, F., & Sherman, M. (1984) Athletic similarity and attitudes towards women as factors in the perceived physical attractiveness and liking of a female varsity athlete. *Perceptual and Motor Skills, 59,* 511–518.

Michener, J. A. (1976) *Sports in America*. New York: Fawcett Crest.

Mouratidis, J. (1984) Heracles at Olympia and the exclusion of women from the ancient Olympic games. *Journal of Sport History, 11*(3), 41–55.

Myers, A., & Lips, H. (1978) Participation in competitive amateur sports as a function of psychological androgyny. *Sex Roles, 4,* 571–578.

Nicholson, C. (1979) Some attitudes associated with sport participation among junior high school females. *Research Quarterly, 50,* 661–667.

Oglesby, C. A. (1984) Interactions between gender identity and sport. In J. M. Silva and R. S. Weinberg (Eds.), *Psychological foundations of sport* (pp. 387–399). Champaign, IL: Human Kinetics.

Osgood, C., Suci, G., & Tannenbaum, P. (1957) *The measurement of meaning*. Urbana: University of Illinois Press.

Ostrow, A. G., Jones, D. C., & Spiker, D. D. (1981) Age role expectations and sex role expectations for selected sport activities. *Research Quarterly for Exercise and Sport, 52,* 216–227.

Pastore, D. L. (1991) The status of female coaches in two-year colleges. *Journal of Physical Education, Recreation and Dance, 62*(2), 22–26.

Patrick, D. (1994) Torrid Torrence warms up quickly for important week. *USA Today,* Aug. 15, 12C.

Pensinger, M. (1992) Personal communication, December 16.

Pivarnik, J. M. (1994) Maternal exercise during pregnancy. *Sports Medicine, 18,* 215–217.

Plowman, S. A. (1989) Exercise and puberty: Is there a relationship for the female athlete? In D. Nudel (Ed.), *Pediatric sports medicine*. New York: PMA Publishing.

Pufahl, A. (1987) Title IX: Boon or bust to intramural programs. *NIRSA Journal, 11*(2), 48–51.

Ransom, K. & Weinberg, R. S. (1985) Effect of situation criticality on performance of elite male and female tennis players. *Journal of Sport Behavior, 8,* 144–148.

Rees, C., & Andres, F. (1980) Strength differences: Real and imagined. *Journal of Physical Education and Research, 2,* 61.

Reiss, M., & Taylor, J. (1984) Ego-involvement and attribution for success and failure in a field setting. *Personality and Social Psychology Bulletin, 10,* 536–543.

Rintala, J., & Burrell, S. (1984) Fair treatment for the active female: A content analysis of *Young Ath-*

lete magazine. *Sociology of Sport Journal, 1,* 231–250.

Riordan, C., Thomas, J., & James, M. (1985) Attributions in a one-on-one sports competition: Evidence for self-serving biases and gender differences. *Journal of Sport Behavior, 8,* 42–53.

Robinson, R. S. (1955) *Sources for the history of Greek athletics.* Cincinnati, OH: Published by author.

Russell, G. (1972) Premenstrual tension and psychogenic amenorrhea: Psychological interactions. *Journal of Psychosomatic Research, 16,* 279–287.

Ryckman, R. M., Robbins, M. A., Thornton, B., & Cantrell, P. (1982) Development and validation of a physical self-efficacy scale. *Journal of Personality and Social Psychology, 42,* 891–900.

Sage, G. H., & Loudermilk, S. (1979) The female athlete and role conflict. *Research Quarterly, 50,* 88–96.

Sanborn, C. F. (1986) Etiology of athletic amenorrhea. In J. L. Puhl & C. H. Brown (Eds.), *The menstrual cycle and physical activity.* Champaign, IL: Human Kinetics.

Sanborn, C. F., Albrecht, B. H., & Wagner, W. W. (1987) Athletic amenorrhea: Lack of association with body fat. *Medicine and Science in Sports and Exercise, 19,* 207–212.

Sasiene, G. (1983) Secondary amenorrhea among female athletes: Current understandings. *Journal of Physical Education, Recreation and Dance, 54*(6), 61–63.

Scanlan, T. K., & Passer, M. W. (1978) Factors related to competitive stress among male youth sport participants. *Medicine and Science in Sports, 10,* 103–108.

Scanlan, T. K., & Passer, M. W. (1979) Sources of a competitive stress in young female athletes. *Journal of Sport Psychology, 1,* 151–159.

Scanlan, T. K., & Passer, M. W. (1980a) The attributional responses of young female athletes after winning, trying, and losing. *Research Quarterly for Exercise and Sport, 51,* 675–684.

Scanlan, T. K., & Passer, M. W. (1980b) Self-serving biases in the competitive sport setting: An attributional dilemma. *Journal of Sport Psychology, 2,* 124–136.

Segal, J., & Weinberg, R. S. (1984) Sex, sex role orientation, and competitive trait anxiety. *Journal of Sport Behavior, 7,* 153–159.

Shifflett, B., & Revelle, R. (1994) Gender equity in sports media coverage: A review of the *NCAA News. Journal of Sport and Social Issues, 18,* 144–150.

Siegel, D., & Newhof, C. (1984) The sports orientation of female collegiate basketball players participating at different competitive levels. *Perceptual and Motor Skills, 59,* 79–87.

Silva, J. M. (1982) An evaluation of fear of success in male and female athletes and nonathletes. *Journal of Sport Psychology, 4,* 92–96.

Snyder, E. E., & Kivlin, J. (1975) Woman athletes and aspects of psychological well-being and body image. *Research Quarterly, 46,* 191–199.

Snyder, E. E., Kivlin, J., & Spreitzer, E. A. (1975) The female athlete: An analysis of objective and subjective role conflict. In D. Harris and R. Christina (Eds.), *Psychology of sport and motor behavior* (pp. 165–180). University Park: Pennsylvania State University.

Snyder, E. E., & Spreitzer, E. A. (1973) Family influence and involvement in sports. *Research Quarterly, 44,* 249–255.

Snyder, E. E., & Spreitzer, E. A. (1978) Socialization comparisons of adolescent female athletes and musicians. *Research Quarterly, 49,* 342–350.

Snyder, E. E., & Spreitzer, E. A. (1983) Change and variation in the social acceptance of female participation in sports. *Journal of Sport Behavior, 6,* 3–8.

Spears, B. (1978) Prologue: The myth. In C. A. Oglesby (Ed.), *Women and sport: From myth to reality* (pp. 3–15). Philadelphia, PA: Lea & Febiger.

Spears, B. (1984) A perspective of the history of women's sport in ancient Greece. *Journal of Sport History, 11*(2), 32–45.

Spears, B., & Swanson, R. A. (1983) *History of sport and physical activity in the United States.* Dubuque, IA: Wm. C. Brown.

Spence, J., Helmreich, R., & Stapp, J. (1974) The Personal Attributes Questionnaire: A measure of sex role stereotypes and masculinity-femininity. *Journal Supplement Abstract Service Catalog of Selected Documents in Psychology, 4,* 43. (Ms. No. 617)

Spence, K., Helmreich, R., and Stapp, J. (1975) Ratings of self and peers on sex-role attributes and their relation to self esteem and concepts of masculinity and femininity. *Journal of Personality and Social Psychology, 32,* 29–39.

Sternfeld, B., Quesenberry, C. P., Eskenazi, B., & Newman, L. A. (1995) Exercise during pregnancy and pregnancy outcome. *Medicine and Science in Sports and Exercise, 27,* 634–640.

Suinn, R. (1988) *Fundamentals of abnormal psychology* (updated). Chicago: Nelson-Hall.

Sullivan, R. (1992) Toughening Title IX. *Sports Illustrated,* March 28, 10.

Sundgot-Borgen, J. (1994) Eating disorders in female athletes. *Sports Medicine, 17,* 176–188.

Survey: Pay lower for women's coaches. (1995) *USA Today,* April 3, 5C.

Swain, A., & Jones, G. (1991) Gender role endorsement and competitive anxiety. *International Journal of Sport Psychology, 22,* 50–65.

Tharp, L. R. (1994) The effect Title IX has had on intramural sports. *NIRSA Journal, 18*(1), 29–31.

The Babe: A record of achievement. (1993) Beaumont, TX: Babe Didrikson Zaharias Foundation, Inc.

Theberge, N. (1991) A content analysis of print media coverage of gender, women, and physical activity. *Journal of Applied Sport Psychology, 3,* 36–48.

The end. (1995) *USA Today,* March 10, 7C.

Thorngren, C. M. (1990) A time to reach out—Keeping the female coach in coaching. *Journal of Physical Education, Recreation and Dance, 61*(3), 57–60.

van Keuren, K. (1992) Title IX 20 years later: Has sport really changed? *The CSSS Digest,* Summer, 9.

Vare, R. (1974) *Buckeye: A study of coach Woody Hayes and the Ohio State Football Machine.* New York: Harper.

Vickers, J., Lashuk, M., & Taerum, T. (1980) Differences in attitude toward the concepts "male," "female," "male athlete," and "female athlete." *Research Quarterly for Exercise and Sport, 51,* 407–416.

Walberg, J. L., & Johnston, C. S. (1991) Menstrual function and eating behavior in female recreational weight lifters and competitive body builders. *Medicine and Science in Sports and Exercise, 23,* 30–36.

Wakat, D., & Sweeney, K. (1979) Etiology of athletic amenorrhea in cross country runners. *Medicine and Science in Sport, 11*(1), 91.

Wark, K., & Wittig, A. (1979) Sex role and sport competition anxiety. *Journal of Sport Psychology, 1,* 248–250.

Webb, J., Millan, D., & Stolz, C. (1979) Gynecological survey of American female athletes competing at the Montreal Olympic Games. *Journal of Sports Medicine, 19,* 405–412.

Weinberg, R. S., Richardson, P., & Jackson, A. V. (1981) Effect of situation criticality on tennis performances of males and females. *International Journal of Sport Psychology, 12,* 253–259.

Weinberg, R. S., Richardson, P., Jackson, A. V., & Yukelson, D. (1983) Coming from behind to win: Sex differences in interacting sport teams. *International Journal of Sport Psychology, 14,* 79–84.

Weiss, M., & Knoppers, A. (1982) The influence of socializing agents on female collegiate volleyball players. *Journal of Sport Psychology, 4,* 267–279.

Whatta woman. (1947) *Time,* March 10, 69–70.

Wieberg, S. (1992) Universities discover good intentions not enough. *USA Today,* June 8, 10C.

Wittig, A. F., Duncan, S. L., & Schurr, K. T. (1987) The relationship of gender, gender-role endorsement, and perceived self-efficacy to sport competition anxiety. *Journal of Sport Behavior, 10,* 192–199.

Woolum, J. (1992) *Outstanding women athletes: Who they are and how they influenced sports in America.* Phoenix, AZ: Oryx Press.

Yates, A., Leehey, K., & Shisslak, C. M. (1983) Running—an analogue of anorexia? *New England Journal of Medicine, 308,* 251–255.

Zaharieva, E. (1965) Survey of sportswomen at the Tokyo Olympics. *Journal of Sports Medicine and Physical Fitness, 5,* 215–219.

Zaharieva, E., & Sigler, J. (1963) Maternidad y deporte. *Tokogenic Pract.,* 144–149.

Zuckerman, M., & Allison, S. (1976) An objective measure of fear of success: Construction and validation. *Journal of Personality Assessment, 40,* 422–430.

Youth Sport

When I was a small boy in Kansas a friend
of mine and I went fishing and as we sat
there in the warmth of a summer afternoon
on a river bank we talked about what we
wanted to do when we grew up. I told him
that I wanted to be a real major league
baseball player, a genuine professional like
Honus Wagner. My friend said that he'd like
to be president of the United States. Neither
of us got our wish.

> Dwight D. Eisenhower, thirty-fourth
> president of the United States

Whatever happened to the good old days
when if you felt like playing baseball you
would round up your buddies, get a bat and
a ball and would go out and play. What do
we do now? We dress up our kids in
uniforms, give them professional equipment,
tell them where to play, when to play,
organize their games for them, give them
officials, and put them in the hands of a
coach who doesn't know the first thing about
the sport or what's good for an eight year
old.

> Joe Paterno, football coach, Penn State,
> cited in Harris (1973)

INTRODUCTION

Perhaps no area of physical activity is as controversial as youth sport. On the one hand, early
participation in sport is widely held to serve as
a mechanism for building character, encouraging sportsmanship, and promoting overall personality development. On the other hand, this
early sport involvement has also been viewed as
an emotional pressure cooker in which children
are subjected to a host of undesirable stresses.
Where the truth actually lies, of course, is a matter of conjecture.

Most agree that youth sport is high drama.
The cast is varied and includes the following
actors: (1) *The athletes.* Some are very young participants who are merely striving to acquire the
most rudimentary skills. Others, perhaps at a
level somewhat beyond entry status, are trying
to have fun and meet a variety of social and
physical needs. At a more advanced level, others
are working on perfecting skills that will allow
them to continue participation at points far
beyond their current states of sophistication.
(2) *The coaches.* These volunteers come in all
sizes, shapes, and descriptions and are vital to
the immediate enjoyment and later involvement
of their young athletes. Probably most mean well
but too few are prepared to provide for meaningful sport experiences for young athletes. Much
remains to be done in training these volunteers,
and some of the more innovative approaches in
this connection are discussed later in chapter 12.
(3) *Extras.* Foremost among these actors are parents and other spectators, though program
administrators are also vital cogs in the youth
sport network. Mix this varied cast of charac-
ters together and what unfolds is the intense
drama known as youth sport.

A BRIEF HISTORY

Youth sport as an organized entity is a relatively
new phenomenon. By the second decade of the
1900s, sport had attained a firm foothold in the
fabric of everyday America, and this movement
was to have significant effects on youth sport.
A second significant force in this sport awakening was an increasing awareness throughout society of the rights of children. Prior to the 1900s,
children were exploited in the workplace and
were accorded little status generally. A third positive agent of change with regard to the youth
sport movement was the emergence of social
agencies such as the Boy Scouts, the Boys Club,
and the YMCA. These youth-oriented organizations took it upon themselves to provide a

Social agencies such as the YMCA have contributed greatly to the development of youth sports in the United States. Summer camps, an early and important part of YMCA work, were part of a broad array of programs designed to keep boys off the streets and out of trouble.

broad array of programming aimed at constructive use of leisure time. Prominently displayed were organized athletic activities, which were believed to be useful in keeping young people off the streets and out of trouble. Also, these social agencies saw character building as a significant duty, and sports were thought to facilitate this process. The impact of all of these agencies was further enhanced because the public schools largely took the view that sports prior to age twelve were too physically and mentally strenuous; as a consequence, little was offered to meet the sporting needs of the preadolescent. This philosophy was to gradually change in the 1940s and 1950s, and a significant force in this alteration in point of view was Little League baseball, which began in Williamsport, Pennsylvania, in 1939.

Little League Baseball

A Pennsylvania businessman, Carl Stotz, was the architect of *Little League baseball*. So popular was his product that by 1954 there were four thousand leagues nationwide (Hale, 1956) involving some 70,000 young men (Skubic, 1955). Today, Little League has grown to what Franklin (1989, p. 64) has called an "amiable monster" of some 2.5 million youngsters playing on more than 42,000 teams in thirty countries. However, this meteoric growth in the popularity of youth baseball has not always been smooth. Critics in the early years were vociferous in the opposition to the Little League program, and their views were reflective of concern among educators, physical educators, and laymen over possible mental and physical harm that might result from early, intense athletic competition.

Slowly but surely, many of the critics of youth baseball were quieted by research extolling the benefits of organized competition. The first of these research efforts was reported by Scott (1953) in a paper in *Research Quarterly*, which was to publish a series of articles over the next decade that generally were supportive of Lit-

tle League baseball. Scott suggested, based on results of a questionnaire, that parents of Little League players approved of their sons' participation. Skubic (1955), in an attempt to debunk the claim that intense competition was too physically strenuous for young athletes, carried out an interesting study of players and nonplayers. Skubic observed 206 boys, ages nine through fifteen (75 Little Leaguers, 51 Middle Leaguers, and 80 nonplayers) in several stress conditions and measured their responses through Galvanic Skin Response (GSR). Based on her observations, Skubic concluded that GSR variations were not significant regardless of whether boys were competing in league games, championship contests, or games generated in physical education classes. To put the results in her own words, Skubic said, "Insofar as the GSR can be taken to be a valid measure of the emotional excitation of boys of this age level, the results of the present study suggest that youngsters were no more stimulated by competition in league games than they were by competition in physical education games" (pp. 350–351).

In 1956, Skubic reported results of four questionnaires aimed at ascertaining parental attitudes toward Little League play. In general, parental attitudes were quite positive toward the activity, though some concern was expressed that not all boys got to play in league games. Other results from her study showed that Little League participants were higher achievers in school and showed better overall personal adjustment than did nonparticipants. These positive findings were corroborated by Seymour (1956) in a study of five leagues in Atlanta, Georgia.

Interest in the Little League games had grown to the point that, in 1947, a national championship playoff was created. The Little League World Series has continued and now has an international flavor and considerable press and television coverage.

All of the early reports centered around the benefits of sport participation for young boys.

However, Little League baseball was not exempt from the effects of the growing women's movement of the 1970s. In 1973, a young girl from Hoboken, New Jersey, named Marie Pepe attempted to become the first girl to compete in Little League baseball. Though Maria Pepe's efforts were rebuffed, she paved the way for Amy Dickinson to become the first female Little Leaguer. According to Jennings (1981, p. 81), Amy Dickinson was characterized as follows: "First player selected in town draft in 1974; All-Star for three years; 1976—starting pitcher (4-2 record including a 1-hitter and another game with 13 strikeouts) and shortstop; excellent at completing the double play; .382 batting average."

Though the Dickinson case was a breakthrough for girls wishing to participate in Little League activities, there has been no landslide in that direction. Schreiber (1990) cites 1989 statistics indicating that there is about one girl per organized league in Little League baseball. On the other hand, some 700,000 girls participate in Little League's popular softball program.

Concerns about Youth Fitness

A second historical force that served to promote youth sport and fitness resulted from research conducted in the early 1950s in which American children were shown to be generally

---

Little League Baseball Comes to Russia

Highlight 11.1

In 1992, baseball officially became a part of the Olympic Games. This prospect led the then-Soviet Union to petition Little League baseball and its president, Creighton J. Hale, to set up a franchise agreement with that country. As of 1988, there were thirty teams of college-age competitors and two teams of youngsters between the ages of eight and twelve years. To further this involvement in baseball, Hale sought financial support from corporations in the United States with the intent of building a number of fields in and around Moscow. Because of the demise of the Soviet Union and the ensuing political instability, it is difficult to get a reading on the success of the attempt to bring Little League baseball to Russia. It is known, however, that there was a single league of unspecified size in Moscow as of 1992; their Little League tournament team participated in the European Regional tournament at Ramstein Air Force Base in Germany, and their Big League tournament team for sixteen- to eighteen-year-olds won the European Regional Tournament and took part in the Big League World Series in Fort Lauderdale, Florida. It should be noted that all of the satellite countries of the former Soviet Union have chartered leagues under Little League jurisdiction.

Sources: Gutierrez (1988); "Soviets in Little League" (1988); Personal Correspondence, Creighton J. Hale, 1992.

unfit when compared with similar samples of European youth. Kraus and Hirschland (1954) were the prime architects of this legendary research, and their findings were ultimately brought to the attention of President Dwight Eisenhower. Alarmed at the fitness gap presented to him, Eisenhower convened a 1955 meeting aimed at responding to this crisis. Out of these deliberations involving 149 national educational and fitness leaders and chaired by Vice President Richard Nixon came, among other things, the President's Council on Youth Fitness (now known as the President's Council on Physical Fitness and Sports), which has served since that time as a moving force behind national youth fitness.

In addition to generating a national-level concern with youth fitness, Eisenhower's actions led the American Alliance for Health, Physical Education and Recreation (AAHPER) to develop its Youth Fitness Test. As the components of the AAHPER test make clear, physical educators at that time viewed fitness in a motoric sense, and this philosophy was to dominate thinking for the next twenty years. In the mid-1970s an awareness was reached that fitness involved more than speed, strength, or endurance. Flexibility, body composition, and cardiorespiratory fitness came to be a part of the fitness formula (Blair, Falls, and Pate, 1983). This transition from the Kraus-Weber approach of the 1950s to the more modern definitions of fitness can be seen in table 11.1.

The concern with youth fitness and its measurement have not resulted in concomitant rises in fitness, however. Although the overall picture is probably better than that reported to President Eisenhower, much remains to be accomplished.

Irrespective of the debate surrounding youth fitness, the impetus given the youth sport movement by the data from the 1950s clearly has been considerable. Most significantly, it sent out an alert that emphasized the need for constructive exercise and physical activity, thereby serving as

a significant force in shaping our views of the interaction between sport and fitness in children.

MOTIVES FOR PARTICIPATING IN SPORT

Estimates are that 23 million young people between the ages of five and sixteen are involved in nonschool sponsored sports programs and yet another 6 million take part in activities that are school-sponsored (Brady, 1989). According to Chambers (1991), these figures account for nearly 50 percent of all youth in this age bracket. What, then, is it that prompts this fascination with sport? To arrive at a reasonably authoritative answer to this question, let's examine studies conducted with diverse youth groups by the Athletic Footwear Association ("American Youth," 1990), Gill, Gross, and Huddleston (1981), Gould, Feltz, Weiss, and Petlichkoff (1982), Griffin (1978), Sapp and Haubenstricker (1978), and the University of California at Los Angeles (UCLA) Sport Psychology Laboratory (Sewell, 1992). Of these various research efforts, that of the Athletic Footwear Association (AFA) merits special consideration, particularly in view of its depth, breadth, and contemporaneity. Martha Ewing and Vern Seefeldt of the Youth Sport Institute at Michigan State University were commissioned by the AFA to look at variables contributing to staying with or dropping out of sport. These investigators asked 10,000 young people between the ages of ten and eighteen to complete questionnaires they had devised. This sample of young people was made up of respondents from eleven cities representing diverse geographical locations and demographic factors. The cities involved were: Hartford, Connecticut; Atlanta, Georgia; Lawrence, Kansas; Baltimore, Maryland; Lansing, Michigan; Cortland, New York; Akron-Kent, Ohio; Arlington, Texas; Brownsville, Texas; and Yakima, Washington. Factors of significance that were predictive of continuation

Table 11.1

Comparison of 1958 and 1976 Youth Fitness Tests With AAHPERD Physical Best Test (1988) and the President's Challenge (1991)

Test Item	Fitness Components
AAHPERD youth fitness test (1958)	
Pull-ups (boys) or modified pull-ups (girls)	Muscular strength/endurance
Sit-ups	Muscular strength/endurance
Shuttle run	Agility/speed
Standing broad jump	Power
50-yard dash	Speed
Softball throw	Skill/muscular strength
600-yard run-walk	Cardiorespiratory endurance/speed
AAHPERD youth fitness test (1976)	
Flexed-arm hang	Arm and shoulder girdle strength/endurance
1-minute bent-knee sit-ups	Abdominal strength/endurance
AAHPERD shuttle run	Agility in running/changing directions
Standing long jump	Leg power
50-yard dash	Speed
600-yard run	Cardiorespiratory function
AAHPERD Physical Best (1988)	
1-mile walk/run	Aerobic endurance
Triceps and calf skinfold measurement	Body composition
Sit-and-reach	Lower back/hamstring flexibility
1-minute bent-knee sit-ups	Abdominal strength/endurance
Palm forward pull-ups	Upper body strength/endurance
The President's Challenge (1991)	
Curl-ups	Abdominal strength/endurance
AAHPERD shuttle run	Speed and agility
1-mile run/walk	Heart/lung endurance
Pull-ups or flexed-arm hang	Upper body strength/endurance
V-sit reach or sit-and-reach test	Lower back/hamstring flexibility

Sources: *AAHPERD Youth Fitness Test Manual* (1980); *AAHPERD Physical Best* (1988); Pate (1983); *The President's Challenge Physical Fitness Program* (1991).

of sport experience among youth in the AFA study, as well as the others to varying degrees, were having fun, skill improvement, fitness benefits, socialization, and a host of miscellaneous and less salient positive variables.

Having Fun

In the middle portion of this century, Skubic (1956) found that a high priority for youth participating in sport was to have fun. Little has transpired in the interim to alter this perception. For example, the 1990 AFA report indicated that the highest-rated reason among eleven possible

For this teen golfer, skill improvement seems to be the primary motivation for participating in the sport.

participation motives was to have fun; on a five-point scale, having fun received a 4.5 from the respondents. These results are very similar to those of Sapp and Haubenstricker in their 1978 research with youngsters in the state of Michigan.

Sapp and Haubenstricker looked at the participation objectives of 579 boys and 471 girls ages eleven to eighteen, participating in eleven non–school-related sports, and found that the most common reason for participation in their sample was to have fun. Gould, Feltz, Weiss, and Petlichkoff (1982) studied 365 swimmers from ages eight to nineteen. Fun was first in importance out of thirty variables studied. Sex differences were noted; girls rated having fun as significantly more important. Scanlan and Lewthwaite (1986), in a study of youth wrestlers from ages nine to fourteen, found sport enjoyment to be closely linked to parental and coach satisfaction, with a lack of maternal pressure and negative reactions to performance, and positive adult involvement in their sport. Perhaps Kleiber (1981, p. 83) said it best: "Winning is important, but fun is more important—at least for children."

Skill Improvement

Another reason that young people choose sport participation is to improve their skills. The AFA study indicated that skill improvement ran a close second to having fun with their sample. In the Sapp and Haubenstricker report, skill improvement was second only to "having fun" and was mentioned by 80 percent of the respondents. Other studies have not accorded skill development quite as lofty a state, but nevertheless are supportive. Wankel and Kreisel (1985), in a study of 310 soccer, 338 hockey, and 174 baseball participants, found that youth in all three groups rated improving game skills as fourth in importance. On a related note, however, comparing their skills with those of others was rated highest of ten enjoyment factors by soccer and baseball players and second by the hockey contingent. Gould et al. (1985), in their study of youth swimmers, also found the skill development factor to be ranked fourth of fourteen factors studied. No appreciable differences were noted by either sex or age considerations in the Gould et al. (1985) sample.

One study in which personal performance was paramount was conducted by McElroy and Kirkendall (1980). More than two thousand participants in the summer portion of the 1979 National Youth Sports Program (average age 11.9 years) responded to a questionnaire about their reasons for taking part in sport. A particularly pertinent question asked of the subjects was:

> In playing a sports game, which of the following is most important?
>
> (a) to defeat your opponent or the other team (winning orientation)
> (b) to play as well as you can (personal performance)
> (c) to play fairly, by the rules at all times (fair play)
> (d) everyone on the team should get to play (total participation)

The results of the responses to this question are summarized in table 11.2.

Clearly, to play as well as one can was overwhelmingly most important in this investigation. Other points of interest include the fact that a winning orientation was endorsed by less than 10 percent of the total sample.

In summary, its relative rank can be argued, but skill development obviously is an important aspect of youth sports, and coaches and others should be alert to its significance with children.

Fitness Benefits

The AFA study indicated that staying in shape was fourth of eleven variables in terms of importance to their sample. The UCLA sample ranked feeling fit fourth of seven variables, but

Table 11.2
Competitive Orientation among Youth Sport Participants

	Males (N = 1236)	Females (N = 1096)
Winning orientation	13.5%	4.6%
Personal performance	51.0	48.3
Fair play	24.4	37.6
Total participation	11.0	9.4
	100.0%	100.0%

Source: McElroy and Kirkendall (1980).

still gave it a higher priority than winning. Fifty-six percent of the Sapp and Haubenstricker respondents saw fitness benefits as an important aspect of sport participation, thereby ranking it third behind having fun and skill development. Gould, Feltz, Weiss, and Petlichkoff (1982), in their study of competitive youth swimmers, reported that their subjects actually saw fitness benefits as a close second to having fun. Others who have stressed the fitness aspect in their research include Gill et al. (1981), Gould et al. (1985), and Griffin (1978).

Team Atmosphere

Team membership and interaction was particularly significant in the UCLA sample, ranking second in importance. The AFA report was less enthusiastic in this regard, but still accorded team involvement some status. Sapp and Haubenstricker (1978) found team atmosphere to be fourth in importance with their respondents. Wankel and Kreisel (1985) found that being on a team was fifth in importance for each of the sport groups in their study. Closely allied with this aspect is the social dimension of making friends, and this is a consistent finding across virtually all of the studies. Clearly, the social dimension of youth sport participation cannot

Motives for Youth Sport Participation

An interesting sidelight related to the study conducted by the Athletic Footwear Association (AFA) relates to a categorization scheme for analyzing
sport participation motives. Accordingly, youth may be viewed as *Reluctant Participants, Image-Conscious Socializers,* or *Competence-Oriented
Participants.* Of the respondents, the Socializers make up the majority,
accounting for 40 percent of all participants; of the remainder, those youth
who are competence-oriented make up 35 percent, and those who take part
reluctantly account for the remaining 25 percent of the picture. In terms
of make-up, the three groups look as follows:

Socializers. Sports are important to this group, but their behavior is
maintained greatly by what others think of them, being made to feel important, and winning trophies and other tangible rewards.

Competence-Oriented Participants. This group is motivated by skill
improvement, and their behavior is maintained by intrinsic rather than
extrinsic reward. As a consequence, this group is more likely to stay with
sport and physical fitness after the adolescent years are over.

Reluctant Participants. Being with or making new friends, winning
peer approval, and staying fit are strong motivaters for this group. However,
if their chosen sport becomes quite demanding and/or peer approval lessens, the physical fitness benefits are not likely to be a strong enough incentive for them to continue sport participation.

Interestingly, the focus on winning is about the same for all three
groups: of twenty-five possible responses as to why they might participate
in sport, the Reluctant Participants ranked winning thirteenth, the
Socializers had it tenth, and the Competence-Oriented Participants ranked
it seventh. While there are some differences placed on winning by these
three groups, it remains clear that it is does not carry a high priority with
youth athletes.

Other key findings from the AFA report indicate the Competence-
Oriented Participants and the Image-Conscious Socializers are quite similar
in perceived athletic ability, importance placed on team membership, and
perceived sport enjoyment. However, the Reluctant Participants rate themselves far below their teammates (and, hence, the other two groups discussed herein) in athletic ability, place a lower value on team membership,
and report much less participation satisfaction.

Source: Athletic Footwear Association, *Teenagers' Motivations for Sports Participation
Help Predict Lifelong Habits* (1990).

be overlooked by those who are in the business of providing sport experience for young people.

Other Reasons

In addition to the reasons for participating already cited, others are perhaps less salient but nevertheless worth mentioning. Among them are sportsmanship, excitement or challenge, travel, and such extrinsic rewards as trophies, citations in the newspapers, and feeling important.

A Final Note

Having fun in sports has generally been accorded a lofty position in the hierarchy of reasons why young people play sports. At the same time, fun has an elusive quality to it. For a minority of youth, winning is the only way to have fun. For others, playing well, achieving fitness, or being part of a team is paramount. In an attempt to arrive at just what it is that constitutes fun, a study by Wankel and Sefton (1989) is instructive. They had fifty-five females and sixty-seven males ages seven to fifteen fill out questionnaires prior to and after ringette and hockey games at various points in their respective seasons. Fun was parsimoniously assessed on a five-point Likert scale from 1 (no fun at all) to 5 (a lot of fun). Other variables studied included age, sex, pre- and postgame affect, motivation mood states, how well one expected to play, confidence in team outcome, and how well one played. Positive postgame affect was the most powerful predictor of fun, followed less saliently by how well one played and level of challenge of the competition. This research strongly suggests that having fun is not a unidimensional concept, but rather is a quite complex phenomenon. Nevertheless, having fun remains a major reason why youth take part in athletic events.

MOTIVES FOR DISCONTINUING PARTICIPATION IN SPORT

Clearly, youth sport is immensely popular and participation is multidimensionally determined. However, it is not rewarding to equal degrees for all who take part. As a consequence, a formidable dropout problem is associated with the various youth sports. Among the primary reasons why youngsters drop out of sport include not having fun, concerns about coaching, and conflict of interest with other life activities. Secondary motives for discontinuing sport involvement include stresses generated by parents or peers, an overemphasis on winning, and not getting to play enough. Each of these concerns will be addressed in turn.

Primary Concerns

Not Having Fun

Up to adolescence, fun is the main reason why young people participate in sport. This fact, in turn, should dictate that all involved in setting up youth programs must do their best to guarantee that fun is awarded the highest priority when planning takes place. Although this is easy to say, the doing is more complicated. The "win at all cost" mentality tends to dominate.

Concerns about Coaching

The potential for misperception of what the coach may be trying to accomplish is considerable. Also, the potential for poor coaching procedures is equally possible. Not enough has been done in terms of training coaches to work with youth; coaches are often very interested in young people and have the best of intentions but simply lack the interpersonal and sport-related skills to be successful. Also, a minority are probably frustrated Vince Lombardis living out some sort of fantasy through the use of strong-arm methods, badgering of officials, and other tactics used or perceived to have been used by their coaching idols. Young people deserve coaches who have the best training available, those with an appreciation of the principles of child development, and those with a soft touch in dealing with people. Many of the other reasons for dropping out could be avoided or greatly buffered by an informed and sensitive coach.

Conflict of Interest with Other Life Activities

One of the more consistent findings with regard to why young people drop out of sports is conflict with other life demands. It is unreasonable to think that sports is the be-all and end-all for everyone, and it would be naive to assume that other priorities do not exist. In the earliest years of athletic performance, little else is available to do and parents pretty much dictate the course of organized activities, sporting or otherwise. However, with increasing maturation comes a rather natural progression toward some degree of independence. This greater independence is reflected in a number of ways, not the least of which is dropping out of sport. The skill selection process is partly responsible, but equally powerful are the pulls of growing social needs, academic pursuits, part-time employment, debating, drama, music, and an endless array of other valuable activities.

A number of studies have substantiated the significance of this conflict of interest finding. For instance, Fry, McClements, and Sefton (1981), in a study of two hundred hockey dropouts in Canada, found that 31 percent reported conflicts as the number one reason for dropping out of their sport. Similarly, Orlick (1974), in his study of five sports reported earlier, found that 31 percent cited general life conflict as the reason for dropping out of their respective sports. In a study by Gould et al. (1985), even stronger results were found with swimmers in the age range of ten to eighteen. "Other things to do" was cited by 84 percent of their subjects.

Burton and Martens (1986) address this issue in a study of youth wrestlers, ages seven to seventeen, and their parents and coaches. The dropouts in their study reported conflict of interest problems as paramount in importance. However, Burton and Martens suspect that threats to perceived ability were the actual culprits in the dropouts in their study. Despite the caveat provided by Burton and Martens, a major factor in dropping out of sport is simple conflict of interest with other activities, a not altogether unhealthy reason. However, the fact that dropping out is so tied in with increasing age does little to ameliorate the aggravations associated with dropping out in the earlier age groups, such as eight through twelve. The younger the participants, the more vulnerable they appear to be to the kinds of things over which the adult leadership has some degree of control, namely, getting to play, having fun, and developing skills with the help of an informed and sensitive coach.

Making Youth Sport More Enjoyable

The answer to making youth sport more enjoyable is most likely embedded in the results published by the AFA in their survey of 10,000 youth ("American youth," 1990). When asked the most important prompt, "Changes you would make for more enjoyment or to stay involved in a sport you dropped," the top eleven responses of the youth surveyed were nested under two major areas, conflict with other activities (4) and coaching (7). By way of elaboration, the following concerns and the ranking of each response were expressed as follows (T = tie in the rankings):

Conflict with other activities
Schedule didn't conflict with studies (#2)
Schedule didn't conflict with social life (#3T)
Games/practice schedule were changed (#7T)
It didn't take so much time (#10T)

Coaching

Practices were more fun (#1)
Coaches understood players better (#3T)
I could play more (#3T)
Coaches were better teachers (#6)
Coach understood the sport better (#T7)
There was less emphasis on winning (#9)
Coach didn't yell so much (#10T)

The preceding points appear to possess considerable validity and should be taken by all of us as legitimate expressions of concerns that young people have about sport participation. Obviously, administrators, coaches, sport scientists, and parents would do well to take these suggestions to heart in future planning of youth sport activities.

As a final aside, it is interesting to again note the importance of fun that is manifested in the preceding responses, with making practices more fun the number one suggestion that young people would make in terms of improving their own sport experience. At all levels of inquiry, the theme of fun pervades virtually every study of youth sport.

Secondary Concerns

Too Much Pressure from Parents and Peers
Youth participants are greatly swayed by parents and peers in both initiating and discontinuing sport involvement. Probably everyone is

"Please, Mrs. Enright, if I let you pinch-hit for Tommy, all the mothers will want to pinch-hit."

Ideally, sport activities should be rewarding events for children rather than vicarious experiences for their parents.

familiar with the parent who reacts to every sport event in which his or her child plays as if it were the Super Bowl and the World Series wrapped into one. Undoubtedly, the chemistry at work here is part ego and part genuine concern for the happiness and well-being of the child. Irrespective of where the true motivation lies, this parental reaction serves as a potential source of stress for the child involved (and for those around him or her, too). The issue of the role of the spectators has been the subject of more than one heated debate in both lay and professional groups. Martens and Seefeldt (1979), reacting to the problems caused by overzealous parent/spectators, have suggested a number of steps that can be taken to curb potentially stress-inducing and embarrassing displays. Among the suggested steps are (1) requiring parents to remain seated in the specified spectator viewing area during all contests; (2) restricting the yelling of instructions, and more particularly criticisms, during the events; (3) not allowing parents to make any derogatory comments to opposing players, officials, and league administrators; and (4) brooking no parental interference with the coach(es) of their children. Parents should have the character to temporarily relinquish their child to the coach for the duration of the event at hand. Though the measures suggested by Martens and Seefeldt may seem unduly harsh, experience has shown that they are not without justification. Games should always be oriented philosophically toward making sport physically healthy and psychosocially rewarding for the participants rather than as a means for parents to live vicariously through their children.

Too Much Emphasis on Winning or on Competition

As can be seen, the emphasis on winning pervades virtually all of the reasons why sport is not always fun for an all too numerous group of children. Orlick (1974), in a study of sixty dropouts from five sports, noted that 67 percent cited competitive emphasis as the major reason for their discontinuation of competition. Pooley (1981), in a study of youth soccer players, found that 33 percent of his respondents dropped out because of too much emphasis on competition. Gould, Feltz, Horn, and Weiss (1982) found his figure to be 16 percent in a group of dropouts from competitive swimming. Results from these three studies should serve as fair warning that too much emphasis can indeed be placed on the competitive aspects of youth sports.

Not Getting to Play Enough

Because of the emphasis placed on winning by coaches, by parents and by society as a whole, a strong tendency exists to always play the best athletes in order to satisfy the hunger, however misguided, for victory. Lost in the shuffle are the less talented performers. Some of them will never become athletes of any consequence; however, the distressing fact is that a fair number will be turned off long before they ever find out the ultimate verdict on their sport skills. Knowing what we do about the tremendous variability in physical maturation rates, it seems ludicrous to make premature assessments of talent, judgments with far-reaching implications for future sport participation. One can only wonder how many potentially fine athletes have been turned off at an early age because some coach or administrator decided that winning was more important than total participation of all involved.

STRESS AND YOUTH SPORT

Simon and Martens (1979) conducted research involving 749 boys ranging in age from nine to fourteen years with the intent to look at pre-event state anxiety responses in a variety of sport and nonsport situations. Required school activities such as classroom examinations, nonrequired nonsport activities such as band solos, and several nonschool team versus individual and

Adult Verbalizations at Youth Sport Events

Most of us are familiar with the obnoxious sports fan, and nowhere is this person more noticeable than at youth sporting events. Data from a number of studies, however, appear to support the notion that these loud, obnoxious types are actually in the minority. They stand out precisely because they are so vociferous in expressing their dislike for players, coaches, officials, and other fans.

Youth sport studies by Faucette and Osinski (1987) and Walley, Graham, and Forehand (1982) in baseball, Crossman (1986) in hockey, and Randall and McKenzie (1987) in soccer point to a generally well-behaved spectator. In the Faucette and Osinski study, spectators at a youth baseball Mustang World Series served as subjects. During a four-day period, sixty-four spectators attending eleven different games were observed by two trained researchers. Results showed that spectators spend over 80 percent of their time silently watching the proceedings or conversing with friends. When verbal comments were made, they were predominantly neutral or positive in tone. Negative comments accounted for slightly over 1 percent of all verbalizations. Walley et al. found virtually identical behaviors in their observations of youth T-ball spectators. Four male raters observed four fans at eighteen different games; they found that 92 percent of the fans offered no verbalizations and far less than 1 percent of them were of a negative variety. Walley and associates did suggest, however, that negative verbalizations may be a linear function; that is, as the stakes go up, so may negativity.

Crossman (1986) had observers view 272 spectators at ninety-one minor league hockey games in Canada. Spectator behavior varied according to the level of the athletes involved, the importance of the competition, and sex of the onlooker, but did not support the stereotype of the verbally abusive fan. In the Randall and McKenzie (1987) investigation involving youth soccer, nearly 75 percent of the verbalizations made by fans were instructive while 5.8 percent were considered to be negative in tone.

These studies have served to shed light on a fascinating aspect of youth sport, that of spectator behavior. Apparently, the picture they have presented dispels the negative stereotype so often held with regard to spectators at youth sporting events. Most fans are quiet, neutral, or positive, with the negative spectator a statistical rarity.

Sources: Crossman (1986); Faucette and Osinski (1987); Randall and McKenzie (1987); Walley, Graham, and Forehand (1982).

contact versus noncontact sports were studied. One of the more revealing findings of the Simon and Martens effort was that, of eleven activities, band solos evoked more pre-event state anxiety than did any of the sports. Results of their thought-provoking analyses can be seen in figure 11.1.

Results of the Simons and Martens study notwithstanding, youth sport can be stressful for some youngsters, and a number of factors contribute to this situation. Among the stress factors are the general emphasis on winning as the measure of success and the constant pressure of social evaluation provided by coaches, parents,

Figure 11.1: **Children's Precompetitive State Anxiety in Eleven Sport and Nonsport Evaluative Activities**

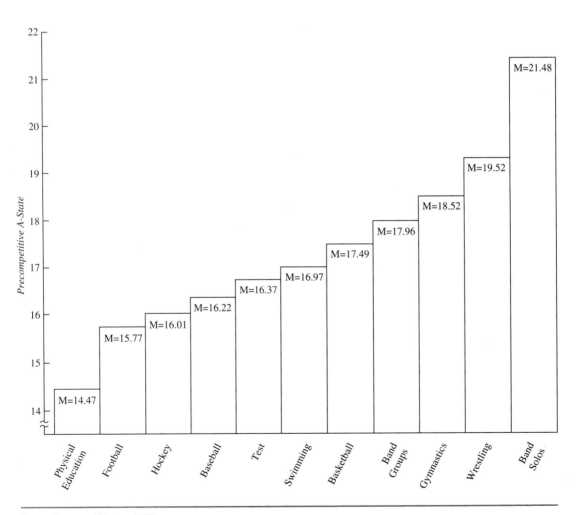

Source: Simon and Martens (1979).

and peers. Also, one's perceived ability, success expectancy, the expectation of negative evaluation, and the expectancy to feel bad in the face of poor performance are additional anxiety producers. We shall deal with each of these issues in an effort to shed light on why it is that youth sport is so stressful for some youth.

Competition: Product or Process?

The word *competition* comes to us from the Latin *com* and *petere,* which collectively mean "to seek together." Clearly, much of sport at all age levels has drifted away from the "seeking together" idea, and youth sport is no exception. Part of the problem in youth sport and sport in general, according to DuBois (1980), is an emphasis on sport as product rather than process. Characteristics of a *product orientation* include: (1) *Winning above all else.* Events in any contest become meaningful in this context so long as they contribute to winning and to the concomitant feeling of domination that goes with beating an opponent. (2) *Tangible awards.* Competition is magnified if a prize of some kind is superordinate to competition itself. (3) *Seeking of adulation.* The product-oriented competitor plays more for the admiration of others than for the intrinsic enjoyment that competition can provide. DuBois suggests that this adulation issue may, in part, explain the difficulties faced by women in their efforts to join the sport subculture. Women have long been viewed as providers or sources rather than recipients of adulation. (4) *Dehumanization of the opponent.* The feeling of domination of an opponent is of primary importance here. Feelings of worth are enhanced not from competing but from domination. At best, this can be viewed as a neurotic sort of motivation for play.

On the other side of the coin, and much more optimistically, the *competition-as-process* approach has much to recommend it. Key to this process point of view are the following: (1) *Par-*

ticipation as an end in itself. Winning is secondary to taking part. *Sport* takes on the trappings of an intrinsically rewarding activity because the players participate for the sake of participation; winning is left to take care of itself. (2) *Striving for personal or team excellence.* Playing as best one can is paramount here. The old cliche, "It's not whether you won or lost, but how you played the game," exemplifies this approach to participation. (3) *Aesthetic sensitivity.* There is absolutely no reason why sport, with all its rough and tumble activities, cannot be viewed as an aesthetic experience. Harmony, "oneness," and rhythm then become integral parts of a sport-as-process experience. (4) *Rapport with competitors.* Competitors are viewed as catalytic agents in the pursuit of mutual goals, namely, excellence in personal and team performance. Without the opponent, no standard exists against which to measure one's own performance. Therefore, the opponent becomes not an enemy but a valued ally.

The competition as process approach is the one we choose to support. Competition as process is not a sentimental notion of what ought to be; it represents an attainable goal toward which all involved with youth sport should be oriented. Not only would youth sport take on new meaning for all concerned, but the lifetime carryover would be significant. We might actually end up with adults with a lifelong interest in sports and physical fitness, adults who also appreciate good ability and effort, sportsmanship, and the aesthetic properties inherent in physical activity.

Competitive Stress

The scientific study of the interaction of youth sport and stress owes a debt of gratitude to the research efforts of Rainer Martens and various associates and the separate and collaborative efforts of Michael Passer and Tara Scanlan. Accordingly, most of what transpires in the next several pages will reflect their substantial efforts in this most important aspect of youth sport.

Researchers generally agree that *competitive stress* is a negative emotional state that is generated when a child feels unable to adequately respond to competitive performance demands, thereby risking failure, subsequent negative evaluation of athletic competence, and resultant loss of self-esteem (Martens, 1977; Passer, 1984; Scanlan, 1984; Scanlan and Passer, 1978; 1981). Vital to understanding competitive stress is an awareness that the entire sequence of events is highly personal and subjective; it is not real or objective failure that matters. What is important is how competitive adequacy is perceived by the child. Also, great individual differences exist in response to competition; not all situations evoke a stress response, and the overall reaction is greatly mediated by a psychologically systemic stress tolerance. Suffice it to say, competitive stress is an incredibly complex phenomenon!

Competitive stress may occur at any time. It may take place at home the day of an important contest or shortly before competition. This is made much more likely where precompetition inadequacies are experienced. A second forum for competitive stress is during actual competition. If an awareness of inability becomes salient, competitive stress becomes a reality. Finally, stress may rise after the fact in situations where game performance may be viewed as inadequate. Giving up a game-winning home run or striking out with the bases loaded in the bottom of the last inning are familiar events for many who have participated in baseball, and postgame competitive stress reactions to such events are common.

Measures of Stress

Scanlan (1984) suggests that stress may be measured through *behavioral, physiological,* or *psychological* means. *Behaviorally,* sleep difficul-ties, appetite loss, digestive disturbances, or self-reports of "nerves" might be used as indices of stress. *Physiologically,* increases in heart rate, respiration, or alterations brought about through activation of the autonomic nervous system could be monitored and used to indicate the presence of stress. An example of physiological monitoring that was touched on earlier involved a Galvanic skin response (GSR) study with Little Leaguers (Skubic, 1955). Yet another effort in physiological monitoring of stress by Hanson (1967) is noteworthy. Also using Little Leaguers, Hanson reported that players' heart rates rose to an average of 166 beats per minute while they were batting. No other game situation evoked anywhere near this much stress. *Psychologically,* the standard stress assessment procedures have been various paper-and-pencil measures, particularly those capable of highlighting state and/or trait anxiety. A general example of the former is Spielberger's *State Anxiety Inventory for Children (SAIC)* (Spielberger, 1973); a sport specific measure of significance is the children's version of the *Competitive State Anxiety Inventory (CSAI-C)* (Martens, Burton, Rivkin, and Simon, 1980). Both of these tests have been used extensively within the youth sport context.

A third important test, and one that has been discussed earlier, is the *Sport Competition Anxiety Test (SCAT)* (Martens, 1977), purportedly a measure of *competitive trait anxiety (CTA).* CTA has been of considerable interest to researchers in sport-related anxiety. Martens' contention is that there will be a significant correlation between high trait anxiety and subsequent state-related anxiety responses to competition. Research by Gill and Martens (1977) and Weinberg and Genuchi (1980) as well as that reported in the various reports by Passer and Scanlan have been most supportive of this line of investigation.

In the various studies conducted on competitive trait anxiety (CTA), at least two preliminary but significant findings emerge. One is that

CTA appears to increase with age, particularly in precollege samples. This increase in anxiety is, no doubt, linked with the increased importance of winning as the athlete grows older and more experienced. A second finding is that CTA is higher in females than in males. Passer (1984) issues several caveats related to these age and gender generalizations, however. One reservation has to do with the cross-sectional rather than longitudinal nature of the differences. It has not been demonstrated over time with groups of athletes that these results would be replicated. Also, laboratory and field studies of state anxiety reactions prior to competition reveal few gender differences (Passer, 1984). Clearly, additional research in the area of age and gender differences in CTA is needed.

Cognitive Aspects of Competitive Stress

Passer (1984) suggests that the extent to which an athlete experiences competitive stress will largely be dictated by at least four cognitive mediators, namely, *perceived ability, success expectancy, expectancy of negative evaluation,* and *expectancy of experiencing negative affect or emotion.*

Perceived Ability

How we perceive our ability is a function of a continuing comparison process that begins in the preschool years and continues throughout the remainder of life. In their earliest years, children have a rather undifferentiated sense of self that is gradually altered by a myriad of environmental events. However, this sense of self eventually must be measured against a multidimensional rather than a unidimensional set of standards. At age four or five years, the evaluative process begins in earnest and thereafter intensifies, perhaps reaching a peak in the adolescent years, that period in which the search for personal identity is so important. One forum that provides much feedback concerning this self-perception

of ability is that of sport. To be selected first (or last) in a pickup baseball game or to be the star (or goat) of an important soccer match has far-reaching consequences for the self-perception of the young athlete. Through a long series of informal and formal events within sports comes a cognitive state that is labeled perceived ability. And with varying perceptions of this ability to compete comes the potential for competitive stress in its various manifestations.

Success Expectancy

Success in youth sport means different things to different people; success may be viewed in terms of winning or losing by some and as playing well and having fun by others. Nevertheless, expectancy for success or failure is an important mediator of competitive stress. Passer (1984) reports that high-CTA youth athletes often feel that they are as physically talented as their low-CTA peers, but consistently report lower expectancy of success. Obviously, CTA is an important part of success expectancy.

Expectancy of Negative Evaluation

The sport situation offers numerous opportunities for self and other appraisal. Home runs and errors, touchdowns and fumbles, and hustling or failing to hustle all are occasions for assessing ability and effort on the part of coaches, parents, and peers. Interestingly, adult significant others appear to be more of a source of competitive stress than are peers (Passer, 1983; 1984). Also, competitive trait anxiety is an integral part of this dimension of competitive stress; high-CTA youngsters do not necessarily expect more disapproval when they perform poorly but they may be more susceptible to negative feedback from significant other adults when such occurrences do transpire.

Expectancy of Negative Affect

High-CTA youth appear to expect the results of their poor performance to be more emotionally aversive than do low-CTA children. Passer (1983), in a study of youth soccer players, found that shame and being generally upset were more common among high-CTA players who performed inadequately. Passer explained these observed feelings of guilt, shame, and dejection in terms of greater expectancy of criticism for poor performance, on an overblown emphasis on success, or on a simple classically conditioned response in which past failures have been paired with negative emotional feelings, thereby eliciting a conditioned negative emotional state related to competing.

Antecedents of Competitive Stress

Obviously there must be antecedent events that create a favorable climate for the development of competitive trait anxiety or competitive stress. While it is likely, as suggested by Martens (1977), that individual variations in experiencing competitive stress have strong roots in recurring competitive sport situations, there must be other predispositional factors to consider. Passer (1984) suggests that parent-child interactions, interactions with other adults and peers, and history of success and failure are three such antecedents.

Parent-Child Interactions

There is sufficient literature both in and outside of sport psychology to suggest that parent-child relationships are a salient factor in the development of personality. Parental use of positive and negative feedback for various behaviors is a most crucial part of this child-rearing process. Children raised with substantial inconsistencies in the use of reinforcement and punishment tend to behave accordingly; they behave erratically because they are not sure just what the exact rules governing the game of life are. This inability, of course, generalizes to the games we play daily.

Children who are raised on a steady diet of punitive measures represent a different issue. They tend to become immune to the effects of punishment and represent discipline problems in school, on the playground, and in the various sport settings. Perhaps a good example can be seen in the personage of George Brett, the multi-talented former major league baseball player. According to Nuwer (1986, p. 64), "Young George looked like a better bet to end up in a reformatory uniform than in trim Kansas City blues." What Nuwer was referring to was the love-hate relationship that existed between Brett and his extremely hard-nosed, demanding father. In speaking of some of the stories that surfaced from time to time concerning their stormy relationship, the elder Brett states, "None of the stories are fun. There was always anger" (p. 64). It was this anger that made young Brett become a bit of a rebel and discipline problem, a boy lacking in academic study habits and general ambition. Despite some early difficulties, however, George Brett developed into an apparently model citizen. Nevertheless, the early negative approach to creating excellence was not without a price. One can only wonder just how many similar cases did not have such a happy ending. The child who is exposed to a balanced ratio of positive and negative sanctions within the family will be most able to cope, whether in sport or in the game of life.

Interactions with Other Adults and Peers

The role of coaches and parents in the creation of competitive stress was discussed earlier, but little has been said about peer pressure. The fact that children spend the majority of their play time in situations not supervised by adults tells us something about the potential for evaluation opportunities on the part of peers. Also, sports, unlike academics, creates such an environment of interdependence that performance failures that affect others must necessarily be viewed with a jaundiced eye by those significant other peers.

History of Success and Failure

Passer (1984) indicates that failure can contribute to competitive trait anxiety in at least two ways. One is that frequent failures enhance the chances for negative adult and peer evaluations. Secondly, repeated failure may lead to the perception of all competition as unduly threatening.

Summary

Clearly, sport can be very stressful for some youngsters. The extent to which sport is stressful will be mediated by a number of interdependent factors, including whether competition is viewed as a product or as a process, the level of generalized and competitive state and trait anxiety experienced, and the extent to which cognitive mediators such as perceived ability, expectancy of success, and expectancy of negative evaluation and emotion are invoked. The role that interactions with coaches, parents, and peers play in this scenario cannot be overestimated.

RECOMMENDATIONS FOR IMPROVING YOUTH SPORT

Youth sport is a positive experience for many who participate. In the best of all possible worlds, it should be so for all youngsters. Developing an appreciation for the skills required within a particular sport, achieving and maintaining a high level of physical fitness, and developing the ability to confront and overcome adversity are all attainable through sport involvement, and these opportunities should be readily available to every participant.

A number of sport scientists have issued calls for improving youth sport. The next several pages will summarize various of these recommendations from the American Academy of Pediatrics (1981), Burke and Kleiber (1976), Duda (1985), Magill (1978), Singer and Gerson (1980), Stewart (1981), and Wood (1983). Their combined reflections cut across several sport science subspecialties including medicine, psychology, and sociology, and they offer much food for thought.

First, the medical aspects of improving youth sport must be addressed. All youth players should be monitored with periodic health status checkups. Also, professional care should be readily available in all competitive settings (including practices, where many injuries occur). The provision of proper equipment, geared to minimize chances for injury, is also important. Particular emphasis here should be on protecting the still-developing joints of the young athlete. It is also important to provide the best in arenas or playing fields. Monetary constraints often force youth activities to take place in less than optimal physical surroundings. However, given the importance we attach to participation, all of us should strive to obtain the best for our youth. Another way to reduce injury is to modify the rules to fit the age and skill level manifested. Instead of tackle football, playing the flag variety is encouraged; baskets are lowered for peewee basketballers; and extremely young pitchers are not allowed to throw the curve ball in baseball. These reasonably simple variants can reduce injury and enhance enjoyment at the same time. Finally, another recommendation that would reduce injury and promote enjoyment is to encourage and provide opportunity for proper sport conditioning for all.

On the psychological side, reinforcement of effort over the old bugaboo, win-loss, is of considerable importance. Coaches who are trained through one of the various youth coaching workshop programs to be discussed in the next chapter, ones who stress the importance of consistent improvement and skill acquisition to both players and parents, would be a most wel-

Positive sport experiences promote healthy self-concept development.

come addition. It would also be important for these coaches to play competitive and social evaluation aspects as low-key as possible. Setting realistic sport mastery goals is another way of shaping positive attitudes and skills. Individualizing the instruction and overall handling of youth would also be helpful. Liberal use of positive reinforcement is called for in dealing with young people; they respond predictably well to positive strokes and generally unpredictably or unsatisfactorily to negativism from coaches, parents, or peers. A clear focus on con-

tinual development of positive feelings about oneself is also recommended. Youth sport should be a big part of self-concept development. Positive sport experiences should result in enhanced feelings of self-worth. Impinging on these feelings of positive self-regard is the concept of locus of control. There are those who maintain that an internal locus of control is psychologically healthy. Singer and Gerson (1980) suggest that evaluating success against the backdrop of individual ability might translate into the development of an internal locus, one in which ability and effort attributions will become dominant. Though argumentative, the Singer and Gerson hypothesis is provocative.

On a more sociological note, a number of recommendations have been made. One is to structure youth sport in such a way that it only vaguely resembles big-time amateur or professional sport. This requires that league officials downplay such things as pep squads, elaborate awards ceremonies, and undue recognition of players or teams through the various media. Inappropriate spectator behavior should not be tolerated by league officials. Aggression and violence on the part of players or spectators, and temper tantrums and similar negative emotional displays on the part of players should not be tolerated. The occasional highly publicized misbehaviors of potential role models at the collegiate or professional level should not be glorified. Finally, positive social behavior on the part of parents might be facilitated by getting them involved in the conduct of some aspects of the action. Manning the concession stand or getting involved in field maintenance and improvement can serve to promote good relations among parents.

As a final note related to the issue of improving youth sport, parents would do well to reinforce involvement in sports other than the "Big Three"—baseball, basketball, and football. Sports such as golf, racquetball, or tennis involve generally lower stakes, are not played in group settings, and parental and peer pressure are less powerful.

If all of the recommendations were to be universally put into effect, the goals and hopes we all have for youth sport would surely be realized. None of the suggestions is pie-in-the-sky. Each of them, with proper urging and support, could be implemented and would insure that our young people would be getting the best that youth sport has to offer.

HEALTH RISKS ASSOCIATED WITH YOUTH SPORT

As part of the hue and cry associated with youth sport since its inception as a formalized entity, critics have pointed the finger at physical risks and psychological trauma. Most certainly there are risks associated with rough and tumble physical activity, whether organized or informal. How many youngsters have broken an arm or a collarbone in a fall from a tree? Or dislocated a finger or injured a knee in a hastily thrown together baseball game in someone's backyard? However, it is our contention that organizers of more formalized youth activities have an opportunity and an obligation to provide proper leadership in reducing the risk of physical injury for the participants. With proper care and supervision, much of the injury potential in organized sport can be brought under control, a situation that does not exist in the unorganized sector. Summarizing the results of several epidemiological studies, Maffulli (1990) indicates that 3 to 11 percent of school-age children are injured each year in sport.

The American Academy of Pediatrics (1981) points to the existence of several problems that increase the likelihood of injury. One potential source of difficulty is that there are such *discrepancies in the physical capabilities* among various youth, partially as a function of the fact that their strength is not proportional to their size. To compound the problem, there are such *variations in maturity* that grouping athletes for competition by chronological age becomes a questionable strategy. Gomolak (1975, p. 96) sums this situation up very well: "At thirteen . . . boys can vary physically from 90 pounds of baby fat and peach fuzz to 225 pounds of muscle and mustache."

A second problem area with young athletes is *impatience with restrictions* on their activities when they are necessary for the diagnosis or treatment of an injury. Running too soon after a leg injury, removing a cast without medical approval and attention, or failure to stay off an injured knee are only a few of the many examples of things young athletes have been known to do.

Yet another troublesome concern has to do with the *musculoskeletal immaturity* of young athletes, which leaves them susceptible to joint and other injuries. A particularly controversial aspect of this problem area concerns what has come to be known as "Little League elbow." Perhaps a brief look at the injury picture in the early days of Little League baseball would set the scene for subsequent discussion.

Highlight 11.4

Would You Want Your Child to Play Tennis?

Data from a *USA Today* survey (Finn, 1987) indicate that tennis at the highly competitive level is an expensive enterprise. Participants at the Omega Easter Bowl tennis tournament in Miami, Florida, perhaps the showcase event for junior tennis players in the United States, were asked to respond to a number of questions related to tennis participation; 336 of 384 competitors responded to the mail survey. Chief among the results were:

1. **85.2 percent reported family income above $40,000 per year; almost 40 percent reported income over $80,000.**
2. **Over 70 percent reported spending in excess of $5,000 per year on tennis alone; 31.3 percent spend over $10,000 annually.**
3. **Only 14.7 percent took up tennis after age ten; an equal number began playing prior to age six.**
4. **Over 59 percent reported practicing from two to six hours daily.**
5. **More than 40 percent reported that their school studies have suffered because of tennis involvement; on the other hand, only 8.3 percent had a grade average in school below a B. Less than 1 percent did not plan to go to college.**
6. **Parents influenced the decision to take up the game of tennis almost equally. Only 7 percent of players cited themselves as the reason.**

If you want your child to be a top tennis player, it is imperative that you allocate the necessary financial resources to the undertaking. Your child would be best advised to pick up the game at an early age if he or she is to be competitive with other top players. Also, it is likely that they will have to devote an inordinate amount of time to the endeavor, and their grades may suffer as a result. Finally, it is important that you be the source of inspiration for taking up the game of tennis.

Source: Finn (1987).

Hale (1961), reacting to criticisms of Little League baseball, showed in a five-year study of nearly 800,000 players a relatively low injury rate. Hale's analysis reported 15,444 injuries requiring medical attention, or an incidence of around 2 percent. Given the number of exposures to potentially injurious situations that are inherent in baseball (Hale indicates that there were 148 million pitched balls alone), Little League does not appear to be especially hazardous. No particular singling out of injuries to the arm or elbow was made by Hale. However, his work arose out of concern about injuries in baseball and laid the foundation for a number of studies over the next quarter century that dealt with arm and elbow problems in particular.

In reviewing the literature as well as following up on 328 former Little Leaguers, Francis, Bunch, and Chandler (1978) assert that injury to the throwing elbow was less common in the Little League players than it was in a matched sample of seventy people who had never played the game of baseball. The injury rate in the form of residual elbow lesions for the ex-Little Leaguers was 1.5 percent whereas it was 2.8 percent for the control group. Overall, there were 7 of 398 total subjects with residual elbow difficulties. Of the 328 ex-Little Leaguers, twenty-eight had gone on to play at the collegiate level; one of these players, a pitcher, had residual damage to the throwing arm. Francis and his associates concluded that psychological trauma might be more of a problem than physical damage in Little League baseball. In any event, the Francis et al. study suggests that "Little League elbow" does exist, but not at the alarming rate suggested by critics of the game.

A fourth problematic issue concerns the possibility of *undiagnosed* or *unrecognized congenital or acquired conditions* that might predispose the athlete to injury or, at the extreme, death. The concern about death is highlighted from time to time by reports in the various media of young, talented, and superbly conditioned high school or college athletes who die on the basketball court or the football field, deaths often attributed by examining medical authorities to covert, undiagnosed congenital heart conditions.

A fifth problem area has to do with *conditioning*. Considerable evidence suggests that our young people are not in optimal physical condition. The conditioning deficiency has obvious ramifications for sport; too many youngsters are not physically prepared for the demands of their chosen sport and all too often are also not willing to become properly conditioned. These liabilities with regard to fitness enhance injury risk, of course.

An antidote to this fitness deficiency is suggested by Pappas and Zawacki (1991). Their emphasis is on musculoskeletal flexibility, aerobic conditioning, and lower extremity strength and endurance. Though specific to youth baseball, the program suggested by Pappas and Zawacki emphasizes injury prevention through total fitness. It seems reasonable to believe that their approach could easily be adapted and implemented across the majority of the youth sport spectrum.

A sixth area of concern is *protective equipment*. Young athletes are often uninformed, indifferent, or uninterested in the fitting, adjustment, or maintenance of protective equipment.

Finally, youth participants all too often are not provided with *access to the services of qualified athletic trainers*. Less than qualified parents, coaches, or an on-call physician usually provide the services of the qualified trainer, a condition that is less than desirable.

SUMMARY

1. Youth sport is a multifaceted enterprise, one fraught with controversy as to its positive and negative consequences.
2. Sport involvement on a formal basis is a relatively new phenomenon. The growth of

organized sport in general in this country and a concomitant increasing awareness of the rights of children gave considerable impetus to the youth sport movement. Also, the emergence of agencies such as the Boy Scouts, Boys Club, and YMCA pushed youth sport to the forefront of American life. The reluctance of the public schools to provide physical education and sport experiences for youngsters under the age of twelve years made the activities provided by these various agencies even more significant.

3. Little League baseball began in 1939 in Pennsylvania and has experienced meteoric rise, currently serving 2.5 million participants. In its earliest days, Little League baseball met with substantial resistance from a variety of critics who saw the sport as too physically dangerous and psychologically demanding. Research published in the 1950s and 1960s countered many of these claims, and Little League baseball continues to prosper. The equal rights movement led to Amy Dickinson becoming the first female Little Leaguer.

4. A second force that propelled youth sport was an increasing concern about physical fitness. A landmark study conducted in the early 1950s indicated that American youngsters were inferior to their European peers in overall fitness. President Dwight Eisenhower was appalled by this finding, and this led him to convene a panel of 149 education and fitness leaders in an effort to respond to what many regarded as a true national crisis. The President's Council on Youth Fitness, still operative today, and the AAHPER Youth Fitness Test, also still operative but with alterations, were two significant products of this presidential response.

5. Approximately 29 million children under age eighteen participate in nonschool and school-sponsored athletic activities.

6. Having fun consistently appears to be the primary reason why children take part in

sport, followed in no particular order by improving athletic skills, achieving a higher level of fitness, and experiencing the social rewards offered by team sports. Extrinsic rewards, such as trophies or media coverage, appear to be of secondary importance.

7. Just what fun is remains elusive, but in at least one study postgame positive affect, how well one played, and the level of challenge of the competition emerged as predictors of fun. This piece of research suggests that fun is a multidimensional rather than a unidimensional concept in the view of youth athletes.

8. The dropout rate in youth sport is, in the view of some, alarmingly high and constitutes a problem for which too few answers have been found. Significant reasons why youngsters discontinue sport participation include not having fun, conflict of interest with other life activities, concerns about coaching, too much parental and peer pressure, too much emphasis on winning, and not getting to play enough.

9. Sport participation could be made more enjoyable, according to youth respondents in the Athletic Footwear Association (AFA) study, through improvement in two primary areas: minimization of conflicts with other life activities and improvements in the quality of coaching. Of the top eleven suggestions for improving youth sport, all could be subsumed under one of these two areas.

10. Sources of stress in youth sport include too much emphasis on winning and the pressure associated with constant social evaluation by significant others. Also, one's perceived ability and its association with expectancy of success are added sources of competitive anxiety.

11. Competition may be viewed as a product or as a process. In the product orientation, the emphasis is on winning above all else, tangible rewards, seeking of adulation, and

dehumanization of one's opponent. In the process orientation, participation becomes an end in itself, personal or team excellence is sought, the activities are appreciated for their aesthetic properties, and there is respect for the opposition.

12. Competitive stress is a negative emotional state that is generated when a person feels unable to cope with competitive demands. This subjective perception of failure results in negative evaluation of athletic ability and resultant loss of self-esteem.

13. Competitive stress may be measured physiologically, behaviorally, or psychologically. Heart rate changes relate to the physiological dimension, quantified sleep loss relates to the behavioral, and using the Sport Competition Anxiety Test (SCAT) represents a psychological measurement tool.

14. Research has suggested that competitive stress is mediated by at least four cognitive variables: perceived ability, expectancy of success, expectancy of negative evaluation, and expectancy of experiencing negative emotional states.

15. General parent-child interactions, interactions with other adults and peers, and history of success or failure are major antecedents of competitive stress.

16. Recommendations for improving youth sport involve attacking the problem from the medical, psychological, and sociological perspectives. Thorough physical examinations, proper equipment, and adapting the rules to fit various skill levels are a few of many medical recommendations. Psychologically speaking, reinforcement of effort (process) over the win-loss (product) standard is highly recommended. Sociologically, not tolerating inappropriate behavior and reinforcing prosocial efforts among fans and players would be valuable in making youth sport more rewarding.

17. A number of health risk factors that contribute to injury rates have been identified by the American Council of Pediatrics and others. Among these health risk factors are discrepancies in size and skill at various ages, impatience with restrictions when injured, musculoskeletal immaturity, possible undetected congenital predisposers to injury, overall physical conditioning deficits, poor utilization of protective equipment, and limited access to services of qualified trainers.

SUGGESTED READINGS

Cahill, B. R., & Pearl, A. J. (Eds.) (1993) *Intensive participation in children's sports.* Champaign, IL: Human Kinetics.

>This edited reader includes chapters by Martens on stress and self-esteem, Gould on stress and burnout, Weiss on beginning and continuing in youth sport, Coakley on intensive training, Donnelly on elite athletes, and at least six other articles on injuries and other more sports medicine-oriented topics.

Cratty, B. J., & Pigott, R. (1984) *Student projects in sport psychology.* Ithaca, NY: Mouvement.

>Cratty and Pigott have put together a collection of twenty-one projects that they suggest can be used to assist teachers and students in sport psychology classes. Project 8, the youth in sport, and Project 18, parent-child observation, are particularly relevant to youth sport. Project 8 involves interviewing a child with the goal of ascertaining some of the psychosocial forces that affect performance and enjoyment of sport. In Project 18, using a suggested checklist, the student assesses parental effects on performance and enjoyment of sport through observation of adults at youth sporting events.

Martens, R. (1978) *Joy and sadness in children's sports.* Champaign, IL: Human Kinetics.

>This 360-page book is a classic reading in the literature of youth sport. Martens, a strong proponent of youth sports, primarily attempts to portray the joy of sports but acknowledges the

difficulty of addressing the issues without confronting the down side. The book was created for all who care about youth sport, and it is sufficiently scholarly and readable to be of interest to coaches, parents, and sports professionals alike. Martens chose 36 articles from a broad array of sources to address the many issues in youth sport.

Miller, D. K. (1994) *Measurement by the physical educator: Why and how.* (2d ed.) Dubuque, IA: Brown and Benchmark.

While there is much in this text that is only tangentially germane to sport psychology, chapter 16 addresses the assessment of physical fitness among youth in considerable detail. Programs such as the Prudential FITNESSGRAM (1992), the Manitoba Schools Fitness Test (1989), the South Carolina Physical Fitness Test (1983), Fit Youth Today (1986), the YMCA Physical Fitness Test (1989), AAHPERD Physical Best (1988), the Chrysler Fund-AAU Physical Fitness Program (1991), the President's Challenge (1991), and the AAHPERD Youth Fitness Test (1976) are compared and contrasted in a most readable fashion. Miller also points out that an "agreement to agree" was generated in 1992 by the leadership of the President's Council on Youth Fitness and Sports (PCYFS) and the American Alliance for Health, Physical Education, Recreation and Dance (AAHPERD) with regard to creating *one* test for the assessment of fitness in young people.

Orlick, T., & Botterill, C. (1975) *Every kid can win.* Chicago, IL: Nelson-Hall.

Though a bit dated, this book remains useful to all involved in youth sport. The authors have attempted to bridge the communications gap that exists between people who generate ideas and those who apply them, in this case, coaches, parents, and others who interact with young people in the athletic arena. Practical suggestions are made about how to keep children in sport and how to make the experience as rewarding as possible in the process. A chapter on the female athlete is particularly interesting given the date of the publication of this work.

Rader, B. (1983) *American sports from the age of folk games to the age of spectators.* Englewood Cliffs, NJ: Prentice-Hall.

Rader's informative book has an excellent chapter on the history of youth sport in the United States (see chapter 13). Topics such as muscular Christianity, the emergence of sport fiction, the Young Men's and Women's Christian Associations, prominent historical figures, the role of the public schools, the playground movement, and women's sports are addressed from a historical perspective. Readers looking for an abbreviated but informative discussion of the history of youth sport will find this chapter to their liking.

RQES forum (1992) *Research Quarterly for Sport and Exercise, 63,* 95–136.

This edition of *RQES* contains eight articles addressing various aspects of youth fitness, focusing primarily on such topics as the fitness level of American youth from a variety of vantage points and measurement problems in assessing youth fitness. This collection serves to reinforce and expand upon many of the points made in the text discussion of youth fitness and related concerns.

Schreiber, L. R. (1990) *The parents' guide to kids' sports.* Boston: Little, Brown.

Schreiber's book represents a lively coverage of a wide variety of topics related to youth sports. In addition, he provides a comprehensive listing of approximately sixty organizations complete with addresses, which serves as resources for those interested in youth sport. Sports covered include baseball and softball, field hockey, football, golf, gymnastics, ice hockey, judo, soccer, swimming, tennis, and volleyball. Additionally, fitness organizations, nutrition resources, sport psychology and sport medicine associations, and miscellaneous allied institutions and alliances and their respective addresses are noted. This compilation serves a useful function for the interested parent, coach, youth administrator, or sport scientist.

Thompson, J. (1994) *Positive coaching: Building character and self-esteem through sports.* Portola Valley, CA: Warde Publishers.

This four hundred-page book contains over two hundred practical coaching recommendations based on the extensive experience of the author, a youth and high school coach as well as an administrator at Stanford University. Much emphasis is placed on building self-esteem and character through the provision of informed and inspirational coaching. Also, tips on handling parents, how to make practices fun and productive, and how to learn from losing are other important topics discussed by the author.

REFERENCES

AAHPERD youth fitness test manual. (1980) Reston, VA: American Alliance for Health, Physical Education, Recreation and Dance.

AAHPERD physical best. (1988) Reston, VA: American Alliance for Health, Physical Education, Recreation and Dance.

American Academy of Pediatrics (1981) Injuries to young athletes. *Physician and Sportsmedicine, 9*(2), 107–110.

American youth and sports participation. (1990) North Palm Beach, FL: Athletic Footwear Association.

Blair, S., Falls, H., & Pate, R. (1983) A new physical fitness test. *Physician and Sportsmedicine, 11*(4), 87–95.

Brady, E. (1989) Being heard often leads to disruption. *USA Today,* June 19, 1C-2C.

Burke, E., & Kleiber, D. (1976) Psychological and physical implications of highly competitive sports for children. *Physical Educator, 33,* 63–70.

Burton, D., & Martens, R. (1986) Pinned by their own goals: An exploratory investigation into why kids drop out of wrestling. *Journal of Sport Psychology, 8,* 183–197.

Chambers, S. T. (1991) Factors affecting elementary school students' participation in sports. *The Elementary School Journal, 91,* 413–419.

Crossman, J. E. (1986) Spectator behavior at minor league hockey games. *Perceptual and Motor Skills, 63,* 803–812.

DuBois, P. (1980) Competition in youth sport: Process or product? *Physical Educator, 37,* 151–154.

Duda, J. (1985) Consider the children: Meeting participants' goals in youth sport. *Journal of Physical Education, Recreation and Dance, 56*(6), 55–56.

Faucette, N., & Osinski, A. (1987) Adult spectator verbal behavior during a Mustang League world series. *Journal of Applied Research in Coaching and Athletics, 2,* 141–152.

Finn, R. (1987) Players to hit books as well as serves. *USA Today,* April 16, 12C.

Francis, R., Bunch, T., & Chandler, B. (1978) Little League elbow: A decade later. *Physician and Sportsmedicine, 6*(4), 88–94.

Franklin, K. (1989) Field of dreams: Little League's not so little anymore. *Sport,* Sept., 64–67.

Fry, D., McClements, J., & Sefton, J. (1981) *A report on participation in the Saskatoon Hockey Association.* Saskatoon, Sask., Canada: SASK Sport.

Gill, D. L., Martens, R. (1977) The role of task type and success-failure on selected interpersonal variables. *International Journal of Sport Psychology, 8,* 160–177.

Gill, D. L., Gross, J. B., & Huddleston, S. (1981) Participation motivation in youth sport. *International Journal of Sport Psychology, 14,* 1–14.

Gomolak, C. (1975) Problems in matching young athletes: Body fat, peach fuzz, muscles, and mustache. *Physician and Sportsmedicine, 3*(5), 96–98.

Gould, D., Feltz, D. L., Horn, T., & Weiss, M. (1982) Reasons for discontinuing involvement in competitive youth swimming. *Journal of Sport Behavior, 5,* 155–165.

Gould, D., Feltz, D. L., & Weiss, M. (1985) Motives for participating in competitive youth swimming. *International Journal of Sport Psychology, 16,* 126–140.

Gould, D., Feltz, D. L., Weiss, M., & Petlichkoff, L. M. (1982) Participating motives in competitive youth swimmers. In T. Orlick, J. T. Partington, & J. H. Salmela (Eds.) *Mental training for coaches and athletes* (pp. 57–58). Ottawa: Coaching Association of Canada.

Griffin, L. (1978) *Why children participate in youth sports.* Paper presented at American Alliance for Health, Physical Education and Recreation (AAHPER) Convention, Kansas City, Missouri.

Gutierrez, L. (1988) Soviets ready to build their diamonds in the rough. *USA Today,* January 26, 8C.

Hale, C. J. (1956) Physiological maturity of Little League baseball players. *Research Quarterly, 27,* 276–284.

Hale, C. J. (1961) Injuries among 771,810 Little League baseball players. *Journal of Sports Medicine and Physical Fitness, 1,* 80–83.

Hale, C. J. (1992) Personal communication, College Station, TX.

Hanson, D. (1967) Cardiac response to participation in Little League baseball competition as determined by telemetry. *Research Quarterly, 38,* 384–388.

Harris, D. V. (1973) Physical activities for children: Effects and affects. Paper presented at American Alliance for Health, Physical Education and Recreation (AAHPER) Convention, Minneapolis, Minnesota.

Jennings, S. (1981) As American as hot dogs, apple pie, and Chevrolet: The desegregation of Little League baseball. *Journal of American Culture, 4*(4), 81–91.

Kleiber, D. (1981) Searching for enjoyment in children's sports. *Physical Educator,* May, 77–84.

Kraus, H., & Hirschland, P. (1954) Minimum muscular fitness tests in young children. *Research Quarterly, 25,* 178–188.

Maffulli, N. (1990) Intensive training in young athletes: The orthopaedic surgeon's viewpoint. *Sports Medicine, 9,* 229–243.

Magill, R. A. (1978) Critical periods: Relation to youth sports. In R. A. Magill, M. J. Ash, & F. L. Smoll (Eds.), *Children in sport* (pp. 38–47). Champaign, IL: Human Kinetics.

Martens, R. (1977) *Sport Competition Anxiety Test.* Champaign, IL: Human Kinetics.

Martens, R., & Seefeldt, V. (1979) *Guidelines for children's sports.* Washington, DC: Alliance for Health, Physical Education, Recreation and Dance.

Martens, R., Burton, D., Rivkin, F., & Simon, J. (1980) Reliability and validity of the Competitive State Anxiety Inventory (CSAI). In C. H. Nadeau, W. R. Halliwell, K. M. Newell, & G. C. Roberts (Eds.), *Psychology of motor behavior and sport—1979* (pp. 91–99). Champaign, IL: Human Kinetics.

McElroy, M. A., & Kirkendall, D. R. (1980) Significant others and professionalized sport attitudes.

Research Quarterly for Exercise and Sport, 51, 645–653.

Nuwer, H. (1986) The new improved George Brett. *Inside Sports, 8,* (June), 60–70.

Orlick, T. (1974) The athletic dropout—A high price of inefficiency. *CAHPER Journal,* Nov.-Dec., 21–27.

Pappas, A. M., & Zawacki, R. M. (1991) Baseball: Too much on a young pitcher's shoulders? *The Physician and Sportsmedicine, 19*(3), 107–117.

Passer, M. W. (1983) Fear of failure, fear of evaluation, perceived competence, and self-esteem in competitive-trait-anxious children. *Journal of Sport Psychology, 5,* 172–188.

Passer, M. W. (1984) Competitive trait anxiety in children and adolescents. In J. M. Silva & R. S. Weinberg (Eds.), *Psychological foundations of sport* (pp. 130–144). Champaign, IL: Human Kinetics.

Pate, R. (1983) A new definition of youth fitness. *Physician and Sportsmedicine, 11*(4), 87–95.

Pooley, J. (1981) *Dropouts from sport: A case study of boys' age-group soccer.* Paper presented at American Alliance for Health, Physical Education, Recreation and Dance (AAHPERD) Convention, Boston, Massachusetts.

The president's challenge physical fitness program. (1991) Washington, DC: President's Council on Youth Fitness and Sports.

Randall, L. E., & McKenzie, T. L. (1987) Spectator verbal behavior in organized youth soccer: A descriptive analysis. *Journal of Sport Behavior, 10,* 200–211.

Sapp, M., & Haubenstricker, J. (1978) Motivation for joining and reasons for not continuing in youth sports programs in Michigan. Paper presented at American Alliance for Health, Physical Education, and Recreation (AAHPER) Convention, Kansas City, Missouri.

Scanlan, T. K. (1984) Competitive stress and the child athlete. In J. M. Silva & R. S. Weinberg (Eds.), *Psychological foundations of sport* (pp. 118–129). Champaign, IL: Human Kinetics.

Scanlan, T. K., & Lewthwaite, R. (1986) Social psychological aspects of competition for male youth participants: IV. Predictors of enjoyment. *Journal of Sport Psychology, 8,* 25–35.

Scanlan, T. K., & Passer, M. W. (1978) Factors related to competitive stress among male youth sport participants. *Medicine and Science in Sports, 10,* 103–108.

Scanlan, T. K., & Passer, M. W. (1981) Competitive stress and the youth sport experience. *Physical Educator, 38,* 144–151.

Schreiber, L. R. (1990) *The parents' guide to kids' sports.* Boston: Little, Brown, and Company.

Scott, P. (1953) Attitudes toward athletic competition in elementary schools. *Research Quarterly, 24,* 352–361.

Sewell, D. (1992) Are parents ruining the games? *Youth Sport Coach, Fall, 1,* 16.

Seymour, E. (1956) Comparative study of certain behavior characteristics of participant and non-participant boys in Little League baseball. *Research Quarterly, 27,* 338–346.

Simon, J., & Martens, R. (1979) Children's anxiety in sport and nonsport evaluative activities. *Journal of Sport Psychology, 1,* 160–169.

Singer, R. N., & Gerson, R. (1980) Athletic competition for children: Motivational considerations. *International Journal of Sport Psychology, 11,* 249–262.

Skubic, E. (1955) Emotional responses of boys to Little League and Middle League competitive baseball. *Research Quarterly, 26,* 342–352.

Skubic, E. (1956) Studies of Little League and Middle League baseball. *Research Quarterly, 27,* 97–110.

Soviets in Little League. (1988) *Houston Chronicle,* January 26, Section 2–3.

Spielberger, C. (1973) *Preliminary test manual for the State-Trait Anxiety Inventory for Children.* Palo Alto, CA: Consulting Psychologists Press.

Stewart, M. (1981) Youth sport participation and the physiological functions of the child. *Physical Educator, 38,* 59–64.

Teenagers' motivations for sports participation help predict lifelong habits. (1990) North Palm Beach, FL: Athletic Footwear Association.

Twombly, W. (1976) *200 years of sport in America.* New York: McGraw-Hill.

Walley, P. B., Graham, G. M., & Forehand, R. (1982) Assessment and treatment of adult observer verbalizations at youth league baseball games. *Journal of Sport Psychology, 4,* 254–266.

Wankel, L. M., & Kreisel, P. (1985) Factors underlying enjoyment of youth sports: Sport and age group comparisons. *Journal of Sport Psychology, 7,* 51–64.

Wankel, L. M., & Sefton, J. M. (1989) A season long investigation of fun in youth sports. *Journal of Sport and Exercise Psychology, 11,* 355–366.

Weinberg, R. S., & Genuchi, M. (1980) Relationship between competitive trait anxiety, state anxiety, and golf performance: A field study. *Journal of Sport Psychology, 2,* 148–154.

Wood, R. (1983) Thoughts on reducing the fear of failure in young children. *Physical Educator, 40,* 219–221.

Chapter Twelve

The Coach and Sport Psychology

Dear Coach Rockne:

As you may know, I have been interested for some years in many of the problems of psychology and athletics. I am writing you now because during the past season I heard a few comments about you and your team that were of interest to my work, having always taken the point that men on a team play best when they love the game they are playing. I have said that I did not believe such a team would have to be keyed up to its games. A team that is keyed up is bound to have a slump. Men who are always playing their best because they like the game are far more apt to go through a season without a serious slump. Now the point I am getting at is this: I have heard it said that you do not key your men up to their games: that you select such men as play the game joyously for its own sake and that you try to develop in them as much of this spirit as you can.

I am wondering if you care to tell me directly about these things? I am asking for information only because of my psychological interest in athletic sports.

Cordially yours,
Coleman R. Griffith

Dear Mr. Griffith:

I feel very grateful to you for having written me, although I do not know a great deal about psychology.

I do try to pick men who like the game of football and who get a lot of fun out of playing. I never try to make football hard work. I do think your team plays good football, because they do like to play and I do not make any effort to key them up, except on rare, exceptional occasions. I keyed them up for the Nebraska game this year, which was a mistake, as we had a reaction the following Saturday against Northwestern. I try to make our boys take the game less seriously than, I presume, some others do, and we try to make the spirit of the game one of exhilaration and we never allow hatred to enter into it, no matter against whom we are playing.

Thanking you for your kindness, I am

Yours cordially,
[Knute Rockne]

My dear Mr. Rockne:

Let me thank you most heartily for your comments about the play spirit in football. If you are so inclined, I would like to hear about the plans you make for playing a post-season game and what efforts you have to make to reawaken the interest of the men. I doubt very much whether teams that have to be keyed up to a game will be able to do so well weeks after the season is closed as a team which plays in the spirit in which yours seems to play. I do not mean, of course, to trouble you about this before your trip to the coast but I will be most grateful for any comments you may have to make after you come back.

Cordially yours,
Coleman R. Griffith

Dear Mr. Griffith:

Regarding our trip to the coast, we took it mostly in the way of a pleasure trip and an educational trip, and we made the workouts short and snappy, so as not to make them hard work in any sense of the word. We had just one real hard workout and that was at Tucson, which served to sort of get the boys in a mood for a game. The climate of California sort of took the resiliency and drive out of their legs before the second half began. However, the spirit of play manifested itself and the boys were so alert that they took advantage of every mistake made by Stanford. I think a keyed-up team would have been too tense and too excited to have profited by these opportunities.

From an educational point of view, we had a very profitable trip and the boys missed but one day of classes.

Yours sincerely,
[Knute Rockne]

My dear Mr. Rockne:

I am doubly indebted to you for your letter of February 10. I was almost sure that the plan which you say you followed would bring success. I know that other teams have gone to the coast so keyed-up and excited that their own mental states fought against them.

Cordially yours,
Coleman R. Griffith

INTRODUCTION

The exchange of letters in 1924–1925 between one of college football's most successful coaches, Knute Rockne of Notre Dame, and the father of sport psychology, Coleman Griffith at the University of Illinois, serves as a poignant reminder that the coaching practices of sixty years ago and those of today have little in common (LeUnes, 1986). Coaching at any level, but particularly in the collegiate or professional

ranks, has become a pressure-laden enterprise, one in which win–loss record is generally viewed as the standard by which success is measured. Our quest here is for a better understanding of the kinds of people who choose this enigmatic profession and what psychology has to offer coaches in their pursuit of excellence for themselves and their players.

FEATURES OF COACHING: PROS AND CONS

Undoubtedly, a great many rewards are associated with coaching. Prevailing in one-to-one competition with your peers has a tremendous amount of appeal. Equally attractive is the pride in taking a group of individuals and molding them into a productive and cohesive team. Another source of great satisfaction has to be watching young people master skills and, at the same time, grow up to be useful contributing citizens. For some coaches, substantial monetary rewards and fame accompany such success. Though these various incentives hardly exhaust the myriad possibilities, they serve as reminders that coaching can be a most exhilarating calling.

Fuoss and Troppmann (1981) indicate that coaches will also confront a number of features of their chosen field that fall into the category of hazards of the profession. For one thing, *everyone is an expert on sport!* Few will tell a watchmaker, a welder, and a wizard in electronics how to do their respective jobs, yet most of us are quite willing to tell an athletic coach how to run his or her team. Second-guessing by the so-called Monday-morning quarterback is a well-documented phenomenon in the coaching experience.

Another pitfall comes in the form of *endless work hours.* Coaches put in many arduous hours in their search for the winning formula. Coaches seem to wholeheartedly subscribe to the work ethic, and this is seen in the various slogans they use to guide their own work and that of their players. "The will to win is the will to work," "success is 99 percent perspiration and 1 percent inspiration," "by failing to prepare yourself, you are preparing to fail," "there is no substitute for hard work," "alertness plus hard work equals a winner," and "winners are workers" are slogans that personify the work ethic in coaching. Because these ideas are so deeply ingrained in the coaching mentality, they contribute to the idea that the coach who works longest will prevail over those who are not so diligent. Craig Morton, when coaching the Denver Gold of the now defunct United States Football League, was branded as being not very diligent, because he worked only a forty-hour week. His feeling was that coaches spend far more time at the job than is required. Morton may or may not have been correct, but he violated a time-honored coaching norm that the person who works longest and hardest prevails.

A third occupational hazard of coaching is *constant evaluation,* and this appraisal is largely based on the performance of other people (players). The coach's record is a matter of public record and the pressure to notch wins over losses seems eternal. Few of us in other professions are so unfailingly scrutinized. The college professor's product is difficult to measure; we often operate in a vacuum as to our proficiency. Not so the coach; the win-loss record is out there for all to see.

Another negative feature of the coaching business is its lack of job security. The coach is only as good as last year's record insofar as management is concerned. To quote Norm Sloan, the former head basketball coach at North Carolina State University: "Coaching is the only profession in which you have to prove yourself as much in the thirtieth year as in the first year" (Sloan, 1977, p. 2). Phil Jackson, commenting on the pressures he faced as coach of the 1991 NBA champion Chicago Bulls, puts it succinctly: "I had to win. I knew it was either

win or be gone" (Vancil, 1991, p. 19). The prevailing attitude of management and the fans seems to have a "What have you done for me lately?" flavor to it.

Statistics from four of the big-time team sports for the years 1980 through 1989 tell a poignant story about the fragile nature of coaching tenure. Table 12.1 vividly attests to the brief tenure characterizing the job of head coach/manager in big-time sports.

Other noteworthy statistics that add emphasis to the data in table 12.1 include the following:

- In the NBA in 1990, there were nine first-year coaches, eight second-year coaches, seven third-year coaches, and three coaches with over three years tenure ("New Faces," 1990). At the start of the 1994 season, there were again nine new coaches ("NBA Coaching Changes," 1994).
- From 1969 to 1989, there were 133 head coaches fired in the NFL. As of 1990, only five coaches had more than nine years' tenure with the same team ("NFL Veterans," 1990).
- In college football, things were not much better than in the NFL. One prominent and not atypical example is the Southeastern Conference (SEC), where only three head

Table 12.1

Coaching Tenure in Selected Professional Sports, 1980–1989

League	Number of Changes	Percent Change Annually	Average Tenure in Years
NFL	53	21.0	4.75
NBA	76	36.4	2.75
NHL	96	50.7	1.96
MLB	103	44.0	2.27

Source: "Pro Coaches Won't Find Security" (1989).

coaches had been at the same school for more than three years at the start of the 1991 season (Crothers, 1991).

- In Division 1 of college basketball, forty-nine coaching changes were made during or after the 1988–1989 season ("Division 1," 1989). This represents a 14 percent turnover of head coaching positions. In 1985–1986 and 1986–1987, there were 123 changes made, yielding a two-year turnover figure of over 40 percent ("Changing of the Guard," 1987). For the 1994–1995 season, there were 53 coaching changes made among 302 Division I schools for a turnover rate of 18 percent (Wieberg, 1995).

When one considers the ripple effect created among assistant coaches when the head coach is fired, the unsettled nature of the profession of coaching, at least in the high profile sports, takes on even more significant proportions. Because of the lack of security, frequent moves are common. Also, getting ahead in coaching calls for additional moves that are not dictated by failure to win.

The unsettled nature of the business and the frequent moving brings us to a fifth drawback, and that is that coaching takes a *toll on family life*. Supportive of this position is a study by Sabock and Jones (1978) in which they asked high school coaches' wives to respond to a survey on problems they faced. Chief among the problems cited were excessive time demands that interfered with family life, health problems among their spouses due to job stress, and a generally irregular schedule involving travel, meals, and other family considerations. Hasbrook, Hart, Mathes, and True (1990) surveyed several thousand male and female interscholastic coaches and found that "incompatibility with family life" was ranked high among both sexes as a reason for leaving coaching. These researchers also found that 79 percent of the male coaches in a state survey and 87 percent in a

national survey were married; the figures for female coaches were 53 percent and 42 percent. In this connection, Thorngren (1990) points out that females in coaching may be more susceptible to the effects of job stress by the very fact that they are more likely to be single, and are thereby deprived of the support system that is inherent in a good marriage. A final point made by Hasbrook et al. is that parenting, not marital pressure, may be the biggest culprit in job dissatisfaction among coaches; to date, there are no studies of parenting and coaching satisfaction.

A final concern to be addressed here is *coaching as a terminal career*. Very few coaches actually retire from coaching at the usual retirement age of sixty-five or seventy, and those who coach beyond the usual retirement age are infinitesimally small in number. We must go back to legends such as Amos Alonzo Stagg at Pacific (retired from coaching at the age of eighty-four), John Dorman at Upper Iowa (age eighty-one), George Allen at Long Beach State (who died on the job at the age of seventy-two), and the legendary Eddie Robinson at Grambling (age seventy-two) in order to find examples of older, active coaches. Given the job demands of the profession today, it is unlikely that we will ever see anyone coaching into their seventies or eighties again.

Even the most serious fan among us would be hard-pressed to name five currently employed collegiate head football coaches who are over the age of fifty-five, and the picture is much the same for their assistants.

To put the issue in data-based terms, Fred Jacoby (1978), Commissioner of the Mid-American Conference, found that only six of eighty-four assistant coaches in his league were over fifty years of age; only one of the ten head coaches was over fifty. Clearly, the coaching of football is a young person's game. Parallels are likely to exist in most other sports. It would appear that coaches, like players, should be aware that they are in a career with a short life expectancy and should prepare for that eventuality, both psychologically and financially.

All things considered, individuals who choose coaching stand to reap many rewards, but they should also be aware of another side of the coin. Having to deal with the multiple pressures of many critics, working seemingly endless hours, having the future rest as much on what others do as on what the coach does himself or herself, having little job security, living a sometimes disjointed family life, and being a member of a career with a short life expectancy are things that have to be dealt with in order to persist and thrive in the profession of coaching.

Qualities of a Good Coach

Though there may be a few diehards in the group, the majority of coaches are aware that coaching is more than X's and O's. This is not to downplay the importance of the intellectual side of the world of sports, but more an attempt to underscore the importance of being able to properly motivate athletes to do their best. Perhaps a personal experience from the background of your senior author would be instructive. In the ninth grade, we found ourselves without a football coach, only a short time before fall practice was to start. For whatever reason, a young (and most capable) science teacher named Carl Davidson was assigned the extra duties as junior high football coach. Despite vehement protests based on the fact that he had never touched a football nor even attended a football game, Mr. Davidson took over the coaching reins two weeks prior to the first game. He was referred to several of the ninth graders as resources on what to do, and as a result he read Bud Wilkinson's then very popular book on the split-T formation (Wilkinson, 1952) and installed it as our offense. Despite this inauspicious debut, Mr. Davidson was able to survive and, ultimately, excel. He lost no games that year and only five in the next seven years. He demonstrated that excellence is perhaps achieved more through motivation than sheer knowledge of the game. All in all, I am convinced that I owe my fascination with the psychological side of sport to those serendipitous events of the early 1950s, and am deeply indebted to Carl Davidson for providing invaluable insights into the importance of motivation in athletic performance.

What is it, then, that makes for a good coach? Inasmuch as *coaches are teachers* and, ultimately, all coaching is nothing more than teaching, the coach should be knowledgeable about the activity being taught. Athletes need to be taught the basic skills or fundamentals essential to excellent performance. A technology for accomplishing this skill acquisition has been provided in chapter 3 (Behavior Principles and Applications), and it behooves all coaches to become familiar with the behavioral approach to coaching. Coaches who are methodical in the teaching of skills and who are expert in the proper application of positive reinforcement and punishment (with emphasis on reinforcement) are miles ahead of their lesser informed contemporaries. At the same time, coaches should have sessions in which the knowledge aspects of the game are stressed. For example, sessions on proper utilization of the rules of a particular activity could be most helpful.

In addition to being a good teacher who knows his or her sport, the coach should also be a *good student*. Studying various sport periodicals on how to improve one's product, attending seminars that have the same goals in mind, and attending university courses in sport or in sport psychology are readily accessible activities for the coach who wants to grow and improve.

The successful coach is a *motivator*. Successful coaches are successful wherever they may go. Programs in the doldrums are continually given new life by coaches who have been successful elsewhere. The ability to motivate is part and parcel of this success formula. Getting athletes to run through the proverbial brick wall seems to come far easier for some coaches than others. Clearly, the former group are motivators, people who are able to generate the desire to excel in their athletes. Perhaps Mike Vreeswyk, a former basketball player at Temple University, captures the essence of the coach as motivator in the following quote about his mentor, John Chaney: "If Coach says a flea can pull a plough, we say hitch him up" (Kirkpatrick, 1988, p. 30).

Being aware of *individual differences* in athletes is also an important ingredient in coaching excellence. Some athletes are turned on by yelling, screaming, throwing things, and other emotional displays. Others are turned off by these shows of emotions, preferring a more serene, meditative approach to getting ready to participate. Individualizing motivation becomes important here. Knowing which athletes to pat on the back and which ones to cajole and emotionally exhort to perform is vital to coaching. Also, watching for signs of under- or overarousal is important. As we saw in our discussion of the

Football as Fun: Some Coaches Who Dared to Be Different

Highlight 12.1

John Gagliardi of St. John's (Minnesota), a forty-one-year coaching veteran, has seen his football teams win 269 games and three small-college national championships under his tutelage. All of these achievements have been attained with a unique coaching philosophy that includes such novelties as never using blocking sleds or tackling dummies, no scrimmages, and practices conducted in sweats and/or shorts only. His opposition to the "no pain, no gain" mentality so pervasive among football coaches is legendary; he says he likes to conduct "kinder, more gentle practices," preferring to view football as an exercise in finesse rather than brute strength. Though he has been tendered a number of lucrative offers from big-time football programs, Gagliardi feels that his philosophy is best suited for St. John's.

In a similar vein, the senior author of this text played his final year of high school football many years ago with coaches who instituted a similar philosophy, and has seen its merits up close and personal. Emphasis in practices was on brevity, speed, timing, conditioning, mental preparation, and esprit de corps; there were no scrimmages after two-a-days were over; and pads were seldom worn. The team eventually won eleven of thirteen games, was ranked number one or two in its classification for the entire season, and ended up losing in the quarterfinals of the state playoffs 13–12 to the eventual state runnerup after having a 12–0 lead at the end of the third quarter. Many thanks go to coaches Kester "Tractor" Trent and L. E. "Hooter" Brewer, particularly the latter, for their lessons in unorthodox but fun football!

Source: "St. John's (Minn.): Peculiar practices" (1990).

inverted-U hypothesis in chapter 4, there is an optimum level of arousal that is conducive to good performance. The good coach has a responsibility to acquire some sense of what this optimum level is for the team and for individual players as well. Though numbers cannot be attached to the individual levels of arousal in the sport context, some skillful assessment of the appropriate level for each player can be made by coaches who are tuned in to their performers.

The good coach is also a *good listener,* keeping an eye open and an ear to the ground to achieve a sense of individual and team subtleties and undercurrents. Consistent with being a good listener, the coach should be a sensitive sounding board for problems, complaints, and wishes of the players. Also, the good coach is going to utilize the team leaders as allies in providing keys to more ably working with other participants. Finally, the good coach will be forceful but democratic, allowing for considerable individual input into the everyday management of the sport at hand, whether team or individual. Players certainly should not run the operation, but they should have input because they are invaluable sources of insights and information.

At times, people step out of line, and athletes are not exceptions to the rule. When misbehavior occurs, the coach must become a *disciplinarian.* Players need to adhere to a reasonable set of rules both on and off the field of play, and penalties must be meted out for violations of the conduct code. The good coach clearly states the code of player conduct up front, and adheres to it with reasonable regularity. When violations occur, punishment should be levied. Consistent with the time-honored rules learned in both the animal laboratory and in human research, if punishment is to be successful in changing behavior, it must be *mild, prompt,* and *consistent. Mildness* means that counterproductive emotionality will be minimal, thereby allowing the intended message to get

During his twenty-five years as head football coach at the University of Alabama, the legendary "Bear" Bryant served as mentor for countless players who are now coaches.

through. *Promptness* means that the punishment and behavior will be tied together temporally in such a way that no mixed messages are sent; to wit, this is the transgression and here is the specified penalty. Finally, punishment that is *consistent* conveys a firm message that there are rules, no one is above the law, and all violations will carry a uniform punishment. Athletes, like the rest of us, can live within a punitive policy that is applied only when absolutely necessary and meets the tripartite standards of mildness, promptness, and consistency.

The good coach also *leads by example*. This implies that the coach who demands hard work from others is also a hard worker. It means that the coach who demands fitness is an exemplar of fitness. Obviously, coaches need not be in as good a condition as their players, but they should serve as fitness role models for their athletes. It means that the coach who commands respect should show respect for others. It means that the coach who expects unbridled enthusiasm should be an enthusiastic person. It means that the coach who asks that the players be good listeners also listens when players and assistant coaches are communicating. Finally, though this list is by no means exhaustive, the coach who expects athletics to build character should be a role model and facilitator of the character-building aspects of athletic participation.

Finally, the good coach must be a *goal setter*. Quite a bit of research on goal setting has emerged of late in the sport psychology literature, and the up-to-date coach would do well to incorporate the best of these findings into his or her motivational repertoire.

SETTING PERFORMANCE GOALS IN SPORT

A popular means of motivating people to perform more effectively in a variety of industrial/organizational settings is goal setting, and much of its popularity is due to the efforts of Locke and Latham and their collaborators (Locke, 1968; Locke, Shaw, Saari, and Latham, 1981). Locke's original exposition on goal setting in 1968 was followed by a strong substantiation in the 1981 Locke et al. piece; in brief, the research team found that ninety-nine of 110 studies they reviewed substantiated their major hypothesis that specific but difficult goals, if accepted, are more facilitative of performance than are easy, vague, or no goals. Subsequent meta-analyses by Mento, Steel, and Karren (1987) and Tubbs (1986) have strongly supported the validity of the goal difficulty/specificity proposition of Locke and associates. In 1985, Locke and Latham extended their goal setting work to sport psychology, and have arrived at five conclusions they feel are applicable to sport settings:

1. Specific, difficult goals lead to better performance than vague, easy goals.
2. Short-term goals can facilitate the achievement of long-term goals.
3. Goals affect performance by affecting effort, persistence, and direction of attention, and by motivating strategy development.
4. Feedback regarding progress is necessary for goal setting to work.
5. Goals must be accepted if they are to affect performance. (p. 205)

Using these five general conclusions as a point of departure, Locke and Latham elaborated on ten specific hypotheses of their own, all generated with the overall guiding hypothesis that goal setting theory is as applicable to sport as it is in the business or research laboratory settings.

Chief among their suggestions was the use of *goal setting* in the practice and competitive environments. For example, figure 12.1 contains a suggested list of goals for the development of certain skills within a variety of sporting contexts. Specific suggestions for skill attainment are made; all are clear-cut and, at the same time, attainable. The suggestions also serve as specific feedback sources to coaches and athletes. The results of the goal setting are measurable, and thus the goals are far superior to the sort of general advice so often given: "Let's go hard for ten or fifteen minutes" or "Work on your free throws. You've had trouble with them lately."

Table 12.2 offers concrete ways of assessing performance in football and basketball. Players are provided with measurable and attainable goals that push them to greater performance. This goal setting, in turn, should translate into better overall team performance, an obvious goal of coaches of team sports.

Crucial to the success of goal setting is the concept of *reinforcement,* which was discussed at length in chapter 3. In brief, reinforcement must convey to the athletes that it is contingent on very specific behavior on their part. Reinforcement should be used to accurately portray degrees of skill acquisition.

Figure 12.1: **Examples of Goals for Subcomponents of Skilled Tasks**

Tennis
- 10 backhands in a row down the line
- 10 volleys in a row alternating left and right corners
- 5 first serves in a row in left third of service court; 5 in middle third; 5 in right third
- 5 returns of serve in a row deep to the add court

Football

Wide receiver:
- 5 over-the-head catches in a row of a 40-yard pass
- 5 one-handed catches in a row of a 15-yard pass

Defensive back:
- 5 interceptions in a row with receiver using preannounced route
- 2 or fewer completions allowed out of 5 tries with receiver running unknown route

Kicker:
- 10 field goals in a row from 40-yard line

Baseball
Infielder:
- 10 hard grounders in a row fielded without error, 5 to left and 5 to right

Outfielder:
- 20 fly balls caught on the run without error (5 to left, 5 to right, 5 in back, 5 in front)

Hitter:
- 5 curve balls in a row hit out of infield

Wrestling
- 6 takedowns using at least two techniques against an inferior but motivated opponent in (?) minutes
- 6 escapes using at least 3 different techniques in (?) minutes against same opponent

Basketball
- 20 foul shots in a row
- 30 uncontested lay-ups in a row
- 10 jump shots in a row from 10 feet
- Dribbling 2 minutes man-on-man against best defensive player without losing ball

Soccer
- 10 shots into left corner of goal from 30 feet with goalie not moving from center of goal
- 5 goals out of 10 shots from 20 feet with goalie free to move

Hockey

Goalie:
- stops 10 of 15 shots from 20 feet
- stops 5 of 10 one-on-one situations

Forward:
- passes successfully 8 out of 10 times to open man in front of net with one defender in between

Lacrosse
- Similar to soccer and hockey

Golf
- 6 drives in a row over 200 yards and landing on fairway
- 15 putts in a row of 12 feet
- 10 9-irons in a row onto green from 75 yards

Source: Locke and Latham (1985).

Table 12.2
Concrete Ways of Assessing Performance in Football and Basketball

A. Sample Point System for Defensive Lineman in Football

Point value	Action
20	Touchdown
10	Interception or fumble recovery
5	Cause fumble
5	Sack
3	Block pass
3	Pressure passer (e.g., within 3 feet of passer when ball released)
5	Tackle runner for 5 yard loss or more
4	Tackle runner for 1 to 4 yard loss
3	Tackle runner after gain of 0 to 3 yards
2	Tackle runner after gain of 4 to 5 yards
3	Tackle after lineman runs more than 10 yards
1	Any other tackle
—	Assist on any of above: 1/2 the number of points indicated
—	Bonus points (0 to 20): Any key 4th-quarter play in a winning effort: judgment of coaches

Possible comparison standards for setting goals
  1) Own performance (number of points in previous game and/or against same opponent last time played)
  2) Own best previous performance (same season)
  3) Performance of other team's best lineman in previous week
  4) Average of all defensive linemen on same team in previous week

B. Sample Point System for Basketball Players

Point value	Action
2	Field goal
1	Assist
1	Foul shot
1	Rebound
1	Steal
1	Blocked shot
Number of points held below average	Hold opposing player to less than season average (one-on-one defense)

Possible comparison standards for setting goals

  1) Own season average
  2) Own performance against same opponent that year
  3) Own performance in last 3 games

Source: Locke and Latham (1985).

Before moving on to other topics, it should be noted that all is not utopian in the goal setting literature. Tenenbaum, Pinchas, Elbaz, Bar-Eli, and Weinberg (1991) and Weinberg, Fowler, Jackson, Bagnall, and Bruya (1991) cite a number of difficulties with the Locke and Latham work, namely equivocal results with regard to the goal difficulty/specificity issue. Tenenbaum and his associates feel that the research findings are sufficiently equivocal as to call into serious question the generalization of goal setting results from industry to the sport and exercise setting. In the Weinberg et al. research, subjects in two separate motor tasks showed no decrement in performance irrespective of goal difficulty; that is, subjects placed in unrealistic-goal conditions, while admitting the difficulty of the assigned task, did not show any motivation decrements. This finding, as is intimated by both the Tenenbaum and Weinberg research teams, is suggestive of the fact that much is yet to be done in understanding the role of goal setting in sport performance. Both groups also propose that personality variables probably moderate the effects of goal setting strategies, and additional research of this nature is warranted.

Given that there are points of disagreement about facets of the Locke and Latham approach, it is fair to say that their contribution drawn from the larger body of industrial and organizational literature has made a substantial contribution to our understanding of goal setting in sport and exercise psychology.

ROLES OF THE COACH

Coaches, regardless of whether they are working with individuals or teams, live a pressure-laden, fishbowl kind of existence. Coaches are expected to win, be a positive reflection on the organization for which they toil, build character in young athletes, and make money for the organization. Frank Kush, while head football coach at Arizona State University, said: "My job is to win football games. I've got to put people in the stadium, make money for the university, keep the alumni happy, and give the school a winning reputation. If I don't win, I'm gone" (Michener, 1976). The coach, in this context, becomes a slave to many masters.

A glance at figure 12.2 will afford some additional insight into the role complexity facing the typical coach. There are multiple pressures impinging on the coach, and success in large part will depend on how well these pressures are handled.

At the *administrative level,* the coach must get along with owners, general managers, athletic directors, and other administrators, depending on the level at which the coaching is being done. This serving of many masters is no small task; often, much money and even bigger egos are involved, greatly increasing the pressure to win at all costs. Also, the prerogatives of the coach can be measurably circumvented by a meddling administrator. For example, chronic failures to win among several organizations in professional baseball, basketball, and football are testimonials to mismanagement. One needs little imagination to figure which organizations these are.

Players are another demand on the resources of the coach. If the coach is not successful in dealing with the players, the other roles are largely inconsequential. The coach must care about the athletes, must be able to motivate them, and must be concerned with their overall welfare. Equally important, the players must sense this commitment to their athletic and personal well-being.

Assistant coaches are also factors to be reckoned with. These aides are invaluable in terms of ultimate success and must be treated accordingly. Assistants should be paid what they are worth in terms of the free market, must be given a free rein to coach their various specialties, and should always be treated as trusted allies. Where

Figure 12.2: **Roles Coaches Are Expected to Play**

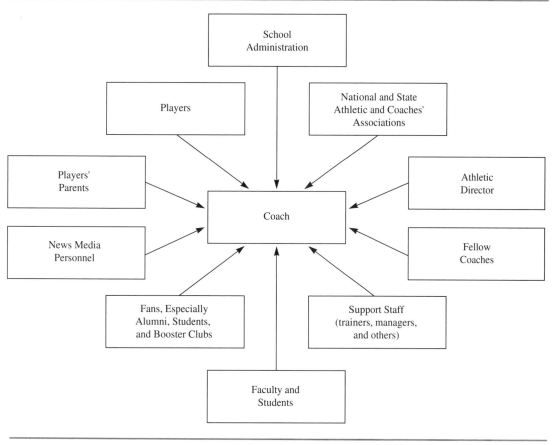

School
Administration

Players

National and State
Athletic and Coaches'
Associations

Players'
Parents

Athletic
Director

Coach

News Media
Personnel

Fellow
Coaches

Fans, Especially
Alumni, Students,
and Booster Clubs

Support Staff
(trainers, managers,
and others)

Faculty and
Students

Source: Coakley (1994).

feasible, they should be groomed for better jobs. It must be very rewarding to look around and see protégés everywhere. In the case of the late football legend Bear Bryant of the University of Alabama, his former players who are now coaches are too numerous to mention, and undoubtedly were a continuing source of immense satisfaction to him. In basketball, Bobby Knight of Indiana had fifteen protégés coaching in major programs at the end of 1986 (Allen, 1987).

The *media* demand yet another role of the coach. Media people are paid to promote listen-ers, viewers, or subscribers for the organizations for which they work and put a lot of pressure on coaches for interesting, salable material. The Monday morning interviews, the pre- and post-game interviews, the midweek interviews, and interviews to explain wins or losses, the inter-views related to exceptional players, and continu-ous media speculation as to team prospects and the ultimate fate of the coaches themselves all require the ability to express oneself under pres-sure. Also, the coaches' diplomacy and tact will be taxed at these times. Media exposure is important to the welfare of the teams and athletes, but the inherent pressures create further role demands for the coaches involved.

Dealing with fans is still another challenge to coaches. There would be few sports if there were not fans, and they can greatly determine the fate of a particular program, either through support or the failure to support it. As a consequence, a good relationship with the fans is important. At the professional level, their support is essential to the financial success of the organization. At the intercollegiate level, this financial dependence is also there in terms of ticket sales, alumni contributions, and overall program support. At the interscholastic level, the fans are often parents with much ego involvement with the activities at hand, and they require a delicate, supportive touch.

Of particular interest in the collegiate area of late has been the *"booster,"* often an overzealous university supporter. Boosters have subverted the very educational goals for which their universities were created through illegal payments to players or prospects, unethical inducements to perform, and, in some cases, blatantly illegal actions, such as plying athletes with cocaine. It is absolutely essential to the academic-athletic balance in universities that these kinds of people not be allowed to function with university sanction, and the coach must be the first to champion the cause of antiboosterism. At the same time, well-meaning alumni have much to offer university athletic programs, and it would not be prudent for the coach to turn these people away. Knowing the good guys from the guys in black unfortunately is not an easy distinction for the coach to make, and no program is available to tell which is which. Needless to say, alumni should be encouraged to support their teams and universities; they should never be encouraged or allowed to subvert the ultimate reason why universities exist, namely academics.

Undoubtedly other role demands are made on coaches, depending on the level at which they function. The roles described here at least create some idea of why coaching is such a demanding profession. By way of summary, perhaps Sabock (1979) says it best when he suggests that the good coach will be all of the following: teacher, disciplinarian, salesperson, public relations specialist, diplomat, organizer, role model, psychologist, leader, judge and jury, mother or father figure, dictator, politician, actor, fundraiser, director, field general, equipment manager, trainer, community citizen, and citizen of the school, university, or organization. With these challenges in mind, it is easy to see why coaches undertake such a career. It is equally easy to see why there are not many old, venerable salts in the sometimes stormy seas of coaching.

COACHING BURNOUT

One possible outcome of prolonged stress associated with coaching is emotional and physical exhaustion; this exhausted state has often been referred to as *burnout*. Burnout is most certainly not unique to the coaching profession; it is a well-documented phenomenon in a variety of work settings. Freudenberger (1974), a psychoanalyst, discussing burnout in the context of clinical settings, has defined burnout as a "state of fatigue or frustration brought about by a devotion to a cause, way of life, or relationship that failed to produce expected reward" (Freudenberger, 1980, p. 13). Maslach (1976) has expanded the work of Freudenberger within the human services arena and, among other things, created the Maslach Burnout Inventory as a measure of the syndrome. To Maslach, burnout is defined as "loss of concern for the people with whom one is working" (p. 16). To Cherniss (1980), burnout takes place when there is an imbalance between demands and available coping resources, thereby causing stress and its numerous by-products. Though there is no clear consensus as to what burnout actually is, most authorities agree that the phenomenon is real.

Smith's Cognitive-Affective Model of Athletic Burnout

In 1986, Ronald Smith introduced the nuances of burnout to sport psychology with an innovative and comprehensive conceptual model. According to Smith, burnout is a reaction to chronic stress and is made up of physical, mental, and behavioral components. The interaction of this assortment of environmental and personal

variables causes burnout. Smith has laid out his model showing the parallel relationships among *situational, cognitive, physiologic,* and *behavioral* components of stress and burnout. This conceptual model can be seen in figure 12.3. Essentially, Smith states that burnout occurs when the available resources are insufficient to meet the demands being placed on the system by the various sources of life stress. Concurrently, there will be a cognitive appraisal of the stress, and the resultant emotional responses will be tempered by how the demands are assessed, an appraisal of what resources are available to deal with the demands, the likely consequences if the demands are not met, and the personal meaning of the

Figure 12.3: **A Conceptual Model for Burnout**

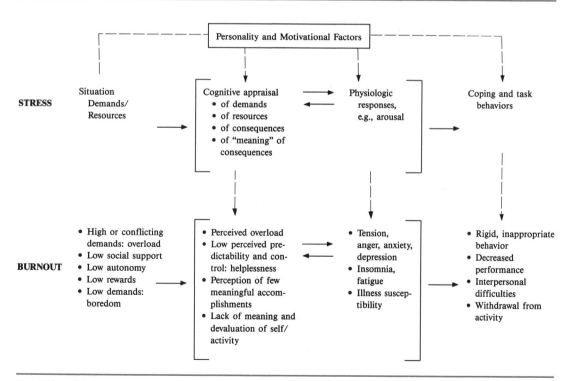

Note: This model shows the parallel relationships assumed to exist among situational, cognitive, physiologic, and behavioral components of stress and burnout. Individual differences in motivation and personality are assumed to influence all of the components.

Source: Smith (1986).

demands for the individual. *Self-efficacy, expectancy of success, self-concept,* and a host of other variables discussed in earlier chapters all come into play at this point in the Smith model. The third part of the model comes into play if danger or harm is feared, and this is the physiologic component. Finally, a variety of coping behaviors, some positive and others counterproductive, will be manifested as moderated by other components of the model. One of these counterproductive behaviors is burnout. In offering his model, Smith has raised some interesting questions concerning the operationalizing of burnout, its measurement, its epidemiological properties, and related causative and moderator variables.

Causes of Burnout

Taking the Job Too Seriously

Probably the single biggest causative factor in coaching burnout is taking oneself too seriously. Coaching is an important challenge, but there is more to life than work. Achieving a balance in life's various demands, and keeping work in perspective, would seem to be a highly preventive first step in avoiding burnout.

Problem Parents

Parents, as stated earlier, constitute a considerable source of stress. When the coach-parent relationship gets out of proportion, stress is generated that can ultimately be a part of coaching burnout.

Problem Athletes

Darrell Royal, a most successful football coach in a winning tradition established at the University of Texas, retired from coaching at a relatively early age, professing symptoms of burnout. One of the contributing factors was the loss of interest in coddling eighteen-year-old prima donnas during recruiting. Getting young people to choose the particular coach's school,

keeping them academically eligible, and getting the most out of their often immense athletic talents is a challenging task, and is made considerably more demanding by problem athletes.

Disenchantment

When the thrill of coaching disappears for whatever reason, burnout cannot be far behind. The notion of a career change becomes prominent in the coach's thoughts.

Pressure to Win

Losing seasons (or strings of them) are frustrating for people with the preexisting fascination with winning that characterizes coaches. Also, a losing season when preseason expectancies have been extremely high is disconcerting.

Other Pressures

Lack of appreciation by administrators, family pressures, too many coaching and teaching duties, little monetary reward, and having to share strained resources with other programs in and out of athletics all take their toll on coaches.

Psychological Factors

In a somewhat different vein, Vealey, Udry, Zimmerman, and Soliday (1992) looked at some of the preceding situational causes of burnout, but added state anxiety to the mix. Vealey and her associates administered the State-Trait Anxiety Inventory (STAI), the Maslach Burnout Inventory (MBI), and a Demographic/Cognitive Appraisal Questionnaire to 381 high school and 467 college coaches in ten different sports; there were 640 males, 201 females, and 7 unknowns in the sample; the average age was 39.16 and mean years as a coach was 14.40. The high school coaches were from Ohio and the college coaches were drawn from a national coaching registry. Data analysis revealed that there was considerable burnout in this sample, perhaps as high as 29 percent of the males and 27 percent of the females. The biggest single predictor of

Pressures Associated with Coaching at the Collegiate and Professional Level

"Fame breeds exhaustion" says Menninger Clinic staff psychologist, Harriet Lerner (Breaking Point, 1995). One arena in which Lerner's sentiment seems to hold true is in big-time collegiate and professional basketball. In 1994 and 1995, a number of college coaches, including Ricky Byrdsong at Northwestern, Tim Grgurich at the University of Nevada at Las Vegas, and Mike Krzyzewski at Duke, were notable casualties of job-related coaching stress. At the professional level, the difficulties in dealing with problem athletes, such as Vernon Maxwell of the Houston Rockets and Dennis Rodman of the San Antonio Spurs, during the 1995 NBA playoffs, illustrate just one of the many stresses facing those coaches and their peers.

The stresses and strains of coaching in college and professional sports increasingly grace the headlines of our sports pages. A partial accounting of the causes for this phenomenon can be ascertained from quotes from prominent basketball coaches who are currently trying to survive the "win-at-all-costs" pressures from administrators, alumni, fans, the media, and owners (quotes from other observers of the basketball scene are also illustrative and have been added for emphasis).

> Why the recent wave of burned-out basketball coaches? Sports gives them tremendous responsibilities but, ultimately, little control. Coaches can only coach; they can't actually run the plays. But if the team loses, they still get fired. (Bureau Report in *Time* magazine)

> I don't want this to sound like I'm comparing what we do to war, because I'm not. But this job is a lot like it was for those guys over in Vietnam. If you're not careful, it can really turn you into somebody else, somebody you don't want to be. (Houston Rockets Coach, Rudy Tomjanovich)

> And I think in a lot of ways, sometimes you have to compromise—compromise your coaching values and your coaching philosophy—just to accommodate people and make things work. And that's the toughest thing about it, the tendency of this job to change you and your losing control of it. (New York Knicks Coach, Pat Riley)

> The problem starts because you've got a lot of young people with huge egos. They are corporations in short pants. And they have been pampered all their lives. (Ex-NBA Coach Chuck Daly)

> There's a certain aspect of coaching a professional team that leads one to paranoia, because there are a lot of times when you feel like there is just you and your dog. (Los Angeles Laker Coach, Del Harris)

(Continued next page)

Highlight 12.2 (Continued)

Pressures Associated with Coaching at the Collegiate and Professional Level

Always there has been pressure on college coaches to win. But never, it seems, have there been so many complications: Pampered and hard-to-handle players, a pile-up of non-coaching responsibilities and unprecedented scrutiny from twenty-four-hour all-sports radio and other media. The toll they're taking is noticeable. (*USA Today* writer, Steve Wieberg)

It's always been a hard job, but it's more difficult now because of the cost of a franchise and the pressure to win. And the players are different—more demanding, more money. It takes a special guy to do a good job. (Golden State Warriors Coach, Don Nelson)

When you're a surrogate father for 14, 15 kids, you're shackled with this mind-boggling responsibility. (University of Virginia Basketball Coach, Terry Holland)

You spend a great part of your time in activities that have nothing to do with coaching, and many times coaches aren't qualified to deal with those areas. You're dealing with drugs, agents, gambling, academics, all the spillovers from everyday society. (Ex-college coach, George Raveling)

Sources: Boeck (1995); "Breaking Point" (1995); "Coaching Exodus Sends Big Eight Reeling" (1994); Sefko (1995); Weiberg (1995); "What They Say About Coaching" (1994); "Working Your Nerves: The Toughest Jobs" (1995).

burnout by far was state anxiety. This finding was particularly salient when male and female coaches were categorized as high or low in burnout as defined by the MBI; high burnout coaches of both sexes reported significantly more state anxiety. Interestingly, actual time spent in coaching was not predictive of burnout, a finding that ran counter to the research hypothesis as well as Maslach's earlier work in other applied settings. Finally, Vealey et al. conclude that their findings are partially supportive of the theoretical framework suggested by Smith.

Another attempt to introduce personality variables into the study of coaching burnout was made by Kelley (1994). Like Vealey et al., Kelley used the MBI to assess burnout in 131 male and 118 female NCAA Division III and NAIA baseball and softball coaches. The psychological variable studied was hardiness, a construct introduced to the literature by Kobasa (Kobasa, 1988; Kobasa, Maddi, and Courington, 1981). Hardiness is characterized by three factors: control, commitment, and challenge. *Control* refers to the tendency of the hardy individual to believe that he or she can influence the course of life events. *Commitment* refers to approaching life with a sense of purpose, a healthy curiosity, and willingness to invest oneself in relationships. As for *challenge,* the hardy personality believes that change rather than stability is the norm; as such, changes are seen as interesting, positive, and an impetus for additional growth. Kobasa's 1988 Third Generation Hardiness Test was used to arrive at a hardiness score for each coach in Kelley's sample. As has been reported elsewhere, coaches in this sample reported high levels of burnout. As for hardiness, it was predictive of burnout; male and female coaches who were low in psychological hardiness reported high levels of burnout and less job satisfaction in general. It was concluded that this research was supportive of the previous work on hardiness, and its efficacy as a personality construct in burnout research was also demonstrated.

The research efforts of Vealey et al. and Kelley are groundbreaking in that they represent an attempt to bring personality variables into play in the understanding of coaching burnout. Obviously, other work linking personality variables and coaching burnout is needed to expand our understanding of the phenomenon.

Effects of Burnout

According to Pate, Rotella, and McClenaghan (1984), the effects of burnout will be seen in the two areas closest to the coach—athletes and family—and the two interact in a circular fashion that multiplies as both relationships deteriorate. Pate et al. further state that *three strategies for coping* with alienation resulting from burnout will become dominant. The first tendency is to *blame the athletes* for the existing problems, looking at them as being low in ability or low in motivation. The second blaming response is to look inward (self-blame), thereby attributing the problems to *lack of coaching ability.* The third available blaming strategy is to point the accusing finger at *the situation itself.* Administrators, lack of overall support, and emphasis on more preferred sport programs become sources of blame for difficulties. The net result of these three blaming strategies is that the coach will sink into despondent mediocrity or

make a career change aimed at restoring motivation and mental well-being.

Prevention of Burnout

A well-rounded life is the key to avoiding burnout. Taking various aspects of one's life equally seriously is most important; letting coaching duties take over to the exclusion of family, friends, and other aspects of life simply will not work in the long run. Burnout in the face of unidimensionality of perspective is, if not inevitable, highly likely.

Maintaining an awareness that *no coach is immune to burnout* is an important preventive measure. Winners and losers alike can burn out; minor sport coaches are not exempt from the burnout so often associated with coaching in major sports; also, burnout is not the exclusive province of collegiate or professional coaches. It can happen at all levels of coaching. Finally, burnout is not an exclusively male phenomenon; Caccese and Mayerberg (1984), in a study of 138 male and 93 female coaches from NCAA and AIAW Division I, found that female coaches reported significantly higher levels of emotional exhaustion and lower levels of personal accomplishment than did members of a comparable male sample. Clearly, female coaches are susceptible to coaching burnout, perhaps even more so than their male counterparts.

Keeping one's *physical health* at an optimal level is an important inoculation against burnout. Coaches who are healthy and fit are likely to feel good, radiate enthusiasm, and serve as an inspiration to their athletes. This overall sense of well-being is contagious; others sense their enthusiasm, take it in, return it to them, and a cycle of enthusiasm is generated and reinforcement of good health is provided on a good maintenance schedule.

Having *associations with others* who understand the coaching situation is important. Other coaches know only too well what the individual

Highlight
12.3

A Measure of Burnout

Maslach and Jackson have developed a measure of burnout, the Maslach Burnout Inventory (MBI) (Maslach and Jackson, 1981), that has received much attention in assessing the presence of the condition among coaches and athletes. The MBI is composed of twenty-two items designed to measure both frequency and intensity of feelings, and consists of three subscales: Emotional Exhaustion (EE), Depersonalization (D), and Personal Accomplishment (PA). By reversing the direction of the scoring of PA, which is the inverse of EE and D, the result is that the higher the score, the greater the degree of burnout on all three subscales. Studies aimed at demonstrating the reliability and validity of the MBI from the standpoint of psychometric theory have been conducted by Abu-Hilal and Salameh in Jordan (1992) and Walkey and Green (1992) in New Zealand. In both studies, the factorial validity of the MBI was supported with only minor caveats.

Early studies in the area of burnout and coaching in which the MBI has been used with favorable results were reported by Caccese and Mayerberg (1984), Capel (1986), and Capel, Sisley, and Desertrain (1987). Caccese and Mayerberg indicated that female coaches in their study reported significantly higher levels of emotional exhaustion (EE) and significantly lower levels of personal accomplishment (PA) than did the male coaches they surveyed. The largest gender differences were found on the item, "I feel frustrated by my job," insofar as frequency was concerned. In terms of intensity, "I feel burned out by my job" showed the largest difference. Overall, however, none of the two groups reported any excessive amount of burnout. Capel studied athletic trainers using the MBI and found little evidence for burnout among these allied professionals. Capel, Sisley, and Desertrain, in a study of high school basketball coaches from six western states, found burnout to be at a low to medium level. Nevertheless, there were burned out coaches in the Capel et al. sample.

Smith (1986), pointing to other successful sport-specific measures that have been outgrowths of assessment devices aimed at nonsport populations, has issued a call for a sport-specific conceptualization and measurement of burnout.

Sources: Abu-Hilal and Salameh (1992); Caccese and Mayerberg (1984); Capel (1986); Capel, Sisley, and Desertrain (1987); Maslach and Jackson (1981); Smith (1986); Walkey and Green (1992).

coach is going through, and they can serve as sources of tension release. Pate et al. (1984) calls this "blowing out," referring to the process as one whereby coaches selectively release tension by letting out frustrations and stresses in the presence of others who will understand these occasional outbursts.

Maintaining a sense of humor is crucial to preventing burnout. Being able to laugh at oneself and the frailties and foibles of others in and out of athletics can be a real tension reducer. There is much humor in athletics, and athletes and coaches are rich sources of such material. Daily quotes and numerous books on the lighter side of sports are commonplace. The coach who contributes to this literature and who appreciates it when coined by others has to be a step up in burnout avoidance.

Undoubtedly, other ingredients of the mentally healthy person merit discussion. Suffice it to say, however, that the points covered here are basic to keeping one's head on the old shoulders when all others around seem to be losing theirs, and the end result will be an enjoyable athletic experience for players, coaches, and fans alike.

PERSONALITY OF THE COACH

In all frankness, little is known about the personality of coaches. Early studies of the subject have taken two directions, one having to do with the supposed authoritarian nature of coaches and the other with Machiavellianism or their tendency to be manipulative in social situations.

Authoritarianism

Ogilvie and Tutko (1966) started the ball rolling with their study of sixty-four coaches from the four major American sports: football, basketball, baseball, and track. Based on his

earlier work with Ogilvie, Tutko and an associate (Tutko and Richards, 1971), identified five types of coaches, one being the hard-nosed or authoritarian coach. Gallon (1980) summarizes the authoritarian coach of Tutko and Richards as follows:

> These coaches leave no doubt about who is boss. They possess well-formulated goals, know exactly what they are trying to achieve, and expect and demand certain responses from those under them. They take the credit or blame for both achievement and mistakes. The advantages and disadvantages of authoritarianism are the same as those for any dictatorship. Most coaches fall into this category (P. 19)

The veracity of Gallon's assertions is subject to question, but the last statement about most coaches being authoritarians has been a popularly accepted one for many years.

Scott (1971) has stated that the relaxed and understanding coach is far outnumbered by those who are rigid and authoritarian. He also indicates that extensive psychological testing has shown coaches to be among the most authoritarian vocational groupings, often outscoring policemen and career military officers on measures of the trait. The "extensive psychological testing" alluded to by Scott refers to conclusions drawn from Ogilvie's and Tutko's 1966 work cited earlier. However, many conclusions from Ogilvie and Tutko's work have been overdrawn and may not be at all representative of coaches beyond the sixty-four in their study.

Research by LeUnes and Nation (1982) may have relevance to the issue of coaching authoritarianism. One source of coaches are the players who choose to enter the profession upon graduation. Our 1982 study of one group of collegiate football players shows that, when compared with non-football-playing peers, the football players are overwhelmingly authoritarian. These data are presented in table 12.3.

Table 12.3
Authoritarian Dimensions: Mean Scores Across Groups

F-Scale Factor	Groups		
	Nonathletes	High School Athletes	College Athletes
Conventionalism	11.25_A	12.20_B	12.77_B
Authoritarian Submission	22.32_A	23.34_B	25.00_B
Authoritarian Aggression	22.75_A	26.29_B	26.52_B
Anti-Intraception	10.87_A	$11.56_{A,B}$	11.91_B
Superstition and Stereotypy	15.42_A	16.02_A	18.07_B
Power and Toughness	20.58_A	$21.64_{A,B}$	22.79_B
Destructiveness and Cynicism	6.28_A	6.15_A	6.84_B
Projectivity	13.00_A	13.05_A	16.18_B
Sex	8.57_A	9.61_B	10.13_B
Total Score	131.17_A	139.95_B	149.84_C

Note: Row means with different subscripts are significantly different ($p < .05$).

Source: LeUnes and Nation (1982).

If one assumes that a potential coaching pool is represented in the sample of football players, it follows that the likelihood that such a personality is authoritarian is fairly high. On the other hand, there were a number of low-authoritarian players in the sample, and these players may go into coaching rather than the authoritarian ones. For the time being, it seems sufficient to say that the stereotype of a coach as an authoritarian personality is not strongly supported, but the issue warrants further investigation.

Machiavellianism

Christie and Geis (1970) are responsible for furthering scientific interest in the *Machiavellian personality*. Drawing from the writings of Machiavelli (*The Prince* and *The Discourses*), Christie and Geis devised a scale purporting to measure Machiavellianism, or what Robinson and Shaver (1973, p. 590) see as "a person's strategy for dealing with people, especially the degree to which he feels other people are manipulable in interpersonal situations." Scott (1971) has stated that coaches as a group are rather insensitive in their dealings with others and are prone to manipulate players and others in order to win. This assertion has been challenged by Sage in a pair of studies conducted in the mid-1970s. In the first study (Sage, 1972a), Sage administered the Machiavellian Scale to 496 college and high school coaches and a sample of male college students from fourteen different universities. No significant differences were found among the various coaching groups and the university students except on age and years of experience; interestingly, the relationship was negative with older more experienced coaches scoring lower than their younger contemporaries. Additionally, there was no indication of even a mild relationship between win-loss record and Machiavellianism, a finding also substantiated by Walsh and Carron (1977) in their survey of a Canadian coaching sample.

Sage's second study (Sage, 1972b) took a slightly different tack, with the Machiavellian measure being replaced by the Polyphasic Values

Inventory (PVI) (Roscoe, 1965), a scale designed to assess conservatism on a variety of philosophical, political, economic, educational, social, religious, and personal-moral issues. A group of randomly selected coaches (n = 246) were then compared with large numbers of college students (n = 4,005) and businessmen (n = 479). Coaches were found to be considerably more conservative than the college students and generally more liberal than the businessmen. Sage concluded that coaches are in fact conservative but probably no more so than males in most other professions.

When all is said and done, coaches are probably a bit authoritarian and conservative, but probably no more so than members of a number of other professions. Also, being authoritarian may not be all bad. At times, one firm hand has to be in control of things. The meetings between coaches and players at critical times in athletic contests call for someone taking control, and that person often is and should be the coach. Finally, coaches may be authoritarian or conservative in the job situation because it serves them well, but they may not be that way at all in dealings with others outside of work.

The preceding discussion summarizes two avenues of research into the coaching personality and are not compelling in terms of conclusiveness. Also, *authoritarianism* and *Machiavellianism* represent only two of many personality dimensions that characterize coaches and saliently point up the need for much more extensive research in the area of personality and coaching.

COACHING AND YOUTH SPORT

Much of the discussion up to this point has centered around the male coach working at a fairly sophisticated level in the male-dominated major team sports. However, there are other demanding coaching situations not involving older male

players and coaches. One of the more prominent of these situations is the *coaching of children.* Youth athletes have become more significant in the sport world, and good coaching is vital to their successful participation.

Lombardo (1986) indicates that there are more than 4 million youth coaches in the United States, many of whom are not qualified to properly deal with children regardless of how well intentioned they may be. To quote Lombardo: "Many leagues are totally dependent upon volunteers and, short of being a convicted felon, are all welcomed" (p. 199). Perhaps things are not quite so grim as portrayed by Lombardo, but his position probably contains an element of truth.

The Coaching Behavior Assessment System (CBAS)

In an effort to reduce the magnitude of the problem of well-intentioned but poorly prepared coaches in youth sport, a number of coaching improvement schemes have been developed. One of the leaders in coaching improvement is the innovative *Coaching Behavior Assessment System (CBAS)* developed by Smith, Smoll, and Hunt (1977). The CBAS was developed to allow for direct observation and subsequent coding of coaching behaviors. The twelve behavioral categories in the CBAS were divided into two subcategories, *reactive or elicited* and *spontaneous or emitted behaviors.* The *reactive category* refers generally to player behaviors whereas the *spontaneous category* refers primarily to game-related or game-irrelevant acts. These various behaviors can be seen in detail in table 12.4.

Smoll and Smith (1984) have summarized the later research on the CBAS. After refining the CBAS, Smoll and Smith used it in a study of fifty-one male coaches and 542 players in the Seattle, Washington, area. Trained observers coded an average of 1,122 behaviors per coach over a four-game period. Results indicated, among other things, that two-thirds of the coaches' behaviors fell within the three instructional and support categories, and the rate of punitive behaviors was generally quite low. The correlation between coaches' ratings of the frequency with which they used a particular behavior and their awareness of the fact was low and insignificant except for the category of punishment. Coaches do seem aware of their use of punitive approaches but are less aware of other behaviors.

Other conclusions drawn from the Smoll and Smith study were that players evaluated their teammates and the sport of baseball more posi-

Table 12.4
CBAS Response Categories

Class I. Reactive Behaviors	
Responses to desirable performance	
Reinforcement	A positive, rewarding reaction, verbal or nonverbal, to a good play or good effort
Nonreinforcement	Failure to respond to a good performance
Responses to mistakes	
Mistake-contingent encouragement	Encouragement given to a player following a mistake
Mistake-contingent technical instruction	Instructing or demonstrating to a player how to correct a mistake
Punishment	A negative reaction, verbal or nonverbal, following a mistake
Punitive technical instruction	Technical instruction that is given in a punitive or hostile manner following a mistake
Ignoring mistakes	Failure to respond to a player mistake
Response to misbehavior	
Keeping control	Reactions intended to restore or maintain order among team members
Class II. Spontaneous Behaviors	
Game-related	
General technical instruction	Spontaneous instruction in the techniques and strategies of the sport (not following a mistake)
General encouragement	Spontaneous encouragement that does not follow a mistake
Organization	Administrative behavior that sets the stage for play by assigning duties, responsibilities, positions, etc.
Game-irrelevant	
General communication	Interactions with players unrelated to the game

Source: Smoll and Smith (1984).

Behavioral Guidelines of Youth Sports Coaches

Ron Smith and Frank Smoll have generated some of the more useful research in the area of coaching youth participants. One important outcome of their work has been the creation of a set of guidelines for working with young athletes that are everyday, sensible applications of behavioral principles discussed earlier in chapter 3.

I. *Reactions to player behaviors and game situations:*
   A. *Good plays*
      Do: Reinforce! Do so immediately. Let the players know that you appreciate and value their efforts. Reinforce effort as much as you do results. Look for positive things, reinforce them, and you'll see them increase. Remember, whether the kids show it or not, the positive things you say and do stick with them.
      Don't: Take their efforts for granted.
   B. *Mistakes, screw-ups, boneheaded plays, and all the things that pros seldom do*
      Do: Encourage immediately after mistakes. That's when the kid needs encouragement most. Also, give *corrective instruction* on how to do it right, but always do so in an encouraging manner. Do this by emphasizing not the bad thing that just happened, but the good things that will happen if the kid follows your instruction (the "why" of it). This will motivate the player positively to correct the mistake rather than motivate him/her negatively to avoid failure and your disapproval.
      Don't: Punish when things go wrong. Punishment isn't just yelling at kids; it can be any indication of disapproval, tone of voice, or action. Kids respond much better to a positive approach. Fear of failure is reduced if you work to reduce fear of punishment.
   C. *Misbehaviors, lack of attention*
      Do: Maintain order by establishing clear expectations. Emphasize that during a game all members of the team are part of the game, even those on the bench. Use reinforcement to strengthen team participation. In other words, try to prevent misbehaviors from occurring by using the positive approach to strengthen their opposites.
      Don't: Constantly nag or threaten the kids in order to prevent chaos. Don't be a drill sergeant. If a kid refuses to cooperate, quietly remove him or her from the bench for a while. Don't use physical

(Continued next page)

Highlight 12.4 (Continued)

Behavioral Guidelines of Youth Sports Coaches

measures (e.g., running laps). The idea here is that if you establish clear behavioral guidelines early and work to build team spirit in achieving them, you can avoid having to repeatedly *keep control.* Remember, kids want clear guidelines and expectations, but they don't want to be regimented. Try to achieve a healthy balance.

II. *Getting positive things to happen:*
Do: Give instruction. Establish your role as a teacher. Try to structure participation as a learning experience in which you're going to help the kids develop their abilities. Always give instruction in a positive fashion. Satisfy your players' desire to become the best athletes they can be. Give instruction in a clear, concise manner; if possible, demonstrate how to do it.
Do: Give encouragement. Encourage effort; don't demand results. Use it selectively so that it is meaningful. Be supportive without acting like a cheerleader.
Do: Concentrate on the game. Be "in the game" with the players. Set a good example for team unity.
Don't: Give either instruction or encouragement in a sarcastic or degrading manner. Make a point, then leave it. Don't let "encouragement" become irritating to the players.

Source: Smoll and Smith (1984).

tively if they played for coaches who used high levels of reinforcement and support, self-esteem was enhanced by the positive coaches, positive coaches were liked much better than the more punitive ones, and win-loss record was generally unrelated to the youngster's feelings about their coaches.

The most recent research from Smoll and Smith examined the impact of coaching behaviors on self-esteem in Little League baseball players (Smoll, Smith, Barnett, and Everett, 1993). In this study, Smoll et al. compared the

results of behavioral training of eight baseball coaches with that of a no-treatment control group of ten coaches. Consistent with previous findings, the trained coaches were evaluated more positively by their players and the players reported having more fun despite no differences in win-loss records when compared with controls. Also, boys with low self-esteem (as determined by a preseason assessment) who played for a trained coach demonstrated significant increases in self-esteem over the season. Unfortunately, low self-esteem boys playing for the untrained coaches did not show concomitant improvements in self-esteem. The efficacy of the Smoll and Smith methodology appears to be incontrovertibly supported, and should be implemented immediately, with slight local variations where necessary, in all youth sport programs. There appears to be no substitute for good training of coaches in terms of enhancing the youth sport experience.

The logical outgrowth of this research was the creation of a training program for youth coaches; Smoll and Smith have labeled their training program *Coach Effectiveness Training (CET)*. To validate the effectiveness of CET, a three-hour program, thirty-one Little League baseball coaches were randomly assigned to an experimental (training) group and to a control group that did not receive the purported benefits of CET. Interviews with 325 players at the end of the season were supportive of CET. The trained coaches used more reinforcement and less punishment, were liked better by the players, and were seen as better teachers. Additionally, self-esteem gains were seen in the players who had CET-trained coaches. Significantly, there were no differences in win-loss records of the two groups, indicating that the gains afforded by CET are primarily expressed in the psychosocial domain.

Coach training programs such as that developed by Smoll and his associates can be influential in improving coaching success at the youth level. As a result, there have been a number of other systems developed to improve youth coaching, and we shall discuss them now.

Other Approaches to Improving Youth Coaching

Murphy (1986) mentions four other programs besides the CET. One of these is the *National Youth Sporting Coaches Association (NYSCA)*, founded in 1981 and headquartered in West Palm Beach, Florida. The NYSCA, an agency of the United Way, involves five to six hours of training through the use of videotapes. Items such as first aid, the psychology of children, and how to organize effective practices are only a few of the topics covered by NYSCA. As of 1989, more than 150,000 youth coaches have participated in the NYSCA training.

Another well-received training program is the American Sport Education Program (ASEP), originally known as the American Coaching Effectiveness Program (ACEP). Founded at the University of Illinois in 1981 by Rainer Martens, ASEP's motto is "Athletes first, winning second." Attesting to the popularity of ASEP, it is used by more than one thousand high schools, two hundred colleges and universities, 250 youth organizations, and forty national sport organizations and governing bodies. ASEP offers courses in three areas: the *volunteer level* for those who work in some capacity with youth sport, *leader level* for those in interscholastic sport, and *master level* for those who have completed the second level program and want advanced training. Goals for ASEP coaching programs include developing a sportsmanship-based coaching philosophy, improving coach-athlete communication, planning and teaching improvement of sport skills, teaching about risk management, and improving first aid skills.

The *Youth Sport Institute (YSI),* an outgrowth of the 1978 Senate-mandated Michigan study concerning youth sport mentioned in chapter 11, is located at Michigan State University. YSI sponsors the Program for Athletic Coaches' Education (PACE), an educational enterprise created specifically for interscholastic coaches.

In Canada, the *Canadian National Certification Program (CNCP)* serves as an invaluable source of guidance for coaches of youth. CNCP is a five-level program ranging from Level 1, the grass roots level, to Level 5, in which youth are being trained to represent their home country in international competition. Emphasis at all levels is placed on theory, technique, and application.

More and more provinces and municipalities in Canada are requiring CNCP training for youth coaches.

It is apparent that a healthy movement is afoot in the United States and Canada to insure that young people are provided with as good an early sport experience as is possible. Training of volunteer coaches through the various available programs is a necessary step in the process of improving youth sport. It is hoped that all youth coaches in the not too distant future will be graduates of one of the training programs in operation today.

THE FEMALE COACH

Two events greatly shaped the face of women's sports in the 1970s. One was an explosion of participation on the part of young females at both the interscholastic and intercollegiate levels. By the mid-1980s, 1.8 million women were competing at the interscholastic level (Perry, 1986). These participation figures represent a five- to sixfold increase from 1970 to the mid-1980s. To put these data in another perspective, the percentage of high school athletes who were female rose during this fifteen-year time period from 7 to 36 (Eitzen and Pratt, 1989). Perry (1986) indicates that another 150,000 females participated in athletics at the intercollegiate level.

A second factor in promoting female sport involvement was the implementation of the Title IX legislation in the early 1970s. Though the intent of the legislation was to assist in the achievement of parity between men and women across the broad spectrum of life activities to include sport, a reverse effect has been generated for female coaches who find themselves on the outside looking in with regard to career options in the coaching field. As you will remember, these unintended consequences of Title IX were discussed at some length in chapter 10.

The Female Interscholastic/ Intercollegiate Coach

At the interscholastic level, Hart and Mathes (1982) reported that the percentage of women coaching girls' teams in Wisconsin dropped from 92 in 1975 to 46 in 1981. In assessing the situation in Colorado, Schafer (1984) reported that 89 percent of coaches of women's high school teams in 1973–1974 were themselves women, whereas this figure dropped to 41 percent by 1983–1984. In a study conducted in Virginia, Heishman, Bunker, and Tutwiler (1990) report a 271 percent increase from 1972 to 1987 in coaching opportunities for women's sport; at the same time, the number of female coaches declined from 80 percent to slightly under 44 percent during that fifteen-year period. A research effort by True (1983) isolated similar trends; data from eight states indicated a 40 to 50 percent decrease in women coaches depending on which state was being considered. Acosta and Carpenter (1985), in reviewing the coaching situation in the states of Illinois, Kansas, Nebraska, and Wisconsin, found nearly identical declines, generally in the 40 to 50 percent range.

A comparable trend toward a reduction in the number of female coaches at the intercollegiate level was first noted by Holmen and Parkhouse (1981), who found that the number of female coaching positions in colleges and universities increased by 37 percent from 1974 to 1979. However, during the same time period the number of female coaches dropped by 20 percent. Interestingly and perhaps prophetically, the number of male coaches coaching female athletic teams grew by a whopping 137 percent. Data from Brewington and White (1988) offer little consolation; since the early 1970s, the number of female coaches has dropped from 90 to 50 percent. Accompanying data indicate that the number of female sports administrators had declined during the same time period from 90 to 15 percent.

While there is no denying that female coaches have been supplanted by males in substantial numbers over the past several decades, it does appear that things may be stabilizing or

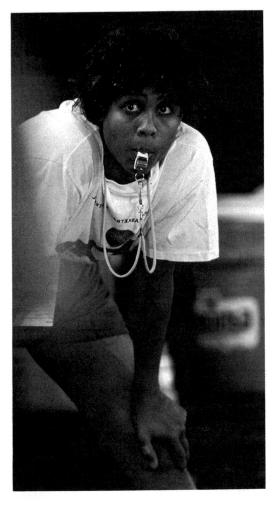

Ranked by many as the finest women's basketball player in history, Cheryl Miller was head coach of the women's basketball team at the University of Southern California. A four-time NCAA All-American as a player on the USC team, she was also an Olympic gold medalist in 1984. In May of 1994, she was inducted into the Basketball Hall of Fame.

even improving. Herwig (1994) indicates a 1.3 percent gain for female coaches at the collegiate level from 1992 to 1994; at the same time, there has been a 4.2 percent gain during the same time period in number of females administering women's sports programs. Also encouraging is the increase in the number of sports offered for women per NCAA school; in 1978, the average number of female sports per school was 5.61; in 1992, it was 7.02 percent, and an all-time high of 7.22 was reached in 1994.

Clearly, there have been some unintended shifts in the career patterns for female coaches over the past two decades. Their numbers have steadily declined at both the interscholastic and intercollegiate levels, though there is some evidence that the picture may be reversing itself ever so slightly. There can be no disputing the fact, however, that 79 percent of all athletic administrators involved in women's athletics are male, as are 50.6 percent of the coaches (Herwig, 1994). An inspection of some of the variables that may have led to this situation is therefore warranted.

Reasons for the Decline in the Number of Female Coaches

As we have seen, in the early 1970s most coaches of girls' or women's teams were female. According to Sisley and Capel (1986), this situation arose as a natural outgrowth of the existing girls' physical education classes and athletic associations. However, as these programs expanded in terms of popularity, finances, and public visibility, the number of women filling the existing coaching slots decreased and their positions were taken over by males. Why has this picture of declining female involvement in the coaching of other females evolved? One of the more credible explanatory proposals is that of Hart, Hasbrook, and Mathes (1986); it is their contention that one or a combination of each of the following factors is at the heart of the issue: (1) role conflict, (2) incomplete occupational socialization, and (3) outright sex discrimination.

Role conflict is an appealing, common sense explanatory mechanism because we would all agree that balancing the multiple demands of teacher, coach, wife, and mother represents quite a challenge for any woman. However, research by Locke and Massengale (1978) and Massengale (1980, 1981a, 1981b) suggests that role conflict is not the exclusive domain of female coaches; in fact, male coaches find the varying demands on their time and energy to be quite conflicting and stressful. Results of a survey of over four thousand high school coaches by Hasbrook, Hart, Mathes, and True (1990) found that males felt more affected by time constraints and resultant conflicts due to family responsibilities than did the females in their sample. "Incompatibility with family life" was the fourth most common reason for leaving coaching for males in their sample and sixth most common for the females. Interestingly, 87 percent of the male coaches were married and 42 percent of the females. The latter statistic may account for the role conflict difference noted by Hasbrook et al. In any event, it is plausible that role conflict is an important issue for both male and female coaches. As such, it probably serves only a minor role in explaining the partial decline of the female coach.

It has been suggested that failure in various work settings may be a function of incomplete occupational socialization, a concept proposed by Burlingame (1972). In this model, the individuals involved simply have not acquired the knowledge, skills, and values to be successful at their jobs. The lack of expectancy of becoming a coach, the dearth of female role models for coaching, and a shortage of top competitive experience all contribute to the failure of female coaches to acquire the fundamental knowledge, skills, and values so critical to success. Though appealing at an intellectual level, there is some evidence to suggest that at least part of this model is not true. For example, studies by Anderson and Gill (1983), Eitzen and Pratt (1989), and Hasbrook et al. (1990) indicate that, at least for the sport of basketball, female coaches at both the interscholastic and collegiate levels had more varsity playing experience than did male coaches. However, Sisley and Capel did not find this difference to be a factor for a variety of other sport coaches they sampled in Oregon. These conflicting results may be due to a host of extraneous variables, but they do point out the need for research in this aspect of the coaching experience. Also, playing experience is only one relatively small aspect of occupational socialization for coaching, and there is much to ponder regarding Burlingame's notion as it relates to the profession of coaching.

The third possible explanation, *sex discrimination,* is also an attractive one, but little again has been done to substantiate or refute such a position. Mathes (1982) reported that female coaches feel restricted to minor sports, believe their mobility to be limited in terms of becoming head coaches or athletic directors, and generally see coaching as a limited source of job opportunity. Mathes also reported other areas in which inequities are seen, particularly in pay, general support, and facilities.

Evidence in several of the areas cited by Mathes indicates that sex discrimination is alive and well in interscholastic and intercollegiate sport, particularly but not exclusively in hiring and retention practices. For example, Heishman, Bunker, and Tutwiler (1990), in their study of coaching changes from 1971–1972 to 1986–1987 in Virginia, found that the sports where males replaced female coaches at the highest rates were track and field, basketball, and softball, in that order. On the other hand, female coaches were much less likely to be replaced in sports such as field hockey, gymnastics, volleyball, and tennis. Stangl and Kane (1990) found a strong relationship between sex of the athletic director and sex of coaches who were hired, resulting in what they call "homologous reproduction." Knoppers, Meyer, Ewing, and Forrest (1989) provide support for this relationship; they suggest that since athletic directors hire coaches, they serve as the "gatekeepers to the profession of coaching" (p. 358). Additional evidence bearing on this point is provided by Herwig (1994), who cites statistics indicating that 57 percent of coaches of NCAA programs are female when the athletic director is also a female.

The intimations of Knoppers et al. and Stangl and Kane give rise to the suspicion that a "good old boy" network may be operating in the hiring and retention of coaches and could account for some of the decline in numbers of female coaches. Conversely, Pastore and Meacci (1994) emphasize that the situation is exacerbated by the absence of a "good old girl" network. The data on other issues related to sex discrimination are less clear, but there is ample evidence that such practices do occur in interscholastic and intercollegiate sports.

A Final Note

A final point concerns male and female coaches and how they are perceived by athletes. Parkhouse and Williams (1986), in a study of eighty male and eighty female interscholastic basketball players in California, found a substantial sex bias favoring male coaches. Though this discovery of possible sex bias is somewhat at variance with earlier research (Cottle, 1982; Rikki and Cottle, 1984; Weinberg, Reveles, and Jackson, 1984), it may suggest that the decline in the number of female coaches is partially due to a "male is better" bias in evaluating coaching ability.

THE BLACK COACH

Black coaches are a rarity at all levels of competition, but their absence is most noticeable in the high profile world of the major collegiate and professional sports. In an early report, Yetman, Berghorn, and Thomas (1980) indicated that slightly over 5 percent of the head coaches in NCAA Division I college basketball were black. Another early summary ("Black Head Coaches," 1982) showed only thirty black head coaches in all major sports at predominantly white universities. Similarly, Latimer and Mathes (1985) studied the racial composition of forty-seven Division I colleges and found a total of eighty black coaches, only one of whom was a head coach. Interestingly, the social and educational background of these black coaches were similar to those of a comparable sample of white coaches. Also, the black coaches were almost always employed as coaches of athletes playing peripheral as opposed to central positions, a finding not inconsistent with results reported in some detail in chapter 9. More recent statistics ("Black Hiring," 1987) reveal that only 4.2 percent of 1,102 men's and women's programs in the top three NCAA divisions of intercollegiate football, basketball, baseball, and track had black head coaches. Even more recent statistics ("There's No Question," 1990) indicate that there were thirty-two black head coaches in predominantly white schools and seventeen others at predominantly black schools among the 293 Division I men's basketball programs. The basketball data are particularly striking when we consider the fact that less than 17 percent of the coaches are black in a sport where the ratio of black to white players is approximately 60–40. In women's collegiate basketball, of the sixty-four teams making the NCAA Division I playoffs in 1994, five were coached by a black male and five by black females ("Women's Hoops Scene," 1994). Interestingly, thirty-eight others were coached by white females; when the five black female coaches and one Asian female coach are added to this total, this means that forty-four of the final sixty-four teams were coached by females. Thus, the percentage of female coaches was 69

Slogans: An Alternate Way of Communicating with Athletes?

Coaches are well-known dispensers of slogans or aphorisms designed to push their charges to greater heights with regard to athletic performance. It is a rare coach who does not employ them around the locker room or in pregame speeches. We have attempted, however arbitrarily, to categorize some of our favorites gleaned from personal experience, talking with athletes and coaches, or reading the related literature.

EMPHASIS ON WINNING

Triumph is when try meets umph.
To explain a triumph, start with the first syllable.
Winning isn't everything, it's the only thing.
Winning beats anything that comes in second.

ATTITUDE/BELIEF IN WHAT YOU ARE DOING

You must believe to achieve.
It's the attitude, not the aptitude, that carries you to the altitude.
By failing to prepare yourself, you are prepared to fail.
Don't make excuses . . . make good.

MENTAL PREPARATION

Keep on your toes and you won't get caught flatfooted.
Good luck is what happens when preparation meets opportunity.
Landing on your feet sometimes requires that you use your head.
It takes a cool head to win a hot game.
Tough times never last, tough people do.

WORK ETHIC

The harder I work, the luckier I get.
If you can't put out, get out.
More sweat in training, less blood in combat.
It's easy to be ordinary, but it takes guts to excel.
Good, better, best; never rest until your good is better and your
    better best.

(Continued next page)

Highlight 12.5 (Continued)

Slogans: An Alternate Way of Communicating with Athletes?

TEAM ORIENTATION

There is no "I" in team.

There is no "U" in team.

Remember the banana . . . every time it leaves the bunch, it gets skinned.

A player doesn't make the team, the team makes the player.

United we stand, divided we fall.

ANIMAL EXHORTATIONS/COMPARISONS

Any nag can start, but it takes a thoroughbred to finish.

It's not the size of the dog in the fight, but the size of the fight in the dog.

A hungry dog hunts best.

You can't run a zoo without the animals.

He who flies with the owls at night cannot keep up with the eagles during the day.

---

percent, a figure quite a bit above what one would predict based on earlier discussion of the male-female coach issue.

At the professional level of play, a similar overall picture emerges. As of 1992, ("Baseball Gets 'C,'" 1993), black head coaches were 26 percent of the total in the NBA, 7 percent in the NFL, and 7 percent in major league baseball. Given the percentage of black athletes in these three sports (77, 68, and 17 percent respectively), there is clear underrepresentation of black coaches. A similar picture exists at all levels of the front offices of these same organizations.

The focus to this point has been entirely on the collegiate and professional levels involving the more visible sports. We are not aware at this point in time of any meaningful summary related to black coaches operating at the interscholastic level; this group might well be a research gold mine in terms of expanding the knowledge base concerning this most important issue.

COMMUNICATION AND COACHING

In all likelihood, the coach who communicates best is most often the winner in athletic contests. Traditional theory in the psychology of communication indicates that there are *four elements in the communication process:* the source, the message, the channel, and the receiver. The *source* is the person originating the communication, the coach in this case. The effectiveness of the coach will depend on such factors as credibility with his or her players, perceived competence, personal and psychological attractiveness, status, and power. The *message* pertains to the meaning being conveyed and may involve shrugs, facial expressions, vocal influences, and the use of sarcasm or sincerity. The *channel* refers to the method used, either verbal or nonverbal. The *receiver* obviously is the target for whom the message is intended, and such variables as intelligence, motivation, and personality will dictate how much and what is perceived. A representation of the interaction of these four components of communication can be seen in figure 12.4.

Mehrabian (1971) has indicated that message transmission is only slightly weighted by what is actually said; he says that any message is *7 percent verbal, 38 percent vocal emphasis,* and *55 percent facial expression.* Coaches should be aware that a lot of what they transmit to their players is nonverbal. Such things as *kinesics* (body language), *proxemics* (social distance or territoriality), and *paralanguage* (inflection or tone) become significant determinants of what is communicated. With regard to *kinesics,* visual gaze, posture, facial gestures, and hand movements are involved; in *proxemics,* personal space issues are paramount; in *paralanguage,* slow speech, fast speech, high pitch, sarcasm, and variable use of phrases are manipulated for

For this Little-League coach, kinesics (body language) and proxemics (social distance or territoriality) are important nonverbal components of communicating to his players.

desired effect. The effective coach motivates and educates through verbalizations, but is also aware of the strategic use of the various elements of kinesics, proxemics, and paralanguage.

THE COACH AND THE SPORT PSYCHOLOGIST

The role of the sport psychologist in assisting coaches is a highly ambiguous one. Traditionally, coaches have been skeptical of psychology in general. Others who have had contact with well-intentioned sport psychologists who were not able to produce or with outright charlatans using the title have added fuel to the anti-psychologist fire. However, coaches are becoming increasingly aware of the role of psychological

Figure 12.4: Interaction of Four Components of Communication

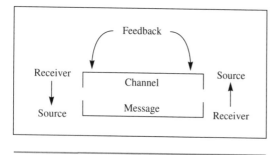

factors in physical performance and are also admitting that they do not have all the answers in this area. At the same time, sport psychologists have increasingly become attuned to their own assets and liabilities, and are offering their services to coaches and athletic teams in areas in which they can truly produce. Also, sport psychologists are increasingly cognizant of the need for extreme diplomacy in dealing with coaches and athletes. All of these attitudinal improvements should result in much more cooperation in the future between coaches and sport psychologists.

A necessary first step in the process of providing sport psychology services is *establishing credibility* with coaches. Lanning (1980) and Suinn (1986) offer a number of suggestions for effectiveness in the sport environment. The guidelines that follow are a synthesis of their various suggestions:

1. The interest of the sport psychologist in the problems of sport should be clearly evident.
2. The ability to objectively evaluate sport situations is critical to success.
3. An awareness is needed that, as the level of performance escalates, the problems of the coach and the sport psychologist concurrently increase.
4. The sport psychologist, as an outsider to athletes and coaches, must prove his or her skills to them.
5. The sport psychologist can have a substantial impact on assistant coaches, athletes, and others related to a team; diplomacy in dealing with these various persons is necessary.
6. A realization that each player and team is unique should guide the efforts of the sport psychologist.
7. Maximization of strengths and recognition of limitations is essential to effective functioning.
8. The role of the sport psychologist is always as psychologist and not as coach.

9. The sport psychologist serves as consultant, not as expert; he or she is a collaborator with others involved with the team or individual athlete.
10. The ability to listen is one of the most valuable tools of the sport psychologist.

If these guidelines are followed in a consistent fashion, the sport psychologist should increasingly become a contributing member in the attainment of athletic excellence. The future can be bright for the sport psychologist working hand in hand with coaches in an effort to make sport even more fun through increased standards of performance.

SUMMARY

1. With so much premium placed at all levels on winning, coaching has become a pressure-laden profession. The many pluses are offset by occupational hazards. Second-guessing by everyone who feels he or she is an expert on sport, the endless work schedule, the pressures of constant evaluation, the lack of job security, the strain on family life, and the fact that coaching is a terminal career are all drawbacks to entering and staying in the coaching business.
2. The qualities of the good coach include being knowledgeable about the sport, being a student of the game, having the ability to motivate athletes, being aware of individual differences in athletes, being a good listener, exercising discipline when necessary, leading by example, and being a goal setter.
3. Roles of the coach include getting along with management, being committed to the athletes, having a good working relationship with assistant coaches and being an advocate in their behalf, establishing contact with the various media, dealing with parents, fans, and boosters, and meeting a broad variety of

other demands necessary to success in coaching. The role of the coach in goal setting is a most important one.

4. Burnout is a common problem in many vocations, and the coaching profession is not exempt from the phenomenon.

5. Taking the job too seriously, having to deal with problem parents and problem athletes, losing the thrill of coaching, feeling the constant pressure always to win, and being underpaid and underappreciated are some of the more prominent situational causes of coaching burnout. Recently, psychological factors such as state anxiety and psychological hardiness have also been linked to burnout. High state anxious coaches and those low in hardiness appear to be susceptible to burnout. These two efforts represent an attempt to link burnout in coaches to psychological constructs, whereas the preponderance of the existing research has looked largely at situational variables.

6. The cognitive-affective model of athletic burnout proposed by Smith represents an attempt to add sophistication to the definition and assessment of the phenomenon.

7. Athletes and the immediate family will be most seriously affected by the burnout of a coach, and the two interact to exacerbate the problem.

8. Living a broadly based, rewarding life outside of work is an important preventive measure related to coaching burnout. Being aware that burnout can happen to anyone regardless of level of coaching or sex of the coach, keeping one's physical health at an optimum level, having friends with whom one can release tension, and maintaining a sense of humor are other important preventive measures.

9. Coaches have been widely assumed to be authoritarian, dogmatic, and Machiavellian. Research conducted in the 1970s and 1980s has not supported this widely accepted contention. Coaches appear to be generally conservative but probably are no more so than adults of similar age and education in a number of other vocations.

10. Many of the more than 4 million youth coaches in the United States are poorly qualified for the duties of coaching youth, but several programs have been created to improve the situation.

11. The Coaching Behavior Assessment System (CBAS) has been developed with the ultimate goal of upgrading youth coaching. An outgrowth of the CBAS research with Little League coaches and players in Seattle, Washington, was Coach Effectiveness Training (CET). CET was tried with a sample of coaches matched with a group of coaches who were not given CET. Results indicated that the trained coaches used more reinforcement and less punishment when coaching, were liked better by their players, and were seen as better teachers. Self-esteem gains were noted in their players, though no win-loss advantage occurred as a result of training.

12. Other approaches to improving youth coaching include the National Youth Sport Coaches Association (NYSCA) in Florida, Rainer Martens' American Sport Education Program (ASEP), the Program for Athletic Coaches' Education (PACE) sponsored by the Youth Sport Institute at Michigan State University, and the Canadian National Certification Program (CNCP), a program with five levels ranging from instructing novice athletes to coaching the elite youth of Canada.

13. Approximately two million girls participated in interscholastic sports in 1983–1984, and 150,000 women competed at the intercollegiate level. Although female sport participation is on a substantial upswing, female coaches are not faring nearly so well. Their numbers decreased at a rate as high as 40

to 50 percent in many states in a recent fifteen year period. Role conflict, incomplete occupational socialization, and sex discrimination have all been cited as possible explanations for this decline in the number of women in coaching.

14. Black coaches at the highest levels of the sport of football are rare, particularly as head coaches. The picture is somewhat brighter in basketball, though baseball also lags behind. Black coaches, like black athletes, are overrepresented at the peripheral and underrepresented at the central positions.

15. Communication in and out of coaching involves four components: the source, the message, the channel, and the receiver. The source originates the communication, the message refers to meaning being conveyed by a communication, the channel refers to verbal or nonverbal mechanisms in communication, and the receiver is the target of the communication. By becoming more familiar with the nuances of communication theory, coaches could substantially improve their ability to relate to players and others.

16. Sport psychologists can be of considerable service in supplementing the efforts of a coach. Areas of expertise in the repertoire of a skilled psychologist are found to varying degrees in coaching, and coaches could profit from taking advantage of these capabilities. The insightful sport psychologist should make his or her interest in sport very clear, should be capable of objective evaluation of problems to be solved, should be aware of psychological demands at all levels of competition, should be aware that he or she is an outsider to coaches and athletes and must exert measures to change this perception, should be aware that his or her impact extends beyond the head coach to the assistants, should appreciate the unique aspects and commonalities among athletes and coaches, should maximize strengths and

recognize limitations, should always be cognizant of the fact that his or her role is as psychologist, not as coach, should be a collaborator, not an expert, and should be a constantly tuned-in listener.

SUGGESTED READINGS

Anshel, M. H. (1994) *Sport psychology: From theory to practice* (2d ed.). Scottdale, AZ: Gorsuch Scarisbrick, Publishers.

> Chapters 8 and 9 of Anshel's book center on communication and counseling of athletes. Down-to-earth techniques based on Anshel's intuition, experience, and an integration of the sport psychology literature all make this useful material. Chapter 11 on the coaching of youth athletes is also well done, and provides a framework for working with young competitors.

Gould, D. (1993) Goal setting for peak performance. In J. M. Williams (Ed.), *Applied sport psychology: Personal growth to peak performance* (2d ed.) (pp. 158–169). Palo Alto, CA: Mayfield.

> In addition to providing an excellent summary of goal setting research and theory, Gould discusses a goal setting system for coaches and some common problems in setting goals. Among the latter are setting too many goals too soon, failing to be cognizant of individual differences, setting goals that are too general, failing to modify unrealistic or outdated goals, failing to set performance goals, and failing to create an environment conducive to goal attainment.

Horn, T. S. (1993) The self-fulfilling prophecy theory: When coaches' expectations become reality. In J. M. Williams (Ed.). *Applied sport psychology: Personal growth to peak performance* (pp. 68–81). Palo Alto, CA: Mayfield.

> Horn illustrates how Rosenthal and Jacobson's 1968 research study on self-fulfilling prophecy can be turned to the advantage of the youth coach. Emphasis is placed on how the expectations set at the beginning of a sport season by youth coaches can become reality. Additionally, behavioral

recommendations that will assist coaches in the expectancy-performance process are delineated.

Martin, G. L., & Lumsden, J. A. (1987) *Coaching: An effective behavioral approach*. St. Louis: Times Mirror/Mosby.

Martin and Lumsden have written a book on coaching that incorporates the best of what is known about basic behavioral principles into the process. Such topics as assessing behavioral baselines, rewarding desirable sport behaviors, things to consider in pre- and postseason goal setting, increasing motivation to succeed, sport psyching, and strategies for decreasing problem behaviors are skillfully addressed. Also "nuts and bolts" kinds of issues such as budgets, equipment, facilities, conditioning, nutrition, ethics, and public relations are also discussed. This book would be quite useful for students hoping to become coaches as well as for those already entrenched in the profession who simply desire to become more effective in dealing with the multiple demands they face.

Mechikoff, R. A., & Kozar, B. (Eds.) (1983) *Sport psychology: The coach's perspective*. Springfield, IL: Charles C. Thomas.

Twenty-two prominent amateur and professional coaches and athletic administrators from seven different sports have contributed articles on how their use of psychological tactics relates to their particular coaching philosophies. The purpose of the volume overall is not to enhance theory or research but to give a view of the practice of psychology within the sporting domain.

Smoll, F. L. (1993) Enhancing coach-parent relationships in youth sport. In J. M. Williams (Ed.), *Applied sport psychology: Personal growth to peak performance* (pp. 58–67). Palo Alto, CA: Mayfield.

Smoll attempts to outline the objectives of youth sport, the role and responsibilities of parents in the process, and the relationship of the coach to parents and young sport participants. Coaches are offered suggestions for handling problem parents, including those who are disinterested, overcritical, screamers, overprotective, or prone to try to assume the prerogatives of the coach. It is shown how they can facilitate understanding through coach-parent meetings. This reading, though brief, provides many useful tips for youth coaches.

REFERENCES

Abu-Hilal, M. M., & Salameh, K. M. (1992) Validity and reliability of the Maslach Burnout Inventory for a sample of non-western teachers. *Educational and Psychological Measurement, 52,* 161–169.

Acosta, R., & Carpenter, L. (1985) Women in athletics: A status report. *Journal of Physical Education, Recreation and Dance, 56*(7), 30–34.

Allen, K. (1987) Coaches too close to go head-to-head too often. *USA Today,* March 20, 4C.

Anderson, D. F., & Gill, K. S. (1983) Occupational socialization patterns of men's and women's interscholastic basketball programs. *Journal of Sport Behavior, 6,* 105–106.

Basketball coaches shift jobs at a record pace: !23 in top division have moved in 2 years. (1986) *Chronicles of Higher Education, 33*(13), 27.

Becker, D., & Herwig, C. (1994) Women's hoops scene not all serene. *USA Today,* March 30, 1C–2C.

Black head coaches: Taking charge on major campuses. (1982) *Ebony,* May, 57–62.

Black hiring issue subject to scrutiny. (1987) *USA Today,* Sept. 28, 2C.

Boeck, G. (1995) Hospital stay shows Nelson he must change. *USA Today,* Jan. 31, 2C.

Breaking point. (1995) *Time,* March 6, 56–61.

Brewington, P., & White, C. (1988) Women fight to keep the door from closing. *USA Today,* Feb. 4, 1C.

Burlingame, M. (1972) Socialization constructs and the teaching of teachers. *Quest, 18* (Winter), 40–56.

Caccese, T., & Mayerberg, C. (1984) Gender differences in perceived burnout of college coaches, *Journal of Sport Psychology, 6,* 279–288.

Capel, S. A. (1986) Psychological and organizational factors related to burnout in athletic trainers. *Athletic Training, 21,* 322–327.

Capel, S. A., Sisley, B. L., & Desertrain, G. S. (1987) The relationship of role conflict and role ambiguity to burnout in high school basketball coaches. *Journal of Sport Psychology, 9,* 106–117.

Changing of the guard. (1987) *USA Today,* Jan. 22, p. 7C.

Cherniss, C. (1980) *Staff burn-out: Job stress in the human services.* Beverly Hills, CA: Sage.

Christie, R., & Geis, F. (1970) *Studies in Machiavellianism.* New York: Academic Press.

Coaching exodus sends Big Eight reeling. (1994) *Bryan-College Station (TX) Eagle,* Nov. 24, C6.

Coakley, J. J. (1994) *Sport in society: Issues and controversies* (5th ed.) St. Louis, MO: Times Mirror/Mosby College Publishing.

Cottle, S. (1982) Sex bias and professional status level effects in the evaluations of coaching ability. Unpublished master's thesis, California State University, Fullerton.

Crothers, T. (1991) Conference independents. *Sports Illustrated, 75*(9), 89–97.

Division I men's basketball coaching changes since 1980. (1989) *USA Today,* Jan. 30, 1C.

Dodd, M. (1994) Baseball gets "C" on "racial report card." *USA Today,* July 9, 1C–2C.

Eitzen, D. S., & Pratt, S. R. (1989) Gender differences in coaching philosophy: The case of female basketball teams. *Research Quarterly for Exercise and Sport, 60,* 152–158.

Freudenberger, H. J. (1980) *Burn-out: How to beat the high cost of success.* New York: Bantam Books.

Fuoss, D., & Troppmann, R. (1981) *Effective coaching: A psychological approach.* New York: Wiley.

Gallon, A. (1980) *Coaching: Ideas and ideals.* Boston: Houghton-Mifflin.

Hart, B., Hasbrook, C., & Mathes, S. (1986) An examination of the reduction in the number of female interscholastic coaches. *Research Quarterly for Exercise and Sport, 57,* 68–77.

Hart, B., & Mathes, S. (1982) Women coaches—Where are they? Paper presented at 1982 Wisconsin Association for Health, Physical Education and Recreation, Glendale, Wisconsin.

Hasbrook, C. A., Hart, B. A., Mathes, S. A., & True, S. (1990) Sex bias and the validity of believed differences between male and female interscholastic athletic coaches. *Research Quarterly for Exercise and Sport, 61,* 259–267.

Heishman, M. F., Bunker, L., & Tutwiler, R. W. (1990) The decline of women leaders (Coaches and Athletic Directors) in girls' interscholastic sport programs in Virginia from 1972 to 1987. *Research Quarterly for Exercise and Sport, 61,* 103–107.

Herwig, C. (1994) NCAA programs hiring more female coaches and administrators. *USA Today,* June 29, 12C.

Holmen, M., & Parkhouse, B. (1981) Trends in the selection of coaches for female athletes: A demographic inquiry. *Research Quarterly for Exercise and Sport, 52,* 9–18.

Jacoby, F. (1978) Where is your next job? *Summer Manual,* American Football Coaches Association, 73–75.

Kelley, B. C. (1994) A model of stress and burnout in collegiate coaches: Effects of gender and time of season. *Research Quarterly for Exercise and Sport, 65,* 48–58.

Kirkpatrick, C. (1988) Freshman at work. *Sports Illustrated,* Feb. 1, 28–31.

Knoppers, A., Meyer, B. M., Ewing, M., & Forrest, L. (1989) Gender and the salary of coaches. *Sociology of Sport Journal, 6,* 348–361.

Kobasa, S. C. (1988) *The Hardiness Test.* New York: Hardiness Institute.

Kobasa, S. C., Maddi, S. R., & Courington, S. (1981) Personality and constitution as mediators in the stress-illness relationship. *Journal of Health and Social Behavior, 22,* 368–378.

Lanning, W. (1980) Applied psychology in major college athletics. In R. M. Suinn (Ed.), *Psychology in sports: Methods and applications* (pp. 362–367). Minneapolis, MN: Burgess.

Latimer, S., & Mathes, S. (1985) Black college football coaches' social, educational, athletic, and career pattern characteristics. *Journal of Sport Behavior, 8,* 149–162.

LeUnes, A. (1986) A sport psychologist and a football legend discuss the psychology of coaching: Coleman Griffith and Knute Rockne. *Journal of Applied Research in Coaching and Athletics, 1,* 127–134.

LeUnes, A., & Nation, J. R. (1982) Saturday's heroes: A psychological portrait of college football players. *Journal of Sport Behavior, 5,* 139–149.

Locke, E. (1968) Toward a theory of task motivation and incentives. *Organizational Behavior and Human Performance, 3,* 157–189.

Locke, E., & Latham, G. (1985) The application of goal setting to sports. *Journal of Sport Psychology, 7,* 205–222.

Locke, E., & Massengale, J. (1978) Role conflict in teacher/coaches. *Research Quarterly, 49,* 162–174.

Locke, E. A., Shaw, K. N., Saari, L. M., & Latham, G. P. (1981) Goal setting and task performance: 1969-1980. *Psychological Bulletin, 90,* 125-152.

Lombardo, B. F. (1986) The behavior of youth sport coaches: Crisis on the bench. In R. E. Lapchick (Ed.), *Fractured focus: Sport as a reflection of society* (pp. 199-205). Lexington, MA: D.C. Heath.

Maslach, C. (1976) Burned-out. *Human Behavior, 5,* 16-22.

Maslach, C., & Jackson, S. E. (1981) The measurement of experienced burnout. *Journal of Occupational Behavior, 2,* 99-113.

Massengale, J. (1980) Role conflict and the occupational milieu of the teacher/coach: Some real working world perspectives. In *National Association for Physical Education in Higher Education Proceedings, II,* 47-52.

Massengale, J. (1981a) Researching role conflict. *Journal of Physical Education, Recreation and Dance, 52*(9), 23.

Massengale, J. (1981b) Role conflict and the teacher/coach: Some occupational causes and considerations for the sport sociologist. In S. Greendorfer and A. Yiannakis (Eds.), *Sociology of sport: Diverse perspectives* (pp. 149-157). West Point, NY: Leisure Press.

Mathes, S. (1982) Women coaches: Endangered species? Paper presented at the American Alliance for Health, Physical Education, Recreation and Dance National Convention, Houston, Texas.

Mehrabian, A. (1971) *Silent messages.* Belmont, CA: Wadsworth.

Mento, A. J., Steel, R. P., & Karren, R. J. (1987) A meta-analytic study of the effects of goal setting on task performance: 1966-1984. *Organizational Behavior and Human Decision Processes, 39,* 52-83.

Michener, J. A. (1976) *Sports in America.* New York: Fawcett Crest.

Murphy, P. (1985) Youth sport coaches: Using hunches to fill a blank page. *Physician and Sportsmedicine, 13*(4), 136-142.

NBA coaching changes. (1994) *Bryan-College Station (TX) Eagle,* August 30, B1.

New faces on the bench. (1990) *USA Today,* November 30, 2C.

NFL veterans. (1990) *USA Today,* October 26, 1C.

Ogilvie, B. C., & Tutko, T. A. (1966) *Problem athletes and how to handle them.* London: Pelham Books.

Parkhouse, B. L., & Williams, J. M. (1986) Differential effects of sex and status on evaluation of coaching ability. *Research Quarterly for Exercise and Sport, 57,* 53-59.

Pastore, D. L., & Meacci, W. G. (1994) Employment process for NCAA female coaches. *Journal of Sport Management, 8,* 115-128.

Pate, R., Rotella, R., & McClenaghan, B. (1984) *Scientific foundations of coaching.* Philadelphia, PA: Saunders.

Perry, J. (1986) Five-on-one. Should men coach women's sports? *Journal of Physical Education, Recreation, and Dance, 57*(3), 62-63.

Pro coaches won't find security. (1989) *Inside Sports, 11,* 11-12.

Rikki, R., & Cottle, S. (1984) Sex bias in evaluation of coaching ability and physical performance research. *Perspectives, 6,* 32-41.

Robinson, J., & Shaver, P. (1973) *Measures of social psychological attitudes.* Ann Arbor, MI: Institute for Social Research.

Roscoe, J. (1965) The construction and applications of the Polyphasic Values Inventory. Unpublished doctoral dissertation, Colorado State College.

Sabock, R. (1979) *The coach.* Philadelphia, PA: Saunders.

Sabock, R., & Jones, D. (1978) The coaching profession: Its effects on the coaches' family. *Athletic Journal, 58*(9), 42, 44-45, 62.

Sage, G. H. (1972a) Machiavellianism among college and high school coaches. *Seventy-fifth Proceedings of the National College Physical Education Association for Men,* pp. 45-60.

Sage, G. H. (1972b) Value orientations of American college coaches compared to male college students and businessmen. *Seventy-fifth Proceedings of the National College Physical Education Association for Men,* pp. 174-186.

Schafer, S. (1984) *Sports needs you. A working model for the equity professional.* Denver, CO: Colorado Department of Education.

Scott, J. (1971) *The athletic revolution.* New York: Macmillan.

Sefko, E. (1995) Professional hazards take toll on coaches. *Houston Chronicle,* January 24, 1B, 4B.

Sisley, B., & Capel, S. (1986) High school coaching: Filled with gender differences. *Journal of Physical Education, Recreation and Dance, 57*(3), 39–43.

Sloan, N. (1977) Opinions out loud. *NCAA News, 14*(7), 2.

Smith, R. E. (1986a) Consultation in sport psychology. *Consulting Psychology Bulletin, 38*(1), 17–20.

Smith, R. E. (1986b) Toward a cognitive-affective model of athletic burnout. *Journal of Sport Psychology, 8,* 36–50.

Smith, R. E., Smoll, F. L., & Hunt, E. (1977) A system for the behavioral assessment of athletic coaches. *Research Quarterly, 48,* 401–407.

Smoll, F. L., & Smith, R. E. (1984) Leadership research in youth sport. In J. M. Silva & R. S. Weinberg (eds.), *Psychological foundations of sport* (p. 375). Champaign, IL: Human Kinetics.

Smoll, F. L., Smith, R. E., Barnett, N. P., & Everett, J. J. (1993) Enhancement of children's self-esteem through social support training for youth sport coaches. *Journal of Applied Psychology, 78,* 602–610.

Stangl, J. M., & Kane, M. J. (1991) Structural variables that offer explanatory power for the underrepresentation of women coaches since Title IX: The case of homologous reproduction. *Sociology of Sport Journal, 8,* 47–60.

St. John's (Minn.): Peculiar practices. (1990) *USA Today,* August 22, 10C.

Suinn, R. M. (1986) Consultation in sport psychology. *Consulting Psychology Bulletin, 38*(1), 17–20.

Tenenbaum, G., Pinchas, S., Elbaz, G., Bar-Eli, M., & Weinberg, R. (1991) Effect of goal proximity and goal specificity on muscular endurance performance: A replication and extension. *Journal of Sport and Exercise Psychology, 13,* 174–187.

There's no question we can do the job. (1990) *USA Today,* March 7, 1C–2C.

Thorngren, C. M. (1990) A time to reach out—keeping the female coach in coaching. *Journal of Physical Education, Recreation and Dance,* March, 57–60.

True, S. (1983) *Data on the percentage of girls' high school athletic teams coached by women.* Kansas City, MO: National Federation of State High School Associations.

Tubbs, M. E. (1986) Goal setting: A meta-analytic examination of the empirical evidence. *Journal of Applied Psychology, 71,* 474–483.

Tutko, T. A., & Richards, J. W. (1971) *Psychology of coaching.* Boston, MA: Allyn and Bacon.

Vancil, M. (1991) Phil Jackson. *Inside Sports, 13,* 19–23.

Vealey, R. S., Udry, E. M., Zimmerman, V., & Soliday, J. (1992) Intrapersonal and situational predictors of coaching burnout. *Journal of Sport and Exercise Psychology, 14,* 40–58.

Walkey, F. H., & Green, D. E. (1992) An exhaustive examination of the replicable factor structure of the Maslach Burnout Inventory. *Educational and Psychological Measurement, 52,* 309–323.

Walsh, J., & Carron, A. V. (1977) Attributes of volunteer coaches. Paper presented at the annual meeting of the Canadian Association of Sport Sciences, Winnipeg, Canada.

Weinberg, R., Fowler, C., Jackson, A., Bagnall, J., & Bruya, L. (1991) Effect of goal difficulty on motor performance: A replication across tasks and subjects. *Journal of Sport and Exercise Psychology, 13,* 160–173.

Weinberg, R. S., Reveles, M., & Jackson, A. (1984) Attitudes of male and female athletes toward male and female coaches. *Journal of Sport Psychology, 6,* 448–453.

What they say about coaching. (1994) *USA Today,* December 21, 5C.

Wieberg, S. (1995) Burnout is consequence of new age. *USA Today,* January 31, 1C–2C.

Wilkinson, C. (1952) *Oklahoma Split T football.* New York: Prentice-Hall.

Working your nerves: The toughest jobs. (1995) *Time,* March 6, 60.

Yetman, N., Berghorn, F., & Thomas, F. (1980) Racial participation and integration in intercollegiate basketball, 1958–1960. Paper presented at the annual program of the North American Society for the Sociology of Sport, Denver, Colorado.

Sport and Physical Activity for All

INTRODUCTION

Thus far, the more formalized aspects of sport for men, women, and children have been the center of attention. However, a number of sport psychologists have devoted their time and energy to promoting an understanding of fitness apart from the orthodox world of athletics. Of primary concern in this chapter will be issues of general fitness, exercise adherence, prevention or alleviation of anxiety and depression through exercise, and peak experiences related to physical activity. Of secondary interest will be discussions of an admixture of athletes, including runners and elderly citizens interested in competition and fitness.

Our collective fascination with physical fitness has led to a rush of activity that can be measured, informally at least, by a concurrent explosion of facilities dedicated to fitness, fitness equipment and paraphernalia, television shows demonstrating or extolling the virtues of fitness, and other related fitness enterprises.

The available statistics on adherence to the various exercise regimens are not particularly reassuring. Why exercise adherence is poor and some recommendations to improve it will be discussed. Various models used to explain adherence will also be advanced along with pros and cons of each.

The relationship of exercise and fitness to mood states constitutes a third area of considerable fascination to psychologists, including those with an interest in sport and fitness. There are many advocates of the use of fitness activities for the prevention or alleviation of anxiety and depression.

Finally, the psychological aspects of participation by various populations of fitness seekers will be discussed. These selected populations include runners and senior participants. The runners who will be scrutinized are recreational joggers, marathon runners, and ultramarathoners. Much interest of late has been generated in the exercise habits of senior citizens; a discussion of their involvement in sport and fitness is warranted.

PHYSICAL FITNESS

Much excitement was generated in the 1980s about a fitness boom in North America. It appeared that everyone was jogging, working out at a fitness center, swimming, walking, or otherwise "getting in shape." One index of the collective penchant for fitness was the sales of related paraphernalia. Legwold (1985) cited 1983 statistics that indicated that annual sales of activewear reached $8 billion, exercise equipment $1 billion, athletic footwear $1 billion, and books concerned with fitness and diet $50 million. An additional $5 billion was spent by corporate fitness centers' and health clubs' programming and fitness paraphernalia.

Statistics from a variety of sources supported the notion that a fitness boom was indeed taking place. Silva and Weinberg (1984) reported that the National Running and Fitness Association had 30 million members in the early 1980s and had experienced a 50 percent growth in membership from 1980 to 1981. Dishman (1984) combined data from a National Center for Health Statistics survey with that of a Harris Poll and placed the number of exercisers in the United States at 50 to 60 million; Legwold (1985) placed the number at 85 million in 1983, a 14 percent increase over the preceding year.

Even in the 1980s, there were skeptics with regard to the fitness revolution. It was Dishman's opinion that probably only about one-third of exercisers engaged in workouts that were conducive to increasing fitness (Dishman, 1983). Less optimistically, Stephens (1985) placed the figure at 20 percent. Data such as these suggest that the fitness movement of the 1980s may have been more apparent than real. What, then, is the picture in the 1990s?

Sales statistics again are suggestive of a fascination with fitness. Random statistics from a number of editions of *USA Today* in 1994 and 1995 are revealing; in excess of $10 billion is spent annually on active-wear, footwear, and exercise equipment. Nike sold two hundred pairs of shoes every minute in 1993, or a total of 100 million pairs. In his first year of operation (1964), Nike owner Phil Knight sold 1,300 pairs of shoes. Nike profits are now such that tennis star Jim Courier just signed a four-year endorsement deal with the shoe company which will pay him $26 million over the life of the contract. Shoe sales from other competing companies will push the sales figure for all running shoes above $4 billion annually. It is interesting to note that the average American spends $193 annually on sports apparel, with the thirteen to seventeen age group spending the most ($311) and the fifty-five and up group spending the least ($155). In another sport, golf, 34,000 sets of clubs are sold every day in the United States; golf balls are sold at the rate of half a million every twenty-four hours.

In terms of actual exercisers, data are not especially encouraging. Data from the Centers for Disease Control indicate that fewer than 10 percent of all Americans exercise enough to attain fitness benefits (Westcott, 1995). Data reported by Caspersen and Merritt (1995) based on responses of almost 35,000 adults in twenty-six states are supportive of Westcott's observation; they report that less than one person in ten in their study was regularly active in intensive exercise. A statement by Brown (1993, p. 2C) summarizes the state of the fitness movement at this time: "The fitness boom hasn't exactly pooped out, but it's definitely taking a rest." It is clear from the preceding data and observations that the fitness movement is in need of new life. The challenge to do so is a big one for health and sport psychologists interested in fitness.

A Definition of Physical Fitness

Physical activity, exercise, and physical fitness tend to be used interchangeably by professionals and laymen alike. However, Caspersen (1985) suggests that the three terms actually connote quite different things and should be treated accordingly. To Caspersen, physical activity refers to any bodily movement produced by the skeletal muscles that results in an expenditure of energy. Physical activity may be expended as a function of exercise, but the housewife chasing after three young children and the meter reader attempting to elude a dog are also expending energy. Hence, physical activity is not at all synonymous with the other two terms under present consideration. *Exercise* is a subset of physical activity characterized by planned, organized, and repetitive components aimed at improving or maintaining physical fitness. Finally, *physical fitness* refers to a set of attributes that are either health- or skill-related. According to a position stand on the part of the American College of Sports Medicine (ACSM), the following standards constitute the essence of a good cardiorespiratory fitness, body composition, and muscular strength and endurance program:

1. Frequency of training:
   Three to five days per weeek.
2. Intensity of training:
   60 to 90 percent of maximum heart rate or 50 to 85 percent of VO2 Max.
3. Duration of training:
   Twenty to sixty minutes each time, depending on the type of activity.
4. Mode of activity:
   Any activity that uses large muscle groups that can be maintained over time and is rhythmic and aerobic in nature.
5. Resistance training:
   Strength training of a moderate intensity.

Subsequent discussion in this chapter will be guided by the definitional distinctions suggested by Caspersen and ACSM.

Benefits of Physical Fitness

Proponents of physical fitness are adamant in their claims about the benefits to be gained from physical activity in the sport and exercise context. Many authorities point to a host of both physical and psychological benefits.

Physical Benefits

Silva and Weinberg (1984) mention several physical benefits associated with physical fitness. They include increased blood flow to the heart, lowered blood pressure, increased lung capacity which allows for more efficient delivery of oxygenated blood to all parts of the body, and lower blood lactate levels. Several authorities (e.g., LaPorte, Dearwater, Cauley, Slemenda, and Cook, 1985; Powell, 1985; Siscovick, 1985) add to the list by citing control of hypertension, diabetes mellitus, and osteoporosis. Williams and Long (1983) suggest that digestive and excretory functioning may be enhanced by being physically fit, and that weight control may also be a decided benefit for many who exercise regularly. Legwold (1985) suggests a fourth fitness benefit in terms of one's sex life, a notion also mentioned by Williams and Long (1983).

Finally, increased longevity may actually accrue as a function of fitness. For example, Lee, Hsieh, and Paffenbarger (1995) reported that vigorous but not nonvigorous physical activity is associated with longevity. Their claims were based on the results of the Harvard Alumni Health Study conducted on over 17,000 Harvard University Alumni who entered the university as undergraduates in the years 1916 through 1950. Physical activity was assessed by asking alumni about flights of stairs climbed, city blocks walked, types of sports and recreational activities engaged in, and the amount of time devoted

Many people find physical fitness a convenient way to meet others. How many of us who exercise regularly maintain our routine by working out with a group of friends?

each week to these sports and recreational activities. Mortality statistics were gathered from the Harvard Alumni Office, which keeps weekly rosters of deceased alumni. Statistical analyses indicated a very strong relationship between vigorous physical activity and longevity in this sample. Lee et al. make an additional point of importance — nonvigorous exercise is preferable to sedentariness in terms of overall health if not longevity.

A physical fitness benefit often cited (Silva and Weinberg, 1984; Williams and Long, 1983) that does not appear to be a benefit after all is a lowered resting heart rate. Authorities such as LaPorte et al. (1985), Legwold (1985), and Rogers (1985) argue that there is little or no evidence that a low resting heart rate is an indicator of superior cardiac functioning, and it probably tells us nothing more about the person than that he or she is still alive.

Psychological Benefits

Among the psychological gains associated with physical fitness, a number of investigators point to anxiety- or stress-reduction (Folkins and Sime, 1981; Powell, 1985; Williams and Long, 1983), a topic we shall discuss in detail later. Also, there may be benefits in terms of socialization, that is, meeting new people and creating new friendships and acquaintances and maintaining old ones. How many of us who exercise regularly have our exercise behavior maintained by getting to work out with a friend or several friends? And how many of us would continue our exercise regimen if our partner(s) suddenly stopped going?

A final psychological benefit for the more serious fitness buff is the thrill of competition. All one has to do to see this quality in action is to line up any Saturday in the nearest 10-kilometer or marathon run. One of the virtues of such events is that they serve as a showcase for most of the other physical and psychological benefits of fitness. Unfortunately, fitness can also serve as a forum for inappropriate proving behavior. We shall attend to this issue a bit later.

EXERCISE ADHERENCE

One of the more interesting paradoxes associated with fitness is the issue of exercise adherence. Perhaps as many as 20–25 million people in the United States exercise on a regular basis and most extol its many physical, psychological, and social virtues. Substantial numbers of others would like

---

Rest and Meditation: Good as Exercise?

Highlight
13.1

Many sport (and health) psychologists are of the opinion that exercise causes a reduction in tension. Raglin and Morgan (1985) suggest that the distraction or diversion associated with exercise may account for the purported anxiety reduction. In an earlier test of this hypothesis, Bahrke and Morgan (1978) randomly assigned seventy-five males to three conditions, one involving *aerobic exercise*, another *meditation*, and a third *quiet rest*. Predictions were that the aerobic exercise and meditation conditions would result in reduced state anxiety as measured by the State-Trait Anxiety Inventory (STAI); in fact, both treatments resulted in reduced anxiety. Surprisingly, however, the quiet rest group experienced similar reductions in state anxiety.

Morgan and his associates point out that their findings may suggest a *quantitative* difference in state anxiety that in no way addresses the *qualitative* issues associated with exercise. A number of physiological changes, such as lowered blood pressure, may not occur as a result of quiet rest or meditation. Also, it is likely that the desirable effects associated with exercise may be much more long-lasting than those related to meditation or rest.

Sources: Bahrke and Morgan (1978); Raglin and Morgan (1985).

to obtain the alleged benefits of exercise but cannot stay with a program long enough to do so. This inability to stick with an exercise regimen is one of the more perplexing problems facing professionals in the various health-related enterprises.

Statistics from a number of adherence studies indicate that about 50 percent of the individuals who start a fitness campaign will drop out in six months or less (Dishman, 1986; Shephard, 1985). These statistics refer to individuals with no known cardiovascular problems. In individuals with a documented history of cardiovascular problems, adherence rates to postmyocardial infarction exercise prescriptions are equally poor. Sanne (1973) studied 148 post-MI patients in Sweden and found that 29 percent of the group never began prescribed exercise programming; at the end of two years, 29 percent of the original 148 patients were working out under a hospital administered exercise program (another 17 percent said they were working out at home on their own). By the four-year mark, 14 percent were still working out at the hospital and 18 percent reported exercising on their own, an overall adherence rate for four years of 32 percent. In another study, Andrew, Oldridge, Parker, Cunningham, Rechnitzer, Jones, Buck, Kavanagh, Shephard, Sutton, and McDonald (1981) found an exercise noncompliance rate of over 44 percent in their longitudinal study of 728 postcoronary men in Ontario, Canada. While some of the patients in each of these studies either never started or dropped out of prescribed exercise due to valid medical contraindications, the adherence rate in MI patients appears to be less than satisfactory. Overall, Oldridge (1988) indicates that 40 to 50 percent of referred patients will drop out of cardiac rehabilitation programs in twelve months or less from the time of initial physician referral.

Inasmuch as adherence rates are low for both "healthy" individuals and those with a history of heart problems, it seems worthwhile at this point to take a look at predictors of exercise adherence, why people fail to comply with exercise programs, and some ways that exercise adherence might be improved.

Predictors of Exercise Adherence

There are a number of physical, psychological, and social predictors of exercise adherence. Perhaps the most salient of these predictors is *physical proximity to the exercise area,* which, as Roth (1974) points out, underscores the importance of practical considerations in exercise adherence. Studies in which geographical proximity to the exercise area has been cited include Teraslinna, Partanen, Koskela, Partanen, and Oja (1969) with Finnish business executives; Andrew et al. (1981) with Canadian heart patients; and Hanson (1977) with American college professors. In each of the studies, proximity was important to the continuance of exercise; in the Teraslinna et al. study, proximity was the single biggest determinant.

While an individually tailored prescription is important in exercise therapy, the therapeutic benefits of a group should not be overlooked.

Another finding is that *spousal support* is important in exercise adherence. McCready and Long (1985) point to a positive though not overwhelming correlation between spousal support and continuance in exercise programs. Dishman (1984, p. 425) states that "a spouse's attitude toward a participant's involvement is a greater influence in the participant's behavior than is his or her own attitude."

It has been suggested that *exercising in small as opposed to large groups* is conducive to exercise continuance (Dishman, 1984). It seems logical that most of the reinforcement associated with exercise should be realized when groups are small and attention from instructors and peers is maximized. Shephard (1985) indicates that many people are intimidated by mixed classes, so provisions should be made in certain instances to have male and female groupings for exercise.

Another mild indicator of exercise adherence is apparently *socioeconomic status.* That exercise may not be reaching an optimal number of people is a challenge issued by Shephard (1985), who states that greater targeting of blue-collar workers and people at the lower end of the white-collar work strata should be carried out by the exercise leadership.

At a psychological level, preliminary and thus tentative research data has implicated an *internal locus of control* as a correlate of exercise adherence. Levenson (1981) has intimated that subjects engaged in health-related activities tend to be more internal on her IPC scale (discussed at several other points in this book), a finding corroborated by McCready and Long (1985) and Noland (1981).

Why People Drop Out of Exercise Programs

A number of negative predictors of exercise adherence have been identified. From the discussion of positive predictors, it seems clear that poor accessibility to the exercise area, a lack of spousal support, and exercising in large and potentially impersonal groups have considerable impact on whether one complies with an exercise regimen. Beyond these problems, *time* appears to be a significant determinant of exercise adherence (Andrew et al., 1981; Dishman, 1986; Gettman, Pollock, and Ward, 1983; Oldridge, 1982; Shephard, 1985). Combining time and accessibility probably constitutes a grouping that accounts for much of the variance in exercise adherence. The extent to which the time-accessibility interaction is true, however, remains to be determined. Sime, Whipple, Stamler, and Berkson (1978) found that dropouts in their study perceived time and accessibility to be problems even though they actually lived closer to their workout environment than did the exercise compliers with whom they were compared.

Another problem in exercise adherence concerns *smoking.* Several authorities have noted the tendency of smokers to drop out of exercise programs (e.g., Massie and Shephard, 1971) and, at the other extreme, the equal tendency on the part of nonsmokers to comply (McCready and Long, 1985).

A third negative predictor concerns *poor choice of exercise.* Persons beginning an exercise program should weigh the merits of various forms of exercise and choose one that is within their physical capabilities and their general interests. A poorly chosen exercise program is destined to fail. A listing of some of the more popular forms of exercise and their benefits and costs can be seen in table 13.1.

Related to choice of exercise is the issue of *injury.* All too often, the beginning exerciser is looking for a "quick fix," and this misplaced emphasis often results in an injury that, in turn, dampens enthusiasm for further exercise. Poor choice of type of exercise, a misguided emphasis on too much exercise too soon, and poor equipment selection all interact to produce the injury effect. The beginning exerciser should

Table 13.1

Benefits and Costs of Some Popular Forms of Physical Activity

Activity	Benefits						Costs		
	Aerobics	Fat Loss	Strength	Muscle Endurance	Flexi-bility	Total	Injury Rate	Workout Time (min.)	Start-Up Costs
Maximum Score	★★★★	★	★★	★★	★	10			
Swimming	★★★★	★	★	★★	★	9	Low	30	$20–$975*
Cross-Country Skiing (Outdoors)	★★★★	★	★	★★	½	8.5	Medium	25	$100–$200
Circuit Weight Training	★★½	½	★★	★★	½	7.5	Medium	30	$200–$675*
Running	★★★★	★	½	★½		7	High	25	$40–$85
Aerobic Dance	★★★	★	★	★½	½	7	High	35	$30–$675*
Cycling (Outdoors)	★★★½	★	★	★		6.5	High†	35	$150–$750
Rowing Machine	★★★	★	★	★½		6.5	Medium	35	$100–$400
Walking	★★★½	★	½	★		6	Low	45	$40–$85
Stair Climbing (Machine)	★★★½	★	½	★		6	Low	25	$120–$2,000
Golf (Carrying Clubs)	★★½	★	½	★½	½	6	Low	45	$200–$725
Rope Skipping	★★★½	½	½	★		5.5	Medium	25	$45–$80
Racquetball/Squash	★★★	★	½	½	½	5.5	Medium	35	$70–$815*
Basketball/Soccer	★★★	½	½	★		5	High	40	$30–$125
Weight Training	★		★★	★½	½	5	Medium	60	$130–$675*
Tennis (Singles)	★★½	½	½	½	½	4.5	Medium	45	$80–$315
Calisthenics	★½		★	★	★	4.5	Low	60	$40–$55

*Upper range includes club fees   †Includes collisions without helmet

Source: "Health and Fitness" (1990).

choose appropriate exercise, opt for a proper workout environment (to include proper instruction), and select suitable equipment.

Two psychological constructs that, like the locus of control dimension of internality mentioned earlier, have been positively though weakly linked to the exercise adherence literature are the *Type A personality* and *extraversion*. The Type A personality is associated with an aggressive, hard-driving, hard-working, time-pressured, and highly competitive individual who is prone, among other things, to being at high risk for coronary heart disease (Friedman and Rosenman, 1974). According to research reported by Oldridge, Wicks, Hanley, Sutton, and Jones (1978), Type A individuals appear to have relatively poor exercise adherence rates. Dishman (1984) interprets the results reported by Oldridge and his colleagues as reflective of either a lack of patience with the seemingly slow pace of the typical fitness program or as a result of setting other competing goals that eventually take priority over exercise because these competing activities provide the more immediate feedback necessary to the psychological sustenance of the Type A personality.

As for *extraversion,* at least two studies have mentioned higher compliance rates for extraverted as opposed to introverted personalities (Blumenthal, Williams, Wallace, Williams, and Needles, 1982; Massie and Shephard, 1971). Inasmuch as extraverts derive much reinforcement from group interactions, exercise groups readily meet the affiliative needs of these typically outgoing people.

While the conceptions of the Type A personality and the extravert are interesting ones, they are in need of further research. Any number of other personality dimensions surely are pertinent to exercise compliance, and studies should be undertaken with the goal of expanding our knowledge base about psychological constructs and fitness.

Improving Exercise Adherence

Dishman (1984, 1991) has reviewed fifty-six studies that used behavior modification procedures, and much of the ensuing discussion will be based on his synthesis of the research. Dishman suggests that while we may have little or no control over situational variables such as spousal support, socioeconomic class, professional or blue-collar status, and so forth, we must live within these multiple realities and work within the constraints they provide. It follows that we should concentrate on events over which we actually have some degree of control to help us adhere to our chosen physical fitness regimen.

One of the approaches suggested by Dishman is *behavioral contracting.* In this situation, exercise specifics are spelled out with the cooperation of both the person doing the exercise and the person(s) supervising it. Once the details are worked out to the satisfaction of all parties, a behavioral contract is signed that more or less publicly binds the exerciser to the mutually determined agreement.

Lotteries represent a second behavioral technique for maximizing exercise adherence. Exercise is determined on a daily basis through a lottery system, or what might be referred to as "luck of the draw." Various exercise programs might be thrown into the lottery formula, and the person using this approach would simply work out according to what was drawn on any particular day. Here an attempt is being made in the case of the lottery to reward the exerciser on a random basis, which should relieve some of the boredom found in more ritualistic programs of exercise.

Self-monitoring and stimulus-cueing are two *goal setting techniques* that have much to recommend them. In *self-monitoring,* objective records are kept that serve as highly identifiable reinforcers for exercise. Variables such as weight loss and heart rate or blood pressure can be monitored for feedback purposes. Examples of event-specific items include mileage in jogging and resistances, repetitions, and sets in weight programs. *Stimulus-cueing* involves exercising using the same activity at the same time and place every day. There is much to be said for the adherence potential in such regimentation; exercise can then become a part of everyday activities. Thompson and Wankel (1980) have pointed out that ritualistic approaches to exercise may have their drawbacks. These authorities have found evidence counter to the general theme of the various goal-setting techniques, which points up the problems in exercise adherence at both the research and the practice levels.

Crucial to an understanding of the various behavioral approaches is the concept of reinforcement or reward. The more reinforcement that can be brought to bear on persons who are exercising, the more likely they are to repeat the

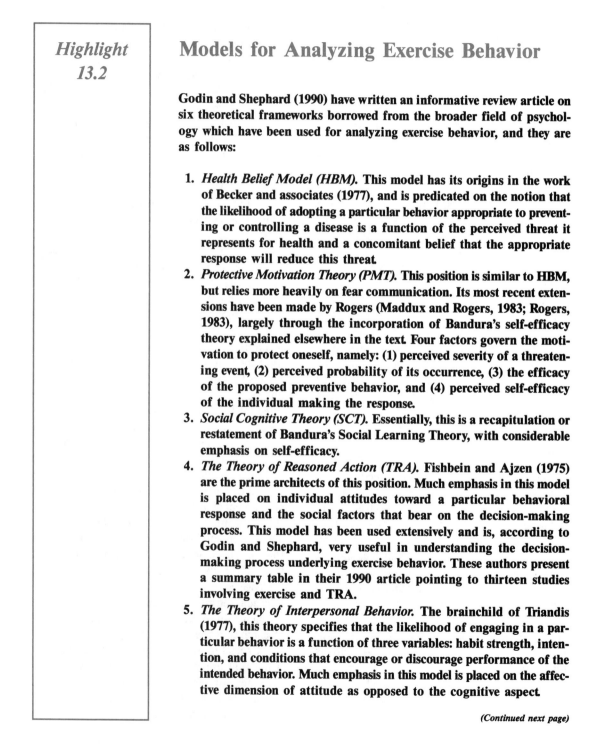

Models for Analyzing Exercise Behavior

Godin and Shephard (1990) have written an informative review article on six theoretical frameworks borrowed from the broader field of psychology which have been used for analyzing exercise behavior, and they are as follows:

1. *Health Belief Model (HBM).* This model has its origins in the work of Becker and associates (1977), and is predicated on the notion that the likelihood of adopting a particular behavior appropriate to preventing or controlling a disease is a function of the perceived threat it represents for health and a concomitant belief that the appropriate response will reduce this threat.

2. *Protective Motivation Theory (PMT).* This position is similar to HBM, but relies more heavily on fear communication. Its most recent extensions have been made by Rogers (Maddux and Rogers, 1983; Rogers, 1983), largely through the incorporation of Bandura's self-efficacy theory explained elsewhere in the text. Four factors govern the motivation to protect oneself, namely: (1) perceived severity of a threatening event, (2) perceived probability of its occurrence, (3) the efficacy of the proposed preventive behavior, and (4) perceived self-efficacy of the individual making the response.

3. *Social Cognitive Theory (SCT).* Essentially, this is a recapitulation or restatement of Bandura's Social Learning Theory, with considerable emphasis on self-efficacy.

4. *The Theory of Reasoned Action (TRA).* Fishbein and Ajzen (1975) are the prime architects of this position. Much emphasis in this model is placed on individual attitudes toward a particular behavioral response and the social factors that bear on the decision-making process. This model has been used extensively and is, according to Godin and Shephard, very useful in understanding the decision-making process underlying exercise behavior. These authors present a summary table in their 1990 article pointing to thirteen studies involving exercise and TRA.

5. *The Theory of Interpersonal Behavior.* The brainchild of Triandis (1977), this theory specifies that the likelihood of engaging in a particular behavior is a function of three variables: habit strength, intention, and conditions that encourage or discourage performance of the intended behavior. Much emphasis in this model is placed on the affective dimension of attitude as opposed to the cognitive aspect.

(Continued next page)

Highlight 13.2 (Continued)

Models for Analyzing Exercise Behavior

6. *The Theory of Planned Behavior.* **Ajzen (1985), in a departure from the TRA model of Ajzen and Fishbein (1980), suggests that TRA is useful in explaining volitional behaviors, but is less so with those in the less voluntary category. Perceived behavioral control, an essential component of this theory, represents an extension of facets of TRA and has much in common with Bandura's notion of self-efficacy. At this time, few investigators have employed this model as a vehicle for conducting their research.**

A partial test of three of these models has been made by Yordy and Lent (1993). They compared the reasoned action, planned behavior, and social cognitive models in explaining exercise intentions and behavior by asking 284 introductory psychology students to respond to scenarios related to each of the models. At the same time, previous exercise activity and future exercise intentions and actual behaviors were assessed. Results showed support for the reasoned action and social cognitive models in predicting intentions and behaviors; less support was found for the reasoned action model. Though the Yordy and Lent study had acknowledged possible methodological flaws and dealt with only three of the six competing models, we expect this sort of research to accelerate over the next several years, thereby lending insights into exercise behavior.

Sources: Ajzen (1985); Becker, Haefner, Kasl, Kirscht, Maiman and Rosenstock (1977); Fishbein and Ajzen (1975); Godin and Shephard (1990); Maddux and Rogers (1983); Triandis (1977); Yordy and Lent (1993).

desired response of exercise adherence. This relationship between reinforcement and response, of course, is at the heart of conditioning and learning, discussed in detail in chapter 3. Shephard (1985), at a very practical level, suggests that exercise rewards may be *symbolic* (badge, T-shirt), *material* (money, time off from work), or psychological (friendship, recognition). Regardless of how the various rewards may be structured and dispensed, they are essential in some form or fashion if the goal of exercise adherence is to be achieved.

COGNITIVE AND AFFECTIVE CONSEQUENCES OF EXERCISE

A regular program of exercise is thought to have positive cognitive and affective consequences for both normal and clinical populations. The actual data bearing on this important and complex issue of fitness and its psychological benefits are less compelling. Not all research has found the purported benefits, and many of the existing studies have been plagued with a host of theoretical and methodological ills. The end result is a cloudy picture concerning the relationship between fitness and psychological well-being.

In the next several pages, an attempt will be made to shed light on what is known about exercise and its consequences for cognitive and affective functioning. Much of what will follow is an amalgamation of review articles by Folkins and Sime (1981) and Tomporowski and Ellis (1986).

Effects of Exercise on Cognitive Processes

The pioneering work of Jean Piaget (1936) on the relationship between motor development and cognitive development in children has sparked considerable research in various areas of psychology for more than sixty years. More recently within the psychology and exercise domain, Folkins and Sime (1981) reviewed the available literature on the relationship between exercise and cognitive functioning and concluded that while success has been achieved with geriatric mental patients, the picture was much less clear with normal children and adults, where conflicting results dominate. Tomporowski and Ellis (1986) have reviewed several dozen studies and have generally arrived at the same conclusions as Folkins and Sime. In their review, Tomporowski and Ellis categorized the available studies in one of four ways: (1) very brief, high-intensity anaerobic exercise; (2) short duration, high-intensity anaerobic exercise; (3) short duration, moderate-intensity aerobic exercise; and (4) long duration aerobic exercise.

Very Brief, High-Intensity Anaerobic Exercise

By the very nature of the type of exercise used in anaerobic studies, the physical measures involved a variety of strength tests (e.g., hand dynamometers, weights suspended on pulleys). Most of the research was aimed at testing the inverted-U hypothesis. Results generally indicated

that moderate levels of anaerobic exercise facilitate cognitive performance as measured by such things as addition problems, digit-span tests, perception of geometric figures, and paired-associate learning. High and low levels of tension, on the other hand, did not facilitate cognitive functioning.

Short Duration, High-Intensity Anaerobic Exercise

The results here are most inconclusive. Six of eleven studies surveyed showed no effects; several showed facilitation of cognitive functioning up to ten or fifteen minutes of exercise, at which time impaired performance became dominant. One additional study showed cognitive impairment at all points. Bicycle pedaling, step-up tasks, or treadmill running were paired with discrimination or arithmetic tasks in these various studies.

Short Duration, Moderate-Intensity Aerobic Exercise

Calisthenics, step-up tasks, bicycle pedaling, treadmill running, and run-jog-walk tasks were used as exercises, and a host of cognitive tasks were employed in this group of studies. Studies in which moderate levels of exercise were used tended to report improved cognitive functioning with increases in arousal. Also, highly fit subjects performed better than less physically fit people on cognitive tasks that were administered in the moderate intensity exercise condition.

Long Duration Aerobic Exercise

Tomporowski and Ellis cited only three studies within this category. A marathon race, a five-mile march carrying a 40-pound pack, and a treadmill task to fatigue were used as long duration aerobic events, with signal detection, perceptual organization, and a free-recall memory test serving as the cognitive measures. Facilitation was found in two studies (Gliner, Matsen-Twisdale, Horvath, and Maron, 1979;

Lybrand, Andrews, and Ross, 1954) and no effect was found in the third (Tomoporowski, Ellis, and Stephens, 1985). Clearly, there is a dearth of research related to assessing the effects of long-duration aerobic exercise and cognitive functioning.

The inability of the available research to arrive at a consensus concerning exercise and cognitive functioning has been brought about by a variety of problems. Little of what has been done has been tied to theory, and methodological flaws are numerous. For example, selection bias is found in many studies; that is, subjects are volunteers who are often physically fit and highly motivated prior to any interventions. These volunteers are often compared with themselves or with control groups who differ greatly in fitness, motivation, and many other attributes. Folkins and Sime (1981, p. 386) sum up the selection bias problem as follows: "Self-selected, motivated volunteers may demonstrate improvement in psychological functioning simply because they are motivated for overall self-improvement. It is therefore necessary to arrange for control groups that have time exposure equal to that of trainees, as well as equal and justified expectations for benefit."

Both Folkins and Sime and Tomporowski and Ellis enumerate proposals for improving future research in fitness and cognitive functioning. One suggestion is to pay more attention to the measurement of the physical effects brought about by exercise. An example would be the measurement of lactic acid produced by exercise (Fox, 1984). Another is employment of the perceived exertion methodology of Borg (1973). Yet a third measure of precision is cardiovascular functioning. A fourth improvement suggestion has to do with assessing preintervention levels of fitness. Comparing highly fit, highly motivated subjects with less fit, perhaps even unmotivated individuals undoubtedly contributes little to our understanding of the important issues at hand. Fifth, greater attention should be devoted to sys-

tematic analysis of the intensity and duration of exercise and the placement of the measures of cognitive functioning (that is, during or after exercise), a point noted by Flory and Holmes (1991) in their study of acute bouts of aerobic exercise and subsequent cognitive functioning. Finally, the veritable smorgasbord of cognitive tests used across the variable research studies has contributed to the currently inconclusive picture of the exercise-cognition issue. In all likelihood, many dimensions of cognition have been tapped in the past, and greater selectivity in choosing future cognitive tasks might yield more valid results.

Effects of Exercise on Mood

Affect and mood have long been used synonymously in the psychological literature, and they shall be used interchangeably in the ensuing discussion of the relationship between exercise and affective states. Of the various mood states, two that have come under considerable scrutiny in the exercise literature are anxiety and depression, and we shall confine our discussion to the relevant findings concerning each construct.

Exercise and Anxiety

One of the generally assumed outcomes of exercise is anxiety reduction, and the literature is supportive of this claim. Folkins and Sime (1981) cite fourteen studies dealing with exercise and affect and thirteen of them reported improvement in mood. Of the thirteen positive reports, seven dealt with anxiety and all pointed to improvement related to that particular affective dimension.

As noted earlier, one of the more popular measures of anxiety has been the *State-Trait Anxiety Inventory (STAI)* (Spielberger, Gorsuch, and Lushene, 1970), and the STAI has been used widely in the exercise and affective state research. For example, Long (1984) studied sixty-one volunteers from a selected community using the STAI, among other things. Long's subjects were administered the STAI prior to being assigned to an aerobics conditioning program involving jogging, a waiting list control group, or a stress inoculation training group that was treated for ten weeks in accordance with the system popularized by Meichenbaum (1977). A post-treatment

and a three-month follow-up testing session were also used in Long's research. Results indicated that self-report statements concerning anxiety (the STAI) decreased in both the jogging and the stress inoculation training groups. These changes were still in effect for both groups at the three-month measurement. In a fifteen-month follow-up study, Long (1985) reported data from forty-

---

Highlight 13.3

Hypotheses Used to Account for Anxiety Reduction Associated with Exercise

Morgan (1985) and Raglin and Morgan (1985) have suggested that the purported anxiolytic properties of exercise may be associated with at least four factors:

1. *The Distraction Hypothesis.* This hypothesis hinges on the proposition that various exercise strategies serve to divert or distract subjects from anxiety-producing stressors. It thus serves as a psychological explanation for the anxiety-reducing properties of exercise.
2. *The Endorphin Hypothesis.* Here, the emphasis is on the release of "morphine-like" chemicals within the pituitary gland and the brain that serve to reduce the painful effects while concurrently enhancing the euphoric aspects of exercise. Reports by Droste, Greenlee, Schreck, and Roskamm (1991) in Germany and Kraemer, Dzewaltowski, Blair, Rinehardt, and Castracane (1990) in the United States in which the endorphin hypothesis has not been substantiated casts suspicion on its validity. Nevertheless, the hypothesis remains intriguing and will undoubtedly continue to spawn future research.
3. *The Thermogenic Hypothesis.* In essence, the tension reduction associated with exercise is thought to be produced by the elevation of body temperature. Among other things, this hypothesis works in favor of the tension-reducing properties of, for example, sauna baths.
4. *The Monoamine Hypothesis.* Largely a model based on research with animals, the monoamine hypothesis asserts that anxiety reduction is brought about by exercise through its alteration of various neurotransmitter substances within the brain, namely norepinephrine and serotonin.

Sources: Morgan (1985); Raglin and Morgan (1985); Droste, Greenlee, Schreck, and Roskamm (1991); Kraemer, Dzewaltowski, Blair, Rinehardt, and Castracane (1990).

five of her original sixty-one subjects, and continued reports of less anxiety were noted. Consistent with data reported earlier in this chapter, only 40 percent of the jogging treatment group were still working out at the time the fifteen-month follow-up was conducted. Generally supportive of Long's findings is the work of Berger (1987), who found decreases in state but not trait anxiety in a study of individuals trying to achieve fitness through swimming. Similar decreases in anxiety have been noted by Boutcher and Landers (1988) with regular runners and by Roth (1989) with both active and inactive subjects working on a stationary cycling regimen.

It thus appears that anxiety reduction can be achieved through a regular program of exercise. However, some critics point either to negative findings found elsewhere but not reported here or to research flaws in the studies reporting positive effects. Accordingly, Raglin and Morgan (1985) assert that it would be best to view the relationship between exercise and anxiety reduction as correlational. Their view is that "physical activity of a vigorous nature is *associated* with improved mood state but available research does not support the commonly held view that exercise *causes* their observed alterations in mood" (p. 182). Until such time as causative links are clearly delineated, it seems appropriate to accept the Raglin and Morgan caveat as illustrative of the current state of the art related to exercise and anxiety reduction.

Additional testimony to the fragile nature of the anxiety and exercise relationship is offered by Desharnais, Jobin, Cote, Levesque, and Godin (1993), who indicate that there may be a strong placebo effect associated with exercise. Desharnais et al. placed forty-eight healthy adults engaged in a ten-week exercise program into two equal groups, experimentals and controls. They led the experimental subjects to believe that their regimen was specifically designed to facilitate psychological well-being. No such intervention was made with the second group. Subsequent measures of fitness indicated improvements for both groups over the ten-week exercise program; however, the experimental subjects improved significantly with regard to scores on a measure of self-esteem when compared with the controls. While these findings need replication, they are further testimony to the tenuous nature of the anxiety and exercise connection.

Exercise and Depression

Depression is a well-documented source of human suffering. According to data from the President's Committee on Mental Health, one of every four Americans suffers from depression at any given time (Monahan, 1986). Depression is, as might be expected, at the root of most suicides, with perhaps 80 percent or more being depression related (Monahan, 1986). Depression is characterized by withdrawal, inactivity, and feelings of hopelessness and loss of control. By acting on each of these symptoms, physical exercise has become popular as a therapeutic intervention in depression.

The use of physical exercise as part of the treatment of depression received much impetus in the late 1970s from a scientific report by Greist, Klein, Eischens, and Faris (1978) and from popular books extolling the virtues of running as a means of promoting overall mental and physical well-being (Fixx, 1977).

The popularity of running as a therapeutic intervention has been propelled to the forefront of the exercise-as-therapy literature through a number of research efforts. This is certainly not intended to suggest that other exercises might not be useful, but merely that running has received the most favorable press. Greist et al. are quick to point out that while other exercise modalities are probably quite useful, they used only running in their treatment and research programs. Bearing on this point, Brown, Ramirez, and Taub (1978) found decreases in depression in their study of high school and college students with wrestling, mixed exercise, and jogging. Tennis produced marginal but positive effects, while softball had no effect at all on depression scores. The greater reduction in depression in the Brown et al. study was in the subjects who engaged in a ten-week program of jogging that required the subjects to work out five times per week.

Considering the pivotal role the work of Greist and his associates has played in the exercise-as-therapy for depression movement, a brief elaboration on their work seems timely. In their study, subjects (men and women) who had been diagnosed as clinically depressed were assigned to one of three groups, a time-limited psychotherapy group (n = 9), a time-unlimited psychotherapy group (n = 7), and a running treatment group (n = 8). The time-limited psychotherapy group received ten therapy sessions emphasizing immediate change strategies; the time-unlimited group was given psychodynamic-oriented therapy; and the eight runners met with a running therapist (not a psychologist or psychiatrist). Stretching, thirty to forty-five minutes of walking and running, discussions while exercising with little emphasis on the depression itself, and further stretching characterized the intervention for the running group. According to Greist and his colleagues, six of the eight patients were essentially well at the end of three weeks, another at the end of the sixteenth week, and one neither improved nor deteriorated although her overall fitness level improved. The overall conclusion was that running was as successful as traditional psychotherapy and at a considerable saving in terms of money and time for the clients. Though the Greist et al. study is not above criticism, the work has been well-received concerning the possible utility of exercise as a means of dealing with depression. Brown (see Monahan, 1986, p. 197), in a burst of enthusiasm, says, "It's almost too good to be true. If you could bottle it and sell it over the counter, you'd make hundreds."

Despite the strength of the research findings and the exuberance of the various testimonials by practitioners, the depression research suffers from many of the same problems as does that in the area of anxiety. Better use of theory and more focused attention to methodological issues is clearly called for. Also, the link between exercise and depression is, as was the case in anxiety discussed earlier, more correlational than causal at this point. More research is needed to establish the supposed causal link between the two.

Considerations in Using Exercise as Therapy for Anxiety or Depression

A number of issues need to be addressed when prescribing exercise as therapy for either anxiety or depression, and a careful delineation of these concerns has been made by Buffone (1984). One issue brought up is that of proper psychological diagnosis and a corresponding *individually tailored exercise prescription*. Choice of type of exercise enters in here, as does the notion of combining running with other possible therapeutic modalities, such as stress inoculation training mentioned earlier in the Long studies (1984, 1985). A second issue to consider is the *proficiency of the exercise therapist*. This person should have mental health training as well as skill in conducting proper exercise. Also, this individual should serve as a *model* for the advantages of exercise and ideally possess expertise in the prevention and treatment of exercise-related injuries. Finally, *reinforcement of exercise behaviors* must be a concern of all involved parties. Care in this area should be exercised to insure that the exercise regimen, once introduced, becomes a positive therapeutic force and not a negative addiction for the client. The consequences of negative addiction to exercise may be such that the client ends up merely trading one problem for another.

Additional caveats with regard to the exercise-as-therapy movement are offered by Martinsen (1990) and Raglin (1990). Both authorities suggest that exercise may be more useful with certain types of mood disorders, and may be of limited utility with others. If such a supposition is true, it would behoove the exercise professional to select clients with the most potential to profit from physical activity.

Raglin goes on to indicate that, in those cases where exercise exerts a beneficial effect on mood, it may be sufficient to merely exercise; that is, fitness as it is usually defined is not necessary for exercise to generate the desired effects on anxiety or depression. As an aside, Raglin also indicates that too vigorous an exercise regimen is quite capable of producing undesirable mood swings in people with heretofore stable emotional patterns. Thus, care should be taken to avoid creating problems in so-called normals when there is such a crying need for competent and effective treatment of individuals with genuine mood-related problems.

SPECIAL FITNESS POPULATIONS

The intent of this section is to address some of the remaining important issues within sport and fitness. Runners, marathoners, and ultramarathoners will be discussed within the context of the notions of positive and negative addiction. Also, there has been an explosion of interest of late in exercise, fitness, and competitive activities for *senior citizens,* and we shall survey what is going on with this increasingly numerous segment of our population.

The Runner

Whatever the explanation, running has become quite popular as a means of achieving fitness. Some people approach running (and other forms of exercise) with reason, and this is referred to as a *positive addiction to exercise.* Other exercisers seem to lose sight of what exercise is all about, and the rabidity with which they pursue the elusive goal of fitness is so notice-

ably excessive that *negative addiction* can be readily inferred.

Sachs (1982) has addressed this addiction issue by suggesting that if exercise addiction does in fact exist, it might be viewed as a continuum in which exercise for the negatively addicted individual has gone from mere importance to a controlling factor that dominates other life choices. To put it another way, Sachs says that the positively addicted individual controls the activity and the negatively addicted person is controlled by the activity.

Pierce (1994) has expanded our insights into the exercise addiction issue by introducing the term *exercise dependence,* which describes the symptoms previously mentioned. Other terminology that has been used to account for the addictive qualities of exercise and, most particularly running, are obligatory running (Yates, Leehey, and Shisslak, 1983), morbid exercising (Waldstreicher, 1985), and compulsive jogging (Veale de Coverley, 1987). Though these assorted terms are provocative and have much in common with addictions, we will confine ourselves for the present to discussing positive and negative addiction as popularized by psychiatrist William Glasser.

Positive Addiction

Glasser (1976) discusses his notion of positive addiction in a book by the same name; he suggests that running, among all possible exercises, is most likely to result in the highly prized positive addiction. To quote Glasser (p. 104):

> I believe that running creates the optimal condition for positive addiction because it is our most ancient and still most effective survival mechanism. We are descended from those who ran to stay alive, and this need to run is programmed genetically into our brains. When we have gained the endurance to run long distances easily, then a good run reactivates the ancient neural program. As this occurs, we reach a state of mental preparedness

that leads to a basic feeling of satisfaction that is less-critical than any other activity that we can do alone.

Though there are many who would argue with Glasser as to the origin of our propensity to run, he does make a compelling case for his point of view with regard to the positive and addictive qualities of running.

Just what is this quality known as positive addiction to running/exercise? Positive addiction is characterized, first of all, by an element of controllability; that is, the person involved controls the exercise regimen. Beyond the control factor, the positively addicted person carefully programs exercise into his or her daily life. Careful organization of competing activities takes place so as to reduce possible sources of interference with the exercise program. Exercise is blended in with work and family life in such a way as to add to rather than detract from those important life dimensions. As one becomes more positively addicted, feelings of control, competence, and physical and psychological well-being increase. Conversely, if the positively addicted person is forced by scheduling conflicts, illness, or injury to miss working out, there is a sense of loss, guilt, and physical and mental discomfort. One runner who responded to Glasser summed up his feelings about missing his running workouts as follows: "When I miss my workouts I feel as though I have let myself down. My personal integrity suffers a blow. Guilt feelings mount continuously until I run again. . . . I am glad, however, that I feel this way because it is the watchdog that makes sure I do my running." If all potential exercisers could arrive at such a point of positive addiction, exercise adherence would rapidly become a nonissue.

One of the first studies aimed at substantiating the positive addictive qualities of running was conducted by Carmack and Martens (1979). These researchers administered a Commitment to Running Scale to 250 male and 65 female runners of various competence and experience levels, and support for both the validity of the scale and the positive addiction notion was demonstrated.

Similar results have been reported by Chapman and DeCastro (1990); these researchers found that addiction to running was associated with positive personality characteristics. Anshel (1991), in looking at addicted and nonaddicted runners, found that the former group demonstrated those characteristics suggested by Glasser. Of particular interest, and important in terms of distinguishing between positive and negative addiction, was the finding that addicted runners in the Anshel study were likely to run despite injury or illness, but were realistic when faced with the reality that occasional health setbacks would occur and periodically interfere with their running propensities.

Negative Addiction

If exercise is viewed as bipolar, as suggested by Sachs (1984), noncompliance would represent one end of the continuum and addiction the other. In turn, addiction might also be viewed as bipolar, with the range running from the positive to the negative dimensions. All of us who have exercised for any length of time have been exposed to persons for whom exercise has become their master. Their behavior is so out of the ordinary that it is noticeable to all observers. They run until they drop. Their life is dominated by running. They fail to use good judgment as to their strengths and weaknesses as a runner. They run to the detriment of their health, career, family, and interpersonal relationships.

Research and speculation about negative addiction was initiated by Morgan (1979), who felt that such a state had been reached when the person believed that running was necessary in order to cope with everyday life and if withdrawal symptoms emerged when running was withdrawn.

One index of running gone awry is found in injury statistics. Diekhoff (1984), in a study of sixty-eight committed male and female runners, administered a Type A/B Scale, an Addiction to Running Scale, and a Commitment to Running Scale. He found that those who had suffered injuries while running tended to be Type A personalities, addicted to running, committed to running, ran more miles, and were more likely to run in fun runs and races than were the noninjured runners. A significant correlation was found between addiction to running and number of doctor visits and between the use of drugs or physical therapy and commitment to running. Layman and Morris (1986) studied more than one thousand runners of all levels of ability and experience and found a highly significant relationship between addiction to running and injuries. Almost 60 percent of the runners in their study reported running-related injuries in the preceding twelve months. Sixty percent of the injured runners considered themselves to be addicted to running. Hailey and Bailey (1982), as part of their attempt to validate the Negative Addiction Scale, found a linear relationship between years of running and negative addiction; addiction scores on their scale were significantly higher for runners who had run from one to four years than for those who had been running for less than a year.

Mood and Running

Perhaps the most consistent research effort related to runners of various persuasions is found in seventeen studies that used the *Profile of Mood States (POMS)*. A summary of these studies can be found in table 13.2. Several conclusions about runners can be drawn from the various studies. One is that running appears to have a facilitative effect on mood. In all studies in which runners were compared with groups of nonrunners, there were clear differences in mood state in favor of the runners. Second, the two studies in which an attempt was made to tease out the role of endogenous opiates (endorphins) were equivocal, which is representative of the overall literature on the exercise-endorphin relationship. Finally, it appears that runners of all levels of competence share somewhat equally in the mood benefits associated with their selected exercise medium. The research on this latter point, however, is scant, and any conclusions drawn at this time should be considered as tentative.

Runner's High

Much interest has been shown among runners and sport scientists alike concerning what, for lack of a better term, has come to be known as the "runner's high." The runner's high is characterized by an unexpected and heightened sense of well-being that may vary from runner to runner in frequency, intensity, and duration. It apparently occurs only in distance runners and probably will not be experienced by runners who log only six to ten miles per week (Weltman and Stamford, 1983). Wagemaker and Goldstein (1980) indicate that the runner's high will occur only in individuals who run for twenty-five or thirty minutes. Sachs (1984) says that at least thirty minutes of running is necessary; in addition, he thinks that distances of six miles or more are required. There is lively argumentation as to whether many distance runners experience the phenomenon at all. James Menegazzi, an exercise researcher and avid runner, believes that the runner's high is a function of endorphin infusion that only takes place at high intensity. As a consequence, Menegazzi has altered his own weekly workout schedule from fifty miles at a moderate clip to twenty-five miles of hard running ("Scanning Sports," 1989).

Estimates of the occurrence of the runner's high range from 9 to 10 percent of all runners (Weinberg, 1980) to 77 or 78 percent (Lilliefors, 1978; Sachs, 1980). As Sachs (1984) has pointed

Table 13.2
Mood State Profiles of Runners

Researcher(s)	Subjects	Results
Cockerill, Nevill, and Byrne (1992)	40 females in high intensity training studied for link between training, mood, and menstrual period	POMS sensitive in picking up mood changes in amenorrheic & non-amenorrheic (eumenorrheic or oligomenorrheic) distance runners and inactive controls
deGeus, Lorenz, van Doornen, and Orlebeke (1993)	62 subjects in 3 experimental conditions, 1 control group for aerobic fitness study	Weak link noted between fitness and mood states
Durtschi and Weiss (1986)	18 elite, 48 non-elite marathon runners, males and females	Few differences in two groups of marathoners; Iceberg Profile not substantiated
Dyer and Crouch (1987)	20 beginning, 20 advanced, 19 control undergraduate runners	Both running groups significantly more positive mood profiles than controls; running had positive effect on both groups of runners
Farrell, Gates, Maksud, and Morgan (1982)	6 experienced distance runners	Mood states improved after treadmill task
Gondola and Tuckman (1982)	348 nonelite marathoners, 856 college students	Marathoners less tense, depressed, fatigued, confused, more vigorous than college sample
Gondola and Tuckman (1983)	68 marathoners, 210 10-Kers, 186 aspiring 10-Kers	10-Kers less tense, depressed than other two groups; 10-Kers less angry, fatigued than marathoners; 10-Kers more vigorous, less confused than aspiring 10-Kers
Joesting (1981)	50 sailors, 130 runners	Male runners less depressed, angry, fatigued than male sailors; female runners less fatigued than female sailors
Kraemer, Dzewaltowski, Blair, Rinehardt, and Castracane (1990)	13 trained, 10 untrained males and females on treadmill	Mood improved after treadmill task for both groups; no endorphin changes were noted
Markoff, Ryan, and Young (1982)	11 male, 4 female marathoners	Less anger and depression on pre- and post-running POMS administration
Morgan and Pollock (1977)	World class middle and long distance runners, world class marathoners, college middle distance runners	Athletes less tense, depressed, fatigued, confused, higher vigor than norm group from POMS manual; elite and college runners not different

Table 13.2 *(Continued)*

Researcher(s)	Subjects	Results
Porter (1985)	Average female runners	Profiles similar to those of young elite male runners
Tharion, Strowman, and Rauch (1988)	56 male ultramarathon runners	Ultramarathoners had Iceberg Profile at initial testing; vigor reduced, fatigue elevated after race
Thaxton (1982)	24 male, 9 female experienced runners	Mood changes noted with even slight changes in training regimen
Thomas, Zebas, Bahrke, Araujo, and Etheridge (1983)	24 college distance runners, 20 jumpers and sprinters	Similar profiles for both groups; overall profile similar to elite performers in other sports
Williams, Krahenbuhl, and Morgan (1991)	10 trained runners	Running efficiency positively related to mood states
Wilson, Morley, and Bird (1980)	10 marathoners, 10 joggers, 10 nonexercisers	Both exercise groups less depressed, angry, confused, more vigorous than nonexercisers; marathoners less depressed, angry, confused, more vigorous than joggers

out, a range of 9 to 78 percent indicates that we have much to learn about the mysterious phenomenon of the runner's high.

The diversity of descriptive terms used to flesh out the runner's high illustrates just how complex and elusive the phenomenon is. To Csikszentmihalyi (1975), the runner's high is described as "flow." To Henderson (1977) it is a "natural laxative" that throws off the waste in the body and mind. "Transcendence" and "euphoric sensation" are descriptive terms used by Sachs (1980, 1984). Peoples (1983) talks in terms of "steady state stimulation." For Ravizza (1984), the runner's high is merely one example of "peak experience" associated with sport. Johnsgard (1985) draws parallels between the runner's high and the tranquil state often thought to be a part of transcendental meditation, and he uses terms like "centering state" and "existential drift" for purposes of enhancing his explanation. Murray Allen, a physician and kine-

siologist, says that "runner's calm" brought about by the quieting as opposed to excitatory effects is the key descriptor (Hopson, 1988). Masters (1992), in a study of thirty male and female marathoners, indicated that 73 percent of his sample had experienced runner's high at some point, and 66 percent experienced it during the marathon under scrutiny. The most common term applied to the runner's high for Masters' sample was "general happiness"; on the other hand, "total euphoria" was the least descriptive term used in his study.

Agreement exists that the runner's high is a real but esoteric phenomenon that almost defies description. Problems in operationally defining the experience are a result of this verbal richness, and research in the area is thereby hampered. Nevertheless, further investigation into the runner's high is warranted in view of the fascination it has provided individuals who have been fortunate enough to have had the experience.

Marathon Runners

Tradition has it that the marathon event was named in honor of the city of Marathon, some twenty-six miles from Athens and the scene of one of the most significant battles between the Greeks and the invading Persians in the year 490 B.C. The Greeks inflicted a great defeat on the numerically superior Persian forces, and the news of the victory was carried from Marathon to Athens by a runner named Pheidippides. Pheidippides reportedly died of exhaustion after his victory announcement (Howell, 1983). Grogan (1981), in a bit of a disclaimer, suggests that the legendary runner was probably named Pheidippides, may or may not have run from Marathon to Athens, and most probably did not die after his victory announcement because he was an accomplished ultramarathoner. Well-documented accounts indicated that Pheidippides had run from Athens to Sparta and back, a distance of two hundred miles, in three or four days, in search of support troops for the upcoming battle at Marathon shortly before his relatively short run from Marathon to Athens.

Arguments as to the origin of the marathon aside, it was a part of the first modern Olympics in 1896, with a field of twenty-five entrants. Only nineteen ran in 1900 and fourteen finished the event in 1904. With each successive Olympics, however, the number of runners has increased. Women participated in the marathon for the first time in the 1984 Olympics in Los Angeles.

Several studies related to personality variables have pointed to marathoners being introverted

---

<table>
<tr><td>

Highlight 13.4

</td><td>

Runner's High: A Case Study

JRN and I visited Bruce Ogilvie for three days in 1981 at his home in Los Gatos, California. On the morning of the second day, we joined Bruce and several of his friends for a six-mile run at 5:30 A.M. The first two miles of the chosen course involved the ascent of a steep incline, most certainly what would be called a mountain in most of our home state of Texas, and the toll extracted on a sore knee left me far behind the pack. Eventually, I lost sight of the other joggers. In the process, I missed a critical turn up the side of a mountain that ultimately led back down to the starting point in Los Gatos. This error added an additional five or six miles to the overall trip. Somewhere along the way, a mixture of exhaustion, cool early morning air, the excitement of the trip to California, the beauty of the landscape, the smell of anise, and an unscheduled running tour of the various wineries along the way produced what must have been the elusive "runner's high" so often referred to by runners and researchers. Though the distance covered far exceeded anything I had covered before, the feeling at the end was one of light-headed giddiness as well as disappointment and frustration because no one wanted to continue the run. Was this the "runner's high"? I suspect so, and I doubt that it will ever happen again. I'm just glad I was there to be a part of what may be, for most of us, a once-in-a-lifetime experience.

Source: Sachs (1984).

</td></tr>
</table>

as opposed to extraverted personalities (e.g., Clit-some and Kostrubala, 1977; Gontang, Clitsome, and Kostrubala, 1977; Morgan and Costill, 1972; Silva and Hardy, 1986). Others have pointed to low anxiety levels (Morgan and Costill, 1972; Silva and Hardy, 1986). Still others have found superior mood profiles, primarily using the POMS (Gondola and Tuckman, 1982; Markoff, Ryan, and Young, 1982; Morgan and Pollock, 1977; Silva and Hardy, 1986; Tharion, Strow-man, & Rauch, 1988; Wilson, Morley, and Bird, 1980). Although the evidence is insufficient at this time in terms of creating a marathon run-ner personality profile, a number of psycholog-ical benefits appear to be associated with such an undertaking, a finding that is consistent with claims made about the positive effects of run-ning and exercise in general.

The most comprehensive summary to date with regard to motives to participate in mara-thon running is that of Masters, Ogles, and Jol-ton (1993). Based on a thorough review of the literature and conclusions drawn from their own research, these investigators have identified four major reasons for running marathons: psycho-logical, physical, social, and achievement. Each of these four major variables is then broken into subcomponents, and they can be seen in the general model provided in figure 13.1.

In addition to presenting a workable model to guide future research on the "mind" of the marathoner, Masters et al. have created an instru-ment to assess motives for competing in mara-thons called the Motivations of Marathoners Scales (MOMS). A subsequent study of 472 run-ners of varying degrees of marathon experience in which the MOMS was used has lent further validity to the scale (Masters and Ogles, 1995). In the Masters and Ogles study, the MOMS suc-cessfully differentiated among the motivations of experienced, mid-level experienced, and rookie marathoners.

In view of the success of the MOMS and the marathoner model, Masters and his col-leagues will undoubtedly play an active role in guiding future research in this intriguing area of inquiry within sport psychology.

Ultramarathoners

McCutcheon and Yoakum (1983) define an ultramarathon as any race that exceeds the offi-cial marathon distance of 26 miles, 385 yards. Maron and Horvath (1978) divide ultramara-thons into those that require repetitive days of running long distances and those that are con-tinuous for distances up to 100 miles. Maron and Horvath, in a study of runners participating in the first type of ultramarathon, were interested in physiological variables only. The race in ques-tion was run in 1928, and involved running the 3,484 miles between Los Angeles and New York City. The twenty-five entrants who finished the event averaged 41 miles a day for eighty-four con-secutive days; interestingly, few and only minor physiological problems were found at the end of the grueling competition.

In an ultramarathon race similar to the 1928 one described by Maron and Horvath, Lewis (1992) describes the trials and tribulations of a trek from California to New York, an event won by David Warady of Huntington Beach, Califor-nia, who completed the 3,000 miles in 521 hours and 35 minutes spaced over sixty-four days. One of the competitors, Al Howie of Scotland, had recently run 4,500 miles across Canada, averag-ing 62 miles per day in the process. Unlike the results reported by Maron and Horvath, Howie and fifteen other runners eventually dropped out of the competition, most due to injury.

A study of the second type suggested by Maron and Horvath involved six hundred par-ticipants in a fifty-four mile race run annually in South Africa. No physiological problems of consequence were noted in the participants.

Psychological descriptions of ultramarathon-ers (increasingly being referred to as ultrarunners) are scant. Folkins and Wieselberg-Bell (1981), in a study of entrants in what they consider to be

Figure 13.1: **Model of Motives for Running Marathons**

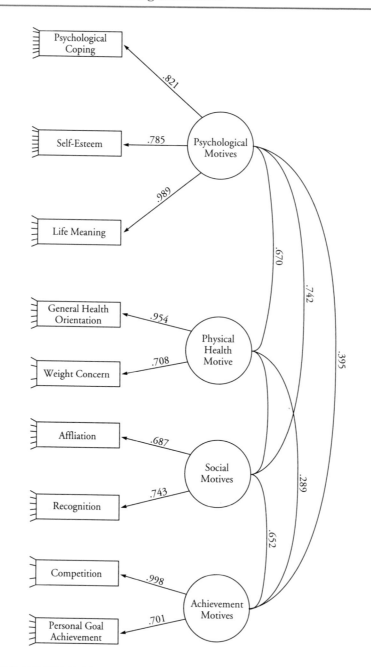

Source: Masters, Ogles, and Jolton (1993).

the toughest endurance run in the United States (a hundred-mile trail over the crest of the Sierra Nevada mountains known as the Western States Endurance Run), found deviant MMPI scores on several subscales in comparisons of finishers and nonfinishers. The finishers had higher Psychopathic deviate (Pd), Depression (D), and Schizophrenia (Sc) scores. On the whole, however, Folkins and Wieselberg-Bell concluded that the ultramarathoners as a group appeared to be reasonably normal, and they interpreted the deviant MMPI scores as being perhaps necessary for completion of basically what may be a deviant task. Another study of ultramarathoners by McCutcheon and Yoakum (1983) revealed no personality differences between their subjects and a matched group of runners who had never competed at distances over ten miles.

An interesting variant related to the mental composition of the ultramarathoner has been provided by Bull (1989). In a comprehensive case study of one competitor, Bull administered four psychometric tests and developed a training, evaluation, and crisis intervention program to assist the runner in question through a gruelling twenty-day run across the 500-mile perimeter of the Mojave Desert in California. Tests administered included the Sixteen Personality Factor Questionnaire (16PF), the Tennessee Self-Concept Scale (TSCS), the State-Trait Anxiety Inventory (STAI), and the Sport Competition Anxiety Test (SCAT). Test results indicated that the ultramarathoner in question was generally within the normal range on the traits measured by the 16PF, was highly trait-anxious on both the STAI and the SCAT, and was slightly below the population mean on self-concept score. Overall, however, little of the deviance suggested by Folkins and Wieselberg-Bell was found in this runner.

Clearly, little is known about the psychological makeup of these interesting athletes. Perhaps future research will be directed toward gaining an understanding of a phenomenon that may,

as suggested by Folkins and Wieselberg-Bell, require a little deviance.

Exercise and Competition for Senior Citizens

How old would you be if you didn't know how old you was?

Satchel Paige, legendary baseball pitcher

A 1987 front page graphic in *USA Today* indicated that the median age of the American population was 31.7 years in 1986 and will rise to 41.6 by the year 2050. One repercussion of this "graying of America" has to do with the role of fitness and competition as a means of adding to the quality of life for senior citizens. Fitness advocates and sport scientists have spent very little time studying the physical fitness and competitive needs, wishes, and talents of people forty-five years of age and older. More attention will be paid to these older citizens in the future, with the goal of improving the quality if not the quantity of life.

Myths permeate the literature concerning the effects of exercise on the aging process. In the next several pages, we shall look at what we know about exercise and competition for senior citizens.

Fitness Issues for Seniors

Veschi (1963) has quoted Rousseau, the eighteenth century French philosopher: "When a body is strong, it obeys; when it is weak, it gives orders." Perhaps this observation is nowhere more applicable than to our generally less-fit seniors. We have all seen an older person who shuffles, a characteristic related to the inevitable shrinkage of connective tissue that so greatly limits length and resiliency of stride. One can go on and on about other examples of the effects of sedentary living; suffice it to say that many of these results of physical deterioration could have been fended off or ameliorated with a good physical activity program.

We have some measure of control over the biological dimension of the aging process. We can apparently moderate the effects of aging through diet, exercise, and prudence in everyday matters. Smith and Gilliam (1983) and Stamford (1984) all indicate that 50 percent of the physical decline associated with age is due to disuse rather than senescence. Substantiation of this point about aging and exercise is offered by Steinhaus, Dustman, Ruhling, Emmerson, Johnson, Shearer, Latin, Shigeoka, and Bonekat (1990). This research team monitored a four-month fast walking or jogging and stretching exercise regimen for twenty-eight sedentary males and females, ages fifty-five to seventy, and found significantly improved aerobic capacity and other indicators of fitness among their subjects. A four-year follow-up showed a 64 percent exercise adherence rate for the group. Similarly, Morey, Cowper, Feussner, DiPasquale, Crowley, and Sullivan (1991), using a two-year exercise regimen, found significant gains in cardiovascular fitness and flexibility in a group of elderly subjects residing in a Veteran's Administration Hospital in North Carolina. Looking at gains in muscle strength as an indicator of fitness, Fiatarone, Marks, Ryan, Meredith, Lipsitz, and Evans (1990) studied a most unusual sample, namely men and women ages eighty-six to ninety-six. These researchers placed six women and four men with extreme sedentary habits and significant health problems on an eight-week strength program of progressive resistance involving the lower leg only. An average strength gain across all subjects of 174 percent was noted over the eight-week exercise period. The authors conclude that much of the strength loss associated with aging is modifiable through exercise. Also, safety concerns about weight training with senior citizens were greatly allayed.

In a most interesting follow-up to her earlier work, Fiatarone and several colleagues (Fiatarone, O'Neill, Ryan, Clements, Solares, Nelson,

Diet and exercise have been shown to positively affect the aging process.

Roberts, Kehayias, Lipsitz, and Evans, 1994) randomly assigned one hundred frail nursing home residents to one of four groups for a ten-week experiment designed to see if weakness and immobility in these individuals could be partially allayed. Three times a week, group one received resistance training for thigh and hip muscles. Groups two and three received vitamin-fortified, 360-calorie drinks. Group four received none of these potentially helpful aids. Positive results were found in the muscle resistance training group: gait velocity in exercisers improved nearly 12 percent, stair-climbing power improved over 28 percent, and thigh muscle size grew by 2.7 percent. As an added extra, four members of the weight training group were able to get out of their walkers and begin using a cane. All gains noted were achieved irrespective of initial frailty, age, gender, or medical condition.

All wishes to the contrary aside, there are legitimate physiological changes associated with

The Interplay Between Exercise and Aging

Highlight 13.5

Waneen Wyrick Spirduso has carved out a most significant research niche in the area of aging and exercise. In a comprehensive survey of the available literature up to 1980, she concluded that, methodological shortcomings aside, there is indirect evidence to suggest that the decline in some aspects of brain functioning in the motoric sense may be substantially allayed by chronic exercise. Inasmuch as it is largely inexpensive, unobtrusive, and self-imposed, exercise may actually offer significant intervention in the aging process, according to Spirduso. The psychological and societal ramifications of this assertion are considerable and merit further attention.

It would appear that simple reaction time as measured by response to a visual stimulus is affected not so much by age as physical condition. Spirduso and Clifford (1978) looked at young runners, young racket-sports competitors, older racket-sports competitors, older runners, young in-actives, and older inactives (young was defined as twenty to thirty years of age, while older was fifty to seventy). The linear relationship between extent of physical involvement and simple reaction and movement time is graphically displayed in figure 13.2.

The significant differences are most noticeable between inactive young and old people and the other four groups. This suggests that differences in simple reaction and movement time are more a function of fitness level than of age.

Sources: Spirduso (1980, 1983); Spirduso and Clifford (1978).

Figure 13.2: Age, Physical Fitness, and Reaction Time*

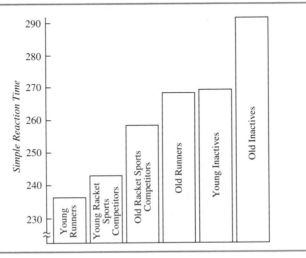

*Ordinal values are in milliseconds.

Source: Spirduso and Clifford (1978).

age and we would be remiss to ignore them. There are unassailable declines in muscle mass and increases in weight and body fat due to a slowing of basal metabolism. Flexibility is affected by aging, as is bone mineral content. Cardiovascular changes involving the heart, the blood vessels, lung surface area, and elasticity are real (Smith and Zook, 1986). These must all be taken into account when drawing up an exercise prescription for an older client. At the same time, we should encourage lifelong fitness as a means for altering the course of deterioration of these various bodily systems.

At the psychological level, little is known about people who either have exercised throughout their lives or have only recently begun such a program. Physical benefits have been found in the case of people who have begun an exercise regimen after age sixty (e.g., Sager, 1984; Sidney and Shephard, 1976). The comparable data on psychological benefits of such efforts is scant. Supposition of improved well-being and higher self-esteem are easily invoked, but actual supportive data are rare. Sidney and Shephard (1976) did find a decrease in anxiety levels in a sample of men and women over sixty years of age who underwent a fourteen-week conditioning program. Much more research needs to be conducted to help substantiate the notion that there are, in fact, psychological benefits to exercise for senior citizens.

The Competitive Senior

Beyond accounts found largely in the popular press, not a great deal more is known about competitive seniors—those athletes who choose to enter various sporting events for the thrill and challenge provided. Rudman (1986), in an attempt to assess how sports are viewed by three different age groups (eighteen to thirty-four, thirty-five to fifty-four, fifty-five plus), queried 1,319 subjects about their participation in fourteen different athletic events. Age, marital status, income, occupational status, and geographic location served as independent variables in the Rudman study. Among the more notable, though not surprising, results was a clear age-related bias in sport involvement. A steady age-related decrease was found; only golf was exempt from differential participation as a function of chronology. The largest drop-off in sport involvement occurred between the eighteen to thirty-four and the thirty-five to fifty-four age groups, suggesting that discontinuation from competition takes place fairly early in life.

A most fascinating exception to the preceding rule is former Olympic sprint star Thane Baker of Dallas, Texas. Baker won a silver medal in the 1952 Olympics and a silver in the 100 meters, a bronze in the 200 meters, and a gold as a member of the winning 400-meter relay team in the 1956 Olympic Games. He continued competing in track over the years and set world records in the 100 meters for men aged forty to forty-four (10.7), forty-five to forty-nine (11.0), and fifty to fifty-four (11.3) as well as the world mark in the 200 meters for ages fifty to fifty-four (23.4). As a fifty-two-year old in 1986, he ran a 10.99 (100 yards) in an all-comers meet at Southern Methodist University (SMU). Of his time at SMU, Baker said: "I hasten to add that I had a pretty good tailwind when I did it, but I am fully aware that it might be the last time I break 11 seconds, so I'll take it any way I can get it" (Vernon, 1984, p. 2C).

An interesting approach to fostering competition among senior athletes over the age of fifty-five has been put together by the fitness coordinator for Baltimore (Maryland) County and described by Zeigler and Michael (1985). The competition, known as the Maryland Senior Olympics, was instituted in 1980 with three hundred entrants, a figure that doubled by the 1984 games. Thirty events encompassing seventeen different sports comprise the games, with separate male and female competition, except for the three coeducational activities: square dancing and doubles in tennis and badminton. Continual

Hundreds of Maryland residents over fifty-five gather annually to compete in over thirty events in the state's Senior Olympics.

revamping of the competition has been done to stay within reasonable safety limits that might be specific to seniors. Games such as those of Baltimore County offer fun and safe competition for older athletes.

Competitions such as the Maryland Games have blossomed into the United States National Senior Olympics, which have been held every two years since 1987. Well over 3,500 competitors compete in fifteen different sports, and they are selected from a talent pool of some 200,000 individuals over the age of fifty-five who have taken part in one of the fifty-five sanctioned games all over the country. Tom Bill, a gymnast in the 1956 Olympic Games, now competes at the senior level in badminton, where he is a multiple medal winner. In an effort to capture the essence of the Senior Olympics, Bill ("Sports Camaraderie," 1989, p. 8C) says: "In '56, we were competing for fame and glory. Now, whether we win or lose comes second to having fun. There is great camaraderie here."

A Final Note

As sport scientists, we can ignore the needs and wishes of our older citizens for fitness and competitive outlets or we can respond to the challenges at hand. More research is needed to help gain insight into our older citizens so that a greater quality of life can be provided through carefully chosen exercise or physical activity. Increasingly, professionals in the health business are reassessing the fascination with running and superior cardiovascular functioning as the major indicators of fitness. Brisk walking, ardent gardening, enthusiastic carpentry, or physical activity of any kind may be as healthy for those who enjoy them as jogging, calisthenics, or aerobic dancing are for others. Much remains to be done in tailoring exercise or physical activity to individuals' needs, wishes, and capabilities.

SUMMARY

1. The continuing fascination with fitness has led to much speculation and research aimed at promoting a better understanding of exercise and its relationship to mental and physical fitness. Why people value fitness, why others cannot adhere to fitness regimens, and the consequences of exercise for prevention and alleviation of anxiety and depression are

The Retired Athlete

Retirement from athletics can occur at a number of junctures and for several reasons. One popular point of departure for discussing career termination is retirement from intercollegiate athletics and another is termination of a professional career. In turn, these retirements may occur for at least three reasons – the selection process, chronological age, or incapacitating injury (Ogilvie and Howe, 1986).

The selection process is particularly brutal. According to Paul Dietzel (1983), a former head football coach and athletic director, only 1 out of every 235 high school players will ever "start" for a Division 1 college team. Even more remote is the possibility of a professional football career; only 1 out of each 5,635 (.018 percent) high school football players will play for a professional team. To compound this problem, only a few of those who make it into the professional ranks will stay long. The average career in the National Football League is 4.2 years; in the National Basketball Association, the statistics are even more grim. The career expectancy of an NBA player is 3.4 seasons. Making it to the professional level is a long shot at best, and survival in such a "Darwinian sports world" (Ogilvie and Howe, 1986, p. 366) is a gargantuan undertaking in its own right. Another view of the selection process discussed so far is provided by Ogilvie and Howe (1986, p. 366):

	Basketball	*Football*
High school	700,000	1,300,000 +
College (NCAA today)	15,000	75,000
Draft	200 (NBA)	320 (NFL)
Final selection	50	150

What becomes of people who retire from sport? The answer to this question is best understood in terms of two perspectives, that of the collegiate athlete who is terminating an athletic career and that of the professional player who is leaving what may amount to a lifetime of sports involvement.

THE COLLEGIATE ATHLETE

Two studies (Greendorfer and Blinde, 1985; Kleiber, Greendorfer, Blinde, and Samdahl, 1987) have generated some understanding of the dynamics concerning the collegiate athlete who "hangs it up" after expiration of

(Continued next page)

Highlight 13.6 (Continued)

The Retired Athlete

eligibility. Reviewing these two research efforts, we can draw several conclusions. One is that termination of athletics at this level is far from traumatic for the majority of athletes involved. In the Greendorfer and Blinde study of 1,123 male and female athletes, 89 percent of the 697 females and 90 percent of the 426 males looked forward to life after college; additionally, 55 percent of the women and 57 percent of the men indicated that they were quite or extremely satisfied with themselves upon career termination; also, 75 percent of the athletes were still participating in their sport at some less formal level. Finally, 81 percent of the men and 55 percent of the women continued to follow their respective sports through the media on a "regular" or "religious" basis.

A second conclusion from the two studies is that there were no sex differences in adjustment to termination. Past research has completely neglected the adjustment of female athletes to career termination, so these two studies represented a significant point of departure concerning research about this issue.

Third, career termination by way of injury resulted in a feeling of less life satisfaction for those athletes. Apparently, a sense of unfulfilled promise permeated the mentality of these injured athletes, resulting in less life satisfaction scores on the measure used. Finally, a shifting of priorities over the collegiate years took place in the majority of the athletes, with sport becoming less significant in their lives and education assuming an increasingly prominent role. These data support the earlier findings of Haerle (1975), who studied professional baseball players and found a strong relationship between amount of education and postplaying occupational achievement.

THE PROFESSIONAL ATHLETE

Presumably, the adjustment to career termination is more complex at the professional level because the stakes are higher. The money involved is substantially greater, with the average 1995 salary in the NBA at $1.9 million and that of the NFL $737,000. Also, the "sports only" identification is probably more operational at this stratified performance level. Partial support for the unidimensionality of professional athletes is provided by Ogilvie and Howe (1986), who indicate that only 20 percent of NBA players and 32 percent of NFL athletes had a college degree.

(Continued next page)

Highlight 13.6 (Continued)

The Retired Athlete

The popular literature is rife with reports of brain-damaged boxers, football players who cannot get out of bed without assistance, and athletes from all sport persuasions who are wife-battering, drug-addicted, alcoholic deadbeats. It is all too easy to infer from these sensationalized accounts that adjustment problems are rampant among ex-athletes. Little, of course, is made of the ex-athlete who quietly goes to work and becomes an adjusted and contributing citizen. Few statistics are available with which to accurately arrive at a composite of what the retired professional athlete is really like.

One of the first studies of athletic termination, and one with problems of extrapolation to U.S. professional athletes, was conducted by Mihovilovic (1968) with retired Yugoslavian soccer players. Ninety-five percent of these athletes were forced to retire and 53 percent reported missing the camaraderie afforded by team members; 39 percent took up smoking for the first time and 16 percent increased their alcohol consumption upon retirement.

Adaptation to family life constitutes another challenge to athletic retirement; Ogilvie and Howe (1986) cite statistics from the NFL Players Association in which 50 percent of all marriages of ex-NFL players end in divorce. Mihoces (1988) sets this divorce figure at 33.5 percent, still a high number. Inability to adjust to serious injury associated with sports is also a consideration that affects the overall adjustment to retirement. Taylor and Ogilvie (1994), in summarizing six studies of a variety of athletes, place the career-ending injury rate at a conservative 14 to 32 percent. In professional football, Mihoces indicates that 66 percent of all NFL players retire with permanent injury. Underwood (1979, p. 80), in discussing football injuries, poignantly portrays the plight of the seriously injured retiree: "Statistics do not show, however, how many ex-pros can no longer tie their shoe laces, or curl their fingers about a golf club. Statistics do not show many can't sleep without narcotics and have to call their wives for help to get out of bed."

Though we have much to learn about the adjustment of professional athletes to retirement, it seems obvious that all is not a bed of roses. Inadequate education, a paucity of job skills beyond those necessary to athletic performance, physical infirmity, and interpersonal difficulties variously contribute to the problems facing all too many retired athletes. Athletic administrators, counselors, agents, coaches, sport psychologists, and the

(Continued next page)

Highlight 13.6 (Continued)

The Retired Athlete

athletes themselves all have a vested interest in doing all they can to smooth the transition from what clearly is a brief career as an athlete to the more long-term endeavor of a contributing human being. Perhaps Dietzel (1983, p. 162) sums the situation up best: "The 'average' NFL player will have 42.4 years remaining after his playing career. That means that even if he does 'make it' in the pros, he will have to earn a living for the remaining two-thirds of his life. He has a .018 percent chance of being a pro but he has a solid 100 percent chance of being a 'breadwinner' for the overwhelming majority of his life."

Sources: Dietzel (1983); Greendorfer and Blinde (1985); Haerle (1975); Kleiber, Greendorfer, Blinde, and Samdahl (1987); Mihoces (1988); Mihovilovic (1968); Ogilvie and Howe (1986); Taylor and Ogilvie (1994); Underwood (1979).

some of the more significant issues confronting health professionals. The psychology of running and the exercise and competitive needs of senior citizens have sparked interest among sport and exercise scientists.

2. An apparent fitness boom of major proportions has seen 50 to 60 million Americans involved in some kind of exercise. However, a large number of so-called exercisers may not work out regularly enough to realize the possible gains in level of fitness. The commitment to fitness may be more verbal than behavioral.

3. Caspersen (1985) suggests that there are differences among physical activity, exercise, and physical fitness, and these distinctions have served as a guiding philosophy for the present discussion.

4. Among the more prominent physical benefits of physical fitness are increased blood flow to the heart, lowered blood pressure, increased lung capacity, lower blood lactate levels, more effective digestive and excretory functioning, improved sex life, and weight control. Whether or not a lowered resting heart rate is actually a benefit remains contentious.

5. The psychological benefits of exercise are less well documented but are thought to include reductions in anxiety and depression, increased socialization, self-confidence, and the thrill of competition against oneself, external standards, or other competitors.

6. Statistics on exercise adherence are generally not good. Exercise dropout rates of up to 50 percent are seen in both exercisers with no history of coronary problems who want to become more fit and those who are post-myocardial infarction patients.

7. Predictors of exercise adherence include geographical proximity to the exercise area, support from the spouse, exercising in small as opposed to large groups, higher socioeconomic status, and, more tentatively, an internal locus of control.

8. Negative predictors of adherence include lack of time, accessibility, being a smoker,

poor choice of exercise, early injury, Type A personality, and being more introverted.

9. A number of behavioral approaches to increase exercise compliance that have been used with some success are behavioral contracts, lotteries, self-monitoring, stimulus-cueing, and reinforcement of exercise behavior.

10. Concerned professionals have shown much interest in the contribution of exercise to cognitive and affective functioning.

11. Many studies have been conducted concerning various kinds of exercise as they relate to cognitive functioning, and the results are highly equivocal at this point. This is generally true for both anaerobic and aerobic exercise conducted at varying degrees of intensity and time. Flaws in methodology and a failure to tie the research to any theoretical base have hampered studies.

12. Exercise is thought to have an impact on both anxiety and depression, two affective states that have been of considerable interest to scientists across many professional fields.

13. In an extensive review of the literature, Folkins and Sime (1981) cite studies pointing to improved affective functioning as a result of exercise. Evidence also suggests that reductions in anxiety can be achieved by pairing exercise with other approaches, such as stress inoculation training.

14. Depression is a major mental health problem in the United States, and a variety of approaches have been used in an attempt to deal with the condition. Greist and his colleagues (1978) brought the use of running as therapy for depression to the forefront from the scientific perspective, whereas Fixx (1977) served the same function for the larger community with his popular book on the many virtues of running. Like the link between anxiety and exercise, the one involving depression is best thought of as correlational as opposed to causative at this point.

More research is needed to make the desired causal connection between exercise and improved affect.

15. In using exercise as therapy for anxiety or depression, first priority should be given to making an accurate psychological diagnosis of the client(s). Exercises should be carefully tailored to the individual and should be performed under the guidance of a skilled exercise therapist who serves as an adjustment and fitness model. The therapy situation requires liberal use of reinforcement.

16. Runners and senior citizens represent two populations of interest to sport and exercise professionals.

17. Much has been made, and with some justification, about the merits of running as a means of promoting physical fitness. Some runners (and other exercisers) form a positive addiction and others a negative addiction to their exercise regimen.

18. The notion of positive addiction was popularized in 1976 by psychiatrist William Glasser. To Glasser, the positively addicted person has a healthy attitude toward exercise, has it worked nicely into everyday life, and does not let exercise control his or her life. Evidence from a number of sources supports a generally healthy psychological state among runners, who Glasser would say are most likely to become positively addicted because they are using the exercise of choice.

19. The negatively addicted person has relinquished control of exercise. Work, family life, and health may be sacrificed for the sake of the search for fitness. Injury statistics indicate that addicted runners are at higher risk of injury while working out or competing.

20. The phenomenon of the "runner's high" is generally agreed to exist, but attempts to operationalize it have not been successful. Estimates indicate that from 9 percent to 78

percent of all runners have experienced the "runner's high."

21. The marathon event was named after a small Greek town in which a prominent battle was fought between the Greeks and the Persians in 490 B.C. The marathon was introduced as an Olympic event in 1896, and its popularity has increased ever since. The event was added to the slate of activities for women in the 1984 Olympics. Studies of marathoners suggest that they are introverts, have low anxiety levels, and have superior mood profiles in general.

22. Ultramarathoners run distances above the 26 miles, 385 yards found in the marathon event. Ultramarathons may involve long distances over several days or weeks or distances up to 100 miles in a given day. Little is known about the psychology of ultramarathoners. Highly preliminary evidence suggests that they are generally psychologically healthy with just enough personality deviance to help them run what may itself be a deviant event.

23. There will be an increase in the median age of the typical American of ten years by the year 2050. This "graying of America" is a phenomenon that will place added pressure on a variety of services, not the least of which is exercise and fitness for senior citizens.

24. Chronological age is unalterable; biological age can be modified to an unknown extent, and it remains the task of the exerciser and the exercise and fitness specialists to determine just what this limit is. It seems likely that exercise offers one point of intervention in this biological aging issue.

25. Seniors who still have a competitive streak are increasingly being provided with outlets for their energies and talents. One such example is the Maryland Senior Olympics, a thirty-event competition for men and women over age fifty-five.

26. Although exercise may represent one way to achieve fitness, physical activities of any kind that keep people occupied, interested, and moving about may be just as productive in promoting health.

SUGGESTED READINGS

Brown, D. R., Wang, Y., Ward, A., Ebbeling, C. B., Fortlage, L., Puleo, E., Benson, H., & Rippe, J. M. (1995) Chronic psychological effects of exercise and exercise plus cognitive strategies. *Medicine and Science in Sports and Exercise, 27,* 765–775.

> This research paper presents results of a variety of exercise treatment conditions on psychological well-being of healthy, sedentary adults (sixty-nine females, sixty-six males). Four groups took part in the experiment: a control group (C), a moderate intensity walk group (MW), a low-intensity walking plus relaxation group (LWR), and a mindful exercise (ME) group engaging in Tai-Chi meditation. Greatest mood changes as measured by the Profile of Mood States (POMS) were for women in the ME group. Women in the MW group reported the greatest changes in attitudes about physical attributes. The authors conclude that fitness programs without a competitive component are less effective than those possessing such an inclusion.

Fimrite, R. (1989) The second time around. *Sports Illustrated,* January 9, 110–121.

> This article gives a positive twist to the retirement from sport literature by highlighting the post-retirement lives of five once-famous athletes. Brief vignettes describe the lives of Jim Ridlon, NFL defensive back turned professor of visual arts; Craig Swan, major league baseball player turned Rolfing expert (a health promotion or healing technique); Madeline Manning Mims, Olympic track gold medalist turned gospel singer and minister; Dr. Bill McColl, professional football player turned orthopedist and leprosy expert; and Bob Love, NBA basketball star turned corporate fitness director. These minicase histories of successful adaptation to retirement from sports serves to balance the picture of the down-and-

out ex-jock who has failed to handle life after sports in a rewarding and productive manner.

Kendzierski, D., & DeCarlo, K. J. (1991) Physical Activity and Enjoyment Scale: Two validation studies. *Journal of Sport and Exercise Psychology, 13,* 50–64.

In this article, the authors present two studies on a sport/exercise-specific scale. After refinements generated from data from the first study, Kendzierski and DeCarlo ended up with an eighteen-item measure that employs a seven-point Likert scale. Analyses gathered during study 2 indicate that the Physical Activity and Enjoyment Scale (PACES) possesses good reliability based on high internal consistency and test-retest procedures. The PACES was also able to discriminate between activity choices of the subjects, thereby providing some validity data. Finally, the PACES was not susceptible to social desirability problems as measured by the Marlowe-Crowne. The PACES appears to have utility as a brief, reliable, and valid assessment device for research in exercise settings.

Physical activity and psychological benefits: A position statement from the International Society of Sport Psychology. (1992) *International Journal of Sport Psychology, 4,* 94–98.

ISSP has reviewed the research and adopted the following stance with regard to the potential psychological benefits of regular physical exercise: (1) exercise can be associated with reduced state anxiety; (2) exercise can be associated with a decreased level of mild to moderate depression; (3) long-term exercise is usually associated with reductions in neuroticism and anxiety; (4) exercise may be an adjunct to the professional treatment of severe depression; (5) exercise can result in the reduction of various stress indices; and (6) exercise can have beneficial emotional effects across all ages and both genders.

Robison, J. I., & Rogers, M. A. (1994) Adherence to exercise programmes. *Sports Medicine, 17,* 39–52.

This comprehensive paper summarizes a good deal of the research on why people adhere to and drop out of exercise programs, including personal, environmental and program factors. As such, it both supports and extends our discussion in this chapter. Other important topics include theories of behavior change and behavioral strategies to improve adherence. The authors also point out limitations in the existing research on exercise adherence and outline an agenda for future efforts at improving exercise. This is a state-of-the-art article and will go a long way toward bringing the reader up to date on these important topics.

Shephard, R. J. (1994) *Aerobic fitness and health.* Champaign, IL: Human Kinetics.

Shephard, one of the leading authorities on exercise and health behavior, has compiled a book that authoritatively summarizes the existing literature on the interaction among physical activity, aerobic fitness, and health. Topics discussed include physiological determinants of aerobic fitness; fitness issues of youth, adults, and the elderly; and the health outcomes of a regular program of exercise. There are over 1,300 references in Shephard's book. As such, this book is the state of the art in the area of aerobic fitness and health.

Stein, G. L., Kimiecik, J. C., Daniels, J., & Jackson, S. A. (1995) Psychological antecedents of flow in recreational sport. *Personality and Social Psychology Bulletin, 21,* 125–135.

In a series of three studies involving weekend tennis competitors, college activity class basketball players, and country club golfers, the authors examined the concept of flow as advanced by Csikszentmihalyi. Though no conclusive statements can be made as a result of these three studies, the review of the literature and related discussion of obtained results point out the elusiveness of the concept of flow and peak experience in sport in general.

Weinstein, N. D. (1993) Testing four competing theories of health-protective behavior. *Health Psychology, 12,* 324–333.

Weinstein provides a contemporary and comprehensive review of four models of health belief models, or what he and others call health-protection models: the health belief model, the subjected expected utility model, protective motivation theory, and the theory of reasoned action.

In addition to providing a summary of the status of the various models, Weinstein examines some methodological and testing issues. This article will assist the reader in understanding more about health behavior.

Weyerer, S., & Kupfer, B. (1994) Physical exercise and psychological health. *Sports Medicine, 17,* 108–116. This article reviews much of what has been reported elsewhere, but there is a particularly good discussion of the psychological mechanisms at work in creating the benefits of regular exercise.

REFERENCES

Ajzen, I. (1985) From intention to actions: A theory of planned behavior. In J. Kuhl & J. Beckman (eds.), *Action-control: From cognition to behavior.* Heidelberg: Springer.

Ajzen, I., & Fishbein, M. (1980) *Understanding attitudes and predicting social behavior.* Englewood Cliffs, NJ: Prentice-Hall.

Andrew, G., Oldridge, N., Parker, J., Cunningham, D., Rechnitzer, P., Jones, N., Buck, C., Kavanagh, T., Shephard, R., Sutton, J., & McDonald, W. (1981) Reasons for dropout from exercise programs in post-coronary patients. *Medicine and Science in Sports and Exercise, 13,* 164–168.

Anshel, M. H. (1991) A psycho-behavioral analysis of addicted versus non-addicted male and female exercisers. *Journal of Sport Behavior, 14,* 145–154.

Bahrke, M. S., & Morgan, W. P. (1978) Anxiety reduction following exercise and meditation. *Cognitive Therapy and Research, 2,* 323–333.

Becker, M. H., Haefner, D. P., Kasl, S. V., Kirscht, J. P., Maiman, L. A., & Rosenstock, I. M. (1977) Selected psychosocial models and correlates of individual health-related behaviors. *Medical Care, 15,* 27–46.

Berger, B. (1987) Swimmers report less stress: A series of investigations. In W. P. Morgan & S. E. Goldston (Eds.), *Exercise and mental health* (pp. 139–143). New York: Hemisphere Pub.

Blumenthal, J., Williams, R., Wallace, A., Williams, R., & Needles, T. (1982) Physiological and psychological variables predict compliance to prescribed exercise therapy in patients recovering from myocardial infarction. *Psychosomatic Medicine, 44,* 519–527.

Borg, G. (1973) Perceived exertion: A note on history and methods. *Medicine and Science in Sports, 5,* 90–93.

Boutcher, S., & Landers, D. M. (1988) The effects of vigorous exercise on anxiety, heart rate, and alpha activity of runners and nonrunners. *Psychophysiology, 25,* 696–702.

Brown, B. (1993) Keeping fit on decline. *USA Today,* April 13, 2C.

Brown, R., Ramirez, D., & Taub, J. (1978) The prescription of exercise for depression. *Physician and Sportsmedicine, 6*(12), 35–45.

Buffone, G. W. (1984) Exercise as a therapeutic adjunct. In J. M. Silva & R. S. Weinberg (Eds.), *Psychological foundations of sport* (pp. 445–451). Champaign, IL: Human Kinetics.

Bull, S. J. (1989) The role of the sport psychology consultant: A case study of ultra-distance running. *The Sport Psychologist, 3,* 254–264.

Carmack, M. A., & Martens, R. (1979) Measuring commitment to running: A survey of runners' attitudes and mental states. *Journal of Sport Psychology, 1,* 25–42.

Caspersen, C. J. (1985) Physical activity, exercise, and physical fitness: Definitions and distinctions for health-related research. *Physician and Sportsmedicine, 13*(5), 162.

Caspersen, C. J., & Merritt, R. K. (1995) Physical activity trends among 26 states, 1986–1990. *Medicine and Science in Sports and Exercise, 27,* 713–720.

Chapman, C. L., & DeCastro, J. M. (1990) Running addiction: Measurement and associated psychological characteristics. *Journal of Sports Medicine and Physical Fitness, 30,* 283–290.

Clitsome, T., & Kostrubala, T. (1977) A psychological study of 100 marathoners using the Myers-Briggs Type indicator and demographic data. In P. Milvey (Ed.), *The marathon: Physiological, medical, epidemiological, and psychological studies. Annals of the New York Academy of Sciences, 301,* 1010–1019.

Cockerill, I. M., Nevill, A. M., & Byrne, N. C. (1992) Mood, mileage and the menstrual cycle. *British Journal of Sports Medicine, 26,* 145–150.

Csikszentmihalyi, M. (1975) *Beyond boredom and anxiety.* San Francisco, CA: Jossey-Bass.

deGeus, E. J. C., Lorenz, J. P., van Doornen, L. J. P., & Orlebeke, J. F. (1993) Regular exercise and aerobic fitness in relation to psychological make-up and physiological stress reactivity. *Psychosomatic Medicine, 55,* 347–363.

Desharnais, R., Jobin, J., Cote, C., Levesque, L., & Godin, G. (1993) Aerobic exercise and the placebo effect: A controlled study. *Psychosomatic Medicine, 55,* 149–154.

Diekhoff, G. (1984) Running amok: Injuries in compulsive runners. *Journal of Sport Behavior, 7,* 120–129.

Dietzel, P. (1983) There is life after football. *Physical Educator, 40,* 161–162.

Dishman, R. K. (1984) Motivation and exercise adherence. In J. M. Silva & R. S. Weinberg (Eds.), *Psychological foundations of sport* (pp. 420–434). Champaign, IL: Human Kinetics.

Dishman, R. K. (1986) Exercise compliance: A new view for public health. *Physician and Sportsmedicine, 14*(5), 127–145.

Dishman, R. K. (1991) Increasing and maintaining exercise and physical activity. *Behavior Therapy, 22,* 345–378.

Droste, C., Greenlee, M. W., Schreck, M., & Roskamm, H. (1991) Experimental pain thresholds and plasma beta-endorphin levels during exercise. *Medicine and Science in Sports and Exercise, 23,* 334–342.

Durtschi, S., & Weiss, M. (1986) Psychological characteristics of elite and nonelite marathon runners. In D. V. Landers (Ed.), *Sport and elite performers.* Champaign, IL: Human Kinetics.

Dyer, J. B., & Crouch, J. G. (1987) Effects of running on mood: A time series study. *Perceptual and Motor Skills, 64,* 783–789.

Farrell, P., Gates, W., Maksud, M., & Morgan, W. (1982) Increases in plasma B-endorphin/B-lipotropin immunoreactivity after treadmill running in rats. *Journal of Applied Psychology, 52,* 1245–1249.

Fiatarone, M. A., Marks, E. C., Ryan, N. D., Meredith, C. N., Lipsitz, L. A., & Evans, W. J. (1990) High-intensity strength training in nonagenarians: Effects on skeletal muscle. *Journal of the American Medical Association, 263,* 3029–3034.

Fiatarone, M. A., O'Neill, E. F., Ryan, N. D., Clements, K. M., Solares, G. R., Nelson, M. E., Roberts, S. B., Kehayias, J. J., Lipsitz, L. A., & Evans, W. J. (1994) Exercise training and nutritional supplementation for physical frailty in very elderly people. *The New England Journal of Medicine, 330,* 1769–1775.

Fishbein, M., & Ajzen, I. (1975) *Belief, attitude, intention, and behavior.* Don Mills, NY: Addison-Wesley.

Fixx, J. (1977) *The complete book of running.* New York: Random House.

Flory, J. D., & Holmes, D. S. (1991) Effects of an acute bout of aerobic exercise on cardiovascular and subjective responses during subsequent cognitive work. *Journal of Psychosomatic Research, 35,* 225–230.

Folkins, C., & Sime, W. (1981) Physical fitness training and mental health. *American Psychologist, 36,* 373–389.

Folkins, C., & Wieselberg-Bell, N. (1981) A personality profile of ultramarathon runners: A little deviance may go a long way. *Journal of Sport Behavior, 4,* 119–127.

Fox, E. (1984) *Sports physiology.* Philadelphia, PA: Saunders.

Friedman, M., & Rosenman, R. (1974) *Type A behavior and your heart.* New York: Knopf.

Gettman, L., Pollock, M., & Ward, A. (1983) Adherence to unsupervised exercise. *Physician and Sportsmedicine, 11*(10), 56–66.

Glasser, W. (1976) *Positive addiction.* New York: Harper & Row.

Gliner, J. A., Matsen-Twisdale, J. A., Horvath, S. M., & Maron, M. B. (1979) Visual evoked potentials and signal detection following a marathon race. *Medicine and Science in Sports, 11,* 155–159.

Godin, G., & Shephard, R. J. (1990) Use of attitude-behavior models in exercise promotion. *Sports Medicine, 10,* 103–121.

Gondola, J., & Tuckman, B. (1982) Psychological, mood states in "average" marathon runners. *Perceptual and Motor Skills, 55,* 1295–1300.

Gondola, J., & Tuckman, B. (1983) Extent of training and mood enhancement in women runners. *Perceptual and Motor Skills, 57,* 333–334.

Gontang, A., Clitsome, T., & Kostrubala, T. (1977) A psychological study of 50 sub-3 hour marathoners.

In P. Milvey (Ed.), *The marathon: Physiological, medical, epidemiological, and psychological studies. Annals of the New York Academy of Sciences, 301,* 1020–1046.

Greendorfer, S., & Blinde, E. (1985) Retirement from intercollegiate sport: Theoretical and empirical considerations. *Sociology of Sport Journal, 2,* 101–110.

Greist, J., Klein, M., Eischens, R., & Faris, J. (1978) Running out of depression. *Physician and Sportsmedicine, 6*(12), 49–56.

Grogan, R. (1981) Run, Pheidippides, run! The story of the battle of Marathon. *British Journal of Sports Medicine, 15,* 186–189.

Haerle, R. K. (1975) Career patterns and career contingencies of professional baseball players: An occupational analysis. In D. W. Ball & J. W. Loy (eds.), *Sport and social order* (pp. 461–519). Reading, MA: Addison-Wesley.

Hailey, B. J., & Bailey, L. (1982) Negative addiction in runners: A quantitative approach. *Journal of Sport Behavior, 5,* 150–153.

Hanson, M. (1977) Coronary heart disease, exercise, and motivation in middle aged males. Doctoral dissertation, University of Wisconsin, Madison, 1976. *Dissertation Abstracts International, 37,* 2755B.

Health and fitness. (1990) *Changing Times,* August, 64–66.

Henderson, J. (1977) Running commentary. *Runner's World, 13*(9), 15.

Hopson, J. L. (1988) A pleasurable chemistry. *Psychology Today,* July–August, 28–33.

Howell, R. (1983) History of the Olympic marathon. *Physician and Sportsmedicine, 11*(11), 153–158.

Joesting, J. (1981) Comparison of personalities of athletes who sail with those who run. *Perceptual and Motor Skills, 52,* 514.

Johnsgard, K. (1985) The motivation of the long distance runner: I. *Journal of Sports Medicine, 25,* 135–143.

Kleiber, D., Greendorfer, S., Blinde, E., & Samdahl, D. (1987) Quality of exit from university sports and life satisfaction in early adulthood. *Sociology of Sport Journal, 4,* 28–36.

Kraemer, R. R., Dzewaltowski, D. A., Blair, M. S., Rinehardt, K. F., & Castracane, V. D. (1990) Mood alteration from treadmill running and its relationship to beta-endorphin, corticotropin, and growth hormone. *Journal of Sports Medicine and Physical Fitness, 30,* 241–246.

LaPorte, R., Dearwater, S., Cauley, J., Slemenda, C., & Cook, T. (1985) Physical activity or cardiovascular fitness: Which is more important for health? *Physician and Sportsmedicine, 13*(3), 145–150.

Layman, D., & Morris, A. (1986) Addiction and injury in runners: Is there a mind-body connection? Paper presented at the annual convention of the North American Society for the Psychology of Sport and Physical Activity, Scottsdale, Arizona.

Lee, I., Hsieh, C., & Paffenbarger, R. S. (1995) Exercise intensity and longevity in men: The Harvard Alumni Health Study. *Journal of the American Medical Association, 273,* 1179–1184.

Legwold, G. (1985) Are we running from the truth about the risks and benefits of exercise? *Physician and Sportsmedicine, 13*(5), 136–148.

Levenson, H. (1981) Differentiating among internality, powerful others, and chance. In H. Lefcourt (Ed.), *Research with the locus of control construct: Assessment methods* (Vol. 1, pp. 1–39). New York: Academic Press.

Lewis, B. (1992) The long and winding road. *Runner's World, 27*(2), 82–89.

Lilliefors, F. (1978) *The running mind.* Mountain View, CA: World Publications.

Long, B. C. (1984) Aerobic conditioning and stress inoculation: A comparison of stress-management interventions. *Cognitive Therapy and Research, 8,* 517–542.

Long, B. C. (1985) Stress-management interventions: A 15-month follow-up of aerobic and stress inoculation training. *Cognitive Therapy and Research, 9,* 471–478.

Lybrand, W. A., Andrews, T. G., & Ross, S. (1954) Systematic fatigue and perceptual organization. *American Journal of Psychology, 67,* 704–707.

Maddux, J. E., & Rogers, R. W. (1983) Protection motivation and self-efficacy: A revised theory of fear appeals and attitude change. *Journal of Experimental and Social Psychology, 19,* 469–479.

Markoff, R., Ryan, P., & Young, T. (1982) Endorphins and mood changes in long-distance running. *Medicine and Science in Exercise and Sport, 14,* 11–15.

Maron, M., & Horvath, S. (1978) The marathon: A history and review of the literature. *Medicine and Science in Sports, 10,* 137–150.

Martinsen, E. W. (1990) Benefits of exercise for the treatment of depression. *Sports Medicine, 9,* 380–389.

Massie, J., & Shephard, R. (1971) Physiological and psychological effects of training: A comparison of individual and gymnasium programs, with a characterization of the exercise 'drop-out.' *Medicine and Science in Sports, 3,* 110–117.

Masters, K. S. (1992) Hypnotic susceptibility, cognitive dissociation, and runner's high in a sample of marathon runners. *American Journal of Clinical Hypnosis, 34,* 193–201.

Masters, K. S., & Ogles, B. M. (1995) An investigation of the different motivations of marathon runners with varying degrees of experience. *Journal of Sport Behavior, 18,* 69–79.

Masters, K. S., Ogles, B. M., & Jolton, J. A. (1993) The development of an instrument of measure motivation for marathon running: The Motivations of Marathoners Scales (MOMS). *Research Quarterly for Exercise and Sport, 64,* 134–143.

McCready, M., & Long, B. C. (1985) Locus of control, attitudes toward physical activity, and exercise adherence. *Journal of Sport Psychology, 7,* 346–359.

McCutcheon, L., & Yoakum, M. (1983) Personality attributes of ultramarathoners. *Journal of Personality Assessment, 47,* 178–180.

Meichenbaum, D. (1977) *Cognitive-behavior modification: An integrated approach.* New York: Plenum.

Mihoces, G. (1988) Less-visible players find little glory after football. *USA Today,* May 10, 12C.

Mihovilovic, M. A. (1968) The status of former sportsmen. *International Review of Sport Sociology, 3,* 73–93.

Monahan, T. (1986) Exercise and depression: Swapping sweat for serenity? *Physician and Sportsmedicine, 14*(9), 192–197.

Morey, M. C., Cowper, P. A., Feussner, J. R., DiPasquale, R. C., Crowley, G. M., & Sullivan, R. J. (1991) Two-year trends in physical performance following supervised exercise among community-dwelling older veterans. *Journal of American Geriatric Society, 39,* 549–554.

Morgan, W. P. (1979) Negative addiction in runners. *Physician and Sportsmedicine, 7*(2), 56–70.

Morgan, W. P., & Costill, D. (1972) Psychological characteristics of the marathon runner. *Journal of Sports Medicine and Physical Fitness, 12,* 42–46.

Morgan, W. P., & Pollock, M. (1977) Psychologic characterization of the elite distance runner. In P. Milvey (Ed.), *The marathon: Physiological, medical, epidemiological, and psychological studies. Annals of the New York Academy of Sciences, 301,* 382–403.

Noland, M. (1981) The efficacy of a new model to explain leisure exercise behavior. Unpublished doctoral dissertation, University of Maryland.

Ogilvie, B., & Howe, M. (1986) The trauma of termination from athletics. In J. M. Williams (ed.), *Applied sport psychology: Personal growth to peak experience* (pp. 365–382). Mountain View, CA: Mayfield.

Oldridge, N. (1982) Compliance and exercise in primary and secondary prevention of coronary heart disease: A review. *Preventive Medicine, 11,* 56–70.

Oldridge, N. (1988) Cardiac rehabilitation exercise programme. Compliance and compliance-enhancing strategies. *Sports Medicine, 6,* 42–55.

Oldridge, N., Wicks, J., Hanley, R., Sutton, J., & Jones, N. (1978) Noncompliance in an exercise rehabilitation program for men who have suffered a myocardial infarction. *Canadian Medical Association Journal, 118,* 361–375.

Peoples, C. (1983) A psychological analysis of the "runner's high." *Physical Educator, 40,* 38–41.

Piaget, J. (1936) *The origins of intelligence in children.* New York: New York University Press.

Pierce, E. F. (1994) Exercise dependence syndrome in runners. *Sports Medicine, 18,* 149–155.

Porter, K. (1985) Psychological characteristics of the average female runner. *Physician and Sportsmedicine, 13*(5), 171–175.

Powell, K. (1985) Workshop on epidemiologic and public health aspects of physical activity and exercise. *Physician and Sportsmedicine, 13*(3), 161.

Raglin, J. (1990) Exercise and mental health. *Sports Medicine, 6,* 323–329.

Raglin, J., & Morgan, W. P. (1985) Influence of vigorous exercise on mood state. *Behavior Therapist, 8,* 179–183.

Ravizza, K. (1984) Qualities of the peak experience in sport, In J. M. Silva & R. S. Weinberg (Eds.), *Psychological foundations of sport* (pp. 452–461). Champaign, IL: Human Kinetics.

The recommended quantity and quality of exercise for developing and maintaining cardiorespiratory and muscular fitness in healthy adults. (1990) *Medicine and Science in Sports and Exercise, 22,* 265–274.

Rogers, C. (1985) Of magic, miracles, and exercise myths. *Physician and Sportsmedicine, 13*(5), 156–166.

Rogers, R. W. (1983) Cognitive and physiological processes in fear appeals and attitude change: A revised theory of protection change. In J. T. Cacciopo and R. E. Petty (eds.), *Social psychology: A sourcebook.* New York: Guilford.

Roth, W. (1974) Some motivational aspects of exercise. *Journal of Sports Medicine, 14,* 40–47.

Roth, W. (1989) Acute emotional and psychophysiological effects on aerobic exercise. *Psychophysiology, 26,* 593–602.

Rudman, W. (1986) Sport as a part of successful aging. *American Behavioral Scientist, 29,* 453–470.

Sachs, M. (1980) On the trail of the runner's high—A descriptive and experimental investigation of characteristics of an elusive phenomenon. Unpublished doctoral dissertation, Florida State University.

Sachs, M. (1982) Compliance and addiction to exercise. In R. C. Cantu (ed.), *The exercising adult.* Boston, MA: Collamore Press.

Sachs, M. (1984) Psychological well-being and vigorous physical activity. In J. M. Silva & R. S. Weinberg (Eds.), *Psychological foundations of sport* (pp. 435–444). Champaign, IL: Human Kinetics.

Sager, K. (1984) Exercises to activate seniors. *Physician and Sportsmedicine, 12*(5), 144–151.

Sanne, H. (1973) Exercise tolerance and physical training of non-selected patients after myocardial infarction. *Acta Medica Scandinavica, 551,* 1–124.

Scanning sports. (1989) *Physician and Sportsmedicine, 17,* (2), 21.

Shephard, R. (1985) Motivation: The key to exercise compliance. *Physician and Sportsmedicine, 13*(7), 88–101.

Sidney, K., & Shephard, R. (1976) Attitudes toward health and physical activity in the elderly. Effects of a physical training program. *Medicine and Science in Sports, 4,* 246–252.

Silva, J., & Hardy, C. (1986) Discriminating contestants at the United States Olympic marathon trials as a function of precompetitive anxiety. *International Journal of Sport Psychology, 17,* 100–109.

Silva, J. M., & Weinberg, R. S. (1984) Exercise and psychological well-being. In J. M. Silva & R. S. Weinberg (Eds.), *Psychological foundations of sport* (pp. 415–419). Champaign, IL: Human Kinetics.

Sime, W. E., Whipple, I. T., Stamler, J., & Berkson, D. M. (1978) Effects of long-term (38 months) training on middle-aged sedentary males: Adherence and specificity of training. In F. Landry & W. A. R. Orban (Eds.), *Exercise and well-being: Exercise physiology* (pp. 456–464). Miami, FL: Symposium Specialists.

Siscovick, D. (1985) The disease-specific benefits and risks of physical activity and exercise. *Physician and Sportsmedicine, 13*(3), 164.

Smith, E. L., & Gilliam, C. (1983) Physical activity prescription for the older adult. *Physician and Sportsmedicine, 11*(8), 91–101.

Smith, E. L., & Zook, S. K. (1986) The aging process: Benefits of physical activity. *Journal of Physical Education, Recreation and Dance,* January, 32–34.

Spielberger, C., Gorsuch, B., & Lushene, R. (1970) Manual for the *State-Trait Anxiety Inventory.* Palo Alto, CA: Consulting Psychologists Press.

Spirduso, W. W. (1980) Physical fitness, aging, and psychomotor speed: A review. *Journal of Gerontology, 35,* 850–865.

Spirduso, W. W. (1983) Exercise and the aging brain. *Research Quarterly for Exercise and Sport, 54,* 208–218.

Spirduso, W. W., & Clifford, P. (1978) Neuromuscular speed and consistency of performance as a function of age, physical activity level and type of physical activity. *Journal of Gerontology, 33,* 26–30.

Sports camaraderie: The fit will frolic. (1989) *USA Today,* June 19, 8C.

Stamford, B. (1984) Exercise and longevity. *Physician and Sportsmedicine, 12*(6), 209.

Steinhaus, L. A., Dustman, R. E., Ruhling, R. O., Emmerson, R. Y., Johnson, S. C., Shearer, D. E., Latin, R. W., Shigeoka, J. W., & Bonekat, W. H. (1990) Aerobic capacity of older adults: A training study. *Journal of Sports Medicine and Physical Fitness, 30,* 163–172.

Stephens, T. (1985) A descriptive epidemiology of leisure-time physical activity. *Physician and Sportsmedicine, 13*(3), 162.

Taylor, J., & Ogilvie, B. C. (1994) A conceptual model of adaptation to retirement among athletes. *Journal of Applied Sport Psychology, 6,* 1–20.

Teraslinna, P., Partanen, T., Koskela, A., Partanen, K., & Oja, P. (1969) Characteristics affecting willingness of executives to participate in an activity program aimed at coronary heart disease prevention. *Journal of Sports Medicine and Physical Fitness, 9,* 224–229.

Tharion, W. J., Strowman, S. R., & Rauch, T. M. (1988) Profile and changes in moods of marathoners. *Journal of Sport and Exercise Psychology, 10,* 229–235.

Thaxton, L. (1982) Physiological and psychological effects of short-term exercise addiction on habitual runners. *Journal of Sport Psychology, 4,* 73–80.

Thomas, T., Zebas, C., Bahrke, M., Araujo, J., & Etheridge, G. (1983) Physiological and psychological correlates of success in track and field athletes. *British Journal of Sports Medicine, 17,* 102–109.

Thompson, C., & Wankel, L. (1980) The effects of perceived activity choice upon frequency of exercise behavior. *Journal of Applied Social Psychology, 10,* 436–444.

Tomporowski, P. D., & Ellis, N. R. (1986) Effects of exercise on cognitive processes: A review. *Psychological Bulletin, 99,* 338–346.

Tomoporowski, P. D., Ellis, N. R., & Stephens, R. (1985) The immediate effects of strenuous exercise on free-recall memory. *Ergonomics, 30,* 121–129.

Triandis, H. C. (1977) *Interpersonal behavior.* Monterey, CA: Brooks/Cole.

Underwood, J. (1979) *The death of an American game.* Boston: Little, Brown.

Veale de Coverley, D. M. W. (1987) Exercise dependence. *British Journal of Addictions, 82,* 735–740.

Vernon, R. (1984) Baker says trials changed for better. *Dallas Morning Times,* June 22, 2C.

Veschi, R. (1963) Longevity and sport. *Journal of Sports Medicine and Physical Fitness, 3,* 44–49.

Wagemaker, H., & Goldstein, L. (1980) The runner's high. *Journal of Sports Medicine, 20,* 227–228.

Waldstreicher, J. (1985) Anorexia nervosa presented as morbid exercising. *Lancet, 1,* 987.

Weinberg, R. S. (1980) Relationship of commitment to running scale to runners' performances and attitudes. In *Abstracts: Research papers 1980 AAHPERD Convention.* Washington, DC: AAHPERD.

Weltman, A., & Stamford, B. (1983) Psychological effects of exercise. *Physician and Sportsmedicine, 11*(1), 175.

Westcott, W. (1995) Converting couch potatoes to fitness fans. *Perspective, 21*(4), 22–25.

Williams, R., & Long, J. (1983) *Toward a self-managed lifestyle* (3rd ed.). Boston: Houghton-Mifflin.

Williams, T. J., Krahenbuhl, G. S., & Morgan, D. W. (1991) Mood state and running economy in moderately trained male runners. *Medicine and Science in Sports and Exercise, 23,* 727–731.

Wilson, V., Morley, N., & Bird, E. (1980) Mood profiles of marathon runners, joggers, and nonexercisers. *Perceptual and Motor Skills, 50,* 117–118.

Yates, A., Leehey, K., & Shisslak, C. M. (1983) Running—An analogue for anorexia? *New England Journal of Medicine, 308,* 251–255.

Yordy, G. A., & Lent, R. W. (1993) Predicting aerobic exercise participation: Social cognitive, reasoned action, and planned behavior models. *Journal of Sport and Exercise Psychology, 15,* 363–374.

Zeigler, R. G., & Michael, R. H. (1985) The Maryland Senior Olympic Games: Challenging older athletes. *Physician and Sportsmedicine, 13*(8), 159–163.

Author Index

Subject Index

Photo Credits